Lecture Notes in Computer Science   2813
Edited by G. Goos, J. Hartmanis, and J. van Leeuwen

T0142084

Springer
Berlin
Heidelberg
New York
Hong Kong
London
Milan
Paris
Tokyo

Il-Yeol Song   Stephen W. Liddle
Tok Wang Ling   Peter Scheuermann (Eds.)

Conceptual
Modeling – ER 2003

22nd International Conference on Conceptual Modeling
Chicago, IL, USA, October 13-16, 2003
Proceedings

Springer

Volume Editors

Il-Yeol Song
Drexel University, College of Information Science and Technology
Philadelphia, PA 19104, USA
E-mail: song@drexel.edu

Stephen W. Liddle
Brigham Young University, Marriott School
School of Accountancy and Information Systems
Provo, UT 84602-3087, USA
E-mail: liddle@byu.edu

Tok Wang Ling
National University of Singapore, Dept. of Computer Science
3 Science Drive 2, Singapore 117543
E-mail: lingtw@comp.nus.edu.sg

Peter Scheuermann
Northwestern University, Dept. of Electrical and Computer Engineering
Evanston, IL 60208-3118, USA
E-mail: peters@ece.northwestern.edu

Cataloging-in-Publication Data applied for

A catalog record for this book is available from the Library of Congress

Bibliographic information published by Die Deutsche Bibliothek
Die Deutsche Bibliothek lists this publication in the Deutsche Nationalbibliografie;
detailed bibliographic data is available in the Internet at <http://dnb.ddb.de>.

CR Subject Classification (1998): H.2, H.4, F.4.1, I.2.4, H.1, J.1, D.2, C.2

ISSN 0302-9743
ISBN 3-540-20299-4 Springer-Verlag Berlin Heidelberg New York

Springer-Verlag Berlin Heidelberg New York
a member of BertelsmannSpringer Science+Business Media GmbH

http://www.springer.de

© Springer-Verlag Berlin Heidelberg 2003
Printed in Germany

Typesetting: Camera-ready by author, data conversion by PTP-Berlin GmbH
Printed on acid-free paper   SPIN 10950005   06/3142   5 4 3 2 1 0

Foreword

The 22nd International Conference on Conceptual Modeling (ER 2003) returned to Chicago after an absence of 18 years. Chicago, a city well known for its trendsetting and daring architecture, has met the new century with a renewed commitment to open public spaces and human interaction. Thus it provided a fitting venue for ER 2003, the scope of which was expanded to encompass all aspects of conceptual modeling in order to deal with constantly changing information technology and business practices and to accommodate a new openness in connecting systems to each other and to human users.

The ER 2003 Program Co-chairs, Il-Yeol Song, Stephen Liddle, and Tok Wang Ling, along with an outstanding Program Committee assembled one of the finest technical programs of this conference series. In keeping with the tradition of previous ER conferences, the program for ER 2003 also included four preconference workshops, two preconference tutorials, two conference tutorials, two panels, and a demos and poster session. The Program Co-chairs, as well as Manfred Jeusfeld and Óscar Pastor (Workshop Co-chairs), Ee-Peng Lim and Tobey Teorey (Tutorial Co-chairs), Avigdor Gal and Elisa Bertino (Panel Co-chairs), and Heinrich Mayr (Demos and Poster Chair), deserve our appreciation for an excellent job. It was a pleasure working with all of them.

I was extremely lucky to work with Kathi Hogshead Davis, the Organizing Chair, who along the road also took on the role of Treasurer, and gracefully ended up doing more work then she originally contracted for. Bamshad Mobasher was an energetic Local Arrangements Chair, and Rokia Missaoui gave very helpful service as Publicity Chair. I thank them and all the other members of the Organizing Committee for their dedication and professionalism.

I also express my sincere appreciation to the members of the ER Steering Committee, in particular to David Embley (Chair), Bernhard Thalheim (Vice-Chair), Jacky Akoka (ER2003 Liaison), and Peter Chen (Emeritus) for their continuing advice and vision.

Thanks are due too to all the sponsors for their support. And to all the attendees who contributed to the success of this conference, I am confident that you found the program of ER 2003 to be exciting and that our meeting, combined with the city of Chicago, provided a memorable experience for all of you.

October 2003   Peter Scheuermann

Preface

The 22nd International Conference on Conceptual Modeling (ER 2003) was held in Chicago, Illinois, October 13–16, 2003. The annual ER conference provides a forum for presenting and discussing current research and applications in which conceptual modeling is the major emphasis. Since its inception in 1979, the ER conference has become the most prestigious scientific conference covering conceptual modeling research and applications. The theme of ER 2003 was "conceptual modeling for the future." The purpose of the conference was to identify challenging problems facing conceptual modeling of future information systems and to shape future research directions by soliciting and reviewing high-quality applied and theoretical research contributions. We solicited forward-looking and innovative papers that identified promising areas for future conceptual modeling research as well as traditional approaches to analysis and design theory for information systems development.

The call for papers resulted in 153 excellent submissions of research papers from more than two dozen countries. Due to space limitations, we were only able to accept 38 papers from 19 countries, for an acceptance rate of 24.8%. Inevitably, many good papers had to be rejected. The accepted papers covered topics such as ontologies, patterns, workflow, metamodeling and methodology, innovative approaches to conceptual modeling, foundations of conceptual modeling, advanced database applications, systems integration, requirements and evolution, queries and languages, Web application modeling and development, schema and ontology integration, and data mining.

We were pleased with the quality of this year's program, from the keynote speeches to the workshops, panels, tutorials, industrial papers, and research papers. Many people helped make ER 2003 successful. We appreciated the outstanding keynote addresses by the renowned scholars Erich Neuhold, Stuart Madnick, and Michael Carey, and we thank James Odell for his excellent industrial keynote speech. We appreciate the diligent work of the organizing committee. Most of all, we are extremely grateful to the program committee members of ER 2003 who generously spent their time and energy reviewing submitted papers. We also thank the many external referees who helped with the review process. Finally, we thank the authors who wrote strong research papers and submitted them to ER 2003.

October 2003

Il-Yeol Song
Stephen W. Liddle
Tok Wang Ling

ER 2003 Conference Organization

Conference Chair
Peter Scheuermann, Northwestern University, USA

Organizing Chair and Treasurer
Kathi Hogshead Davis, Northern Illinois University, USA

Program Co-chairs
Il-Yeol Song, Drexel University, USA
Stephen W. Liddle, Brigham Young University, USA
Tok Wang Ling, National University of Singapore, Singapore

Workshop Co-chairs
Manfred Jeusfeld, Tilburg University, The Netherlands
Óscar Pastor, Polytechnic University of Valencia, Spain

Tutorial Co-chairs
Ee-Peng Lim, Nanyang Technological University, Singapore
Toby Teorey, University of Michigan, USA

Industrial Co-chairs
Terry Halpin, Northface Learning, USA
Peter Aiken, Virginia Commonwealth University, USA

Publicity Chair
Rokia Missaoui, University of Quebec, Canada

Panel Co-chairs
Avigdor Gal, Technion, Israel
Elisa Bertino, University of Milan, Italy

Demos and Posters Chair
Heinrich C. Mayr, University of Klagenfurt, Austria

Local Arrangements Chair
Bamshad Mobasher, DePaul University, USA

Registration Chair
Eugene Sheng, Northern Illinois University, USA

Steering Committee Representatives
Chair: David W. Embley, Brigham Young University, USA
Vice-Chair: Bernhard Thalheim, Brandenburg Technical University
at Cottbus, Germany
ER 2003 Liaison: Jacky Akoka, CNAM & INT, France
Emeritus: Peter P. Chen, Louisiana State University, USA

Program Committee

Jacky Akoka, CNAM & INT, France
Hiroshi Arisawa, Yokohama National University, Japan
Paolo Atzeni, University of Rome, Italy
Elisa Bertino, DSI, Italy
Mokrane Bouzeghoub, University of Versailles, France
Marco A. Casanova, Catholic University of Rio de Janeiro, Brazil
Tiziana Catarci, University of Rome, La Sapienza, Italy
Stefano Ceri, Milan Politechnic, Italy
Ye-Sho Chen, LSU, USA
Roger H.L. Chiang, University of Cincinnati, USA
Wesley Chu, UCLA, USA
Olga De Troyer, Free University of Brussels, Belgium
Lois Delcambre, OGI/OHSU, USA
Debabrata Dey, University of Washington, USA
Ramez Elmasri, University of Texas, Arlington, USA
David W. Embley, Brigham Young University, USA
Andreas Geppert, Credit Suisse, Switzerland
Don Goelman, Villanova University, USA
Paul Grefen, Eindhoven University of Technology, The Netherlands
Nicola Guarino, National Research Council ISTC-CNR, Italy
Jean-Luc Hainaut, University of Namur, Belgium
Terry Halpin, Northface Learning, USA
Hyoil Han, Drexel University, USA
Wook-Shin Han, Kyungpook National University, Korea
Brian Henderson-Sellers, University of Technology, Sydney, Australia
Howard Ho, IBM, Almaden Lab, USA
Xiaohua Tony Hu, Drexel University, USA
Paul Johannesson, Stockholm University, Sweden
Hannu Kangassalo, University of Tampere, Finland
Alberto Laender, Federal University of Minas Gerais, Brazil
Byung S. Lee, University of Vermont, USA
Dongwon Lee, Pennsylvania State University, USA
Jeong-Joon Lee, KPU, Korea
Mong Li Lee, National University of Singapore, Singapore
Ling Liu, Georgia Institute of Technology, USA
Leszek Maciaszek, Macquarie University, Australia
Sal March, Vanderbilt University, USA
Heinrich C. Mayr, University of Klagenfurt, Austria
William McCarthy, Michigan State University, USA
Elisabeth Metais, University of Versailles, France
Rokia Missaoui, University of Quebec, Canada
Takao Miura, Hosei University, Japan
Wai Yin Mok, University of Alabama, Huntsville, USA
Daniel Moody, Univerzita Karlova v Praze, Czech Republic

External Referees

Samuil Angelov
Maria Bergholtz
Stefano Borgo
Sven Casteleyn
Li Chen
Wan-Sup Cho
Cecil Eng Huang Chua
Daniela Damm
Michael Derntl
Pascal van Eck
Li Feng
Renato Ferreira
George Feuerlicht
Ed Glantz
Matteo Golfarelli
Mathias Goller
Cesar Gonzalez Guido Governatori
Ramanathan Guha
Giancarlo Guizzardi
Farshad Hakimpour
Sari Hakkarainen
Jean Henrard
Mauricio Hernandez
Teruhisa Hochin
Anne Hoffmann
Zhengrui Jiang
Zoubida Kedad
Maurice van Keulen
Vijay Khatri
Henry Kim
Stephen Kimani
Subodha Kumar
Juliano P. Lage
Stephan Lechner
Sang-Ho Lee
Maurizio Lenzerini
Jiuyong Li
Xue Li
Yun Lin

Chengfei Liu
Zhenyu Liu
Federica Mandreoli
Renata de Matos Galante
Raimundas Matulevicius
Ibrahim Mescioglu
Gillian Miller
Ralf Muhlberger
Jeffrey Parsons
Vanessa de Paula Braganholo
Vicente Pelechano
Günter Preuner
Shazia Sadiq
Jennifer Sampson
Giuseppe Santucci
Monica Scannapieco
Isamu Shioya
Masataro Shiroiwa
Anastasiya Sotnykova
Darijus Strasunskas
Markus Stumptner
Hong Su
Yong Tan
Philippe Thiran
Takashi Tomii
Arvind Tripathi
Karthikeyan Umapathy
Petko Valtchev
Yannis Velegrakis
Csaba Veres
Fusheng Wang
Melanie Weis
Lingling Yan
Liang-Huai Yang
Li Xu
Jeffrey Xu Yu
Yijun Yu
Zhongju Zhang
Huimin Zhao

Tutorials

Object-Process Methodology and Its Application to the Visual Semantic Web
Dov Dori, Technion, Israel and MIT, USA

Data Modeling Using XML
Murali Mani, UCLA, USA
Antonio Badia, University of Louisville, USA

Understanding Metamodeling
Brian Henderson-Sellers, Sydney University of Technology, Australia

Data Analytics for Customer Relationship Management
Jaideep Srivastava, University of Minnesota, USA

Workshops

eCOMO 2003
4th International Workshop on Conceptual Modeling Approaches for E-Business
Co-chairs: Heinrich C. Mayr, University of Klagenfurt, Austria
Willem-Jan van den Heuvel, Tilburg University, The Netherlands

IWCMQ 2003
International Workshop on Conceptual Modeling Quality
Co-chairs: Marcela Género, University of Castilla-La Mancha, Spain
Jim Nelson, Ohio State University, USA
Geert Poels, Ghent University, Belgium

AOIS 2003
5th International Workshop on Agent-Oriented Information Systems
Co-chairs: Paolo Giorgini, University of Trento, Italy
Brian Henderson-Sellers, University of Technology, Sydney

XSDM 2003
International Workshop on XML Schema and Data Management
Chair: Sanjay K. Madria, University of Missouri-Rolla, USA

See LNCS vol. 2814 for the workshop proceedings.

Table of Contents

Metamodeling and Methodology

Views and XQuery Approaches

Web Application Modeling and Development

Requirements and Evolution

Data Warehousing and OLAP

Conceptual Modeling Foundations

Data Mining

Innovative Approaches to Conceptual Modeling

Queries

Schema and Ontology Integration

Industrial Abstracts

Semantic Web Application Modeling

Erich Neuhold

Fraunhofer Institute for Integrated Publication and Information Systems (IPSI)
Darmstadt, Germany
neuhold@ipsi.fhg.de

Abstract. The Semantic Web and the Web service paradigm are currently the most important trends on the way to the next generation of the Web. They promise new opportunities for content and service provision, enabling manifold and flexible new applications and improved support for individual and cooperative tasks. The use of the Web service paradigm in the development of Web applications, that typically couple application databases with user dialogs, is quite obvious. The development of Web applications that can be operated effectively in the Semantic Web context (*Semantic Web Applications*), however, imposes some challenges. Two main challenges towards extended (conceptual) modeling support are addressed in this talk:

1. In the Semantic Web, Web applications move from a purely human user community towards a mixed user community consisting of humans as well as of software agents; this results into new requirements towards models for Web applications' *user* interfaces;

2. Automatic interpretation of content, one of the main building blocks of the Semantic Web, is based on interlinking local models with globally defined interpretation schemes like vocabularies and ontologies; this has to be reflected by the conceptual application domain models of Semantic Web Applications.

Conceptual Modeling for Web applications, thus, has to be revisited in the context of the new Web trends looking for adequate *Semantic Web Application Models*.

In Web applications dialog-oriented (in most cases form-based) user interface models are state-of-the art for the interaction with users. The requirement of representing interaction with humans as well as with software agents is best met by a user interface model that describes the dialogs with the system on a conceptual level that can be dynamically translated into a (user) interface language adequate for the respective "user" (human or agent). The upcoming Web standard XForms for the next generation of form-based user interfaces is a good example of such a conceptual user interface model. For the linking of globally defined concepts with local domain model concepts one of the most popular models in the context of the Semantic Web is provided by the Resource Description Framework (RDF). The systematic integration of Uniform Resource Identifiers (URIs) into the model facilitates references to vocabularies and ontologies defined e.g. as RDF Schema or OWL ontology. However, for using RDF in Web applications a coupling between these "semantic" data models and the more traditional data models underlying the application data is necessary.

I.-Y. Song et al. (Eds.): ER 2003, LNCS 2813, pp. 1–2, 2003.

In addition to the aforementioned requirements, models, and approaches, the talk discusses a framework for the development of semantic-enabled Web applications designed at Fraunhofer IPSI. This approach combines semi-automatically extracted RDF-based domain models with an XForms-based conceptual user interface model, and application logic encoded in Web services. Within a corresponding application development framework, so-called Web application authoring tools support general model management, definition and management of domain model views and the definition and automatic run-time operazionalization of flexible couplings between the domain model, conceptual UI model, and application logic, i.e. between the components of the semantic web application model.

Oh, so That Is What You Meant! The Interplay of Data Quality and Data Semantics

Stuart Madnick

Massachusetts Institute of Technology
Sloan School of Management and School of Engineering
Cambridge, MA 02139
smadnick@mit.edu

Abstract. Data quality issues have taken on increasing importance in recent years. In our research, we have discovered that many "data quality" problems are actually "data misinterpretation" problems – that is, problems with data semantics. In this paper, we first illustrate some examples of these problems and then introduce a particular semantic problem that we call "corporate householding." We stress the importance of "context" to get the appropriate answer for each task. Then we propose an approach to handle these tasks using extensions to the COntext INterchange (COIN) technology for knowledge storage and knowledge processing.

Keywords: Data Quality, Data Semantics, Corporate Householding, COntext INterchange, Knowledge Management.

1 Introduction

Data quality issues have taken on increasing importance in recent years. In our research, we have discovered that many "data quality" problems are actually "data misinterpretation" problems – that is, problems with data semantics. To illustrate how complex this can become, consider Figure 1. This data summarizes the P/E ratio for Daimler-Benz obtained from four different financial information sources – all obtained on the same day within minutes of each other. Note that the four sources gave radically different values for P/E ratio.

Source	P/E Ratio
ABC	11.6
Bloomberg	5.57
DBC	19.19
MarketGuide	7.46

Fig. 1. Key Financials for Daimler-Benz

The obvious questions to ask are: "Which source is correct?" and "Why are the other sources wrong – i.e., of bad data quality?" The possibly surprising answer is: they are all correct!

The issue is, what do you really mean by "P/E ratio". Some of these sites even provide a glossary which gives a definition of such terms and they are very concise in

I.-Y. Song et al. (Eds.): ER 2003, LNCS 2813, pp. 3–13, 2003.

saying something like "P/E ratio" is "the current stock price divided by the earnings". As it turns out, this does not really help us to explain the differences. The answer lies in the multiple interpretations and uses of the term "P/E ratio" in financial circles. It is for the entire year for some sources but for one source it is only for the last quarter. Even when it is for a full year, is it:

- the last four quarters?
- the last calendar year?
- the last fiscal year? or
- the last three historical quarters and the estimated current quarter (a popular usage)?

This can have serious consequences. Consider a financial trader that used DBC to get P/E ratio information yesterday and got 19.19. Today he used Bloomberg and got 5.57 (low P/E's usually indicate good bargains) – thinking that something wonderful had happened be might decide to buy many shares of Daimler-Benz today. In fact, nothing had actually changed, except for changing the source that he used. It would be natural for this trader (after possibly losing significant money due to this decision) to feel that he had encountered a data quality problem. We would argue that what appeared to be a data quality problem is actually a data misinterpretation problem.

To illustrate the significance of this issue, consider the vignettes displayed in Figures 2(a) and 2(b). In the case of Figure 2(a), the emissaries of the Austrian and Russian emperors thought that they had agreed on the battle being October 20th. What they had not agreed upon was <u>which</u> October 20th! This kind of semantic misunderstandings do not only resided hundred of years in the past, consider Figure 2(b) where a similar mishap also had dramatic consequences for the Mars Orbiter satellite.

(a) The 1805 Overture

> In 1805, the Austrian and Russian Emperors agreed to join forces against Napoleon. The Russians promised that their forces would be in the field in Bavaria by **Oct. 20**. The Austrian staff planned its campaign based on that date in the **Gregorian calendar**. Russia, however, still used the ancient **Julian calendar**, which lagged 10 days behind. The calendar difference allowed Napoleon to surround Austrian General Mack's army at Ulm and force its surrender on Oct. 21, well before the Russian forces could reach him, ultimately setting the stage for Austerlitz.
>
> Source: David Chandler, *The Campaigns of Napoleon*, New York: MacMillan 1966, pg. 390.

(b) The 1999 Overture

> **Unit-of-Measure mixup tied to loss of $125 Million Mars Orbiter**
>
> "NASA's Mars Climate Orbiter was lost because engineers did not make a simple conversion from English units to metric, an embarrassing lapse that sent the $125 million craft off course ... The navigators [JPL] **assumed metric units** of force per second, or newtons. In fact, the numbers **were in pounds** of force per second as supplied by Lockheed Martin [the contractor]."
>
> Source: Kathy Sawyer, *Boston Globe*, October 1, 1999, pg. 1.

Fig. 2. Examples of consequences of misunderstood context

It should be apparent from these examples, and many more, that such "data quality" problems can have significant consequences. But in all these cases, the data source did not make any "error," the data that it provided was exactly the data that it intended to provide – it just did not have the meaning that the receiver expected.

Before going any further, it should be noted that if all sources and all receivers of data always had the exact same meanings, this problem would not occur. This is a desirable goal – one frequently sought through standardization efforts But these standardization are frequent unsuccessful for many reasons[1]. Consider Figure 3; is it a picture of an old lady or a young lady? The point here is that some will see it one way, some will see it the other way, and most be able to see both images – but only one at a time[2]. This is the situation that we often face in real life. There is often no "right" answer and different people will continue to see things in different ways. Merely saying that everyone should see it the same way does not change the reality that multiple different legitimate, and often essential, views exist.

Fig. 3. Old woman or young woman?

2 Corporate Householding

In our research we have studied many of examples of these "data quality" problems caused due to differences in data semantics. In this section we will introduce an interesting category of these problems, which we call the "corporate householding problem."

The rapidly changing business environment has witnessed widespread and rapid changes in corporate structure and corporate relationships. Regulations, deregulations, acquisitions, consolidations, mergers, spin-offs, strategic alliances, partnerships, joint ventures, new regional headquarters, new branches, bankruptcies, franchises … all these make understanding corporate relationships an intimidating job. Moreover, the same two corporation entities may relate to each other very differently when marketing is concerned than when auditing is concerned. That is, interpreting corporate structure and corporate relationships depends on the task at hand.

Lets us consider some typical, simple, but important questions that an organization, such as IBM or MIT, might have about their relationships:

[MIT]: "How much did we buy from IBM this year?"
[IBM]: "How much did we sell to MIT this year?"

---

[1] A full discussion of all the difficulties with standardization is beyond the scope of this paper. It is worth noting that the "Treaty of the Meter" committing the U.S. government to go metric was initially signed in 1875.

[2] If you are unable to see both, email me and I will send clues for seeing each.

The first question frequently arises in the Procurement and Purchasing departments of many companies, as well as at more strategic levels. The second question frequently arises in the Marketing departments of many companies and is often related to Customer Relationship Management (CRM) efforts, also at more strategic levels. Logically, one might expect that the answers to these two questions would be the same – but frequently they are not, furthermore one often gets multiple different answers even within each company.

These types of questions are not limited to manufacturers of physical goods, a financial services company, such as Merrill Lynch, might ask:

> [Merrill Lynch]: "How much have we loaned to IBM?"
> [IBM]: "How much do we owe Merrill Lynch?"

On the surface, these questions are likely to sound like both important and simple questions to be able to answer. In reality, there are many reasons why they are difficult and have multiple differing answers, as discussed in the next section.

2.1 A Typology of Corporate Householding Problems

At least three types of challenges must be overcome to answer questions such as the ones illustrated above: (a) identical entity instance identification, (b) entity aggregation, and (c) transparency of inter-entity relationships. These challenges provide a typology for understanding the Corporate Householding issues, as illustrated in Figure 4 and explained below.

Identical entity instance identification. In general, there are rarely complete unambiguous universal identifiers for either people or companies. Two names may refer to the same physical entity even though they were not intended to create confusions in the beginning. For example, the names "James Jones", "J. Jones", and "Jim Jones" might appear in different databases, but actually be referring to the same person. Although identifiers such as Social Security numbers are helpful, they might not always be available or feasible. For example, what is the SS# of a French citizen who works in one of IBM's European divisions?

The same problems exist for companies. As shown in Figure 4(a), the names "MIT", "Mass Inst of Tech", "Massachusetts Institute of Technology", and many other variations might all be used to refer to the exact same entity. They are different simply because the users of these names choose to do so. Thus, we need to be able to identify the same entity correctly and efficiently when naming confusion happens. We refer to this problem as *Identical Entity Instance Identification* [7]. That is, the same identical entity might appear as multiple instances (i.e., different forms) – but it is still the same entity.

Entity aggregation. Even after we have determined that "MIT", "Mass Inst of Tech", "Massachusetts Institute of Technology" all refer to the same entity, we need to determine what exactly is that entity? That is, what other unique entities are to be included or aggregated into the intended definition of "MIT." For example, the MIT Lincoln Lab, according to its home page, is "the Federally Funded Research and Development Center of the Massachusetts Institute of Technology." It is located in Lexington and physically separated from the main campus of MIT, sometimes refer to

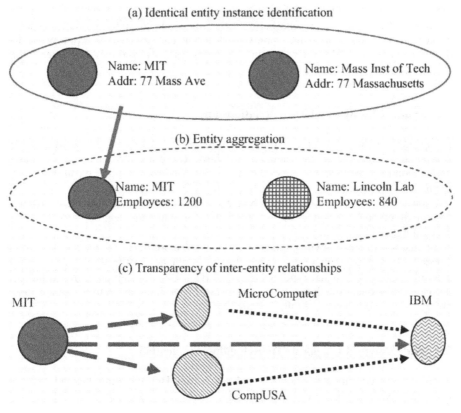

(a) Identical entity instance identification

Name: MIT
Addr: 77 Mass Ave

Name: Mass Inst of Tech
Addr: 77 Massachusetts

(b) Entity aggregation

Name: MIT
Employees: 1200

Name: Lincoln Lab
Employees: 840

(c) Transparency of inter-entity relationships

MIT

MicroComputer

IBM

CompUSA

Fig. 4. Typology for Corporate Householding

as the "on-campus MIT," which is in Cambridge. Lincoln Lab has a budget of about $500 million, which is about equal to the rest of MIT.

Problem arises when people ask questions such as "How many employees does MIT have?", "How much was MIT's budget last year?", or our original question – for IBM: "How much did we sell to MIT this year?" In the case illustrated in Figure 4(b), should the Lincoln Lab employees, budget, or sales be included in the "MIT" calculation and in which cases they should not be? Under some circumstances, the MIT Lincoln Lab number should be included whereas in other circumstances they should not be. We refer to these differing circumstances as *contexts*. To know which case applies under each category of circumstances, we must know the context. We refer to this type of problem as *Entity Aggregation*.

Transparency of inter-entity relationships. A relationship between entities might involve multiple layers. Under what circumstances should these layers be collapsed? Let us consider our original questions again: [MIT] "How much did we buy from IBM this year?" and [IBM]: "How much did we sell to MIT this year?" As illustrated in Figure 4(c), MIT buys computers from IBM both directly and through local computer stores (e.g., MicroCenter and CompUSA). This is the classic case where a seller sells its products to a broker (and maybe directly also), and then the broker sells them to the ultimate buyer. Whether we are interested in the interface between the seller and the broker or the one between the seller and the ultimate buyer (via the broker) also depends upon the context – different answers will be appropriate for different contexts. We refer to this problem as *Transparency of Inter-Entity Relationships*.

2.2 Types of Entities and Their Relationships

In considering the issue of entity aggregation, we need to consider what types of "corporate" entities exist and their relationships. There are obvious examples based on location (e.g., *branches*), scope (e.g., *divisions*), and ownership (e.g., *subsidiaries*). Even these may have variations, such as wholly-owned subsidiaries compared with fractional ownership – sometimes 66%, 51%, and 50% ownerships have different special significance regarding entity aggregation in matters of legal control, taxation, accounting, and bankruptcy.

In addition to these obvious types of entities, there are many others that need to be considered, such as *joint ventures*, which also might be fractional. Referring to our example in Figure 4, what type of entity is MIT's Lincoln Lab and how would one define its relationship with the other parts of MIT? Defining the "atoms" of corporate entities is an important part of this research effort.

2.3 Wide Range of Corporate Householding Applications

There is a wide range of examples of Corporate Householding beyond the few examples used to illustrate the framework above. For example, if an agent is to determine a quote for business owner protection insurance for IBM, he must know how many employees IBM has [5]. To do so, he has to figure out what the rules are to decide what entities are part of IBM as far as business owner protection insurance is concerned. Does Lotus Development Corporation, a wholly-owned subsidiary of IBM, fall under the IBM umbrella? Similarly, if MIT buys a company-wide license for a piece of software, such as IBM's Lotus Notes or Microsoft's Office, does that automatically include Lincoln Lab – or not?

The concerns regarding Corporate Householding play an important role in both purchasing, and marketing activities. We have encountered many other specialized applications in discussing these matters with executives. For example, especially in consulting or auditing practices, you might agree with a client to not also do business with one of its competitors – but how is the "client" defined and how are its "competitors" defined?

3 Role of Context

We have used the term "context" earlier. To put this issue in perspective, consider a traditional family household. As family structures evolve, such as the increasing number of single families, families with no children, or husband and wife with different last name, it becomes more difficult to define and identify "household" [4].

For example, are grandparents or visiting cousins living at same address to be considered part of the same household? Are two unmarried people living together a household? The important point to note is that there is no single "right" answer; the answer depends upon the intended purpose of the question – which is what we mean by the context.

Similarly, a corporate household would also be different depending on different contexts such as a financial perspective, legal perspective, and the reporting structure. Identifying those contexts and representing the right structure for the right task is critical and can provide important competitive advantage.

Furthermore, it is important to note that corporate householding often changes over time; thus, the context also changes over time. For example, at one point Lotus Development Corporation was a separate corporation from IBM. When doing a historical comparison of growth or decline in "number of employees" of IBM, should current Lotus employees be counted in a total as of today? Should the Lotus employees in 1990, when it was a separate corporation, be added with the IBM employees of 1990 to make a meaningful comparison? Thus, temporal context often must be considered.

4   Using Context Interchange (COIN) Technology for Storage and Processing of Corporate Householding Knowledge

COntext INterchange (COIN) [3] is a knowledge-based mediation technology that enables meaningful use of heterogeneous databases where there are semantic differences. For example, attributes that represent money, such as "price", may be expressed in "US dollars" in a USA database but in "Chinese RMB" in a Chinese database. Though the two attributes may have the same name, the semantic conflict has to be addressed before a correct query result involving the attributes can be obtained (e.g., "which price is less expensive?"). We refer to these semantic meanings as being the "context" of each source or *source context*. Furthermore, different users, also called "receivers," may have different contexts or *receiver contexts* (e.g., I might want the answer in "Euros"). There are many parallels between the traditional COIN applications and the needs of Corporate Housekeeping where each source has its own Corporation Housekeeping context (e.g., "in this database, data on IBM includes all subsidiaries, such as Lotus") and each user's query has a context (e.g., "employee count for liability insurance purposes.")

The overall COIN project [3, 9, 10] includes not only the mediation infrastructure and services, but also wrapping technology and middleware services for accessing the source information and facilitating the integration of the mediated results into end-users applications. The wrappers are physical and logical gateways providing a uniform access to the disparate sources over the network [3].

The set of Context Mediation Services comprises a Context Mediator, a Query Optimizer, and a Query Executioner. The Context Mediator is in charge of the identification and resolution of potential semantic conflicts induced by a query. This automatic detection and reconciliation of conflicts present in different information sources is made possible by general knowledge of the underlying application domain, as well as informational content and implicit assumptions associated to the receivers and sources. These bodies of declarative knowledge are represented in the form of a domain model, a set of elevation axioms, and a set of context theories respectively.

The result of the mediation is a mediated query. To retrieve the data from the disparate information sources, the mediated query is then transformed into a query execution plan, which is optimized, taking into account the topology of the network of sources and their capabilities. The plan is then executed to retrieve the data from the various sources; results are composed as a message, and sent to the receiver.

The COIN approach allows queries to the sources to be mediated, i.e., semantic conflicts to be identified and solved by a context mediator through comparison of contexts associated with the sources and receivers concerned by the queries. It only requires the minimum adoption of a common Domain Model, which defines the domain of discourse of the application.

The knowledge needed for integration is formally modeled in a COIN framework [3] as depicted in Figure 5. The COIN framework is a mathematical structure offering a sound foundation for the realization of the Context Interchange strategy. The COIN framework comprises a data model and a language, called COINL, of the Frame-Logic (F-Logic) family. The framework is used to define the different elements needed to implement the strategy in a given application:

- The Domain Model is a collection of rich types (semantic types) defining the domain of discourse for the integration strategy (e.g., "Length");
- Elevation Axioms for each source identify the semantic objects (instances of semantic types) corresponding to source data elements and define integrity constraints specifying general properties of the sources;
- Context Definitions define the different interpretations of the semantic objects in the different sources or from a receiver's point of view (e.g., "Length" might be expressed in "Feet" or "Meters").

Finally, there is a conversion library which provides conversion functions for each modifier to define the resolution of potential conflicts. The conversion functions can be defined in COINL or can use external services or external procedures. The relevant conversion functions are gathered and composed during mediation to resolve the conflicts. No global or exhaustive pair-wise definition of the conflict resolution procedures is needed.

Both the query to be mediated and the COINL program are combined into a definite logic program (a set of Horn clauses) where the translation of the query is a goal. The mediation is performed by an abductive procedure which infers from the query and the COINL programs a reformulation of the initial query in the terms of the component sources. The abductive procedure makes use of the integrity constraints in a constraint propagation phase which has the effect of a semantic query optimization. For instance, logically inconsistent rewritten queries are rejected, rewritten queries containing redundant information are simplified, and rewritten queries are augmented with auxiliary information. The procedure itself is inspired by the Abductive Logic Programming framework and can be qualified as an abduction procedure. One of the main advantages of the abductive logic programming framework is the simplicity in which it can be used to formally combine and to implement features of query processing, semantic query optimization and constraint programming.

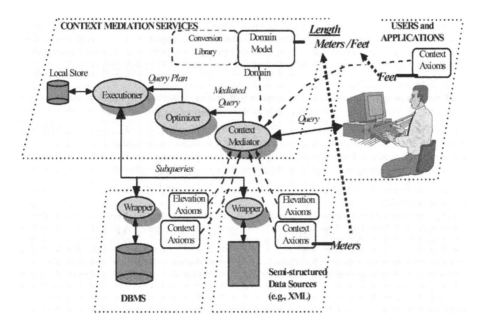

Fig. 5. The Architecture of the Context Interchange System

COIN was designed originally to address database queries in the face of disparate semantics in different sources. We have recently adapted the COIN system so that it can be applied to corporate householding, which – in a certain sense – is to determine which attributes in different databases should be united or viewed as the same. In this implementation, the Domain Model stores general corporate householding knowledge. It decides how the relationships between entity instances should be decided when a certain task is concerned. The Elevation Axioms and Context Axioms describe the context associated with each specific database and specific application. The Context Mediator manages the interactions between Domain Model, Elevation Axioms, and Context Axioms. It is the interactions between the three that determine how the data stored in a database can be interpreted in terms of corporate household.

Such an implementation makes it much easier to answer questions such as "What is IBM's total global asset worth for purposes of bankruptcy insurance?", which involves both corporate householding knowledge processing and data semantics knowledge processing.

5   Conclusions and Future Research

We are in the midst of exciting times – the opportunities to access and integrate diverse information sources, most especially the enormous number of sources provided over the web, are incredible but the challenges are considerable. It is sometimes said that we now have "more and more information that we know less and less about." This can lead to serious "data quality" problems caused due to improperly understood or used data semantics. The effective use of semantic metadata and context knowledge processing is needed to enable us to overcome the challenges described in this paper and more fully realize the opportunities. A particularly interesting aspect of the context mediation approach described is the use of context metadata to describe the <u>expectations of the receiver</u> as well as the <u>semantics assumed by the sources</u>.

In this paper, we present a framework for understanding corporate householding problems. We then proposed that much of the burden of corporate householding could be reduced through the use of a corporate householding engine. We proposed an integrated method to accomplish the goal using COntext INterchange (COIN) to store and apply the captured knowledge. COIN builds on previous research, and is intended to maximally automate corporate householding with specially designed software modular – once the underlying source and receiver corporate household knowledge has been acquired.

Our future research plans include the following. First, we will continue to collect field data to determine the types of corporate householding knowledge needed. Second, we will explore the role of COIN in corporate householding. We plan to continue to extend our COIN-based system to further facilitate the process of capturing, storing, maintaining, and applying the corporate householding knowledge.

Acknowledgements. Work reported herein has been supported, in part, by Banco Santander Central Hispano, Citibank, Defense Advanced Research Projects Agency (DARPA), D & B, Fleet Bank, FirstLogic, Merrill Lynch, MITRE Corp., MIT Total Data Quality Management (TDQM) Program, PricewaterhouseCoopers, Singapore-MIT Alliance (SMA), Suruga Bank, and USAF/Rome Laboratory. We also wish to thank the participants of the MIT Summer Data Quality course (15.56s) and the MIT workshops on corporate householding for their helpful feedback and comments on the ideas that lead to the current paper. Information about the Context Interchange project can be obtained at http://context2.mit.edu.

References

[1]   Brown, J.S. and P. Duguid, Organizational learning and communities of practice: toward a unified view of working, learning, and innovation. Organization Science, 1991. 2(1): p. 40–57.

[2]   Constant, D., L. Sproull, and S. Kiesler, The kindness of strangers: The usefulness of electronic weak ties for technical advice. Organizational Science, 1996. 7(2): p. 119–135.

[3]   Goh, C.H., et al., Context Interchange: New Features and Formalisms for the Intelligent Integration of Information. ACM Transactions on Information Systems, 1999. 17(3): p. 270–293.

[4]   Kotler, P., Marketing Management: Analysis, Planning, Implementation, and Control. 9th ed. 1997: Prentice Hall.

[5]   Madnick, S., et al. Corporate Household Data: Research Directions. in AMCIS 2001. 2001. Boston, Massachusetts.

[6]   Madnick, S., et al. Improving the Quality of Corporate Household Data: Current Practices and Research Directions. in Sixth International Conference on Information Quality. 2001. Cambridge, MA.

[7] Madnick, S. and R. Wang, The Inter-Database Instance Identification Problem in Integrating Autonomous Systems. in Fifth International Data Engineering Conference February 1989. Los Angeles, CA.
[8] Nonaka, I., A Dynamic Theory of Organizational Knowledge Creation. Organization Science, 1994. 5(1): p. 14–37.
[9] Siegel, M. and Madnick, S. Context Interchange: Sharing the Meaning of Data. SIGMOD RECORD, Vol. 20, No. 4, December 1991, p. 77–78.
[10] Siegel, M. and Madnick, S. (1991). A metadata approach to solving semantic conflicts. in Proc of the 17th International Conference on Very Large Data Bases, 1991, pp. 133–145.

Enterprise Information Integration – XML to the Rescue!

Michael J. Carey

BEA Systems, Inc.
2315 North First Street
San Jose, CA 95131
mcarey@bea.com

Abstract. The database field has been struggling with the data integration problem since the early 1980's. We've named and renamed the problem – heterogeneous distributed databases, multi-databases, federated databases, mediator systems, and now enterprise information integration systems – but we haven't actually solved the problem. Along the way, we've tried data model after data model – functional, relational, object-oriented, logical, semi-structured, you name it, we've tried it – and query language after query language to go with them – but we still haven't solved the problem. A number of startups have died trying, and no major software vendor has managed to hit a home run in this area. What's going on? Is the problem too hard? Should we just declare it impossible and give up?

In this talk, I'll explain why I believe now would be exactly the wrong time to give up. After a brief look at history, I'll make the case that we are finally on the verge of finding a real solution to this problem. I'll define the enterprise information integration problem as I see it and then explain how the XML and Web Services revolutions that are in progress – based on SOAP, WSDL, XML Schema, XQuery, and so on – relate to the problem and its solution. I'll describe the path that we are on at BEA to deliver a solution, and finally I'll leave the audience with my thoughts on some open problems where the database field, especially the "modeling crowd", can contribute.

I.-Y. Song et al. (Eds.): ER 2003, LNCS 2813, p. 14, 2003.
© Springer-Verlag Berlin Heidelberg 2003

Workflow Using AUML and Agents

James J. Odell

James Odell Associates,
3646 West Huron River Drive, Ann Arbor
MI 48103-9489 USA
email@jamesodell.com
http://www.jamesodell.com

Introduction

Workflow provides a way to standardize processes and processing. For those organizations that have predefined ways of performing activities, workflow is a useful approach. Currently most workflow systems, however, employ a centralized form of coordination. For small systems, such an approach is possible; for large systems, centralized control would quickly paralyze the organization. One way to enable scalability of workflow systems is by using a distributed mechanism such as agents. This presentation describes how to develop agent-based workflow systems using UML – for analysis, design, and execution. In other words, it describes a model-driven approach (MDA) for distributed workflow.

The Traditional Approach

Traditionally, most IT systems employ a centralized approach. Database transactions were controlled by code that invoked the database operations in a careful, premeditated manner. In OO, behavior is invoked by sending messages to objects. In other words, objects are usually implemented as passive processors waiting to by awakened by something that is supposed to know when to send the appropriate request.

A centralized form of process control is very useful for certain kinds of problems. For example, organizing a D-Day style surprise attack would be close to impossible to accomplish any other way. In organizations whose business is fairly predictable and orderly, top-down control of workflow is an efficient technique. Software structures that exhibit similar characteristics can also use an *uber*-controller to manage the way applications process their work. However, for processing systems that must be adaptable and highly scalable, central control can be more of a liability than an asset. Furthermore, when a control node fails, entire systems can be brought to their knees.

An Agent-Based Approach

Multiagent systems operate as lots of distributed processing entities that can coordinate their efforts in some way. An increasingly popular application of agents is

I.-Y. Song et al. (Eds.): ER 2003, LNCS 2813, pp. 15–16, 2003.
© Springer-Verlag Berlin Heidelberg 2003

in scheduling discrete manufacturing systems. Currently, I am focusing on architectures like AARIA [1, 2] that assign agents to manufacturing entities (most prominently, orders, parts, and resources) rather than functions or clusters of tasks. A common feature of this approach is financial negotiation between orders moving through the plant and the resources that they must visit in order to be processed. Orders are given a budget to "get themselves manufactured" when they are released into the plant, and operate as cost centers. They ask for processing bids from the resources able to provide the processes they need, and accept bids from the least expensive resources that meet their requirements. Resources are profit centers, seeking to stay busy while maximizing the fees they earn from the orders they process. Management prioritizes orders by varying the budgets they are given. Orders with high budgets can outbid other orders for access to scarce resources.

In such an architecture, resources maintain a record of the tasks they have currently accepted in order to make intelligent bids for new work. Van Parunak [3] calls this record the resource's "dance card" in his DESK (Density-based Emergent Scheduling Kernel) approach [4]. The dance card should satisfy several requirements.

- It should permit the resource to add tasks incrementally, rather than requiring that all tasks be presented concurrently at the start of the day. Incremental arrival is more common in the kinds of industrial applications to which DESK is likely to be applied than the "all at once" framework assumed by many theoretical scheduling studies.
- It should enable the resource to estimate its load as a function of time, so that it can offer preferential pricing to tasks that will fit in periods where it might be underutilized, and charge a premium for its services during busy periods.
- It should permit the resource to adjust the precise timing of tasks already scheduled as new opportunities arise, and to offer preferential price treatment to tasks that provide it the latitude for such adjustment.
- In support of the two previous requirements, it should support a continuous model of time. Work to date in market-based scheduling defines the commodities being traded as fixed time slots.

Based on the initial experience with this approach, it can be also used to support workflow in general – within a distributed environment that requires a service-oriented architecture. Furthermore UML can be employed to specify such an approach.

References

[1]   A. D. Baker, H. V. D. Parunak, and K. Erol. Agents and the Internet: Infrastructure for Mass Customization. *IEEE Internet Computing*, 3(5 (September–October)):62–69, 1999.

[2]   H. V. D. Parunak, A. D. Baker, and S. J. Clark. The AARIA Agent Architecture: From Manufacturing Requirements to Agent-Based System Design. *Integrated Computer-Aided Engineering*, Forthcoming, 1999. Available at http://www.erim.org/~van/icaa98.pdf.

[3]   S. J. Clark and H. V. D. Parunak. Density-Based Emergent Scheduling System. USA Patent # 5,953,229, Environmental Research Institute of Michigan, 1999.

[4]   H.V.D. Parunak, J. Sauter, J. Goic, J. Schneider, N.S. Merchawi. *Temporal Pheromones for Agent-Based Scheduling*. Report, Altarum, 1999.

Statistical Analysis as Methodological Framework for Data(base) Integration*

Evguenia Altareva and Stefan Conrad

Institute of Computer Science – Database Systems
Heinrich–Heine–University Düsseldorf
D–40225 Düsseldorf, Germany
{altareva,conrad}@cs.uni-duesseldorf.de

Abstract. We propose a methodological framework for building a statistical integration model for heterogeneous data sources.
We apply the latent class analysis, a well-established statistical method, to investigate the relationships between entities in data sources as relationships among dependent variables, with the purpose of discovering the latent factors that affect them. The latent factors are associated with the real world entities which are unobservable in the sense that we do not know the real world class memberships, but only the stored data.
The approach provides the evaluation of uncertainties which aggregate in the integration process. The key parameter evaluated by the method is the probability of the real world class membership. Its value varies depending on the selection criteria applied in the pre-integration stages and in the subsequent integration steps. By adjusting selection criteria and the integration strategies the proposed framework allows to improve data quality by optimizing the integration process.

1 Introduction

The major aim of the DIAsDEM project[1] is the integration of heterogeneous data sources, including structured data from relational databases and semi-structured data. Such an integration is a vital necessity for many real life applications, in particular when information sources containing semantically related data and designed for different purposes need to be used as one, although they have different data models, data manipulating languages and, in consequence, have no common database management system.

The whole integration process consists of many subsequent integration steps. Nowadays there exist many methods allowing to solve each of the specific problems representing these steps. But a prerequisite of most of these methods is "perfect" and exact input knowledge which in practice is a rare case. More often the input is supported with certain confidence level. Consequent application

---

* Part of this work has been supported by the German Science Foundation DFG (grant no. CO 207/13-1).

[1] project DIAsDEM: Data Integration for Legacy Systems and Semi-Structured Documents Employing Data Mining Techniques

I.-Y. Song et al. (Eds.): ER 2003, LNCS 2813, pp. 17–30, 2003.

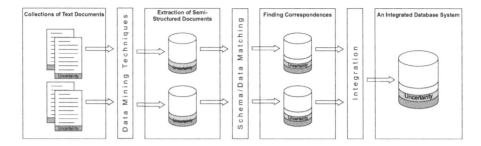

Fig. 1. The integration process

of these methods will distort the final result more and more. That is why the conceptual model for the evaluation of the whole integration process result is needed.

In this paper we consider the process of integration represented by consequently employing various techniques in different stages of integration, as shown in figure 1.

In real life, sources to be integrated are often not fully structured and their semantics is not completely known, for instance sources containing text documents, XML documents, etc. In the first integration step their structures need to be derived. At this step various data mining techniques could be employed in order to extract structural properties, functional dependencies and class membership in each data source. The next step is to find correspondences between two input sources. In this step we can use schema matching techniques to determine the correspondences on the schema level (structural correspondences). Then one has to define the correspondences between objects of two data sources. For this purpose numerous methods from the area of data cleaning could be used. Finally, after all the information about each source and correspondences between the sources is collected, the schema integration and then data integration can be carried out.

In general the input data sources already contain uncertain information. The uncertainty increases with every integration step since every method we apply contributes additional uncertainty. These uncertainties can basically be expressed in terms of probability, support, confidence level, etc. The types of uncertainty can be classified with respect to their origins in the integration process as follows (cf. [1]):

◊ uncertainty about the exact structure of data objects,
◊ uncertainty concerning the assignment of data objects to classes,
◊ uncertainty concerning the extensional correspondence between classes from two data sources.

The uncertainty accumulated over all the stages of integration may affect the final result in a crucial and unpredictable way. In [2] we examine some problems caused by these uncertainties occurring in the integration process.

The purpose of this paper is to propose a conceptual model of applying statistical analysis to the integration task in order to take control over uncertainties and their propagation during the integration. In this paper we are not trying to detail the specific techniques which should be applied during the integration (schema matching, data cleaning, etc.) because statistical analysis is indifferent to the nature of these techniques.

The remainder of this paper is organized as follows. We discuss related work in section 2. Then in section 3 we consider the problem of setting up a statistical model for the task of integration. The basic principles of latent variable models will be described in section 4. In section 5 we illustrate the application of latent class analysis by means of a simple integration example. In section 6 we give a brief summary and outlook.

2   Related Work

A major part of the bibliography on the integration of heterogeneous data sources is devoted to the specific problems of the integration process such as schema integration, schema matching, data cleaning, etc.

In [7], [22], [25] various general techniques for *schema integration* are presented. These methods assume that the data to be integrated is exactly defined. A complete knowledge about objects class membership and about class correspondences is a significant requirement. For example, in [23] the authors propose an approach to schema integration that supports an incremental refinement of the integrated schema which is derived from extensional relationships. As a conclusion they emphasize the importance of considering precise extensional relationships as input for a correct and complete schema integration. Therefore, the application of these methods to data sources which contain a large fraction of uncertain information is problematic. In [24] a set of tools for supporting the schema integration process is sketched. The paper reports on an integrated approach to tool support of such important integration aspects as integrity rules, authorization policies and transactional processes.

Various methods of *schema matching* (e.g. MOMIS [5], LSD [8], [9], DIKE [20], Clio [19], [27]) have been developed. A very detailed classification of matching techniques is given in [21]. For example, the approach Cupid [18] combines linguistic and structural matching algorithms. It finds semantically similar schema elements and computes combinations of elements that appear together in a structure. The result of the schema matching procedure is the value of similarity between corresponding schema nodes. Therefore it cannot be considered as an exact input knowledge for a subsequent schema integration.

For finding similarities between objects from different data sources *data cleaning* techniques [10], [12], [17] should be applied. For instance, Record Linkage [11] compares the common object attributes using the selection rules which cannot be exactly derived from the data, but with a certain support.

In order to integrate non- or semi-structured data sources one should apply methods through which all information needed for the integration could be derived from these data sources. Typical examples are data mining methods ([6], [15]). For instance, in [26] a text archive consisting of several text documents is transformed using a markup technique into an archive of semi-structured XML documents. For this XML archive a probabilistic XML document type definition (DTD) is derived using data mining techniques.

On one hand, the heterogeneous data which in principle contains uncertain information can only be integrated after applying the above-mentioned methods. Therefore, the input for integration becomes even more uncertain. Furthermore the uncertainties interact with one another and accumulate over the integration process.

On the other hand, the existing integration techniques require exact input information about the input sources and about the correspondences between them.

Thus, the analysis of uncertainties and their propagation in the integration process is a new task. For this task statistical analysis can be employed. We see the numerous examples of application of statistical methods in the domain of knowledge discovery. For instance, the latent variable models, in particular factor analysis and principal component analysis, are successfully used in data mining for finding a structure and reducing dimensionality. For an overview and further references see [14].

In the integration domain the stated methods have not been employed yet. We see a challenge in developing a methodological framework which extends the application area of statistical methods to the integration domain.

3   Statistical Model of the Integration Task

We propose the analysis of the uncertainties and their propagation from one integration step to another using available statistical methods. Their application requires to build a statistical model of the integration task.

Generally, the integration of k data sources includes two major stages. At the first step we determine the correspondences of schema nodes of these data sources and build the integrated schema. At the next step the correspondences between the objects from corresponding schema nodes (class, subclass) are established. Thus, for each schema node we have a set of n objects and a knowledge (partly uncertain) about their class membership. This information could be presented as a table of the class membership of objects in each data source, shown in figure 2. We denote the class membership with the following values.

$$x_{i,j} = \begin{cases} 0 \text{ missing data} \\ 1 \text{ if object belongs to the class} \\ 2 \text{ if object does not belong to the class} \end{cases}$$

where subscript $i = 1, 2, \ldots, k$ refers to the data source, $j = 1, 2, \ldots, n$ is the object number.

A set of values $x_{i,j}$ forms the n-rows by k-columns $(n \times k)$ matrix X of class membership.

Data Sources

j \ i	1	2	...	k	
1	1	1	...	1	
2	1	1	...	1	I
⋮	⋮	⋮	⋮	⋮	
⋮	1	1	...	1	
⋮	2	1	...	1	
⋮	1	1	...	2	II
⋮	⋮	⋮	⋮	⋮	
⋮	1	2	...	1	
⋮	1	0	...	1	
⋮	0	1	...	0	III
⋮	⋮	⋮	⋮	⋮	
n	1	1	...	0	

Objects

Fig. 2. Class membership table

We do not assign a certain row to a certain object, but assume that the rows can be sorted in order to compose a clear structure of the table. We distinguish three different parts in the table, namely, the definite part (I) which includes the objects which are presented in each data source (equivalence), a so-called random part (II) which includes all the uncertainties, and a part (III) which includes missing data (disjoint).

The random part presents mistakes of two types, when the object belongs to the class but was defined as "2" and the object does not belong to the class being defined as "1". In ideal case, the random part should include the rows with the random combinations of "1" and "2", the rows with only "1" or only "2" are possible as well. Therefore, the random part cannot be mechanically separated from the other parts. A statistical method should be applied for this.

Thus this table is a collection of correct and random data. All three types of uncertainties described in [1] contribute to the values $x_{i,j}$.

The information we deal with has a discrete nature. Every real object is unique and cannot have a partial class membership. On contrary, the statistics does not make any difference between objects and considers a class membership of each object as a single measurement (or trial) of the random variable assigned to this class.

We construct the table based on the data obtained by various methods used in the integration process. In fact it is not possible to identify a certain object with a certain row. The table should be reconstructed using the integral parameters delivered by the applied techniques such as data mining, schema matching, data cleaning, etc.

The support of the object's class membership for each data source is provided by data mining techniques (in particular, classification techniques are well-suited candidates for this task cf. [6]). Therefore, the proportion of values "0", "1", "2" in every column of the class membership table is known.

Schema matching delivers the support of class correspondence. We use this information together with the information obtained by data mining and data cleaning to find the parts of the table which should be disjoint for every pair of data sources.

The value of integral parameter (for example, support of class membership) means that the corresponding column of the table contains a certain number of "1" and "2", but there is no information which row contains "1" and which row contains "2". Therefore, we can sort the values in every column in order to fit the value of the class correspondence support. This integral parameter is responsible for the relative number of combinations "1-2", "2-1", "1-1" and "2-2" for every two columns of the table.

This information may not be sufficient for the complete reconstruction of the class membership table, but this is not really needed for applying statistical methods.

In section 5 we describe how the statistical analysis evaluates various uncertainties. For this we consider a case when the first two columns of the table are assigned to two input data sources and the third column is reserved for the integrated database. The values in this column are of our choice, depending on the integration strategy for which the expert's decisions could be important. Therefore, there could be cases that objects belonging to the classes in the input data sources are not included into the integrated database and vice versa.

Below we describe the basic concepts of Latent Variable Models which we use for the statistical analysis.

4   Latent Variable Models

4.1   Principles of Latent Variable Models

Latent variable models provide an important tool for the analysis of multivariate data. They offer a conceptual framework within which many disparate methods can be unified and a base upon which new methods can be developed. Latent variable models include such methods as factor analysis, clustering and multidimensional scaling, latent class analysis, latent trait analysis, latent profile analysis, etc. [3], [4].

Latent variable models are based on the statistical model and are used to study the patterns of relationship among many dependent variables, with the goal of discovering something about the nature of the latent (unobservable) variables that affect them, even though those latent variables were not measured directly. The latent variables are called factors. Dependent variables used in Latent Variable Models are manifest variables which can be directly observed.

In section 3 we have described the class membership table where the dependent variables are associated with data sources. The values of these variables present the object's class membership. A latent variable corresponds to real world class membership. This membership is unobservable (in the sense that we only have the stored data at hand) and it does determine class membership in both input data sources and in an integrated database.

Generally, both latent and manifest variables could be metrical or categorical. Metrical variables have realized values in the set of real numbers and may be discrete or continuous. Categorical variables assign individuals to one of a set of categories.

The relevant method for the integration task is latent class analysis (LCA), since both latent and manifest variables are categorical.

A typical LCA model suggests answers to three major questions:

1. How many different factors are needed to explain the pattern of relationships among the variables?
2. How well do the hypothesized factors explain the observed data?
3. How much purely random or unique variance does each observed variable include?

Thus, LCA allows us to define which part of our sample is defined by the latent class and which part is a random part. This is equivalent to the decomposition of our sample matrix in two parts, where one part consists only of positive responses (defined by the latent class), and another, random part. There should not be any correlation between the variables for the random part. This is a restriction of the statistical method which is usually used as a measure of goodness for the model applied.

In the next section we present LCA model formally.

4.2   A Theoretical Framework

Mathematical models of LCA are well presented in the literature. Here we follow the definitions in [4].

A collection of categorical manifest variables will be distinguished by subscripts and written as a vector

$$x = (x_1,\ x_2,\ \ldots\ ,x_k)$$

where

$$x_i = \begin{cases} 1 \text{ for the positive outcome of the trial} \\ 2 \text{ for the negative outcome of the trial} \end{cases}$$

for $i = 1, 2, \ldots, k$. The outcome corresponding to the code "1" (positive) and to the code "2" (negative) is defined arbitrary.

Considering m latent classes and k dichotomous random variables (categories) the following notations should be introduced.

π_s – the unobserved probability of being in the sth latent class, $s = 1, 2, \ldots, m$;

p_i – observed proportion of sample points that respond positively to the ith category ($i = 1, 2, \ldots, k$);

p_{ij} – observed proportion of sample points that respond positively to both the ith and jth categories ($i \neq j$, $p_{ij} = p_{ji}$);

$p_{ij\ldots k}$ – observed proportion of sample points that respond positively to the ith, jth, ..., kth, categories ($i \neq j \neq \ldots \neq k$) where permutations of indices are excluded;

ν_{is} – the unobserved conditional probability that a sample point in the sth latent class is also in the ith observed category.

Then the latent class model can be presented as a set of equations:

$$1 = \sum_{s=1}^{m} \pi_s \tag{1}$$

$$p_i = \sum_{s=1}^{m} \pi_s \nu_{is} \tag{2}$$

$$p_{ij} = \sum_{s=1}^{m} \pi_s \nu_{is} \nu_{js} \quad (i, j = 1, 2, \cdots, k) \tag{3}$$

$$p_{ij\cdots k} = \sum_{s=1}^{m} \pi_s \nu_{is} \nu_{js} \cdots \nu_{ls} \quad (i, j, \cdots, l = 1, 2, \cdots, k) \tag{4}$$

where $i \neq j \neq \cdots \neq l$ and permuted subscripts do not appear. Equations (1) - (4) express observed probabilities in terms of unknown probabilities, and represent the general system of normal equations for a latent class model.

A necessary condition for identifiability is

$$\frac{2^k}{k+1} \geq m. \tag{5}$$

The input data for the analysis are the observable variables $p_i, p_{ij}, \ldots, p_{ij\ldots k}$.

5   Applying LCA to the Integration Task

Let us consider a simple case. We have two data sources to integrate and one integrated database. During the integration process we have employed various methods to extract structure information for each input source, to find correspondences between the sources, to reduce redundancy of the data, etc. All this

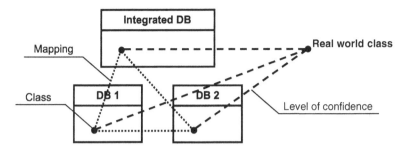

Fig. 3. The integration of two corresponding classes

information is potentially uncertain and we would like to evaluate the result of integration.

Figure 3 presents the single act of integration, the integration of two corresponding classes from two input data sources. Knowing the values of support for object's class membership and support for class correspondences we would like to evaluate how well both the input and the integrated classes correspond to the real world class (RWC). If we get an answer for every class to be integrated, then we can evaluate the whole integration process.

This task can be solved with the help of LCA in the following way.

Applying to our example we get the number of categories $k = 3$. The minimal number of latent classes $m = 2$ reserves for the objects only two possibilities: to be a member of RWC or not to be. According to the condition (5) this is the simplest case that could be considered in the LCA.

At these conditions the LCA model could be represented (according to equations (1) - (4)) as the following system of eight equations with eight variables.

$$1 = \pi_1 + \pi_2$$
$$p_1 = \pi_1 \nu_{11} + \pi_2 \nu_{12}$$
$$p_2 = \pi_1 \nu_{21} + \pi_2 \nu_{22}$$
$$p_{12} = \pi_1 \nu_{11} \nu_{21} + \pi_2 \nu_{12} \nu_{22}$$
$$p_3 = \pi_1 \nu_{31} + \pi_2 \nu_{32}$$
$$p_{13} = \pi_1 \nu_{11} \nu_{31} + \pi_2 \nu_{12} \nu_{32}$$
$$p_{23} = \pi_1 \nu_{21} \nu_{31} + \pi_2 \nu_{22} \nu_{32}$$
$$p_{123} = \pi_1 \nu_{11} \nu_{21} \nu_{31} + \pi_2 \nu_{12} \nu_{22} \nu_{32}$$

To give a solution example of this system we consider the following class membership 108×3 matrix X which does not contain any missing data.

$$X = \begin{bmatrix} 1\ 1\ 1 \\ 1\ 1\ 1 \\ \vdots\ \vdots\ \vdots \\ 1\ 1\ 1 \\ \\ 2\ 1\ 1 \\ 1\ 2\ 1 \\ 1\ 1\ 2 \\ 2\ 2\ 1 \\ 2\ 1\ 2 \\ 1\ 2\ 2 \\ 1\ 1\ 1 \\ 2\ 2\ 2 \end{bmatrix}$$

This matrix consists only of the definite part (100 rows with a pattern "1-1-1") and of the ideally random part which has zero correlation matrix (8 last rows).

An exact solution of the system in this case is shown below.

$\pi_1 = 0.926$ – the unobserved probability of RWC membership.
$\nu_{i1} = 1$ – the unobserved conditional probability that an object from the RWC is also in the ith data source.
$\pi_2 = 0.074$ – the unobserved probability of RWC non-membership.
$\nu_{i2} = 0.5$ – the unobserved conditional probability that an object which is not in RWC is presented in the ith data source.

Thus the LCA gives us an answer to the question how many objects belong to the RWC ($\pi_1 = 0.926$). Indeed, this value demonstrates a confidence with which the integrated class corresponds to RWC.

We see that 7.4% of objects do not belong to RWC. They have equal probability (50%) to be found or not to be found in each data set. This follows from the initial assumptions about statistical nature of our uncertainties.

In real cases the initial data may not fit well to requirements of statistical analysis. They may contain a large fraction of missing data, the random variables may not have the normal distribution, etc. The various LCA realizations (almost in any statistical software package) could be used to work with such data. They use, for example, a likelihood-ratio estimation technique which allows to adopt real data to the statistical model and provides a measure of applicability (goodness of fit). They can deal with several latent classes, disjoint and missing data. For the purposes of this paper, we abstain from going in details of such estimation or appropriation approaches.

6   Conclusion and Future Work

For the integration of heterogeneous data sources it is important to have a methodological integration approach at our disposal. The central problem here

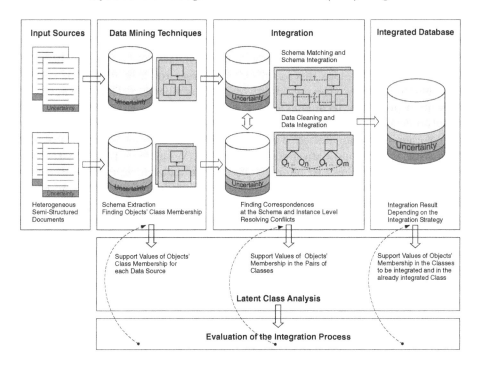

Fig. 4. The integration process with the assistance of LCA

is the evaluation of the degree of the accumulated uncertainty resulted from applying various methods at the consequent integration steps. Careful investigation yielded LCA as the most suitable solution for this problem. The application of statistical methods for the integration task is a novel and promising research approach.

The proposed framework is able to answer the question of the quality of the integrated database or in other words how exact the real world entities are presented in it. We have shown how a statistical model of the integration task can be developed. It can be summarized as follows.

The required input data such as support of object's class membership (p_i), support of class correspondence (p_{ij}) and a result of integration (p_{ijl}) has to be discovered e.g. by data mining, schema matching, data cleaning, schema and data integration methods.

Then the output data associated with the unobservable latent factors such as RWC membership is provided by LCA. The method can be applied to each single step of the integration giving us a propagation of uncertainties in the process of integration.

Figure 4 illustrates how the integration process with applying LCA is realized.

The key parameter is the RWC membership probability (π_1). Its value varies depending on the integration strategy and integration decisions. One can think about maximization of RWC membership probability in order to obtain the highest integration quality. This can be achieved by adjusting the selection criteria used by the methods applied during the integration process.

It is important to emphasize that an integrated database is naturally included in the analysis. Therefore, we can try out various strategies of integration and see how they contribute to the probability of RWC membership. Thus, the approach provides a promising technique for optimization of integration that is a subject to future work.

Another important aspect which should be considered is the problem of evaluating schema and data quality ([13], [16]). With the aid of LCA the proposed framework allows to improve the schema and data quality as the data and schemas during the integration process are implicitly checked for accuracy, completeness, consistency, etc.

The proposed method could also be used for defining a quality measure for query results. Thereby, a user asking queries to the integrated database can get an additional information about the quality of the results of his/her queries. This brings up the question how to represent this measure such that it can be used for query processing.

We are convinced, that our technique is a powerful tool for the analysis of decisions taken at every single integration step, especially in difficult, ambiguous cases.

The proposed approach opens a way for an optimal integration of data sources which contain uncertain information.

References

1. E. Altareva and S. Conrad. The Problem of Uncertainty and Database Integration. In R.-D. Kutsche, S. Conrad, and W. Hasselbring, editors, *Engineering Federated Information Systems, Proceedings of the 4th Workshop EFIS 2001, Oct 9–10, 2001, Berlin (Germany)*, pages 92–99. infix-Verlag / IOS Press, 2001.
2. E. Altareva and S. Conrad. Dealing with Uncertainties during the Data(base) Integration Process. In Gunnar Weber, editor, *Tagungsband zum 14. GI-Workshop Grundlagen von Datenbanken, Strandhotel Fischland, Halbinsel Fischland-Darß-Zingst, Mecklenburg-Vorpommern, 21. bis 24. Mai 2002*, pages 6–10. Fachbereich Informatik, Universität Rostock, 2002.
3. D. Bartholomew and M. Knott. *Latent Variable Models and Factor Analysis*, volume 7 of *Kendall's Library of Statistics*. Arnold, London, 1999.
4. A. Basilevsky. *Statistical Factor Analysis and Related Methods: Theory and Applications*. Wiley and Sons, New York, 1994.
5. D. Beneventano, S. Bergamaschi, F. Guerra, and M. Vincini. The MOMIS Approach to Information Integration. In *ICEIS 2001, Proc. of the 3rd Int. Conf. on Enterprise Information Systems, Setubal, Portugal, July 7–10, 2001*, 2001.
6. M.-S. Chen, J. Han, and P. S. Yu. Data Mining: An Overview from a Database Perspective. *IEEE Transactions on Software Engineering*, 8(6):866–883, 1996.
7. U. Dayal and H.-Y. Hwang. View Definition and Generalization for Database Integration in a Multidatabase System. *IEEE Transactions on Software Engineering*, 10(6):628–644, 1984.

8. A. Doan, P. Domingos, and A. Y. Levy. Learning Mappings between Data Schemas. In *Proceedings of the AAAI-2000 Workshop on Learning Statistical Models from Relational Data, 2000, Austin, TX*, 2000.

9. A. Doan, P. Domingos, and A. Y. Levy. Learning Source Description for Data Integration. In D. Suciu and G. Vossen, editors, *Proc. of the Third International Workshop on the Web and Databases, WebDB 2000, Dallas, Texas, USA, May 18–19, 2000*, pages 81–86, 2000.

10. W. Fan, H. Lu, S. E. Madnick, and D. W.-L. Cheung. Discovering and Reconciling Value Conflicts for Numerical Data Integration. *Information Systems*, 26(8):635–656, 2001.

11. I.P. Fellegi and A.B. Sunter. A Theory for Record Linkage. *Journal of the American Statistical Association*, 64:1183–1210, 1969.

12. H. Galhardas, D. Florescu, D. Shasha, E. Simon, and C.-A. Saita. Improving Data Cleaning Quality Using a Data Lineage Facility. In D. Theodoratos, J. Hammer, M. A. Jeusfeld, and M. Staudt, editors, *Proc. of the 3rd Intl. Workshop on Design and Management of Data Warehouses, DMDW'2001, Interlaken, Switzerland, June 4, 2001*, 2001.

13. M. Gertz and I. Schmitt. Data Integration Techniques based on Data Quality Aspects. In I. Schmitt, C. Türker, E. Hildebrandt, and M. Höding, editors, *FDBS 3. Workshop "Föderierte Datenbanken", Magdeburg, Germany, 1998*, page 1. Shaker Verlag, Aachen.

14. D. Hand, H. Mannila, and P. Smyth. *Principles of Data Mining*. MIT Press, Massachusetts Institute of Technology, USA, 2001.

15. M. Höding and S. Conrad. Data-Mining Tasks in Federated Database Systems Design. In T. Özsu, A. Dogac, and Ö. Ulusoy, editors, *Issues and Applications of Database Technology (IADT'98), Proc. of the 3rd World Conf. on Integrated Design and Process Technology, July 6–9, 1998, Berlin, Germany*, volume 2, pages 384–391. Society for Design and Process Science, 1998.

16. M. Jarke, M. A. Jeusfeld, C. Quix, and P. Vassiliadis. Architecture and Quality in Data Warehouses: An Extended Repository Approach. *Information Systems*, 24(3):229–253, 1999.

17. W. L. Low, M.-L. Lee, and T. W. Ling. A knowledge-based Approach for Duplicate Elimination in Data Cleaning. *Information Systems*, 26(8):585–606, 2001.

18. J. Madhavan, P. A. Bernstein, and E. Rahm. Generic Schema Matching with Cupid. In P. M. Apers, P. Atzeni, S. Ceri, S. Paraboschi, K. Ramamohanarao, and R. T. Snodgrass, editors, *VLDB 2001, Proceedings of 27th International Conference on Very Large Data Bases, September 11–14, 2001, Roma, Italy*, pages 49–58. Morgan Kaufmann, 2001.

19. R. J. Miller, L. M. Haas, and M. A. Hernandez. Schema Mapping as Query Discovery. In A. E. Abbadi, M. L. Brodie, S. Chakravarthy, U. Dayal, N. Kamel, G. Schlageter, and K.-Y. Whang, editors, *VLDB 2000, Proc. of 26th International Conference on Very Large Data Bases, September 10–14, 2000, Cairo, Egypt*, pages 77–88. Morgan Kaufmann, 2000.

20. L. Palopoli, G. Terracina, and D. Ursino. The System DIKE: Towards the Semi-Automatic Synthesis of Cooperative Information Systems and Data Warehouses. In Y. Masunaga, J. Pokorny, J. Stuller, and B. Thalheim, editors, *Proceedings of Chalenges, 2000 ADBIS-DASFAA Symposium on Advances in Databases and Information Systems, Enlarged Fourth East-European Conference on Advances in Databases and Information Systems, Prague, Czech Republic, September 5–8, 2000*, pages 108–117. Matfyz Press, 2000.

21. E. Rahm and P.A. Bernstein. A Survey of Approaches to Automatic Schema Matching. *VLDB Journal*, 10(4):334–350, 2001.

22. I. Schmitt and G. Saake. Merging Inheritance Hierarchies for Database Integration. In *Proc. of the 3rd IFCIS Int. Conf. on Cooperative Information Systems, CoopIS'98, August 20–22, 1998, New York, USA*, Los Alamitos, CA, 1998. IEEE Computer Society Press.

23. I. Schmitt and C. Türker. An Incremental Approach to Schema Integration by Refining Extensional Relationships. In Georges Gardarin, James C. French, Niki Pissinou, Kia Makki, and Luc Bouganim, editors, *Proceedings of the 1998 ACM CIKM International Conference on Information and Knowledge Management, Bethesda, Maryland, USA, November 3–7, 1998*. ACM Press, 1998.

24. K. Schwarz, I. Schmitt, C. Türker, M. Höding, E. Hildebrandt, S. Balko, S. Conrad, and G. Saake. Design Support for Database Federations. In J. Akoka, M. Bouzeghoub, I. Comyn-Wattiau, and E. Métais, editors, *Conceptual Modeling – ER'99 (18th International Conference on Conceptual Modeling, Paris, France, November 15–18, 1999, Proceedings)*, Lecture Notes in Computer Science, Vol. 1728, pages 445–459. Springer-Verlag, 1999.

25. S. Spaccapietra, C. Parent, and Y. Dupont. Model Independent Assertions for Integration of Heterogeneous Schemas. *VLDB Journal*, 1(1):81–126, 1992.

26. K. Winkler and M. Spiliopoulou. Structuring Domain-Specific Text Archives by Deriving a Probabilistic XML DTD. In Tapio Elomaa, Heikki Mannila, and Hannu Toivonen, editors, *Proceedings of the 6th European Conference on Principles and Practice of Knowledge Discovery in Databases (PKDD'02), Helsinki, Finland, August 2002*, volume 2431 of *Lecture Notes in Computer Science*, pages 461–474. Springer, 2002.

27. L.-L. Yan, R. J. Miller, L. M. Haas, and R. Fagin. Data-Driven Understanding and Refinement of Schema Mappings. In W. G. Aref, editor, *ACM SIGMOD Conference 2001: Santa Barbara, CA, USA*. SIGMOD 2001 Electronic Proceedings, http://www.acm.org/sigmod/sigmod01/eproceedings, 2001.

QoM: Qualitative and Quantitative Schema Match Measure

Naiyana Tansalarak and Kajal Claypool

Department of Computer Science,
University of Massachusetts - Lowell
{ntansala,kajal}@cs.uml.edu
http://www.cs.uml.edu/dsl/index.html

Abstract. Integration of multiple heterogeneous data sources continues to be a critical problem for many application domains and a challenge for researchers world-wide. Schema matching, a fundamental aspect of integration, has been a well-studied problem. However researchers have, for the most part, concentrated on the development of different schema matching algorithms, and their performance with respect to the number of matches produced. To the best of our knowledge, current research in schema matching does not address the issue of *quality of matching*. We believe that quality of match is an important measure that can not only provide a basis for comparing multiple matches, but can also be used as a metric to compare as well as optimize existing match algorithms. In this paper, we define the *Quality of Match* (QoM) metric, and provide *qualitative* and *quantitative* analysis techniques to evaluate the QoM of two given schemata. In particular, we introduce a taxonomy of schema matches as a qualitative analysis technique, and a weight-based match model that in concert with the taxonomy provides a quantitative measure of the QoM. We show, via examples, how QoM can be used to distinguish the "goodness" of one match in comparison with other matches.

Keywords: Schema Matching, Schema Integration, Quality of Matching

1 Introduction

Integration of heterogeneous data sources continues to be a critical problem for many application domains and a challenge for researchers world-wide. Today there is a broad spectrum of information that is available in interconnected digital environments such as the Web, each with its own concepts, semantics, data formats, and access methods. Currently, the burden falls on the user to resolve conflicts, integrate the data, and interpret the results, a process that can take on the order of hours and days to accomplish, often leaving data under-exploited and under-utilized. An integral problem underlying this entire process is that of data integration, and in particular that of matching schema entities in an automated/semi-automated manner.

Schema matching is the task of finding semantic correspondences between elements of two schemas [DR02]. Various systems and algorithms have been proposed over the years to automate this process of schema matching. While most approaches address

I.-Y. Song et al. (Eds.): ER 2003, LNCS 2813, pp. 31–44, 2003.
© Springer-Verlag Berlin Heidelberg 2003

the problem for specific domains [BHP94,BCVB01,BM01], there have been a few approaches that tackle the problem independent of the domain [HMN+99,MBR01,DR02]. The proposed approaches exploit various types of schema information such as element names, data types, structural properties, ontologies, domain knowledge as well as characteristics of data instances. Typically, two schemas are provided as input and *matches* between the schemas, denoting correspondences between the entities of the two schemas, are produced as output by the match algorithm. Two entities are said to match if their *similarity value* is above a certain *threshold*. Calculation of the similarity value is largely dependent on the type of match algorithm used. For example, Madhavan et al. [MBR01] define the similarity value for structural matching as the fraction of leaves in the two subtrees that have at least one *strong* link to some leaf in the other subtree. A link in their case is said to be a strong if the similarity value exceeds a pre-set threshold. Thresholds, on the other hand, are typically set in an ad-hoc manner.

Similarity value and threshold together provide a measure of the quality of match that is produced by a system. Unfortunately, in current systems, calculation of the similarity value and the setting of the threshold value are tightly coupled to the individual algorithms, with no metric that can compare matches across the different algorithms. There has been no concerted effort to provide a metric that compares (1) the quality of match across different match algorithms (horizontal comparison); or (2) multiple matches that may be discovered for a given source entity (vertical comparison) via the same match algorithm.

In this paper we define a *Quality of Match* (QoM) metric, and provide *qualitative* and *quantitative* analysis techniques to evaluate the QoM of two given schemata, independent of the actual match algorithm used. In particular, we propose a first of its kind *match taxonomy*, a qualitative analysis technique, that categorizes the structural overlap and hence the information capacity of the given schemata. Our match taxonomy uses UML as its unifying data model, thereby broadening its applicability to relational, XML and OO schemas which can all be expressed in the UML model. However, we find that while the match taxonomy provides a categorization of the matches at a high level, it cannot distinguish between matches within a given category. To enable distinction of matches within a category, we propose a quantitative measurement of QoM via a *weight-based match model*. The match model, based on the structural and informational aspects of a schema, quantitatively evaluates the quality of match, assigning it an absolute numeric value.

Roadmap: The rest of the paper is organized as follows. Section 2 presents a formalization of the UML model. Section 3 presents the match taxonomy, while Section 4 describes the weight-based match model. Section 5 presents related work and we conclude in Section 6.

2   Background: The UML Model

Today, much of the information exists in heterogeneous sources such as relational tables, objects, or XML documents. To integrate information from these heterogeneous sources and to reason over them, we must necessarily unify them in one common data model [RR87,MIR93]. Given the universal acceptance of the UML model and its suitability for modeling all aspects of the relational, object-oriented, and XML data models [CSF00], we have chosen the UML model as our common data model. In this section, we present a brief overview of the UML model, and provide some basic definitions that are used in the later sections of this paper.

UML, the Unified Modeling Language, as defined by Rambaugh, Jacobson, and Booch [Boo94], is a general purpose visual modeling language that can be used to specify, visualize, construct, and document the artifacts of a software system. While UML can model both the static structure and the dynamic behavior of systems, we are primarily interested in capturing schema structures in the static view [Boo94]. Classes, the cornerstone of the UML static view, consist of a class name, attributes, and methods. The attribute, identified by its label, has associated with it a set of properties that define its domain type, its scope, and possibly a set of initial values. A method, on the other hand, is identified by its signature comprising of its scope, return value, and a set of input parameters (possibly empty). In addition, a method has a set of pre-and post-conditions which define its behavior. Note that in the case of XML and relational models, no methods are defined for the classes. Formally, we define an attribute and a method as follows.

Definition 1. *An attribute* a *is defined as a 5-tuple* a $= < \mathcal{L}, \mathcal{A}, \mathcal{T}, \mathcal{N}, \mathcal{I} >$ *where* $\mathcal{L}$ *represents the label,* $\mathcal{A}$ *the set of applicable modifiers,* $\mathcal{T}$ *the domain type, either primitive or user-defined,* $\mathcal{N}$ *the cardinality, and* $\mathcal{I}$ *the list of possible initial value(s) of the attribute.*

Definition 2. *A method* m *is defined as a 5-tuple* m $=< \mathcal{A}, \mathcal{O}, \mathcal{I}, pre, post >$ *where* $\mathcal{A}$ *is the set of applicable modifiers,* $\mathcal{O}$ *the return data type,* $\mathcal{I}$ *a finite set of input parameter data types,* pre *the precondition, and* post *the postcondition.* [1]

In Definitions 1 and 2, the applicable modifiers are the set of modifiers permissible in UML, namely, the access modifiers (private, public, and protected), the class-wide modifiers (static), and the constant modifier (final). Note that not all data models, XML and relational models for example, have a direct mapping to the modifiers. Default values are used when translations are done from these data models.

The UML data model also defines a set of possible relationships (association, aggregation, and generalization and specialization) between classes. In our work, we translate all relationships into attributes of the given class based on the conversion rules [San95]. For example, an association with *one-to-many* cardinality between class A and class B is given by an attribute of the type A on class B. Similarly, a specialized class is represented by the set of all local and inherited attributes and methods. A class is thus defined as follows.

Definition 3. *A class* c *is defined as a 2-tuple* c $=< \mathcal{E}, \mathcal{F} >$ *where* $\mathcal{E}$ *a finite set of all attributes (local and inherited), and* $\mathcal{F}$ *a finite set of all methods (local and inherited).*

Lastly, while the UML model does not specifically define the concept of a schema, we find it useful to define a schema simply as a collection of classes.

Definition 4. *A schema,* $\mathcal{S}$, *is defined as a finite set of classes,* $< \mathcal{C} >$.

---

[1] The first three properties represent a *method signature*, while the last two properties denote a *method specification*.

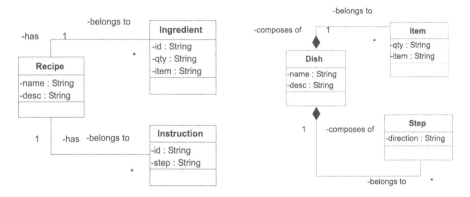

Fig. 1. The Recipe Schema   **Fig. 2.** The Dish Schema

Notation. We use the following notations throughout the rest of the paper. We use the notation S_s and S_t to represent the source and the target schemas respectively. In addition, $\mathcal{C}(S_s)$ denotes a set of valid classes of S_s, $\mathcal{M}(C_s)$ a set of valid attributes and methods of a class $C_s \in S_s$, $|S_s|$ the number of classes (cardinality) of S_s, and $|C_s|$ the number of attributes and methods (cardinality) of C_s. Similar notation is used for the target schema.

3   Qualitative Analysis: Taxonomy of Schema Matching

We define the *quality of match* (QoM) metric as the measure of "goodness" of a given match. In this section, we focus on defining a qualitative measure of this goodness via a well-defined *match taxonomy*.

Schema matching is typically based on the inherent hierarchy present in the schema structure, resulting in the comparison of attributes (and methods for OO schemas) at the lowest level, the comparison of containers (relations, classes, and elements), and the comparison of the schemas themselves. Each level of the comparison is tightly coupled, and hence heavily dependent on its lower level. Based on this hierarchy we now define a *match taxonomy* that categorizes the matches at the attribute (or method), class and the schema levels. We classify theses matches as *micro*, *sub-macro*, and *macro* matches respectively.

3.1   Micro Match

In existing match algorithms [MBR01,DR02,BM01,BHP94,HMN+99], a match between two attributes is typically determined by the similarity (via linguistic matching) of their labels. In addition to label similarity, some algorithms [MBR01,DR02] also consider the domain type of the attributes to determine a match. A match between two methods, on the other hand, is typically done via a matching of the method signatures and/or the matching of method specifications as given by its pre- and post-conditions [ZW95, ZW97,JC95]. Most method matching algorithms do not take the label of the method into account [ZW95,ZW97,JC95]. Based on this existing work and the UML model presented in Section 2, we now define a match between attributes (or methods), termed a *micro match*, as a match of all properties of the attributes (or methods).

The quality of match (QoM) for a micro match is categorized as either *exact* or *relaxed*. A micro match is said to be *exact* if all properties of the two attributes (or methods) as per Definition 1 (Definition 2) are either (a) identical or equivalent. Assuming labels of the attributes are compared using linguistic match algorithms, *identical* labels imply that the two labels are either exactly the same or are synonymous. For all other properties, it implies "exactly the same" semantics. As an example, consider schema *Recipe* and schema *Dish* given in Figures 1 and 2 respectively. Here, the attribute name of class Recipe is an exact match to the attribute name of class Dish as all properties including the label name are identical. On the other hand, the attribute name of class Recipe is not considered an exact match of the attribute qty of class Ingredient as their labels are neither identical nor synonymous (even though the other properties are identical). An *equivalent* match used for method specification implies the logical equivalence of two method specifications. For example, the precondition $count = count + 1$ is equivalent to the precondition $num = num + 1$. Formally, an *exact* match for two attributes or two methods can be defined as follows.

Definition 5. *A match between two attributes $a_s \in C_s$ and $a_t \in C_t$ is said to be* **exact**, $a_s =_E a_t$, *if* $< \mathcal{L}_s, \mathcal{A}_s, \mathcal{T}_s, \mathcal{C}_s, \mathcal{I}_s >=< \mathcal{L}_t, \mathcal{A}_t, \mathcal{T}_t, \mathcal{C}_t, \mathcal{I}_t >$, *where $=$ denotes either an identical or a synonymous match between $\mathcal{L}_s$ and $\mathcal{L}_t$, and identical matches for all other properties.*

Definition 6. *A match between two methods $m_s \in C_s$ and $m_t \in C_t$ is said to be* **exact**, $m_s =_E m_t$, *if (1)* $< \mathcal{A}_s, \mathcal{O}_s, \mathcal{I}_s >=< \mathcal{A}_t, \mathcal{O}_t, \mathcal{I}_t >$, *where $=$ denotes an identical match; and (2)* $< pre_s, post_s >\Leftrightarrow < pre_t, post_t >$, *where $\Leftrightarrow$ denotes an equivalent match.*

A micro match is said to be *relaxed* if (a) the labels of the attributes are related but not identical (approximate). For example, they may be either hyponyms, or may have the same stem; or the properties of an attribute (or a method) are a generalization or a specialization of the other. For example, the access modifier *public* is considered to be a generalization of the modifier *protected*; or (c) for a method match, the pre- and post-conditions of the source method imply the pre-and post-conditions of the target method, or vice versa. For example, the precondition count > 10 implies the precondition count > 5. Consider again the schemas given in Figure 1 and 2. The attribute step of class Instruction has a relaxed match with the attribute direction of class Step as their labels are in the same word hierarchy (hyponym), but are not identical or synonymous. Formally, we define a relaxed match between two attributes (or methods) as follows.

Definition 7. *A match between two attributes $a_s \in C_s$ and $a_t \in C_t$ is* **relaxed**, $a_s =_R a_t$, *if* $< \mathcal{L}_s, \mathcal{A}_s, \mathcal{T}_s, \mathcal{C}_s, \mathcal{I}_s > \approx < \mathcal{L}_t, \mathcal{A}_t, \mathcal{T}_t, \mathcal{C}_t, \mathcal{I}_t >$ *where $\approx$ denotes an approximate match between the labels $\mathcal{L}_s$ and $\mathcal{L}_s$, and either a generalized match $(>)$ or a specialized match $(<)$ for all other properties.*

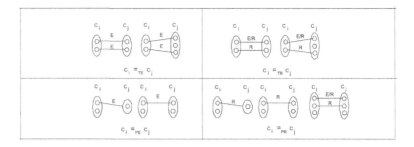

Fig. 3. The QoM for Sub-Macro Matches.

Definition 8. *A match between two methods $m_s \in C_s$ and $m_t \in C_t$ is* **relaxed**, $\mathbf{m_s} =_\mathbf{R} \mathbf{m_t}$, *if (1)* $< \mathcal{A}_s, \mathcal{O}_s, \mathcal{I}_s > \approx_{sig} < \mathcal{A}_t, \mathcal{O}_t, \mathcal{I}_t >$, *where* $\approx_{sig}$ *denotes either a generalized match ($>$) or a specialized match ($<$); and (2)* $< pre_s, post_s > \approx_{spec} < pre_t, post_t >$, *where* $\approx_{spec} = \{\Rightarrow or \Leftarrow\}$ *denotes that one set of pre-and post-conditions can imply the other set of pre-and post-conditions.*

3.2   Sub-macro Match

A class, as per Definition 3, is defined as a set of attributes and methods. Thus, a match between two classes, referred to as the *sub-macro match*, can be compared on the basis of (1) the number of matched attributes (or methods); and (2) the quality of the micro matches. Based on the number of matched attributes (methods) between the source and target classes, the quality of match (QoM) at the *sub-macro* level is given as either a *total* or a *partial* match. In a total match, **all** attributes (or methods) of the source class match **some or all** attributes (or methods) of the target class one-to-one, while in a partial match **some** (but not all) attributes (or methods) of the source class match those in the target class. For example, the class Recipe in Figure 1 has total coverage in the class Dish in Figure 2, while the class Ingredient in Figure 1 has only partial coverage with respect to the class Item in Figure 2.

Definition 9. *A* **total** *match between two classes $C_s \in S_s$ and $C_t \in S_t$, denoted as* $\mathbf{C_s} =_\mathbf{T} \mathbf{C_t}$, *is defined as a total and injective function over attributes and methods* $f : \mathcal{M}(C_s) \to \mathcal{M}(C_t)$.

Definition 10. *A* **partial** *match between two classes $C_s \in S_s$ and $C_t \in S_t$, denoted as* $\mathbf{C_s} =_\mathbf{P} \mathbf{C_t}$, *is defined as an injective function over attributes and methods* $f : \mathcal{M}(C_s) \to \mathcal{M}(C_t)$.

Combining the two criteria, number of matches and the quality of micro match, we define four classifications for the QoM at the sub-macro level: (1) *total exact*, wherein **all** attributes and methods of the source class match **exactly** (exact micro match) the attributes and methods of the target class; (2) *total relaxed*, wherein **all** attributes and methods of the source class have either a **relaxed** micro match, or some combination of exact and relaxed micro matches in the target class; (3) *partial exact*, wherein **some** of the source attributes and methods have an **exact** micro match in the target class; and (4) *partial relaxed*, wherein **some** of the source attributes and methods have either a **relaxed** micro match, or some combination of exact and relaxed micro matches in the target class. Figure 3 diagrammatically depicts the possible QoMs for a sub-macro match. Here E and R denote an exact and a relaxed micro match respectively, while TE, TR, PE, PR denote total exact, total relaxed, partial exact, and partial relaxed matches respectively.

Definition 11. *A* **total exact** *match between two classes* $C_s \in S_s$ *and* $C_t \in S_t$, *denoted as* $\mathbf{C_s} =_{\mathbf{TE}} \mathbf{C_t}$, *is a total and injective function over attributes and methods* $f : \mathcal{M}(C_s) \rightarrow \mathcal{M}(C_t)$ *where* $\forall m_s \in \mathcal{M}(C_s) \wedge \exists m_t \in \mathcal{M}(C_t) \mid (m_s =_E m_t)$.

Definition 12. *A* **total relaxed** *match between two classes* $C_s \in S_s$ *and* $C_t \in S_t$, *denoted as* $\mathbf{C_s} =_{\mathbf{TR}} \mathbf{C_t}$, *is a total and injective function over attributes and methods* $f : \mathcal{M}(C_s) \rightarrow \mathcal{M}(C_t)$ *where* $\forall m_s \in \mathcal{M}(C_s) \wedge \exists m_t \in \mathcal{M}(C_t) \mid (m_s =_R m_t \vee m_s =_E m_t)$ *with at least one relaxed micro match* $(m_s =_R m_t)$.

Definition 13. *A* **partial exact** *match between two classes* $C_s \in S_s$ *and* $C_t \in S_t$, *denoted as* $\mathbf{C_s} =_{\mathbf{PE}} \mathbf{C_t}$, *is an injective function over attributes and methods* $f : \mathcal{M}(C_s) \rightarrow \mathcal{M}(C_t)$ *where* $\exists m_s \in \mathcal{M}(C_s) \wedge \exists m_t \in \mathcal{M}(C_t) \mid (m_s =_E m_t)$.

Definition 14. *A* **partial relaxed** *match between two classes* $C_s \in S_s$ *and* $C_t \in S_t$, *denoted as* $\mathbf{C_s} =_{\mathbf{PR}} \mathbf{C_t}$, *is an injective function over attributes and methods* $f : \mathcal{M}(C_s) \rightarrow \mathcal{M}(C_t)$ *where* $\exists m_s \in \mathcal{M}(C_s) \wedge \exists m_t \in \mathcal{M}(C_t) \mid (m_s =_R m_t \vee m_s =_E m_t)$ *with at least one relaxed micro match* $(m_s =_R m_t)$.

As an example consider once again the schemas in Figure 1 and 2. Here the class `Recipe` (Figure 1) has a total exact match with the class `Dish` (Figure 2). On the other hand, the class `Ingredient` in Figure 1 has only a partial exact match with class `Item` in Figure 2 as there is no match for the attribute `id` of class `Ingredient`. Similarly, the class `Instruction` in Figure 1 has a partial relaxed match with class `Step` in Figure 2 as the class `Instruction` provides only partial coverage for its attributes, and the micro matches are relaxed.

3.3 Macro Match

As per Definition 4 (Section 2), a schema is defined as a collection of classes. Thus, a match between two schemas, referred to as the *macro match*, is dependent on (1) the number of matched classes in the schema; and (2) the quality of the sub-macro matches. Similar to the classification at the sub-macro level, we categorize the quality of match (QoM) at the macro level as either a *total* or a *partial* match based on the number of sub-macro matches between the source and the target schemata. A match is *total* if **all** classes in the source schema match some or all classes in the target schema. Note that this is not a one-to-one correspondence as it is possible that two or more source classes map to one target class. A match is *partial* if **some** (but not all) of the source classes match some of the target classes.

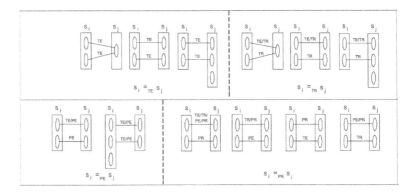

Fig. 4. The QoM for Macro Matches.

Definition 15. *A* **total** *match between two schemas* S_s *and* S_t, *denoted as* $\mathbf{S_s} =_{\mathbf{T}} \mathbf{S_t}$, *is defined as a total function over classes* $f : \mathcal{C}(S_s) \rightarrow \mathcal{C}(S_t)$.

Definition 16. *A* **partial** *match between two schemas* S_s *and* S_t, *denoted as* $\mathbf{S_s} =_{\mathbf{P}} \mathbf{S_t}$, *is defined as a function over classes* $f : \mathcal{C}(S_s) \rightarrow \mathcal{C}(S_t)$.

Combining the two criteria given above, we now classify the QoM at the macro level as (1) *total exact*, wherein **all** classes of the source have a **total exact** sub-macro match in the target schema; (2) *total relaxed*, wherein **all** source classes have a **total match** in the target schema, with at least one **total relaxed** sub-macro match; (3) *partial exact*, wherein either **all** source classes have an **exact** sub-macro match in the target schema with at least **one partial** sub-macro match, or **some** (but not all) of the source classes have either **partial or total exact** sub-macro matches in the target schema; and (4) *partial relaxed* wherein either **all** source classes have a sub-macro match in the target schema with at least **one partial** sub-macro match and **one relaxed** sub-macro match, or **some** (but not all) source classes have a sub-macro match in the target schema with at least **one total relaxed** sub-macro match or **one partial relaxed** sub-macro match. Figure 4 diagrammatically depicts the possible QoMs for a macro match.

Definition 17. *A* **total exact** *match between two schemas* S_s *and* S_t, *denoted as* $S_s =_{TE} S_t$, *is defined as a total function over classes* $f : \mathcal{C}(S_s) \rightarrow \mathcal{C}(S_t)$ *where* $\forall \, C_s \in \mathcal{M}(S_s) \wedge \exists \, C_t \in \mathcal{M}(S_t) \mid (C_s =_{TE} C_t)$.

Definition 18. *A* **total relaxed** *match between two schemas* S_s *and* S_t, *denoted as* $\mathbf{S_s} =_{\mathbf{TR}} \mathbf{S_t}$, *is defined as a total function over classes* $f : \mathcal{C}(S_s) \rightarrow \mathcal{C}(S_t)$ *where* $\forall C_s \in \mathcal{M}(S_s) \wedge \exists C_t \in \mathcal{M}(S_t) \mid (C_s =_{TR} C_t \vee C_s =_{TE} C_t)$ *with at least one total relaxed sub-macro match* $(C_s =_{TR} C_t)$.

Definition 19. *A* **partial exact** *match between two schemas* S_s *and* S_t, *denoted as* $\mathbf{S_s} =_{\mathbf{PE}} \mathbf{S_t}$, *is defined as either (1) a total function over classes* $f : \mathcal{C}(S_s) \rightarrow \mathcal{C}(S_t)$ *where* $\forall C_s \in \mathcal{M}(S_s) \wedge \exists C_t \in \mathcal{M}(S_t) \mid (C_s =_{PE} C_t \vee C_s =_{TE} C_t)$ *with at least one partial exact class match* $(C_s =_{PE} C_t)$, *or (2) a function over classes* $f : \mathcal{C}(S_s) \rightarrow \mathcal{C}(S_t)$ *where* $\exists C_s \in \mathcal{M}(S_s) \wedge \exists C_t \in \mathcal{M}(S_t) \mid (C_s =_{PE} C_t \vee C_s =_{TE} C_t)$.

Definition 20. *A* **partial relaxed** *match between two schemas S_s and S_t, denoted as* $S_s =_{PR} S_t$, *is defined as either (1) a total function over classes* $f : \mathcal{C}(S_s) \rightarrow \mathcal{C}(S_t)$ *where* $\forall C_s \in \mathcal{M}(S_s) \land \exists C_t \in \mathcal{M}(S_t) \mid ((C_s =_{PR} C_t) \lor (C_s =_{TE} C_t) \lor (C_s =_{PE} C_t) \lor (C_s =_{TR} C_t))$ *with at least one partial relaxed sub-macro match* $(C_s =_{PR} C_t)$, *or (2) a function over classes* $f : \mathcal{C}(S_s) \rightarrow \mathcal{C}(S_t)$ *where* $\exists C_s \in \mathcal{M}(S_s) \land \exists C_t \in \mathcal{M}(S_t) \mid ((C_s =_{PR} C_t) \lor (C_s =_{TE} C_t) \lor (C_s =_{PE} C_t) \lor (C_s =_{TR} C_t))$ *with at least one partial relaxed or total relaxed sub-macro match.*

Consider the schemas given in Figure 1 and 2. The schema `Recipe` has a partial relaxed match with the *Dish* schema. However, there is a total relaxed match between the *Dish* schema and the *Recipe* schema if the *Dish* schema is considered to be the source schema.

4   Quantitative Analysis: Weight-Based Match Model

In Section 3, we have presented a qualitative technique for evaluating the quality of match (QoM) between two schemata. Based on the qualitative analysis it can be observed that the QoM for an exact match is typically better than the QoM for a relaxed match. Similarly, the QoM for a total match is generally better than the QoM for a partial match. Moreover, we can observe that in general the quality of match is guaranteed to be better if the match is total exact. However, we find that qualitative analysis alone can not accurately determine the distinction between a total relaxed, a partial exact, or a partial relaxed match. To address this, in this section we now provide a *weight-based match model* that quantitatively determines and ranks the QoM. We define this quantitative model at each level of the match taxonomy.

4.1   Micro Match Model

Micro matches (refer Section 3.1) are classified as either exact or relaxed based on the matches between the properties of the two attributes (or methods). Recall that each property of a source attribute is compared to the corresponding property of the target attribute, and is determined to be either identical $(=)$, equivalent $(\Leftrightarrow)$, or relaxed $(\approx)$, where $\approx = \{>, <, \Leftarrow, \Rightarrow\}$. We term $=$, $\Leftrightarrow$, and $\approx$ the *match operators*. In the match model, we now assign a weight to each of these match operators, with $=$ and $\Leftrightarrow$ receiving a weight of 1.0 to indicate an exact match for the property, and $\approx$ getting a weight of 0.5 to denote a relaxed match at the property level. These weights form the basis of the match model, and represent the *match weight* of a property, denoted as $\mathcal{W}(P_s, P_l)$ where P_s and P_l are properties of the source and target attributes (or methods) respectively.

Based on the match weight of its properties, the QoM for source and target attributes (or methods) is defined as the normalized sum of the match weights of all its properties. Thus, the QoM of a given source attribute $(a_s \in C_s)$ and target attribute $(a_t \in C_t)$, denoted as $QoM(a_s, a_t)$, is given as:

$$QoM(a_s, a_t) = \frac{\mathcal{W}(\mathcal{L}_s, \mathcal{L}_t) + \mathcal{W}(\mathcal{A}_s, \mathcal{A}_t) + \mathcal{W}(\mathcal{T}_s, \mathcal{T}_t) + \mathcal{W}(\mathcal{N}_s, \mathcal{N}_t) + \mathcal{W}(\mathcal{I}_s, \mathcal{I}_t)}{5}$$

$$(1)$$

As an example consider the *Recipe* and *Dish* schemas given in Figures 1 and 2 respectively. The QoM of attribute `name` of class `Recipe` and attribute `name` of class `Dish`, QoM($name_{Recipe}$, $name_{Dish}$), based on Equation 1 is given as $\frac{1.00+1.00+1.00+1.00+1.00}{5} = 1.00$.

Similarly, the QoM for a given source method ($m_s \in C_s$) and target method ($m_t \in C_t$), denoted as $QoM(m_s, m_t)$, is given as:

$$QoM(m_s, m_t) = \frac{QoM_{sig}(m_s, m_t) + (2 * QoM_{spec}(m_s, m_t))}{3} \qquad (2)$$

where $QoM_{sig}(m_s, m_t)$ denotes the quality of match of the method signatures, and $QoM_{spec}(m_s, m_t)$ denotes the quality of match of the method specifications. However, it has been generally recognized in software matching literature [ZW97] that method specification is a more accurate measure of a match between two methods than the method signature. In the match model, we reflect this by assigning a higher weight for the method specification. We further define $QoM_{sig}(m_s, m_t)$ as the normalized sum of the weights of properties that define the method signature, and $QoM_{spec}(m_s, m_t)$ as the normalized sum of the weights of the pre-and post-conditions.

$$QoM_{sig}(m_s, m_t) = \frac{\mathcal{W}(\mathcal{A}_s, \mathcal{A}_t) + \mathcal{W}(\mathcal{O}_s, \mathcal{O}_t) + \mathcal{W}(\mathcal{I}_s, \mathcal{I}_t)}{3} \qquad (3)$$

$$QoM_{spec}(m_s, m_t) = \frac{\mathcal{W}(pre_s, pre_t) + \mathcal{W}(post_s, post_t)}{2} \qquad (4)$$

In an exact match by definition (Definitions 5 and 6) only the match operators $=$ and $\Leftrightarrow$ are valid for property comparisons. Thus, the QoM value for an exact match is `1.0`. However, as all match operators are valid for property comparisons in a relaxed match (Definitions 7 and 8), the QoM for relaxed matches typically ranges between `0.50-0.90`.

4.2 Sub-macro Match Model

As stated in Section 3.2, a sub-macro match is classified based on the quality of match of the micro match, and the ratio of the number of micro matches to the total number of attributes and methods in the source class. Consequently, to provide a quantitative benchmark for the sub-macro QoM we define two measures, *micro match weight*, and *cardinality ratio*. The *micro match weight*, denoted as $\mathcal{R}_W(C_s, C_t)$, is the normalized sum of the QoM of the micro matches for all attributes and methods of the source class C_s. Formally, the micro match weight is given as:

$$\mathcal{R}_W(C_s, C_t) = \frac{\sum QoM(M_s, M_t)}{|C_s|} \qquad (5)$$

The *cardinality ratio* is the ratio of the number of micro matches and the cardinality of the source class, and is given as:

$$\mathcal{R}_S(C_s, C_t) = \frac{|C_s^m|}{|C_s|} \qquad (6)$$

where $|C_s^m|$ is the number of micro matches in C_s. Based on these weights, the quantitative QoM for a sub-macro match is defined as the normalized sum of the micro match weights and the cardinality ratios.

$$QoM(C_s, C_t) = \frac{\mathcal{R}_W(C_s, C_t) + \mathcal{R}_S(C_s, C_t)}{2} \qquad (7)$$

However, we find that in some cases it is desirable to also provide a measure of congruity between the source and the target classes, i.e., to provide an estimate of not only how many of the attributes and methods of the source class match with those in the target class, but to also provide an estimate of the percentage of the target class that matches the source class. For example, consider the source class `Instruction` in Figure 1 and two target classes `Dish` and `Step` in Figure 2. Assuming that the attributes *name* and *direction* are relaxed matches of the attribute *step*, we find
`Instruction` $=_{PR}$ `Dish` and `Instruction` $=_{PR}$ `Step` where
QoM(`Instruction`, `Dish`) $= \frac{\frac{0.90}{2} + \frac{1}{2}}{2} = 0.47$ and QoM(`Instruction`, `Step`) $= \frac{\frac{0.90}{2} + \frac{1}{2}}{2} = 0.47$. However, it can be intuitively concluded from the Figures 1 and 2 that the target class `Step` is a better match for the source class `Instruction`. To account for this in the quantitative QoM measure, we now define the *congruity ratio* as the ratio of the number of the micro matches and the cardinality of the target class, $|C_t|$.

$$\mathcal{R}_T(C_s, C_t) = \frac{|C_s^m|}{|C_t|} \qquad (8)$$

The quantitative QoM for the sub-macro match is now given as:

$$QoM(C_s, C_t) = \frac{\mathcal{R}_W(C_s, C_t) + \mathcal{R}_S(C_s, C_t) + \mathcal{R}_T(C_s, C_t)}{3} \qquad (9)$$

Based on Equation 9, QoM(`Instruction`, `Dish`) $= \frac{\frac{0.90}{2} + \frac{1}{2} + \frac{1}{2}}{3} = 0.48$ and QoM(`Instruction`, `Step`) $= \frac{\frac{0.90}{2} + \frac{1}{2} + \frac{1}{1}}{3} = 0.65$, suggesting that the target class `Step` is a better match.

4.3 Macro Match Model

We now define a quantitative measure for the QoM of a macro match. Recall from Section 3.3 that a macro match is categorized based on the QoM of sub-macro matches, and the ratio of the sub-macro matches to the total number of classes (cardinality) of the source schema. Similar to the quantitative analysis at the sub-macro level, we now define the following three measures: (1) the *sub-macro match weight*, denoted as $\mathcal{R}_W(S_s, S_t)$, that is the normalized sum of the QoM of the sub-macro matches for all matched classes in the source schema; (2) the *cardinality ratio*, denoted as $\mathcal{R}_S(S_s, S_t)$, that is the ratio of the number of sub-macro matches in the source schema and the cardinality of the source schema; and (3) the *congruity ratio*, denoted as $\mathcal{R}_T(S_s, S_t)$, that is the ratio of the number of sub-macro matches and the cardinality of the target schema. That is,

$$\mathcal{R}_W(S_s, S_t) = \frac{\sum QoM(C_s, C_t)}{|S_s|} \qquad (10)$$

$$\mathcal{R}_S(S_s, S_t) = \frac{|S_s^m|}{|S_s|} \tag{11}$$

$$\mathcal{R}_T(S_s, S_t) = \frac{|S_s^m|}{|S_t|} \tag{12}$$

where $C_s \in S_s$, $C_t \in S_t$, $|S_s|$ is the cardinality of S_s, $|S_t|$ the cardinality of S_t, and $|S_s^m|$ the number of sub-macro matches in S_s.

Based on these three ratios, the quantitative measure of the QoM at the macro level is given as:

$$QoM(S_s, S_t) = \frac{\mathcal{R}_W(S_s, S_t) + \mathcal{R}_S(S_s, S_t) + \mathcal{R}_T(S_s, S_t)}{3} \tag{13}$$

Again, consider the source *Recipe* and target *Dish* schemas in Figures 1 and 2 respectively. Here Recipe $=_{TE}$ Dish, Ingredient $=_{PE}$ Item, and Instruction $=_{PR}$ Step with QoM(Recipe, Dish) = 1.00, QoM(Ingredient, Item) = 0.78, and QoM(Instruction, Step) = 0.65. Thus, the quantitative QoM for the two schemas is given as QoM(*RecipeSchema*, *DishSchema*) = $\frac{\frac{1.00+0.78+0.65}{3} + \frac{3}{3} + \frac{3}{3}}{3}$ = 0.94.

5   Related Work

Schema matching has received much interest over the past years. Various systems approaches [BHP94,BCVB01,BM01,HMN⁺99,MBR01,DR02] have been developed to determine schema matches (semi-)automatically, ranging from domain specific approaches to more general domain independent approaches such as CUPID [MBR01] and Clio [HMN⁺99]. These techniques exploit various types of schema information, element names, data types, structural properties, as well as characteristics of data instances. Some approaches also use auxiliary sources such as taxonomies, dictionaries and thesauri. However, it is unlikely that a single technique (while essential) will be able to provide a high degree of match accuracy. For this reason, new approaches look at a *hybrid* and a *composite* combination of individual matchers. CUPID [MBR01] for example, represents a hybrid match approach that combines a name (linguistic) matcher with a structural match algorithm. LSD [DDH01], an example of a composite approach for combining different matchers, uses machine-learning techniques for individual matchers and an automatic but fixed combination of match results via a meta-learner. However, we find that while some of the approaches incorporate a cost model for the matches [MBR01], these are generally regarded as internal implementation for the algorithm. Miller et al [MIR93] has done work on comparing the transformation of one schema to another based on its information capacity. While this work is targeted towards schema transformations the notion of comparing information capacity motivated our work on quality of match metric.

Similar work on matching also exists in the software engineering realm, wherein research has focused on the matching of methods and on the basis of that on the matching of component [ZW95,ZW97,JC95]. In all of these approaches, the state, i.e., the attributes, are largely ignored. In most of these approaches, matching is really divided into two segments, signature matching, wherein comparison is done at the syntactic level [ZW95];

and specification matching wherein the comparison is based on the behavior of the methods as specified by the pre- and post-conditions [ZW97]. This work [ZW95,ZW97,JC95] forms the basis of the micro match for methods as defined in Section 3.

We have found that both in schema matching and method matching, there has been no concerted effort to define a metric for the quality of match. To the best of our knowledge we are the first to now propose a QoM and provide a qualitative and quantitative analysis technique for its measurement.

6   Conclusions

In this paper we define a *Quality of Match* (QoM) metric, and provide a *qualitative* match taxonomy and *quantitative* weight-based match model to evaluate the QoM of two given schemata, independent of the match algorithm that is applied. To the best of our knowledge, ours is the first of its kind work that now provides a metric for comparing different matches based on the combination of the quality (exact, relaxed or not match) and the degree (total or partial) of match.

While we are not proposing any new schema match algorithms, our work compliments existing approaches. Our approach provides a tool set to evaluate the quality of match produced by such algorithms, and enables the optimization of the performance of current schema matching algorithms.

Future work needs to focus on (1) the use of "user input" to define the final matches, (2) the optimization of the schema match process, (3) the quality of match across different schema match algorithms as well as (4) the analysis of QoM for solving real data integration problems.

References

[BCVB01] S. Bergamaschi, S. Castano, M. Vincini, and D. Beneventano. Semantic integration of heterogeneous information sources. *Data and Knowledge Engineering*, 36(3):215–249, 2001.

[BHP94]   M.W. Bright, A.R. Hurson, and S. H. Pakzad. Automated Resolution of Semantic Heterogeneity in Multidatabases. *TODS*, 19(2):212–253, 1994.

[BM01]   J. Berlin and A. Motro. AutoPlex: Automated Discovery of Content for Virtual Databases. In *CoopIS*, pages 108–122, 2001.

[Boo94]   G. Booch. *Object-Oriented Analysis and Design*. Benjamin Cummings Pub., 1994.

[CSF00]   R. Conrad, D. Scheffner, and J.C. Freitag. XML conceptual modeling using UML. In Alberto H. F. Laender, Stephen W. Liddle, and Veda C. Storey, editors, *Conceptual Modeling - ER 2000, 19th International Conference on Conceptual Modeling, Salt Lake City, Utah, USA, October 9-12, 2000, Proceedings*, volume 1920, pages 558–571. Springer, 2000.

[DDH01]   A.H. Doan, P. Domingos, and A. Halevy. Reconciling Schemas of Disparate Data Sources: A Machine-Learning Approach. In *sigmod*, 2001.

[DR02]   Hong Hai Do and E. Rahm. COMA - A System for Flexible Combination of Schema Matching Approaches. In *vldb*, 2002.

[HMN⁺99] L.M. Haas, R.J. Miller, B. Niswonger, M.T. Roth, P. Schwarz, and E.L. Wimmers. Transforming Heterogeneous Data with Database Middleware: Beyond Integration. *IEEE Data Engineering Bulletin*, 22(1):31–36, 1999.

[JC95]   Jun-Jang Jeng and Betty H. C. Cheng. Specification matching for software reuse: A foundation*. In *Proceedings of the 1995 Symposium on Software reusability*. ACM Press, 1995.

[MBR01]   J. Madhavan, P. Bernstein, and E. Rahm. Generic Schema Matching with Cupid. In *vldb*, pages 49–58, 2001.

[MIR93]   R. J. Miller, Y. E. Ioannidis, and R. Ramakrishnan. The Use of Information Capacity in Schema Integration and Translation. In *Int. Conference on Very Large Data Bases*, pages 120–133, 1993.

[RR87]   A. Rosenthal and D. Reiner. Theoretically Sound Transformations for Practical Database Design. In Salvatore T. March, editor, *Entity-Relationship Approach, Proceedings of the Sixth International Conference on Entity-Relationship Approach, New York, USA, November 9-11, 1987*, pages 115–131, 1987.

[San95]   G. Lawrence Sanders. *Data Modeling*. Boyd and Fraser Publishing Company, 1995.

[ZW95]   Amy Moormann Zaremski and Jeannette M. Wing. Signature matching: a tool for using software libraries. In *ACM Transactions on Software Engineering and Methodology (TOSEM)*. ACM Press, 1995.

[ZW97]   Amy Moormann Zaremski and Jeannette M. Wing. Specification matching of software components. In *ACM Transactions on Software Engineering and Methodology (TOSEM)*. ACM Press, 1997.

The Uni-level Description: A Uniform Framework for Representing Information in Multiple Data Models*

Shawn Bowers and Lois Delcambre

OGI School of Science and Engineering at OHSU
Beaverton OR 97006, USA
{shawn,lmd}@cse.ogi.edu

Abstract. One advantage of having several different representation schemes and data models is that users can select the right representation and associated tools for their particular need. However, multiple representations introduce structural, model-based heterogeneity, making it difficult to combine information from different sources and exploit information using generic tools (e.g., for querying or browsing). In this work, we define a uniform representation based on a meta-data-model called the *Uni-Level Description* (ULD) that can accommodate and accurately store information in a broad range of data models. The ULD defines three distinct *instance-of* relationships plus a relationship for modeling *conformance*, which is used to connect (data) constructs to other (schema) constructs and can be constrained to reflect the requirements of the data model. The ULD has been shown to enable powerful, generic transformation rules and simple generic browsing capability over information represented in diverse data models and representation schemes.

1 Introduction

This work is motivated by a simple observation—that most data models and representation schemes use a small set of basic structures such as scalar data, tuple, and collection constructs, composed in various ways, to store information. The basic idea of our work is to describe the constructs of a data model using these basic structures and then instantiate them to describe the schema and data that is present in an information source. The goal of our work is to develop a generic representation that:

- can enable generic tools (i.e., tools that work over multiple data models);
- can describe a variety of data models;
- includes the data, schema(s) if present, and the data model of sources;
- is flat, much like RDF, so that data model, schema, and data can be accessed at the same time, e.g., in the same query;

---

* This work supported in part by NSF grants EIA-99083518 and IIS-9817492.

I.-Y. Song et al. (Eds.): ER 2003, LNCS 2813, pp. 45–58, 2003.

Relational Schema   *RDF Schema*

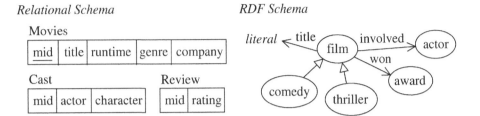

Fig. 1. Similar schemas expressed in the relational and RDF data models.

- permits various descriptions of any particular data model;
- can describe information where the schema is missing, where it is partial (e.g., like an "open" DTD for XML), and where there are multiple levels of schema (e.g., where the type of one topic is another topic, and the type of that topic is yet another topic in a Topic Map);
- permits the definition and use of new, special-purpose data models.

Our representation is called the *Uni-Level Description* (ULD). One of the key characteristics of the ULD is the use of three, distinct *instance-of* relationships plus a *conformance* relationship. That is, the traditional *instance-of* or *type* relationship is not overloaded in the ULD (unlike in knowledge representation models such as RDF). The conformance relationship allows the configurer of a data model to specify the connection between a data construct definition (like the entity construct in the E-R model) with the corresponding schema construct definition (like the entity type construct in the E-R model). More than that, providing constraints on the conformance relation permits accurate description of a wide range of data models.

We focus on structural heterogeneity [11] of data models, as shown in Figure 1 and schemas, as shown in Figure 2. We envision an environment where arbitrary data sources are easily described using the ULD, permitting the use of generic, ULD-based tools that can work over arbitrary information sources, as shown in Figure 3. We have implemented a transformation facility [7] where powerful transformation rules expressed in Datalog can easily convert information from one source to another, in the presence of different schemas or data models. We have also implemented a browser [6], supported by a navigational API against the ULD, that permits both naive users (e.g., users that don't know what an XML element or attribute is) and sophisticated users (e.g., agents or crawlers) to access information sources in a generic manner.

This paper is organized as follows. The ULD is presented in Section 2 with a detailed description of the meta-data-model architecture and *conformance* and *instance-of* relationships. Section 3 describes a language for representing and accessing information sources using the ULD. Related work is presented in Section 4 and conclusions and future work are presented in Section 5.

```
Schema 1:
  <!ELEMENT movie (title+,studio,genre*,actor*)>
  <!ELEMENT title (#PCDATA)>
  <!ELEMENT studio (#PCDATA)>
  <!ELEMENT genre (#PCDATA)>
  <!ELEMENT actor (#PCDATA)>
  <!ATTLIST actor role CDATA #REQUIRED>
Schema 2:
  <!ELEMENT movie (thriller|comedy)>
  <!ATTLIST movie name CDATA #REQUIRED>
  <!ELEMENT thriller (actor*,crew*)>
  <!ELEMENT comedy (actor*,crew*)>
  <!ELEMENT actor (#PCDATA)>
  <!ATTLIST actor role CDATA #REQUIRED>
  <!ELEMENT crew (#PCDATA)>
  <!ATTLIST crew role CDATA #REQUIRED>
```

Fig. 2. Heterogeneous XML DTDs that: (a) overlap, (b) are structurally different, and (c) are schematically different.

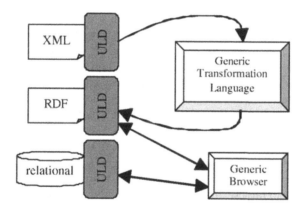

Fig. 3. ULD-enabled environment – generic tools can access information in various data models.

2   The Uni-level Description Framework

The architecture used by most meta-data-model approaches [1,2,3,8,13,9,14] is shown in Figure 4. The architecture consists of four levels representing the meta-data-model, the meta-schema (i.e., the data model), the schema, and source data. A meta-schema represents the set of structural *constructs* provided by a data model; and schemas are represented as instantiations of the meta-schema constructs. For example, the meta-schema to describe the relational model would consist of various data structures for representing relation types, their attribute types, primary and foreign keys, and so on.

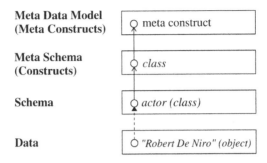

Fig. 4. The typical meta-data-model architecture

A number of architectures use E-R, entity and relationship structures to define meta-schemas and their corresponding schemas [1,2,3,8,13,14]. In this case, meta-schema constructs are defined as patterns, or compositions of entity and relationship types. These types are used to define entities and relationships representing corresponding schema items. With this approach, a meta-schema for the object-oriented data model would contain a class construct represented as an entity type (called *class*) with a name attribute and relationships to other constructs (e.g., that represent class attributes). A particular object-oriented schema is then represented as a set of entities and relationships that instantiate these meta-schema types. We note that in most meta-data-model architectures, data (the bottom level of Figure 4) is not explicitly represented—data is assumed to be stored outside of the system and is not directly represented in the architecture.

Traditional database systems generally require *complete schema* in which all data must satisfy all of the constraints imposed by the schema. Typical meta-data-model approaches assume data models require complete schema, and is reflected in the architecture of Figure 4, which assumes data follows from (only) the schema level.

2.1   The ULD Architecture

In contrast to Figure 4, the ULD uses the three-level architecture shown in Figure 5. The ULD meta-data-model (shown as the top level) consists of *construct types* (i.e., meta-constructs) that denote structural primitives. The middle level uses the structural primitives to define both data and schema constructs as well as possible conformance relationships among them.

The ULD architecture distinguishes three kinds of *instance-of* relationships. Constructs introduced in the middle layer are necessarily an instance (*ct-inst*) of a construct type in the meta-data-model. Similarly, every item introduced in the bottom layer is necessarily an instance (*c-inst*) of a construct in the middle layer. Finally, a data item in the bottom layer can be an instance (*d-inst*) of another data item, as allowed by *conformance* relationships in the middle layer.

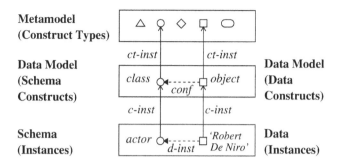

Fig. 5. The ULD meta-data-model architecture.

The ULD is able to represent a wide range of data models using the flexibility offered by the *conf* and *d-inst* relationships. For example, in XML, conformance between elements and element types is optional. Thus, an XML element without a corresponding element type would not have a *d-inst* link to an XML element type as part of a partial or optional schema.

The ULD represents an information source as a *configuration*, which contains the construct types of the meta-data-model, the constructs of a data model, the instances (both schema and data) of a source, and the associated instance-of relationships. Thus, a configuration can be viewed as an instantiation of Figure 5. Each configuration uses a finite set of identifiers for denoting construct types, constructs, and instances as well as a finite set of *ct-inst*, *c-inst*, *conf*, and *d-inst* relationships. Together, the use of identifiers with explicit instance-of relationships allows all three levels of Figure 5 to be stored in a single configuration (i.e., as a single level)—enabling direct and uniform access to all information in a source.

In a configuration, all construct and instance identifiers have exactly one associated value, where a value is a particular instantiation of a structure (e.g., a tuple or collection value). Primitive values such as strings, integers, and Booleans are treated as subsets of the data-item identifiers in a configuration.[1] The primitive structures defined in the ULD meta-data-model include tuples (lists of name-value pairs), collections (set, list, and bag), atomics (for primitive values like strings and integers), and unions (for representing union types, i.e., a non-structural, generalization relationship among types). The construct type identifiers are denoted *set-ct*, *list-ct*, *bag-ct*, *struct-ct*, *atomic-ct*, and *union-ct* representing collection, tuple, atomic, and union structures, respectively.

---

[1] This choice is primarily for enabling a more concise representation—primitive values could also be represented as distinct sets, disjoint from identifiers.

3   The ULD Representation Language

3.1   Representing Data Models in the ULD

Figures 6, 7, and 8 use the language of the ULD to describe the relational, XML, and RDF data models, respectively. Note that there are potentially many ways to describe a data model in the ULD, and these examples show only one choice of representation. As shown, a construct definition can take one of the following forms.

`construct` c = $\{a_1\text{->}c_1, a_2\text{->}c_2, \ldots, a_n\text{->}c_n\}$ `conf(domain=`x`,range=`y`)`:c'
This expression defines a tuple-construct c as a *ct-inst* of construct type *struct-ct*, where a_1 to a_n are unique strings, $n \geq 1$, and c_1 to c_n and c' are construct identifiers. Each expression $a_i = c_i$ is called a *component* of the construct c where a_i is called the component *selector*. If the *conf* expression is present, instances of c may conform (i.e., be connected by a *d-inst* relationship) to instances of c' according to the domain and range constraints on the expression. If the conformance expression is not present, conformance is not permitted for the construct (i.e., there cannot be a *d-inst* relationship between the construct instances). The cardinality constraints on conformance (x and y above) restrict the participation of associated instances in *d-inst* relationships to either exactly one (denoted as 1), zero or one (denoted as ?), zero or more (denoted as *), or one or more (denoted as +) for both the domain and range of the relationship.

`construct` c = `set of` c_1 `conf(domain=`x`,range=`y`)`:c'
This expression defines a set-construct c as a *ct-inst* of construct type *set-ct*. The definition restricts instances of c to sets whose members must be instances of construct c_1. In addition, for instances of c, each member must have a unique identifier. Bag types and list types are defined similarly. These constructs can also contain conformance definitions.

`construct` c = c_1 | c_2 | ... | c_n
This expression defines a union-construct c as a *ct-inst* of construct type *union-ct*, where c_1 to c_n are distinct construct identifiers for $n \geq 2$ such that for all i from 1 to n, $c \neq c_i$. All instances of c_1 to c_n are considered instances of c, however, we do not allow instances of only c directly. A union construct provides a simple mechanism to group heterogeneous structures (e.g., atomics and structs) into a single, union type, as opposed to *isa* relationships, which offer inheritance semantics, and group like structures (e.g., class-like structures).

`construct` c = `atomic conf(domain=`x`,range=`y`)`:c'
This expression defines an atomic type c as a *ct-inst* of construct type *atomic-ct*. These constructs can also contain a conformance definition.

As shown in Figure 6, tables and relation types are one-to-one such that each table conforms to exactly one relation type. Each tuple in a table must conform (as shown by the range restriction 1) to the table's associated relation type. We assume each relation type can have at most one primary key.

```
% schema constructs
construct relation  = {relname->string, atts->attlist}
construct attlist   = list of attribute
construct attribute = {aname->string, attof->relation, domain->valuetype}
construct pkey       = {pkeyof->relation, keyatts->attlist}
construct fkey       = {fkeyof->relation, ref->relation, srcatts->attlist}
% instance constructs
construct table      = bag of tuple conf(domain=1,range=1):relation
construct tuple      = list of value conf(domain=*,range=1):relation
```

Fig. 6. Description of the relational data model in the ULD.

```
% schema constructs
construct pcdata     = atomic
construct cdata      = atomic
construct elemtype   = {name->string, atts->attdefset, cmodel->contentdef}
construct attdefset  = set of attdef
construct attdef     = {name->string, attof->elemtype}
construct contentdef = set of elemtype
% data constructs
construct element    = {tag->string, atts->attset, children->content}
                        conf(domain=*,range=?):elemtype
construct attset     = list of attribute
construct attribute  = {name->string, attof->element, val->cdata}
                        conf(domain=*,range=?):attdef
construct content    = list of node
construct node       = element | pcdata
```

Fig. 7. Simplifed ULD description of the XML/DTD data model.

The XML data model shown in Figure 7 includes constructs for element types, attribute types, elements, attributes, content models, and content, where element types contain attribute types and content specifications, elements can optionally conform to element types, and attributes can optionally conform to attribute types. We simplify content models to sets of element types for which a conforming element must have at least one subelement (for each corresponding type).

Finally, Figure 8 shows the RDF(S) data model expressed in the ULD, and includes constructs for classes, properties, resources, and triples. In RDF, rdf:type, rdf:subClassOf, and rdf:subPropertyOf are considered special RDF properties for denoting instance and specialization relationships. However, we model these properties using conformance and explicit constructs (i.e., with subclass and subprop). Therefore, RDF properties in the ULD represent regular relationships; we do not overload them for type and subclass/subproperty def-

```
construct literal   = atomic
construct resource = {val->uri} conf(domain=*,range=*):class
construct class     = {rid->resource, label->string}
construct prop      = {rid->resource, label->string, domain->class,
                       range->rangeval}
construct rangeval = class | valuetype
construct subclass = {super->class, sub->class}
construct subprop  = {super->prop, sub->prop}
construct triple    = {pred->resource, subj->resource, obj->objval}
                       conf(domain=*,range=*):prop
construct objval    = resource | literal
```

Fig. 8. (Simplified ULD description of the RDF(S) data model.

initions. This approach does not limit the definition of RDF; partial, optional, and multiple levels of schema are still supported.

ULD configurations are populated with default constructs representing typical primitive value types, such as *string, Boolean, integer, url,* etc., as instances of *atomic-ct*. The *valuetype* and *value* constructs are special constructs that work together to provide a mechanism for data models to permit user-defined primitive types (e.g., to support XML Schema basic types or relational domains). The *value* construct is defined as the union (i.e., a union construct) of all defined *atomic-ct* constructs. Thus, when a new *atomic-ct* construct is created, it is automatically added to *value*'s definition. The *valuetype* construct has an instance with the same name (represented as a string value) as each construct of *value*. To add a new primitive type (e.g., a date type), we create a new construct (with the identifier *date*), add it as a member of *value* (recall *value* is a union construct), and create a new *valuetype* instance 'date,' connected by *c-inst*.

3.2   Representing Instances in the ULD

Examples of schema and data expressed in the ULD for XML and RDF are shown in Figures 9 and 10, respectively. Figure 9 gives (a portion of) the first XML DTD of Figure 2 and Figure 10 gives (a portion of) the RDF schema of Figure 1. As shown, expressions for defining instances take the form: i = c v d-inst:$i_1,i_2,\ldots,i_l$, where c is a construct, v is a valid value for construct c, and i_1 to i_l are instance identifiers for $l \geq 0$. The expression defines i as a construct instance (c-*inst*) of c with value v. Further, i is a data instance (d-*inst*) of i_1 to i_l, which must be instances of the construct(s) c conforms to. The d-inst expression is not present if i is not a data instance of another instance (i.e, $l = 0$).

Given the construct c, we say $c \in ct$-$inst(ct)$ is true if and only if c is defined as an instance (ct-*inst*) of construct type ct. Similarly, the expressions $i \in c$-$inst(c)$ and $i \in d$-$inst(i')$ are true if and only if i is defined as an instance (c-*inst*) of construct c and a data instance (d-*inst*) of i'. Finally, the relation $conf(c, c', x, y)$

is true if and only if a conformance relationship is defined from c to c' (i.e., instances of c are allowed to be data instances of c'). The domain constraint of the conformance relationship is x, and the range constraint is y. An instance is *valid* for a configuration if it is both well-formed and satisfies the constraints of its associated construct. We note that each data-level identifier can only be defined once in a configuration, and must have exactly one associated construct (i.e., must be a *c-inst* of exactly one construct). The following constraints are imposed by constructs on their instances.

Value Definition. If i is an instance of construct c (i.e., $i \in$ *c-inst*(c)) and c is a *struct-ct* construct (i.e., $c \in$ *ct-inst*(*struct-ct*)) then the value of i must contain the same number of components as c, each component selector of i must be a selector of c, and each component value of i must be an instance of the associated component construct value for c. Alternatively, if c is a collection construct, then the value of i must be a collection whose members are instances of the construct that c is a collection of, and if c is a set, i's elements must have unique identifiers.

Conformance Definition. If i is an instance of construct c (i.e., $i \in$ *c-inst*(c)), i' is an instance of construct c' (i.e., $i' \in$ *c-inst*(c')), and c can conform to c' (i.e., *conf*(c, c', x, y) is true for some x, y), then i is allowed to be a data instance (*d-inst*) of i'. Further, domain and range cardinality constraints on conformance can restrict allowable data-instance relationships. Namely, if the domain constraint on the conformance relationship is + (i.e., $x = +$), i must participate in at least one data-instance relationship (i.e., there must exist an i' where $i \in$ *d-inst*(i')). For a domain constraint of 1, i must be a data instance of exactly one i'. Similarly, if the range constraint on the conformance relationship is + (i.e., $y = +$), every i' must have at least one associated i (i.e., for each i' there must exist an i where $i \in$ *d-inst*(i')). For a range constraint of 1, exactly one i must be a data instance of i'.

3.3   Querying ULD Configurations

Information can be accessed in the ULD through queries against configurations. A query is expressed as a range-restricted Datalog program (i.e., a set of Datalog rules). A rule body consists of a set of conjoined ULD expressions possibly containing variables. For example, the following query finds all available class names within an RDF configuration. (Note that upper-case terms denote variables and lower-case terms denote constants.)

classes(X) ← C ∈ *c-inst*(class), C.label=X.

The following formulas are allowed in the body of ULD rules. The membership operator ∈ is used to access items in the sets *ct-inst*, *c-inst*, or *d-inst*. For example, the expression C ∈ *c-inst*(*class*) above finds RDF class identifiers C in the given configuration. In addition, the membership operator can access elements in collection structures, where an expression of the form $v \in x$ is true if v is a member of x's value and x is an instance of a set, list, or bag construct. Both

```
movie   = elemtype {name:'movie', atts:nilad, cmodel:moviecm}
nilad   = attdefset []
moviecm = contentdef [title, studio, genre, actor]
title   = elemtype {name:'title', atts:nilad, cmodel:nilcm}
nilcm   = contentdef []
genre   = elemtype {name:'genre', atts:nilad, cmodel:nilcm}
actor   = elemtype {name:'actor', atts:actorat, cmodel:nilcm}
actorat = attdefset [role]
role    = attdef {name:'role', attof:actor}
e1      = element {tag:'movie', atts:nilas, children:e1cnt} d-inst:movie
nilas   = attset []
e1cnt   = content [e2,e3,e4]
e2      = element {tag:'title', atts:nilas, children:e2cnt} d-inst:title
e2cnt   = content ['Usual Suspects']
e3      = element {tag:'genre', atts:nilas, children:e3cnt} d-inst:genre
e3cnt   = content ['thriller']
e4      = element {tag:'actor', atts:e4as, children=e4cnt} d-inst:actor
e4as    = attset [a1]
e4cnt   = content ['Kevin Spacey']
a1      = attribute {name:'role', attof:e4, val:'supporting'} d-inst:role
...
```

Fig. 9. Sample XML data and schema (DTD) expressed in the ULD.

```
film    = resource {val:'#film'}
title   = resource {val:'#title'}
comedy  = resource {val:'#comedy'}
filmc   = class {rid:film, label:'film'}
titlep  = prop {rid:title, label:'title', domain:filmc, range:'literal'}
comedyc = class {rid:comedy, label:'comedy'}
fc      = subclass {super:filmc, sub:comedyc}
f1 = resource {val:'http://.../review.html'} d-inst:comedyc,filmc
t1 = triple {pred:title, subj:f1, obj:'Meet the Parents'} d-inst:titlep
...
```

Fig. 10. Sample RDF(S) data expressed in the ULD.

v and x can be variables (bound or unbound) or constants. Finally, the expression $x.y = v$ (alternatively, $x \rightarrow y = v$) can be used to access data components (component definitions), where x is a data identifier (construct identifier), y is a component selector of x (component selector definition of x), and v is the value of the component (construct of the component definition). The terms x, y, and v can be either variables or constants.

The following query returns the property names of all classes in an RDF configuration. Note that this query, like the previous one, is expressed solely against the schema of the source.

1. elemtypes(X) ← E ∈ *c-inst*(elemtype), E.name=X.
2. atttypes(X,Y) ← A ∈ *c-inst*(attdef), A.name=Y, A.attof=E, E.name=X.
3. movies(X)   ← AT ∈ *c-inst*(attdef), AT.name='title', A ∈ *d-inst*(AT), A.val=X.
4. atts(X)   ← A ∈ *c-inst*(attribute), A.name=X.
5. attvals(X)   ← A ∈ *c-inst*(attribute), A.name='title', A.val=X.

Fig. 11. Example XML queries for schema directly, data through schema, and data directly.

properties(X,Y) ← C ∈ *c-inst*(*class*), P ∈ *c-inst*(*prop*), P.domain=C, C.label=X,
        P.label=Y.

After finding the available classes and properties of the schema, we can then use this information to find data instances. That is, a user could issue the previous query, see that the source contains title properties, and then construct the following query that returns all film titles in the configuration.

films(X) ← P ∈ *c-inst*(*prop*), P.label='title', T ∈ *d-inst*(P), T.obj=X.

ULD queries can access information at various levels of abstraction within an information source, including direct access to data (i.e., accessing data items without first accessing schema), direct access to schema (as shown in the previous queries), and direct access to data-model constructs. For example, the following query is expressed directly against data, and returns the *uri* of all resources used as a property in at least one triple (note that the resource may or may not be associated with schema).

allprops(X) ← T ∈ *c-inst*(*triple*), T.pred=R, R.val=X.

Once this query is issued, a user may wish to find additional information about a particular resource. For example, the following query returns all values of a resource used as a title property of a triple.

propvals(X) ← T ∈ *c-inst*(*triple*), T.pred='#title', T.obj=X.

Figure 11 shows a similar set of queries as those presented here, but for XML sources. The first query finds all available element types in the source, the second finds all available attribute types, the third finds the set of movie titles, the fourth finds the set of attributes (as a data query), and the last query finds the set of values for title attributes in the configuration.

Finally, a query can be posed against a data-model directly to determine the available constructs in a source. For example, the following query returns all constructs that serve as *struct-ct* schema constructs and their component selectors. (Note that conformance relationships are accessed through the *conf* relation defined previously.)

schemastructs(SC,P) ← SC ∈ *inst-ct*(*struct-ct*), *conf*(DC,SC,X,Y), SC→P=C.

3.4 Specifying Additional Rules for Conformance

The ability to query the ULD is not only important for providing uniform access to information sources, but can also be used to specify additional constraints on configurations (i.e., axioms). Here, we consider the use of queries for further defining conformance relationships, beyond cardinality restrictions.

A conformance definition consists of a restricted set of rules. Namely, the head of a conformance-definition is always of the form: $X \in d\text{-}inst(Y)$, which specifies that X can be a data-instance of Y when the conditions specified in the body of the rule are true. For example, according to the definition in Figure 6, tables can conform to relation types, however, the conformance specification given does not provide the necessary conditions to determine when conformance can occur (it states that tables and tuples must conform to relation types). The following two rules elaborate the conformance definitions for the relational model.

$X \in d\text{-}inst(Y) \leftarrow X \in c\text{-}inst(\text{table}),\ Y \in c\text{-}inst(\text{relation}),$
$\qquad forall_{T \in X}(T \in d\text{-}inst(Y)).$
$X \in d\text{-}inst(Y) \leftarrow X \in c\text{-}inst(\text{tuple}),\ Y \in c\text{-}inst(\text{relation}),\ Y.\text{atts=AS},$
$\qquad \text{length}(X,L),\ \text{length}(AS,L),$
$\qquad forall_{V \in X}(\text{memberAt}(V,X,I),\ \text{memberAt}(A,AS,I),$
$\qquad A.\text{domain=D},\ \text{d-inst}(V,D)).$

The first rule states that for a table to conform to a relation type, each tuple in the table must be a data instance of the relation type. Note that we use the shorthand notation *forall* to simulate a universal quantifier in Datalog. The expression can be replaced to create a Datalog rule by using the standard technique of introducing an intensional predicate and double negation.[2] The second rule states that for a tuple to conform to a relation type it must have the same number of values as attributes in the relation type, and each value must be a data instance of the corresponding attribute's domain

Conformance constraints can be used to determine whether the result of transforming one source into another creates a valid (target) configuration. We are interested in investigating how conformance constraints can be further exploited within the ULD and in identifying a general set of concise constraints (much like in description logics) for specifying additional conformance definitions.

4 Related Work

Most approaches for resolving structural heterogeneity focus on schema and assume a common data model (e.g., [4,5,10]). Here, we discuss alternative techniques that consider disparate data models and we discuss their limitations.

A *self-describing* data model [12] describes its own structure to integrate the representation of data, schema, and meta-schema (i.e., a description of the possible schema structurings). Self-describing data models use their own structuring

---

[2] For example, we can rewrite the first rule as:
$\quad X \in d\text{-}inst(Y) \leftarrow X \in c\text{-}inst(\text{table}),\ Y \in c\text{-}inst(\text{relation}),\ \neg\ \text{not-conf}(X,Y).$
$\quad \text{not-conf}(X,Y) \leftarrow T \in X,\ \neg\ T \in d\text{-}inst(Y).$

capability to represent meta-schema and schema information. To access multiple data models, users must still use distinct languages and interfaces for each source. Self-describing data models require conventions to distinguish meta-schema from schema, and schema from data.

Atzeni and Torlone's MDM [1,2,14] uses primitives similar to E-R entity and relationship types and data-model constructs are defined as compositions of these structures. Schemas in MDM are instantiations of these data-model structures and MDM does not consider source data.

In YAT [9], a meta-data-model is used to define XML *tree patterns*, which are DTDs that permit variables. A tree pattern describes a meta-schema, a partially instantiated tree pattern denotes a schema, and a fully instantiated tree pattern represents the content of an information source. YAT's meta-data-model has limited structuring capabilities for representing data-model constructs and schemas, and instead, defines simple conventions to represent source data as hierarchies.

Gangopadhyay and Barsalou use *metatypes*, which are similar to MDM primitive structures, to define data models. A data model is represented as a collection of specialized metatypes, each serving as a specific data model construct. A schema instantiates the associated data-model metatypes, and a database in the federation is assumed to contain instances of the corresponding schema types (metatypes are considered second-order).

5   Conclusions and Future Work

The ULD extends existing meta-data-model approaches by providing richer modeling capabilities for defining data models. In particular, the ULD permits both data and schema constructs with their conformance relationships. The ULD also provides explicit instance-of relationships, which allow uniform representation of data-model constructs, schema, and data, making each level directly accessible and explicitly connected. The framework enables (accurate) representation of a broader range of data models than previous approaches by permitting zero, one, or more levels of schema. In addition, the ULD enables a transformation language [7], which can specify and mix data, schema, and data-model mappings. The transformation language is an extension of the query language presented in this paper. We also have a generic navigation language on top of the ULD to uniformly browse information represented in diverse data models and representation schemes [6].

Our current implementation of the ULD provides converters for RDF(S), XML, and relational sources into the ULD (i.e., into a Prolog knowledge base), where queries and transformations can be executed (via rules expressed in Prolog). We are also developing a Java-based API for the ULD that contains function calls for accessing the various ULD predicates (*ct-inst*, *c-inst*, *d-inst*, and so on) to leave data "in place" (i.e., un-materialized).

References

1. P. Atzeni and R. Torlone. Schema translation between heterogeneous data models in a lattice framework. In *Proceedings of the 6th IFIP TC-2 Working Conference on Data Semantics (DS-6)*, pages 345–364. Chapman and Hall, 1995.
2. P. Atzeni and R. Torlone. Management of multiple models in an extensible database design tool. In *Proceedings of the 5th International Conference on Extending Database Technology (EDBT'96)*, volume 1057 of *Lecture Notes in Computer Science*, pages 79–95. Springer, 1996.
3. T. Barsalou and D. Gangopadhyay. M(DM): An open framework for interoperation of multimodel multidatabase systems. In *Proceedings of the 8th International Conference on Data Engineering (ICDE'92)*, pages 218–227. IEEE Computer Society, 1992.
4. C. Batini, M. Lenzerini, and S.B. Navathe. A comparative analysis of methodologies for database schema integration. *ACM Computing Surveys*, 18(4):323–364, 1986.
5. P.A. Bernstein, A.Y. Halevy, and R. Pottinger. A vision of management of complex models. *SIGMOD Record*, 29(4):55–63, December 2000.
6. S. Bowers and L. Delcambre. JustBrowsing: A generic API for exploring information. In *Demo Session at the 21st International Conference on Conceptual Modeling (ER'02)*, 2002.
7. S. Bowers and L. Delcambre. On modeling conformance for flexible transformation over data models. In *Proceedings of the ECAI Workshop on Knowledge Transformation for the Semantic Web*, pages 19–26, 2002.
8. K. Clapool and E. Rudensteiner. Sangam: A framework for modeling heterogeneous database transformations. In *Proceedings of the 5th International Conference on Enterprise Information Systems*, 2003. To Appear.
9. S. Cluet, C. Delobel, Jérôme Siméon, and K. Smaga. Your mediators need data conversion! In *Proceedings of the 1998 ACM SIGMOD International Conference on Management of Data*, pages 177–188. ACM, 1998.
10. S. B. Davidson and A. Kosky. WOL: A language for database transformations and constraints. In *Proceedings of the 13th International Conference on Data Engineering (ICDE'98)*, pages 55–65. IEEE Computer Society, 1997.
11. J. Hammer and D. McLeod. On the resolution of representational diversity in multidatabase systems. In *Management of Heterogeneous and Autonomous Database Systems*, pages 91–118. Morgan Kaufmann, 1998.
12. L. Mark and N. Roussopoulos. Integration of data, schema and meta-schema in the context of self-documenting data models. In *Proceedings of the 3rd International Conference on Entity-Relationship Approach (ER'83)*, pages 585–602. North-Holland, 1983.
13. OMG. *Meta Object Facility (MOF) Specification*, Sept. 1997. OMG Document ad/97-08-14.
14. R. Torlone and P. Atzeni. A unified framework for data translation over the web. In *Proceedings of the 2nd International Conference on Web Information Systems Engineering (WISE'01)*, IEEE Computer Society, pages 350–358, 2001.

Temporal Conceptual Modelling of Workflows

Carlo Combi[1] and Giuseppe Pozzi[2]

[1] Università di Verona,
strada le Grazie 15, I-37134 Verona - Italy
`carlo.combi@univr.it`
[2] Politecnico di Milano,
P.za L. da Vinci 32, I-20133 Milano - Italy
`giuseppe.pozzi@polimi.it`

Abstract. Business processes require the coordinated execution of simple activities (tasks) by human or automatic executors (agents). Business processes are described in terms of a workflow and their execution is supported by suitable software systems named workflow management systems (WfMS). Several conceptual models for the formal definition of workflows have been defined in the literature. However, a detailed conceptual model enabling the process designer to specify temporal constraints for the activities in a workflow is still lacking.

By this paper we enrich a previously published conceptual model of workflows by adding the definition of three kinds of constraints: task constraints, related to the starting timestamp and to the duration of one single task; schedule-task constraints, related to the time elapsed between the completion of a task and the start of the subsequent task by the entitled agent; inter-task constraints, related to the time elapsed between the execution of a task and of one subsequent task of its. The enriched model enables a WfMS to manage soft real-time processes.

1 Introduction

Workflows are activities involving the coordinated execution of single atomic activities (*tasks*), assigned and executed by processing entities (*agents*) to reach a common goal. Business processes can be modelled by workflows and enacted by suitable software systems (Workflow Management Systems - WfMS). WfMSs assign tasks to executing agents, which can be a human executor or an automatic executor like a software system or a combination of both, according to predefined policies. Conceptual models (*schema*) describe activities, capturing the behavior of the process and providing a formal process model. Several conceptual models were defined in the literature - we mention here [2,12] - and any WfMS proposes its own one: despite the efforts from the Workflow Management Coalition [12] (WfMC), no standard has been achieved yet for the definition of process models and their interoperability among different WfMSs still is far away.

WfMSs organize long running activities which can be mission critical for the organization where the activity is held: in most of these activities the management of time is not critical. Recently, WfMSs have been applied to the management of soft real-time processes featuring a not negligible temporal semantics:

I.-Y. Song et al. (Eds.): ER 2003, LNCS 2813, pp. 59–76, 2003.
© Springer-Verlag Berlin Heidelberg 2003

this widens a new frontier for the research on temporal data management and workflow systems. Indeed, soft real-time processes are processes where temporal deadlines must be matched: they differ from strict real-time processes as in these latter any deadline mismatch leads to unacceptable consequences, like in a nuclear plant or in a military defense system. As an example of a soft real-time process, we consider the typical business process when organizing a conference: invitations to attend the conference must be sent well in advance before the conference opens. Invitations sent out only two weeks before the conference opens will have no effect. As another example, we consider the building management: if a fire sensor sends in an alarm, the controlling system must activate fire extinguishers close to that sensor within a few seconds to achieve the maximum efficiency. Without a strict control over temporal constraints and deadlines for the completion of tasks, a WfMS could hardly manage soft real-time processes.

During the enactment of instances (*cases*) of a process model inside a WfMS, abnormal delays can take place, thus reducing the global performance of the managed business process. If no temporal information can be defined, these exceptional situations are hardly detected or require a complex software system to plug into the WfMS [4]. The definition and the management of temporal information of processes will improve the management of processes by a WfMS and widen the applicability of WfMSs to many different areas, including but not limited to plant management, control of telephone lines, building management, health care management. Specifically, some of the temporal aspects that can be considered aim at defining constraints over data specific of the process managed by the WfMS (e.g. rental date for the business process of a car rental company), over data of the workflow itself and related to starting and ending timestamps of tasks, and over data about agents involved into the processes.

In this paper we focus on the definition of temporal constraints at the very conceptual level, ignoring any implementation aspect. The paper is structured as follows: Sect. 2 introduces an atemporal (timeless) conceptual model for workflows, the architecture of a WfMS, and a motivating example; Sect. 3 considers the aspects of a process model with relevant temporal information, and the constraints that can be defined; Sect. 4 provides a detailed example with some temporal constraints; Sect. 5 considers the related work; finally, Sect. 6 sketches out some conclusions and future directions.

2   Conceptual Modelling

The conceptual model (*schema*) of a workflow describes the normal behavior of the process, identifying the single atomic activities (*tasks*), their activation sequences, and criteria to assign them to performing agents. As the reference conceptual model, we consider the atemporal one by Casati et al. in [2]. The model is not influenced by any particular commercial WfMS and is one of the models closest to the recommendations from the Workflow Management Coalition [12]. After a very short review of the model and of the architecture of a

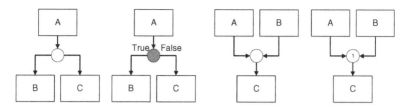

Fig. 1. Graphical symbology for total fork, partial fork, total join, partial join

generic WfMS, we introduce a motivating example showing that temporal aspects of the business process need to be managed and do not fit into that model.

2.1 Atemporal Conceptual Modelling of Workflows

The model by Casati et al. in [2] does not consider temporal aspects, providing an atemporal (timeless) model. Elementary activities, namely task types or more shortly tasks, are described in terms of the following main characteristics:

- name: a unique identifier for the task type. The name must follow the rules typical for a programming language when choosing the name of a variable;
- description: a natural language description of the activity of the task type;
- precondition: a boolean expression which must be true for the task instance to start. If the condition evaluates false, the task instance has to wait and will start only after the condition evaluates true;
- actions: a sequence of statements to manipulate workflow and local temporary data. Workflow data are supposed to be stored into the Database Management System (DBMS) and are manipulated via SQL statements: local temporary variables are read by the get statement and may be copied to workflow data or may be lost at case completion;
- exceptions: abnormal events are detected before the task instance commits by a pair <Exception, Reaction>. Exceptions are detected by the WfMS and may be related to constraints over temporary or workflow data and to the duration of execution of the task instance. Actions can be the forced completion (end) or the cancellation (cancel) of the task instance, a notification to an agent, or the execution of a specific task handling the abnormal situation.

One task, named predecessor, may have one outgoing arc towards a successor: the semantics of this straight connection is very intuitive. One task may have the outgoing arc towards a routing connector, to increase the expressiveness in constructing the flow of execution (see Fig. 1). Routing connectors can be *fork* connectors (*split* according to the WfMC): a total fork states that all the outgoing arcs from the fork connector will be activated; a conditional fork, eventually with mutual exclusion, states that only some of the outgoing arcs from the fork connector will be activated, e.g. according to the values of local or workflow variables. Routing connectors can also be *join* connectors, to synchronize the flow by waiting the completion of two or more predecessor tasks: a total

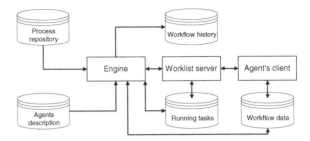

Fig. 2. Generic architecture of a Workflow Management System (WfMS)

join waits for the completion of all the incoming arcs; a partial join waits for the completion of n incoming arcs, being n the parameter of the join connector.

A schema may have some local variables, each case having its own copy of vars: variables can be used to store process data that are not stored into the DBMS and will be lost at case completion. Local variables are used as criteria to select outgoing arcs from a fork connector, typically. A schema also has one start symbol, connected to the first task to be executed, and at least one stop symbol: after any stop symbol is reached, the case is completed and the tasks eventually still running are no longer considered. Tasks can also be grouped into a *supertask* (or subprocess or subworkflow), introducing the notion of modularization. A supertask has the same properties of a task, meaning that the precondition and the exceptions of that supertask are evaluated for the first task of the supertask to start and after the last task of the supertask commits, respectively.

2.2   Reference Architecture of a WfMS

Figure 2 depicts a generic architecture of a WfMS. The workflow engine reads from a process repository the schema of the process to be executed, schedules task executions by assigning them according to criteria and descriptions of the organization stored into the agent description database. As the scheduler, that is a part of the engine, selects the agent suitable for the task to start, it puts the work item into the agent's work list: the agent accesses the work list via a client (mostly, a web browser), performs the task and reads and writes workflow data. After a task is completed, it moves back from the work list to the engine and finally it is stored into the workflow history database.

2.3   A Motivating Example

As an example, we consider a schema managing car accidents for a car rental company: then, we shall add some temporal constraints. Whenever during a car rental a customer experiences a car accident, he/she has to inform immediately the rental company by calling a toll-free number: the answering operator stores data about the rental (RentalID) and about the accident (AccidentDate and AccidentPlace) into the database. Within 24 hours from the phone call, the insurance

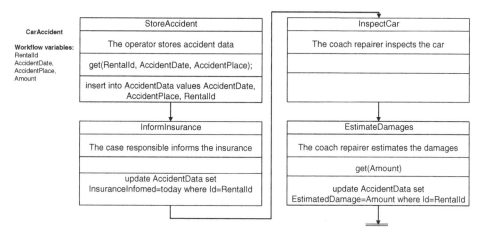

Fig. 3. Schema of the car accident process

company needs to be informed by the rental company about the accident: the entitled agent compiles the form, faxes it to the insurance and stores related data into the database. Within 2 days after the notification of the car accident to the insurance company, the coach repairer selected by the insurance company has to start inspecting the car: after inspection is completed, he/she estimates the amount of damages suffered by the car, and stores it into the database. The schema of the process is depicted in Fig. 3, where for readability reasons preconditions and exceptions are omitted as they are null.

The temporal constraints referred to must be observed, or the insurance policy becomes void and the insurance company will not refund any damage. This schema defines a soft real-time process [11].

3   Temporal Conceptual Modelling of Workflows

The subtended temporal data model considers instants and durations [5] as elementary types. As recommended by the WfMC [12], a finest granularity is adopted: we assume that timestamps are read from the system internal clock at the seconds granularity as the finest one available. Durations are computed as a length on the time axis and can be easily computed if the starting and ending instants are defined at the same granularity level: for instance, this happens for durations of completed tasks. Intervals are derived types and can be defined either as a duration after an instant or as a duration before an instant or as the distance between starting and ending timestamps [5].

Temporal constraints can be defined over the model. Constraints can be divided as task constraints, schedule-task constraints, and inter-task constraints, as detailed in Sect. 3.1. In this paper we do not consider the reactions the system can perform, and how it effectively performs, whenever a temporal constraint is violated: we assume that some temporal constraints are defined inside the conceptual model and that allowed reactions managed directly by the WfMS include the activation of a new case or the notification to an agent by e-mail.

Finally, some information can be provided into the conceptual model at different levels of granularity. One may want to define the maximum allowed time span at the granularity of seconds (e.g. 360 seconds) or of days (e.g. 3 days) or of months (e.g. 4 months). This extends the recommendations of [12], where all the temporal information are defined at the only granularity level allowed.

3.1   Temporal Constraints

We can define a taxonomy of temporal constraints as follows:

i. task constraints: constraints at the single task level may relate to task start or end time (timestamp constraint) and to task duration time (duration constraint). The task start time may be either an absolute timestamp (e.g. on May 24th 2002, 16:10:34) or a periodic timestamp (e.g. every Sunday morning at 2:10:05 a.m.); an end time for the task (e.g. on June 7th 2002, 18:30:00) may also be provided, specifying a deadline for that task, no matter when the task started. Two main attributes, namely ExpectedTaskDuration and MaxTaskDuration may also be defined, fixing some acceptable limit values for the duration of every task;

ii. schedule-task constraints: these constraints consider the ending timestamp of a task and the beginning timestamp of its successor, taking into account also the scheduling time: additional considerations are required (Sect. 3.2) if there is more than one successor due to a fork connector or there is more than one predecessor due to a join connector;

iii. inter-task constraints: these constraints consider the timestamps of a task and the timestamps of its successor: additional considerations are required (see Sect. 3.2) if there is more than one successor due to a fork connector or there is more than one predecessor due to a join connector.

To consider schedule-task and inter-task constraints an example is needed for. We consider an elementary process model with two tasks, A and B, and a straightforward connection. After predecessor A commits, the scheduler selects the successor B, selects its executing agent and puts the task into the agent's work list: the agent will then pick the work item and execute it.

The temporal constraints we may define obviously depend on several factors, including the total workload of the processing system and the scheduling time, i.e. the time required for the execution of the scheduling activity inside the WfMS. While many contributions neglect the scheduling time considering it as null ([10,13]: see Sect. 5), we do not consider that time a negligible one at the conceptual level, as we aim at using WfMSs for soft real-time processes, too[1]. The scheduling time may also be significantly affected by several factors: the

---

[1] Additionally, the scheduling activity can not be considered a task specific of the managed business process, since that activity is performed by the workflow engine.

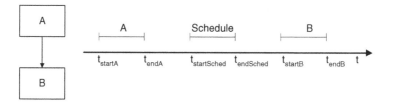

Fig. 4. Temporal constraints can be defined among tasks

execution of a query over a federated DBMS, or more simply the evaluation of a function inside a fork or a join connector, to mention few of them. If the WfMS is run by a company with different sites, we can assume that the execution of a case may require the involvement of agents from different sites: e.g., a car rental company may have one office in Boston, MA, and one office in Buffalo, N.Y., while the unique administrative office is in Syracuse, N.Y. For a given case, the reservation is performed by an agent in Boston while the invoice is sent out by an agent in Syracuse. This implies that the WfMS may assign tasks to agents from different sites: reasonably, data about agents reside on different DBMSs, requiring a distributed or federated query to properly select the executing agent according to resource availability criteria. Additionally, the process instance partially run in Boston by the WfMS in Boston may be transferred to Syracuse to be run by the WfMS in Syracuse. In both situations, distributed or federated queries and the transferring a process instance from one WfMS (in Boston) to another one (in Syracuse) may require additional time to complete: the process model has to enable the process designer to define suitable temporal constraints.

In the following we consider in detail each kind of constraint for a straight-forward connection between task A and its unique successor B as in Fig. 4.

3.1.1 Task Constraints

Timestamp constraints, both absolute and periodical, allow the designer to define when the task has to start. These constraints can be defined at any granularity level and are converted to the finest level adopted by the WfMS. Both times-tamp constraints are directly managed by the WfMS, as well as the violation of constraints are.

Considering duration constraints, the attribute ExpectedTaskDuration defines the expected duration of the task, i.e. the average duration reasonably acceptable for the execution of the task; the attribute MaxTaskDuration defines the maximum allowable duration beyond which an alert must be risen and possibly some compensation is needed for. These two attributes enable the process designer to consider a soft deadline and a firm deadline, according to the requirements of the managed process. The two attributes are similar to those defined in [4]: however, the main difference is that these constraints are defined here at the process model level instead of being defined at the exception manager level. By defining these constraints inside the process model, their management can be mapped into any commercial WfMS as a localized exception [4].

The attributes ExpectedTaskDuration and MaxTaskDuration are semantically a duration. During the execution of the task instance inside the WfMS some alarms are set to detect the exceeding duration. If in the conceptual model the duration is defined at the finest granularity level (e.g. seconds), or at levels that can be precisely converted to the finest granularity level (i.e., minute = 60 seconds, hour = 60×60 seconds, day = 24 hours = 86,400 seconds), at task execution time the attributes are copied from the conceptual model and converted to the finest granularity level. If in the conceptual model the duration is expressed at levels that can not be converted precisely to the finest granularity level (i.e., one month is made up of a variable number of days, $28 \div 31$) at task execution time the attributes are computed according to the current calendar and converted to a variable number of seconds [9]. As an example, if the current date is March 31st and the ExpectedTaskDuration is one month, at task execution time the attribute is computed as April 30th, assuming a 30-day long month: if the current date is April 30th and the ExpectedTaskDuration is three months, at task execution time the attribute is computed as July 30th, totalizing 91 days as 3 months. Leap years are managed, too.

3.1.2 Schedule-Task Constraints

Schedule-task constraints deal with the time between the completion of a predecessor and the beginning of the successor (i.e., A and B in Fig. 4), and include the scheduling time. In the following, we assume that the successor is unique: later on we shall discuss what may happen if the successors are more than one. The following four different constraints enable the WfMS to manage soft real-time processes, and can be defined as:

i. $t_{startSched} - t_{endA} < \epsilon_1$. The scheduler must start operating before a duration ϵ_1 elapses after the completion of the predecessor (i.e., A);

ii. $t_{endSched} - t_{endA} < \epsilon_2$. The scheduler has to select the successor and its executing agent, and to put the task into the agent's work list within a duration ϵ_2 after the predecessor A completed. The total workload of the system, and the difficulty in finding a suitable executing agent may affect this constraint, requiring a long time for the selection: this may happen in a distributed or federated database environment or if the organization does not provide a sufficient number of agents or if most of them will go on holiday before they will have completed the task according to its expected duration;

iii. $t_{startB} - t_{endSched} < \epsilon_3$. The constraint states that the selected agent has to pick the work item from his/her work list and start it before an amount of time ϵ_3 elapses since the end of the scheduling. This constraint aims at verifying how prompt the reply from an agent is;

iv. $t_{startB} - t_{startSched} < \epsilon_4$. The constraint states that the selected agent has to pick the work item from his/her work list and start it before an amount of time ϵ_4 elapses since the beginning of the scheduling.

Observation. Should all of the above constraints be defined over the same couple of tasks, some relationships between the different ϵ_i must be fulfilled, e.g. $\epsilon_1 + \epsilon_4 = \epsilon_2 + \epsilon_3$. Additionally, some other constraints can be defined for the category of schedule-task constraints: they all relate to durations. We mention here $t_{startSched}$ - $t_{startA} < \epsilon$, $t_{endSched}$ - $t_{startA} < \epsilon$, t_{endB} - $t_{startSched} < \epsilon$, t_{endB} - $t_{endSched} < \epsilon$. We believe that these constraints are not needed for in the real application context of most processes and thus we shall not consider them here.

3.1.3 Inter-task Constraints

Inter-task constraints deal with the time between the beginning/completion of a predecessor and the beginning/completion of the successor (i.e., A and B in Fig. 4). As previously, in the following we assume that the successor is unique: later on we shall discuss what may happen if the successors are more than one. The following four different constraints enable the WfMS to manage soft real-time processes, and can be defined as:

i. t_{startB} - $t_{startA} < \delta_1$. The time elapsed between the start of the predecessor and the time when the agent picked the successor from the work list must be smaller than δ_1;

ii. t_{startB} - $t_{endA} < \delta_2$. This constraint states that the successor must start (i.e., the assigned agent has to open the work item from the work list) within a temporal delay of δ_2 after the completion of the predecessor;

iii. t_{endB} - $t_{endA} < \delta_3$. The ending time of the successor must be at a distance smaller than δ_3 from the ending time of the predecessor: thus the successor must be completed within the deadline $t_{endA} + \delta_3$;

iv. t_{endB} - $t_{startA} < \delta_4$. The distance between the time when the agent picked the predecessor from the work list and when the successor was completed must be less than δ_4: thus the maximum amount of time available for the execution of the two tasks is δ_4.

Observation. Should all of the above constraints be defined over the same couple of tasks, some relationships between the different δ_i must be fulfilled, e.g. δ_4 - $\delta_1 = \delta_3$ - δ_2. Moreover, inter-task constraint and schedule-task constraints are bounded: as an example, $\delta_2 = \epsilon_1 + \epsilon_4$.

3.2   Temporal Constraints with Connectors

In this Sect. we extend the considerations about schedule-task and inter-task constraints of Sect. 3.1 to schemata where one predecessor is connected to multiple successors via a fork connector or where more predecessors are connected to one successor via a join connector. In the following we assume that both tasks involved by the constraint will be executed: should any or both of them be skipped due to a conditional execution path, the trigger becomes void. For clarity reasons, we categorize temporal constraints firstly according to the kind of connector, and secondly according to the schedule-task or inter-task feature.

3.2.1 Temporal Constraints with Fork Connectors

Figure 5 depicts a total fork connector. A mutually exclusive fork is immediately reduced at run-time to a straightforward connection like in Fig. 4: if the constraint is defined for one outgoing arc, e.g. from A to B, and the local variable

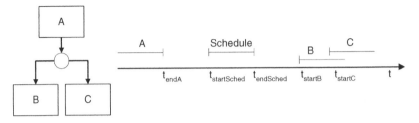

Fig. 5. Temporal constraint in the presence of a total fork connector

does not take that branch, the constraint is void. The same applies if the constraint is defined for the outgoing arc from A to C and the branch taken is the one towards B. Schedule-task and inter-task constraints are thus immediately dealt with as defined in Sect. 3.1, like if no fork connector was defined.

In the presence of a total fork connector, where all the outgoing arcs from A will be activated, the designer may still want to define a temporal constraint C_1 over one specific outgoing arc, e.g. from A to B. This implies that the constraint is defined over that arc only, while no constraint is defined over the outgoing arc from A to C. The designer may also want to define a constraint C_2 on the arc towards C, managing the two constraints in a separate way. Again, schedule-task and inter-task constraints are thus immediately dealt with as in Sect. 3.1, like if no fork connector was defined.

In the following we consider the schemata where the designer wants to define a constraint over all of the outgoing arcs managed globally. As in Fig. 5, after task A ends at time t_{endA} the scheduler during the interval $[t_{startSched}, t_{endSched}]$ selects the executing agents for tasks B and C; the executing agent of task B picks the work item from the work list at time t_{startB} while the executing agent of task C picks the work item from the work list at time t_{startC}. The schedule-task and inter-task temporal constraints are thus redefined in the following.

Schedule-Task Constraints. These constraints are related to the amount of time elapsed after the scheduler started and before the successors are opened. Given a process model $\mathcal{P}$ and the function *Schema* returning the set of tasks of $\mathcal{P}$, the set of tasks T_j successors of task T_i is made of the tasks returned by the function *Succ*:

$$Succ : Schema(\mathcal{P}) \rightarrow 2^{Schema(\mathcal{P})},$$
$$Succ(T_i) = \{T_j \mid T_j > T_i \wedge \neg \exists T_k (T_j > T_k > T_i)\} \tag{1}$$

where the relationship $>$ is a partial order relationship according to the execution time of tasks within a process model. We can now reconsider the schedule-task constraints of Sect. 3.1. We shall consider a new schema as in Fig. 5, where predecessor A has a set of successors $Succ(A)$, namely B and C. Changes apply to schedule-task constraints number iii) and iv) only, as follows:

iii. $\max(t_{startT_j})$ - $t_{endSched} < \epsilon_3$, where $T_j \in Succ(A)$. The constraint states that the selected agents have to pick the work items from their work lists and start all the tasks of the current process before an amount of time ϵ_3 elapses since the end of the scheduling. This constraint aims at verifying that all the tasks are started promptly by their respective agents;

iv. $\max(t_{startT_j}) - t_{startSched} < \epsilon_4$, where $T_j \in Succ(\mathsf{A})$. The constraint states that the selected agents have to pick the work items and start them before an amount of time ϵ_4 elapses since the beginning of the scheduling.

Inter-Task Constraints. These constraints are related to the amount of time elapsed between the predecessor and the successors. Given a process model $\mathcal{P}$, the set of tasks T_j successors of task T_i is made of the tasks for which definition (1) holds. We can now reconsider the inter-task constraints of Sect. 3.1. Changes apply to schedule-task constraints as follows:

i. $\max(t_{startT_j}) - t_{startA} < \delta_1$, where $T_j \in Succ(\mathsf{A})$. The time elapsed between the start of the predecessor and the time when the agents picked all the work items of the current process from the work lists must be smaller than δ_1;

ii. $\max(t_{startT_j}) - t_{endA} < \delta_2$. This constraint states that the successors must start (i.e., the assigned agents have to open the work items of the current process from the work lists) within a temporal delay of δ_2 after the completion of the predecessor;

iii. $\max(t_{endT_j}) - t_{endA} < \delta_3$. The ending time of all the successors must be at a distance smaller than δ_3 from the ending time of the predecessor: thus the successors must be completed within the deadline $t_{endT_i} + \delta_3$;

iv. $\max(t_{endT_j}) - t_{startA} < \delta_4$. The distance between the time when the agent picked the predecessor from the work list and when the successors were completed must be less than δ_4: thus the maximum amount of time available for the execution of the tasks T_i and of all of its successors T_j is δ_4.

3.2.2 Temporal Constraints with Join Connectors

Figure 6 depicts a total join connector. A partial join is parametric on a variable n meaning how many incoming arcs are to be completed for the outgoing arc to be activated. In the presence of a partial join with $n = 1$, the partial join is immediately reduced at run-time to a straightforward connection like in Fig. 4: if the constraint is defined for one incoming arc, e.g. from A to C, and task B completes before A completes, the constraint is void. The same applies if the constraint is defined for the outgoing arc from B to C and A completes first. Schedule-task and inter-task constraints are thus immediately dealt with as defined in Sect. 3.1, like if no join connector was defined.

In the presence of a total join connector or of a partial join with $n \geq 2$, where all or some of the incoming arcs have to be completed, the designer may still want to define a temporal constraint C_1 over one specific outgoing arc, e.g. from A to C. This implies that the constraint is defined over that arc only, while no constraint is defined over the arc from B to C. The designer may also want to define a constraint C_2 on the arc from B, managing the two constraints in a separate way. Again, schedule-task and inter-task constraints are thus immediately dealt with as in Sect. 3.1, like if no join connector was defined.

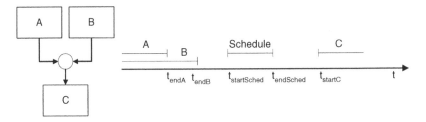

Fig. 6. Temporal constraint in the presence of a total join connector

In the following we consider the schemata where the designer wants to define a constraint over all of the incoming arcs managed globally. As depicted in Fig. 6, after task A ends at time t_{endA} and task B ends at time t_{endB}, the scheduler during the interval $[t_{startSched}, t_{endSched}]$ selects the executing agent for task C; the executing agent of task C picks the work item from the work list at time t_{startC}. The schedule-task and inter-task temporal constraints are thus redefined in the following.

Schedule-Task Constraints. These constraints are related to the amount of time elapsed after the scheduler started and before the successor is opened. Given a process model $\mathcal{P}$, the set of tasks T_i predecessors of task T_j is made of the tasks returned by the function $Pred$:

$$Pred : Schema(\mathcal{P}) \to 2^{Schema(\mathcal{P})},$$
$$Pred(T_j) = \{T_i \mid T_j > T_i \land \neg \exists T_k (T_j > T_k > T_i)\} \tag{2}$$

We can now reconsider the schedule-task constraints of Sect. 3.1. We shall consider a new schema as depicted in Fig. 6, where successor C has a set of predecessors $Pred(C)$, namely A and B.

i. $t_{startSched}$ - $\max(t_{endT_i}) < \epsilon_1$, where $T_i \in Pred(C)$. The scheduler must start operating before a duration ϵ_1 elapses after the completion of all the predecessors (i.e., after the completion of the last predecessor);

ii. $t_{endSched}$ - $\max(t_{endT_i}) < \epsilon_2$. The scheduler has to select the successor and its executing agent, and to put the task into the agent's work list within a duration ϵ_2 after all the predecessors completed, (i.e., after the completion of the last predecessor).

iii. t_{startC} - $t_{endSched} < \epsilon_3$, as described in Sect 3.1;

iv. t_{startC} - $t_{startSched} < \epsilon_4$, as described in Sect. 3.1.

Inter-Task Constraints. These constraints are related to the amount of time elapsed between the predecessors and the successor. We can now reconsider the inter-task constraints of Sect. 3.1. Changes apply to inter-task constraints as:

i. t_{startC} - $\max(t_{startT_i}) < \delta_1$, where $T_i \in Pred(C)$. The time elapsed between the start of all the predecessors and the time when the agent picks the work item of the current process from the work list must be smaller than δ_1;

ii. t_{startC} - $\max(t_{endT_i}) < \delta_2$. This constraint states that the successor must start (i.e., the assigned agent has to open the work item from the work list) within a temporal delay δ_2 after the completion of all the predecessors;

iii. t_{endC} - $\max(t_{endT_i}) < \delta_3$. The ending time of the successor must be at a distance smaller than δ_3 from the ending time of all the predecessors: thus the successor must be completed within the deadline $\max(t_{endT_i}) + \delta_3$;

iv. t_{endC} - $\max(t_{startT_i}) < \delta_4$. The distance between the time when the agent picked the last predecessor (i.e. the last starting one) from the work list and when the successor was completed must be less than δ_4: thus the maximum amount of time available for the execution of the task C and of all of its immediate predecessors (after the last predecessor started) is δ_4.

3.3 Extending Constraints

The above constraints can be extended to a group of tasks and to free couples of tasks, i.e. tasks among which no predecessor or successor relationship exists.

3.3.1 Constraints on a Group of Tasks

Temporal constraints we defined above can be immediately extended to a group of tasks. If we consider supertasks (or subprocesses or subworkflows, see Sect. 2.1), task constraints may define when the first task of the supertask has to start, thus starting the supertask itself, or when the last task has to end, thus ending the supertask itself. Task constraints extend at the supertask level the concepts previously defined and consider the ExpectedTaskDuration and the MaxTaskDuration for the entire supertask, thus limiting the time span between the beginning of the first task and the ending of the last one for that supertask. Inter-task constraints consider the intervals between the first task of the supertask and its predecessor(s), or the last task of the supertask and its successor(s).

Temporal constraints from above can also be immediately extended to arbitrary sequences of tasks. Let us consider a very simple process model where tasks A, B, C, and D are sequentially connected (no fork, no join, but a straightforward connection). Task, schedule-task and inter-task constraints can be defined as from above over couples of subsequent tasks. Additionally, the process designer may also want, for example, to define another trigger limiting to δ the maximum allowed temporal interval elapsed between t_{startB} and t_{endD}: this constraint is an inter-task one that considers one task (B) and one successor of one successor of its (D). The global effect is similar to that of defining a supertask including B, C, and D, featuring a MaxTaskDuration equal to δ.

3.3.2 Constraints on Free Couples of Tasks

Temporal constraints can also be defined for a free couple of tasks, e.g. the couple A and B or the couple C and D of Fig. 7, where the 2 tasks of the couple are being executed at the same time but with no predecessor or successor relationship among them. In this situation only inter-task constraints apply. Constraints between task A and task C or D, or between task B and task C or D

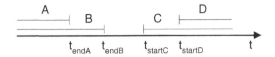

Fig. 7. Temporal constraints between free couples of tasks with no predecessor or successor relationship

of Fig. 7 are extensions of inter-task constraints for a group of tasks as defined above. Constraints between tasks A and B or between C and D need further analysis: one may want to define a constraint between t_{endB} and t_{endA} or even between t_{startD} and t_{startC}.

Let us consider the task couple A and B of Fig. 7, assuming that A ends before B ends: obviously the same applies should task B end before A ends. The constraint we define aims at verifying that the latter task to complete ends within a duration δ after the first task completes. Formally, we say that $t_{endB} - t_{endA} < \delta$. Should the task B end with a delay greater than δ after the completion of task A, the constraint is violated and the WfMS will manage it.

Let us now consider the task couple C and D of Fig. 7, assuming that C starts before D starts: obviously the same applies should task D start before C starts. The constraint we define aims at verifying that the latter task to be opened by the executing agent starts within a duration δ after the first task was opened. Formally, we say that $t_{startD} - t_{startC} < \delta$. Should the task D be opened with a delay greater than δ after the agent opened task C, the constraint is violated and the WfMS will manage it.

These constraints can also be applied to tasks whose executions are started in parallel by a fork connector or are waited for by a join connector. In fact, constraints between tasks A and B of Fig. 7 can be applied to tasks A and B of Fig. 6, to monitor the delay by which the second task of a parallel execution ends before the join connector resynchronizes the execution. Similarly, constraints between tasks C and D of Fig. 7 can be applied to tasks B and C of Fig. 5, to monitor the delay by which the second task is opened by the executing agent after the fork connector. Durations defined inside constraints are computed at case execution time. Should the durations be defined as months (made of a variable number of days and thus of seconds) or years (made of a variable number of days and thus of seconds), criteria to convert durations to the finest granularity level from Sect. 3 apply.

4   A Detailed Example

We now consider the example of Sect. 2.3 and we show how the constraints we previously defined can be adopted. In the motivating example we defined two constraints: the first one (C_1) is related to the notification of the car accident to the insurance company within 24 hours after the customer informed the car rental company; the second one (C_2) is related to the beginning of the inspection of the car within 2 days after the notification to the insurance company. One may also want to add a new constraint (C_3) limiting the duration of the task at the call center, so that the operator invites the customer to provide only the essential data to be stored, avoiding unnecessary descriptions. We shall consider only these three constraints, while obviously some other ones can be defined, e.g. on the maximum duration of the repair of the car, to refund of the damages from the insurance company to the car rental company and many others.

C_1. The constraint limits the time elapsed between the end of the predecessor task that collects data about the car accident from the customer (StoreAccident) and the end of the task that informs the insurance company about the car accident itself (InformInsurance). This constraint is an inter-task one and is formally defined in the process model as follows:

$$t_{endInformInsurance} - t_{endStoreAccident} < 24 \text{ hours}$$

C_2. The constraint limits the time elapsed between the end of the task that informs the insurance company about the car accident (InformInsurance) and the beginning of the task that starts inspecting the car (InspectCar). The car repairer has to open the task from is/her work list within 2 days after the notification to the insurance company. The two tasks involved are linked by an schedule-task constraint which is formally defined in the process model as follows:

$$t_{endInformInsurance} - t_{startInspectCar} < 2 \text{ days}$$

C_3. The constraint fixes the MaxTaskDuration constraint for the task StoreAccident: this is a task constraint related to the duration of one single task. If we assume that the maximum allowable duration for the task is 10 minutes, we define a constraint as:

$$MaxTaskDuration(StoreAccident) = 10 \text{ minutes}$$

At case execution time, the durations of the constraints must be translated to the finest granularity level allowed by the WfMS: for this case, C_1 and C_2 are easily translated to $24 \times 60 \times 60 = 86{,}400$ seconds and to $2 \times 24 \times 60 \times 60 = 172{,}800$ seconds, respectively.

5   Related Work

The topic of the management of temporal aspects in the definition of workflows has been considered by the literature only recently. Currently available WfMSs, both off-the-shelf ones and research prototypes, offer a very limited limited support for defining, managing and detecting temporal constraints over executed tasks: reports from the WfMC [12] do not provide any specification for time modelling. In this Sect. we compare the conceptual model we proposed here with related work from the literature.

Eder et al. in [6] specify the temporal properties for a task (namely, "activity node"), considering the duration, and the earliest finish and latest finish times. The same author et al. in [7] extend the concept by adding the best and worst case of execution to cope with possible conditional branches: thus, for a task they distinguish the earliest best finishing time, the earliest worst finishing time, the latest best finishing time and the latest worst finishing time. Again, Eder et al. in [8] go deeper into that topic investigating, in the presence of conditional execution paths, the inconsistencies among constraints that can be detected at process definition time and at run time. With respect to [6,7,8], we do not limit our investigation to durations and deadlines for tasks, but we provide a conceptual model that considers also the starting time for a task. To extend the use of WfMSs to the management of real-time processes, we also consider as a parameter the scheduling time: in fact, the time spent by the WfMS to look for the executing agent in some particular situations can become critical and should not be neglected. We also remove the limitation to express constraints by relating them to the t_0 instant (the starting of the case) and allow the definition of the constraint over a group of tasks (namely, a supertask) without having to define constraints separately for every composing task. According to Eder et al. a task must always have a constraint delimiting its duration, while in the real word some task may last indefinitely.

Sadiq et al. in [13] cover two main topics: workflow change management, where their contribution extends the contribution of Casati et al. in [3], and time management in workflows. About temporal properties of workflow process models (namely, "meta-models"), the authors briefly list three different types of constraints without going into details: *duration constraint*, defining the expected duration of every task, which can possibly be modified at case execution time according to some local variables or to the workflow history; *deadline constraint*, defining the absolute time for the termination of a task, e.g. June 23rd; *interdependent temporal constraint*, for the definition of task start time and end time related to start/end of another task. With respect to [13], we extend the concepts of constraint duration by distinguishing an ExpectedTaskDuration and a MaxTaskDuration, as in [4]: this way, two different levels of constraint can be defined, providing a soft constraint and a firm constraint for the completion of the task. We define several different types of constraints for interdependencies among tasks, distinguishing them in three categories (see above), and we also consider the constraints for process models which include split and join operators.

Marjanovic et al. in [10] provide a framework for the definition of constraints and some constraint verification algorithms. Temporal constraints are classified as basic temporal, limited duration, deadline, and interdependent temporal. *Basic temporal constraints* define the minimum and the maximum duration of a single task: the concept is then easily extended to a set of tasks connected either via a sequential structure, or via a fork connector, or via a join connector. Set of tasks (named "instance types") feature a cumulative minimum duration (shortest duration) and a cumulative maximum duration (longest duration), computed according to the minimum duration and the maximum duration of every component task, respectively. With respect to basic temporal constraints, our model allows the designer to define an ExpectedTaskDuration and a MaxTaskDuration, obtaining two different levels of warning to detect a possible delayed execution of a task: the ExpectedTaskDuration is not the minimum duration but rather a reasonable duration of the task. We do not limit the minimum duration of a task:

the sooner it finishes, the better. In our model, we also consider the scheduling time as a not negligible aspect, while Marjanovic et al. consider that time as rigorously null. As we aim at extending the use of WfMSs to the management of (soft) real-time processes, the scheduling time has to be considered.

Limited duration constraints define the minimum and maximum duration of an entire workflow enactment. Our model allows the designer to define the Expected TaskDuration and MaxTaskDuration attributes for any set of tasks: according to our model, having defined a set of task as the entire schema, the same above considerations on basic temporal constraints apply.

Deadline constraints define when a task should start or finish in terms of absolute time (e.g., on November 12th 2001). Our model enables the process designer to define deadline constraints at different granularity levels.

Interdependent temporal constraints limit the time distance between two tasks in a workflow. In case of subsequent tasks with a straight connection, the constraint becomes a basic duration one. If the two tasks are neither subsequent nor concurrent, two possible constraints can defined: the minimum distance between the end of one task (A) and the start of the other task (B); the maximum distance between the start of the first task (A) and the end of the second task (B). In our model we do not consider the minimum distance between the execution of tasks. However, the first constraint can be mapped by adding a dummy task in parallel to the sequence A .... The dummy task stays awaiting for the minimum required time distance: only after its completion the enactment of the case can proceed with the execution of task B. The second constraint is a constraint on a group of task (see Sect. 3.3), and again we consider that the scheduling time is a not negligible aspect.

None of the above mentioned proposals allows one to define constraints at different levels of granularity. On the other hand, in the conceptual model here proposed, we allow temporal constraints to be expressed at different granularity levels [5]. Only few other authors consider temporal granularity in WfMSs: Bettini et al. [1] focus on the temporal reasoning aspects related to finding schedules for autonomous agents, when temporal constraints for tasks are given even at different granularities. In [1], temporalities of the conceptual model are not considered nor is the scheduling time.

6 Conclusions

In this paper we enriched a conceptual model for workflows we adopted as reference [2]. We added features to manage temporal aspects that should not be neglected if we aim at controlling a soft real-time process by a workflow management system (WfMS).

In the model, we added the definition of some temporal constraints related to the duration of the single task, to the duration of a couple of tasks linked by a successor/predecessor relationship, and to the duration of more tasks in presence of fork or join connectors activating parallel execution or resynchronizing after parallel execution. We also extended the concepts to cover constraints defined over a group of tasks and over a free couple of tasks, i. e. tasks with no particular relationship of successor/predecessor. We allowed temporal constraints to be defined at any arbitrary level of granularity.

As future directions, we plan to extend the conceptual model to include loops and the workflow definition language (WFDL) from the reference model [2] to include constraint specifications as from the current paper, achieving a temporal workflow definition language (TWFDL). Furthermore, most of the constraint we defined can be mapped onto most commercial WfMSs, by suitably modifying the activity graphs of the processes as designed onto that specific system: in this way, constraints can be added to any existing WfMS without having to modify the core of the system. We also plan to consider aspects related to constraint consistency checking, both at process definition time (static checking) and at run time (dynamic checking), following the direction led by [10] and [1].

References

1. Bettini C, Wang X., Jajodia S., *Temporal Reasoning in Workflow Systems*, Distributed and Parallel Databases, 11(3): 269–306 (2002).
2. Casati F., Ceri S., Pernici B., Pozzi G., *Conceptual Modeling of Workflows*, Entity Relationship Int. Conf., Springer, 1995: 341–354
3. Casati F., Ceri S., Pernici B., Pozzi G., *Workflow Evolution*, Data and Knowledge Engineering, 24(3): 211–238 (1998)
4. Casati F., Ceri S., Paraboschi S., Pozzi G., *Specification and Implementation of Exceptions in Workflow Management Systems*, ACM Transactions on Database Systems, 24(3): 405–451 (1999)
5. Combi C., Pozzi G., *HMAP – A Temporal Data Model Managing Intervals with Different Granularities and Indeterminacy from Natural Language Sentences*, VLDB Journal, 9(4): 294–311 (2001)
6. Eder J., Panagos E., Rabinovich M.: *Time Constraints in Workflow Systems*, Int. Conf. on Advanced Information Systems Engineering, Springer, 1999: 286–300
7. Eder J., Panagos E., Pozewaunig H., Rabinovich M., *Time Management in Workflow Systems*, Int. Conf. on Business Information Systems, Springer, 1999, pp. 265–280
8. Eder J., Gruber W., Panagos E., *Temporal Modeling of Workflows with Conditional Execution Paths*, Database and Expert Systems Applications, Int. Conf., Springer, 2000: 243–253
9. Goralwalla I., Leontiev Y., Özsu M. T., Szafron D., Combi C., *Temporal Granularity: Completing the Puzzle*, Journal of Intelligent Information Systems 16(1): 41–63 (2001)
10. Marjanovic O., Orlowska M. E., *On Modeling and Verification of Temporal Constraints in Production Workflows*, Knowledge and Information Systems, 1(2): 157–192 (1999)
11. Pressman R., *Software Engineering: A Practitioner's Approach*, McGraw-Hill, 5th ed., 2001
12. The WorkFlow Management Coalition, `http://www.wfmc.org`
13. Sadiq S. W., Marjanovic O., Orlowska M. E., *Managing Change and Time in Dynamic Workflow Processes*, International Journal of Cooperative Information Systems 9(1–2): 93–116 (2000)

Towards a Logical Model for Patterns[*]

Stefano Rizzi[1], Elisa Bertino[2], Barbara Catania[3], Matteo Golfarelli[1],
Maria Halkidi[4], Manolis Terrovitis[5], Panos Vassiliadis[6], Michalis Vazirgiannis[4],
and Euripides Vrachnos[4]

[1] DEIS, Univ. of Bologna, Italy
[2] DICO, Univ. of Milan, Italy
[3] DISI, Univ. of Genoa, Italy
[4] Athens Univ. of Economics & Business, Greece
[5] Dept. of Electrical and Computer Engineering,
Nat. Tech. Univ. of Athens, Greece
[6] Dept. of Computer Science, University of Ioannina, Greece

Abstract. Nowadays, the vast volume of collected digital data obliges us to employ processing methods like pattern recognition and data mining in order to reduce the complexity of data management. In this paper, we present the architecture and the logical foundations for the management of the produced knowledge artifacts, which we call *patterns*. To this end, we first introduce the concept of Pattern-Base Management System; then, we provide the logical foundations of a general framework based on the notions of pattern types and pattern classes, which stand for the intensional and extensional description of pattern instances, respectively. The framework is general and extensible enough to cover a broad range of real-world patterns, each of which is characterized by its structure, the related underlying data, an expression that carries the semantics of the pattern, and measurements of how successful the representation of raw data is. Finally, some remarkable types of relationships between patterns are discussed.

1 Introduction and Motivation

The increasing opportunity of quickly collecting and cheaply storing large volumes of data, and the need for extracting concise information to be efficiently manipulated and intuitively analysed, are posing new requirements for DBMSs in both industrial and scientific applications. In this direction, during the last decade we witnessed the progressive spreading and success of data warehousing systems, built on top of operational databases in order to provide managers and knowledge workers with ready-at-hand summary data to be used for decision support. In these systems, the transactional view of data is replaced by a multidimensional view, relying on an *ad-hoc* logical model (the *multidimensional*

---

[*] This work was partially funded by the Information Society Technologies programme of the European Commission, Future and Emerging Technologies under the IST-2001-33058 PANDA project

I.-Y. Song et al. (Eds.): ER 2003, LNCS 2813, pp. 77–90, 2003.

Table 1. Some examples of patterns.

Application	Raw data	Type of pattern
market-basket analysis	sales transactions	item association rules
signal processing	complex signals	recurrent waveforms
mobile objects monitoring	measured trajectories	equations
information retrieval	documents	keyword frequencies
image recognition	image database	image features
market segmentation	user profiles	user clusters
music retrieval	music scores, audio files	rhythm, melody, harmony
system monitoring	system output stream	failure patterns
financial brokerage	trading records	stock trends
click-stream analysis	web-server logs	sequences of clicks
epidemiology	clinical records	symptom-diagnosis correlations
risk evaluation	customer records	decision trees

model [17]) whose key concepts are made first-class citizens, meaning that they can be directly stored, queried, and manipulated.

On the other hand, the limited analysis power provided by OLAP interfaces proved to be insufficient for advanced applications, in which the huge quantity of data stored necessarily requires semi-automated processing techniques, and the peculiarity of the user requirements calls for non-standard analysis techniques. Thus, sophisticated data processing tools (based for instance on data mining, pattern recognition, and knowledge extraction techniques) were devised in order to reduce, as far as possible, the user intervention in the process of extracting interesting knowledge artifacts (e.g., clusters, association rules, time series) from raw data [8,11,13]. We claim that the term *pattern* is a good candidate to generally denote these novel information types, characterized by a high degree of diversity and complexity. Some examples of patterns in different application domains are reported in Table 1.

Differently from the case of data warehousing systems, the problem of directly storing and querying pattern-bases has received very limited attention so far in the commercial world, and probably no attention at all from the database community. On the other hand, we claim that end-users from both industrial and scientific domains would greatly benefit from adopting a *Pattern-Base Management System* (PBMS) capable of modeling and storing patterns, for the following main reasons:

- *Abstraction.* Within a PBMS, patterns would be made first-class citizens thus providing the user with a meaningful abstraction of raw data to be directly analyzed and manipulated.
- *Efficiency.* Introducing an architectural separation between the PBMS and the DBMS would improve the efficiency of both traditional transactions on the DBMS and advanced processing on patterns.
- *Querying.* The PBMS would provide an expressive language for querying the pattern-base in order to retrieve and compare patterns.

In this context, the purposes of the *PANDA* (*PAtterns for Next-generation DAtabase systems* [4]) project of the European Community are: (1) to lay the foundations for pattern modeling; (2) to investigate the main issues involved in managing and querying a pattern-base; and (3) to outline the requirements for building a PBMS.

In this paper we propose a logical framework for modeling patterns, aimed at satisfying three basic requirements:

- *Generality*. The model must be general enough to meet the specific requirements posed in different application domains for different kinds of patterns.
- *Extensibility*. The model must be extensible to accomodate new kinds of patterns introduced by novel and challenging applications.
- *Reusability*. The model must include constructs encouraging the reuse of what has already been defined.

Informally, a pattern can be thought of as a *compact* and *rich in semantics* representation of raw data. In our approach, a pattern is modeled by its *structure*, *measure*, *source*, and *expression*. The structure component *qualifies* the pattern by locating it within a pattern space. The measure component *quantifies* the pattern by measuring the quality of the raw data representation achieved by the pattern itself. The source component describes the raw data which the pattern relates to. The expression component describes the (approximate) mapping between the raw data space and the pattern space.

The paper is structured as follows. In Section 2 we deliver an informal definition of patterns and outline a reference architecture in which a PBMS could be framed. In Section 3 we formally describe our proposal of a logical framework for modeling patterns, while Section 4 discusses some remarkable types of relationships between patterns. In Section 5 we survey some related approaches. Finally, in Section 6 the conclusions are drawn and the future work is outlined.

2   From DBMSs to PBMSs

2.1   Raw Data vs. Patterns

Raw data are recorded from various sources in the real world, often by collecting measurements from various instruments or devices (e.g., cellular phones, environment measurements, monitoring of computer systems, etc.). The determining property of raw data is the vastness of their volume; moreover, a significant degree of heterogeneity may be present.

Clearly, data in such huge volumes do not constitute knowledge *per se*, i.e. little useful information can be deduced simply by their observation, so they hardly can be directly exploited by human beings. Thus, more elaborate techniques are required in order to extract the hidden knowledge and make these data valuable for end-users. The common characteristic of all these techniques is that large portions of the available data are abstracted and effectively represented by a small number of knowledge-carrying representatives, which we call

Fig. 1. Patterns and raw data in the supermarket example.

patterns. Thus, in general, one pattern is related to many data items; on the other hand, several patterns (possibly of different types) can be associated to the same data item (e.g., due to the application of different algorithms).

Example 1. Consider a supermarket database which records the items purchased by each customer within each sales transaction. While this large volume of data is not providing the supermarket management with any clear indication about the buying habits of customers, some knowledge discovery algorithm can be applied to come up with relevant knowledge. In Figure 1 both a clustering technique [15] and an algorithm for extracting association rules [7] have been applied. In the first case, patterns are clusters of customers which share some categories of products. In the second, patterns come in the form of association rules which relate sets of items frequently bought together by customers; the relevance of each rule is typically expressed by statistical measures which quantify its support and confidence. Note that each pattern, besides providing the end-user with some hidden knowledge over the underlying data, can be mapped to the subset of data it is related to.

Patterns, thus, can be regarded as artifacts which effectively describe subsets of raw data (thus, they are compact) by isolating and emphasizing some interesting properties (thus, they are rich in semantics). While in most cases a pattern is interesting to the end-users because it describes a recurrent behaviour (e.g., in market segmentation, stock exchange analysis, etc.), sometimes it is relevant just because it is related to some singular, unexpected event (e.g., in failure monitoring). Note that all the kinds of patterns, besides being somehow related to raw data, also imply some processing in order to either generate them through some learning algorithm or to check/map them against raw data.

We are now ready to give a preliminary, informal, definition for patterns; a formal definition will be given in Section 3.1.

Definition 1 (Pattern). *A pattern is a compact and rich in semantics representation of raw data.*

2.2   Architecture

Patterns can be managed by using a Pattern-Base Management System exactly as database records are managed by a database management system. A Pattern-Base Management System is thus defined as follows.

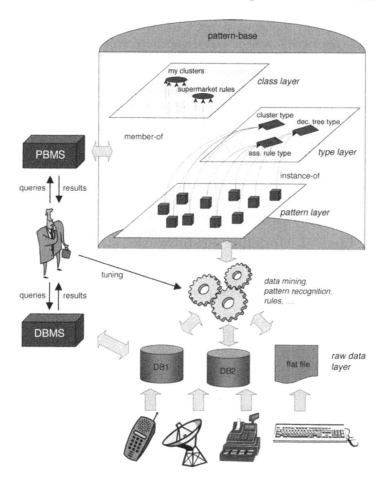

Fig. 2. The PBMS architecture.

Definition 2 (PBMS). *A* Pattern-Base Management System *(PBMS) is a system for handling (storing/processing/retrieving) patterns defined over raw data in order to efficiently support pattern matching and to exploit pattern-related operations generating intensional information. The set of patterns managed by a PBMS is called* pattern-base.

The reference architecture for a PBMS is depicted in Figure 2. On the bottom layer, a set of devices produce data, which are then organized and stored within databases or files to be typically, but not necessarily, managed by a DBMS. Knowledge discovery algorithms are applied over these data and generate patterns to be fed into the PBMS; note that, in our approach, these algorithms are loosely coupled with the PBMS. Within the PBMS, it is worth to distinguish three different layers:

1. The *pattern layer* is populated with patterns.
2. The *type layer* holds built-in and user-defined types for patterns. Patterns of the same type share similar structural characteristics.
3. The *class layer* holds definitions of pattern classes, i.e., collections of semantically related patterns. Classes play the role of collections in the object-oriented context and are the key concept in the definition of a pattern query language.

Besides using the DBMS, end-users may directly interact with the PBMS: to this end, the PBMS adopts ad-hoc techniques not only for representing and storing patterns, but also for posing and processing queries and for efficiently retrieving patterns.

3   The Logical Modeling Framework

In this section we formalize our proposal of a logical framework for modeling patterns by characterizing pattern types, their instances, and the classes which collect them.

3.1   Pattern Types

Though our approach is parametric on the typing system adopted, the examples provided in this paper will be based on a specific, very common typing system. Assuming there is a set of *base types* (including the *root type* $\perp$) and a set of *type constructors*, the set T of types includes all the base types together with all the types recursively defined by applying a type constructor to one or more other types. Types are applied to *attributes*.

Let base types include integers, reals, Booleans, strings, and timestamps; let type constructors include list, set, bag, array, and tuple. Using an obvious syntax, some examples of type declarations are (we use uppercase for base types and type constructors, lowercase for attributes):

- salary: REAL
- SET(INTEGER)
- TUPLE(x: INTEGER, y: INTEGER)
- personnel: LIST(TUPLE(age: INTEGER, salary: INTEGER))

A pattern type represents the intensional form of patterns, giving a formal description of their structure and relationship with source data. Thus, pattern types play the same role of abstract data types in the object-oriented model.

Definition 3 (Pattern type). *A* pattern type *pt is a quintuple $pt = (n, ss, ds, ms, f)$ where n is the* name *of the pattern type; ss, ds, and ms (called respectively* structure schema, source schema, *and* measure schema*) are types in T; f is a* formula, *written in a given language, which refers to attributes appearing in the source and in the structure schemas.*

The first component of a pattern type has an obvious meaning; the remaining four have the following roles:

- The structure schema ss defines the pattern space by describing the structure of the patterns instances of the pattern type. The achievable complexity of the pattern space (hence, the flexibility of pattern representation) depends on the expressivity of the typing system.
- The source schema ds defines the related source space by describing the dataset from which patterns, instances of the pattern type being defined, are constructed. Characterizing the source schema is fundamental for every operation which involves both the pattern space and the source space (e.g., when applying some technique to extract patterns from raw data or when checking for the validity of a pattern on a dataset).
- The measure schema ms describes the measures which quantify the quality of the source data representation achieved by the pattern. The role of this component is to enable the user to evaluate how accurate and significant for a given application each pattern is. Besides, the different semantics of the measure component with reference to the structure can be exploited in order to define more effective functions for evaluating the distance between two patterns [12].
- The formula f describes the relationship between the source space and the pattern space, thus carrying the semantics of the pattern. Inside f, attributes are interpreted as free variables ranging over the components of either the source or the pattern space. Note that, though in some particular domains f may exactly express the inter-space relationship (at most, by allowing all raw data related to the pattern to be enumerated), in most cases it will describe it only approximatively.

Though our approach to pattern modeling is parametric on the language adopted for formulas, the achievable semantics for patterns strongly depends on its expressivity. For the examples reported in this paper, we try a constraint calculus based on polynomial constraints which seems suitable for several types of patterns [16]; still, a full exploration of the most suitable language is outside the scope of the paper.

Example 2. Given a domain D of values and a set of transactions, each including a subset of D, an *association rule* takes the form $A \rightarrow B$ where $A \subset D$, $B \subset D$, $A \cap B = \emptyset$. A is often called the *head* of the rule, while B is its *body* [13]. A possible pattern type for modeling association rules over strings representing products is the following:

$$n : \mathsf{AssociationRule}$$
$$ss : \mathsf{TUPLE(head:\ SET(STRING),\ body:\ SET(STRING))}$$
$$ds : \mathsf{BAG(transaction:\ SET(STRING))}$$
$$ms : \mathsf{TUPLE(confidence:\ REAL,\ support:\ REAL)}$$
$$f : \forall x (x \in \mathsf{head} \vee x \in \mathsf{body} \Rightarrow x \in \mathsf{transaction})$$

The structure schema is a tuple modeling the head and the body. The source schema specifies that association rules are constructed from a bag of transactions, each defined as a set of products. The measure schema includes two common measures used to assess the relevance of a rule: its confidence (what percentage of the transactions including the head also include the body) and its support (what percentage of the whole set of transactions include both the head and the body). Finally, the formula of the constraint calculus represents (exactly, in this case) the pattern/dataset relationship by associating each rule with the set of transactions which support it.

Example 3. An example of a mathematical pattern is a straight line which interpolates a set of samples. In this case, the source schema models the samples, the structure schema includes the two coefficients necessary to determine a line, while the measure schema includes, for instance, a fitting quantifier. The formula which establishes the approximate correspondence between the pattern and the source data is the equation of the line.

$$n : \mathsf{InterpolatingLine}$$
$$ss : \mathsf{TUPLE(a:\ REAL,\ b:REAL)}$$
$$ds : \mathsf{SET(sample:\ TUPLE(x:\ REAL,\ y:\ REAL))}$$
$$ms : \mathsf{fitting:\ REAL}$$
$$f : \mathsf{y = a \cdot x + b}$$

3.2   Patterns

Let raw data be stored in a number of databases and/or files. A *dataset* is any subset of these data, which we assume to be wrapped under a type of our typing system (*dataset type*).

Definition 4 (Pattern). *Let $pt = (n, ss, ds, ms, f)$ be a pattern type. A pattern p instance of pt is a quintuple $p = (pid, s, d, m, e)$ where pid (pattern identifier) is a unique identifier for p; s (structure) is a value for type ss; d (source) is a dataset whose type conforms to type ds; m (measure) is a value for type ms; e is an expression denoting the region of the source space that is related to p.*

According to this definition, a pattern is characterized by (1) a pattern identifier (which plays the same role of OIDs in the object model), (2) a structure that positions the pattern within the pattern space defined by its pattern type, (3) a source that identifies the specific dataset the pattern relates to, (4) a measure that estimates the quality of the raw data representation achieved by the pattern, (5) an expression which relates the pattern to the source data. In particular, the expression is obtained by the formula f in the pattern type by (1) instantiating each attribute appearing in ss with the corresponding value specified in s, and (2) letting the attributes appearing in ds range over the source space. Note that further information could be associated to each pattern, specifying for instance the mining session which produced it, which algorithm was used, which parameter values rule the algorithm, etc.

Example 4. Consider again pattern type AssociationRule defined in Example 2, and suppose that raw data include a relational database containing a table sales which stores data related to the sales transactions in a sport shop: sales (transactionId, article, quantity). Using an extended SQL syntax to denote the dataset, an example of an instance of AssociationRule is:

> $pid : 512$
>> s : (head = {'Boots'}, body = {'Socks', 'Hat'})
>> d : 'SELECT SETOF(article) AS transaction
>>   FROM sales GROUP BY transactionId'
>> m : (confidence = 0.75, support = 0.55)
>> e : {transaction : $\forall x(x \in$ {'Boots', 'Socks', 'Hat'} $\Rightarrow x \in$ transaction)}

In the expression, transaction ranges over the source space; the values given to head and body within the structure are used to bind variables head and body in the formula of pattern type AssociationRule.

Example 5. Let raw data be an array of real values corresponding to samples periodically taken from a signal, and let each pattern represent a recurrent waveshape together with the position where it appears within the dataset and its amplitude shift and gain:

> n : TimeSeries
> ss : TUPLE(curve: ARRAY[1..5](REAL), position: INTEGER,
>   shift: REAL, gain: REAL)
> ds : samples: ARRAY[1..100](REAL)
> ms : similarity: REAL
> f : samples[position $+ i - 1$] = shift + gain $\times$ curve[i],
> $\forall i : 1 \le i \le 5$

Measure similarity expresses how well waveshape curve approximates the source signal in that position. The formula approximatively maps curve onto the data space in position. A possible pattern, extracted from a dataset which records the hourly-detected levels of the Colorado river, is as follows:

> $pid : 456$
>> s : (curve = (y = 0, y = 0.8, y = 1, y = 0.8, y = 0),
>>   position = 12, shift = 2.0, gain = 1.5)
>> d : 'colorado.txt'
>> m : similarity = 0.83
>> e : {samples[12] = 2.0, samples[13] = 3.2, samples[14] = 3.5,
>>   samples[15] = 3.2, samples[16] = 2.0}

3.3   Classes

A class is a set of semantically related patterns and constitutes the key concept in defining a pattern query language. A class is defined for a given pattern type and contains only patterns of that type. Moreover, each pattern must belong to at least one class. Formally, a class is defined as follows.

Definition 5 (Class). *A class c is a triple c* $= (cid, pt, pc)$ *where cid (class identifier) is a unique identifier for c, pt is a pattern type, and pc is a collection of patterns of type pt.*

Example 6. The *Apriori* algorithm described in [7] could be used to generate relevant association rules from the dataset presented in Example 4. All the generated patterns could be inserted in a class called *SaleRules* for pattern type AssociationRule defined in Example 2. The collection of patterns associated with the class can be later extended to include rules generated from a different dataset, representing for instance the sales transaction recorded in a different store.

4   Relationships between Patterns

In this section we introduce some interesting relationships between patterns aimed at increasing the modeling expressivity of our logical framework, but which also improve reusability and extensibility and impact the querying flexibility. For space reasons we will propose here an informal presentation; see [9] for formal details.

4.1   Specialization

Abstraction by specialization (the so-called *IS-A* relationship) is widely used in most modeling approaches, and the associated inheritance mechanism significatively addresses the extensibility and reusability issues by allowing new entities to be cheaply derived from existing ones.

Specialization between pattern types can be defined by first introducing a standard notion of subtyping between base types (e.g., integer is a subtype of real). Subtyping can then be inductively extended to deal with types containing type constructors: t_1 specializes t_2 if the outermost constructors in t_1 and t_2 coincide and each component in t_2 is specialized by one component in t_1. Finally, pattern type pt_1 specializes pattern type pt_2 if the structure schema, the source schema, and the measure schema of pt_1 specialize the structure schema, the source schema, and the measure schema of pt_2.

Note that, if pt_1 specializes pt_2 and class c is defined for pt_2, also the instances of pt_1 can be part of c.

Example 7. Given a set S of points, a clustering is a set of clusters, each being a subset of S, such that the points in a cluster are more similar to each other than points in different clusters [13]. The components for pattern type Cluster, representing circular clusters defined on a 2-dimensional space, are:

$$n : \mathsf{Cluster}$$
$$ss : \mathsf{TUPLE}(\mathsf{radius}: \perp, \mathsf{center}: \mathsf{TUPLE}(\mathsf{cx}: \perp, \mathsf{cy}: \perp))$$
$$ds : \mathsf{SET}(\mathsf{x}: \perp, \mathsf{y}: \perp)$$
$$ms : \emptyset$$
$$f : (\mathsf{x} - \mathsf{cx})^2 + (\mathsf{y} - \mathsf{cy})^2 \leq \mathsf{radius}^2$$

where f gives an approximate evaluation of the region of the source space represented by each cluster. While in Cluster the 2-dimensional source schema is generically defined, clusters on any specific source space will be easily defined by specialization. Thus, Cluster could be for instance specialized into a new pattern type ClusterOfIntegers where cx, cy, x, and y are specialized to integers, radius is specialized to reals, and a new measure avgIntraClusterDistance of type real is added.

4.2 Composition and Refinement

A nice feature of the object model is the possibility of creating complex objects, i.e. objects which consist of other objects. In our pattern framework, this can be achieved by extending the set of base types with pattern types, thus giving the user the possibility of declaring *complex types*. This technique may have two different impacts on modeling.

Firstly, it is possible to declare the structure schema as a complex type, in order to create patterns recursively containing other patterns thus defining, from the conceptual point of view, a *part-of* hierarchy. We will call *composition* this relationship.

Secondly, a complex type may appear within the source schema: this allows for supporting the modeling of patterns obtained by mining other existing patterns. Since in general a pattern is a compact representation of its source data, we may call *refinement* this relationship in order to emphasize that moving from a pattern type to the pattern type(s) that appear in its source entails increasing the level of detail in representing knowledge.

Example 8. Let pattern type ClusterOfRules describe a mono-dimensional cluster of association rules: the source schema here represents the space of association rules, and the structure models one cluster-representative rule. Assuming that each cluster trivially includes all the rules sharing the same head, it is:

$$n : \mathsf{ClusterOfRules}$$
$$ss : \mathsf{representative}: \mathsf{AssociationRule}$$
$$ds : \mathsf{SET}(\mathsf{rule}: \mathsf{AssociationRule})$$
$$ms : \mathsf{TUPLE}(\mathsf{deviationOnConfidence}: \mathsf{REAL}, \mathsf{deviationOnSupport}: \mathsf{REAL})$$
$$f : \mathsf{rule.ss.head} = \mathsf{representative.ss.head}$$

where a standard dot notation is adopted to address the components of pattern types. Thus, there is a refinement relationship between ClusterOfRules and AssociationRule. Consider now that a clustering is a set of clusters: intuitively, also clustering is a pattern, whose structure is modeled by a complex type which aggregates a set of clusters. Thus, there would be a composition relationship between pattern types Clustering and ClusterOfRules.

5   Related Approaches

The most popular efforts for modeling patterns is the Predictive Model Markup Language [6], that uses XML to represent data mining models. Though PMML enables the exchange of patterns between heterogeneous pattern-bases, it does not provide any general model for the representation of different pattern types; besides, the problem of mapping patterns against raw data is not considered.

Among the other approaches, we mention the SQL/MM standard [2]; here, the supported mining models are represented as SQL types and made accessible through the SQL:1999 base syntax. A framework for metadata representation is proposed by the Common Warehouse Model [1], whose main purpose is to enable easy interchange of warehouse and business intelligence metadata between various heterogeneous repositories, and not the effective manipulation of these metadata. The Java Data Mining API [5] addresses the need for procedural support of all the existing and evolving data mining standards; in particular, it supports the building of data mining models as well as the creation, storage, access, and maintenance of data and metadata that represent data mining results. Finally, the Pattern Query Language is an SQL-like query language for patterns [3], assumed to be stored like traditional data in relational tables.

Overall, the listed approaches seem inadequate to represent and handle different classes of patterns in a flexible, effective, and coherent way: in fact, a given list of predefined pattern types is considered and no general approach to pattern modeling is proposed. In contrast, in our framework, the definition of a general model and the possibility of constructing new pattern types by inheritance from a root type allow uniform manipulation of all patterns.

A specific mention is deserved by *inductive databases*, where data and patterns, in the form of rules inducted by data, are represented together to be uniformly retrieved and manipulated [14]. Our approach differs from the inductive database one in different ways:

– While only association rules and string patterns are usually considered there and no attempt is made towards a general pattern model, in our approach no predefined pattern types are considered and the main focus lies in devising a general and extensible model for patterns.
– Patterns are far more complex than the raw data they represent and, we argue, cannot be effectively stored in a relational manner.
– The difference in semantics between patterns and raw data discourage from adopting the same query language for both, rather call for defining a *pattern*

query language capable of capitalizing on the peculiar semantics of each pattern component.
- Differently from [14], we claim that the peculiarities of patterns in terms of structure and behaviour, together with the characteristic of the expected workload on them, call for a logical separation between the database and the pattern-base in order to ensure efficient handling of both raw data and patterns through dedicated management systems.

We close this section by observing that, though our approach shares some similarities with the object-oriented model, there are several specific requirements calling for an ad-hoc model and for a dedicated management system:

- In terms of the logical framework, the discriminating feature is the requirement for a semantically rich representation of patterns, achieved by separating structure and measure on the one hand, by introducing the expression component on the other.
- From a conceptual point of view, the modeling framework adopted entails the refinement relationship between patterns, not directly supported by object-oriented models.
- From the functional point of view, instead of pointer-chasing object-oriented queries, novel querying requirements will presumably arise, including (a) ad hoc operations over the source and pattern spaces and their mapping; (b) pattern matching tests, strengthened by the separation of structure and measure; (c) reasoning facilities based on the expression component of patterns.
- In terms of system architecture, the relevance of queries aimed at evaluating similarity between patterns and the request for efficiency call for alternative storage and query optimization techniques.

6 Conclusions and Future Work

In this paper, we have dealt with the introduction of the architecture and the logical foundations for pattern management. First, we introduced Pattern-Base Management Systems and their architecture. Then, we provided the logical foundations of a general framework, as the basis for PBMS management. Our logical framework is based on the principles of generality, extensibility and reusability. To address the generality goal we introduced a simple yet powerful modeling framework, able to cover a broad range of real-world patterns. Thus, the most general definition of a pattern specifies its structure, the underlying data that correspond to it, an expression which is rich in semantics so as to characterize what the pattern stands for, and measurements of how successful the raw data abstraction is. To address the extensibility and usability goals, we introduced type hierarchies, that provide the PBMS with the flexibility of smoothly incorporating novel pattern types, as well as mechanisms for constructing composite patterns and for refining patterns.

Though the fundamentals of pattern modeling have been addressed, several important issues still need to be investigated. Future research includes both theoretical aspects as well as implementation-specific issues. Implementation issues involve primarily the construction of ad-hoc storage management and query processing modules for the efficient management of patterns. The theoretical aspects include the evaluation and comparison of the expressivity of different languages to express formulas, and the study of a flexible query language for retrieving and comparing complex patterns. In particular, as to query languages, a basic operation is that of comparison: two patterns of the same type can be compared to compute a score assessing their mutual similarity as a function of the similarity between both the structure and the measure components. Particularly challenging is the comparison between complex patterns: in this case, the similarity score is computed starting from the similarity between component patterns, then the obtained scores are aggregated, using an aggregation logic, to determine the overall similarity [10].

References

1. Common Warehouse Metamodel (CWM). http://www.omg.org/cwm, 2001.
2. ISO SQL/MM Part 6. http://www.sql-99.org/SC32/WG4/Progression_Documents/FCD/fcd-datamining-2001-05.pdf, 2001.
3. Information Discovery Data Mining Suite. http://www.patternwarehouse.com/dmsuite.htm, 2002.
4. The PANDA Project. http://dke.cti.gr/panda/, 2002.
5. Java Data Mining API. http://www.jcp.org/jsr/detail/73.prt, 2003.
6. Predictive Model Markup Language (PMML). http://www.dmg.org/pmmlspecs_v2/pmml_v2_0.html, 2003.
7. R. Agrawal and R. Srikant. Fast algorithms for mining association rules. In *Proc. 20th VLDB*, 1994.
8. M. Berry and G. Linoff. *Data mining techniques: for marketing, sales, and customer support*. John Wiley, 1996.
9. E. Bertino et al. A preliminary proposal for the PANDA logical model. Technical Report TR-2003-02, PANDA, 2003.
10. I. Bartolini et al. PAtterns for Next-generation DAtabase systems: preliminary results of the PANDA project. In *Proc. 11th SEBD*, Cetraro, Italy, 2003.
11. U. Fayyad, G. Piatesky-Shapiro, and P. Smyth. From data mining to knowledge discovery: an overview. In *Advances in Knowledge Discovery and Data Mining*, pages 1–34. AAAI Press and the MIT Press, 1996.
12. V. Ganti, R. Ramakrishnan, J. Gehrke, and W.-Y. Loh. A framework for measuring distances in data characteristics. *PODS*, 1999.
13. J. Han and M. Kamber. *Data mining: concepts and techniques*. Academic Press, 2001.
14. T. Imielinski and H. Mannila. A Database Perspective on Knowledge Discovery. *Communications of the ACM*, 39(11):58–64, 1996.
15. A. K. Jain, M. N. Murty, and P. J. Flynn. Data clustering: a survey. *ACM Computing Surveys*, 31:264–323, 1999.
16. P. Kanellakis, G. Kuper, and P. Revesz. Constraint Query Languages. *Journal of Computer and System Sciences*, 51(1):25–52, 1995.
17. P. Vassiliadis and T. Sellis. A survey of logical models for OLAP databases. *SIGMOD Record*, 28(4):64–69, 1999.

Designing Foundational Ontologies

The Object-Centered High-Level Reference Ontology OCHRE as a Case Study

Luc Schneider

Institute for Formal Ontology and Medical Information Science,
University of Leipzig, Härtelstrasse 16-18, D–4109 Leipzig
luc.schneider@ifomis.uni-leipzig.de

Abstract. Foundational ontologies are axiomatic theories about high-level domain-independent categories of the real world. They constitute toolboxes of eminently reusable information modelling primitives for building application ontologies about specific domains. The design of foundational ontologies confronts the conceptual modeller with completely new challenges in respect of their content as well as their formalisation. As a case study, this article outlines the axiomatisation of the Object-Centered High-level REference ontology OCHRE, comparing its basic conceptual modelling choices with those underlying DOLCE, a foundational ontology developed in the Wonderweb project.

1 Introduction

Foundational ontologies are axiomatic theories of domain-independent top-level notions such as *object, attribute, event, parthood, dependence*, and *spatio-temporal connection*. As of late, the need for foundational ontologies has been acknowledged in the conceptual modelling community in at least two respects. First, they have been used to give a real-world interpretation to the primitives of modelling languages such as UML (Guizzardi, Herre and Wagner 2002). Second, they have been proposed as so-called *reference* ontologies, toolboxes of highly general information modelling concepts that can be reused in the design of application ontologies for all sorts of domains (Gangemi et al. 2002). By providing repositories of standardised knowledge representation primitives, they also foster the semantic interoperability in distributed information systems (ibid.).

Ontologies may be used at development time or at run time (Guarino 1998); in the last case, they can be considered as pieces of software themselves. Hence the problem of choosing the right design methodologies and tools may also appear at the level of top-level ontologies. The challenges of conceptual modelling applied to foundational ontologies are singular. Indeed, the design options for top-level ontologies are identical to the ontological choices discussed in classical and contemporary metaphysics, as well as in the research on qualitative reasoning. Although down-to-earth pragmatical considerations on simplicity and contextual applicability help to avoid getting bogged down in spurious details,

I.-Y. Song et al. (Eds.): ER 2003, LNCS 2813, pp. 91–104, 2003.

a good knowledge of the recent advances in metaphysics, as well as in qualitative reasoning, is still necessary to gauge different ontological positions and approaches. Furthermore, the required accuracy of conceptual analysis presupposes a particularly careful axiomatisation of the basic ontological notions.

As an illustration of current approaches to the design of foundational ontologies, the present paper outlines the formalisation of the Object-Centered High-level REference ontology OCHRE, confronting its basic conceptual modelling decisions with those underlying DOLCE, a top-level ontology developed in the Wonderweb project (Masolo et al. 2002, Gangemi et al. 2002). This essay reflects the author's first-hand experience as the designer of OCHRE and a co-designer of DOLCE. Its purpose is to present not only what the author believes to be a particularly elegant basic ontological framework, but also to demonstrate how the quality of a foundational ontology depends on maximal formal elegance and transparency in the limits of descriptive adequacy.

The sections of this article describe the different components of OCHRE. Section 2 treats the theory of parts and wholes, presenting a simple algebraic framework for mereology. Section 3 proposes a qualitative account of objects as bundles of attributes and defines the relation of similarity between individual features. Section 4 outlines a theory of dependence grounding the ontological priority of objects over other entities. Section 5 discusses the problem of change and contends a distinction between objects and their short-lived stages. Spatiotemporal connection between such stages of objects is axiomatised. Section 6 analyses the relations between attributes and objects. Section 7 concludes with a theory of temporal order over object-stages, as well as an account of processes in terms of successive object-stages.

2   Theory of Parts and Wholes

Mereology, the formal theory of parthood, has grown out of early-20th-century mathematical research into a calculus of individuals capturing relations between set-theoretical *urelemente* (Leonard and Goodman 1940). The strongest mereology, namely *General Extensional Mereology (GEM)*, amounts to a Boolean algebra without a null element (Simons 1987, chap. 1; Casati and Varzi 1999, chap. 3). In particular, OCHRE is based on the atomistic version of GEM.

The *parthood* relation is reflexive, antisymmetric and transitive.

MA 1. Pxx *(reflexivity)*

MA 2. $(Pxy \land Pyx) \rightarrow x = y$ *(antisymmetry)*

MA 3. $(Pxy \land Pyz) \rightarrow Pxz$ *(transitivity)*

From the reflexivity of parthood (**MA 1**) it follows that identity implies mutual parthood. In other words, parthood can be regarded as partial identity (Armstrong 1997, p. 17; Lewis 1991, pp. 81-82).

MT 1. $x = y \rightarrow (Pxy \land Pyx)$ *(parthood is partial identity)*

The irreflexive variant of parthood is called *proper parthood*.

MD 1. $PPxy \equiv_{df} Pxy \wedge \neg x = y$ *(proper parthood)*

Two individuals *overlap* iff they have at least one common part.

MD 2. $Oxy \equiv_{df} \exists z\,(\,Pzx \wedge Pzy\,)$ *(overlap)*

An *atom* is an entity that has no proper parts.

MD 3. $Ax \equiv_{df} \neg \exists y\, PPyx$ *(atom)*

Atomistic mereology assumes that everything has atomic parts:

MA 4. $\exists y\,(\,Ay \wedge Pyx\,)$ *(atomicity)*

OCHRE postulates the extensionality of parthood, i.e. that an individual is part of another if every atomic part of the first is also part of the second.

MA 5. $(\,(\,Az \wedge Pzx\,) \rightarrow Pzy\,) \rightarrow Pxy$ *(extensionality)*

The main mereological operation is the *(generalised) sum* or *fusion* of all φ-ers which yields the individual containing the atoms of all entities satisfying the condition φ.

MD 4. $SM(x, \lambda y \varphi y) \equiv_{df} \forall z\,(\,Az \rightarrow (\,Pzx \leftrightarrow \exists w\,(\,\varphi w \wedge Pzw\,)\,)\,)$ *(sum)*

The *General Sum Principle* stipulates that for every satisfiable condition φ, there is a unique sum of all φ-ers.

MA 6. $\exists x \varphi x \leftrightarrow \exists! y\, SM(y, \lambda z \varphi z)$ *(general sum principle)*

As a consequence, there is a least upper bound for parthood, some entity of which everything is a part, namely the the fusion of all self-identical entities.

MD 5. $\mathcal{U}x \equiv_{df} SM(x, \lambda y\,(\,y = y\,)\,)$ *(least upper bound)*

The mereological operations of *(binary) sum*, *product* and *difference* correspond to the set-theoretic operations of union, intersection and set difference:

MD 6. $SM(x, y, z) \equiv_{df} SM(x, \lambda w\,(\,Pwy \vee Pwz\,)\,)$ *(binary sum)*

MD 7. $PR(x, y, z) \equiv_{df} SM(x, \lambda w\,(\,Pwy \wedge Pwz\,)\,)$ *(product)*

MD 8. $DF(x, y, z) \equiv_{df} SM(x, \lambda w\,(\,Pwy \wedge \neg Owz\,)\,)$ *(difference)*

The axiomatisation described above has the advantage of a clear algebraic approach and a great conceptual unity. Nevertheless, the authors of DOLCE adopt two distinct parthood relations: a temporalised parthood for three-dimensional objects and an untemporalised one for four-dimensional entities like processes or events (Masolo et al. 2002). Furthermore, DOLCE does not allow for the extensionality of parthood in *all* cases (ibid.). These choices are motivated by considerations related to the problem of change, especially how to represent the loss and gain of parts, as well as the quandary of coincident entities, such as artifacts and the amounts of matter they are made of (Simons 1987, chap. 3). I will discuss later how these problems can be dealt with in OCHRE.

3   Theory of Similarity

Repeatable and non-repeatable attributes. The crucial ontological choice in an atomistic mereology pertains to the nature of the building blocks of reality. There is a widespread consensus amongst ontologists that the denizens of reality fall into three main categories: *objects* (like quarks, tables, stones, insurance companies and solar systems), *attributes* or particular properties and relations (like the various colour hues on a soap bubble, the mass and velocity of a bullet, your intelligence and your relatedness to your parents) as well as *events* and *processes* (like runnings, hugs, bank transfers, perceptions, and thinkings). In the final section of this paper, I will show that events and processes can be regarded as successions of attribute bundles.

A descriptively adequate ontology has to allow for both *objects* and *attributes*. This does not contradict considerations of conceptual economy that motivate defining references to entities of one category in terms of references to entities of the other. The so-called *Qualitative Account* of objects as bundles of properties and relations enjoys a certain popularity among ontologists, as e.g. Williams (1953), Campbell (1990), Denkel (1996), and Simons (1994), because it avoids the problematic idea of objects as unscrutable blobs which attributes somehow adhere to. Nevertheless it is also true that objects are more than mere sums of their properties. A descriptively adequate ontology has to account for the completeness, independence, and spatio-temporal bulk that objects enjoy in contrast to arbitrary agglomerations of attributes (Denkel 1996, pp. 16–17).

Attributes can be regarded either as *repeatables* or as *non-repeatables* (Armstrong 1997, p. 31). Repeatables, also called *universals*, apply to more than one case; by contrast, non-repeatables, commonly referred to as *tropes* (Williams 1953; Campbell 1990), are single characteristics of individuals. In the terminology of object-oriented conceptual modelling, repeatables correspond to *class attributes* and non-repeatables to pairs of *object attributes* and their respective values. OCHRE endorses the view of Williams, Campbell, and Denkel that the building blocks of reality, the atoms of mereology, are non-repeatables. Note however, that not every non-repeatable has to be atomic: as we shall see, some non-repeatable properties (like colours) and in fact *all* non-repeatable relations (like family relationships) may be regarded as composite. In this article, the term *trope* will denote atomic non-repeatables only.

Obviously, OCHRE has to acknowledge repeatable properties or relations, too, if only the *formal universals* that are the subject matter of any foundational ontology, such as *object, trope, parthood, dependence*, or *similarity*. References to formal properties and relations are made through (lambda-abstractions of) the respective predicates. Semantically, of course, predicates can be interpreted as sets; ontologically, however, there is no need to regard a universal as something outside or above the entities that exemplify it. OCHRE embraces the stance of *Aristotelian realism*, according to which repeatable properties and relations are given or present in their very instances (Aristotle, *Met.*: 1023b; Armstrong 1997, p. 22). For example, in order to know whether an individual is part of another, it is sufficient to inspect both of them.

Intensity, Comparability, and Similarity. An essential feature of tropes is that they constitute families whose members can be compared with each other and (weakly) ordered in terms of their *intensity*. Qualities like mass or density, relations like being-in-love, and dispositions like intelligence or brittleness may vary according to degrees. And even though individual marriages and tropes of magnetic polarity admit no such degrees, they are nonetheless comparable. But there is no way to collate tropes of brightness and hue, or tropes of mass and electrical charge.

The relation of *being more or equally intense* (in symbols: "Ixy") is a reflexive and transitive relation defined over tropes (atoms).

SA 1. $Ixy \rightarrow (\mathcal{A}x \wedge \mathcal{A}y)$ *(restriction)*

SA 2. $\mathcal{A}x \rightarrow Ixx$ *(reflexivity)*

SA 3. $(Ixy \wedge Iyz) \rightarrow Ixz$ *(transitivity)*

Multidimensional variability of intensity as in the case of colours indicates that the attribute in question is in fact composite; colours, for instance, can be resolved into tropes of saturation, brightness, and hue.

Two tropes x and y are *comparable* iff x and y can be ordered in terms of their intensity.

SD 1. $CMxy \equiv_{df} Ixy \vee Iyx$ *(comparability)*

Two tropes x and y are *similar* iff x and y are equally intense. Note that similarity is to be understood as *exact*, not *approximate* similarity.

SD 2. $Sxy \equiv_{df} Ixy \wedge Iyx$ *(similarity)*

Two non-atomic individuals x and y are (exactly) similar iff their respective component tropes can be associated one-to-one with each other such that to every trope of x there corresponds an (exactly) similar trope of y and vice-versa.

References to *material universals*, i.e. kinds of tropes (or trope-bundles) such as *Mass*, *Colour*, or *Humanity* are unavoidable in everyday discourse and thus have to be also allowed for by OCHRE. In particular, the *genus* of any conventionally chosen trope x is defined as the property of being comparable to x and its *species* as the property of being similar to x. As similarity implies comparability, the genus of a trope (like *Mass*) subsumes its species (like *15 kg*).

SD 3. $GE_x y \equiv_{df} \lambda y\, CMyx$ *(genus)*

SD 4. $SP_x y \equiv_{df} \lambda y\, Syx$ *(species)*

In order to capture the genus-species distinction, DOLCE duplicates the attribute category by adopting a bipartite scheme that is akin to a frame-based representation. Indeed, Masolo et al. (2002) and Gangemi et al. (2002) distinguish between slot-like *qualities* (e.g. *colours*, *masses*) and their *qualia* or *quality regions* as their values (e.g. *red*, *15 kg*). As qualia are repeatable, indeed shareable between qualities of different objects, they are actually universals, namely species; however, the authors of DOLCE classify them as non-repeatables. In comparison to OCHRE's trope-view, DOLCE's scheme of qualities and qualia seems to be rather contrived.

4   Theory of Dependence

Even if tropes are regarded as the building blocks of reality, they cannot be conceived of as separate from the objects they characterise. Each trope (e.g. a brittleness) is *dependent* on a particular object (e.g. a glass). Following Strawson (1959, pp. 16–17), dependence can be understood in terms of *identification*. An individual x (say, a trope of mass or velocity) is *identificationally dependent* on an individual y (say, a bullet) – in symbols: "Dxy" – if and only if, in order to identify x, one has to single out y first. In a sense, the entites on which something is dependent are part of its very definition or identity (Fine 1994/1995, p. 275).

The basic difference between objects and dependent entities is that the former can be singled out on their own, while the latter have to be individuated relatively to some object. Hence, one can characterise objects as identificationally self-dependent entities; we suppose that no object is atomic, i.e. a single trope:

DD 1. $Ox \equiv_{df} Dxx$ *(objects)*

DA 1. $Ox \to \neg Ax$ *(non-atomicity of objects)*

As we shall see in section 5, the self-dependent trope-bundles are so-called *thin objects*, the mereological sums of essential features of everyday *thick* objects.

As self-dependent entities, objects are not dependent on any other entity.

DA 2. $Ox \to (Dxy \to x = y)$ *(objects are independent)*

Objects enjoy ontological priority over other particulars since they constitute a framework of reference that serves as a basis for identification. Formally, nothing can depend on an entity that is not self-dependent.

DA 3. $Dxy \to Oy$ *(everything depends on objects)*

Every trope which is part of an object is dependent on the latter.

DA 4. $(Ox \wedge Ay \wedge Pyx) \to Dyx$ *(dependent atomic parts of objects)*

Moreover, if something is not self-dependent, then it depends on anything that one of its atomic parts is dependent on. This rule ensures that by dealing with the dependence of tropes, we determine the dependence of any non-object.

DA 5. $(\neg Ox \wedge Ay \wedge Pyx \wedge Dyz) \to Dxz$ *(dependencies of non-objects)*

Now, every trope is assumed to depend on exactly one object.

DA 6. $Ax \to \exists! y\, Dxy$ *(a trope is dependent on one object)*

Non-repeatable relations (e.g. marriages, or kinships) have been defined as multiply dependent attributes in the literature on ontology (Simons 1995, Mulligan and Smith 1986). Since tropes as atomic attributes are dependent on one object, non-repeatable relations have to be mereological sums of tropes. In fact, an individual marriage just amounts to the mereological sum of the particular rights and duties of the husband and the wife. Similarly, a biological kinship is based on the particular DNA of each member of a family. The theory according to which relations supervene on monadic properties of their relata, such that there are no relational differences without qualitative ones, is called *foundationism* (Campbell 1990, pp. 101, 113). Inspired by a proposal of Mulligan (1998, p. 327), OCHRE adopts foundationism for atomic non-repeatables, but assumes irreducible repeatable relations like the formal relation of parthood.

Masolo et al. (2002) use a more common definition of dependence according to which an entity is dependent on another, if and only if, necessarily, the former cannot exist, provided the latter exists (cf. also Simons 1987, chap. 8). While existential dependence is without a doubt a formal relation worthy of interest, it is too pervasive to demarcate objects. For instance, a body may be *existentially* dependent on the process that is its metabolism, but in terms of identification it is the metabolic process that is dependent on the body and not vice-versa. It is difficult to name one existentially independent entity.

5   Theory of Connection

The Problem of Change; Thin and Thick Objects. The thesis that objects form the basic framework of reference may seem to be undermined by the fact that objects change. Objects apparently lose and gain parts, move around, and exhibit uncompatible properties and relations over time. A solution favoured by many ontologists, e.g. Quine (1960, p. 171), Heller (1990), and Armstrong (1997, pp. 99–107), is to regard objects as space-time worms: incompatible facts just pertain to different phases of such four-dimensional entities. This approach is elegant, but rejects the intuitive distinction between objects and processes.

Alternatively, one can stick to the intuition of objects as three-dimensional entities and temporalise the *assertions* about objects instead. Formal universals, like parthood, have to receive an additional temporal parameter. This approach has been defended, amongst many others, by Simons (1987, chap. 5), and has been adopted by Masolo et al. (2002). However, temporalisation makes reasoning about formal universals like parthood more difficult.

The problem of change emphasises an ambiguity of the ontological concept of object. Varying the terminology of Armstrong (1997, pp. 123–126) and developing intuitions from Simons (1994) and Denkel (1996, p. 108), one has to distinguish between an evanescent whole, the *thick object*, and a core of enduring characteristics, the *thin object*. Thick objects have spatio-temporal bulk and undergo change. More precisely: change consists in the succession of temporary aggregations of tropes shaped by relations of spatio-temporal connection. Thin objects as the enduring cores of thick objects constitute the ultimate referential framework, the ontological backbone of reality. Thick objects are dependent entities; successions of thick objects are held together by thin objects common to all elements in these chains, such as for example by bundles of essential functions in the case of artifacts or organisms. An analogy from software engineering would be the distinction between an software object and its succeeding states.

Our approach to the problem of change is akin to the stage theory proposed by Sider (2001, pp. 1-10, pp. 188-208), Hawley (2001, chap. 2), and Denkel (1996, pp. 101-109), with the main difference that thick objects as stages of thin objects are dependent entities in OCHRE. Successive incompatible states of affairs bear on consecutive thick objects that share the same thin object as a common core. The exchange of colour-tropes in a ripening tomato just pertains to different evanescent wholes centered around the bundle of core characteristics, amongst them the tomato's DNA. That one speaks of the same object through change is grounded in the existence of thin objects. Every temporal attribution of properties and relations to a thin object amounts to the atemporal attribution of these attributes to succeeding thick objects as its stages.

Connection and Thick Objects. As thin objects are the ultimate nodes in a pervading network of dependences, thick objects are nodes in a comprehensive grid of spatio-temporal connections. The formal framework of qualitative space-time reasoning is referred to as *mereotopology* (Casati and Varzi 1999, chap. 4).

Connection is a symmetric and non-transitive relation that is reflexive in all cases it applies at all. Its underlying idea is that of immediate neighbourhood in space and time. For example, France is connected to Germany, and Germany to Poland, but France is not connected to Poland.

CA 1. $Cxy \rightarrow Cxx$ $\hfill$ *(reflexivity)*

CA 2. $Cxy \rightarrow Cyx$ $\hfill$ *(symmetry)*

Thick objects are bundles of tropes exhibiting spatio-temporal connections. No thick object is an independent entity or thin object.

CD 1. $O^*x \equiv_{df} \exists y\, Cxy$ $\hfill$ *(thick object)*

CA 3. $O^*x \rightarrow \neg Ax \wedge \neg Ox$ $\hfill$ *(thick objects are dependent trope-bundles)*

Parthood between thick objects will be called *thick parthood*.

CD 2. $TPxy \equiv_{df} O^*x \wedge O^*y \wedge Pxy$ $\hfill$ *(thick parthood)*

A thick object is *enclosed* in another iff anything connected to the first is also connected to the second. A heart is enclosed in a chest or a fish in a lake.

CD 3. $Exy \equiv_{df} \forall z\, (Czx \rightarrow Czy)$ $\hfill$ *(enclosure)*

Mutual enclosure implies identity. In other words: distinct thick objects cannot be co-located, they compete for space.

CA 4. $(Exy \wedge Eyx) \rightarrow x = y$ $\hfill$ *(mutual enclosure entails identity)*

The formal link between mereology and topology is the axiom of monotonicity (Casati and Varzi 1999, p. 54): thick parthood entails enclosure, but not vice-versa. Since a heart is part of a chest, it is also contained in the latter. However, a fish is enclosed in, but is not part of a lake.

CA 5. $TPxy \rightarrow Exy$ *(monotonicity)*

In contrast to DOLCE, there is no commitment to regions of space and time as a distinct category of particulars in OCHRE. Spatio-temporal relations are considered as (formal) universals that are exemplified by thick objects.

6 Theory of Inherence

Direct Parthood and Essence. Traditionally, the peculiar formal relation between objects and their characteristics has been called *inherence* and the authors of DOLCE follow this usage (Masolo et al. 2002, Gangemi et al. 2002). In OCHRE, however, it is not necessary to provide for inherence as an additional primitive; in fact, the relation between (thin or thick) objects and their attributes can be accounted for in terms of dependence and parthood.

Since a thick object may contain other thick objects as parts, it is necessary to determine whether a trope or a thin object is associated with that thick object or one of its thick parts. For example, one would like to distinguish the weight of a body and the weight of its right arm. Such distinctions can be done through the relation of *direct parthood*. An individual x is a direct part of an entity y iff x is a proper part of y, y is a thick object, and there is no thick proper part z of y such that x overlaps with z. No thick part can be a direct part and vice-versa.

CD 4. $DPxy \equiv_{df} PPxy \wedge O^*y \wedge \neg \exists z \, (TPzy \wedge \neg z = y \wedge Oxz)$ *(direct parthood)*

Every trope is a direct part of some thick object.

IA 1. $Ax \rightarrow \exists y \, DPxy$ *(tropes are direct parts of thick objects)*

No two comparable tropes may be both direct parts of the same thick object. Thus a physical object-stage cannot have more than one mass or kinetic energy.

IA 2. $(DPyx \wedge DPzx \wedge CMyz) \rightarrow y = z$ *(comparability and direct parthood)*

A thin object x that is a direct part of a thick object y is called an *essence* of y. Each thick object has at least one essence.

ID 1. $ESxy \equiv_{df} Ox \wedge DPxy$ *(essence)*

IA 3. $O^*x \rightarrow \exists y \, ESyx$ *(existence of essences)*

In order to fully specify the dependence of entities that are not self-dependent, one further constraint on the dependence of tropes is needed (cf. **DA 5**). The *inherence principle* links atomic direct parthood and dependence by stipulating that, for any trope x, thin object y, and thick object z, if x depends on y and is a direct part of z, then y is an essence of z.

IA 4. $(Ax \wedge Dxy \wedge DPxz) \rightarrow ESyz$ *(inherence principle)*

The presence of a trope in a thick object implies that of the thin object on which it depends.

Coincidence and Guises. Commonsense allows for numerically distinct objects to be spatio-temporally co-located, or *coincident*, e.g., a terracotta statue and the clay it is made of, or a person and her body. Many ontologists, amongst them Simons (1987, chap. 6) and the authors of DOLCE (Masolo et al. 2002, Gangemi et al. 2002), assume such entities to be distinct physical objects of which one (e.g. the clay) *constitutes* the other (e.g. the statue), where *constitution* is a kind of non-extensional composition. This modelling decision implies a serious complication of part-whole reasoning.

In OCHRE, co-location between *thick* objects is excluded; indeed, thick objects have spatio-temporal bulk and thus compete for space. Instead, OCHRE considers coincident entities to be *direct parts* of the same thick object. Thick objects can have more than one essence, each of which has its own periphery of dependent tropes. The mereological sum of a thin object and all the tropes dependent on it represents a qualitative aspect of the thick object, which I call a *guise*, after Castañeda (1985/1986). Formally, some x is a guise of a thick object y with respect to some essence z of y iff x is the mereological sum of all atomic direct parts of y which are dependent on z.

ID 2. $G_z xy \equiv_{df} ESzy \wedge SM(x, \lambda w\,(Aw \wedge DPwy \wedge Dwz\,))$ *(guise)*

A particular thick object that we identify as a terracotta statue made of clay can be regarded to contain two sub-bundles of tropes, namely the statue and the amount of clay, each centered on a particular thin object: the essential functions of the artifact as well as the invariant physico-chemical characteristics of the material. These sub-bundles are not separate spatio-temporal entities, but direct parts of the same thick object representing different aspects of the latter.

7   Theory of Temporal Order

Temporal Anteriority and Essential Succession. As stages of thin objects, thick objects are not only spatio-temporally connected, but also succeed each other in time. Since any computer representation of time has to be granular, time may be regarded as a *discrete* series of atomic intervals.

The theory of temporal order is based on two primitive relations: *direct anteriority* and *simultaneity*, both defined over thick objects. Direct anteriority is irreflexive, asymmetric and intransitive.

TA 1. $DAxy \rightarrow (O^* x \wedge O^* y\,)$ *(restriction)*

TA 2. $\neg DAxx$ *(irreflexivity)*

TA 3. $DAxy \rightarrow \neg DAyx$ *(asymmetry)*

Simultaneity is, of course, an equivalence relation.

TA 4. $SIxy \rightarrow (O^* x \wedge O^* y\,)$ *(restriction)*

TA 5. $O^* x \rightarrow SIxx$ *(reflexivity)*

TA 6. $SIxy \to SIyx$ *(symmetry)*

TA 7. $(SIxy \wedge SIyz) \to SIxz$ *(transitivity)*

Thick parthood may only relate simultaneous thick objects.

TA 8. $TPxy \to SIxy$ *(thick parthood implies simultaneity)*

Thick objects do not temporally overlap, but form discrete and synchronised series of stages that are instantaneous with respect to a certain granularity of time. This is ensured by postulating that all direct temporal antecessors, as well as all direct temporal successors, of a thick object are simultaneous.

TA 9. $(DAyx \wedge DAzx) \to SIyz$ *(simultaneity of direct temporal antecessors)*

TA 10. $(DAxy \wedge DAxz) \to SIyz$ *(simultaneity of direct temporal successors)*

The temporal relation of *(indirect) anteriority* is defined by recursion:

TA 11. $DAxy \to Axy$ *(indirect anteriority: base case)*

TA 12. $(DAxy \wedge Ayz) \to Axz$ *(indirect anteriority: recursive step)*

Any two thick objects x and y can be temporally compared in the sense that either x is an indirect temporal antecessor of y, or y is an indirect temporal antecessor of x, or x and y are simultaneous:

TA 13. $(O^*x \wedge O^*y) \to (Axy \vee Ayx \vee SIxy)$ *(temporal comparability)*

Successive thick objects that are stages of the same thin object stand in a peculiar relation of loose identity: they are not identical, but everything that is true of them is also true, in a temporal sense, of the common thin object. In the following I develop the idea of stage-successions, which is related to Chisholm's (1976, pp. 97–104) account of change in terms of consecutive entities.

A thick object x is the *direct essential successor* of some thick object y *with respect to* a thin object z iff y is directly anterior to x, x and y are spatio-temporally connected, and z is a common essence of x and y.

TD 1. $DS_z xy \equiv_{df} DAyx \wedge Cxy \wedge ESzx \wedge ESzy$ *(direct essential succession)*

Direct essential succession is linear. In other words, distinct thick objects may not be direct essential successors of the same thick object, nor can they share the same direct essential successor.

TA 14. $(DS_z yx \wedge DS_z wx) \to y = w$ *(unicity on the left)*

TA 15. $(DS_z xy \wedge DS_z xw) \to y = w$ *(unicity on the right)*

In order to exclude that thin objects have instantaneous lives, I postulate for each thin object x there are at least two thick objects that are in direct essential succession with respect to x.

TA 16. $Ox \to \exists yz\, DS_x yz$ *(non-instantaneity of thin objects)*

Note that, by extensionality of parthood, there must be at least one atomic part that is not shared between distinct stages of a thin object. Hence there cannot be successive stages with exactly the same proper parts: things change constantly.

Endurants and Perdurants. A central feature of DOLCE is that it acknowledges the common-sense distinction between objects and processes, or, as the philosophical jargon has it, between *endurants* and *perdurants* (Masolo et al. 2002, Gangemi et al. 2002). Endurants have no phases and are present as a whole at each instant they are present at all. Perdurants, on the contrary, consist of different phases at different times (Lewis 1986, p. 202).

It is crucial for a descriptively adequate ontology to respect this distinction. However, this does not mean that both the notion of *endurant* and that of *perdurant* have to be considered as primitive. According to the intuitive definition of endurants, tropes, as well as thin and thick objects, turn out to be endurants. Thin objects are wholly present in each of the thick objects they are part of, and the same trivially applies to tropes, i.e. to atoms. And since a thick object as well as its thick parts are only present in one instant, they too are endurants. We propose regarding perdurants as successions of thick objects, i.e. endurants.

The basic perdurants are events as changes or state-transitions: for example, the change of a tomato's colour from green to red amounts to the succession of a red tomato-stage to a green one. The change of a memory cell from 0 to 1 is the succession of a charged cell-stage to an uncharged one. Some x is an *event in* a thin object y iff x is the mereological sum of two thick objects that are directly essentially succeeding stages of y; we say also that y is the *substrate* of x.

TD 2. $EVxy \equiv_{df} \exists wz\,(\,SM(x,w,z) \wedge DS_y wz\,)$ $\hspace{2cm}$ *(event in)*

TD 3. $\mathcal{E}x \equiv_{df} \exists y\,EVxy$ $\hspace{4cm}$ *(event)*

The definition implies that there are no instantaneous events, which is consistent with the doctrine that perdurants have at least two distinct temporal parts. The instantaneous left and right boundaries of perdurants are endurants, namely thick objects. Hence the *events* that represent the beginning and the ending of a perdurant cannot be instantaneous and always have to involve at least two object-stages.

Perdurants are arbitrary mereological sums of events; they can be recursively characterised with single events as a base case.

TA 17. $\mathcal{E}x \rightarrow \mathcal{P}x$ $\hspace{4cm}$ *(perdurant: base case)*

TA 18. $(\,\mathcal{E}x \wedge \mathcal{P}y \wedge SM(z,x,y)\,) \rightarrow \mathcal{P}z$ $\hspace{1.5cm}$ *(perdurant: recursive step)*

In particular, the life of a thin object is the perdurant that is the sum of all events in this thin object:

TD 4. $Lxy \equiv_{df} SM(x, \lambda z\,EVzy)$ $\hspace{4cm}$ *(life)*

In DOLCE, the relation between perdurants and the (thin) objects involved in them is called *participation* and considered to be a primitive. OCHRE's particular account of perdurants in terms of endurants allows for participation to be defined as a special case of parthood. Indeed, a thin object x *participates in* a process y, iff x is the substrate of an event that is part of y.

TD 5. $PCxy \equiv_{df} \mathcal{O}x \wedge \mathcal{P}y \wedge \exists z\,(\,EVzx \wedge Pzy\,)$ *(participation)*

Thus OCHRE acknowledges the distinction between endurants and perdurants without assuming two separate domains of endurants and perdurants organised by two different parthood and dependence relations.

8   Conclusions

Designing foundational ontologies presents challenges unfamiliar to the conceptual modelling practice for common software artifacts. On the one hand, the need for descriptive adequacy requires an often perplexing subtlety of conceptual analysis. On the other hand, the usability of foundational ontologies depends on the greatest possible formal simplicity and transparency. This paper emphasises a clear and elegant mereological framework that gives a straightforward account of parthood relations between individuals. I have illustrated this point by sketching the formalisation of the ontology OCHRE and by comparing it with the axiomatisation of DOLCE.

DOLCE is a decisive first step towards an expressive top-level ontology. Yet, DOLCE has its problems. By multiplying parthood relations and abandoning extensional mereology, by introducing a non-mereological relation of constitution between objects as well as recurring to an opaque temporalisation of changeable attributes, DOLCE confronts its user with superfluous complications.

OCHRE maintains the descriptively correct distinctions of DOLCE while avoiding its formal intricacies. This is ensured by the following modelling decisions:

1. To account for change in objects, OCHRE acknowledges the ambiguity of references to objects and distinguishes between thin objects and thick objects as their evanescent stages.
2. Events are accounted for in terms of succeeding object-stages.
3. Co-located distinct entities are reconstructed as qualitative aspects or guises of the same thick object.

A classical extensional mereology can be preserved throughout, assuming atomic attributes out of which thick and thin objects are ultimately composed, leaving no space for unscrutable substrates.

This article serves as a comparative case study and attempts to highlight the specific requirements for modelling foundational ontologies. Once these requirements are better understood, more theoretical investigations into measuring the quality of the design of top-level ontologies will be possible.

Acknowledgements. This paper is based on work supported by the Alexander von Humboldt Foundation under the auspices of its Wilhelm Paul Programme. The author is deeply indebted to Pierre Grenon (IFOMIS, Leipzig/Germany), Brandon Bennett (School of Computing, University of Leeds/UK), Claudio Masolo (ISTC-CNR, Trento/Italy), as well as two anonymous reviewers for many helpful suggestions regarding a previous version of this article.

References

Aristotle. *Metaphysics*.

Armstrong, D. M. 1997. *A World of States of Affairs*. Cambridge: Cambridge University Press.

Campbell, K. 1990. *Abstract Particulars*. Oxford: Blackwell.

Casati, R., Varzi, A. 1999. *Parts and Places. The Structures of Spatial Representation*. Cambridge/MA., London: MIT Press.

Castañeda, H. N. 1985/1986. "Objects, Existence and Reference. A Prolegomenon to Guise Theory". *Grazer Philosophische Studien 25/26*: 31–66.

Chisholm, R. 1976. *Person and Object. A Metaphysical Study*. Chicago, La Salle /Ill.: Open Court.

Denkel, A. 1996. *Object and Property*. Cambridge: Cambridge University Press.

Fine, K. 1994/1995. "Ontological Dependence". *Proceedings of the Aristotelian Society 95*: 269–290.

Gangemi A., Guarino N., Masolo C., Oltramari, A., Schneider L., 2002. "Sweetening Ontologies with DOLCE". In Gómez-Pérez, A., Benjamins, V.R., (eds.), *Knowledge Engineering and Knowledge Management. Ontologies and the Semantic Web. Proceedings of the 13th International Conference (EKAW 2002). LNCS 2473*. Heidelberg: Springer, 166–181.

Guarino N. 1998. "Formal Ontology and Information Systems". In Guarino, N. (ed.), *Formal Ontology in Information Science. Proceedings of FOIS'98, Trento, Italy* Amsterdam: IOS Press, 3–15.

Guizzardi G., Herre H., Wagner G., 2002. "On the General Ontological Foundations of Conceptual Modeling". In Spaccapietra, S., March, S.T., Kambayashi, Y., (eds.), *Conceptual Modeling. Proceedings of the 21st International Conference on Conceptual Modeling (ER 2002). LNCS 2503*. Heidelberg: Springer, 65–78.

Hawley, K. 2001. *How Things Persist*. Oxford: Clarendon Press.

Heller, M. 1990. *The Ontology of Physical Objects*. Cambridge: Cambridge University Press.

Leonard, H. S., Goodman N., 1940. "The Calculus of Individuals and Its Uses". *Journal of Symbolic Logic 5*: 45–55.

Lewis, D. 1986. *On the Plurality of Worlds*. Oxford: Blackwell.

Lewis, D. 1991. *Parts of Classes*. Oxford: Blackwell.

Masolo, C., Borgo, S., Gangemi, A., Guarino, N., Oltramari, A., Schneider, L. 2002. "The WonderWeb Library of Foundational Ontologies. Preliminary Report". *WonderWeb Deliverable D17*. Downloadable at *http : //wonderweb.semanticweb.org*

Mulligan, K., Smith, B. 1986. "A Relational Theory of the Act". *Topoi 5*: 115–130.

Mulligan, K. 1998. "Relations – through thick and thin". *Erkenntnis 48*: 325–353.

Quine, W. O. 1960. *Word and Object*. Cambridge/MA: MIT Press.

Sider, T. 2001. *Four-Dimensionalism. An Ontology of Persistence and Time*. Oxford: Clarendon Press.

Simons, P. 1987. *Parts. A Study in Ontology*. Oxford: Clarendon.

Simons, P. 1994. "Particulars in Particular Clothing: Three Trope Theories of Substance". *Philosophy and Phenomenological Research 65*: 553–575.

Simons, P. 1995. "Relational Tropes". In Haefliger, G., Simons, P. (eds.), *Analytic Phenomenology: Essays in Honor of Guido Küng*. Dordrecht: Kluwer.

Strawson, P. 1959. *Individuals. An Essay in Descriptive Methaphysics*. London: Routledge.

Williams, D. C. 1953. "On the elements of being". *Review of Metaphysics 7*: 3–18, 171–192.

An OPM-Based Metamodel of System Development Process

Dov Dori and Iris Reinhartz-Berger

Technion, Israel Institute of Technology
Technion City, Haifa 32000, Israel
{dori@ie,ieiris@tx}.technion.ac.il

Abstract. A modeling and development methodology is a combination of a language for expressing the universal or domain ontology and an approach for developing systems using that language. A common way for building, comparing, and evaluating methodologies is metamodeling, i.e., the process of modeling the methodology. Most of the methodology metamodels pertain only to the language part of the methodologies, leaving out the description of the system development processes or describing them informally. A major reason for this is that the methods used for metamodeling are structural- or object-oriented, and, hence, are less expressive in modeling the procedural aspects of a methodology. In this paper we apply Object-Process Methodology (OPM) to specify a generic OPM-based system development process. This metamodel is made possible due to OPM's view of objects and processes as being on equal footing rather than viewing object classes as superiors to and owners of processes. This way, OPM enables specifying both the structural (ontological constructs) and behavioral (system development) aspects of a methodology in a single, unified view.

1 Introduction

A system modeling and development methodology ideally supports the entire system lifecycle, from initiation (conceiving, initiating, and requirement elicitation) through development (analysis, design, and implementation) to deployment (assimilation, usage, and maintenance) [5]. To enable this diversified set of activities, the methodology should be based on sound ontology, which can be either universal or domain-specific; a language for expressing the ontology; and a well-defined system development process. Developers who follow this process use the language to produce the artifacts that are pertinent for each phase of the system's lifecycle. It should therefore come as no surprise that any system modeling and development methodology worthy of its name is itself a highly complex system, and as such, it ought to be carefully analyzed and modeled.

The concept of metadata is quite widespread. In the context of the Internet, for example, metadata is machine understandable information for the Web. Metamodeling, the process of modeling a methodology, extends the notion of metadata and produces metamodels, i.e., models of methodologies. Metamodels have become important means for building, comparing, and evaluating methodologies and

I.-Y. Song et al. (Eds.): ER 2003, LNCS 2813, pp. 105–117, 2003.

their supporting CASE tools. Hence, it has been the focal point in several efforts to coalesce object-oriented methods and, at the same time, put them on a more rigorous footing [3, 9, 11, 13]. Some of the created metamodels use the methodology being modeled as a tool for describing itself. We refer to this type of metamodeling as **reflective metamodeling** and to the methodology as a **reflective methodology**. A reflective methodology is especially powerful since it is self-contained and does not require auxiliary means or external tools to model itself.

Most of the existing (both reflective and non-reflective) metamodels focus on describing the syntax and semantics of the methodology constructs, leaving out of the metamodel all the procedural and behavioral aspects [4]. These aspects relate to processes that are either part of the language capabilities (such as refinement-abstraction processes) or processes that belong to the development of a system using the methodology. The reason for the lack of procedural modeling is that the techniques used for metamodeling (such as ERD and UML) are structural- or object-oriented. Object-Process Methodology (OPM) overcomes this limitation by supporting the specification of the structural and behavioral aspects of the modeled methodology in a single framework, enabling mutual effects between them.

In this paper, we apply OPM to define a comprehensive lifecycle-supporting system development process. This process follows generic concepts of systems evolution and lifecycle, namely requirement specification, analysis and design, implementation, usage and maintenance, and, as such, it is not specific to OPM-based system development. Nevertheless, applying it in an OPM framework has great benefits as explained latter. In Section 2 we review existing metamodels and criticize their ability to model system development processes. In Section 3 we introduce the foundations of OPM, while the metamodel of an OPM-based development process is presented in Section 4. Finally, in Section 5, we summarize the main benefits of our metamodeling approach and discuss future research directions.

2   Literature Review: Metamodels and Metamodeling

2.1   Metamodel and Metamodeling Definitions

System analysis and design activities can be divided into three types with increasing abstraction levels: real world, model, and metamodel [9, 19]. The real world is what system analysts perceive as reality or what system architects wish to create as reality. A model is an abstraction of this perceived or contemplated reality that enables its expression using some approach, language, or methodology. A metamodel is a model of a model, or more accurately, a model of the modeling methodology [22].

Analogous to modeling, metamodeling is the process that creates metamodels. The level of abstraction at which metamodeling is carried out is higher than the level at which modeling is normally done for the purpose of generating a model of a system [9]. Metamodeling is worth pursuing because of the following reasons:

- With the advent of the Internet, and particularly the Intranet, data integration has become a major concern. Metamodels are the foundation for data integration in software (and even hardware) development. One such major effort is the Resource Description Framework (RDF) [20] which provides a lightweight ontology system to support the exchange of knowledge on the Web.

- Metamodels help abstracting low level integration and interoperability details and facilitate partitioning problems into orthogonal sub-problems. Hence, metamodels can serve as devices for method development (also referred to as method engineering) [1, 2], language modeling, and conceptual definition of repositories and CASE tools [17].
- Defining a methodology is an interactive process, in which a core is defined and then extended to include all the needed concepts. Metamodeling enables checking and verifying the completeness and expressiveness of a methodology through understanding the deep semantics of the methodology as well as relationships among concepts in different languages or methods [10].

The growth of object-oriented methods during the last decade of the 20th century introduced a special type of metamodeling, which we call **reflective metamodeling**. Reflective metamodeling models a methodology by the means and tools that the methodology itself provides. While metamodeling is a formal definition technique of methodologies, reflective metamodeling can serve as a common way to examine and demonstrate the methodology's expressive power.

2.2   Leading Metamodels of Analysis and Design Methods

Metamodels of visual software engineering methods are commonly expressed in ER or class diagrams. These notations model primarily the structural and static aspects of methodologies. ER-based metamodels are also limited in describing constraints, hierarchical structures (i.e., complex objects), explosion, and polymorphism [4] required for specifying complete methodologies or languages.

UML, which is the standard object-oriented modeling language, has several metamodel propositions. The reflective UML metamodel in [13], for example, includes class diagrams, OCL (Object Constraint Language) [21] sentences, and natural language explanations for describing the main elements in UML and the static relations among them. The Meta Object Facility (MOF) [11], which is an OMG standard, extensible four layer metadata architecture, is also applied to metamodel UML. MOF layers are: information (i.e., real world concepts, labeled M0), model (M1), metamodel (M2), and meta-metamodel (M3). The meta-metamodel layer describes the structure and semantics of meta-metadata, i.e., it is an "abstract language" for defining different kinds of metadata (e.g., meta-classes and meta-attributes). The Meta Modeling Facility (MMF) [3] provides a modular and extensible method for defining and using UML. It comprises a static, object-oriented language (MML), used to write language definitions; a tool (MMT) used to interpret those definitions; and a method (MMM), which provides guidelines and patterns encoded as packages that can be specialized to particular language definitions.

These metamodels of UML are incomplete in more than one way. First, UML is only a language, not a methodology, so only the language elements are metamodeled, but not any object-oriented (or other) development process [13]. Second, the consistency and integrity constraints that UML models should follow are not included and formulated in these metamodels. Several "software process models" have been associated with UML to create complete UML-based methods. One such familiar development process is the Rational Unified Process (RUP) [16]. RUP is a configurable software development process pattern that presents the relations between the process lifecycle aspects (inception, elaboration, construction, and transition) and the process disciplines and activities (business modeling, requirements, etc.). While RUP supplies a general framework of development processes, it does not have a precise underlying metamodel.

The Software Process Engineering Metamodel (SPEM) [12] uses UML to describe a concrete software development process or a family of related software development processes. It uses MOF four-layered architecture, where the performing process (the real-world production process) is at level M0 and the definition of the corresponding process (e.g., RUP) is at level M1.

The Object-oriented Process, Environment, and Notation (OPEN) [8, 14] is a methodology that offers a notation, called OPEN Modeling Language (OML) [7], as well as a set of principles for modeling all aspects of software development across the entire system lifecycle. The development process is described by a contract-driven lifecycle model, which is complemented by a set of techniques and a formal representation using OML. The lifecycle process, including its techniques, tasks, and tools, is described in terms of classes and their structural relations.

The above metamodels, as well as other metamodels that use structural- or object-oriented methodologies, emphasize the objects and their relations within the metamodel, while the procedural aspects are suppressed and revealed only through operations of objects and the messages passed among them [4]. While real-world processes require interaction and state diagrams to describe system dynamics and function, metamodels of methodologies use only packages, classes, and associations. The main reasons for this limited usage of UML include the complexity of its vocabulary [18] and its model multiplicity and integration problems [15]. Object-Process Methodology overcomes this shortcoming by recognizing processes as entities beside, rather than underneath, objects.

3 Object-Process Methodology (OPM)

Object-Process Methodology (OPM) [5] is an integrated modeling approach to the study and development of systems in general and information systems in particular. Enabling the existence of processes as stand-alone entities provides for the ability to model a system in a single unified framework, showing in the same diagram type its structure and behavior. These two major aspects co-exist in the same OPM model without highlighting one at the cost of suppressing the other. Hence, OPM provides a solid basis for modeling complex systems, in which structure and behavior are highly intertwined and hard to separate. Involving the modeling process with the ontology elements, system development methodologies are a prime example of such systems.

The elements of the OPM ontology are entities (things and states) and links. A *thing* is a generalization of an *object* and a *process* – the two basic building blocks of any system expressed in OPM. At any point in time, each object is at some *state*, while object states are changed through occurrences of processes. Respectively, links can be structural or procedural. *Structural links* express static relations between pairs of things, where aggregation, generalization, characterization, and instantiation are the four fundamental structural relations. *Procedural links* connect entities to describe the behavior of a system, i.e., how processes transform and use other entities.

Two semantically equivalent modalities, one graphic and the other textual, jointly express the same OPM model. A set of inter-related Object-Process Diagrams (OPDs) constitute the graphical, visual OPM formalism. Each OPM element is denoted in an OPD by a symbol, and rules are defined for specifying correct and consistent ways by which entities are linked. The Object-Process Language (OPL), defined by a grammar, is the textual counterpart modality of the graphical OPD-set. OPL is a dual-purpose language, oriented towards humans as well as machines. Catering to human needs, OPL serves domain experts and system architects engaged in analyzing and designing a system. Designed also for machines, OPL provides a firm basis for automatically generating the designed application. Every OPD construct is expressed by a semantically equivalent OPL sentence or part of a sentence and vice versa.

OPM manages system complexity through three refinement/abstraction mechanisms: *Unfolding/folding*, which is used for refining/abstracting the structural hierarchy of a thing; *In-zooming/out-zooming*, which exposes/hides the inner details of a thing within its frame; and *state expressing/suppressing*, which exposes/hides the states of an object. Using these mechanisms, OPM enables specifying a system to any desired level of detail without losing legibility and comprehension of the resulting specification.

Being both object- and process-oriented, OPM enables explicit modeling of the procedural and dynamic aspects of the development process part of a system analysis and design methodology. In the rest of the paper, we present a graphical OPM model of a generic system development process, which includes requirement specifying, analyzing and designing, implementing, and using and maintaining. The legend of this model is provided in [5] and in Appendix A.

4   An OPM-Based System Development Model

The System Diagram, which is labeled **SD** and shown in 0, is the top-level specification of the OPM metamodel. It specifies **Ontology, Notation,** and the **System Developing** process as the major OPM features (characterizations). **Ontology** includes the basic elements in OPM, their attributes, and the relations among them. For example, objects, processes, states, and aggregations are all OPM elements. The **Notation** represents the **Ontology** graphically (by OPDs) or textually(by OPL sentences). For example, a process is represented graphically in an OPD by an ellipse, while an object is symbolized by a rectangle.

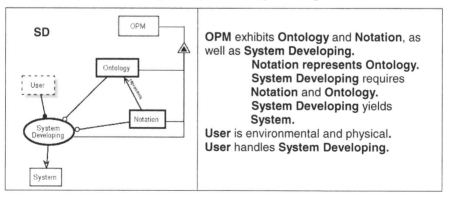

Fig. 1. The top level specification of the OPM metamodel

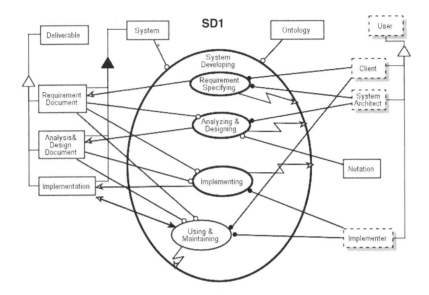

Fig. 2. Zooming into **System Developing**

The **System Developing** process, also shown in **SD**, is handled by the **User**, who is the physical and external (environmental) object that controls (is the agent of) the process. This process also requires **Ontology** and **Notation** as instruments (inputs) in order to create a **System**.

The OPL paragraph, which is equivalent to **SD**, is also shown in 0. Since OPL is a subset of English, users who are not familiar with the graphic notation of OPM can validate their specifications by inspecting the OPL sentences. These sentences are automatically generated on the fly in response to the user's draws of OPDs [6]. Due to space limitations and the equivalence of OPM graphical and textual notations, we use only the OPD notation in the rest of the paper.

Zooming into **System Developing**, **SD1** (0) shows the common sequential[1] stages of system developing processes: **Requirement Specifying**, **Analyzing & Designing**, **Implementing**, and **Using & Maintaining**. All of these processes use the same OPM **Ontology**, a fact that helps narrowing the gaps between the different stages of the development process. **SD1** shows that the **Client** and the **System Architect**, who, along with the **Implementer**, specialize **User**, handle the **Requirement Specifying** sub-process. **Requirement Specifying** takes OPM **Ontology** as an input and creates a new **System**, which, at this point, consists only of a **Requirement Document**. The termination of **Requirement Specifying** starts **Analyzing & Designing**, the next sub-process of **System Developing**.

---

[1] The time line in an OPD flows from the top of the diagram downwards, so the vertical axis within an in-zoomed process defines the execution order. The sub-processes of a sequential process are depicted in the in-zoomed frame of the process stacked on top of each other with the earlier process on top of a later one. Analogously, subprocesses of a parallel process appear in the OPD side by side, at the same height.

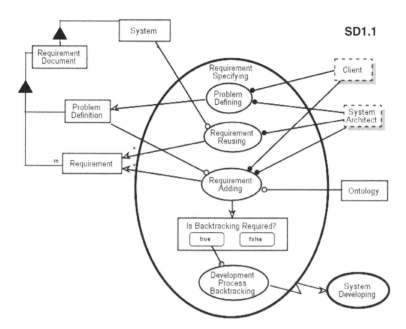

Fig. 3. Zooming into **Requirement Specifying**

The agent of the **Analyzing & Designing** stage is the **System Architect**, who uses the **Requirement Document** and OPM **Notation** to create a new part of the system, the **Analysis & Design Document**. When the **Analyzing & Designing** process terminates, the **Implementer** (programmer, DBA, etc.) starts the **Implementing** phase, which uses the **Requirement Document** and the **Analysis & Design Document** in order to create the **Implementation**. Finally, the **Implementer** changes the system **Implementation** during the **Using & Maintaining** stage, while the **Client** uses the **System**.

As the invocation links in **SD1** denote, each **System Developing** sub-process can invoke restarting of the entire development process, which potentially enables the introduction of changes to the requirements, analysis, design, and implementation of the **System**. These invocations give rise to an iterative development process, in which an attempt to carry out a sub-process reveals faults in the deliverable of a previous subprocess, mandating a corrective action.

4.1 The Requirement Specifying Stage

In **SD1.1** (0), **Requirement Specifying** is zoomed into, showing its four subprocesses. First, the **System Architect** and the **Client** define the problem to be solved by the system (or project). This **Problem Defining** step creates the **Problem Definition** part of the current system **Requirement Document**. Next, through the **Requirement Reusing** sub-process, the **System Architect** may reuse requirements that fit the problem at hand and are adapted from any existing **System** (developed by the organization). Reuse helps achieve high quality systems and reduce their development and debugging time. Hence, when developing large systems, such as Web applications or real-time systems, it is important to try first to reuse existing artifacts adapted from previous generations, analogous systems, or commercial off-the-shelf (COTS) products that fit the current system development project. Existing, well-phrased requirements are often not trivial to obtain, so existing relevant requirements should be treated as a potential resource no less than code. Indeed, as the OPD shows, reusable artifacts include not only components (which traditionally have been the primary target for reuse), but also requirements.

After optional reuse of requirements from existing systems (or projects), the **System Architect** and the **Client**, working as a team, add new **Requirements** or update existing ones. This step uses OPM **Ontology** in order to make the **Requirement Document** amenable to be processed by other potential OPM tools, and in particular to an OPL compiler. The bi-modal property of OPM, and especially the use of OPL, a subset of natural language, enables the **Client** to be actively involved in the critical **Requirement Specifying** stage. Moreover, since the **System Architect** and the **Client** use OPM **Ontology** in defining the new requirements, the resulting **Requirement Document** is indeed expressed, at least partially, in OPL in addition to explanations in free natural English. Such structured OPM-oriented specification enables automatic translation of the **Requirement Document** to an OPM analysis and design skeleton (i.e., a skeleton of an OPD-set and its corresponding OPL script). Naturally, at this stage the use of free natural language beside OPM seems mandatory to document motivation, alternatives, considerations, etc.

Finally, the **Requirement Adding** process results in the Boolean object "**Is Backtracking Required?**", which determines whether **System Developing** should be restarted. If so, **Development Process Backtracking** invokes the entire **System Developing**. Otherwise, **Requirement Specifying** terminates, enabling the **Analyzing & Designing** process to begin.

4.2   The Analyzing and Designing Stage

During the **Analyzing & Designing** stage, shown in **SD1.2** (0), a skeleton of an **OPL Script** is created from the **Requirement Document** for the current system. As noted, in order to make this stage as effective and as automatic as possible, the **Requirement Document** should be written using OPM, such that the resulting OPL script can be compiled. The **System Architect** can then optionally reuse analysis and design artifacts from previous systems (projects), creating a basis for the current system analysis and design. Finally, in an iterative process of **Analysis & Design Improving** (which is in-zoomed in **SD1.2.1**, 0), the **System Architect** can engage in **OPL Updating, OPD Updating, System Animating, General Information Updating**, or **Analysis & Design Terminating**.

Any change a user makes to one of the modalities representing the model triggers an automatic response of the development environment software to reflect the change in the complementary modality. Thus, as **SD1.2.1** shows, **OPD Updating** (by the **System Architect**) affects the **OPD-set** and immediately invokes **OPL Generating**, which changes **OPL Script** according to the new **OPD-set**. Conversely, **OPL Updating** (also by the **System Architect**) affects the **OPL Script**, which invokes **OPD Generating**, reflecting the OPL changes in the **OPD-set**.

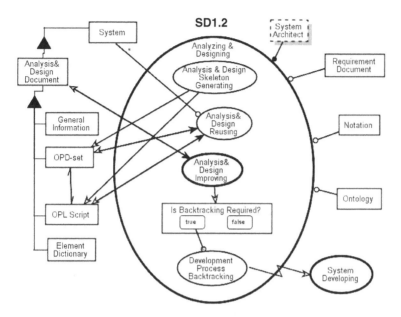

Fig. 4. Zooming into **Analyzing & Designing**

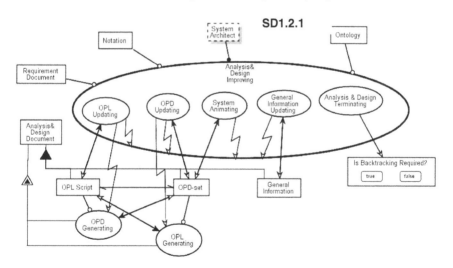

Fig. 5. Zooming into **Analysis & Design Improving**

Since OPM enables modeling system dynamics and control structures, such as events, conditions, branching, and loops, **System Animating** simulates an **OPD-set**, enabling **System Architects** to dynamically examine the system at any stage of its development. Presenting live animated demonstrations of system behavior reduces the number of design errors percolated to the implementation phase. Both static and dynamic testing help in detecting discrepancies, inconsistencies, and deviations from the intended goal of the system. As part of the dynamic testing, the simulation enables designers to track each of the system scenarios before writing a single line of code. Any detected mistake or omission is corrected at the model level, saving costly time and efforts required within the implementation level. Avoiding and eliminating design errors as early as possible in the system development process and keeping the documentation up-to-date contribute to shortening the system's delivery time ("time-to-market").

Upon termination of the **Analysis & Design Improving** stage, if needed, the entire **System Developing** process can restart or the **Implementing** stage begins.

SD1.3

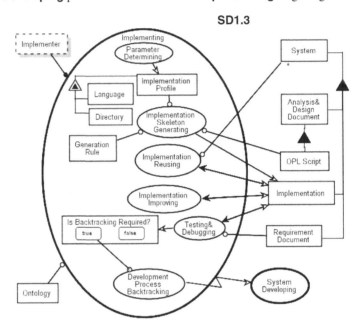

Fig. 6. Zooming into **Implementing**

4.3   The Implementing Stage

The **Implementing** stage, in-zoomed in **SD1.3** (0), begins by defining the **Implementation Profile**, which includes the target **Language** (e.g., Java, C++, or SQL) and a default **Directory** for the artifacts. Then, the **Implementation Skeleton Generating** process uses the **OPL Script** of the current system and inner **Generation Rules** in order to create a skeleton of the **Implementation**. The **Generation Rules** save pairs of OPL sentence types (templates) and their associated code templates in various target **Languages**.

The initial skeleton of the **Implementation**, which includes both the structural and behavioral aspects of the system, is then modified by the **Implementer** during the **Implementation Reusing** and **Implementation Improving** steps. In the **Testing & Debugging** stage, the resulting **Implementation** is checked against the **Requirement Document** in order to verify that it meets the system requirements defined jointly by the **Client** and the **System Architect**. If any discrepancy or error is detected, the

System Developing process is restarted, else the system is finally delivered, assimilated and used. These sub-processes are embedded in the **Using & Maintaining** process at the bottom of **SD1** (0). While **Using & Maintaining** takes place, the **Client** collects new requirements that are eventually used when the next generation of the system is initiated. A built-in mechanism for recording new requirements in OPM format while using the system would greatly facilitate the evolution of the next system generation [5].

5   Summary and Future Work

We have presented a complete and detailed model of a system for developing systems as part of the OPM reflective metamodel. This system development model follows generic concepts of systems evolution and lifecycle, and as such, it is not specific to OPM-based system development. Nevertheless, applying this process in an OPM framework has great benefits: it narrows the gap between the various development steps and enables semi-automated generations. The elaborate backtracking options of this model, which are built-in at all levels, make it flexible enough to represent a variety of information system development approaches, ranging form the classical waterfall model through incremental development to prototyping.

Although object-oriented system development methods have been augmented to include models that enable specification of the system's behavioral aspects (e.g., UML sequence, collaboration, and Statechart diagrams), formal metamodels of these methods relate only to their language aspects. More specifically, the widely accepted object-oriented approach, which combines UML as the language part with RUP as the system development part, provides a formal metamodel only of the static aspects. Conversely, since OPM inherently combines the system's structural and behavioral aspects in a unifying, balanced framework, it can reflectively metamodel both the language and the development process parts of any methodology. This ability to model equally well structural and procedural system aspects is indicative of OPM's expressive power, which is a direct result of its balanced ontology. Recognizing objects and processes as prime ontological constructs of equal status provides for faithful modeling of systems, regardless of their domain, while OPM's abstraction-refinement capabilities enable systems' complexity management.

The system development process specified in this work is designed to accompany the development of any system that involves a combination of complex structure and behavior. The model of this development process provides a theoretical foundation for improving the current version of OPCAT [6], Object Process CASE Tool, that supports OPM-based systems development. **System Animating**, **OPD Updating**, and **OPL Updating** are already implemented as OPCAT services, while **Implementation Skeleton Generating** is in progress. We also plan to implement and incorporate all the other **System Developing** sub-processes into OPCAT in order to make it a fully Integrated System Engineering Environment (I SEE).

References

1. Brinkkemper, S., Lyytinen. K., and Welke, R. Method Engineering: Principles of Method Construction and Tool Support, Kluwer Academic Publishers, 1996.
2. Brinkkemper, S., Saeki, M., and Harmsen. F. A Method Engineering Language for the Description of Systems Development Methods. 13th Conference on Advanced Information Systems Engineering (CaiSE'2001), Lecture Notes in Computer Science 2068, pp. 473–476, 2001.
3. Clark, T., Evans, A., and Kent, S. Engineering Modeling Languages: a Precise Meta-Modeling Approach. http://www.cs.york.ac.uk/puml/mmf/langeng.ps
4. Domínguez, E., Rubio, A.L., Zapata, M.A. Meta-modelling of Dynamic Aspects: The Noesis Approach. International Workshop on Model Engineering, ECOOP'2000, pp. 28–35, 2000.
5. Dori, D. Object-Process Methodology – A Holistic Systems Paradigm, Springer Verlag, Berlin, Heidelberg, New York, 2002.
6. Dori, D. Reinhartz-Berger, I. and Sturm A. *OPCAT* – A Bimodal Case Tool for Object-Process Based System Development. 5th International Conference on Enterprise Information Systems (ICEIS 2003), pp. 286–291, 2003. Software download site: http://www.objectprocess.org
7. Firesmith, D., Henderson-Sellers, B., and Graham, I. The OPEN Modeling Language (OML) – Reference Manual. Cambridge University Press, SIGS books, 1998.
8. Graham, I., Henderson-Sellers, B., and Younessi, H. The OPEN Process Specification. Addison-Wesley Inc., 1997.
9. Henderson-Sellers, B. and Bulthuis, A. Object-Oriented Metamethods, Springer Inc., 1998.
10. Hillegersberg, J.V., Kumar, K. and Welke, R.J. Using Metamodeling to Analyze the Fit of Object-Oriented Methods to Languages. Proceedings of the 31st Hawaii International Conference on System Sciences (HICSS'98), pp. 323–332, 1998.
11. Object Management Group (OMG). Meta Object Facility (MOF) Specification. OMG document formal/02-04-03, http://cgi.omg.org/docs/formal/02-04-03.pdf
12. Object Management Group (OMG). Software Process Engineering Metamodel (SPEM), version 1.0, OMG document formal/02-11-14, http://www.omg.org/technology/documents/formal/spem.htm
13. Object Management Group (OMG). UML 1.4 – UML Semantics. OMG document formal/01-09-73, http://cgi.omg.org/docs/formal/01-09-73.pdf
14. OPEN web site, http://www.open.org.au/
15. Peleg, M. and Dori, D. The Model Multiplicity Problem: Experimenting with Real-Time Specification Methods. IEEE Transaction on Software Engineering, 26 (8), pp. 742–759, 2000.
16. Rational Software. Rational Unified Process for Systems Engineering – RUP SE1.1. A Rational Software White Paper, TP 165A, 5/02, 2001, http://www.rational.com/media/whitepapers/TP165.pdf
17. Talvanen, J. P. Domain Specific Modelling: Get your Products out 10 Times Faster. Real-Time & Embedded Computing Conference, 2002, http://www.metacase.com/papers/Domain-specific_modelling_10X_faster_than_UML.pdf
18. Siau, K. and Cao, Q. Unified Modeling Language (UML) – A Complexity Analysis. Journal of Database Management 12 (1), pp. 26–34, 2001.
19. Van Gigch, J. P. System Design Modeling and Metamodeling. Plenum press, 1991.
20. W3C Consortium. Resource Description Framework (RDF). http://www.w3.org/RDF/
21. Warmer, J. and Kleppe, A. The Object Constraint Language – Precise Modeling with UML. Addison-Wesley, 1999.
22. What is metamodelling, and what is a metamodel good for? http://www.metamodel.com/

Appendix A: Main OPM Concepts, Their Symbols, and Their Meaning

Concept Name	Symbol	Concept Meaning
Informatical object		A piece of information
Environmental, physical object		An object which consists of matter and/or energy and is external to the system
Process class		A pattern of transformation that objects undergo
State		A situation at which an object can exist for a period of time
Characterization		A fundamental structural relation representing that an element exhibits a thing (object/process)
Aggregation		A fundamental structural relation representing that a thing (object/process) consists of one or more things
General structural link		A bidirectional or unidirectional association between things that holds for a period of time
Condition link		A link denoting a condition required for a process execution
Agent link		A link denoting that a human agent (actor) is required for triggering a process execution
Instrument link		A link denoting that a process uses an entity without changing it. If the entity is not available, the process waits for its availability.
Effect link		A link denoting that a process changes an entity. The black arrowhead points towards the process that affects the entity.
Consumption link		A link denoting that a process consumes an (input) entity
Result link		A link denoting that a process creates an (output) entity
Invocation link		A link denoting that a process triggers (invokes) another process when it ends

A Unified Approach for Software Policy Modeling: Incorporating Implementation into a Modeling Methodology

Junho Shim[1], Seungjin Lee[2], and Chisu Wu[2]

[1] Department of Computer Science
Sookmyung Women's University
Seoul 140-742, Korea
jshim@sookmyung.ac.kr
[2] School of Comp. Sci. & Engineering
Seoul National University
Seoul 151-742, Korea
{lsj,wuchisu}@selab.snu.ac.kr

Abstract. Works in some software project domains consist of many small projects of which development cycles are relatively quite short and numerous. In such domains, the software development policy such as the work assignment policy needs not only its modeling but also needs the prompt implementation of the model. However, incorporating the implementation into the modeling methodology has not been paid great attention to in the areas of software process. Each organization may have different situations in human resources and tasks as well as practical constraints, and it may not be feasible to devise a single model to cover all policies. In this paper, we do not focus on presenting a universal model for the work assignment policy. Instead, we provide a meta-model based methodology which enables us to develop an extensible model for an organization. In our modeling methodology, the model for the work assignment policy and its implementation are incorporated. We employ UML and ConceptBase. We highlight how a model illustrated in UML is generated in ConceptBase codes. And finally, we introduce our experience from the use of a prototype system in actual software project field.

1 Introduction

The software process has been vigorously researched in both industry and academia, since it has been known as a critical parameter to determine the quality and cost of a final software product [2,3]. An important element which should be represented in a software process model is the *work assignment policy*. The work assignment policy is, in its simple explanation, a policy to determine who would perform which work (or task). Since the human resource in an organization is limited, how to assign a task to whom is of importance in the software process.

A Web site maintenance project, for example, usually consists of multiple subprojects of which development life cycles are quite short, i.e., within a few months. A subproject in turn consists of many short-duration works, of which an

I.-Y. Song et al. (Eds.): ER 2003, LNCS 2813, pp. 118–130, 2003.

example is to update a set of JSP (Java Server Page) codes within hours. Within ordinary software development projects, the maintenance phase usually kicks off only after completing several months or years of development phase. Within a Web site development project, however, the initial product (web site) is developed in quite short period of time, and then the maintenance tasks consisting of numerous short subprojects are carried out simultaneously to improve the product.

It is also not unusual within a Web site development project that a team member for the project simultaneously participates in many different projects, and that the members are shared across the projects. The work assignment for a project, then, may affect the development schedules of other projects. And the unclear expectation to the final outcome of the Web site may often incur the frequent changes of its development schedule. Therefore, it is desirable to identify the on-going situation of several projects and to perform more prompt work assignments in order to keep the project schedules on time. From our experience in the field, for example, assigning works by weekly offline meetings is not sufficient. At the same time, it is not either desirable or practical to hold more recurrent meetings than weekly based ones within a development team with large number of members.

This motivates our work that develops a tool to help the project managers perform the online work assignment. For this purpose, we develop a modeling methodology which help the project managers to model the software process for the work assignment policy and then to automatically implement the models within the tool.

1.1 An Example of the Work Assignment Policy

To illustrate the motivation why it is necessary to develop our modeling methodology for such areas as the Web site maintenance, we present an example of the work assignment policy for the *change management process* [12]. The change management process, in UML Activity Diagram [8], is shown in Fig. 1, and its short explanation is as following.

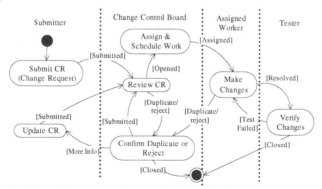

Fig. 1. Change Management Process illustrated in UML Activity Diagram

A project member may submit a CR (Change Request) which is reviewed by CCB (Change Control Board). If CCB regards the CR appropriate, they determine whether the CR should be included on current product release. They may confirm the CR duplicate to another, or reject the CR if they find it inappropriate. If more information is needed or the CR is rejected, then the submitter is notified. The submitter, then later, may submit an updated CR. Once the CR is approved (opened) by CCB, and then project manager assigns workers and schedules work to perform the CR. Workers make changes according to the work schedule. Then the resolved CR goes through a verification process in which testers verify changes, after which the CR becomes closed.

Within a Web site maintenance project, change requests occur quite frequently compared to other traditional projects, and most of them need relatively short development hours. Therefore in the context of Web site maintenance how to effectively model and implement the change management process may be of much importance in practice [11]. For example, let us consider a work assignment policy for the change management process as following: *i) Updating a CR should be assigned to the worker who submitted the CR.*

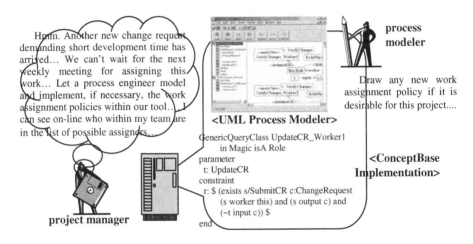

Fig. 2. Models in UML and Implementation in ConceptBase

A new change request has arrived to a project manager who has been so busy to care for a large number of small projects. (Fig. 2) If the project requires one or multiple new or updated work assignment policies, then to model and implement the policies is necessary. The manager, then, may ask a process engineer to model and implement the policies. The process engineer represents the policies in UML Process Modeler, and then the corresponding ConceptBase codes to implementing the model are automatically generated. Then, the manager can see who within his team are available for the request within a modeling tool; an output interface of running a ConceptBase query class. Note that the tool provides the manager with a set of workers eligible for the work, rather than optimally assigning an individual or group of workers to the work. The actual decision is made by the manager. This paper describes how this entire process works within our approach.

In addition to the policy *i)*, we see that such work assignment policies as following can be frequently found in the Web site maintenance.

ii)   CCB (Change Control Board) consists of Configuration Manager, Project Manager, and Architect.

iii) *Different level of review formality may be applied to a CR for each phase of the software process lifecycle. For example, Architect may informally review a CR during inception phase as CCB should formally review the CR during other phases such as elaboration, construction, or transition phase*

iv) *If a CR is originally submitted by a QA (Quality Assurance) engineer, then the task of verifying changes must be assigned to the QA. Otherwise, the task of verifying changes is assigned to any QA.*

v) *Coding a HTML page should be assigned to the worker who has a skill of HTML coding.*

vi) *Assigning a work should take into account of the workload of workers.*

In order to model those policies, we should represent in the model multiple and extensible views (or aspects). In this paper we show that modeling with the following four aspects are desirable to implementing the above policies: 1) *organization aspect* to represent the structure of a team or the role of member, 2) *process aspect* to represent the lifecycle phases, the task hierarchy, or the role eligible to perform a task, 3) *product aspect* to represent the input or output artifact, or the role responsible for an artifact, and 4) *project aspect* to represent the project schedule, staffing plan, or the worker's skill and workload. Note that we do not say that the above four-views is the only necessary and sufficient set of views to cover the entire work assignment policies in the software process. The four-views is exemplary to feature our modeling methodology and provides a complete set of views just for the above six policies.

The rest of this paper is organized as follows. Section 2 provides the related work. Section 3 illustrates how we view work assignment policy modeling in such aspects as organization, process, product, and project, and shows how models by meta-modeling methodology can be refined for each view. Section 4 illustrates how we implement our model and discusses some features of our implementation. Section 5 explains a field study. And finally, Section 6 draws the conclusion.

2   Related Work and Our Contribution

In this paper, we present a modeling methodology into which the implementation is incorporated. We illustrate the need of our methodology in the domain of the work assignment process modeling. A work assignment process, in general, may consist of the following two phases: 1) determine a set of workers who are eligible to perform a task. 2) then, among the set of eligible workers, assign an individual or group of workers to the task. The optimal assignment for 2) step is known as a resource constrained scheduling problem, which can be reduced to a NP problem in [1]. Note that the optimal assignment is beyond the scope of this paper.

Traditionally, the role concept has been extensively used for the work assignment policy in the software process modeling [2,3]. In a role-based model, a work is assigned only by the role of a worker. However, we see that such role as Designer or Tester should not be an only element to represent a work assignment policy. It is not difficult to see that work assignment only by role information is not sufficient to represent the above exemplary policies *i)* to *vi)*. A work assignment policy model should represent in detail any necessary criteria for the given work. As long as the authors' knowledge, we are the first to present such a methodology in which such work assignment policies described as in the exemplary policies are implemented.

The modeling and its implementation are not separated in our methodology. Instead, models represented in UML [8] are automatically generated into the codes in ConceptBase [5], an object oriented logical database system. We claim that this approach may not only help the automation of the above 1) step, but also help to decrease the size of the set of eligible workers, which may help 2) step to be more efficiently performed in practice.

Software process is inherently creative and includes inconsistency in itself [3]. There may be different sets of eligibility criteria for a work assignment policy from an organization to another. We need an extensible model which can provide in a model from a basic set consisting of core modeling elements for simple process to an extensive set containing various modeling elements for complex process. We in this paper offer such extensibility through meta modeling approach.

[9,12,6] employs UML and meta modeling to model software process. [9] illustrates how to verify the consistency of a model. [12] focuses on defining the modeling elements and proposing the standard UML notations for software process. [6] is our initial work to demonstrate an idea that UML and meta-modeling can be employed for the task assignment policy. However, its scope is limited in that it lacks of various modeling aspects, and that implementation details and case study are not covered. For the viewpoint of project management, the Web project differs to the traditional project in a way that the former contains uncertainty in many phases, continuously changes, and rapidly develops [7,10]. Finally, we in this paper show how we develop a prototype based on the illustrated modeling methodology and furthermore perform a case study in the Web project field.

3 Modeling

Each organization may have different situations in human resources and tasks as well as practical constraints, and it may not be feasible to devise a single model to cover all policies. We need an extensible model which can provide from a basic set of core modeling elements for simple process to an extensive set for complex process. Within our modeling methodology we offer such extensibility through meta modeling. We define in a meta model the classes of modeling elements which are used in conceptual model. For example, a simplest meta model for the work assignment policy is illustrated in Fig. 3. There are three meta classes: M2Role, M2Artifact, and M2Task, which is, respectively, the meta class of role, artifact, and task classes in conceptual model. The eligibility to perform a task is represented by worker association, and the responsibility for an artifact is represented by owner association. The relationship between task and artifact is represented by input or output association.

In the following subsections, we illustrate how we develop such work assignment policies as i) to vi) in Section 1 within our meta-modeling methodology where we represent the policies in four different views: organization, process, product and project.

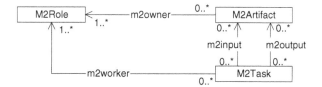

Fig. 3. A simple meta model for the work assignment policy

3.1 Organization Model

Organization model represents the organizational information. It shows worker's role such as Architect, Project Member, or Configuration Manager, and the hierarchical structure of roles. It also shows the team structuring policy; for example, how to structure CCB. Fig. 4 shows an organization model. In order to represent the policy *ii)* in Section 1; *CCB (Change Control Board) consists of Configuration Manager, Project Manager, and Architect,* the previous meta model shown in Fig. 3 is not sufficient, since there is no modeling elements to represent a team structuring policy in it. Therefore we expand the meta model into the one in Fig. 4-a). In Fig. 4-a) we have M2Person and M2Team sub meta classes of M2Worker, and m2consistOf meta association between M2Team and M2Role.

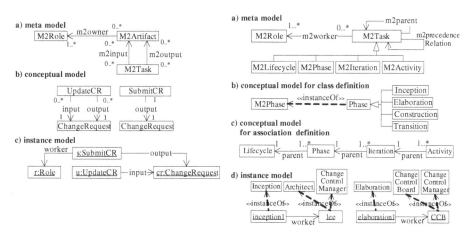

Fig. 4. Organization model   **Fig. 5.** Process model

Based on the expanded meta model, we can represent in conceptual model the CCB team structuring policy. (Fig. 4-b) In the figure, we represent that CCB class should consist of ConfigurationManager, ProjectManager, and Architect classes. The association between CCB and each role class is defined as leader, member1, or member2, respectively.

Then an instance model for each project can be constructed based on conceptual model. (Fig. 4-c) In the figure, lee is defined as a Person who has Architect role. And lee is also a member of CCB.

3.2   Process Model

In process model, we represent the software process lifecycle such as inception, elaboration, construction, or transition phase; task hierarchies such as parent or child relationships between tasks; and role information to show which roles are eligible to perform a task.

In order to represent the lifecycle of a project in a meta model, the meta model shown in Fig. 3 can be expanded into the one in Fig. 5-a). In the figure, M2Task meta class has sub meta classes like M2Lifecycle, M2Phase, M2Iteration, and M2Activity. Then a conceptual model can be constructed. (Fig. 5-b) The Phase class, an instance of M2Phase meta class, has as lifecycle phases Inception, Elaboration, Construction, and Transition sub phase classes. We may then have parent associations between Lifecycle and Phase, and between Phase and Iteration, since they are all tasks. (Fig. 5-c)

A process instance model shows the policy *iii)* in Section 1; *Different level of review formality may be applied to a CR for each phase of the software process lifecycle.* (Fig. 5-d) In the figure, lee, an Architect and ChangeControlManager, works during task Inception phase, while CCB works during Elaboration task phase.

3.3   Product Model

In product model, we represent input or output artifact of task, and role information to show who is responsible for an artifact. Fig. 6 shows a product model. The figure shows how the work assignment policies *i)* in Section 1 are modeled. The policy *i)*: *Updating a CR should be assigned to the worker who submitted the CR;* is represented in c) in a way that UpdateCR task has input association with ChangeRequest artifact which has output association with SubmitCR task. Therefore a worker who has the role for submit a CR should have the role for update the CR.

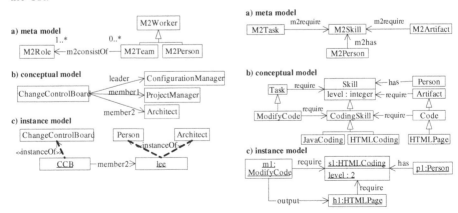

Fig. 6. Product model   **Fig. 7.** Project model - capability of worker

3.4 Project Model

In project model, we represent the capability and workload of worker. Fig. 7 is a project model to illustrate the capability of worker. The figure shows the work assignment policy stated as *v)* in Section 1: *Coding a HTML page should be assigned to the worker who has a skill of HTML coding.* What skill is necessary for a given task depends on what artifact is output (modified) by the task. For example, HTML page h1 requires HTML coding skill s1. Then ModifyCode m1 which outputs h1 should require s1. The worker p1 has the HTML coding skill can be assigned the task m1.

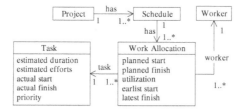

Fig. 8. Project model - workload

Fig. 8 is a project conceptual model to represent the work assignment policy *vi)* in Section 1: *Assigning a work should take into account of the workload of workers.* In the figure, the workload of a worker is illustrated by the work allocation to the worker. A project has one or multiple schedules, and a schedule has one or multiple work allocations each of which has a task and a worker.

4 Implementation

A novelty of our modeling methodology is on automating the model implementation. In our modeling methodology, the ConceptBase codes are just the textual representation of a UML model, i.e., a modeling element in UML can be mapped to its corresponding ConceptBase codes. Note however that this does not mean that we cover the full set of UML. We currently employ only the subset of UML class diagram and its corresponding subset of the ConceptBase language, which are just enough for modeling and implementing the work assignment policies presented in the paper. For example, the constraint formula for a query class is limited to the *disjunctive normal form.* (see Section 4.1)

In general, it does not require complex scheme to translate a work assignment policy model in UML into the ConceptBase codes. Technically, the *meta class, class, object, association, instanciation, generalization,* and *template class* in UML is mapped respectively to the *meta class, simple class, token, attribute, in* relationship, *isa* relationship, and *generic query class* in ConceptBase. (Fig. 9-b) For example, M2Artifact meta class and Package class shown in Fig. 6-b) can be coded in ConceptBase as following in Fig. 9-a).

```
MetaClass M2Artifact with
attribute, "to(1..*)"
    m2owner : M2Role
end

SimpleClass Package in M2Artifact
    with m2owner, "to(1..*)"
    owner : PackageTeam
end
```

UML	ConceptBase
meta class	meta class
class	simple class
object	token
association	attribute
instanciation	in relationship
generalization	isa relationship
template class	generic query class

Fig. 9-a) ConceptBase codes for Fig. 6-b   **Fig. 9-b)** UML vs ConceptBase mapping

Some UML modeling elements with no proper corresponding constructs in ConceptBase are handled in case by case. For example, we define "from(1)", "from(1..*)", "to(1)", and "to(1..*)" attribute objects to implement the multiplicity constraint in UML. "from(1)" or "to(1)" represents 1 multiplicity constraint at starting end or at ending end, respectively. Similarly, "from(1..*)" or "to(1..*)" represents 1..* multiplicity constraint at starting end or at ending end, respectively. 0..* multiplicity can be ignored since it does not constrain at all. In Fig. 9-a), m2owner meta association and m2owner have "to(1..*)" since they have 1..* multiplicity constraint in Fig. 6.

In the following subsections, we illustrate some highlights on our modeling implementation.

4.1   Query for Work Assignment Policy

As mentioned in Section 1.2, finding a smaller set of workers who are eligible to perform a given task is quite important in practice. For this purpose, we create our own UML stereotype, called *queryClass*.

The queryClass extends the semantic of template class which is a modeling element in UML. A template class is a class with parameters as inputs. An example of queryClass, RolePlayer, is shown in Fig. 10-a). Fig. 10-b) is a code for RolePlayer in ConceptBase. How to translate a query class graph in UML into a query class tree in ConceptBase is summarized as following. A node like r (in Fig. 10-a) with multiple parents can be duplicated in order to transform a graph into a tree. Any child of the root in the tree should be this, i.e., each subtree of a query class should have this as its root. Each subtree represents a constraint formula, and constraints are connected by OR logical connectives, while within a subtree constraints are connected by AND logical connectives. In other words, the constraint formula of a query class follows the disjunctive normal form. For a parameter variable such as t or r appearing in the formula, we put ~ character before the variable name. A non-parameter variable such as m is quantified by exists operator if it begins with a lower case letter, otherwise by forall operator.

RolePlayer has two parameters t and r where t is an instance of Task class and r is an instance of M2Role meta class. RolePlayer finds out the instances of r role class which has worker association with ancestor task of t task. In Fig. 5, for example, `RolePlayer<t,ChangeControlManager>` finds lee as `RolePlayer` if t is a subtask of `inception1`, or finds CCB if t is a subtask of `elaboration1`.

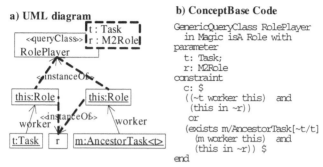

Fig. 10. An example of queryClass and its representation in ConceptBase

Using `RolePlayer` queryClass, we show how to find a proper worker based on the policy *iv)* in Section 1: *If a CR is originally submitted by a QA (Quality Assurance) engineer, then the task of verifying changes must be assigned to the QA. Otherwise, the task of verifying changes is assigned to any QA.* In Fig. 11, `VerifyChange_Worker1` is defined as a queryClass of which input is t `VerifyChanges` task. At first, it needs to find out the input c `ChangeRequest` of t. And it finds out s `SubmitCR` which outputs c. Then, it finds out the worker who performs s. In other words, combined with `RolePlayer<t,QAEngineer>`, `VerifyChange_Worker1` finds out the worker who submit the same CR for verification if he is a QAEngineer. `VerifyChange_Worker2` is a different queryClass to `VerifyChange_Worker1` in a way that the former finds out workers who play `QAEngineer`.

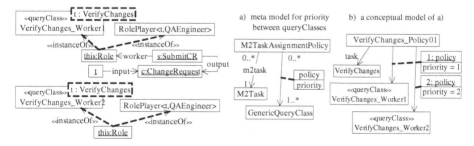

Fig. 11. Two queryClasses for the policy *iv)*   **Fig. 12.** An implementation of the policy *iv)*

Combining two queryClasses and a meta model to provide the priority between queryClasses, we can find a proper worker as shown in Fig. 12. In a meta model, policy association contains a priority attribute to indicate that a queryClass associated with higher priority value is chosen rather than the other queryClass associated with lower value. In other words, `VerifyChange_Worker1` is chosen if there is an instance to satisfy, or `VerifyChange_Worker2` is chosen otherwise.

4.2 An Extension of the Model: Towards Considering the Worker's Capability

One of the advantages of our approach is that if necessary we may extend the model by adding new elements. For example, we can extend the work assignment policy implemented in Section 4.1 so that we take into account of the worker's capability modeled in Section 3.4.

```
GenericQueryClass RolePlayer in Magic isA Agent with
parameter
    task: Task;
    role: M2Role
constraint
c2: $ forall s1/Skill (~task require s1) =>
        (exists S/M2Skill s2/Skill
        (s1 in S) and (s2 in S) and (this has s2)) $
end
```

The code shows that we add a constraint c2 to the RolePlayer shown in Fig. 11. The constraint c2 is for taking into account of the worker's capability. The c2 defines that for any skill instance required by a task instance, both instances s1 and s2 of Skill should be the instances of the Skill class S. The c2 constrains that only the workers who have the skill required by a task can be assigned to the task. It checks whether the class of Skill coincides but it ignores whether the level value, an attribute of skill, coincides. Our experience on the Web project shows that it is better to provide the project manager with the flexibility of considering the skill-level value.

5   Case Study Using a Prototype

In order to evaluate the usefulness of our approach in the field, we developed a prototype. The architecture of our prototype is shown in Fig. 13. The *UML Process Modeler* implemented in Visual C++ and Visual Basic enables a process engineer to construct a model for the software process and the work assignment policy (Fig. 14). The model is sent by the socket communication to the *Knowledgebase* which employs ConceptBase and Java codes. During the construction of a model, the *Model Advisor* implemented in CLIPS expert system [4] guides the engineer to avoid semantic as well as syntactic errors. The Model Advisor is in the form of Windows DLL(Dynamic Link Library) and is run-time bound to the UML Process Modeler.

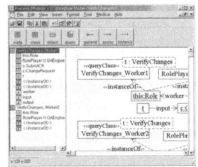

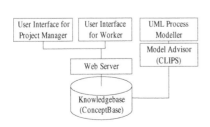

Fig. 13. The architecture of our prototype   **Fig. 14.** A snapshot of UML Process Modeler

5.1 Field Experience

We applied the prototype to the Web site maintenance projects carried by a IT division of a major news-media company in Korea. The division has about 80 workers consisting of graphic designers, software engineers, copywriters, system operators, and managers. A major duty of the division is to implement a series of change requests which very frequently occur due to the change of surrounding IT techniques and business environment. Approximately 50 percent of change requests turn out to take less than one man-week to be implemented. The number of change requests, however, is quite large; on average one thousand requests per a month.

Within the division, to meet deadline of a change request often failed due to the difficulty in the project management. Let us say that a change request related to a Web page style is initiated. Then the manager of graphic design team would assign the work to the member whose current or projected workload is light. However, it is not easy for her to see the workload of each member since most her members are involved in multiple projects which are managed by different managers but herself. Project members such as graphic designers have little or no experience in the software process, and they often fail to perform the task by its priority.

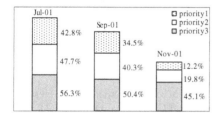
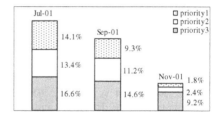

Fig. 15-a) The average ratio of the job-queuing time to the total time (lower priority number means higher priority)

Fig. 15-b) Deadline miss-ratio (lower priority number means higher priority)

Fig. 15-a) shows the average ratio of the job-queuing time which takes from the submission of a change request and to the assignment of the request, to the total time which takes from the submission and to the closing of the request. Before we used the prototype, the ratio of the job-queuing time was high; more than 40 percent even for the jobs with the highest priority (priority-1). The reason is that the division held a weekly off line meeting to assign jobs to workers while the majority of jobs are such small as requiring two to three-man-day. Since September when the division began to apply our tool, the project managers were able to assign works online and the ratio became decreasing.

In addition to decreasing the average job-queuing time, the tool also enables the project managers to analyze more precisely the information such as the workload and schedule of team members. The team members can also easily identify the priorities and delayed times of assigned tasks, which helps them to perform the tasks accordingly. This leads to decreasing the deadline miss-ratio as shown in Fig. 15-b).

6 Conclusion

We introduce a software process modeling methodology for the work assignment policy. Within our modeling methodology the implementation in ConceptBase is incorporated into the modeling in UML. Meta modeling approach enables us to perform the modeling with flexibility and extensibility.

In the area of software process, verifying the usefulness of a model is another subject of equal importance to developing and implementing the model. We developed a prototype and conducted a case-study which shows how our methodology presented in the paper benefits in practice.

The user interface to input the data in the current prototype employs the Web, which requires the developers to voluntarily input the data. Developers, however, often delayed or sometimes neglected to input the data. It may be necessary to integrate the prototype with other software development tools and to automatically extract the data from the tools. For example, the division our prototype was applied to also carries out another pilot project to employ the CMS(Content Management Server). The CMS manages the information of developers, products, and work processes. Should the prototype be integrated with the CMS, we can possibly make use of necessary data from the CMS.

References

1. U. Belhe and A. Kusiak, "Dynamic scheduling of design activities with resource constraints," IEEE Transactions on Systems, Man and Cybernetics, Part A, 27(1), IEEE Computer Society, 1997.
2. J.C. Derniame, B.A. Kaba and D. Wastell (ed.), Software Process: Principles, Methodology, and Technology, Springer, 1999.
3. A. Fuggetta and A. Wolf, Software Process, John Wiley & Sons, 1996.
4. J.C. Giarratano, CLIPS User's Guide (Version 6.0), NASA Lyndon B. Johnson Space Center, Information Systems Directorate, Software Technology Branch, 1993.
5. M. Jarke, R. Gallersorfer, M.A. Jeusfeld and M. Staudt, "ConceptBase-A Deductive Object Base for Meta Data Management", Journal of Intelligent Information Systems, 4(1), 1995.
6. S. Lee, J. Shim and C. Wu, "A Meta Model Approach using UML for Task Assignment Policy", Proceedings of the 9th Asia-Pacific Software Engineering Conference, IEEE Computer Society, 2002.
7. R.S. Pressman, "What a Tangled Web We Weave," IEEE Software, 17(1), IEEE Computer Society, 2000.
8. J. Rumbaugh, I. Jacobson and G. Booch, The Unified Modeling Language Reference Manual, Addison Wesley, 1999.
9. A. Schleicher and B. Westfechtel, "Beyond stereotyping: metamodeling approaches for the UML," Proceedings of the 34th Annual Hawaii International Conference on System Sciences, IEEE Computer Society, 2001.
10. K. Wiegers, "Software Process Improvement in Web Time," IEEE Software, 16(4), IEEE Computer Society, 1999.
11. J. Wright, D. Wilkin and N. Newton, "Managing the matrix," Engineering Management Journal, 11(1), Feb. 2001.
12. The Object Management Group, Software Process Engineering Metamodel Specification (adopted draft), http://www.omg.org, Dec. 2001.

Deriving Use Cases from Business Process Models

Jan L.G. Dietz

Delft University of Technology
P.O. Box 5031, NL-2600GA Delft
j.l.g.dietz@its.tudelft.nl

Abstract. Use cases are intended to capture the functional requirements of an information system. The problem of identifying use cases is however not satisfactorily resolved yet. The approach presented in this paper is to derive use cases from the business system models that are produced by applying DEMO (Demo Engineering Methodology for Organizations). These models have three attractive properties: essence, atomicity and completeness. Essence means that the real business things are identified, clearly distinguished from informational things. Atomic means that one ends up with things that are units from the business point of view. Complete means that no business things are overlooked and that the models do not contain irrelevant things. A three-step procedure is proposed for deriving use cases from these models, such that they do possess the same properties of essence, atomicity and completeness.

1 Introduction

A use case is a construct for the definition of the behavior of a system without revealing its internal structure [6]. In [16] it is defined more specifically as a description of the complete *course of events* initiated by an actor and of the *interaction* between the actor and the (future) system. By system is meant an information system or computer application, and by actor is meant a particular role of the user(s) of the system. In addition to introducing use cases, Jacobson introduced the use case diagram to represent them [16]. Although not exclusively meant for that purpose, use cases are mostly applied in engineering methods that are based on the UML, like the ones described in [15] and [1]. The strong point of these methods is, that once the use cases are identified, the development of the application software goes smoothly. The weak point however is the identification of use cases itself. To be fair, this is not specifically a drawback of the UML based engineering methods. Requirements elicitation is the weakest link in all methods, although the past decades have shown progress. In the former days, the common approach to requirements elicitation was in fact the so-called 'waiter strategy': the information analyst or architect just asked the future users what services they wanted the system to provide. Currently, many methods start with modeling the business domain that has to be supported by the information system. Business domain models offer a more objective criterion for evaluating the requirements as listed by the future users.

Unfortunately, the modeling of the business domain is in danger to become the next weakest link because many people appear to conceive business processes as

I.-Y. Song et al. (Eds.): ER 2003, LNCS 2813, pp. 131–143, 2003.

some kind of information processes. Business systems/processes are not yet treated as a serious and independent field of study, next to and independent of information systems/processes. Consequently, business process modeling languages are often provided as an 'extension' of a language for modeling information processes. A striking example is the UML itself. Booch, Jacobson and Rumbaugh [3] indicate that the UML offers a standard way to write a systems blueprint including "conceptual things such as business processes". First, business processes are not "conceptual things" but concrete things. The classification "conceptual" rightly fits information processes. Second, because of its foundation in O-O software development, we argue that the UML is primarily an information system modeling language and not a language that is appropriate for expressing business process models. Despite the ambition or even claim of many people, and even despite proposed extensions to the UML, like in [11], an information system is basically a system in the category of rational systems (if one abstracts from its implementation), whereas a business process (better: system) is a system in the category of social systems. The problem of confusing business systems with information systems is a major problem addressed in this paper.

In order to prevent the modeling of the business domain from becoming the next weakest link but instead to gain real benefit from it, we argue that a use case should satisfy the next requirements:

- It should make a clear and well-founded distinction between the *essential* business actions and informational actions. The latter are exactly the things that have to be reconsidered when developing an information system. For example, requesting a supplier to deliver articles is essential, but computing the amount of articles is informational (it is no new fact, only the outcome of a computation).
- It should have the right granularity or level of detail. "Right" means in this respect: finding the actions that are *atomic* from the business point of view. They may be composite only in their implementations. For example, the request to a supplier is atomic from the business point of view, but to perform a request by postal mail, a number of non-essential actions have to be taken like mailing the order form, transporting it and delivering it to the supplier.
- It should be *complete*, i.e. it should contain everything that is necessary and it should not contain anything that is irrelevant. As will be shown in the sequel, this requirement is probably the most hard to satisfy since it is common practice in most organizations to perform several kinds of coordination acts tacitly, according to the rule "no news is good news".

A reliable approach to satisfy these requirements seems to be to base the use cases on a model of the business domain that is essential, atomic and complete. According to our observations, very few business process-modeling approaches satisfy these requirements; one of them is DEMO (Demo Engineering Methodology for Organizations). DEMO is a methodology that is developed particularly for the purpose of modeling the essential business processes, abstracting completely from their realization [7,8,9,25]. DEMO fits in a fairly new and promising perspective on business processes and information systems, called the Language/Action Perspective, or LAP for short. The theoretical foundation of this new perspective is constituted by Speech Acts Theory [2,21], and the Theory of Communicative Action [14]. The major difference between DEMO and other LAP approaches, like the ones described in [13] and [18], is that it builds on two additional theoretical pillars next to the LAP, namely

Organizational Semiotics [23] and Systems Ontology [4,5]. We report in this paper about the application of DEMO for identifying and specifying use cases. Comparable research is reported in [12] and [20]. However, the approaches presented in these papers do not seem to satisfy all of the three requirements proposed above.

The outline of the paper is as follows. Section 2 provides a summary of the relevant parts of DEMO, necessary and sufficient for understanding the rest of the paper. In section 3, the DEMO model of a library is presented and explained as an example. From this model a set of use cases is derived in section 4 that constitute the starting point for the development of information systems, using e.g. one of the mentioned UML-based engineering methods. Section 5 contains the conclusions that can be drawn from this exercise.

2 Summary of the DEMO Theory

This section contains a brief description of the theory behind the DEMO methodology. The readers that are not (yet) familiar with DEMO may be tempted to consider the terminology queer and unnecessarily different from what they are used to. However, it is not. To deal seriously with business processes as phenomena that are fundamentally different from information processes, it is necessary to develop a dedicated terminology. It would only be misleading and confusing to use the terminology from the information systems area.

An organization consists of social individuals (people) or *subjects* that perform two kinds of acts. By performing *production acts*, the subjects fulfill the mission of the organization. A production act (P-act for short) may be material (e.g. a manufacturing or transportation act) or immaterial (e.g. approving an insurance claim, or electing someone president). By performing *coordination acts* (C-acts for short), subjects enter into and comply with commitments. In doing so, they initiate and coordinate the execution of production acts. To abstract from the particular subject that performs an action, and to concentrate on the organizational role of the subject in performing that action, the notion of *actor role* is introduced. An actor role is a particular, atomic 'amount' of authority, viz. the authority needed to perform precisely one kind of production act. A subject in his/her fulfillment of an actor role is called an *actor*.

The result of successfully performing a P-act is a *production fact* or P-fact. P-facts in a library include "membership M has started to exist" and "the late return fine for loan L is paid". The variables M and L denote an instance of membership and loan respectively. All realization issues are fully abstracted out. Only the facts as such are relevant, not how they are achieved. Examples of C-acts are requesting and promising a P-fact (e.g. requesting to become member of the library).

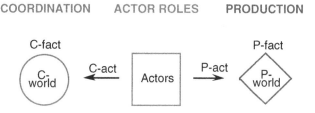

Fig. 1. The white-box model of an organization

The result of successfully performing a C-act is a *coordination fact* or C-fact (e.g. the being requested of the production fact "membership #387 has started to exist"). Again, all realization issues are ignored (e.g. whether the request is made by a letter or e-mail or via a website). Just as we distinguish between P-acts and C-acts, we also distinguish between two worlds in which these kinds of acts have effect: the *production world* or P-world and the *coordination world* or C-world respectively (Fig. 1). An *event* is the creation of a fact (e.g. "membership #387 has started to exist"). C-facts serve as agenda (plural of agendum) for actors. Actors constantly loop through a cycle in which they try to deal with their agenda. Dealing with an *agendum* means selecting the corresponding action rule, gathering information (if needed), and then performing the act.

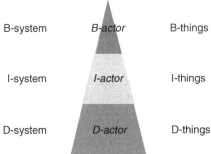

B-system	B-actor	B-things
I-system	I-actor	I-things
D-system	D-actor	D-things

Fig. 2. The three levels of abstraction

Concerning P-acts and -facts, three levels of abstraction are distinguished (Fig. 2). These levels may be understood as 'glasses' for viewing an organization. Looking through the *essential* glasses, one observes the core business actors, who perform P-acts that result in original (non-derivable) facts, and who directly contribute to the organization's function (e.g. approving a membership application, or diagnosing a patient's medical problems). These essential acts and facts are collectively called *B-things* (from Business). Looking through the *informational* glasses, one observes intellectual actors, who execute informational acts like collecting, providing, recalling and computing knowledge about business acts and their results. Informational acts and facts are collectively called *I-things* (from Information and Intellect). Looking through the *documental* glasses, one observes documental actors, who execute documental acts like gathering, distributing, storing, copying, and destroying documents containing the aforementioned knowledge. Documental acts and facts are collectively called *D-things* (from Documents and Data).

The three kinds of actors are called B-actors, I-actors and D-actors. They are the elements of three corresponding aspect systems of an organization: the B-system, the I-system, and the D-system. The starting point and emphasis in DEMO is the B-system. Only in the B-system may new original facts be created. The corresponding I-system and D-system are part of the realization of the B-system, and so can be designed only after the B-system is designed. Information and communication technology can be applied without any risk or harm to the I-system and the D-system. However, one must be cautious in applying it to the B-system, to prevent falling into the 'AI-trap' that machines could take over the responsibility of B-actors. One can only mimic or simulate B-systems. The triangular shape of the levels in Fig. 2 shows that there is nothing 'above' the B-system, and that generally the amount of D-things in an organization is much more than the amount of I-things, and that the amount of I-things is much more than the amount of B-things.

P-acts and C-acts appear to occur in generic recurrent patterns, called *transactions*. A transaction has three phases: the order phase (O-phase), the execution phase (E-phase), and the result phase (R-phase). It is carried through by two actors, who alternately perform acts. The actor who starts the transaction and eventually completes it, is called the *initiator*. The other one, who actually performs the production act, is called the *executor*. The O-phase is a conversation that starts with a request by the initiator and ends (if successfully) with a promise by the executor. The R-phase is a conversation that starts with a statement by the executor and ends (if successfully) with an acceptance by the initiator. In between these two conversations there is the E-phase in which the executor performs the P-act.

Fig. 3 exhibits the standard pattern of a transaction. A white box represents a C-act type and a white disk represents a C-fact type. A gray box represents a P-act type and a gray diamond a P-fact type. The initial C-act is drawn with a bold line, as is every terminal C-fact. The gray colored frames, denoted by "initiator" and "executor" represent the *responsibility areas* of the two partaking actor roles. As an illustrating example we take the buying of a loaf at the bakery's store. The customer plays the role of initiator; the baker plays the role of executor. The process starts with the request by the customer for delivering a loaf. The result is the C-fact that the delivery is requested ("rq"). This C-fact is drawn between the two actor roles to show that it is a fact in their *intersubjective world* (cf. [14]). The C-fact "rq" is an agendum for the executor (the baker). As the outcome of dealing with the agendum, the baker may promise to deliver the requested loaf or decline it. If he promises, the process reaches the state promised (the C-fact "pm"). This fact is an agendum for the baker. In dealing with it, the baker produces the P-fact. The P-act consists of the decision by the baker to sell the requested loaf to the customer. The reason for coloring P-act types and P-fact types gray is to emphasize that they belong to the *subjective world* of the executor. Next, the baker states that the loaf has been delivered, resulting in the C-fact "st". This fact is an agendum for the customer. If he responds to it by accepting the produced P-fact, the process reaches the successful terminal state "ac". This coincides by definition with the *P-event* in which the P-fact comes actually into existence.

The standard pattern must always be passed through for establishing a new P-fact. A few comments are in place however. First, performing a C-act does not necessarily mean that there is oral or written communication. Every (physical) act may count as a C-act. Second, C-acts may be performed *tacitly*, according to the rule "no news is good news" as mentioned in the introduction. In particular the promise and the acceptance are often performed tacitly. Third, next to the standard transaction pattern, four cancellations patterns are identified [9]. Together with the standard pattern they constitute the complete transaction pattern. This complete pattern is represented by the construct in the lower part of Fig. 3. This construct is the basis for the Construction Model (cf. Fig. 4).

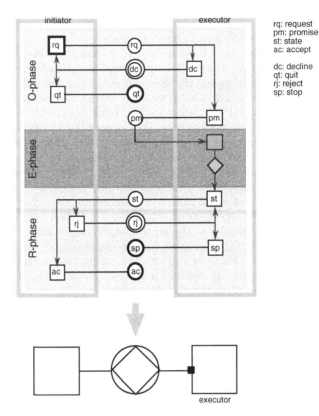

rq: request
pm: promise
st: state
ac: accept

dc: decline
qt: quit
rj: reject
sp: stop

Fig. 3. The standard pattern of a transaction

3 The Business Domain Model of a Library

The complete model of the B-system of an organization in DEMO is called the *essential model* of the organization. It consists of an integrated set of four aspect models: the *Construction Model* (CM), the *Operation Model* (OM), the *State Model* (SM), and the *Process Model* (PM). The CM shows the actor roles and the transaction types in which they partake (as initiator and/or executor), as well as the external information banks (containing P-facts) and the corresponding usage links. The OM specifies the action rules that the actors apply in carrying through transactions. The PM shows how transactions are causally and conditionally related, and the SM models the fact types that are created and/or used in carrying through transactions. Fig. 4 shows the CM of a part of the activities in a library. Only the registration of members is considered. The next excerpt from [10] holds for this part:

Anyone who wants to be registered as member of the library has to apply with Lisa. She writes the data needed on a registration form. These forms are collected daily by someone from the central office. Within a few days, the new member receives a letter welcoming him/her as new member and informing him/her about the library rules. The letter also contains the fee to be paid, and the message that the membership card can be collected at the branch office. By default, this fee is the standard annual fee as determined by the library board. Exceptions may be made for people without means. In that case, Lisa applies in writing to the library board for the reduced fee. Of course, she has to wait for the board's decision, which she also gets in writing, before the membership can be registered. One gets the membership card after cash payment of the fee.

A DEMO analysis of this example yields three essential transaction types. They are listed in the table in Fig. 4 (Note. The limited size of the paper prevents us from explaining how they are identified and why all other things in the description seem to be neglected). Accordingly, only three P-event types are identified. The diagram in Fig. 4 shows the actor roles, transaction types, and the relationships between them (i.e. which actor roles are initiator and/or executor of which transaction types). The same basic symbols are used as the ones in Fig. 1. An actor role is represented by a box; the transaction symbol is a diamond (the symbol for production) embedded in a disk (the symbol for coordination). The small black box denotes which actor role is the executor of a transaction type. The gray-lined open box represents the boundary of the considered part of the library. The actor role inside the boundary is an elementary actor role; it is the executor of exactly one transaction type. Actor roles outside the boundary are (by definition) non-elementary, so-called system actor roles; they are colored gray. Outside the boundary are also two (external) fact banks, EB01 and EB02. They contain the P-facts of transactions that are external to the modeled part of the library. However, their contents are needed by the modeled part. A dotted line indicates that an actor has access to a fact bank.

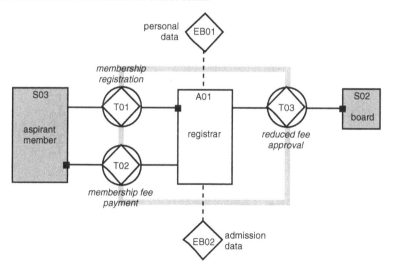

transaction type	resulting P-event type
T01 membership_registration	PE01 *membership M has started to exist*
T02 membership_fee_payment	PE02 *the fee for membership M in year Y has been paid*
T03 reduced_fee_approval	PE03 *the reduced fee for membership M in year Y has been approved*

Fig. 4. Part of the Construction Model of the Library

Fig. 5 exhibits the Process Model that corresponds with the CM of Fig. 4. The pattern of each of the three transaction processes resembles the one in Fig. 3, but is condensed: every C-act is taken together with its resulting C-fact in a combined symbol, called coordination step or *C-step* for short (a disk in a box). For example, the C-step "T01 rq" represents the C-act "request T01" as well as the resulting C-fact "T01 is requested". The same holds mutatis mutandis for the (gray-colored) *P-step*.

One can quite easily recognize in Fig. 5 the transaction patterns of each of the transactions (Note. For the sake of simplicity, only the success patterns of the transactions are shown). The relationships between them can be explained as follows. In dealing with the agendum "T01 is promised", actor A01 performs (or tries to perform) three acts: the P-act of T01, the request of T02 and the request of T03. The latter is optional (indicated by the cardinality range 0..1). It expresses that not everyone applies for a reduced fee. The dotted arrows are wait conditions. So, the P-step of T01 has to wait for the completion of T02 (the C-fact "T02 is accepted"). Likewise, the request of T02 has to wait for the completion of T03. Note that this condition is optional because the initiation of T03 was optional.

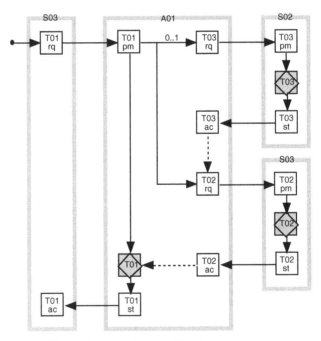

Fig. 5. Part of the Process Model of the Library

4 Deriving Use Cases for a Membership Application

In this section, we will explain how the set of use cases that capture the interactions between the actors and an information system is derived from an essential DEMO model. This research builds on earlier work, presented in [17] and [22]. As an example, we take a membership application, i.e. an information system that supports the part of the library as modeled in section 3. The use cases are derived in a three-step-procedure. The first step is a straightforward transformation from the Process Model to the use case diagramming technique [24]. A little problem pops up now. The definition of the use case in this technique is not quite precise; in fact, anything that is represented by an oval is called a use case. This definition does not necessarily correspond with the definition in [16] that we quoted in section 1. To avoid any misunderstanding, we will refer to the ovals in the diagrams as *components* and to the collective contents of a box as a *use case*. Fig. 6 exhibits the use case that is the result of the first step.

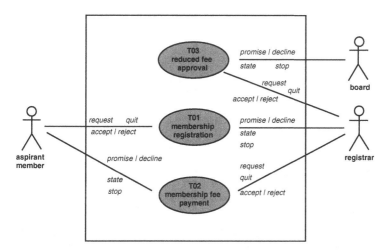

Fig. 6. First step in developing the Use Case for the Library

Three components are identified, corresponding with the three transaction types. To emphasize that these components are (essential) *business components*, they are colored red. Also, the same actor roles are identified (Note. The notion of actor in use cases appears to correspond very well with notion of actor role in DEMO). Next to the interaction lines between actors and components, the main actions to be taken by the actor are mentioned, in correspondence with the standard transaction pattern (cf. Fig. 3). The interaction between the actors and the components has to be understood as follows (taking the carrying through of a transaction T01 as example). The aspirant member activates the component T01 by the request. The component then prompts the registrar for performing the promise or the decline and waits for one of the two inputs. Suppose the promise is made. The component then prompts the registrar again but now for the state act. If this has happened, the aspirant member is prompted for either accepting or rejecting. If he gives the accept input, the component creates a new membership.

The second step consists firstly of considering the kind of relationships between the business components. It appears, according to the UML rules, that T02 is included by T01, and that T03 is an extension of T01. Next, all *informational components* are added, i.e. the components that serve to provide the information needed by the business components. The informational components are straightforwardly identified on the basis of the Operation Model (which is not shown because of lack of space). Two informational components are identified, which correspond with the external fact banks in Fig. 4. To emphasize their informational nature, they are colored green. They are connected to the business components by include relationships. Fig. 7 shows the result of the second step.

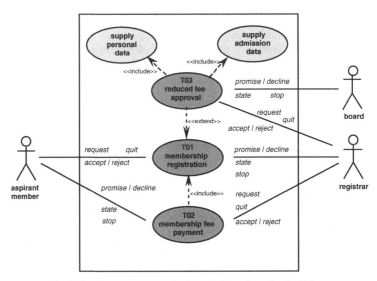

Fig. 7. Second step in developing the Use Case for the Library

In the third step one decides which business components will be 'automated', i.e. mimicked by an informational component. Let us assume that it is decided that T01 and T02 will be. This is similar to saying that the registrar will be 'automated'. Fig. 8 exhibits this final situation.

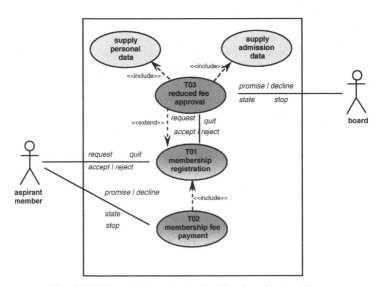

Fig. 8. Third step in developing the Use Case for the Library

To emphasize that the two business components are 'automated', they are colored red and green. The logical consequence of 'automating' the registrar is that that action rules from the Operation Model become algorithmic procedures (methods in the O-O terminology) in the information system to be built. Likewise, the interactions between the registrar and the components T01, T02 and T03 in Fig. 8 must now be contained in the new informational components. The final use case appears to be a very appropriate point of departure for the development of a supporting system. It satisfies all three requirements, mentioned in the introduction

5   Conclusions

We have reported on a successful approach to resolving several aspects of the problem of requirements elicitation. A major cause of this problem is the misconception that a business system (process) is a kind of information system (process). Instead, they are systems in different categories: social and rational respectively. We have introduced the DEMO methodology and we have demonstrated that applying DEMO yields a model of the business domain from which use cases can be derived straightforwardly. This new field of application of DEMO is currently explored practically in a large Dutch insurance company. A three-step procedure has been presented for arriving at high quality use cases, which means that the use cases satisfy three requirements: essence, atomicity and completeness.

The *essence* of an organization lies in the entering into and the complying with commitments by authorized and responsible subjects. This constitutes the working principle of any organization. Most current approaches to modeling business processes however do not embody an appropriate understanding of the notion of business process, and consequently do not provide an effective help, DEMO being one of the few exceptions. Because DEMO abstracts completely from the way in which the essential model of an organization is realized, one has the right design freedom for thinking about its realization. Otherwise said, one is in the right position to think of applying modern information and communication technology in an optimal way.

The requirement of *atomicity* means that the lowest level interaction steps between actors and use cases are atomic from the business point of view. The steps in a DEMO transaction meet this requirement and therefore do have the right granularity. These transactions therefore can be considered as the molecular building blocks of business processes. This way of structuring business activities yields very transparent models, as we have demonstrated for a small example case in section 3. The atomic business acts can straightforwardly be transformed to interaction acts between actors and use cases.

A DEMO model is said to be *complete* in two respects. First, because of the extensiveness of the transaction pattern, it is very unlikely that one would overlook a transaction type completely. It is sufficient to find just one business act during the analysis of the business domain, e.g. a request, to be sure that a complete transaction has been identified. Second, the transaction pattern also contains those acts that are often performed tacitly and therefore are a potential source of mistakes in practice. Fortunately, modern information and communication technology offers the possibility to perform them explicitly. More and more web-based applications appear to do this.

Additional research is needed to provide substantial evidence that the use of DEMO as a basis for requirements elicitation is indeed a major improvement. One line of research is to pursue the comparative analysis of the proposed approach with current (best) practices. Another one is to investigate more profoundly the connection of use cases with component-based system development. The confusion about the notion of use case, as revealed in section 4, must be resolved. A third line of research is the investigation of the identification of (business) object classes. This is another not yet satisfactorily resolved problem (cf. [19]).

A comment is in place regarding the rather special position that is assigned to DEMO in this paper, while there are so many other approaches currently applied for deriving use cases. In particular workflow-modeling methods seem to do a similar job as DEMO does. Unfortunately however, one has to assess that none of them is able to separate business processes from the supporting information processes. This explains the exceptional position of DEMO. Consequently, it does not seem to make much sense to conduct extensive comparisons between DEMO and these other approaches; that would really be comparing apples and pears.

References

1. Apperly, H., et.al., Service- and Component-based Development: Using the Select Perspective and UML, Addison-Wesley Longman, 2003.
2. Austin, J.L., How to do things with words, Harvard University Press, Cambridge MA, 1962
3. Booch, G., I. Jacobson, J. Rumbaugh, 'The Unified Modeling Language User Guide', Addison-Wesley, Reading, 1999
4. Bunge, M.A., Treatise on Basic Philosophy, vol.3, D. Reidel Publishing Company, Dordrecht, The Netherlands, 1977.
5. Bunge, M.A., Treatise on Basic Philosophy, vol.4, D. Reidel Publishing Company, Dordrecht, The Netherlands, 1979
6. Cockburn, A., Structuring Use Cases with Goals, Journal of Object-Oriented Programming, Sept–Oct 1997 and Nov–Dec 1997.
7. Dietz, J.L.G., Understanding and Modeling Business Processes with DEMO, in: Proceeding ER Conceptual Modeling, Paris, 1999.
8. Dietz, J.L.G 2003, 'The Atoms, Molecules and Fibers of Organizations', *Data & Knowledge Engineering*, 2003.
9. Dietz, J.L.G. 2003, 'Generic recurrent patterns in business processes', Proc. International Conference on Business Process Management, Lecture Notes in Computer Science 2678, Springer-Verlag, 2003.
10. Dietz, J.L.G., T. Halpin, Combining DEMO and ORM – an investigation of mutual benefits, Proc. EMSSAD workshop, Velden, Austria, 2003, (downloadable from www.demo.nl).
11. Eriksson, H.E., M. Penker, Business Modeling with UML, John Wiley & Sons Inc., 2000
12. Garcia, J., et.al., On Business Towards Use Case and Conceptual Models through Business Modeling, Proc. 19th International Conference on Conceptual Modeling (ER2000), 2000.
13. Goldkuhl, G. 1996. Generic business frameworks and action modelling. In: Dignum, F., J. Dietz, E. Verharen, H. Weigand (Eds.), (1996). *Communication Modeling – The Language/Action Perspective, Proceedings of the First International Workshop on Communication Modeling*, Electronic Workshops in Computing Springer. http://www.springer.co.uk/ewic/workshops/CM96/

14. Habermas, J., Theorie des Kommunikatives Handelns, Erster Band, Suhrkamp Verlag, Frankfurt am Main, 1981.
15. Jacobson, I., G. Booch, J. Rumbaugh, The Unified Software Development Process, Addison-Wesley, 1999.
16. Jacobson, I., M. Christerson, P. Jonsson, G. Övergaard, Object-Oriented Software Engineering: A Use Case Driven Approach, Addison-Wesley, 1992.
17. Mallens, P., J. Dietz, B-J Hommes, The value of Business Process Modeling with DEMO prior to Information Systems Modeling with UML, Proc. EMMSAD'01, 2001.
18. Medina-Mora, R., T. Winograd, R. Flores, F. Flores, The Action Workflow Approach to Workflow Management Technology. In: J. Turner, R. Kraut (Eds.), *Proceedings of the 4th Conference on Computer Supported Cooperative Work.* ACM, New York, pp. 281–288.
19. Meyer, B. Object Oriented Software Construction, 2nd edition, Prentice-Hall Inc., 1998.
20. Sadiq, W., M.E. Orlowski, On Business Process Model Transformations, Proc. 19th International Conference on Conceptual Modeling (ER2000), 2000.
21. Searle, J.R., Speech Acts, an Essay in the Philosophy of Language, Cambridge University Press, Cambridge MA, 1969
22. Shishkov, B., J.L.G. Dietz, Analysis of suitability, appropriateness and adequacy of Use Cases combines with Activity Diagrams for Business Systems Modeling, Proc. ICEIS'01, 2001.
23. Stamper, R.K., Applied Semiotics, in: Proc. of the ICL/University of New Castle Seminar 'Information', New castle, 1993
24. UML Specification version 1.3, to be found on http://www.rational.com/uml/
25. Van Reijswoud, V.E., J.B.F. Mulder, J.L.G. Dietz, Speech Act Based Business Process and Information Modeling with DEMO, Information Systems Journal, 1999

Order-Sensitive View Maintenance of Materialized XQuery Views

Katica Dimitrova, Maged El-Sayed, and Elke A. Rundensteiner

Department of Computer Science, Worcester Polytechnic Institute
Worcester, MA 01609, USA
{katica,maged,rundenst}@cs.wpi.edu

Abstract. In this paper we present the first approach for incremental order-preserving maintenance of XQuery views. Our technique is based on an algebraic representation of the XQuery view query called XAT. The XML algebra has ordered bag semantics; hence most of the operators logically are order preserving. We propose an order-encoding mechanism that migrates the XML algebra to (non-ordered) bag semantics, no longer requiring most of the operators to be order-aware. This way operators become distributive over update operations. This transformation brings the problem of maintaining XML views closer to the problem of maintaining views in other (unordered) data models. We have implemented our view maintenance technique on top of RAINBOW, the XML data management system developed at WPI. Our experimental results confirm that incremental XML view maintenance is significantly faster than complete recomputation.

1 Introduction

View Maintenance Problem. XML views are a popular technique for integrating data from heterogeneous data sources. Many systems employing XML views, often specified by the XML query language XQuery [20], have been developed in recent years [11,23,24]. Materialization of the view content has important applications including providing fast access to complex views, optimizing query processing based on cashed results, and increasing availability. This raises the issue of how to efficiently refresh the content of views in this new context of XML in response to base source changes. For relational views it is often cheaper to apply incremental view maintenance instead of full recomputation [7]. However the problem of incremental maintenance of XQuery views has not yet been addressed. Incremental XML view maintenance poses unique challenges compared to the incremental maintenance of relational or even object-oriented views. [12] classifies XML result construction into non-distributive functions which in general are not incrementally computable. Also, unlike relational or even object-oriented data, XML data is ordered. Supporting XML's ordered data model is crucial for applications like content management, where document data is intrinsically ordered and where queries may need to rely on this order [17]. In general, XQuery expressions return sequences that have a well-defined order [20]. The

I.-Y. Song et al. (Eds.): ER 2003, LNCS 2813, pp. 144–157, 2003.

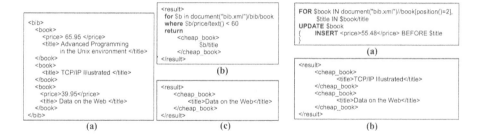

Fig. 1. Example (a) XML data, (b) XQuery view definition and (c) initial extent of view

Fig. 2. (a) Update XQuery and (b) extent of the view defined in Figure 1.b after the update in (a)

resulting order is defined both by the implicit XML document order possibly overwritten by other orders explicitly imposed in the XQuery definition by the Order By clauses or by nested subclauses [20]. As a consequence, a view has to be refreshed correctly not only concerning its view values but also its view order.

Motivating Example. We use the XML document bib.xml shown in Figure 1.a as running example. It contains a list of book titles and optionally their prices. The XQuery definition, which lists the titles of all books that cost less than $60, is shown in Figure 1.b, and the initial view content in Figure 1.c. The update as in Figure 2.a is specified to insert a price element with value $55.48 for the second book. The affected book now passes the selection condition and should be inserted into the view extent (Figure 2.b). Even though the view definition does not explicitly refer to the document order, this new book has to be inserted before the one already in the view to preserve document order.

Algebraic View Maintenance. Early work on relational view maintenance [2,8] when considering rather simple views utilized an algorithmic fixed procedure. Later efforts on more complex view definitions including duplicates [6] or aggregations [14] and also object-oriented views often have instead taken an algebraic approach. Unnesting and restructuring of data is core even in the simplest XQuery view definitions due to the nested structure of XML data. Thus any practical solution for XQuery views should support a rather large set of complex operations including unnesting, aggregation and tagging. The algebraic approach is therefore the appropriate foundation for tackling incremental view maintenance in the XML context. Advantages of an algebraic approach to view maintenance include [6]: (1) It is independent from the view definition language syntax. (2) The modularity enables us with ease to extend our algebra with more operators. (3) Propagation rules for operator that also occur in other data models can be reused here. (4) The algebraic approach naturally leads itself towards establishing a proof of correctness [4].

Our Approach. In this paper, we propose an algebraic XML view maintenance strategy that covers the core subset of the XQuery language, namely FLWR expressions without recursion. Our approach is based on the XML algebra XAT [24]. For each operator in the algebra and for each type of update, we define update propagation rules that specify the modification of the operator's output as a response to the modification of its input. Unlike [5], we now address the problem of maintaining order using a scalable order-preserving strategy. Contributions of this work include: (1) we identify new challenges imposed to incremental view maintenance by the ordered hierarchical nature of XML, (2) we propose an order-encoding mechanism that migrates the XML algebra from ordered bag to non-ordered bag semantics, thus making most of the operators distributive with respect to the bag union, (3) we give the first order-sensitive algebraic solution for incremental maintenance of XML views defined with XQuery, (4) we have implemented our proposed solution in the XML data management system Rainbow, and (5) we conducted an experimental study.

Outline. In the next section we review related research. Section 3 introduces the XML algebra XAT. Section 4 describes our strategy for maintaining order in the presence of updates. In Section 5 we present the order-sensitive incremental view maintenance strategy for XQuery views. Section 6 describes our experimental evaluation while Section 7 concludes the paper.

2   Related Work

The incremental maintenance of materialized views has been extensively studied for relational databases [2,8,6,14]. In [6] an algebraic approach for maintaining relational views with duplicates, i.e., for bag semantics, has been proposed. [12] proposes an algorithm that maintains views whose definition includes aggregate functions that are not distributive over all operations. They perform selective recomputation to maintain such views. To a lesser degree, view maintenance has also been studied for object-oriented views. In the MultiView solution [10, 9] incremental maintenance of OQL views exploits object-oriented properties such as inheritance, class hierarchy and path indexes. Maintenance for materialized views over semi-structured data based on the graph-based data model OEM is studied in [1]. They do not consider order. In [13], maintenance for materialized views for XML based on XPath was proposed, thus excluding result restructuring. The problem of encoding XML structure as well as XML order has been studied for the purpose of storing XML documents. Several explicit order encoding techniques have been proposed [16,3].

3   Background: XML Query Model

We adopt standard XML [19] as data model. XML nodes are considered duplicates based on equality by node identity denoted by $n1 == n2$ [18]. We use $\uplus$ to denote bag union of sequences of XML nodes, $\dot{-}$ to denote monus (bag difference) and $\bigcup$ to denote union of sequences of XML nodes. Given m sequences of XML nodes, where $seq_j = (n_{1j}, n_{2j}, ..n_{k_j j})$, $1 \leq j \leq m$, $k_j \geq 0$, n_{ij} is an XML node, $1 \leq i \leq k_j$, we define **order-sensitive bag union** of such sequences as:

$\overset{\circ}{\biguplus}_{j=1}^{m} seq_j \overset{def}{=} (n_{11}, n_{21}, ...n_{k_1 1}, n_{12}, ...n_{k_2 2}, ..., n_{1m}, ...n_{k_m m})$. When a single XML node appears as argument for $\overset{\circ}{\biguplus}$, $\bigcup$, $\biguplus$ or $\overset{\cdot}{-}$ it is treated as a singleton sequence [21]. We use the term **path** to refer to a path expression [20] consisting of any combination of forward steps, including $//$ and $*$. **Position** refers to a path that uniquely locates a single node in an XML tree, containing the element names and the ordering positions of all elements from the root to that node, e.g., $bib[1]/book[3]/title[1]$. The sequence of XML nodes arranged in document order and located by the path $path$ starting from each of the nodes in the sequence seq is denoted as $\overset{\circ}{\phi}(path : seq)$. The notation $\phi(path : seq)$ stands for the corresponding unordered sequence. For a position pos and a path $path$, we use the notation $pos \trianglerighteq path$ to denote that pos is "contained" in the node set implied by $path$. More precisely, an ancestor of the node n located by pos or the node n itself must be among the nodes located by $path$, if both pos and $path$ are applied on the same XML data, e.g., $/book[1]/author[2]/name[1] \trianglerighteq /book/author$ and $/book[2]/author[2]/phone[1] \trianglerighteq //author$. When $pos \trianglerighteq path$, we define $pos - path$ as the remainder position that starts from n's ancestor located by $path$.

We use XQuery [20], a W3C working draft for an XML query language, as the view definition language. The XQuery expression is translated into an XML algebraic representation called XAT [24]. Typically, an XAT operator takes as input one or more XAT tables and produces an XAT table as output. An *XAT table* R is an order-sensitive table of tuples t_j (e.g., $t_j \in R$), where the column names represent either a variable binding from the user-specified XQuery, e.g., $\$b$, or an internally generated variable name, e.g., $\$col_1$. Each cell c_{ij} in a tuple can store an XML node or a sequence of nodes. To refer to the cell c_{ij} in a tuple t_j that corresponds to the column col_i we use the notation $t_j[col_i]$. The XAT algebra has order sensitive bag semantics: (1) The order among the tuples t_j is of significance, (2) The order among the XML nodes contained in a single cell is of significance. In general, an XAT operator is denoted as $op_{in}^{out}(s)$, where op is the operator type's symbol, in represents the input parameters, out the newly produced output column and s the input source(s), typically XAT table(s). We restrict ourselves to the core subset of the XAT algebra operators [24]. XAT operators include the relational equivalent operators, including *Select* $\sigma_c(R)$, *Theta Join* $\bowtie_c (R, P)$, *Distinct* $\delta(R)$, and *Order By* $\tau_{col[1..n]}(R)$, where R and P denote XAT tables. Those operators are equivalent to their relational counterparts, with the additional responsibility to reflect the order among the input tuples to the order among the output tuples.

Source $S_{xmlDoc}^{col'}$, a leaf node in an algebra tree, takes the XML document $xmlDoc$ and outputs an XAT table with a single column col' and a single tuple $tout_1 = (c_{11})$, where c_{11} contains the entire XML document.

Navigate Unnest $\phi_{col,path}^{col'}(R)$ unnests the element-subelement relationship. For each tuple tin_j from the input XAT table R, it creates a sequence of m output tuples $tout_j^{(l)}$, where $1 \leq l \leq m$, $m = |\phi(path : tin_j[col])|$, $tout_j^{(l)}[col'] = \overset{\circ}{\phi}(path : tin_j[col])[l]^1$.

Navigate Collection $\Phi_{col,path}^{col'}(R)$ is similar to *Navigate Unnest*, except it places all the extracted children in a single cell. For each tuple tin_j from R, it creates a single output tuple $tout_j$, where $tout_j[col'] = \overset{\circ}{\phi}(path : tin_j[col])$, see Figure 3.

Combine $C_{col}(R)$ groups the content of all cells corresponding to col into one sequence (with duplicates). Given the input R with m tuples tin_j, $1 \leq j \leq m$, *Combine* outputs one tuple $tout = (c)$, where $tout[col] = c = \overset{\circ}{\underset{j=1}{\uplus}}^{m} tin_j[col]$.

Tagger $T_p^{col}(R)$ constructs new XML nodes by applying the tagging pattern p to each input tuple. A pattern p is a template of a valid XML fragment [19] with parameters being column names, e.g., $<result>\$col2</result>$. For each tuple tin_j from R, it creates one output tuple $tout_j$, where $tout_j[col]$ contains the constructed XML node obtained by evaluating p for the values in tin_j.

Expose $\epsilon_{col}(R)$ appears as a root node of an algebra tree. Its purpose is to output the content of column col into XML data in textual format.

By definition, all columns from the input table are retained in the output table of an operator (except for the *Combine* operator), plus an additional one may be added. Such schema is called *Full Schema (FS)*. However, not all the columns may be utilized by operators higher in the algebra tree. *Minimum Schema (MS)* of an output XAT table is defined as a subsequence of all columns, retaining only the columns needed later by the ancestors of that operator [24]. The process of determining the Minimum Schema for the output XAT table of each operator in the algebra tree, called Schema Cleanup, is described in [24]. For two tuples in an XAT table, we define the expression $before(t_1, t_2)$ to be $true$ if the tuple t_1 is ordered before the tuple t_2, $false$ if t_2 is before t_1 and $undefined$ if the order between the two tuples is irrelevant.

4   The Rainbow Approach for Maintaining Order

4.1   Preserving Order in the Context of the XML Algebra

Order makes the maintenance of XML views significantly different from the maintenance of relational views. The basic idea behind incrementally maintaining relational select-project-join views is that such views are distributive with regard to the union. For example, for any two relations R and Q, any joining condition c and any delta set ΔQ of inserted tuples into Q, the equation $R \bowtie_c (Q \cup \Delta Q) = (R \bowtie_c Q) \cup (R \bowtie_c \Delta Q)$ holds. Due to having to maintain the order among the tuples, the XAT operators are not distributive over any update operation, as due to an update tuples may be inserted at arbitrary positions. For example, assume a new j-th tuple tin_j is inserted in the input XAT table R of the operator *Navigate Unnest*. As a result, a sequence of new zero or more

---

[1] Tuples $tout_j^{(l)}$ are ordered by major order on j and minor order on l.

XAT tuples $tout_j^{(l)}$ may have to be inserted in the output XAT table. However, these tuples must be placed after the tuples derived from all tin_i, $i < j$ and before the tuples derived from all tin_k, $k > j$. A similar issue arises due to the requirement of maintaining order among XML nodes contained in a single cell. Thus an explicit order encoding technique suitable for both expressing the order among the XAT tuples and among XML nodes within one cell in the presence of updates is needed. Intuitively, the obvious solution of consecutively number- ing the XAT tuples and the members of sequences would not be practical, as insertions and deletions would lead to frequent renumbering, extra processing and distributiveness over update operations would again not be achieved.

4.2   Using Node Identity for Encoding Order

We note that the concept of node identity can serve the dual purpose of en- coding order, if the node identity encodes the unique path of that node in the tree and captures the order at each level along the path. Most existing tech- niques for encoding order in XML data may require numbering in the presence of inserts [16]. Such renumbering is clearly undesirable for view maintenance. In [3] a lexicographical order encoding technique called **LexKey**-s that does not require reordering on updates is proposed. It is analogous to the Dewey order- ing [16][2], except rather than using numbers in the encoding, it uses variable length strings. The identity of each node is equal to the concatenation of all lexicographical nodes keys of its ancestor nodes and of that node's own key (see Figure 4 for example). This encoding is thus well suited for our purpose of view maintenance. It does not require reordering on updates, identifies a unique path from the root to the node and embeds the relative order on each level. We use the notation $k_1 \prec k_2$ to note that LexKey k_1 lexicographically precedes LexKey k_2. If k_1 and k_2 are the LexKeys of nodes n_1 and n_2 respectively, then (1) $k_1 \prec k_2$ if and only if n_1 is before n_2 in the document and (2) k_1 is a prefix of k_2 if and only if n_1 is an ancestor of n_2. It is always possible to generate a LexKey for newly inserted nodes at any position in the document without updating existing keys. The deletion of any node does not require modification of the LexKeys of other existing nodes. We use LexKeys for encoding the node identities of all nodes in the source XML document. We also use LexKeys to encode the node identity of any constructed nodes either in intermediate states of the view alge- bra structure or in the final view extent. The LexKeys assigned to constructed nodes are algebra-tree-wide unique. They can be reproduced by the operator ($Tagger$) that created them initially based on information about the input tuple they were derived from. Rather than instantiating the actual XML fragments in our system, we only store a *skeleton* representing their structure and instead reference through LexKeys the other source data or constructed nodes that are included in the newly constructed node, e.g., $<cheap\_book>b.t.r</cheap\_book>$.

---

[2] Where each node is assigned a vector of numbers that represent the path from the root to the node and at the same time the node order.

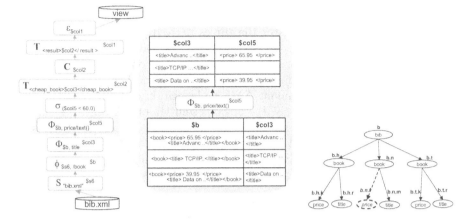

Fig. 3. The algebra tree (XAT) for the running example   **Fig. 4.** Lexicographical ordering of the XML document presented in Figure 1

For reducing redundant updates and avoiding duplicated storage we only store references (that is LexKeys) in the XAT tables rather than actual XML data. This is sufficient as the LexKeys serve as node identifiers (and thus are references to the base data) and capture the order. For maintaining order different than document order in sequences of XML nodes we treat keys as symbols and compose them into higher-level keys. For example the LexKey $k = $ "$b.c..c.d$" is a composition of the LexKeys $k1 = $ "$b.c$" and $k2 = $ "$c.d$" and "$..$" is used as delimiter. We denote this by $k = compose(k1, k2)$.

4.3   Maintaining Order Using LexKeys

The order among the tuples in an XAT table can now be determined by comparing the LexKeys stored in cells corresponding to some of the columns. For example, consider the tuples $t_1 = (b.h, b.h.r)$ and $t_2 = (b.n, b.n.m)$ in the input XAT table of the operator $\Phi^{\$col3}_{\$b,/title}$ in Figure 6. Here t_1 should be before t_2, that is $before(t_1, t_2)$ is true. This can be deduced by comparing the LexKeys in $t_1[\$b]$ and $t_2[\$b]$ lexicographically given that the relative order among the tuples in an XAT table is encoded in the keys contained in certain columns and can be determined by comparing those LexKeys. We call these columns *Order Schema*.

Definition 41 *The **Order Schema** $OS_R = (on_1, on_2, ...on_m)$ of an XAT table R in an algebra tree is a sequence of column names on_i, $1 \leq i \leq m$, computed following the rules in Figure 5 in a postorder traversal of the algebra tree.*

These rules guarantee that cells corresponding to the Order Schema never contain sequences, only single keys [4].

Cat.	Operator op	OS_Q^*
I	$T_p^{col}(R)$ $\Phi_{col,path}^{col'}(R)$ $\sigma_c(R)$	OS_R
II	$S_{xmlDoc}^{col'}$ $C_{col}(R)$ $\delta_{col}(R)$ $\gamma_{col[1..n]}(R, fun)$	$\varnothing$
III	$\times(R, P)$ $\bowtie_c(R, P)$ $\bowtie_{L_c}(R, P)$	$(on_1^{(R)}, on_2^{(R)}, ...on_{ml}^{(R)},$ $on_1^{(P)}, on_2^{(P)}, ...on_{mr}^{(lr_{in})})$ $mr = |OS_R|, ml = |OS_P|$
IV	$\phi_{col,path}^{col'}(R)$	$(on_1^{(R)}, on_2^{(R)}, ...on_p^{(R)}, col')$ if $on_m^{(R)} = col$ then $p = m - 1$, else $p = m$.
V	$\tau_{col[1..n]}(R)$	$(col''), col''$ is new column[3]
VI	$\epsilon_{col}(R)$	N/A
*	$Q = op_{in}^{out}(R), OS_R = (on_1^R, on_2^R, ...on_m^R)$	

Fig. 5. Rules for computing Order Schema

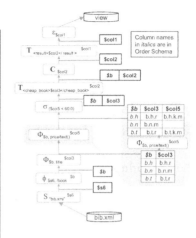

Fig. 6. Order Schema computation example

Definition 42 *For two tuples t_1 and t_2 from an XAT table R with $OS_R = (on_1, on_2, ...on_m)$, the comparison operation $\prec$ is defined by: $t1 \prec t2 \Leftrightarrow (\exists j, 1 \leq j \leq m)(((\forall i, 1 \leq i < j)(t_1[on_i] == t_2[on_i])) \wedge (t_1[on_j] \prec t_2[on_j]))$*

Theorem 41 *For every two tuples $t_1, t_2 \in R$, where R is any XAT table in an XAT, with $before(t_1, t_2)$ defined as in Section 3, (I) $before(t_1, t_2) \Rightarrow (t_1 \prec t_2)$, and (II) $(t_1 \prec t_2) \Rightarrow (before(t_1, t_2) \vee (before(t_1, t_2) = undefined))$.*

Proof *The proof is omitted for space reasons, it can be found in [4].*

Theorem 41 shows that the relative position among the tuples in an XAT table is correctly preserved by the cells in the Order Schema of that table. This enables more efficient order-sensitive view maintenance because for most operators insertions and deletions of tuples in their output XAT table can be performed without accessing other tuples, nor performing any reordering.

Maintaining Order in Sequences of XML Nodes. For sequences of XML nodes contained in a single cell that have to be in document order (as those created for example by the *Navigate Collection*), the LexKeys representing the nodes accurately reflect their order. However, the *Combine* operator creates a sequence of XML nodes that are not necessarily in document order and whose relative position depends on the relative position of the tuples in the input XAT table that they originated from. To represent this order that is different than the one encoded in the LexKey k serving as the node identity of the node, we attach an additional LexKey to k (called *Overriding Order*) which reflects the node's proper order. We denote that as $k.overridingOrder$ and we use $order(k)$ to refer

---

[3] The column col'' by definition is responsible for holding keys such that (I) and (II) hold.

to the order represented by k. If the overriding order of k is set, then $order(k) = k.overridingOrder$, otherwise $order(k) = k$. When the LexKey $k1$ has overriding order $k2$ it is also noted as $k1[k2]$. For the *Combine* operator, given that the input R contains p tuples tin_j, $1 \leq j \leq p$, the output of *Combine* $C_{col}(R)$ can now be noted as $C_{col}(R) = tout = (\biguplus_{j=1}^{p} combine(tin_j[col], tin_j, col))$ [4].

5   Rules for Incremental Maintenance of XML Views

5.1   Update Operations and Format of the Delta

While an update XQuery is being applied to one input source, a sequence of XML updates as presented in Table 1 is produced [4]. An insertion or deletion of a complex element is specified as a single XML update. The absolute order is substituted with the LexKeys of the corresponding nodes in the position *pos* to which an XML update refers to. The LexKey k represents the root element of the document affected by the update. As illustration, the update presented in Figure 2 is specified as $Insert(b.n.f, book[b.n]/price[b.n.f], b)$. We also define a set of update operations over XAT tables, referred to as *delta*, see Table 2. Each tuple t in each XAT table R is assigned an integer identifier, *tid*, unique within that table. Even though here we use $\bigtriangledown R$ to represent the deleted tuples, the actual update only carries the *tid*-s of the deleted tuples.

Table 1. XML Update operations (δk)

Update Operation	Description	Notation
Insert *(n, pos, k)*	Insert node with LexKey n at position *pos* into node with LexKey k	$\delta_{n,pos}^{+} k$
Delete *(n, pos, k)*	Delete node with LexKey n at position *pos* from node with LexKey k	$\delta_{n,pos}^{-} k$
Replace *(old, new, pos, k)*	Replace value *old* at position *pos* with *new* from node with LexKey k	$\delta_{pos,old \to new}^{r} k$

Table 2. The format of the intermediate updates

Intermediate XAT Updates		
$u(\triangle R)$	Insertion of tuples $\triangle R$ into XAT table R	$R^{new} \leftarrow R \uplus \triangle R$
$u(\bigtriangledown R)$	Deletion of tuples $\bigtriangledown R$ from XAT table R	$R^{new} \leftarrow R \dot{-} \bigtriangledown R$
$u(\triangle c, col, tid)$	Insertion of LexKeys into a single cell	$c^{new} \leftarrow c \uplus \triangle c, c = t[col]^4$
$u(\triangledown c, col, tid)$	Deletion of LexKeys from a single cell	$c^{new} \leftarrow c \dot{-} \triangledown c, c = t[col]$
Intermediate XML Updates		
$u(\delta k, col, tid)$	Modification of LexKey k in cell $t[col]$ by δk, δk is any updates from Table 1	

---

[4] In this section, we consistently use t for the tuple identified by tuple identifier *tid*

5.2   Update Propagation Algorithm

Our propagation algorithm performs a bottom-up postorder traversal of the tree, invoking each operator with a sequence of updates. The *Source* operator accessing the updated XML document is invoked first (by Table 1 update). It then translates the update into an intermediate update (Table 2). From there on, each node in the algebra tree, having the knowledge about the algebra operator it represents, processes one intermediate update at a time and translates it into a sequence of zero or more intermediate output updates. After the node has processed the entire sequence of its input updates, it outputs the sequence of updates it has generated. After all nodes have been visited at most once the view is refreshed. For this, we define update propagation rules for pairs of each algebra operator and each type of update. Some operators can process any update without requiring additional information. But for certain operators, the output *delta* cannot be calculated using only the input *delta* [4]. In this case our system stores the needed columns of the input or the output XAT tables derived during computing the view as auxiliary views. These auxiliary views only store LexKeys, thus are compact.

5.3   Propagation of Updates through XAT SQL Operators

The migration from ordered bag semantics to bag semantics makes our XAT SQL operators equivalent to their relational counterparts, i.e., relational bag algebra [6,14]. We can now adopt the update propagation rules for those SQL-like operators from the respective relational view maintenance work ([6], [14]). Thus for space reasons we do not discuss them here further.

5.4   Propagation of Updates through XAT XML Operators

Propagating Insertions and Deletions of Tuples. All XAT XML operators become distributive over insertions and deletions of tuples. In particular, if *op* is any of the operators *Tagger, Navigate Collection, Navigate Unnest, XML Union, XML Intersect* or *XML Difference*, the following propagation equations hold:
$op_{in}^{out}(R \uplus \triangle R) = op_{in}^{out}(R) \uplus op_{in}^{out}(\triangle R)$ and
$op_{in}^{out}(R \dot{-} \triangledown R) = op_{in}^{out}(R) \dot{-} op_{in}^{out}(\triangledown R)$.

The *Combine* operator has the equivalent property, but at the cell level. Let $tout^{old} = (c^{old})$ and $tout^{new} = (c^{new})$ denote the results of $C_{col}(R)$ and $C_{col}(R^{new})$ correspondingly. Then:
$C_{col}(R \uplus \triangle R) = tout^{new} = (c^{new}) = (\Pi_{col}C_{col}R \uplus \Pi_{col}C_{col} \triangle R) = (c^{old} \uplus \Pi_{col}C_{col} \triangle R)$, and $C_{col}(R \dot{-} \triangledown R) = tout^{new} = (c^{new}) = (\Pi_{col}C_{col}R \dot{-} \Pi_{col}C_{col} \triangledown R) = (c^{old} \dot{-} \Pi_{col}C_{col}(\triangledown R))$.

The propagation rules for the XML operators on insertions and deletions of tuples can be directly deduced from these maintenance equations. For example, if the output of an $\phi_{col,path}^{col'}(R)$ is denoted as $Q = \phi_{col,path}^{col'}(R)$, then on $u(\triangle R)$, the operator $\phi_{col,path}^{col'}(R)$ propagates $u(\triangle Q)$, where $\triangle Q = \phi_{col,path}^{col'}(\triangle R)$.

Table 3. Propagation rules for the XML operators on $u(\triangle c, col, tid)$

Operator	Propagate	Info Accessed
$\phi_{col,path}^{col'}(R)$	$u(\triangle Q)\mid(\forall t' \in \triangle Q)(\forall cn \in RS_Q \mid cn \neq col')(t'[cn] = t[cn]) \wedge$ $(\forall n \in \phi(path : \triangle c))(\exists! t' \in \triangle Q)(t'[col'] = n)$	t
$\Phi_{col,path}^{col'}(R)$	$u(\triangle c', col', tid)\mid \triangle c' = \phi(path : \triangle c)$	none
$T_p^{col'}(R)$	$(\forall ppath \mid \phi(ppath : p) = col)(\forall n \in \triangle c)\ u(\delta_{n,ppath}^+ k', col', tid)$ k' is the key reproduced from tid	none
$C_{col}(R)$	$u(\triangle c', col, 1)\mid \triangle c' = combine(\triangle c, t, col)$	$(\forall on \in OS_R)t[on]$
$\overset{x\,col'}{\cup_{col1,col2}}(R)^5$	$u(\triangle c', col, tid)\mid \triangle c' = \{n \mid (n \in \triangle c) \wedge (n \notin \Pi_{col}t' \mid t' = Q.getTuple(tid))\}$	$t'[col]$

Propagating Insertions and Deletions of LexKeys in a Cell. The rules for propagating $u(\triangle c, col, tid)$ when col is among the input columns of the corresponding operator are shown in Table 3. They are directly derived from the corresponding maintenance equations and can be proven correct [4]. For example, consider the rule for $\Phi_{col,path}^{col'}(R)$ when col in $u(\triangle c, col, tid)$ matches column col, which is input column for $\Phi_{col,path}^{col'}(R)$. Let $t = (c_1, c_2, ..c, ..c_n)$ and $t^{new} = (c_1, c_2, ..c \uplus \triangle c, ..c_n)$ be the state of the tuple t before and after the update. Let $tout$ and $tout^{new}$ be the corresponding derived tuples in the output table, where $tout^{new}$ is obtained by recomputation over t^{new}. Let the last cells of $tout$ and $tout^{new}$ correspond to col'. Then:

$$tout = \Phi_{col,path}^{col'}(t) = \Phi_{col,path}^{col'}(c_1, c_2, ..c, ..c_n) = \Pi_{RS}(c_1, c_2, ..c, ..c_n, \phi(path : c))$$

$$tout^{new} = \Phi_{col,path}^{col}(t^{new}) = \Phi_{col,path}^{col'}(c_1, c_2, ..c \uplus \triangle c, ..c_n) = \Pi_{RS}(c_1, c_2, ..c \uplus \triangle$$
$$c, ..c_n, \phi(path : c \uplus \triangle c)) = \Pi_{RS}(c_1, c_2, ..c \uplus \triangle c, ..c_n, \phi(path : c) \uplus \phi(path : \triangle c))$$

By comparing $tout$ and $tout^{new}$, we can conclude that on $u(\triangle c, col, tid)$, $\Phi_{col,path}^{col'}(s)$ should propagate $u(\triangle c', col', tid)$, where $\triangle c' = \phi(path : \triangle c)$. In addition, the original update $u(\triangle c, col, tid)$ should be propagated if col is in the Minimum Schema of the output table. In this case, the propagation can be done without any additional information. By associating parent-child relationships between the tuples in the input table R with the tuples in the output XAT table Q we are able to identify the tid of the tuple(s) in the output table given the tid of the tuple that it is derived from. We denote that as $Q.getDerived(tid)$. For most operators this relationship is implicit, that is $tid = Q.getDerived(tid)$. The rules for $u(\triangledown c, col, tid)$ are similar and can be found in [4].

Propagating Intermediate XML Updates. The intermediate XML update operations only affect the XAT operators *Navigate Collection* and *Navigate Unnest* that require accessing keys at a level deeper than the updated node k. The propagation rules for these operators on $u(\delta_{n,pos}^+ k, col, tid)$ are given in Table 4. The rules for $u(\delta_{n,pos}^- k, col, tid)$ and $u(\delta_{pos,old->new}^c k, col, tid)$ are similar and can be found in [4].

Exposing the Updated View. When a sequence of update operations reaches the root *Expose* node of the algebra tree, a partial reordering is performed to

---

[5] See our technical report [4] for the rules for the other two XML set operators $\overset{x\,col}{\cap_{col1,col2}}(R)$ and $\overset{x\,col}{-_{col1,col2}}(R)$.

Table 4. Propagation rules for the XML operators on $u(\delta^{+}_{n,pos}k, col, tid)$

Operator	Cases	Propagate	Info Accessed
$\phi^{col'}_{col,path}(R)$	$pos \lhd path$	$u(\triangle Q)\|(\forall t' \in \triangle Q)(\forall cn \in RS_Q\|cn \neq col')(t'[cn] = t[cn]) \wedge$ $(\forall n' \in \phi(path - pos : n))(\exists! t' \in \triangle Q)(t'[col'] = n')$	t
	$pos \unrhd path$	$u(\delta^{+}_{n,pos-path}k', col', tid')\|(tid' \in Q.getDerived(tid)) \wedge$ $(t' = Q.getTuple(tid')) \wedge (t'[col'] = k')$	tid index $\Pi_{col'}Q$
$\Phi^{col'}_{col,path}(R)$	$pos \lhd path$	$u(\triangle c', col', tid)\| \triangle c' = \phi(path - pos : n)$	none
	$pos \unrhd path$	$u(\delta^{+}_{n,pos-path}k', col', tid)$	none
When $pos \unrhd path$, k' is name of the first forward step in pos that is not in $pos - path$.			

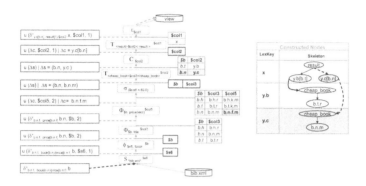

Fig. 7. Update propagation for the running example

determine the absolute positions of the updates. The reordering is done only for correctly placing the nodes that have been added (or whose order has been modified) among their siblings. Thus the overhead of preserving order is greatly minimized.

5.5   Propagation Example

Figure 7 shows the update propagation for our running example[6]. $S^{s6}_{"bib.xml"}$ transforms the incoming update into an intermediate update. $\phi^{\$b}_{\$s6,/book}$ compares the position $book[b.n]/price[b.n.f]$ to its path $(/book)$, and as $book[b.n]/price[b.n.f] \unrhd /book$, it rewrites the position in the output update. When the update reaches $\Phi^{\$col5}_{\$b,/price/text()}$, which extracts the prices of the books, the update is translated into an intermediate XAT update specifying modification of the cell containing the prices of the book with LexKey $b.n$. The newly inserted price now makes the corresponding book pass the selection condition. Thus a tuple insertion is generated by $\sigma(col5 < 60)$. The new title is tagged, and the constructed node is assigned the LexKey $y.c$. The overriding order of this key is set by C_{col2}. When the final *Tagger* receives this update, it updates

---

[6] Not all of the XAT tables shown in Figure 7 are materialized. Their content is shown for clarifying the explanation.

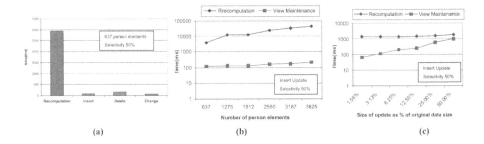

Fig. 8. Experimental evaluation

the result to include the new title. When the final update is passed to ϵ_{col1}, it refreshes the view by reordering the $y.c[b.n]$ and $y.b[b.t]$, thus placing the new node before the one already in the view. The correctness of our the propagation strategy is given in [4].

6 Evaluation

Our system has been implemented in Java on top of the XQuery engine Rainbow [23,22]. We have performed a performance evaluation of our solution on a Pentium III PC with 512MB of RAM running Windows 2000 with data and queries from the XMARK benchmark [15]. The queries extract data from "person" elements. Figure 8.a shows that incremental maintenance significantly outperforms recomputation for all three types of updates. Figure 8.b compares the performance of our solution to recomputation when a new person element is inserted for different base XML data sizes. The cost of recomputation follows the growth of the data size. While the cost of incremental maintenance also increases, it does so at a much lower rate. Figure 8.c shows that incremental maintenance is much faster even for large updates. In that figure, the number of inserted "person" elements ranges from 1% to being over 50% of the number of "person" nodes already in the database. As the size of the inserted nodes increases, the cost of view maintenance approaches the cost of recomputation. We have measured the overhead of maintaining order, by also running the system in a non-order-sensitive mode and found it to be not noticeable compared to the overall cost of incremental view maintenance.

7 Conclusion

We have presented the first solution for order-preserving incremental maintenance of XQuery views. We show how, by using our order encoding schema, the XML algebra can be transformed from ordered bag to (non-ordered) bag semantics, thus enabling efficient view maintenance. Our experiments have confirmed that our solution outperforms recomputation even for large updates.

References

1. S. Abiteboul and et al. Incremental maintenance for materialized views over semistructured data. In *VLDB*, pages 38–49, 1998.
2. J. A. Blakeley, P. Larson, and F. W. Tompa. Efficiently updating materialized views. In *SIGMOD*, pages 61–71, 1986.
3. K. W. Deschler and E. A. Rundensteiner. MASS: A Multi-Axis Storage Structure for Large XML Documents. Technical Report WPI-CS-TR-02-23, Computer Science Department, Worcester Polytechnic Institute, 2002.
4. K. Dimitrova, M. El-Sayed, and E. A. Rundensteiner. Order-sensitive view maintenance of materialized XQuery views. Technical Report WPI-CS-TR-03-17, Computer Science Department, Worcester Polytechnic Institute, 2003.
5. M. El-Sayed and et al. An algebraic approach for incremental maintenance of materialized XQuery views. In *WIDM*, pages 88–91, 2002.
6. T. Griffin and L. Libkin. Incremental maintenance of views with duplicates. In *SIGMOD*, pages 328–339, 1995.
7. A. Gupta and I. S. Mumick. Maintenance of materialized views: problems, techniques, and applications. In *Bulletin of the Tech. Com. on Data Eng., 18(2)*, pages 3–18, 1995.
8. A. Gupta, I. S. Mumick, and V. S. Subrahmanian. Maintaining views incrementally. In *SIGMOD*, pages 157–166, 1993.
9. H. A. Kuno and E. A. Rundensteiner. Using object-oriented principles to optimize update propagation to materialized views. In *ICDE*, pages 310–317, 1996.
10. H. A. Kuno and E. A. Rundensteiner. Incremental maintenance of materialized object-oriented views in MultiView: strategies and performance evaluation. In *IEEE Trans. on Data and Knowledge Eng.*, volume 10(5), pages 768–792, 1998.
11. M. Fernandez and et al. Publishing relational data in XML: the SilkRoute approach. *IEEE Trans. on Computers*, 44(4):1–9, 2001.
12. T. Palpanus, R. Sidle, R. Cochrane, and H. Pirahesh. Incremental maintenance for non-distributive aggregate functions. In *VLDB*, pages 802–813, 2002.
13. L. P. Quan, L. Chen, and E. A. Rundensteiner. Argos: Efficient refresh in an XQL-based web caching system. In *WebDB*, pages 23–28, 2000.
14. D. Quass. Maintenance expressions for views with aggregation. In *SIGMOD*, pages 110–118, 1996.
15. A. R. Schmidt, F. Waas, M. L. Kersten, M. J. Carey, I. Manolescu, and R. Busse. Xmark: A benchmark for xml data management. In *VLDB*, pages 974–985, 2002.
16. I. Tatarinov and et al. Storing and querying ordered XML using a relational database system. In *SIGMOD*, pages 204–215, 2002.
17. I. Tatarinov, Z. G. Ives, A. Y. Halevy, and D. S. Weld. Updating XML. In *SIGMOD*, pages 413–424, 2001.
18. W3C. XML Query Data Model. http://www.w3.org/TR/query-datamodel.
19. W3C. XML^{TM} . http://www.w3.org/XML.
20. W3C. XQuery 1.0: An XML Query Language. http://www.w3.org/TR/xquery/.
21. W3C. XQuery 1.0 Formal Semantics. http://www.w3.org/TR/query-semantics/.
22. X. Zhang, K. Dimitrova, L. Wang, M. El-Sayed, B. Murphy, B. Pielech, M. Mulchandani, L. Ding, and E. A. Rundensteiner. Rainbow: Mapping-Driven XQuery Processing System. In *SIGMOD Demonstration*, page 671, 2003.
23. X. Zhang and et al. Rainbow: Mapping-Driven XQuery Processing System. In *SIGMOD Demo*, page 614, 2002.
24. X. Zhang, B. Pielech, and E. A. Rundensteiner. Honey, I shrunk the XQuery! – An XML algebra optimization approach. In *WIDM*, pages 15–22, 2002.

Automatic Generation of XQuery View Definitions from ORA-SS Views

Ya Bing Chen, Tok Wang Ling, and Mong Li Lee

School of Computing
National University of Singapore
{chenyabi,lingtw,leeml}@comp.nus.edu.sg

Abstract. Many Internet-based applications have adopted XML as the standard data exchange format. These XML data are typically stored in its native form, thus creating the need to present XML views over the underlying data files, and to allow users to query these views. Using a conceptual model for the design and querying of XML views provides a fast and user-friendly approach to retrieve XML data. The Object-Relationship-Attribute model for SemiStructured data (ORA-SS) is a semantically rich model that facilitates the design of valid XML views. It preserves semantic information in the source data. In this paper, we develop a method that automatically generates view definitions in XQuery from views that have been designed using the ORA-SS model. This technique can be used to materialize the views and map queries issued on XML views into the equivalent queries in XQuery syntax on the source XML data. This removes the need for users to manually write XQuery expressions. An analysis of the correctness of the proposed algorithm is also given.

1 Introduction

XML is rapidly emerging as the standard for publishing and exchanging data for Internet-based business applications. The ability to create views over XML source data, not only secures the source data, but also provides an application-specific view of the source data [1]. Major commercial database systems provide the ability to export relational data to materialized XML views [18] [19] [20]. Among them, Microsoft's SQL server is the only one that supports querying XML views by using XPath. SilkRoute [13] [14] adopts two declarative language RXL and XML-QL to define and query views over relational data respectively. XPERANTO [5] [6] [12] uses a canonical mapping to create a default XML view from relational data, and other views can be defined on top of the default view. In addition, XQuery [17] is adopted to issue query on views of relational data in [15]. Xyleme [10] defines an XML view by connecting one abstract DTD to a large collection of concrete DTDs with an extension of OQL as the query language. ActiveView [2] [3] defines views with active features, such as method calls and triggers, on ArdentSoftware's XML repository using a view specification language. In addition, XML views are also supported as a middleware in integration systems, such as MIX [4], YAT [9] and Agora [21].

I.-Y. Song et al. (Eds.): ER 2003, LNCS 2813, pp. 158–171, 2003.

All these systems exploit the potential of XML by exporting their data into XML views. However, they have the following drawbacks. First, semantic information is ignored when presenting XML views in these systems. It is useful to preserve semantic information since it provides for checking of the validity of views [8] and query optimization. Second, users have to write complex queries to define XML views by using their own language in these systems. Although XPERANTO adopts XQuery [17], which is a standard query language for XML, it is not a user-friendly language as the XQuery expression can be long and complex.

In contrast, we propose a novel approach to design and query XML views based on a conceptual model. We adopt the Object-Relationship-Attribute model for SemiStructured data (ORA-SS) [11] as our data model because it can express more semantics compared to the DTD, XML schema or OEM. In our approach, XML files are first transformed into the ORA-SS source schema with enriched semantics. Valid ORA-SS views can be defined over the ORA-SS source schema via a set of operators such as select, drop, join and swap operators [8]. A graphical tool that allows users to design XML views graphically using these query operators has been developed in [7]. The validity of these views can be checked based on the semantics in the underlying source data.

In this paper, we examine how view definitions in XQuery can be generated automatically from the valid views that have been defined using the operators above based on the ORA-SS model. Thus, users do not have to manually write XQuery expression for views, which can be complex compared to simply manipulating a set of query operators. The generated view definitions can be directly executed against the source XML files to materialize the XML views. Further, users can use the same set of query operators to issue queries on ORA-SS views, which are subsequently mapped into equivalent XQuery queries on XML source data. Here, we develop a method to automatically generate view definitions in XQuery. This method can be used to materialize XML view documents, and map queries issued on ORA-SS views into equivalent queries in XQuery on the source XML data. The correctness of the proposed method is also provided.

The rest of the paper is organized as follows. Section 2 briefly reviews the ORA-SS data model and the importance of its expressiveness. Section 3 introduces a motivating example to illustrate why the automatic generation of XQuery view definitions is desirable. Section 4 presents the details of the algorithm to generate correct view definitions in XQuery from valid ORA-SS views. Section 5 describes how XML views can be queried using our approach, and we conclude in Section 6.

2   ORA-SS Data Model

The Object-Relationship-Attribute model for Semi-Structured data (ORA-SS) [12] comprises of three basic concepts: *object classes*, *relationship types* and *attributes*. An object class is similar to an entity type in an Entity-Relationship diagram or an element in XML documents. A relationship type describes a relationship among object classes. Attributes are properties that belong to an object class or a relationship type.

Fig. 1 depicts two ORA-SS schema diagrams *s1* and *s2* that have been transformed from two XML files. Each schema diagram contains several object classes, denoted by a labeled rectangle in the ORA-SS schema. Attributes of an object class are shown as circles in the schema. The key attribute of an object class is denoted by a filled circle. We observe that the value of the attribute *price* is determined by both *supplier* and *part*. It is an attribute of relationship type (*sp, 2, 1:n, 1:n*), where *sp* denotes the name of the relationship type, 2 indicates the degree of the relationship type, the first (*1:n*) is the participation constraint of the parent object class (*supplier* in this case), and the second (*1:n*) is the participation constraint of the child object class (*part* in this case) in the relationship type. Fig. 1 also shows a key-foreign key reference from *project* to *project'*, implying that each key value of *project* must appear as a key value of *project'*. In general, we assume that key-foreign key references do not exist within one ORA-SS schema. This assumption is reasonable because in most cases an object class usually refers to another object class in another schema.

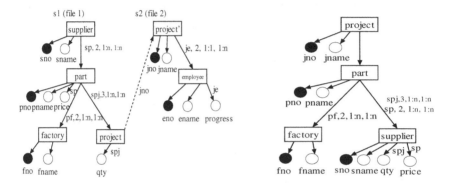

Fig. 1. An ORA-SS source schema transformed from XML files.

Fig. 2. An ORA-SS view of Fig. 1.

We observe that ORA-SS not only reflects the nested structure of semistructured data, but it also distinguishes between object classes, relationship types and attributes. Such semantics are lacking in existing semistructured data models including OEM, XML DTD and XML Schema [16]. In designing XML views, these semantics are critical in ensuring that the designed views are valid [8], that is, the views are consistent with the source schema in terms of semantics. Note we use four operators to design valid XML views: the select operator imposes some where conditions on attributes; the drop operator removes object classes or attributes; the join operator combines two object classes together; and the swap operator interchanges two object classes in a path. The following example illustrates how we use these operators to design valid views.

Example. Fig. 2 shows an ORA-SS view obtained by applying several query operators to the schemas in Fig. 1. First, we apply a join operator on *project* and *project'*: $join_{s1//project \to s2//project'}$, where *s1* and *s2* are the two source schemas. The attributes of *project'*, such as *jno* and *jname* can be grafted below *project* as its attributes. In addition, we can also graft the object class *employee* below *project* and maintain the relationship type *je* and its attribute, since we do not violate any semantics in the source schema. Following the join operator, we apply a swap operator to swap *supplier* and *project* and drop *employee*: $swap_{s//supplier \leftrightarrow s//supplier/part/project} \ drop_{s//employee}$, where *s* indicates the current view schema. Since *price* is an attribute of the relationship type *sp*, *price* cannot be placed below the object class *part* after the swap operator is applied. Instead, it will be placed automatically below *supplier* in our system as shown in the new view schema. Without the semantics captured in the ORA-SS schema diagram, we may design an invalid view in which the attribute *price* still remains with the object class *part*, thus resulting in inconsistency with the semantics in the original schema.

3 Motivating Example

After designing the views using the four operators, the next step is to generate view definitions in XQuery that can be executed to materialize these views. A naive solution is to write the view definitions manually according to the ORA-SS views. However, view definitions in XQuery can be very complex, as we will illustrate.

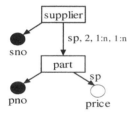
Fig. 3. An ORA-SS source schema

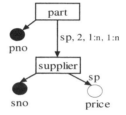
Fig. 4. An ORA-SS view schema

```
1. let $pno_set := distinct-values          9.   satisfies (exists($p1[@pno=$p_no])
      ($in//part/@pno)                            and (exists($p1
2. let $sno_set := distinct-values                [ancestor::supplier/@sno=$s_no]))
      ($in//supplier/@sno)                 10.   let $s :=$in//supplier[@sno=$s_no]
3. return <db>                             11.   return <supplier sno="{$s_no}">
4. for $p_no in $pno_set                   12.         {$s/part[@pno=$p_no]/price}
5. let $p := $in//part[@pno=$p_no]         13.         </supplier>
6. return <part pno="{$p_no}">             14.   }
7.    {for $s_no in $sno_set              15. </part>
8.    where some $p1 in $in//part         16. </db>
```

Fig. 5. View definition in XQuery expression

Consider the ORA-SS source schema in Fig. 3. Fig. 4 shows a view that has been designed using a swap operator on the object classes *supplier* and *part*, that is, $swap_{s/supplier \leftrightarrow s/supplier/part}$. Note that the attribute *price* does not move up with *part*, because it is an attribute of the relationship type *sp*. The swap operator is able to handle this automatically. Fig. 5 shows the XQuery expression for the view in Fig. 4. The variable *$in* represents the XML file corresponding to the source schema in Fig. 3.

It is clear that the XQuery expression is much more complex than the swap query operator that generates the view. In general, the complexity and length of XQuery view definitions increases dramatically as the number of object classes increases. The likelihood of introducing errors in the view definitions also increases if users are to manually define such views in XQuery. This problem can be addressed using our approach which provides a set of query operators for users to define views from which XQuery expressions can be automatically generated.

4   Generation of XQuery View Definitions

The main idea in the proposed algorithm is to generate the definition of each object class individually and then combine all the definitions together according to the tree structure of the view. The definition of an object class comprises of a FLWR expression in XQuery. The FLWR expression consists of *for, let, where* and *return* clauses. Basically, the algorithm first generates a where clause to restrict the data instances represented by the object class (say *o*). Then it generates a *for* clause to bind a variable to iterate over each distinct key value of *o* that are qualified by the *where* clause. Finally, it generates a *return* clause to construct the instances of *o*.

While it is relatively straightforward to generate the *for* and *return* clauses for each object class in a view, it is not a trivial task to generate the condition expressions in the *where* clause, which restrict the instances of the object class in the view. This is because there may exist relationship sets among the object classes. Thus, many different object classes may exert influences on a given object class in the view. In order to generate the correct condition expressions for an object class in a view, we use the following intuition, that is, the data instances for an object class in a view are determined by all the object classes in the path from the root to the object class.

Definition. Given an object class *o* in an ORA-SS view, the path from the root of the view to *o* is called the *vpath* of *o*. Object classes that occur in *vpath* of *o*, except for the root and *o* itself, determine all condition expressions for object class *o* in the view.

By analyzing the object classes in the vpath of an object class *o*, we can capture all their influences on *o* in a series of where conditions. In the next subsection, we first determine the possible types of object class that can appear in a *vpath*. Then we provide a set of generic rules to guide the generation of where conditions for each type of object class.

4.1   Analyzing Vpath

There are three types of object classes in the *vpath* of an object class *o* in any views designed by the 4 operators mentioned before. The object classes in a *vpath* are classified based on their origin in the source schema.

Type I: For any object class *o* in a view schema, a Type I object class in its *vpath* originates from some *o*'s ancestor or descendant in the source schema.

Type II: For any object class *o* in a view schema, a Type II object class in its *vpath* originates from some descendant of some *o*'s ancestor in the source schema. In other words, Type II object classes in *o*'s *vpath* are *o*'s siblings, descendants of o's siblings, o's ancestors' siblings, or descendants of o's ancestors' siblings in the source schema.

Type III: For any object class o in a view schema, a Type III object class in its *vpath* originates from the object classes in another source schema, whose ancestor or descendant has a key-foreign key reference with o's ancestor or descendant in o's source schema. They are generated in the *vpath* by a single join operator only, or a single join operator and a series of swap operators together.

The three object types introduced above include all the object classes in the vpath of a given object class.

Example. Fig. 6 illustrates the three different object types. We design a valid view in Fig. 6(b) based on the source schema in Fig. 6(a) using our operators [8]. Consider the *vpath* of object class O in the view. The object classes B and P are the ancestor and descendant of O respectively in the source schema (see Fig. 6(a)). Therefore, B and P are Type I object classes in the *vpath* of O. On the other hand, the object class J is O's ancestor B's descendant in the source schema. Therefore, J is a Type II object class in the *vpath* of O. Finally, the object class K is from the source schema 1 in Fig. 6(a), whose parent F has a key-foreign key reference with D, which is the parent of O. Therefore, K is a Type III object class in O's *vpath* that is obtained by first applying a join operator to D and F so that K can be grafted below D as its child, and then applying swap operators so that K can become a parent of O.

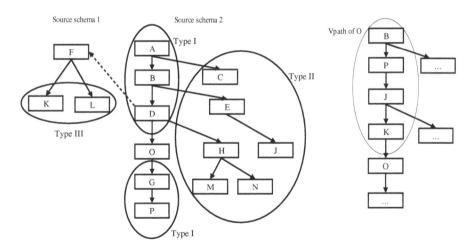

Fig. 6 (a). Two simplified ORA-SS source schema

Fig. 6 (b). A simplified ORA-SS view schema

4.2 Generating Where Conditions

Next, we present a set of rules to guide the generation of *where* conditions for each type of object class. The generated *where* conditions, in bold, reflect the influence the object classes exerts on o. We will use the notation *vo* to an arbitrary object class in o's *vpath* in the view. Note that *vo* is not the root of the views in the following figures. To simplify discussion, we just present a path of the views that contains *vo* and *o*. The key attributes of the two object classes will be referred to as *o_no* and *vo_no* respectively in the following rules. Since *vo* is an ancestor of *o* in the view, and a depth first search is employed to generate the query expression for each object class in the view, the query expression for *vo* is generated before *o*. The variable *$vo_no* denotes the current qualified key value of *vo*, and *$in* represents the XML source file.

Rule Type I_A. If *vo* is an ancestor of *o* in the source schema (see Fig. 7(a)), then Fig. 7(b) defines the *where* condition (in bold) to generate.

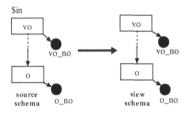

let $o_no_set := distinct-values($in//o/@o_no)
for $o_no in $o_no_set
where **some $vo1 in $in//vo satisfies (**
        exists($vo1[@vo_no=$vo_no]) and
        exists($vo1[descendant::o/@o_no=$o_no]))

Fig. 7(a). Case for Rule Type I_A   **Fig. 7(b).** Condition generated by Rule Type I_A

To understand the context for the *where* condition, we have also shown the *let* and *for* clauses. Note that the let and for clauses are generated for the object class *o* only once. The entire *where* conditions for the object classes in the *vpath* of *o* are linked together using "*and*" in a single *where* clause. The *where* condition generated by Rule Type I_A indicates if an instance of *o* with key value *$o_no* is selected as a child of an instance of *vo* with the current qualified key value *$vo_no* in the view, then there must exist an instance of *vo* in the source that has a key value *$vo_no* and has a descendant instance of *o* with key value *$o_no*.

Rule Type I_B. If *vo* is a descendant of *o* in the source schema (see Fig. 8(a)), then Fig. 8(b) defines the *where* condition to generate.

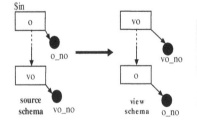

let $o_no_set := distinct-values($in//o/@o_no)
for $o_no in $o_no_set
where **some $vo1 in $in//vo satisfies (**
        exists($vo1[@vo_no=$vo_no]) and
        exists($vo1[ancestor::o/@o_no=$o_no]))

Fig. 8(a). Case for Rule Type I_B   **Fig. 8(b).** Condition generated in Rule Type I_B

Rule Type I_B is similar to Rule Type I_A except that the axis before *o* is an ancestor, instead of a descendant in the generated *where* condition.

In the case where *vo* is a Type II object class in *o*'s *vpath*, *vo* has no ancestor-descendant relationship with *o*. However, it still has influence on *o* through an intermediate object class – the Lowest Common Ancestor of *vo* and *o*. Consider

Figure 9. If an instance of *vo*, say *vo1*, appears in the *vpath* of o in the view document, then *vo1* must be under an instance of the Lowest Common Ancestor of vo and o, say *lca1*, in the source document, which actually determines a set of instances of o, say (*o1, o2, ...on*), under *lca1* in the source document. Therefore, *vo1* determines (*o1, o2, ...on*) through *lca1*. The reason why we use the lowest common ancestor of the two object classes as the intermediate object class is that it correctly reflects the restriction of *vo* on *o*. Otherwise, we may introduce a wider range of instances of *o*, some of which are not determined by *vo*. We have the following two rules for Type II object classes.

Rule Type II_ A. If *vo* is a Type II object class in *o*'s *vpath* and the Lowest Common Ancestor of *vo* and *o*, say LCA, is also in the *vpath* of *o* in the view schema (see Fig. 9), then there is no need to generate a where condition for the restriction of *vo* on *o*.

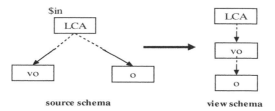

Fig. 9. Case for Rule Type II_A

Rule Type II_A states that we do not need to consider the influence of *vo* on *o* when the Lowest Common Ancestor of *vo* and *o* is also in the *vpath* of *o*. This is because this influence will be considered when the algorithm processes the Lowest Common Ancestor (LCA) as another object class in the *vpath* of *o*.

Rule Type II_B. If vo is a Type II object class in o's *vpath* and the Lowest Common Ancestor of *vo* and *o*, say LCA, is not in the *vpath* of *o* in the view schema (see Fig. 10 (a)), then Fig. 10 (b) defines the where condition generated.

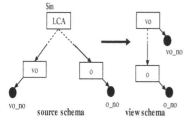

```
let $o_no_set := distinct-values($in//o/@o_no)
for $o_no in $o_no_set
where some $LCA in $in//LCA satisfies (
      exists($LCA//o[@o_no=$o_no]) and
      exists($LCA//vo[@vo_no=$vo_no]) )
```

Fig. 10(a). Case for Type II_B   **Fig. 10(b).** Condition generated in Rule Type II_B

Rule Type II_B presents the *where* condition in the case where the LCA does not occur in the *vpath* of *o*. The condition states that if an instance of *o* with key value *$o_no* is selected in the view under the instance of *vo* with the current qualified key value *$vo_no*, then there must exist an instance of LCA in the source that has both a descendant instance of *o* with key value *$o_no* and a descendant instance of *vo* with key value *$vo_no*. In other words, the instances of *vo* and *o* must have a common ancestor instance of LCA.

Next, we process the case where *vo* is a Type III object class in the *vpath* of *o*. We have *vo* and *o* that are linked together by the referencing and referenced object classes of a join operator. Consider Figure 11 (a). We assume that *vo* and *o* originates from two different schemas (*$in1* and *$in2*). The influence of *vo* on *o* is as follows: an instance of *vo*, say *vo1*, has an ancestor instance of the referenced object class, say *referenced₁*, which in turn determines an instance of the referencing object class, say *referencing₁*, which refers to the *referenced₁* by key-foreign key reference. As a descendant of *o*, the instance of the referencing object class must determine an instance of *o*, say *o1*. In this way, an instance of *vo* (*vo1*) determines an instances of o (*o1*) through the referencing and referenced object classes together.

Rule Type III_A. If *vo* is a descendant of the referenced object class and o is an ancestor or descendant of the referencing object class in the source schema, and the referencing object class is in *o*'s vpath in the view schema (see Fig. 11), then there is no need to generate a where condition.

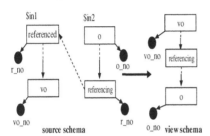 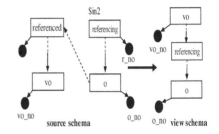

Fig. 11(a). O as an ancestor of the referencing in Rule Type III_A

Fig. 11(b). O as a descendant of the referencing in Rule Type III_A

Since the influence of *vo* on *o* will be considered when processing the referencing object class, we do not need to generate a *where* condition for the restriction of *vo* on *o*. In this case, o can be an ancestor or descendant of the referencing object class.

Rule Type III_B. If *vo* is a descendant of the referenced object class and *o* is an ancestor of the referencing object class in the source schema, and the referencing object class is not in *o's vpath* in the view schema (see Fig. 12(a)), then Fig. 12(b) defines the *where* condition generated.

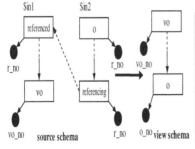

```
let $o_no_set := distinct-values($in//o/@o_no)
for $o_no in $o_no_set
where some $referenced in $in1//referenced satisfies
(exists
    ($referenced[descendant::vo/@vo_no=$vo_no]) )
and
    some $referencing in $in2//referencing satisfies (
    exists($referencing[@r_no=$referenced/@r_no])
and
    exists($referencing[ancestor::o/@o_no=$o_no]) )
```

Fig. 12(a). Case for Rule Type III_B   **Fig. 12(b).** Condition generated in Rule Type III_B

Rule III_B states that if an instance of *o* with key value o_no is selected under the instance of *vo* with the current qualified key value vo_no, then there must exist an instance of the referenced object class in source 1 ($in1$) that has a descendant *vo* with key value vo_no. Moreover, there must exist an instance of referencing object class in source 2 ($in2$) that has a key value equal to the instance of the referenced object class's key value and has an ancestor instance of *o* with key value equal to o_no.

Rule Type III_C. If *vo* is a descendant of the referenced object class and o is the referencing object class itself in the source schema(see Fig. 13 (a)), then Fig. 13 (b) defines the where condition generated.

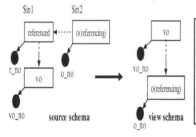

Fig. 13(a). Case for Rule Type III_C   **Fig. 13(b).** Condition generated in Rule Type III_C

Rule Type III_C states that if an instance of *o* with key value o_no is selected under the instance of *vo* with the current qualified key value vo_no, then there must exist an instance of the referenced object class, which has a key value equal to o_no and a descendant instance of *vo* with key value vo_no.

Rule Type III_D. If *vo* is a descendant of the referenced object class and *o* is a descendant of the referencing object class in the source schema, and the referencing object class is not in *o's vpath* in the view schema (see Fig. 14 (a)), then Fig. 14 (b) defines the where condition generated.

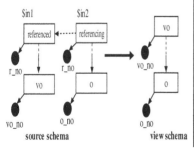

Fig. 14(a). Case for Rule Type III_D   **Fig. 14(b).** Condition generated in Rule Type III_D

Rule Type III_D is similar rule as Rule Type III_B except that *o* is now not an ancestor, but a descendant of the referencing object class.

Note the above set of rules for Type III object class handles the cases where *vo* is always a descendant of the referenced object class in the source schema. A similar set of rules can be derived for the cases where *vo* is an ancestor of the referenced object class in the source schema. However, these sets of rules are not enough for all cases where *vo* is a Type III object class in the vpath of *o* in the view. Note these rules consider the case where vo is from the schema of the referenced object class and o is from the schema of the referencing object class. We observe that *vo* can also originate from the schema of the referencing object class and *o* from the schema of the referenced object class according to the definition of Type III in Section 4.1. In this case, similar set of rules can still be derived to generate the *where* condition of *vo* on *o*.

4.3 Algorithms

Fig. 15 presents the details of the algorithm Generate_View_Definition to generate view definitions in XQuery. The inputs are valid ORA-SS views. The algorithm first generates a set of let clauses for all object classes in the view using a depth first search method. Each of these clauses binds a global variable to all possible distinct key values of a different object class. Next, it generates a root element for the view because each XML document must have a root element. The root is above the first object class in the ORA-SS views. By default, this root element is not shown as an object class in the ORA-SS views. Finally, for each child object class of the root, say *o*, it calls the algorithm Generate_ObjectClass_Definition to generate a definition for *o* and all its descendants. Each of the definition is contained in a pair of curly brackets, indicating that they are sub-elements of the root element.

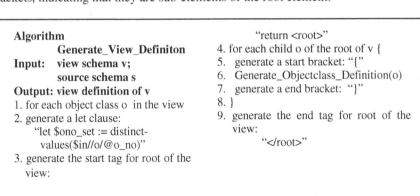

Algorithm
        Generate_View_Definiton
Input: **view schema v;**
        source schema s
Output: view definition of v
1. for each object class o in the view
2. generate a let clause:
    "let $ono_set := distinct-
    values($in//o/@o_no)"
3. generate the start tag for root of the
    view:

        "return <root>"
4. for each child o of the root of v {
5.   generate a start bracket: "{"
6.   Generate_Objectclass_Definition(o)
7.   generate a end bracket: "}"
8. }
9. generate the end tag for root of the
    view:
        "</root>"

Fig. 15. Algorithm to generate view definition

Generate_ObjectClass_Definition (Fig. 16) returns the view definition of *o* and all its descendants in *v*. The functions ProcessTypeI, ProcessTypeII and ProcessTypeIII take *vo* and *o* as inputs and generate where conditions that reflect the restriction of *vo* on *o* based on the rules described in the previous section. Note attributes that are below *o* and shown as sub elements of *o* in the source file are generated as sub-elements of *o* (line 16-18). For each child of *o,* the same algorithm is invoked recursively until all the descendants of *o* have been processed (line 24-28).

```
Algorithm
  Generate_ObjectClass_Definition
Input:    object class o
Output: view definition of o and its
          descendants
1. generate a for clause
     "for $o_no in $o_no_set"
2. generate an empty where clause
     for o;
3. for each object class vo in the
     vpath of o{
4. if vo belongs to type I
5.     ProcessTypeI(vo, o)
6. if vo belongs to type II
7.       ProcessTypeII(vo, o)
8. if vo belongs to type III
9.       ProcessTypeIII(vo, o)
10. append the generated condition
     in the where clause;
11.}
12. if there is any selection operator
     applied to o
13.     generate a where condition
          for all the operators in the
          where clauses

14. generate a let clause:
     "let $o := $in//o[@o_no = $o_no]"
15. generate a return clause:
     "return <o o_no="{$o_no}"
              distinct($o/@attributes)>"
16. for each attribute of o shown as a
     sub element of o in the source file {
17.    generate it as a sub element of o:
          "{distinct($o/@attribute)}"
18. }
19. if o has no child {
20.    generate an end tag for o: "</o>"
21.    return the generated definition;
22. }
23. else {
24.    for each child object class co of o{
25.       generate a start bracket: "{"
26.       Generate_View_Definition(co)
27.       generate an end bracket: "}"
28. }
29.    generate an end tag for o: "</o>"
30.    return the generated definition;
31. }
```

Fig. 16. Algorithm to generate object class definition

4.4 Correctness of Algorithm

The intuition behind Generate_ObjectClass_Definition is that the data instances represented by an object class in an ORA-SS view are determined by all the object classes in its *vpath*. A pre-condition for the algorithm is: o is an object class of an ORA-SS view and the number of the descendants of o in the view is n ($n \geq 0$). After executing the algorithm with o as input, we have *result* = Generate_Objectclass_Definition(o). Then a postcondition states what is to be true about the generated result which is given by *result* = XQuery expression of a sub tree rooted at o. The proof of correctness takes us from the precondition to the postcondition.

(a) $n = 0$. This is the base case where o has no children. For each object class in the *vpath* of o, we generate the *where* condition according the rules that correspond to the object type. A return clause is generated to construct the result of o. Thus, the algorithm generates and returns the correct XQuery expression for o itself.

(b) $n > 0$. In this inductive step, o will have children. We have an inductive hypothesis that assumes Generate_Objectclass_Definition(o,v) returns the correct XQuery expression of a sub tree rooted at o for all the object class o such that $0 \leq j \leq$ n-1 where j is the number of descendants of o. From the base case, the algorithm first generates the correct XQuery expression for o itself. Then it processes each child of o, say c. By the inductive hypothesis, GenerateViewDefinition(c) will return the correct XQuery expression of a sub tree rooted at c since $0 \leq j \leq$ n-1 where j is the number of descendants of c. By combining the query expressions of o and its children, the algorithm returns the correct XQuery expression of a subtree rooted at o.

5   Querying ORA-SS Views

Having automatically generated the view definition in XQuery, we can now execute it against XML files using existing XQuery engines. This allows users to browse the materialized view documents. In this section, we demonstrate how this approach can be used to support queries on the ORA-SS views.

In general, users may only be interested in a particular item of the view with some selection conditions. That is, the queries on views consist of only selection operations. We can compose these queries with the generated XQuery view definition to rewrite the query on the view. Specifically, we insert the conditions into the corresponding where clauses in the view definition. Then we execute the rewritten query against source XML files to generate the query result.

In situations where users issue more complex queries involving swap or join operators, we will directly apply the query to the view and generate the ORA-SS result tree of the query, which is treated as an ORA-SS view in our system. We can then use the same proposed algorithm to generate its view definition in XQuery, which is in fact the rewritten query on source XML files. Thus, we map any query on ORA-SS views into an equivalent XQuery on source XML files.

A query that is composed of several operators typically requires a rather complex XQuery expression. Compared to approaches that directly employ XQuery or other query languages to issue queries on views, we offer a much simpler solution with our approach that exploits a conceptual model and a set of query operators.

6   Conclusion

In this paper, we have described a method to automatically generate XQuery view definitions from views that are defined using the ORA-SS conceptual model. The proposed technique can be used to materialize the views and map queries issued on XML views into the equivalent queries in XQuery syntax on the source XML data. This removes the need for users to manually write XQuery expressions. Although visual query languages proposed for XQuery language such as XML-GL [22] also aim to solve the problem, these visual query languages do not have a mechanism that guarantees that the constructed views are valid. In contrast, our approach provides such a facility based on ORA-SS data model. To the best of our knowledge, this is the first work to employ a semantic data model for the design and query of XML views. Using a conceptual model for the design and querying of XML views provides a fast and user-friendly approach to retrieve XML data. Ongoing work aims to generate query definitions for ORA-SS views in the case where XML source data are stored into an object-relational database by employing the semantics in the source data.

References

1.   S. Abiteboul. On views and XML. 18th ACM Symposium on Principles of Database Systems, pp. 1–9, 1999.
2.   S. Abiteboul, S. Cluet, L. Mignet, et. al., "Active views for electronic commerce", VLDB, pp.138–149, 1999.
3.   S. Abiteboul, V, Aguilear, S, Ailleret, et. al., "XML repository and Active Views Demonstration", VLDB Demo, pp.742–745, 1999.
4.   C. Baru, A. Gupta, B. Ludaescher, et. al., "XML-Based Information Mediation with MIX", ACM SIGMOD Demo, 1999.
5.   M. Carey, J. Kiernan, J. hanmugasundaram, et. al., "XPERANTO: A Middleware for Publishing Object-Relational Data as XML Documents", VLDB, pp. 646–648, 2000.
6.   M. Carey, D. Florescu, Z. Ives. et. al., "XPERANTO: Publishing Object-Relational Data as XML", WebDB Workshop, 2000.
7.   Y.B. Chen, T.W. Ling, M.L. Lee, "A Case Tool for Designing XML Views", DIWeb Workshop, 2002.
8.   Y.B. Chen, T.W. Ling, M.L. Lee, "Designing Valid XML Views", ER Conference, 2002
9.   V. Christophides, S. Cluet, J. Simeon,"On Wrapping Query Languages and Efficient XML Integration", SIGMOD, pp. 141–152, 2000.
10. S. Cluet, P. Veltri, D. Vodislav, "Views in a large scale xml repository", VLDB, pp. 271–280, 2001.
11. G. Dobbie, X.Y Wu, T.W Ling, M.L Lee, "ORA-SS: An Object-Relationship-Attribute Model for SemiStructured Data", Technical Report TR21/00, School of Computing, National University of Singapore, 2000.
12. C. Fan, J. Funderburk, H. Lam, Et. al., "XTABLES: Bridging Relational Technology and XML", IBM Research Report, 2002.
13. M. Fernandez, W. Tan, D. Suciu, "Efficient Evaluation of XML Middleware Queries", ACM SIGMOD, pp. 103–114, 2001.
14. M. Fernandez, W. Tan, D. Suciu, "SilkRoute: Trading Between Relations and XML", World Wide Web Conference, 1999.
15. J. Shanmugasundaram, J. Kiernan, E. Shekita, et. al., "Querying XML Views of Relational Data", VLDB, pp. 261–270, 2001.
16. "XML Schema", W3C Recommendation, 2001.
17. "XQuery: A Query Language for XML", W3C Working Draft, 2002.
18. Microsoft Corp. http://www.microsoft.com/XML.
19. Oracle Corp. http://www.oracle.com/XML.
20. IBM Corp. http://www.ibm.com/XML.
21. I. Manolescu, D. Florescu, D. Kossmann, "Answering XML Queries over Heterogeneous Data Sources", VLDB Conf, 2001, pp.241–25
22. S. Ceri, S. Comai, E. Damiani, et. al., "XML-GL: a graphical language of querying and restructuring XML documents", WWW Conf, pp. 151–165, 1999

Automaton Meets Query Algebra: Towards a Unified Model for XQuery Evaluation over XML Data Streams

Jinhui Jian, Hong Su, and Elke A. Rundensteiner

Department of Computer Science, Worcester Polytechnic Institute
Worcester, MA 01609, USA
{jian,suhong,rundenst}@cs.wpi.edu

Abstract. In this work, we address the efficient evaluation of XQuery expressions over continuous XML data streams, which is essential for a broad range of applications including monitoring systems and information dissemination systems. While previous work has shown that automata theory is suited for on-the-fly pattern retrieval over XML data streams, we find that automata-based approaches suffer from being not as flexibly optimizable as algebraic query systems. In fact, they enforce a rigid data-driven paradigm of execution. We thus now propose a unified query model to augment automata-style processing with algebra-based query optimization techniques. The proposed model has been successfully applied in the Raindrop stream processing system. Our experimental study confirms considerable performance gains with both established optimization techniques and our novel query rewrite rules.

1 Introduction

XML has been widely accepted as the standard data representation for information exchange on the Web. Two camps of thoughts have emerged on how to deal with ubiquitous data. The "load-and-process" approach preloads the data (e.g., a complete XML document) into a persistent storage and only thereafter starts processing. The "on-the-fly" approach instead processes the data while it is being received. In this work, we adopt the second approach and address the efficient evaluation of XQuery expressions over continuous XML data streams. Such capability is essential for a broad range of applications, including monitoring systems (e.g., stock, news, sensor, and patient information) and information dissemination systems.

While previous work [2,8,14,11] has shown that automata theory is suited for XPath-like pattern retrieval over token-based XML data streams, we find these automata-based approaches suffer from being not as flexibly optimizable as, for example, traditional database systems that are based on query algebras [3,6]. We thus now propose a unified model to augment automata-style processing with algebra-based query optimization techniques. It is our goal to exploit the respective strength inherent in these two paradigms and to bring them together into one unified query model.

I.-Y. Song et al. (Eds.): ER 2003, LNCS 2813, pp. 172–185, 2003.

We shall focus on flexible integration of automata into query algebras. To the best of our knowledge, we are the first to tackle this flexible integration problem. Previous work applies automata techniques such as NFAs or DFAs in a rather fixed fashion that impairs the potential of query optimization. For example, [11] treats the whole automaton, which is used to scan all XPath-like patterns, as one single query operator, that is, as a "black box" with multiplexed yet fixed functionality. This has some disadvantages. First, it disallows or at least hinders pulling out some of the pattern scans from the automaton. In fact, the trade-off between moving query functionality into and out off the automata is one theme of this paper. Second, because multiple pattern scans are encoded in one single operator, the relationship between these scans is hidden from the topology of a logical plan. Hence traditional query optimization techniques such as equivalent rewriting [3,6] are not directly applicable. In contrast, we attempt to open the "black box" and create a logical "view" within our algebraic framework. The key advantage of our approach is that it allows us to refine automata in the same manner as refining an algebraic expression (i.e., with equivalent rewriting).

We have implemented a prototype system based on the proposed query model to verify the applicability of established optimization techniques [3,6] in the context of query plans with automata constructs. We have devised a set of query rewriting rules that can flexibly move query functionality into and out off the automata. All these optimization techniques allow us to reason about query logic at the algebraic level and only thereafter play with the implementation details. Our experimental study confirms considerable performance gains achievable from these optimization techniques.

The rest of the paper is organized as follows. Section 2 summarizes related work. Section 3 presents the overall approach. Sections 4, 5, and 6 describe the three layers in our model, respectively. Section 7 presents the experimental results and our analysis. Section 8 summarizes our conclusion and possible future work.

2   Related Work

The emergence of new applications that deal with streaming XML data over the Internet has changed the computing paradigm of information systems. For example, dissemination-based applications [2] now require a system to handle user queries on-the-fly. [2,8] have adopted automata-based data-driven approaches to deal with this new requirement. Following this data-driven paradigm, [11] employs a set of Finite Machines, [5] employs a *Trie* data structure, and [14] employs Deterministic Finite Automata (DFA) to perform pattern retrieval over XML streams. These recent works all target some subset of XPath [16] as the query language. With the XQuery language [17] emerging as the *de facto* standard for querying XML data, however, more and more XML applications adopt XQuery to express user requests. This more complex language raises new challenges that must be met by new techniques.

[13] applies the concept of an *extended transducer* to handle XQuery. In short, an XQuery expression is mapped into an XSM (XML Stream Machine). The XSM is consequently translated into a C program and compiled into binary code. The incoming data is then streamed through this system at run time. Note that the data-driven nature of execution is retained. We speculate that this rigid-mapping approach has scalability and optimization problems. For example, it is not clear how such a model can be flexibly extended to support multiple queries. It is also unstudied what query optimization techniques can be applied to this rigid automata-based model.

On the other hand, the traditional database literature [7,3,6,9] has advocated algebraic systems as the suitable foundation for query optimization and evaluation. While a number of recent papers have proposed algebras for XML query evaluation [4,19,18,12,11], none address flexible integration of automata theory into query algebras. [4,19,18] focus on querying XML views over relational databases. [12] queries native XML data. Neither can process streaming data. [11] applies automata theory but integrates the automata in a rather fixed fashion, as discussed in Section 1.

3   The Raindrop Approach

Our approach faces an intricate trade-off. On the one hand, we want to exploit automata theory to process streaming XML data on-the-fly. On the other hand, we need to overcome the limitations imposed by the automata model and instead exploit query algebra for optimization.

While a number of recent papers [2,8,11,14,13] have shown that automata theory is suitable for XML stream processing, we now analyze the limitations of automata in terms of query optimization. Automata such as NFA, DFA, and transducer models enforce data-driven execution, which implies an underling token-based data model. In the XML context, a token is typically represented as a piece of XML data, such as an open tag, a close tag, or a piece of character data (PCDATA). This token-based data model is different from the one adopted in the XQuery language, which instead is a sequence of node-labeled trees [17] or a collection of tree fragments [12]. This mismatch is two-fold. First, tokens are sequential and discrete, while trees are connected and have an internal structure. Second, tokens and trees have different granularities in terms of abstraction.

From the query optimization point of view, mixing these heterogeneous models complicates the optimization. First, the design of operators is more complex because the operators now must process more complex mixed-typed objects. Second, the search for optimal plans may be more expensive because this new mixed data model introduces a new dimension to the search space. Third, different operators may require data types in different data models, which impairs the uniformity of the query model.

Considering the need for both data models and the limitations of arbitrarily mixing them, we now propose a three-layer hierarchical model to resolve this dilemma. The top layer represents the semantics of query plans and thus is

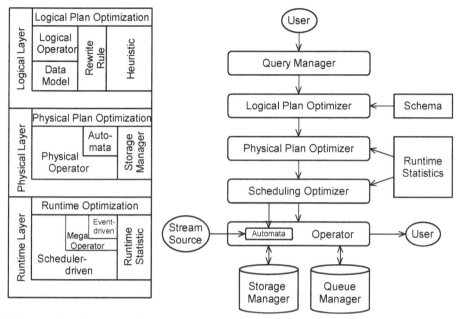

Fig. 1. Three layers in the unified query model

Fig. 2. System components

called logical layer (see Section 4. It serves specifically as the basis for plan optimization, i.e., to find efficient query plans. We adopt the tuple model in this layer to simplify the design of operators and particularly to leverage various established query optimization techniques developed specifically for the tuple model [3,6]. Note that while the token model is hidden from this layer, the automata flavor of the system is still embodied in, for example, the Extract operators in Figure 4. Hence, we can refine the automata in the same manner as we refine algebraic query plans, thus overcoming the limitations imposed by automata techniques.

The physical layer refines the logical query plan by specific algorithms to implement the functionalities of logical operators (see Section 5. In particular, the physical layer describes how automata techniques are used to implement the *automata operators* such as Extract and Structural Join. The token-based data model, which is hidden from the logical layer, is made explicit inside each *automata operator*. Note that this is a hierarchical design where the logical layer describes the overall query plan and the functionality of each operator, while the physical plan describes the internal implementation of each individual operator. Although the token model is made explicit in the physical layer, it is restricted to being exposed only inside each individual operator. It does not impair the homogeneity of the data model at the logical layer.

The runtime layer describes the overall execution strategy for a query plan. It specifies the control and coordination for each physical operator. In particular, we devise a two-level control mechanism that integrates the data-driven execution strategy common for automata with more flexible execution strategies such as the the traditional iterator-based evaluation strategy or the more recently proposed scheduler-driven strategies. We employ the concept of *mega operator* to bridge these two execution levels, as explained in Sectionruntime.

4   The Logical Layer

4.1   The Data Model

Because [17] has defined the *XQuery data model* for query evaluation, we now first explain why we in addition need yet another data model. According to [17], a data model defines the logical view of (1) the source data and (2) the intermediate data of query expressions (i.e., the inputs and outputs of query operators). In the *XQuery data model*, source data is defined as node-labeled trees augmented with node identity, while intermediate data is defined as a sequence of zero or more items, each either a node or an atomic value.

We cannot directly adopt the *XQuery data model* to query streaming XML data. First, streaming XML data can be more naturally viewed as a sequence of discrete tokens, where a token can be an open tag, a close tag, or a PCDATA. In fact, the node-labeled tree view of an XML data stream is incomplete until after the stream is wholly received and parsed.

Second, the *XQuery Data Model* is not suitable for pipelining the execution. To make it clear, we shall draw a comparison with the *relational data model* [7], which is based on sets of tuples. A relational algebraic query plan usually ignores whether it will be executed in a pipelining fashion or in an iterative fashion. In other words, the execution strategy is left out off the logical query model. This design is feasible, however, only because the *relational data model* has a natural atomic execution unit, i.e., a tuple. A query plan executor can choose whatever execution strategy without breaking this atomic unit. In the XML realm, however, such an atomic unit is not directly available because of its arbitrarily nested structure. In fact, many approaches such as the one suggested by the *XQuery data model* consider the complete XML document as a unit, and thus exclude the possibility of pipelined execution. Going to another extreme, [13] considers each XML data token as an atomic unit. As discussed in previous sections, this purely token-based approach is rigid and at times too low-level.

Based on the above observations, we now define our logical data model. We shall adopt <tag> to denote XML tags, [...] for a list (or a sequence), ⟨...⟩ for a *tuple*, with each *field* in the *tuple* bound to an *attribute name* (i.e., the *named perspective* in [1]). We shall use ∘ for *tuple concatenation* and π for *tuple projection*.

1) We define the source XML streams to be sequences of *tokens*, where a *token* can be an open tag, a close tag, or a piece of *character data* (PCDATA). Formally, we define $\mathcal{T}$, the domain of *tokens*, as:

$$\mathcal{T} = \{<x> | x \in \mathcal{E}\} \cup \{</x> | x \in \mathcal{E}\} \cup \{d | d \in \mathcal{D}\}$$

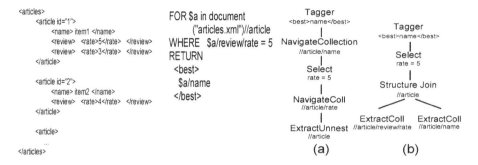

Fig. 3. Example document and query   **Fig. 4.** Two equivalent query plans

where $\mathcal{E}$ is the domain of *XML element names* and $\mathcal{D}$ is the domain of *character data* (strings).

2) We define intermediate data of query expressions (i.e., the inputs and outputs of query operators) to be a sequence of zero or more *tuples*, with each *field* in a *tuple* being a sequence of zero or more *items*. Each *item* is either an *XML node* or an *atomic value*. Formally, we define $\mathcal{P}$, the domain of *tuples* as:

$$\mathcal{F} = \{ \, [v_1, ..., v_n] \mid v_i \in \mathcal{A} \cup \mathcal{X}, n \text{ is the size of a field}\}$$
$$\mathcal{P} = \{\langle f_1, ..., f_n\rangle | f_i \in \mathcal{F}, n \text{ is the arity of a tuple}\}$$

where $\mathcal{F}$ is the domain of *fields*, $\mathcal{A}$ is the domain of *atomic values*, and $\mathcal{X}$ is the domain of *XML nodes*.

4.2   The Logical Operators

Following the data model defined above, every logical operator accepts a sequence of tuples as input and produces a sequence of tuples as output. We distinguish between two classes of operators. The *pattern retrieval operators*, such as Navigate, Extract, and Structural Join, are designed to locate XML elements specified by XPath expressions. The *filtering and construction operators*, such as Select, Join, and Tagger, are designed to filter data and construct nested data fragments. Considering the limitation of space, here we only show details of the *pattern retrieval operators*. For the *filtering and construction operators*, readers are referred to [19]. For illustrative purposes, we shall follow a simple running example as shown in Figures 3 and 4.

NavigateUnnest. $\Phi_{ep,path}(\, T \,) = [\, t \circ \langle f \rangle \mid t \leftarrow T, f \leftarrow follow(\pi_{ep}(t), path) \,]$

The *follow* operation denotes the "descendant" relation in [16] and returns a sequence of descendent elements of the first argument. The NavigateUnnest operator finds all descendants of the *entry point* ep in *tuple* t that conform to the XPath expression *path*. An output tuple is constructed for each such descendant by inserting the descendant as a field into the input tuple. For example, let tuple list $T = [\langle article \rangle]$, where "article" is the first article element in Figure 3, and let \$a denote the attribute name of "article", then $\Phi_{\$a,//article/rate}(T) = [\langle article, r_1 \rangle, \langle article, r_2 \rangle]$, where "r1" and "r2" are the two "rate" descendants of "article".

NavigateCollection. $\phi_{ep,path}(T) = [t \circ \langle f \rangle \mid t \leftarrow T, f = [f' \mid f' \leftarrow follow(\pi_{ep}(t), path)]]$

This operator again finds all descendants of the *entry point* ep in *tuple* t that conform to the XPath expression *path*. One collection, constructed from all descendent elements, is then concatenated to the input tuple as a field. Following the above example, $\phi_{\$a,//article/rate}(T) = [\langle article, [r_1, r_2] \rangle]$.

ExtractUnnest. $\Psi_{str,path}( ) = [\langle n \rangle \mid n \leftarrow follow(str, path)]$

This operator identifies from the input data stream *str* (i.e., the root element) all XML elements that conform to the given XPath expression *path*. A new tuple is generated for each matched element. For example, let the stream name of the document in Figure 3 be "articles.xml", $\Psi_{"articles.xml",//article/review/rate}( ) = [\langle r_1 \rangle, \langle r_2 \rangle, ..., \langle r_n \rangle]$, where $r_1, r_2, ...r_n$ are "rate" elements conforming to "//article/review/rate".

An *ExtractUnnest* operator does not take in any input tuples. Instead, as will be further explained in the physical layer, the operator's internal mechanism, namely its associated automaton, is responsible for analyzing the input stream and extracting the desired data. This association with the automaton does not affect the semantics of the operator; it is simply an implementation issue. Hence optimization techniques such as query rewriting are not restricted by the data model and the execution strategy that are imposed by automata theory.

ExtractCollection. $\psi_{str,path}( ) = [\langle n \rangle \mid n = [n' \mid n' \leftarrow follow(str, path)]]$

This operator identifies from the input data stream *str* all XML elements that conform to the XPath expression *path*. A collection, composed of all such elements, is then used as the only field for the output tuple. For example, $\Psi_{"articles.xml",//article/review/rate}( ) = [\langle [r_1, r_2, ..., r_n] \rangle]$. Similar to an *ExtractUnnest* operator, an *ExtractCollection* operator does not take in any input tuples, but instead generates the output using its internal mechanism.

Structural Join. $X \bowtie_{path} Y = [t_x \circ t_y \mid t_x \leftarrow X; t_y \leftarrow Y; precede(t_x, path) = precede(t_y, path)]$

The *precede* operation denotes the "ancester" relation in [16]. The Structural Join operator concatenates input tuples based on their structural relationship such as common ancestor. For example, $[\langle [r_1, r_2, r_3] \rangle] \bowtie_{//article} [\langle [n_1, n_2] \rangle] = [\langle [r_1, r_2], n_1 \rangle, \langle r_3, n_2 \rangle]$

Although a *Structural Join* operator can be implemented like a traditional join, i.e., by value comparisons, it can be more efficiently implemented using an associated automaton. Again this association does not affect the operator's formal semantics. Hence we can take advantage of automata theory without being restricted by its implied limitations in terms of optimization.

4.3   The Potential Query Rewriting

Now we discuss the optimization opportunity provided by the proposed algebra. Due to the space limitation here we only discuss rewrites on *pattern retrieval operators*. Readers are are referred to [19] for other rules. The two plans in Figure 4 are equivalent. Plan 4(a) uses an Extract operator to grab "article" elements and two Navigate operators to identify proper descendants of the "article". This is a top-down dissection process in which higher level XML nodes are first grabbed and then lower level XML nodes are identified by navigating into the higher lever node. In contrast, two Extract operators in plan 4(b) first grab lower level nodes and a Structural Join operator then joins the lower level nodes by matching their common parent. This can be viewed as a bottom-up construction process.

Formally, Plan 4(a) can be transfromed into Plan 4(b) using the following rules:

$$\phi_{\$a,p_1}(\phi_{\$a,p_2}(\psi_{str,p_3})) = \psi_{str,p_1} \bowtie_{p_3} \psi_{str,p_2}$$

$$\sigma_{cond}(\phi_{\$a,p}) = \phi_{\$a,p}(\sigma_{cond})$$

where the attribute name $\$a$ denotes the output of ψ_{str,p_3}, the XPath expression p_3 is the common prefix of p_1 and p_2, str is an XML data stream, σ denotes a Select operator, and the condition *cond* is independent of the attribute $\$a$.

5   The Physical Layer

5.1   Applying Automata

We resort to NFA to implement the *automata operators* such as Extract and Structural Join. Each *automata operator* is associated with an NFA. Each NFA is constructed to recognize one given XPath expression. All related NFAs, i.e., whose XPath expressions are based on the same input stream, are merged into one single NFA for sharing computation. Such NFA construction and merging is a well-studied topic in the literature [8]. We differ from previous work, however, in the operations undertaking by the sequence of accepting events.

Figure 5 shows a partial plan with its associated NFA (after merging). State 3 together with all its preceding states is constructed to recognize the expression "//article/name". For each "name" element, State 3 will be activated twice, one for the open tag "<name>" and the other for the close tag "</name>". The associated operator (i.e., the one connected to State 3 as shown in Figure 5) is invoked by the close tag. This seemingly simple scheme is actually very powerful when multiple operators are invoked in a specific order, as will be shown below.

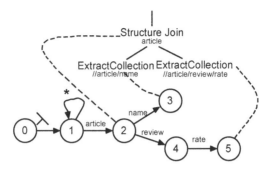

Fig. 5. Physical operators and their associated automaton

5.2   Implementing Physical Operators

Extract. An Extract operator has two steps: first assembling input tokens that conform to a given XPath expression into XML elements and second encapsulating the elements into tuples. Although each Extract operator may look for elements conforming to different XPaths, these elements may often overlap. Take the document in Figure 3 for example. There may be an Extract operator looking for "//article" and another for "//article/review/rate", i.e., the former element contains the latter. It is naive to store them separately. Hence we adopt a centralized approach to perform the first step.

An XML element can be viewed as a token connected to other tokens. Hence the assembly process is a matter of connecting proper tokens. Take the plan in Figure 5 for example. Suppose the open tag "<article>" comes from the stream, and we are now at state 2. It is easy to conclude that whatever next open tag is encountered, it must be a child of "article". In general, a *context node* is maintained during runtime and is set to the document root at the initialization. Every incoming open tag is connected to the *context node* and becomes the new *context node*; every incoming close tag resets the *context node* to the previous *context node* by referring to a *context stack*.

The second step, i.e., encapsulating proper elements into tuples, is performed by the Extract operators. Recall that *automata operators* are invoked by close tags. Take Figure 5 as example. The Extract operator at the left hand side is associated with state 3, which will invoke the operator when a "</name>" arrives. Note that all descendent tokens of a particular "name" element, e.g., its *Text*, must come between "<name>" and the corresponding "</name>" tags. Hence before invoking the Extract operator, we would have assembled a complete "name" element by the first step. This element will be passed to the operator and will be put into a tuple.

Structural Join. [12] points out that "an efficient implementation of structural join is critical in determining the overall performance of an XML query processing system". While naive structural join algorithms would take a high-order polynomial time, we now propose the JIT (Just-In-Time) Structural Join algorithm. This join algorithm exploits the sequentiality of stream tokens and takes linear time.

The algorithm is simple. When a Structural Join operator is invoked by its associated NFA, it makes a cross product out of all its inputs. The cross product is guaranteed to be the correct output. The trick is the timing of invocation. Take the document in Figure 3 and the plan in Figure 5 as example. The Structural Join is first invoked on the first "</article>". At this time, the output of the left Extract is $\langle n_1 \rangle$, and the output of the right Extract is $\langle [\, r_1, r_2 \,] \rangle$, where n_1, r_1, and r_2 are defined in Section 4.2. It is obvious that n_1, r_1, and r_2 are descendants of the first "article" element. Hence the cross product $\langle n_1, [\, r_1, r_2 \,] \rangle$ is the correct output. Similarly, every consequent invocation of the Structural Join must have descendants of the current "article" element as input, because descendants of the previous "article" element would have been consumed by the previous invocation of the Structural Join and descendants of future "article" elements have not yet come. Because no value comparison is involved, the complexity of the JIT join is equal to the complexity of output tuple construction, hence linear in the output size.

Other Operators. Other operators such as Join, Select, and Navigate are rather generic and can be found in other XQuery engines [19,18]. We skip further description here.

6   The Runtime Layer

A general assumption in stream systems is that data arrival is unpredictable [15]. This characteristic makes the demand-driven execution strategies [10] not directly applicable in the stream context. One solution is to let the incoming data "drive" the execution, which leads to a purely data-driven (or event-driven) execution strategy. This approach is adopted by for example [13]. The disadvantage is its rigidity: every incoming data token will trigger a fixed sequence of operations immediately. This rigidity excludes the possibility of deferring certain operations and then batching their processing, which may be more efficient because the cost of context switching between operators can be reduced.

Another solution [15] uses a *global scheduler* who calls the *run* methods of query operators based on a variety of scheduling strategies. The disadvantage is its over generality. In principle the scheduler-driven strategy subsumes the data-driven strategy, i.e., the general strategy can simulate the rigid one. It is easy to conceive, however, that this simulation may be less efficient than directly applying the data-driven strategy because of the cost in making such scheduling decisions.

In this paper, we adopt a hierarchical approach to integrate both the data-driven and the scheduler-driven strategies by employing a *mega operator*. We organize a physical operator plan into two levels as shown in Figure 6. The top level plan is composed of all *non-automata operators*, while the bottom level is

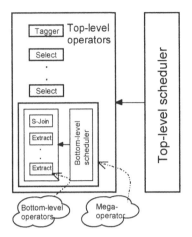

Fig. 6. Two-level scheduling

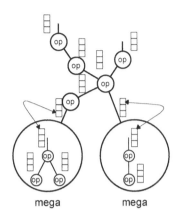

Fig. 7. Two-level data passing

composed of *automata operators*. A *mega operator* encapsulates a set of automata operators at the bottom level and represents this subplan as one operator at the top level, as shown in Figure 7. Each bottom level plan is controlled by an NFA, while the top level plan is flexibly governed by the global scheduler. When a *mega operator* is invoked by the global scheduler, it takes the outputs from the bottom level plan and transfers them to the top level plan.

7   Experimental Evaluation

Our evaluation studies the trade-offs between moving query functionality into and out off the automata. This is to be compared with previous work [8,11] which offers no such flexibility and instead assumes (or even advocates) maximal pattern retrieval push-down.

We have implemented our prototype system with Java 1.4. All experiments are conducted on a Pentium-III 800Mhz processor with 384 MB memory running Windows 2000. The JVM is initialized with 256 MB heap space. Garbage collection is explicitly invoked to avoid interference. Every experiment is repeated at least 10 times.

The test data is synthetically generated similar to the document in Figure 3. The data size is 9.0 MB. The user queries are similar to the one in Figure 3, with slight modifications on the *RETURN* clause to include more path bindings. Accordingly, the query plans are similar to those in Figure 4. We call plan (a) "bottom-most navigation only"(BMNO), and plan (b) "all navigation"(AN). We make another plan using equivalent rewrite rules to push the selection into the automata, which is called "all navigation and selection"(ANS).

Our first experiment compares the three push-down strategies. Figures 8 and 9 illustrate their performances in different settings, i.e., different workloads and selectivities. BMNO wins in Figure 8 (i.e., the output rate is higher and

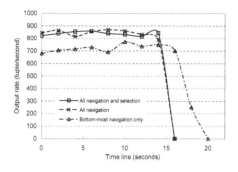

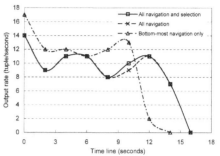

Fig. 8. Output rate with low workload and high selectivity

Fig. 9. Output rate with high workload and low selectivity

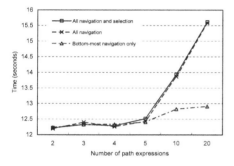

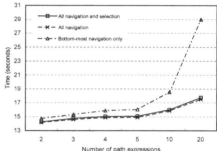

Fig. 10. Comparing different workloads with selectivity = 5%

Fig. 11. Comparing different workloads with selectivity = 90%

the finishing time is shorter) while AN and ANS win in Figure 9. Clearly both workload and selectivity affect the result. This justifies our effort to allow for flexible query rewriting even in this new automata context.

Our second experiment analyzes the three strategies in terms of different workloads, in particular, different numbers of path expressions in a query. Figures 10 and 11 illustrate the same interesting pattern as the first experiment. But this time we see that with low selectivity (Figure 10), BMNO outperforms AN and ANS. In fact, higher workloads further enlarge the gap between them. In contrast, with high selectivity (Figure 11), AN and ANS outperform BMNO. The gap also increases with a higher workload. Intuitively, this is because automata are efficient in pattern retrieval, especially when the retrieval of several patterns is encoded into one automaton. Hence in Figure 11 the more aggressive push-down strategies (AN and ANS) outperform the less aggressive one (BMNO). However, evaluating all bindings together in the automaton disallows for early selection, a well-established optimization technique in the database literature. For example, in the query plan shown in Figure 4 (b), the Selection is evaluated before the top-most Navigation. Hence we can reduce the cost of Navigation to

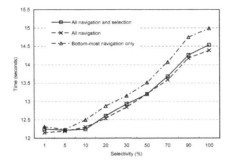 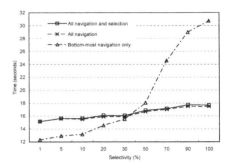

Fig. 12. Comparing different selectivity with numBinding = 2)

Fig. 13. Comparing different selectivity with numBinding = 20

all "articles" elements without a "rate-5" review. When selectivity is low, such optimization can save a lot of work, as illustrated in Figure 10.

We now look more closely at the relationship of selectivity and performance. With low workloads, Figure 12 shows that the performance difference is small. But with higher workloads, this difference is enlarged, as in Figure 13. We can see clearly that with a selectivity less than 40%, BMNO outperforms the other two. The smaller the selectivity, the larger the difference. With a selectivity greater than 40%, both AN and ANS outperform BMNO. Their difference also increases when the selectivity becomes larger. This is the trade-off we expect and which our unified framework is empowered to exploit.

8   Conclusion

We have presented a unified model for efficient evaluation of XQuery expressions over streaming XML data. The key feature of this model is its power in flexibly integrating automata theory into an algebraic query framework. Unlike any of the previous work, this power facilitates various established query optimization techniques to be applied in the automata context. It also allows for novel optimization techniques such as rewrite rules that can flexibly change the functionality implemented by the automata-based operators. Our experimental study confirms that these optimization techniques indeed result in a variety of interesting performance trade-offs that can be exploited for efficient query processing. However, this paper serves only as the first step towards a full-fledged framework for XML stream systems. It is a solid foundation for making various optimization techniques possible in the XML stream context.

References

1. S. Abiteboul, R. Hull, and V. Vianu. *Foundations of Databases*. Addison Wesley, 1995.
2. M. Altinel and M. J. Franklin. Efficient filtering of XML documents for selective dissemination of information. In *The VLDB Journal*, pages 53–64, 2000.
3. M. Astrahan et al. System R: a relational approach to database management. *ACM Trans. on Database Systems*, pages 97–137, 1976.
4. M. J. Carey, D. Florescu, Z. G. Ives, Y. Lu, J. Shanmugasundaram, E. J. Shekita, and S. N. Subramanian. XPERANTO: Publishing object-relational data as XML. In *WebDB*, pages 105–110, 2000.
5. C. Y. Chan, P. Felber, M. N. Garofalakis, and R. Rastogi. Efficient filtering of XML documents with XPath expressions. In *Proc. ICDE*, pages 235–244, 2002.
6. S. Chaudhuri. An overview of query optimization in relational systems. In *Proc. Seventeenth Annual ACM Symposium on Principles of Database Systems*, pages 34–43, June 1998.
7. E. Codd. A relational model of data for large shared data banks. *Communications of the ACM*, 13(6):377–387, 1970.
8. Y. Diao, P. Fischer, M. J. Franklin, and R. To. YFilter: Efficient and scalable filtering of XML documents. In *Proc. of ICDE*, pages 341–344, 2002.
9. L. Fegaras, D. Levine, S. Bose, and V. Chaluvadi. Query processing of streamed XML data. In *CIKM*, pages 126–133, 2002.
10. G. Graefe. Query evaluation techniques for large databases. *ACM Computing Surveys*, pages 73–170, June 1993.
11. Z. G. Ives, A. Y. Halevy, and D. S. Weld. An XML query engine for network-bound data. *VLDB Journal*, 11(4), 2002.
12. H. Jagadish, S. Al-Khalifa, L. Lakshmanan, A. Nierman, S. Paparizos, J. Patel, D. Srivastava, and Y. Wu. TIMBER: A native XML database. *VLDB Journal*, 11(4):274–291, 2002.
13. B. Ludascher, P. Mukhopadhyay, and Y. Papakonstantinou. A Transducer-Based XML Query Processor. In *Proc. VLDB*, pages 215–226, 2002.
14. G. Miklau, T. J. Green, M. Onizuka, and D. Suciu. Processing xml streams with deterministic automata. In *ICDT*, pages 173–189, 2003.
15. R. Motwani et al. Query processing, approximation, and resource management in a data stream management system. In *Proc. CIDR*, pages 245–256, 2003.
16. W3C. XML path language (xpath) version 1.0. http://www.w3.org/TR/xpath, November 2002.
17. W3C. XQuery 1.0: An XML query language. http://www.w3.org/TR/xquery/, November 2002.
18. X. Zhang, K. Dimitrova, L. Wang, M. EI-Sayed, B. Murphy, B. Pielech, M. Mulchandani, L. Ding, and E. A. Rundensteiner. Rainbow II: Multi-XQuery optimization using materialized xml views. In *SIGMOD Demonstration*, page 671, June 2003.
19. X. Zhang, B. Pielech, and E. A. Rundensteier. Honey, I shrunk the XQuery! – an XML algebra optimization approach. In *Proceedings of the fourth international workshop on Web information and data management*, pages 15–22, Nov 2002.

Querying Heterogeneous XML Sources through a Conceptual Schema

Sandro Daniel Camillo[1], Carlos Alberto Heuser[1], and
Ronaldo dos Santos Mello[2]

[1] Universidade Federal do Rio Grande do Sul
Instituto de Informática
Caixa Postal 15064 Av. Bento Goncalves, 9500 - Bloco IV - Prédio 43412
CEP: 91501-970 - Porto Alegre - RS - Brazil
{camillo,heuser}@inf.ufrgs.br
[2] Universidade Federal de Santa Catarina
Centro Tecnológico Departamento de Informática e de Estatística
Campus Universitário Trindade
Caixa Postal 476 CEP: 88040-900 - Florianópolis - SC - Brazil
ronaldo@inf.ufsc.br

Abstract. XML is a widespread W3C standard used by several kinds
of applications for data representation and exchange over the *web*. In the
context of a system that provides semantic integration of heterogeneous
XML sources, the same information at a semantic level may have different
representations in XML. However, the syntax of an XML query depends
on the structure of the specific XML source. Therefore, in order to obtain
the same query result, one must write a specific query for each XML
source. To deal with such problem, a much better solution is to state
queries against a global conceptual schema and then translate them into
an XML query against each specific data source. This paper presents
CXPath (Conceptual XPath), a language for querying XML sources at
the conceptual level, as well as a translation mechanism that converts a
CXPath query to an *XPath* query against a specific XML source.

1 Introduction

XML is a common W3C standard for semi-structured data representation, being used by *web* applications for data exchange [1,2]. In this paper, we focus
on the problem of performing queries on heterogeneous XML data sources related to some specific domain. Examples of applications that require solutions
to such problem are federated information systems [3] and semantic *web* applications [4]. In this context, the main challenge is to deal with different XML
representations of semantically equivalent data. To manage this problem, it is
necessary to provide [5]:

1. a global (unified) representation for all XML source schemata, avoiding that
   the user must know the schema of each source to formulate queries;

I.-Y. Song et al. (Eds.): ER 2003, LNCS 2813, pp. 186–199, 2003.

2. a translation mechanism to convert a global query into queries in accordance to the schema of each XML source, avoiding that several queries must be formulated against each XML source;

3. an instance integration mechanism to unify query results coming from several XML sources into a single query result in accordance to the global schema.

This paper particularly focuses on the second point. We propose a mechanism to deal with the problem of translating global queries to XML sources. This mechanism is supported by:

- a *global schema* that is a *conceptual abstraction* of several XML schemata (such a conceptual schema is constructed by a semantic integration process that is out of the scope of this paper [6]);
- a *language* to formulate queries over this conceptual model, called *CXPath (conceptual XPath)*;
- *mapping information* for concepts at the conceptual schema level into concepts at the XML level.

We adopt a *conceptual* model for defining a global schema instead of the *logical* XML model, because the XML model is unable to abstract several XML schemata at the same time. This is due to the inherent hierarchical nature of XML data. The schema of an XML source must define a specific hierarchical structure for representing relationships between XML elements. Therefore, heterogeneous XML sources belonging to a same application domain may define different hierarchical representations for the same many-to-many relationship. Considering the example of a library, a many-to-many relationship between *article* and *author* may be represented by two different XML schemata: (i) one *article* (ancestor element) associated to many *authors* (descendent elements); or (ii) one *author* (ancestor element) associated to many *articles* (descendent elements). A global XML schema would be able to represent only one of these possibilities. However, a conceptual model directly represents many-to-many relationships (many *articles* associated to many *authors*, and vice-versa), without imposing a strict navigation order between them.

This paper defines the query language used at the conceptual level. During the definition of this language we had two objectives in mind: (i) to simplify the process of translation of a query at the conceptual level to a query at the XML level; and (ii) to simplify the learning process of the language to those acquainted with the query languages of the XML standard (*XPath* and XQuery) [7].

One way to simplify the process of translation between two languages is to narrow the semantic gap between these languages. The target language *XPath 1.0* is based on the concept of *path expression* for navigating through the hierarchical relationships of an XML instance. Thus, we have chosen for the conceptual level a language that is also based on the concept of path expression, and discarded languages like *entity-relationship* algebras [8,9] and *SQL* [10] that are based on the *join* operation.

Examples of query languages that are based on the concept of *path expression* are OQL for the object-oriented model [11], *Lorel* for semi-structured data [12] and *XPath* for the XML model. As we aim at simplifying the process of learning of the proposed language for those acquainted with the XML, we chose to base the conceptual level query language on the *XPath 1.0* language [13].

We defined *CXPath (Conceptual XPath)* as a variant of *XPath 1.0* [13]. The main difference between *CXPath* and *XPath 1.0* is that, whereas in *XPath 1.0* a path expression specifies the navigation through hierarchical relationships, in *CXPath* a path expression specifies the navigation through a web of relationships among entities in a graph-based conceptual base.

The translation process of a *CXPath* query to an *XPath 1.0* query is based on mapping information associated to each concept and relationship in the conceptual schema. A mapping information is an *XPath path expression* that maps each conceptual construct into an XML source. For a concept at the conceptual schema, this expression specifies how to reach the corresponding XML construct (element or attribute) in the source. For a relationship at the conceptual schema, this expression specifies the traversal path in terms of the XML source that corresponds to the traversal of the relationship at the conceptual level. The use of the same language as the target language and as the language for expressing mapping information further simplifies the process of query translation from the conceptual into the XML level.

The *CXPath* language and the proposed translation mechanism may be applied to the context of mediation-based systems that provides integrated access to heterogeneous XML sources related to a same application domain [14,15,16, 17]. Such systems are responsible for the semantic integration of XML schemata and global query processing to XML sources. A semantic integration module generates the conceptual schema and the mapping information. A query processing module receives a *CXPath* query based on the conceptual schema, translates it to *XPath* queries for each XML source and performs the integration of query results.

This paper is organized as follows. Section 2 presents the *CXPath* language: its syntax, the considered conceptual model and some query examples. Section 3 presents the adopted approach to represent the mapping information between the conceptual and the XML levels. Section 4 describes the *CXPath* into *XPath* translation mechanism, providing some examples of query translation. Section 5 is dedicated to the conclusion. The Appendix contains the *CXPath* grammar.

2   CXPath

CXPath (Conceptual XPath) is a language for querying a conceptual base that results from the integration of XML sources. The considered conceptual model is based on ORM/NIAM [18] and defines *concepts* and *relationships* between concepts. We use this model because it is the model used in the schema integration module that we have developed in previous work [19,20]. However, the language and the translation process do not depend on this particular data model and should be easily adapted to other variants of the ER model. Two types of concepts are supported in this model: lexical and non-lexical. A *lexical concept*

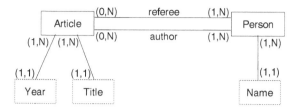

Fig. 1. An example of a conceptual schema

models information that has an associated textual content, like #PCDATA elements and attributes. A *non-lexical concept* models information that is composed by other information, like elements that have sub-elements. An *association relationship* is a binary relationship with cardinality constraints. Relationship names and roles may be optionally defined on it.

Figure 1 shows a conceptual schema for a domain of bibliographical references. Article is a non-lexical concept (solid rectangle), being composed by information about *Title, Year* and *Person* (authors and referees). *Title, Year* and *Name* are lexical concepts (dotted rectangles), holding textual information. An association relationship is defined between *Article* and *Year*, denoting that an article has one associated year information, and a year is associated to one or more articles. A named association relationship *referee* is defined between *Article* and *Person*, denoting that a person may be a referee of several articles.

A *CXPath* query specifies an *XPath 1.0*-like *path expression* to reach information that must be retrieved, with optional selection predicates that may be defined on this path. Although they are based on the *XPath 1.0* syntax, *CXPath* and *XPath 1.0* have different semantics because they are applied to different data models. *XPath 1.0* is suitable for navigating in XML documents that are tree-based structures, whereas *CXPath* is suitable for navigating in the conceptual base that is a graph based structure. These differences in the data model impose several differences on the languages, as described below.

– *concept names instead of element names*
  In *XPath*, XML elements are referred by their labels (element names). In *CXPath*, concept names are used instead of element names. A concept name refers to all instances of that concept in the conceptual base.

– *root element and absolute path expressions*
  An XML instance has a *root element*. An *XPath* expression that begins with slash (an *absolute* path expression) starts navigating from the root element. The conceptual base does not have this root element. The *CXPath* semantics for the absolute path expression is that the navigation source is the entire conceptual base, i.e. the navigation may start at any concept in the conceptual base.

Example 1. Retrieve all instances of concept Article:

/Article

- *navigation operator (slash operator) and relative path expressions*
  In *XPath*, the slash operator, when not appearing at first place in a path expression, has the semantics of "navigate to the child elements". As the conceptual base is a graph and not a tree, this semantics has been changed to "navigate to the related elements".

Example 2. Retrieve all instances of concept Title that are related to the instances of concept Article:

/Article/Title

Further, in *XPath* a path expression may contain other path expressions. For example, the path expression /Article[Year = "2003"]/Title contains the path expression Year. This is a *relative* path expression. In *XPath* the context of evaluation of a relative path expression is the set of child elements of an Article instance. As with the slash operator, in *CXPath* the context of evaluation in which a relative path expression is evaluated has been changed from "all child elements" (*XPath*) to "all related elements" (*CXPath*).

Example 3. Retrieve all instances of concept Title that are related to those instances of concept Article that are related to instances of concept Year with value 2003:

/Article[Year = "2003"]/Title

In this path expression, the context of evaluation of the path expression Year is the set of all concepts related to *Article*. Thus, Year refers to the set of all *Year* instances that are related to *Article* instances.

- *qualified navigation operator - relationship name*
  When more than one relationship relates two concepts, the identification of a specific relationship to be navigated may be needed. For example, the expression /Article/Person refers to all instances of Person that are related to instances of Article, thus including authors and referees. If a specific relationship (author or referee in the example) is to be navigated, the name of the relationship may appear in curly brackets after the slash operator.

Example 4. Retrieve all names of persons that are authors of articles produced in the year 2003:

/Article[Year = "2003"]/{author}Person/Name

In this example, the qualified navigation operator "/{author}" specifies the navigation to only those instance that are related through the relationship named author.

- *qualified navigation operator - role name*
  In the case of self-relationships, the *role name* may be needed to indicate the direction of navigation.

Example 5. Consider the conceptual schema depicted in Figure 2.
The following *CXPath* query retrieves the names of all husbands in current marriages:

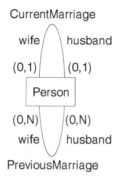

Fig. 2. Examples of self-relationships in a conceptual schema

`/Person/{CurrentMarriage.husband}Person/Name`

– *hierarchical operators*

All *XPath* operators that refer explicitly or implicitly to the navigation to ancestors (e.g.: ".." or "ancestor" operator) or descendents (e.g.: "//" operator) do not appear in *CXPath*. As stated before, just the *XPath* slash operator remains, but its semantics has been changed from "navigate to the child elements" to "navigate to the related elements".

The production rules of the *CXPath* grammar are shown in the Appendix. This grammar does not contain all language operators but only those that are relevant to the understanding of the proposed approach.

3 Mapping Information

In order to translate a *CXPath* query to an *XPath* query, mapping information between the conceptual and XML schemata is required. In the literature of database integration, two approaches are usually employed to define mapping information: a *mapping catalog* or *views* [5]. In the mapping catalog approach, constructs in the global schema are mapped into constructs in the logical schema. In the view approach, a query statement (view) for each global concept and relationship is defined describing which corresponding data must be retrieved from local sources. We chose the view approach. For each construct at the conceptual level an *XPath* query that retrieves the set of instances in the XML source is defined. This approach was chosen because it simplifies the translation mechanism, as each reference to a concept in a *CXPath* query is directly replaced by the corresponding *XPath* expression.

XPath expressions are associated to each *concept* and to each *traversal direction of each relationship* in the conceptual schema. One *XPath* expression is associated to each XML source.

Table 1. Mapping information to the conceptual schema of Figure 1

Concept/Relationship	Mapping to XML Source 1	Mapping to XML Source 2
Article	/references/paper	/publications/author/article
Person	/references/paper/* [local-name(.)='author' or local-name(.)='referee']	/publications/author
Title	/references/paper/@title	/publications/author/ article/heading
Year	*not applicable*	/publications/author/ article/year
Name	/references/paper/* [local-name(.)='author' or local-name(.)='referee']/name	/publications/author/name
Article$^{\{author\}}\rightarrow$Person	Author	..
Article$\leftarrow^{\{author\}}$Person	[local-name(.) = "author"]/..	article
Article$^{\{referee\}}\rightarrow$Person	Referee	*not applicable*
Article$\leftarrow^{\{referee\}}$Person	[local-name(.) = "referee"]/..	*not applicable*
Article$\rightarrow$Title	@title	heading
Article$\leftarrow$Title	..	..
Article$\rightarrow$Year	*not applicable*	year
Article$\leftarrow$Year	*not applicable*	..
Person$\rightarrow$Name	name	name
Person$\leftarrow$Name	..	..

To exemplify the mapping between *CXPath* and *XPath*, consider that the conceptual schema of Figure 1 is a unified abstraction of the XML sources 1 and 2, shown at Figure 3 (a) and (b), respectively.

Table 1 depicts the mapping information from concepts and relationships of the conceptual schema to the XML sources 1 and 2.

The mapping information from a *concept* to an XML source is an absolute *XPath* expression that defines the hierarchy of elements that must be searched to reach the corresponding element or attribute. The mappings from *Article* and *Title*[1] to the XML source 1 are examples (see Table 1). When a concept has more than one corresponding element or attribute in an XML source, the *XPath* mapping expression must refer to the union of the corresponding elements. One example is the concept *Person* that matches *author* and *referee* in XML source 1 (the `local-name` function returns the name of an element). Another example is the mapping of the concept *Name* to the XML source 1.

The mapping information from a *relationship* C_1-C_2 to an XML source is a *relative XPath expression* that denotes how to navigate from the element corresponding to concept C_1 to the element corresponding to concept C_2 (and vice-versa) in this source. Mappings for both traversal directions are defined. The mapping of the relationship *Person-Name* to the XML source 2 is an example. In this source, the element `name` (corresponding to concept *Name*) is a sub-element of the element `author` (corresponding to concept *Person*). The Person$\rightarrow$Name navigation direction is mapped to this XML source by the relative path `"name"`. This path expression allows the navigation to *name* elements, when the context is an `author` element. Analogously, the *Person$\leftarrow$Name* navigation direction is mapped to `".."`. This path expression allows the navigation in the reverse order, i.e., to `author` elements, when the context is a `name` element.

---

[1] A reference to an attribute A in *XPath* is denoted by $@A$

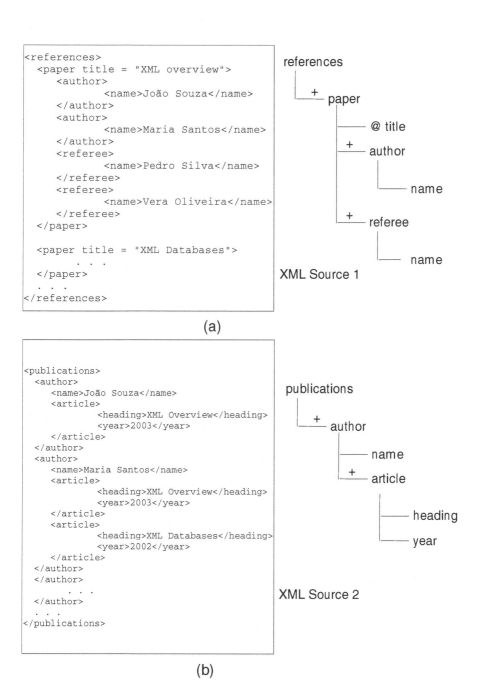

Fig. 3. An example of two XML sources (a) and (b): document and schema

A special case on the mapping definition is a concept C that has more than one corresponding element in an XML source S, one for each relationship R_i it takes part. A mapping from a relationship $C \rightarrow^{\{Ri\}} C_x$ to S must select only those elements in S that correspond to C and take part of relationship R_i. One example is build by concept *Person* and the relationships *referee* and *author* when source 1 is considered. In this source the concept *Person* maps into two elements, `author` and `referee`. A *Person* instance that maps to an `author` element takes part of the *author* relationship, whereas a *Person* instance that maps to an `referee` element takes part of the *referee* relationship. If a navigation starts at an element representing *Person*, the *XPath* expression must assure that the correct element (in the example, an `author` or a `referee`) is used as the source of the navigation. This is achieved by the *XPath* function local-name(), that results in the name of an element. Then, the mapping from $Article^{\{referee\}} \leftarrow Person$ to XML source 1, as shown in Table 1, is the following *XPath* expression:

$$\texttt{[local-name(.) = "referee"]/..}$$

This predicate guarantees that the source element of the navigation is an element of type referee, before navigating to the *paper* element (that represents to concept *Article*).

In general, *XPath predicates* must be defined in a mapping information every time a specific semantic intention must be checked to provide a correct relationship mapping. To exemplify another situation, suppose that a concept *Person* has two relationships with a concept *Address* named *Home* and *Office* (home and office addresses of a person, respectively). If an XML source defines an element `person` with two sub-elements `address`, where the first one is the home address, the mapping from the relationship $Person^{\{home\}} \rightarrow Address$ to this source should be `Address[position() = 1]`. The *XPath* function `position()` verifies if the occurrence of the sub-element `Address` to be searched is equal to 1.

We assume that the mapping information for the XML sources is semi-automatically generated by a *semantic integration module* when the XML schemata of these sources are integrated. Such a module is discussed elsewhere [19, 20].

4   CXPath to XPath Translation

The *CXPath* to *XPath* translation applies a *rewriting strategy*, i.e., each reference to a concept as well as each relationship traversal found in the *CXPath* expression are replaced by their corresponding mapping information to the considered XML source.

The translation process of an input *CXPath* query to an output *XPath* query for an XML source basically proceeds as follows:

- The input is analyzed from left to right.
- Tokens found in the input are written to the output, with some exceptions:

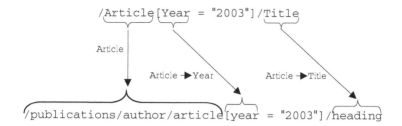

Fig. 4. Example of *CXPath* to *XPath* query translation (I)

- the first slash of an absolute *CXPath* expression is not written to the output;
- each *concept* found in the input will be substituted by an *XPath* expression as shown below;
- a qualified navigation operator in the form /{*Rel*} or /{*Rel.role*} is substituted in the output by the slash operator.

- When the first concept C_a of an *absolute CXPath* expression is found, the *XPath* expression that maps the concept C_a to the source is written to the output. This is always an absolute expression.
- Each other concept C_r found in the input has a context, i.e., it is *relative* to some other concept C_c. When such a relative concept C_r is found in the input, the *XPath* expression that maps the traversal of the relationship from the context concept C_c to the relative concept C_r ($C_c \rightarrow C_r$) is written to the output. If the concept C_r is preceded by an expression in the form {*Rel*} or {*Rel.role*}, this expression is used to select which mapping expression will be used.

In the following, some examples of query translations are presented. Such examples take into account the mapping information shown in Table 1.

Translation 1. The *CXPath* query defined in Figure 4 retrieves titles of articles from the 2003 year. This translation is performed to XML source 2.

The left-to-right analysis of the *CXPath* expression starts with the concept *Article*. As *Article* is the first concept in an absolute *CXPath* path expression, the *XPath* expression /publications/author/article that maps the concept *Article* is written to the output. In the sequence, the construct "[" is written to the output and the concept *Year* is found. *Year* is a relative concept and its context is *Article*. Thus, the mapping for the relationship navigation *Article→Year* (year) is written to the output. The remaining tokens of the predicate are written to the output, as well as the construct "/" that follows. Finally, the relative concept *Title* is found. The context of this concept is still *Article*. Therefore, the mapping of the relationship navigation *Article→Title* (heading) is written to the output.

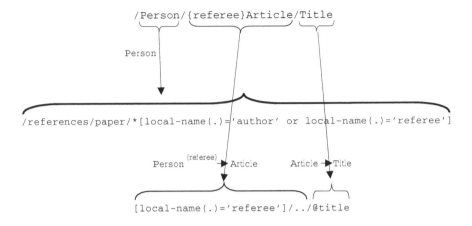

Fig. 5. Example of *CXPath* to *XPath* query translation (II)

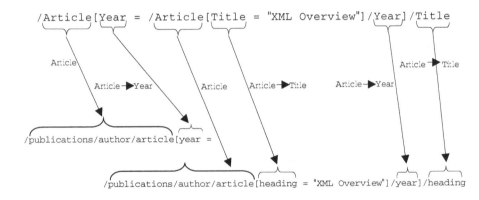

Fig. 6. Example of *CXPath* to *XPath* query translation (III)

Translation 2. A more complex example of query translation is shown in Figure 5. It illustrates the translation of a *CXPath* query that contains a qualified navigation expression (/{referee}). This *CXPath* query retrieves titles of refereed articles. This query is translated to the XML source 1.

The query translation starts with the mapping of the absolute *CXPath* path expression /**Person**. When the relative concept *Article* is found, the context concept is *Person*. As the concept *Article* is preceded by the qualification **referee** the mapping for the relationship navigation $Person^{\{referee\}} \rightarrow Article$ is written to the output.

Notice in this example the use of the local-name(.) function as described in Section 3.

Translation 3. This last example of query translation, shown at Figure 6, illustrates the recursive translation of an embedded absolute *CXPath* query. The presented query retrieves titles of articles that were written in the same year of the article with title *"XML Overview"*. This query is translated to the XML source 2.

Initially, the absolute *CXPath* path expression `/Article` is identified and the mapping of the concept *Article* is performed. In the sequence, the "[" operator is written to the output and the relationship *Article→Year* is identified and mapped to XML source 2. At this point, the embedded absolute *CXPath* expression `/Article[Title = "XML Overview"]/Year` is identified. Thus, the translation process is recursively applied to it.

5   Conclusion and Future Work

This paper proposes an approach to deal with the problem of querying several XML sources through a conceptual schema that unifies the schemata of these sources. The contributions of this work are the following:

- *CXPath*, an *XPath* based language for building queries over a conceptual schema that is an abstraction of several XML sources;
- a strategy for defining mapping information related to concepts and relationships of the conceptual schema that is also based on *XPath* views; and
- a translation mechanism from *CXPath* queries to *XPath* queries that deals with the problem of schematic heterogeneity when a high level query over a conceptual schema must be converted to a query over an XML source.

However, other issues related to the problem of querying heterogeneous data sources through a global unified schema are still open.

In this paper, the translation process considers a single XML source. The problem of *query decomposition*, i.e., the problem of deciding how a query against a global schema that unifies several XML sources is translated to queries against those several sources must be investigated.

The *XPath* query generated by the translation of a *CXPath* query is not optimized. For example, the *XPath* query which results from the translation process in Figure 5:

```
/references/paper/*[local-name(.)='author' or local-name(.)=
        'referee'][local-name(.)="referee"]/../@title
```

could be optimized to:

```
/references/paper/referee/../@title.
```

Another future work is the application of W3C *XQuery* [7] or a variant of it as the language for querying the conceptual schema. *XPath* itself is more a language to refer to parts of XML documents than properly a query language able to build new XML instances. This role is played in the W3C standard by *XQuery*. As *XQuery* embeds *XPath*, the use of *XQuery+CXPath* as the conceptual level language should be investigated.

References

1. *Extensible Markup Language* – XML. Available at: *http://www.w3.org/XML.*
2. Bradley, N. The *XML Companion.* Addison-Wesley Longmann Limited, 2ed., 2000. 435p.
3. Busse, S.; Kutshce R.; Leser, U.; Weber, H. *Federated Information Systems: Concepts, Terminology and Architectures.* Technical Report 99–9, Universität Berlin, 1999.
4. *W3C Semantic Web.* Available at: *http://www.w3.org/2001/sw.*
5. Elmagarmid, A.; Rusinkiewicz, M.; Sheth, *A. Management of Heterogeneous and Autonomous Database Systems.* Morgan Kaufmann Publishers, Inc., 1999. 413p.
6. Mello, R.S.; Heuser, C.A. A Bottom-Up Approach for Integration of XML Sources. In: *International Workshop on Information Integration on the Web (WIIW'2001),* pp. 118–124, Rio de Janeiro, Brazil, apr, 2001.
7. *XQuery 1.0 and XPath 2.0 Data Model.* Available at: *http://www.w3.org/TR/query-datamodel.*
8. Parent, C.; Spaccapietra S. An Entity-Relationship Algebra. *In: 1st International Conference on Data Engineering (ICDE),* pp. 500–507, Los Angeles, USA, IEEE Computer Society, apr, 1984.
9. Campbell, D. M.; Embley, D. W.; Czejdo, B. D. A Relationally Complete Query Language for an Entity-Relationship Model. In: *4th International Conference on Entity-Relationship Approach,* pp. 90–97, Chicago, USA, North-Holland, oct, 1985.
10. *ANSI/ISO/IEC 9075-2* – Information Technology – Database Languages – SQL. 1999.
11. ODMG Home Page. Available at: *http://www.odmg.org.*
12. Abiteboul, S.; Quass, D.; McHugh, J.; Widom, J.; Wiener, J. L. The Lorel Query Language for Semistructured Data. *International Journal on Digital Libraries,* v.1, n.1, 1997, pp. 68–88.
13. *XML Path Language* – *XPath.* Available at: *http://www.w3.org/TR/xpath.*
14. Rodriguez-Gianolli, P.; Mylopoulos, J. A Semantic Approach to XML-Based Data Integration. In: *20th International Conference on Conceptual Modeling (ER'2001),* pp. 117–132, Yokohama, Japan, Springer-Verlag, nov, 2001.
15. Bergamaschi, S.; Castano, S.; Beneventano, D.; Vincini, M. Semantic Integration of Heterogeneous Information Sources. *Data Knowledge Engineering,* v.36, n.1, mar, 2001, pp. 215–249.
16. Vdovjak, R.; Houben, G. RDF-Based Architecture for Semantic Integration of Heterogeneous Information Sources. In: *International Workshop on Information Integration on the Web (WIIW'2001),* pp. 51–57, Rio de Janeiro, Brazil, apr, 2001.
17. Jensen, M.R.; Moller, T.H.; Pedersen, T.B. Converting XML Data to UML Diagrams for Conceptual Data Integration. In: *1st International Workshop on Data Integration over the Web (DIWeb) at 13th Conference on Advanced Information Systems Engineering (CAISE'01),* Interlaken, Switzerland, jun, 2001.
18. Halphin, T. Object-Role Modeling (ORM/NIAM). *Handbook on Architectures of Information Systems.* Springer-Verlag, 1998. p. 81–102.
19. Mello, R.S.; Heuser, C.A. A Rule-Based Convertion of a DTD to a Conceptual Schema. In: *20th International Conference on Conceptual Modeling (ER'2001),* pp. 133–148, Yokohama, Japan, Springer-Verlag, nov, 2001.
20. Mello, R.S.; Castano, S.; Heuser, C.A. A Method for the Unification of XML Schemata. *Information and Software Technology,* v.44, n.4, mar, 2002, pp. 241–249.

Appendix: CXPath Grammar

This appendix contains the syntax of the *CXPath* language. The initial symbol of grammar is *CXPathExpr*. The names of the majority of productions rules are identical to those used in the *XPath 1.0* grammar available at the W3C site *(http://www.w3.org/TR/xpath)*

```
CXPathExpr ::= ("/" RelativePathExpr?) | RelativePathExpr
RelativePathExpr ::= StepExpr ("/" StepExpr)*
StepExpr ::= (ForwardStep) Predicates
ForwardStep ::= ("{"RelationshipName(("}")|("." RoleName "}"))?
                NodeTest
Predicates ::= ( "[" (CXPathExpr) (GeneralComp
                                   (literal|CXPathExpr))? "]" )  *
GeneralComp    ::=    "=" |  "!=" |  "<" |  "<=" |  ">" |  ">="
Literal ::= NumericLiteral | StringLiteral
NumericLiteral ::= IntegerLiteral | DecimalLiteral | DoubleLiteral
StringLiteral ::= ('"'(('"' '"')|[^"])*'"')|("'"(("'"'"
               "'")|[^'])*"'")
IntegerLiteral ::= Digits
DecimalLiteral ::= ("." Digits) |  (Digits "." [0-9]*)
DoubleLiteral ::= (("." Digits)|(Digits("."[0-9]*)?))("e"|
                "E")("+" | "-")? Digits
Digits ::= [0-9]+
NodeTest ::= QName
RelationshipName ::= QName
RoleName ::= QName
VarName ::= QName
QName ::= (Letter) (NCNameChar)*
NCNameChar ::= Letter | Digit | "_"
Letter ::= [a-z|A-Z]+
```

Analysis of Web Services Composition Languages: The Case of BPEL4WS

Petia Wohed[1*], Wil M.P. van der Aalst[2,3], Marlon Dumas[3], and Arthur H.M. ter Hofstede[3]

[1] Department of Computer and Systems Sciences
Stockholm University/The Royal Institute of Technology, Sweden
`petia@dsv.su.se`
[2] Department of Technology Management
Eindhoven University of Technology, The Netherlands
`w.m.p.v.d.aalst@tm.tue.nl`
[3] Centre for Information Technology Innovation
Queensland University of Technology, Australia
`{m.dumas,a.terhofstede}@qut.edu.au`

Abstract. Web services composition is an emerging paradigm for application integration within and across organizational boundaries. A landscape of languages and techniques for web services composition has emerged and is continuously being enriched with new proposals from different vendors and coalitions. However, little effort has been dedicated to systematically evaluate the capabilities and limitations of these languages and techniques. The work reported in this paper is a step in this direction. It presents an in-depth analysis of the Business Process Execution Language for Web Services (BPEL4WS) with respect to a framework composed of workflow and communication patterns.

1 Introduction

Web Services is a rapidly emerging paradigm for architecting and implementing business collaborations within and across organizational boundaries. In this paradigm, the functionalities provided by business applications are encapsulated within web services: software components described at a semantic level, which can be invoked by application programs or by other services through a stack of Internet standards including HTTP, XML, SOAP, WSDL, and UDDI [7]. Once deployed, web services provided by various organizations can be inter-connected in order to implement business collaborations, leading to *composite web services*.

Business collaborations require long-running interactions driven by explicit process models [1]. Accordingly, it is a natural choice to capture the logic of a composite web service using business process modeling languages tailored for web services. Many such languages have recently emerged, including WSCI [20], BPML [6], BPEL4WS [8], BPSS [19], and XPDL [23], with little effort being

---

* Research conducted while at the Queensland University of Technology.

I.-Y. Song et al. (Eds.): ER 2003, LNCS 2813, pp. 200–215, 2003.
© Springer-Verlag Berlin Heidelberg 2003

dedicated to their evaluation with respect to common benchmarks. The comparative evaluation of these languages would contribute to ongoing standardization and development efforts, by identifying their relative strengths and weaknesses, delimiting their capabilities and limitations, and detecting ambiguities.

As a step in this direction, this paper analyses one of these emerging languages, namely BPEL4WS. An evaluation of BPML can be found in [2] and is briefly summarized in Section 4. Similar evaluations of other languages for web services composition will be conducted in the future.

Approach. The analysis is based on a set of *patterns*: abstracted forms of recurring situations encountered at various stages of software development [12]. Specifically, the analysis framework brings together a set of *workflow patterns* documented in [5], and a set of *communication patterns* documented in [16].

The workflow patterns (WPs) have been compiled from an analysis of workflow languages. They capture typical *control flow* dependencies encountered in workflow modeling. More than 12 commercial Workflow Management Systems (WFMS) as well as the UML Activity Diagrams notation, have been evaluated in terms of their support for these patterns [5,10]. Since the functionalities abstracted by the WPs are also required for capturing interactions between web services, these patterns are arguably suitable for analysing languages for web services composition.

The Communication Patterns (CPs) on the other hand, relate to the way in which system modules interact in the context of Enterprise Application Integration (EAI). Given the strong overlap between EAI and web services composition, both requiring the representation of *communication flows* between distributed processes, the communication patterns defined for EAI provide an arguably suitable framework for the analysis of web services composition languages.

The evaluation framework therefore focuses on the control-flow and the communication perspectives. In particular, it excludes the data manipulation and the resource allocation perspectives (e.g. partner selection). The argument is that data manipulation and resource allocation can be treated separately from control-flow and communication, and that a separate framework could be designed for evaluating languages with respect to these other perspectives. Although data manipulation (e.g. counters and boolean variables used as flags) can be used for capturing control-flow aspects, this is undesirable, not only because it breaks the principle of separation of concerns, but more importantly, because it hinders the applicability of verification and analysis techniques to the resulting process models [13].

Overview of BPEL4WS. BPEL4WS builds on IBM's WSFL (Web Services Flow Language) and Microsoft's XLANG. Accordingly, it combines the features of a block structured process language (XLANG) with those of a graph-based process language (WSFL). BPEL4WS is intended for modeling two types of processes: executable and abstract processes. An *abstract process* is a business protocol specifying the message exchange behavior between different parties without revealing the internal behavior of any of them. An *executable process* specifies the execution order between a number of constituent *activities*, the *partners* involved, the *messages* exchanged between these partners, and the *fault* and *exception handling* mechanisms.

A BPEL4WS process specification is a kind of flow-chart. Each element in the process is called an *activity*. An activity is either *primitive* or *structured*. The primitive activity types are: invoke (to invoke an operation of a web service described in WSDL); receive (to wait for a message from an external source); reply (to reply to an external source); wait (to remain idle for some time); assign (to copy data from one data *variable* to another); throw (to indicate errors in the execution); terminate (to terminate the entire service instance); and empty (to do nothing).

To enable the representation of complex structures the following *structured activities* are provided: sequence, for defining an execution order; switch, for conditional routing; while, for looping; pick, for race conditions based on events; flow, for parallel routing; and scope, for grouping activities to be treated by the same fault-handler. Structured activities can be nested. Given a set of activities contained within the same flow, the execution order can further be controlled through (control) links, which allow the definition of dependencies between two activities: the target activity may only start when the source activity has ended. Activities can be connected through links to form directed acyclic graphs.

Related Work. BPEL4WS was originally released together with two other specificatons: WS-Coordination (WS-C) and WS-Transaction (WS-T). However, WS-C and WS-T deal with issues orthogonal to control-flow and communication and hence fall outside the scope of this paper. Indeed, WS-C and WS-T are concerned with the coordination of distributed processes, in particular for the purpose of performing ACID and long-running transactions. A comparison of WS-C and WS-T with a competing proposal, namely the Business Transaction Protocol (BTP), is reported in [9].

Existing frameworks for comparing process modeling languages [11,18,17] are coarse-grained and syntactical in nature, addressing questions such as: "does a language offer more operators than another and which ones?", or "does it integrate a given ontological construct?". This contrasts with the functional nature of the workflow patterns approach which addresses questions such as: "does a language provide a given functionality and how?". The analysis presented in this paper is therefore complementary to the above ones.

2   The Workflow Patterns in BPEL4WS

Web services composition and workflow management are related in the sense that both are concerned with executable processes. Therefore, much of the functionality in workflow management systems [3,15] is also relevant for web services composition languages like BPEL4WS, XLANG, and WSFL. In this section, we consider the 20 workflow patterns presented in [5], and we discuss how and to what extent these patterns can be captured in BPEL4WS. Most of the solutions are presented in a simplified BPEL4WS notation, which is rich enough for capturing the key ideas of the solutions, while avoiding irrelevant coding details.

The description of the first pattern, namely **Sequence**, is ommitted since it is trivially supported by the BPEL4WS construct with the same name.

WP2 Parallel Split. A point in a process where a single thread of control splits into multiple threads which can be executed in parallel, thus allowing activities to be executed simultaneously or in any order [21]. **Example:** After activity *new cellphone subscription order*, the activity *insert new subscription* in Home Location Registry application and *insert new subscription* in Mobile answer application are executed in parallel.

WP3 Synchronization. A point in the process where multiple parallel branches converge into a single thread of control, thus synchronizing multiple threads [21]. This pattern assumes that after an incoming branch has been completed, it cannot be completed again while the merge is still waiting for other branches to be completed. Also, it is assumed that the threads to be synchronized belong to the same process instance. **Example:** Activity *archive* is executed after the completion of both activity *send tickets* and activity *receive payment*. The *send tickets* and *receive payment* relate to the same client request.

Solutions, WP2 & WP3. The flow construct combined with the sequence construct (for expressing the synchronisation after the flow) provide a straightforwad way to capture these patterns (see Listing 1).

An alternative approach is to use control links inside a flow as shown in Listing 2. In this listing, two links L1 and L2 are defined between two activities A1 and A2 (to be executed in parallel) and an activity B (to be executed after the synchronisation). Note that the joinCondition of the links is of type AND. This ensures that B is only executed if both A1 and A2 are executed.

Listing 1
```
1 <sequence>
2   <flow>
3     activityA1
4     activityA2
5   </flow>
6   activityB
7 </sequence>
```

Listing 2
```
1 <flow name="F">
2   <links>
3     <link name="L1"/>
4     <link name="L2"/>
5   </links>
6   activityA1
7     <source linkName="L1"/>...
8   activityA2
9     <source linkName="L2"/>...
10  activityB
11    joinCondition="L1 AND L2"
12    <target linkName="L1"/>
13    <target linkName="L2"/>...
14 </flow>
```

Listings 1 and 2 illustrate the two styles of process modeling supported by BPEL4WS. Listing 1 shows the "XLANG-style" of modeling (i.e., routing through structured activities). Listing 2 shows the "WSFL-style" of modeling (i.e., using links instead of structured activities). It is also possible to mix both styles by having links crossing the boundaries of structured activities.[1] An example is given in Listing 3, where the sequences Sa and Sb are defined to run in parallel. The definition of link L (lines 3, 7 and 13) implies that activity B2 (which follows B1) can be executed only after activity A1 has completed. In other words, link L captures an intermediate synchronization point between the parallel threads Sa and Sb. This inter-thread synchronization cannot be expressed using structured activities only (for a proof see [14]), so that the solution of the pattern that uses links, is more general than the one without. Figure 1 illustrates the example in graphical form.

Listing 3

```
 1 <flow name="F">
 2   <links>
 3     <link name="L"/>
 4   </links>
 5   <sequence name="Sa">
 6     activityA1
 7       <source linkName="L"/>
 8     activityA2
 9   </sequence>
10   <sequence name="Sb">
11     activityB1
12     activityB2
13       <target linkName="L"/>
14   </sequence>
15 </flow>
```

Figure 1

WP4 **Exclusive Choice.** A point in the process where, based on a decision or control data, one of several branches is chosen. **Example:** The manager is informed if an order exceeds $600, otherwise not.

WP5 **Simple Merge.** A point in the workflow process where two or more alternative branches come together without synchronization. It is assumed that the alternative branches are never executed both in parallel (if it is not the case, then see the patterns Multi-Merge and Discriminator). **Example:** After the payment is received or the credit is granted, the car is delivered to the customer.

Solutions, WP4 & WP5. As in the previous patterns, two solutions are proposed. The first one relies on the activity switch inherited from XLANG (Listing 4). The second solution uses control links (see Listing 5 and Figure 2). The different conditions (C1 and C2 in the example) are specified as transitionConditions, one for each corresponding link (L1 or L2). This implies that the activities specified as targets for these links (A1 and A2 in the example) will be executed

---

[1] However, in order to prevent deadlocks, links are not allowed to cross the boundaries of while loops, serializable scopes, or compensation handlers.

only if the corresponding conditions are fulfilled. An empty activity is the source of links L1 and L2, implying that conditions C1 and C2 are evaluated as soon as the flow is initiated. Activity C is the target of links L1s and L2s whose sources are A1 and A2 respectively, thereby capturing the Simple Merge pattern.

Listing 4

```
1 <switch>
2     <case condition="C1">
3         activityA1
4     </case>
5     <case condition="C2">
6         activityA2
7     </case>
8 </switch>
9 activityC
```

Figure 2

Listing 5

```
1 <flow>
2   <links>
3     <link name="L1"/>
4     <link name="L2"/>
5     <link name="L1s"/>
6     <link name="L2s"/>
7   </links>
8   <empty>
9     <source linkName="L1"
10        transitionCondition="C1"/>
11    <source linkName="L2"
12        transitionCondition="C2"/>
13   </empty>
14   activityA1
15     <target linkName="L1">
16     <source linkName="L1s">
17   activityA2
18     <target linkName="L2">
19     <source linkName="L2s">
20   activityC
21     joinCondition="L1s OR L2s"
22     <target linkName="L1s">
23     <target linkName="L2s"> ...
24 </flow>
```

A difference between these two solutions is that in the solution of Listing 4 only one activity is triggered, the first one for which the specified condition evaluates to true. Meanwhile, in the solution of Listing 5 multiple branches may be triggered if more than one of the conditions evaluate to true.

WP6 Multi-Choice. A point in the process, where, based on a decision or control data, a number of branches are chosen and executed as parallel threads. **Example:** After executing the activity *evaluate damage* the activity *contact fire department* or the activity *contact insurance company* is executed. At least one of these activities is executed, and it is possible that both need to be executed.

WP7 Synchronizing Merge. A point in a process where multiple paths converge into a single one. Some of these paths are executed and some are not. If only one path is executed, the activity after the merge is triggered as soon as this path completes. If more than one path is executed, synchronization of all executed paths needs to take place before the next activity is triggered. It is an assumption of this pattern that a branch that has already been executed, cannot be executed again while the merge is still waiting for other branches to complete. **Example:** After one or both of the activities *contact fire department* and *contact insurance company* have completed (depending on whether they were executed at all), the activity submit report needs to be performed (exactly once).

Solutions, WP6 & WP7. The solution of WP6 and WP7 are identical to the WSFL-style solutions of WP4 and WP5 (Listing 5). This follows from the *dead-path elimination* principle, according to which the truth value of an incoming link is propagated to its outgoing link. In the example of Listing 5, if condition C1 (C2) evaluates to true, activity A1 (A2) receives a positive value and is therefore executed. On the other hand, if condition C1 (C2) evaluates to false, activity A1 (A2) receives a negative value, and it is not executed but still propagates the negative value through its outgoing link L1s (L2s). In particular, both A1 and A2 are executed if the two conditions C1 and C2 evaluate to true. In any case, the OR joinCondition attached to C, ensures that C is always executed, provided that one of the activities A1 or A2 is executed.

WP8 Multi-Merge. A point in a process where two or more branches reconverge without synchronization. If more than one incoming branch is executed, the activity following the merge is started once for each completion of an incoming branch. **Example:** Two activities *audit application* and *process applications* running in parallel should both be followed by an activity *close case*. Activity *close case* should be executed twice if both activities *audit application* and *process applications* are executed.

Solution, WP8. BPEL4WS offers no direct support for WP8. Neither XLANG nor WSFL allow multiple (possibly concurrent) activations of an activity following a point where multiple paths converge. In the example, the *close case* activity cannot be activated once after completion of *audit application*, and again after completion of *process applications*.

WP9 Discriminator. A point in the workflow process that waits for one of the incoming branches to complete before activating the subsequent activity. From that moment on it waits for all remaining branches to complete and 'ignores' them. Once all incoming branches have been triggered, it resets itself so that it can be triggered again (which is important otherwise it could not really be used in the context of a loop). **Example:** To improve query response time a complex search is sent to two different databases over the Internet. The first one that comes up with the result should proceed the flow. The second result is ignored.

Solution, WP9. This pattern is not directly supported in BPEL4WS. Neither is there a structured activity construct which can be used for implementing it, nor can links be used for capturing it. The reason for not being able to use links with an OR joinCondition is that a joinCondition is only evaluated when the status of all incoming links are determined and not, as required in this case, when the first positive link is determined.

WP10 Arbitrary Cycles. A point where a portion of the process (including one or more activities and connectors) needs to be "visited" repeatedly without imposing restrictions on the number, location, and nesting of these points.

Solution, WP10. This pattern is not supported in BPEL4WS. The while activity can only capture structured cycles, i.e. loops with one entry point and one exit point. On the other hand, the restrictions made in BPEL4WS that links should not cross the boundaries of a loop, and that links should not create cycles, entail that it is not possible to capture arbitrary cycles using control links. Note that there exist non-structured cycles that cannot be unfolded into structured ones [14], unless process variables are used to encode control-flow aspects.

WP11 Implicit Termination. A given subprocess terminates when there is nothing left to do (without having to specify an explicit termination activity).

Solution, WP11. The pattern is directly supported since in BPEL4WS there is no need to explicitly specify a termination activity.

WP12 MI without Synchronization. Within the context of a single case multiple instances of an activity may be created, i.e. there is a facility for spawning off new threads of control, all of them independent of each other. The instances might be created consecutively, but they will be able to run in parallel, which distinguishes this pattern from the pattern for Arbitrary Cycles. **Example:** When booking a trip, the activity *book flight* is executed multiple times if the trip involves multiple flights.

Solution, WP12. Multiple instances of an activity can be created by using the invoke activity embedded in a while loop (see Listing 6). The invoked process, i.e., process B, has to have the attribute createInstance within its receive activity assigned to "yes" (see Listing 7).

WP13-WP15 MI with Synchronization. A point in a workflow where a number of instances of a given activity are initiated, and these instances are later synchronized, before proceeding with the rest of the process. In WP13 the number of instances to be started/synchronized is known at design time. In WP14 the number is known at some stage during run time, but before the initiation of the instances has started. In WP15 the number of instances to be created is not known in advance: new instances are created on demand, until no more instances are required. **Example of WP15:** When booking a trip, the activity *book flight* is executed multiple times if the trip involves multiple flights. Once all bookings are made, an invoice is sent to the client. How many bookings are made is only known at runtime through interaction with the user.

Solutions, WP13-WP15. If the number of instances to be synchronized is known at design time (WP13), a solution is to replicate the activity as many times as it needs to be instantiated, and run the replicas in parallel by placing them in a flow activity. The solution becomes more complex if the number of instances to be created and synchronized is only known at run time (WP14), or not known (WP15) – see Listing 8. In this solution a pick activity within a while loop is used, enabling repetitive processing triggered by three different messages: one indicating that a new instance is required, one indicating the completion of a previously initiated instance, and one indicating that no more instances need to be created. Depending on the message received an activity is performed/invoked in each iteration of the loop. However, this is only a work-around solution since the logic of these patterns is encoded by means of a loop and a counter: the counter is incremented when a new instance is created, and decremented each time that an instance is completed. The loop is exited when the value of the counter is zero and no more instances need to be created.

Listing 6
```
1 <processA>
2   <while cond="C1">
3     <invoke processB ... >
4     </invoke>
5   </while>
6 </process>
```

Listing 7
```
1 <processB>
2   <receive processA ...
3     createInstance="yes">
4   </receive>
5 </process>
```

Listing 8
```
1 moreInstances:=True
2 i:=0
3 <while moreInstances OR i>0>
4   <pick>
5     <onMessage StartNewActivityA>
6       invoke activityA
7       i:=i+1
8     </onMessage>
9     <onMessage ActivityAFinished>
10      i:=i-1
11    </onMessage>
12    <onMessage NoMoreInstances>
13      moreInstances:=False
14    </onMessage>
15  </pick>
16 </while>
```

WP 16 Deferred Choice. A point in a process where one among several alternative branches is chosen based on information which is not necessarily available when this point is reached. This differs from the normal exclusive choice in that the choice is not made immediately when the point is reached, but instead several alternatives are offered, and the choice between them is delayed until the occurrence of some event. **Example:** When a contract is finalized, it has to be reviewed and signed either by the director or by the operations manager. Both the director and the operations manager would be notified and the first one who is available will proceed with the review.

Solution, WP16. This pattern is directly supported by the pick construct, which effectively waits for an occurence of one among several possible events before continuing the execution according to the event that occurred.

WP 17 Interleaved Parallel Routing. A set of activities is executed in an arbitrary order. Each activity in the set is executed exactly once. The order between the activities is decided at run-time: it is not until one activity is completed that the decision on what to do next is taken. In any case, no two activities in the set can be active at the same time. **Example:** At the end of each year, a bank executes two activities for each account: *add interest* and *charge credit* *card costs.* These activities can be executed in any order. However, since they both update the account, they cannot be executed at the same time.

Solution, WP17. It is possible to capture this pattern in BPEL4WS using the concept of serializable scopes (see Listing 9). A serializable scope is an activity of type scope whose variableAccessSerializable attribute is set to "yes", thereby guaranteeing concurrency control on shared variables. The activities to be interleaved are placed in different variables which all write to a single shared variable (variable C in Listing 9). Since the activities are placed in different variables, they can potentially be executed in parallel. On the other hand, since the serializable scopes that contain the activities write to the same variable, no two of them will be "active" simultaneously, but instead, they will be executed one after the other. Three things are worth pointing out with respect to this solution. Firstly, the semantics of serializable scopes in BPEL4WS is not clearly defined. The BPEL4WS specification only states that this semantics is "similar to the standard isolation level 'serializable' of database transactions", but it does not specify where the similarity stops (e.g. how does the underlying transaction model deal with or prevent serialization conflicts?). Secondly, it is not possible in this solution to externally influence (at runtime) the order in which the activities are executed: instead, this order is fixed by the transaction manager of the underlying BPEL4WS engine. Finally, since serializable scopes are not allowed to be nested, this solution is not applicable if one occurrence of the interleaved parallel routing pattern is embedded within another occurrence.

To overcome these limitations, a work-around solution using deferred choice (i.e. pick) as proposed in [5] can be applied (see Listing 10). The drawback of this solution is its complexity, which increases exponentially with the number of activities to be interleaved.

Listing 9

```
1 <flow>
2   <scope name=S1
3     variableAccessSerializable:="yes">
4     <sequence>
5        write to variable C
6        activityA1
7        write to variable C
8     </sequence>
9   </scope>
10  <scope name=S2
11    variableAccessSerializable:="yes">
12    <sequence>
13       write to variable C
14       activityA2
15       write to variable C
16    </sequence>
17  </scope>
18 </flow>
```

Listing 10

```
1 <pick>
2   <onMessage m1>
3     <sequence>
4        activity A1
5        activity A2
6     </sequence>
7   </onMessage>
8   <onMessage m2>
9     <sequence>
10        activity A2
11        activity A1
12     </sequence>
13   </onMessage>
14 </pick>
```

WP18 Milestone. A given activity E can only be enabled if a certain milestone has been reached which has not yet expired. A milestone is a point in the process where a given activity A has finished and a subsequent activity B has not yet started. **Example:** After having placed a purchase order, a customer can withdraw it at any time before the shipping takes place. To withdraw an order, the customer must complete a withdrawal request form, and this request must be approved by a customer service representative. The execution of the activity *approve order withdrawal* must therefore follow the activity *request withdrawal*, and can only be done if: (i) the activity *place order* is completed, and (ii) the activity *ship order* has not yet started.

Solution, WP18. BPEL4WS does not provide direct support for capturing this pattern. Therefore, a work-around solution using deferred choice, as proposed in [5], has to be applied.

WP19 Cancel Activity & WP20 Cancel Case. A cancel activity terminates a running instance of an activity, while canceling a case leads to the removal of an entire workflow instance. **Example of WP19:** A customer cancels a request for information. **Example of WP20:** A customer withdraws his/her order.

Solutions, WP19 & WP20. WP20 maps directly to the basic activity terminate, which is used to abandon all execution within a business process instance. All currently running activities must be terminated as soon as possible without any fault handling or compensation behavior. WP19 is supported through fault and compensation handlers.

3   The Communication Patterns in BPEL4WS

In this section we evaluate BPEL4WS with respect to the communication patterns presented in [16]. Since communication is realized by exchanging messages between different processes, it is explicitly modeled by sending and receiving messages. Two types of communications are distinguished, namely synchronous and asynchronous communication.

3.1   Synchronous Communication

CP1 Request/Reply. Request/Reply communication is a form of synchronous communication where a sender makes a request to a receiver and waits for a reply before continuing to process. The reply may influence further processing on the sender side.

CP2 One-Way. A form of synchronous communication where a sender makes a request to a receiver and waits for a reply that acknowledges the receipt of the request. Since the receiver only acknowledges the receipt, the reply is empty and only delays further processing on the sender side.

Solutions, CP1 & CP2. The way in which synchronous communication is modeled in BPEL4WS is by the invoke activity included in the requesting process, process A (see Listing 11) and a couple of receive and reply activities in the responding process, process B (see Listing 12). Furthermore, two different variables need to be specified in the invoke activity within process A: one input-Variable, where the outgoing data from the process is stored (or input data for the communication); and one outputVariable, where the incoming data is stored (or the output data from the communication). The One-Way pattern differs from Request/Reply only by B sending its reply (i.e., confirmation) immediately after the message from A has been received.

Listing 11

```
1 <process name="processA">
2   <sequence>
3     . . .
4     <invoke partner="processB" ...
5       inputVariable="Request"
6       outputVariable="Response">
7     </invoke>
8     . . .
9   </sequence>
10 </process>
```

Listing 12

```
1 <process name="processB"> ...
2   <sequence>
3     <receive partner="processA" ...
4       variable="Request">
5     </receive>
6     . . .
7     <reply partner="processA" ...
8       variable="Response">
9     </reply>
10  </sequence>
11 </process>
```

CP3 Synchronous Polling. Synchronous Polling is a form of synchronous communication where a sender dispatches a request to a receiver, but instead of blocking, continues processing. At intervals, the sender checks to see if a reply has been received. When it detects a reply it processes it and stops any further polling. **Example:** During a game session, the system continuously checks if the customer has terminated the game.

Solution, CP3. This pattern is captured through two parallel flows: one for the receipt of the expected response, and one for the sequence of activities not depending on this response (Listing 13, lines 4–7). The initiation of the communication is done beforehand through an invoke action (line 3). To be able to proceed, the invoke action is specified to send data and not wait for a reply. This is indicated by omitting the specification of an outputVariable. The communication for the responding process is the same as for the previous pattern (Listing 12).

Listing 13

```
1 <process name="A"
2   <sequence>
3     <invoke partner="processB" ... inputVariable="Request"...></invoke>
4     <flow>
5       <sequence> ... </sequence>
6       <receive partner="processB" ... variable="Result" ...></receive>
7     </flow>
8     access variable "Result" ...
9   </sequence>
10 </process>
```

3.2   Asynchronous Communication

CP4 Message Passing. Message passing is a form of asynchronous communication where a request is sent from a sender to a receiver. When the sender has made the request it continues processing. The request is delivered to the receiver and is processed. **Example:** When an order is received, a log is notified, before the system executes the order.

Solution, CP4. The solution for this pattern has already been demonstrated as part of the solution for CP3, namely an invoke activity with an inputVariable only (line 3 in Listing 13).

CP5 Publish/Subscribe. A form of asynchronous communication where a request is sent by a process and the receivers are determined by a previous declaration of interest. **Example:** An organization offers information about products to its customers. If the customers are interested in receiving such information, they have to notify a system, which keeps track of interested customers. When product information is going to be distributed to the customers, the organization requests the current list, including the customers' addresses.

CP6 Broadcast. A form of asynchronous communication in which a request is sent to all participants, the receivers, of a network. Each participant determines whether the request is of interest by examining the content. **Example:** Before a system is shut down for maintenance, every client connected to it is informed about the situation.

Solutions, CP5 & CP6. Publish/Subscribe and Broadcast are not directly supported in BPEL4WS. They could be encoded by introducing a service (possibly encoded in BPEL4WS) that acts as a broker between senders and receivers, providing operations for subscribing and posting messages.

4   Discussion

A comparison of BPEL4WS with BPML, WSCI, and XPDL is given in Table 1. The ratings for BPEL4WS are based on the discussions in this paper, those for BPML and WSCI are taken from [2] and those for XPDL are based on a preliminary evaluation. A '+' in a cell of the table refers to direct support (i.e. there is a construct in the language which directly supports the pattern). A '–' indicates that there is no direct support. This does not mean though that it is not possible to realize the pattern through some work-around solution. In fact, any of the patterns can be realized using a standard programming language but this is irrelevant.[2] Sometimes there is a feature that only partially supports a pattern, e.g. a construct that directly supports the pattern but imposes some restrictions on the structure of the process. The support is then rated '+/–'.

---

[2] BPEL4WS, XPDL, and BPML are all Turing complete. They can be used to emulate a Turing machine, and therefore, can theoretically do any calculation. However, this observation is not relevant in the context at hand: Any programming language is

Table 1. Comparison of BPEL4WS, BPML, WSCI, and XPDL using workflow and communication patterns.

pattern	product/standard			
	BPEL	BPML	WSCI	XPDL
Sequence	+	+	+	+
Parallel Split	+	+	+	+
Synchronization	+	+	+	+
Exclusive Choice	+	+	+	+
Simple Merge	+	+	+	+
Multi-Choice	+	−	−	+
Synchronizing Merge	+	−	−	−
Multi-Merge	−	+/−	+/−	+/−
Discriminator	−	−	−	−
Arbitrary Cycles	−	−	−	+
Implicit Termination	+	+	+	+
MI without Synchronization	+	+	+	+
MI with Design Time Knowledge	+	+	+	+
MI with Runtime Knowledge	−	−	−	−
MI without A Priori Runtime Knowledge	−	−	−	−
Deferred Choice	+	+	+	−
Interleaved Parallel Routing	+/−	−	−	−
Milestone	−	−	−	−
Cancel Activity	+	+	+	−
Cancel Case	+	+	+	−
Request/Reply	+	+	+	−[3]
One-Way	+	+	+	−[3]
Synchronous Polling	+	+	+	−[3]
Message Passing	+	+	+	−[3]
Publish/Subscribe	−	−	−	−
Broadcast	−	−	−	−

The following observations can be made from the table:

- As the first five patterns correspond to the basic routing constructs, they are directly supported by all languages.
- BPEL4WS, in contrast to the other language, offers direct support for the Multi Choice and Synchronizing Merge. This is a consequence of the "dead-path elimination" characteristic inherited from WSFL.
- BPEL4WS does not support the Multi-Merge pattern, while BPML directly supports it with some restrictions. This is due to the fact that BPML, unlike BPEL4WS, supports invocation of sub-processes.
- BPEL4WS, BPML, and WSCI support the Deferred Choice. This distinguishes them from many mainstream workflow languages (and from XPDL).
- BPEL4WS, through the concept of serializable scope, is the only language in the table (partially) supporting the Interleaved Parallel Routing pattern.
- None of the compared languages supports *arbitrary* cycles.

Turing-complete, but this does not imply suitability for web services composition. Hence, we consider "direct support" rather than Turing-completeness.

[3] Not supported by XPDL itself, but could be captured using Wf-XML [22].

BPEL4WS is an expressive language when compared to state-of-the-art languages for business process modeling. In particular, languages supported by existing workflow management systems generally provide direct support for only less than half of the workflow patterns [5] and do not provide direct support for inter-process communication. On the negative side, BPEL4WS is a complex language in the sense that it offers many overlapping constructs (i.e. it lacks orthogonality). This is reflected in the multiplicity of possible solutions for the basic patterns, i.e. "XLANG–style" solutions, "WSFL–style" solutions, and solutions combining both styles. In addition, the semantics of BPEL4WS is not always clear, especially for advanced constructs such as control links and serializable scopes. A simplification of the language and a mapping to a formal language (e.g. π–calculus or Petri nets) are therefore desirable. We sugggest that BPEL4WS should be revisited in order to minimise (or eliminate) the overlap between the structured activity constructs (e.g. switch and sequence) on the one hand, and the concept of control-links on the other. This should however be done in such a way as to preserve (or increase) the expressiveness of the language.

An alternative approach to design a language for Web service composition would be to start from a formal process modelling language supporting all the patterns that are relevant for Web service composition, and to refine it in order to incorporate other requirements not captured by the patterns (e.g. interfacing with WSDL and having an XML syntax). In the setting of workflow modelling, this idea is being pursued by the YAWL initiative [4].

BPEL4WS is a communication-oriented language in the sense that all the basic activities supported (except for the assign) are for sending and receiving messages. The communication patterns used in our analysis are directly borrowed from a previous proposal [16]. An analysis based on a more refined set of communication patterns which explicitly take into account aspects such as process creation and correlation is a possible direction for future work.

References

1. W.M.P. van der Aalst. Don't go with the flow: Web services composition standards exposed. *IEEE Intelligent Systems*, 18(1):72–76, January/February 2003.
2. W.M.P. van der Aalst, M. Dumas, A.H.M. ter Hofstede, and P. Wohed. Pattern-Based Analysis of BPML (and WSCI). Technical Report FIT-TR-2002-05, Faculty of IT, Queensland University of Technology, Brisbane, Australia, 2002. www.citi.qut.edu.au/pubs/technical/pattern_based_analysis_BPML.pdf.
3. W.M.P. van der Aalst and K.M. van Hee. *Workflow Management: Models, Methods, and Systems*. MIT press, Cambridge, Massachusetts, 2002.
4. W.M.P. van der Aalst and A.H.M. ter Hofstede. YAWL: Yet Another Workflow Language. Technical Report FIT-TR-2002-06, Faculty of IT, Queensland University of Technology, Brisbane, Australia, 2002. tmitwww.tm.tue.nl/research/patterns/download/yawl_qut_report_FIT-TR-2002-06.pdf.
5. W.M.P. van der Aalst, A.H.M. ter Hofstede, B. Kiepuszewski, and A.P. Barros. Workflow patterns. *Distributed and Parallel Databases*, 14(1):5–51, July 2003.

6. BPML.org. Business Process Modeling Language. Accessed November 2002 from `www.bpmi.org/`, 2002.
7. F. Curbera, M. Duftler, R. Khalaf, W. Nagy, N. Mukhi, and S. Weerawarana. Unraveling the Web Services Web: An Introduction to SOAP, WSDL, and UDDI. *IEEE Internet Computing*, 6(2):86–93, March 2002.
8. F. Curbera, Y. Goland, J. Klein, F. Leymann, D. Roller, S. Thatte, and S. Weerawarana. Business Process Execution Language for Web Services version 1.1. `http://dev2dev.bea.com/techtrack/BPEL4WS.jsp`.
9. S. Dalal, S. Temel, M. Little, M. Potts, and J. Webber. Coordinating Business Transactions on the Web. *IEEE Internet Computing*, 7(1):30–39, January/February 2003.
10. M. Dumas and A.H.M. ter Hofstede. UML Activity Diagrams as a Workflow Specification Language. In M. Gogolla and C. Kobryn, editors, *Proc. of the 4th Int. Conference on the Unified Modeling Language (UML01)*, volume 2185 of *LNCS*, pages 76–90, Toronto, Canada, October 2001. Springer Verlag.
11. P. Green and M. Rosemann. An Ontological Analysis of Integrated Process Modelling. In *Proc. of the 11th International Conference on Advanced Information Systems Engineering (CAiSE)*, pages 225–240, Heidelberg, Germany, June 1999. Springer Verlag.
12. Hillside.net. Patterns Home Page. `http://hillside.net/patterns`, 2000–2002.
13. B. Kiepuszewski. *Expressiveness and Suitability of Languages for Control Flow Modelling in Workflows*. PhD thesis, Queensland University of Technology, Brisbane, Australia, 2003. Available via `http://www.tm.tue.nl/it/research/patterns`.
14. B. Kiepuszewski, A.H.M. ter Hofstede, and C. Bussler. On Structured Workflow Modelling. In B. Wangler and L. Bergman, editors, *Proc. of the 12th Int. Conference on Advanced Information Systems Engineering (CAiSE00)*, volume 1789 of *LNCS*, pages 431–445, Stockholm, Sweden, June 2000. Springer Verlag.
15. F. Leymann and D. Roller. *Production Workflow: Concepts and Techniques*. Prentice-Hall PTR, Upper Saddle River, New Jersey, 1999.
16. W.A. Ruh, F.X. Maginnis, and W.J. Brown. *Enterprise Application Integration: A Wiley Tech Brief*. John Wiley and Sons, Inc, 2001.
17. R. Shapiro. A Comparison of XPDL, BPML and BPEL4WS. Accessed February 2003, `http://xml.coverpages.org/Shapiro-XPDL.pdf`.
18. E. Söderström, B. Andersson, P. Johannesson, E. Perjons, and B. Wangler. Towards a framework for comparing process modelling languages. In *Proceedings of the 14th International Conference on Advanced Information Systems Engineering (CAiSE)*, volume 2348 of *LNCS*, Toronto, Canada, May 2002. Springer.
19. UN/CEFACT and OASIS. ebXML Business Process Specification Schema (Version 1.01). Accessed November 2002 from `www.ebxml.org/specs/ebBPSS.pdf`, 2001.
20. W3C. Web Service Choreography Interface (WSCI) 1.0. Accessed November 2002 from `www.w3.org/TR/wsci/`, 2002.
21. WfMC. Terminology and Glossary. Document WFMC-TC-1011 Issue 3.0, February 1999 `http://www.wfmc.org`.
22. WfMC. Workflow Standard – Interoperability Wf–XML Binding. Document Number WFMC-TC-1023, Final Draft, accessed March 2003 from `http://www.wfmc.org/standards/docs/Wf-XML-11.pdf`, November 2001.
23. WfMC. Workflow Process Definition Interface – XML Process Definition Language. Accessed November 2002 from `www.wfmc.org/standards/docs/TC-1025_10_beta_xpdl_073002.pdf`, 2002.

Extending Conceptual Models for Web Based Applications*

Phillipa Oaks, Arthur H.M. ter Hofstede, David Edmond, and Murray Spork

Centre for Information Technology Innovation
Faculty of Information Technology
Queensland University of Technology
GPO Box 2434, Brisbane, QLD 4001, Australia
{p.oaks,a.terhofstede,d.edmond,m.spork}@qut.edu.au

Abstract. The next phase envisioned for the World Wide Web is auto-mated ad-hoc interaction between intelligent agents, web services, data-bases and semantic web enabled applications. Although at present this appears to be a distant objective, there are practical steps that can be taken to advance the vision. We propose an extension to classical concep-tual models to allow the definition of application components in terms of public standards and explicit semantics, thus building into web-based applications, the foundation for shared understanding and interoperabil-ity. The use of external definitions and the need to store outsourced type information internally, brings to light the issue of object identity in a global environment, where object instances may be identified by multiple externally controlled identification schemes. We illustrate how traditional conceptual models may be augmented to recognise and deal with multiple identities.

1   Introduction

The world wide web (WWW) has already made interaction between people and web pages possible. The next wave of interaction promised by the web is be-tween software applications operating without the need for human intervention. These web-based applications could be federated databases, intelligent agents, grid services, Web services and other kinds of distributed applications.

This vision for web applications involves *loosely coupled* applications operat-ing on different platforms and *interoperating without prior agreements* in place. There are several problems to be solved before the vision can become a reality.

The words, terminology and definitions used to describe a software appli-cation, by its designers and developers, are naturally biased towards their own context and naming conventions. This local terminology may not be understood by users outside of this environment. Shared understanding is a major problem

---

* This work was supported by the Australian Research Council SPIRT Grant "Self-describing transactions operating in a large, open, heterogeneous, and distributed environment" involving QUT, UNSW and GBST Holdings Pty Ltd.

I.-Y. Song et al. (Eds.): ER 2003, LNCS 2813, pp. 216–231, 2003.

for ad-hoc interaction between web applications. One solution is to *reuse* common external definitions, standards and specifications to describe some aspects of an application. For example, the ISO 8601 standard can be used to describe and represent dates.

Unfortunately, universally accepted definitions such as ISO 8601 do not exist for all the things that can be described by web applications. There are efforts underway[1] to create specifications for "universal" descriptions of various aspects of web based business applications but it is unlikely that these one-size-fits-all specifications will be useful for all users in all contexts[2]. In addition, there will be many web applications that are not business related.

It is more likely that vendors and user interest groups will generate many similar standards and specifications that suit their own needs. In this case, web application providers risk a problem similar to vendor lock-in. By selecting one particular standard over another, application providers reduce their user base to those that use the same standard.

A better approach would be to create local definitions similar to application profiles [1,2] that refer to all the standards and specifications that seem to be appropriate in the application context. In this way, applications can be made available to a wide range of users and the reliance on any one particular standard is reduced. These local definitions, based on external definitions and standards, can evolve to incorporate new standards as they are developed and to reflect changes in existing standards and the application environment. At present there are no explicit methods for developing conceptual models for web-based applications that take into account external definitions and specifications.

In this paper we introduce *outsourced types*, an extension to conceptual models. Outsourced types ensure web applications are developed from the conceptual level with the capability to use and understand information specified elsewhere. An outsourced type is an abstraction mechanism that allows the conceptual modeler to delegate (or outsource) responsibility for the definition of the internal structure of the type. The modeler can also attach requirements for external services to the outsourced type, thus providing the ability to manipulate and query an instance of the outsourced type without having to understand its internal representation.

In the next section we present a conceptual model to describe a relatively complex case study to show how outsourced types can be used in a global financial services context. Sections 3.1 to 3.3 motivate the need for outsourced type descriptions with the main focus on how to provide unique identities for instances of outsourced types in a global context. Section 4 introduces a meta-model for outsourced types. In section 5 we suggest some simple questions that can be used to identify the kinds of objects that may be candidates for outsourcing and illustrate how conceptual models may be augmented to allow the generation of relational schemas for the storage of entities with multiple identities. Related work is discussed in section 7.

---

[1] www.oasis-open.org/committees/ubl/ and www.rosettanet.org
[2] lists.ebxml.org/archives/ebxml-dev/200106/msg00038.htm

2   Case Study

Object Role Modeling (ORM)[3] is a visual conceptual data modeling technique, mainly used for the design of relational databases. It is used to describe object types and their relationships in a particular application domain. ORM has an associated modeling methodology, the Conceptual Schema Design Procedure (CSDP). ORM and CSDP were selected to model the case study because of their ability to produce robust and graphic models that "rigorously capture the semantic nuances of an information system" (John Zachman in [3]).

We briefly describe some of the main concepts of ORM is to assist the reader to interpret the schema presented in figure 1. The ellipses represent entity types (e.g. *Request*), while the boxes represent roles. A fact type consists of one or more roles and can play a role itself in other fact types (e.g. the fact type *Collateral*). Double arrows represent uniqueness constraints (e.g. a *Request* plays or takes at most one role), while solid dots represent mandatory role constraints (e.g. every *Request* plays or takes a *Role*). When a string is put in parenthesis below the name of an entity type (e.g. *(id)*) this indicates the presence of a value type with a name which is the concatenation of that entity type name and that string. In this case instances of the value type uniquely identify instances of that entity type (e.g. *Requestid* is a value type providing identification for entity type *Request*). The schema in figure 1 also contains a sample population shown below the fact types.

The case study is drawn from the field of securities[3] lending. In this domain, the owners of securities can lend those securities in exchange for cash collateral or other securities. Depending on the type of collateral, the owner will be recompensed by interest on the deposit of cash collateral, or a flat fee for non-cash collateral. Borrowers may have any one of several reasons to borrow securities, traditionally the most common, is to cover short sales[4]. Lenders usually participate in the transaction to generate additional income from their securities investments.

The model (figure 1) shows the information necessary to describe a request that borrowers or lenders could place in a market to indicate a willingness to borrow or lend securities. The request itself is not a web service but provides the *context* for several associated services such as *Placing* and *Retrieving* loan requests. Requests could be constructed in many ways depending on the capabilities of the applications making and taking the request. A stored request could be revealed as a web accessible form [4], serialized in XML [5,6], RDF/RDFS[5], or OWL[6] documents, or it could be revealed gradually as part of an interactive information service.

The shaded ellipses in the figure represent outsourced types. Outsourced types are necessary for this application, designed to operate in a global environ-

---

[3] Financial instruments or securities, in this context, are those traded on stock exchanges such as the NYSE, the LSE or the ASX.

[4] Short sale - the sale of a security before it is purchased.

[5] www.w3.org/RDF/

[6] www.w3.org/2001/sw/WebOnt/

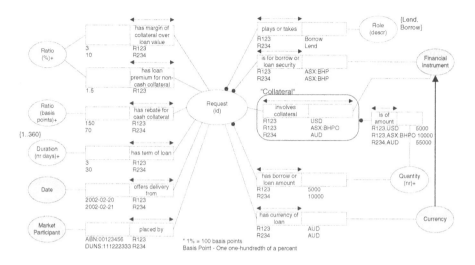

Fig. 1. Securities lending conceptual model

ment, for several reasons. The Date type (based on ISO 8601 [7]) is outsourced because date representations differ from country to country for example 10/7/03 represents October 7 in the USA and July 10 in Australia. The Currency type (based on the ISO 4217 standard for currency codes [8]) ensures there is no confusion when applications deal with money outside of their national borders.

Financial instruments are treated as outsourced types because they are subject to many different identification schemes and we want to ensure that all parties are talking about the same thing. This is especially relevant in the context of cross border securities trading where failed trades, due to mistaken identity, cost millions of dollars every year [9]. In addition, outsourced types allow service requirements to be attached to the financial instrument type for operations such as the retrieval of the name of its issuer, without having to have that information explicitly defined in the local model.

The population in the model (figure 1) captures two requests. The request (*R123*) is to *Borrow* the *borrow or loan amount* of *5000* of the *Financial instrument* identified as *ASX:BHP* shares[7]. The request offers two types of *Collateral*, the *Currency USD* (US dollars cash) and the *Financial instrument* identified as *ASX:BHPO* shares. The *margin of collateral over loan value* is how much more collateral, over and above the loan value, is required by the lender. The lenders return is the *loan premium for non-cash collateral* of *1.5%* on the ASX:BHPO shares and the *rebate for cash collateral* of *150* basis points[8] on the cash value for a 3 day loan.

Over the duration of a securities loan, the value of the loan and the consequent value of the collateral required will fluctuate depending on the value of

---

[7] ASX = Australian Stock Exchange, www.asx.com.au
[8] Basis Point - One one-hundredth of a percent

the financial instrument and the current exchange rate between Australian and US dollars. The runtime re-calculation of the value of the loan means several operations are required to provide this information, a requirement for a service to retrieve the current market price of shares can be attached to the *Financial instrument*, and a requirement for an exchange rate conversion service can be attached to the *Currency* type.

3   Outsourced Types

3.1   Information Sources

A web-based application should be able to provide clarification of the terms it uses by referring to definitions, ontologies and other sources of information. The association of other sources of information with the outsourced type is primarily for the benefit of inference tools and mediators [10], it allows modelers to explicitly provide the semantics of the terms used in this context. As application terminology is often unique to a particular designer or software provider, support for dynamic runtime disambiguation and inferencing must be provided by the service itself. In addition, the use of common type systems such as external standards for the internal representation of data provides interoperability with all the other programs using the same standards. References to type definitions and alternative sources of information will enable inference engines to disambiguate the terms used in this context and is a practical step towards the goal of global interoperability.

The outsourced type *Date* demonstrates how external sources of information can be used. The outsourced type definition can refer directly to the ISO 8601 Date specification, or it can take advantage of the XML Schema Datatypes specification or schemas developed for use with RDF such as the Dublin Core (DC) element set[9] both of which are based on ISO8601. For those applications that are not aware of the ISO standard or its syntax (ccyy-mm-dd), the outsourced type definition can also specify the requirements for services to translate dates to and from ISO format.

3.2   Service Descriptions and Capability Oriented Modeling

The lack of prior agreements between interaction partners means that there may be mismatches between the data required for a web service invocation and the data available. In this case service descriptions can be used to describe the operational capabilities that must be provided by or for the outsourced type in this context. Some of the operational capabilities will be generic, such as *creating instances, comparison, format translation* and *getting* and *setting* values, others will be specific to the type, such as retrieving the current market price from a financial instrument. A service description may also describe non-functional requirements and constraints. A description of these can be found in

---

[9] dublincore.org/documents/1999/07/02/dces

[11]. At present, it is not possible to specify this kind of service requirement in ORM models [12]. Outsourced type definitions allow the specification of service requirements at a conceptual level, where the description is in terms of *what* is required (capabilities) rather than *who* by, or *how* the operations should be provided (implementation).

The delegation of tasks to external services is a natural extension of the object oriented and component programming paradigms. This kind of modularisation allows applications to concentrate on core competencies and delegate less relevant concerns to specialist services in non-core areas. At the conceptual level the modeler is only responsible for providing a description of what a service is required to do or provide. At runtime, the choice of which service implementation to use should be based on how well the service fulfils the required functional and non-functional constraints; rather than (as now) the functionality that can be inferred from a WSDL[10] service description.

3.3   Identification Schemes

In the global environment there is often more than one externally controlled identification scheme and entities may have valid identities in several schemes. In the past, each application could provide its own unique identification mechanism for the local application context but it is difficult to maintain uniqueness constraints over relationships when the same entity may have several valid identifiers in different schemes.

Here we address the issue of entity or object identity rather than the issue of personal identity on the web covered by products such as the Microsoft Passport and frameworks such as [13,14]. In UML models in particular, the identity of entities and objects is implicit rather than explicit as in ORM. The advantage of providing explicit identification is the ability to identify specific instances in terms that are meaningful outside of the system being modeled. An extension to the UML meta-model to allow explicit identity has been proposed in [15].

In ORM each instance of an entity must have an explicit unique identifier. An application that has outsourced entity types must be able to use different identification schemes *while ensuring that different identities for the same instance are recognised*, and the opposite case where the same identifier in different schemes, identifies different instances. The use of external identification schemes means the responsibility for enforcing constraints such as, a constraint that *identities within a scheme must be unique*, is delegated to the schemes' controller.

Each identification scheme will be owned or controlled by a different organization and each will have different rules and jurisdiction over the target group. The coverage of identification schemes may range from fully disjoint to fully overlapping depending on which aspects/properties/roles of the entity that the scheme is interested in. Similarly the scope of schemes may not be equivalent, for example the Australian ABN scheme [16] simply states that an Australian business exists and is registered (to pay tax), whereas a D-U-N-S[11] implies some

---

[10] www.w3.org/2002/ws/desc/
[11] www.dnb.com

rating or assessment has taken place before the identifier is issued. Identification schemes themselves may have properties such as trustworthiness, accessibility, reliability and quality.

It may be necessary for some applications to limit the identification schemes that can be used; either by limiting the number of schemes, or by specifying acceptable schemes by name or by specifying the scope of acceptable schemes. The limitations on schemes could also be instance dependent, for example, if a Person is involved in a relationship "pays tax" and the person is from USA then only accept USA TFN's or USA SSN's to identify that Person.

In some cases it may not be possible to determine if an instance has an identity in a particular scheme, due to limitations on access to information without payment of a subscription or because of security concerns. Security is also an issue when it is necessary to pass identity information to downstream[12] services, there may be user constraints on whom the information can be passed to, or how the information can be used.

There are two conceptual modeling issues related to multiple identities that are a consequence of outsourcing types in a global context. The first issue is that there may not be an *exhaustive* list of all the possible identification schemes to start with, hence the model will not "know" about new schemes introduced after the modeling process is complete. Consequently a form of schema evolution is required to introduce new identity schemes. In terms of our meta-model (figure 2), an evolution mechanism for the introduction of new identification schemes would require information about the organization that controls, owns or publishes the scheme; whether or not its origin is based upon some other published information, such as a standard or law; and a source of information about the scheme itself.

The second modeling issue concerns ensuring the uniqueness *constraints* described in the base model are not violated when using instances of outsourced types. There are several options to prevent constraint violations at the implementation level. One option is to choose one or more of the external identification schemes to act as the canonical representation within the local application. A cover constraint is a requirement that all possible instances can be identified by the selected identification scheme or schemes. Therefore the schemes should be selected to maximise the coverage of instances and minimise the possibility of overlapping identities. The schemes should also have a similar interest in aspects of the instances they identify.

In terms of the case study, we could choose the ISO 15022 standard for International Security Identification Numbers (ISIN) [17] as it is an internationally agreed standard for the identification of securities. In practice we cannot use it on its own yet as it is not implemented in all countries. This means we would have to use ISIN along with all the identification schemes used in all the countries not yet covered by the ISIN scheme.

---

[12] Upstream services are users or clients, downstream services are providers of functionality.

Another option is to create an internal canonical identification scheme, and map identities from multiple external schemes to the canonical identifier, typically with the help of external conversion services. In most applications, including the case study, it will be necessary to record which identification scheme a client prefers to enable the reverse mapping back to the representation the client understands. A mechanism to do this is discussed more fully in section 6.

The advantage of this approach is that complete coverage can be guaranteed, at least internally. Complete coverage ensures the single canonical identification of any instance; and any instance previously unknown can be assigned a new identifier in the local scheme. The use of a single (locally) controlled canonical identifier also ensures that the constraints concerning the outsourced types are satisfied.

The identification of Financial Instruments is just one example of the multiplicity of identification schemes in the global context. In the first case above, several existing schemes could be chosen to provide complete coverage. However it will be difficult to find a manageably small number of schemes so that this can be done without overlapping identities. For this reason we tend to prefer the second option of a single canonical representation. The single canonical representation can be managed by a single party that has the ability to: ensure uniqueness constraints are preserved, include new identification schemes, and generate new identifiers when appropriate.

4   Meta Model

Figure 2 is a populated ORM meta-schema for outsourced types. Outsourced object types are a subtype of ORM Unnested Entity Types as defined in the ORM meta-schema [18]. They participate in three relationships which match the three types of information identified in section 3.

The first is the mandatory role *has instances governed by identification scheme*. The mandatory constraint means that there must be a way of identifying the scheme that issued the outsourced types' instance identifier. This rule makes explicit the entity identification rules inherited from ORM while recognising that instance identifiers may come from different identification schemes.

The second role is *has additional information*, this allows other information to be associated with the type, such as a definition in a thesaurus or ontology. The information is intended to be used to aid the comprehension of the syntax and semantics of the type and its roles in this context.

The central element in the meta-schema is *Information source*. The value constraint attached to *is of* shows an Information source can be of many different types. One type in particular, the *Service description*, is shown as a subtype of Information source because we want to indicate that it contains a particular kind of information and provides a link to the third role played by outsourced types, *has associated service description*. This relationship allows various requirements for downstream services to be associated with an outsourced type and its instances.

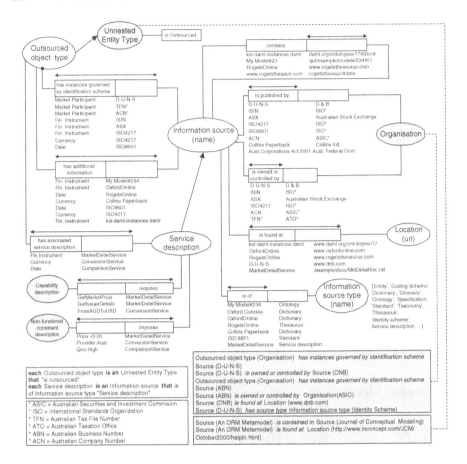

Fig. 2. Meta-model of outsourced object types

Information sources may also have other properties: they can contain or be contained within another source, they can be found at a particular location and information sources are published and/or controlled by some organisation.

The meta model describes the abstract syntax of the proposed extension. An abstract syntax captures concepts and their interrelations but does not deal with aspects of concrete representation. The shaded boxes provide a sample of a concrete representation. A concrete representation appropriate for web application descriptions is necessary but outside the scope of this paper.

5   Identifying Outsourced Types

Although ORM already has the *external type* construct to represent information found in another ORM model, outsourced types allow ORM models to include external descriptions from many other sources in a similar manner to RDF or OWL ontologies and topic maps[13].

The Conceptual Schema Design Procedure (CSDP) is a seven step procedure to transform facts related to the domain of interest into a well defined conceptual schema. Steps 1 to 3 are concerned with identifying entity types, value types and fact types. Steps 4 to 7 of the CSDP are when the constraints on entity types and the roles they play in relationships, are identified and incorporated into the schema diagram. The decision to use outsourced types can be taken when all the elements in the domain model have been identified, therefore the decision comes after step 3 of the CSDP.

Three questions help to decide whether an entity type should be defined as an outsourced type. At the conceptual level the concerns are to manage complexity, to reuse external definitions when they are appropriate and to prepare for interaction as a web-based application.

Elementary types: The first question is trivial and asks whether the object type represents an elementary or complex type. Elementary objects representing a number such as *Quantity* in figure 1 will not be treated as outsourced types. However, to promote interoperability elementary types could be defined in terms of an external definition such as XML Schema Part 2: Datatypes[14].

Imported definitions: The second question asks whether there already exists a definition for this object type. These definitions can come from any model, schema or definition that is not the current model.

At the beginning of our investigation, we assumed all imported definitions should be treated as external, that is, supplied with an outsourced type definition for onward exposure to clients of the application being modeled. However as we have developed the meta-model, this requirement has become blurred. On one hand an imported element could be treated as an outsourced type only if it is also exposed to users. On the other hand, outsourced types can be used as a guide for software developers in the way an element should be implemented because the more external information is reused in local models, the greater will be the basis for shared understanding and interoperability. Reuse of publicly accessible information provides cost effectiveness, consistency and interoperability both within an organisational context and in the global world of web applications.

Exported definitions: The final question asks if the object type is to be exported or exposed to clients of this model. Exposure can either be direct or indirect. Direct exposure happens when objects are shared as part of the normal operation of an application, such as function names, parameters, return values or message components. Indirect exposure happens when up or downstream services require clarification of the semantics of the terms used by the application. For example a user of the securities lending request, may ask "what is a financial instrument?", and the application could return the URI of a dictionary definition, or an ontology entry, or a list of alternative terms.

---

[13] www.topicmaps.org/xtm
[14] www.w3.org/XML/Schema

Outsourced types provide a means to describe entities in terms of external information, however web-based applications will need to store this information locally. In the next section we bridge the gap between the extension to the conceptual model and databases to store information about outsourced types. We illustrate how traditional ORM models must be modified to recognise multiple identity schemes.

6   Realisation

The existence of multiple external identity schemes is not evident from the representation of outsourced types in the local ORM model. This means the relational mapping procedure (Rmap) [3], used to convert an ORM model to a database schema, will be unaware of the multiple identities that may be associated with an instance of an outsourced type. The following examples illustrate how the model must be augmented as a precursor to Rmap. The augmentation procedure substitutes a canonical identifier for each external identifier and its associated identification scheme, while retaining information about which scheme is being used in each role. There are many cases that could be considered, each representing a different relationship (and its constraints) that an outsourced type can participate in with other outsourced and non-outsourced types. In this section we illustrate two sample cases that represent different uniqueness constraints on *binary* relationships between an outsourced and a non-outsourced entity type.

The augmentation process is done in two stages. In the first stage, a canonical identifier is introduced in place of an external identifier and its associated identification scheme. To retain knowledge about the relationship between: the canonical identifier, the external identifier, and its associated identification scheme, a ternary relationship (henceforth called the identity catalogue) is created. The identity catalogue is attached to the outsourced type, which now uses the canonical identifier as its primary reference scheme.

The identity catalogue is used to record *all* the identifiers and schemes that are known or can be found for a particular canonical identifier. There are two ways to build this list of schemes and their identifiers. The first option is to actively search for alternative identities and schemes when the database table is first created; the second option is to check and add new schemes when they are introduced to the application. The options represent a trade-off between the possibly lengthy time taken to populate the table when it is created and quick updates; or a longer time taken to make updates while new information is checked and incorporated into the table.

In the second stage, a new binary relation is introduced to make explicit the association of the canonical identifier and the identification scheme used in a specific role. The association of this new relation with the entities in the model depends upon the uniqueness constraints governing the whole relationship. This is illustrated below in relation to the one to many and many to many relationships.

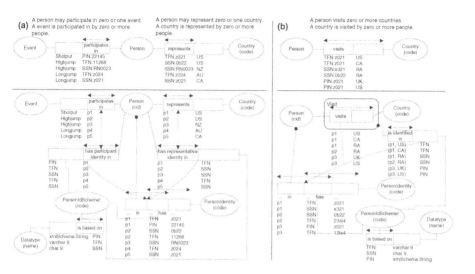

Fig. 3. One to Many and Many to Many relationships

Configuring a One to Many relationship. Figure 3(a) is in two parts, the top section shows the original relationships between an outsourced type (Person) and local entity types (Event and Country). A problem with this model is the identification scheme for *Person* is a combination of the name of an identification scheme and a value in that scheme. In the example, a Person may only represent one country but we are unable to determine from the identifiers, TFN:z024 and SSN:z021, that these really are different people. For this reason we introduce a canonical identifier (cid) for each outsourced entity instance and substitute the cid for the composite identification in the original *participates in* and *represents* roles.

The lower part of the figure is extended with an identity catalogue, to make the relationships between the cid, and all its related identification schemes and identities explicit. The identity catalogue is subject to two uniqueness constraints. The first is over the external identifier and its identification scheme. This constraint states that each identifier is unique within its identification scheme. The second constraint states that each combination of cid and identification scheme is unique. The combination of these two constraints means that a person with identities in different identification schemes can be uniquely identified by a single cid.

The next stage in the translation procedure is to make explicit the relationship between the cid and the identification scheme used in a particular role. The equality constraint between *participates in* and *has participant identity in* ensures that when a cid appears in the *participates in* relation, then this cid and the identification scheme used for this role are recorded in the new relation *has participant identity in*. This relation records which specific scheme, amongst potentially many schemes, is relevant for the *participates in* relation. Similarly a new relation, *has representative identity in*, is constructed to represent the relevant identities and schemes for the *represents* relation. In both cases, as *Person* is on the "one side" of the one to many relation we attach the new relationships to *Person*.

Configuring a Many to Many relationship. Figure 3(b) shows a visitation relationship between People and Countries. The primary concern in this case is to ensure that each row of the visits/visited by relationship is unique. In the original schema we would be unable to enforce this constraint given the current information. For example, *TFN:z021* and *SSN:x321* are different identity codes, but are alternative identifiers for the same Person instance (p1).

Although there are alternative ways to prepare the many to many conversion for Rmap, we have elected to introduce an objectified relation *Visit* to represent the necessary information. The uniqueness constraint over the *Visit* roles ensures the original uniqueness requirement (that there are no duplicate rows) is maintained. A join subset constraint is placed over the roles involving a *Person* and a *PersonIdScheme* with the corresponding roles in the identity catalogue. This constraint means that for every fact in which a certain Person is used in conjunction with a Person Id Scheme, we should have information about this combination in the identity catalogue.

7   Related Work

There are two main strands of interest and activity in the Web services area. The first strand is the focus of several industry organizations including the Web services Interoperability Organization[15] and the World Wide Web Consortium (W3C) Web services Activity[16] which includes the Web services Architecture and Web services Description working groups. This strand is largely based upon the SOAP , WSDL and UDDI specifications. These services will, in the main, require off-line agreement between the parties over the semantics of WSDL interfaces and the message flow pattern before they can be used for automated interaction.

Web Services Description Language (WSDL) defines a grammar for describing Web service operations in terms of input and output messages. It has become the de-facto standard for the description of Web services and is currently (February 2003) in the process of being updated and revised by the World Wide Web Consortiums' Web services Description Working Group[17]. WSDL does not provide facilities for referring to external information to describe the semantics of terms used in a Web service description.

The UDDI specification[18] provides a mechanism primarily to advertise Web service providers and the services they offer. UDDI does not contribute to the description of a service but it does provide "pointers" to tModels which represent technical documents such as specifications, protocols and categorisation schemes. Outsourced type definitions could be registered as tModels in a UDDI registry.

---

[15] www.ws-i.org
[16] www.w3.org/2002/ws
[17] www.w3.org/2002/ws/desc/
[18] www.uddi.org/

The second strand are semantic web services [19,20], these services are on the boundary between the Semantic Web and Web services where semantic content and some intelligence are used in conjunction with the specifications listed above to provide a greater range of automated invocation and usability. In these services the interaction sequence will be determined by the goals of the user rather than the internal processes of the service provider.

The Web Service Modeling Framework (WSMF) [10,21] is one of the interesting proposals in the area of semantic web services. The WSMF is based on two principles, the de-coupling of the various components that make up a Web service, and the use of mediators to translate between heterogeneous data representations and interaction styles. The information provided by outsourced types provides an explicit declaration of the semantics intended by the service provider, thus reducing the cognitive workload on mediators.

In the more general area of data modeling of web applications, Atzeni et. al. [22,23] draw data from HTML web pages, and selectively rearrange and amalgamate it for presentation as new HTML pages. In contrast, outsourced types selectively draw information from a wide variety of sources in order to be able to describe aspects of a web application to users. This outsourced type information could be packaged and presented to users according to the methods described in [24,25,26]. The focus of that work is on providing context sensitive data and navigation options to human users but could also be applied in the area of machine to machine interaction.

Ontologies have been the subject of much work recently [27,28] and they can provide high level views of a domain or lower level context specific views. One advantage of our method of extending conceptual models is that the ORM model can be used as the basis of a local ontology [29] or an application profile [2] that ties the local context to the global context via outsourced types. ORM provides the assurance of a methodology and modeling language that have been proven with time and experience to assist in building well formed conceptual models. The building of valid and useable ontologies will be better accomplished by using this accepted and proven conceptual modeling methodology.

8   Conclusion

In this paper we have introduced outsourced types, an extension to classical conceptual models. Outsourced types are a practical step towards achieving the goal of automated ad-hoc interaction between web-based applications.

Outsourced types provide several benefits. Firstly, they allow designers and developers to *reuse* existing definitions from local and global sources. Outsourced type definitions can also be reused as they are defined at a conceptual level outside of the scope of programming language, application and enterprise boundaries.

Outsourced types help to reduce the reliance on particular representations by allowing the use of alternative definitions (standards, specifications and ontologies) thus helping to avoid problems such as vendor lock-in. Another advantage of alternative definitions is that there will be a greater probability of interaction partners understanding at least one of the offered definitions. Alternative definitions also provide redundancy in a possibly unreliable web environment.

The outsourced type definition also provides the basis for downstream service composition by allowing specific statements of what capabilities the outsourced type is expected to provide for the local model.

The definition and creation of outsourced types will place a greater work load on web service providers but we believe the benefits will ultimately outweigh any increased costs.

References

1. Baker, T., Dekkers, M., Heery, R., Patel, M., Slokhe, G.: What Terms Does Your Metadata Use? Application Profiles as Machine Understandable Narratives. Journal of Digital Information 2 (2001)
2. Dekkers, M.: Application Profiles, or how to Mix and Match Metadata Schemas (2001) Cultivate Interactive, issue 3. Available from:
   http://www.cultivate-int.org/issue3/schemas/, (20 August 2002).
3. Halpin, T.: Information Modeling and Relational Databases: from conceptual analysis to logical design. Morgan Kaufmann Publishers, San Diego, CA, USA (2001)
4. Dumas, M., Aldred, L., ter Hofstede, A.: From conceptual models to constrained web forms. In: Real-World Semantic Web Applications. IOS Press (2002) 50–68
5. Demey, J., Jarrar, M., Meersman, R.: A markup Language for ORM Business Rules (2002) International Workshop on Rule Markup Languages for Business Rules on the Semantic Web, Sardinia (Italy) in conjunction with the First International Semantic Web Conference (ISWC2002).
6. Bird, L., Goodchild, A., Halpin, T.A.: Object Role Modelling and XML-Schema. In: Proceedings of the 19th International Conference on Conceptual Modeling (ER), Salt Lake City, Utah, USA, Springer-Verlag (2000) 309–322
7. International Organization for Standardization: ISO 8601:2000 Data elements and interchange formats – Information interchange – Representation of dates and times (2000) Available at: http://www.iso.org, (25 February 2002).
8. International Organization for Standardization: ISO 4217:2001 Codes for the representation of currencies and funds. (2001) Available at: http://www.iso.org, (25 February 2002).
9. London Stock Exchange: Exchange to introduce new global numbering system (2002) Press release, 7 November 2002, available from:
   http://www.londonstockexchange.com/newsroom/releases,
   (28 November 2002).
10. Fensel, D., Bussler, C.: The Web Service Modeling Framework WSMF. Electronic Commerce Research and Applications 1 (2002) 113–137
11. O'Sullivan, J., Edmond, D., ter Hofstede, A.: What's in a service? Towards accurate description of non-functional service properties. Distributed and Parallel Databases Journal – Special Issue on E-Services 12 (2002) 117–133
12. Weber, R., Zhang, Y.: An analytical evaluation of NIAM's grammar for conceptual schema diagrams. Information Systems Journal 6 (1996) 147–170
13. OneName Corporation: Requirements for a global identity management service a position paper (2001) Presented to W3C Workshop on Web Services, San Jose, CA USA.

14. Hodges, J.: Liberty Architecture Overview, v1.0 (2002) Available from: `http://www.projectliberty.org/specs/liberty-architecture-overview-v1.0.pdf`, (10 October 2002).
15. Cranefield, S., Purvis, M.: Generating Ontology-Specific Content Languages. Information Science Discussion Paper 2001/08, University of Otago, Otago, New Zealand (2001) ISSN 1172-6024.
16. Australian Securities and Investment Commission: What's in a name? business names, company names, domain names and trade marks (2001) `http://www.asic.gov.au/asic/asic.nsf`, (11 July 2002).
17. von Rochow, I.B., Yous, N.: ISO 6166: Securities – International securities identification numbering system (ISIN) (2001) Information available from: `http://www.anna-web.com/`, (4 September 2002).
18. Halpin, T.: An ORM Metamodel. Journal of Conceptual Modeling **16** (2000)
19. Bussler, C., Fensel, D., Payne, T., Sycara, K.: Tutorial (T3): Semantic Web Services (2002) More information available at: `http://www.daml.ri.cmu.edu/tutorial/iswc-t3.html`, (15 October 2002).
20. Ankolekar, A., Burstein, M., Hobbs, J.R., Lassila, O., Martin, D.L., McIlraith, S.A., Narayanan, S., Paolucci, M., Payne, T., Sycara, K., Zeng, H.: DAML-S: Semantic Markup For Web Services. In: Proceedings of SWWS' 01 The First Semantic Web Working Symposium, Stanford University, CA, USA (2001) 411–430
21. Bussler, C., Fensel, D., Maedche, A.: A Conceptual Architecture for Semantic Web Enabled Web Services. SIGMOD Record, Special Section on Semantic Web and Data Management **31** (2002)
22. Atzeni, P., Mecca, G., Merialdo, P.: To weave the web. In Jarke, M., Carey, M.J., Dittrich, K.R., Lochovsky, F.H., Loucopoulos, P., Jeusfeld, M.A., eds.: VLDB'97, Proceedings of 23rd International Conference on Very Large Data Bases, Athens, Greece, Morgan Kaufmann (1997) 206–215 ISBN 1-55860-470-7.
23. Atzeni, P., Mecca, G., Merialdo, P., Sindoni, G.: A Logical Approach to Metadata in Web Bases. In: XI ERCIM Database Working Group Workshop: Metadata in Web Databases, Sankt Augustin, Germany, ERCIM (1998)
24. Ceri, S., Fraternali, P., Matera, M.: Conceptual Modeling of Data-Intensive Web Applications. IEEE Internet Computing **6** (2002) 20–30
25. Feyer, T., Kao, O., Schewe, K.D., Thalheim, B.: Design of Data-Intensive Web-Based Information Services. In: Proc. 1st International Conference on Web Information Systems Engineering (WISE 2000), Hong Kong, IEEE CS Press (2000) 462–467
26. Schwabe, D., Esmeraldo, L., Rossi, G., Lyardet, F.: Engineering Web Applications for Reuse. IEEE Multimedia **8** (2001) 20–31
27. McGuinness, D.L.: Ontologies and Online Commerce. IEEE Intelligent Systems **16** (2001) 9–10
28. Das, A., Wu, W., McGuinness, D.L.: Industrial Strength Ontology Management. In Cruz, I., Decker, S., Euzenat, J., McGuinness, D., eds.: The Emerging Semantic Web. Volume 75 of Frontiers in Artificial Intelligence and Applications. IOS Press (2002)
29. Meersman, R.: Ontologies and Databases: More than a Fleeting Resemblance (2002) in d'Atri A. and Missikoff M. (eds), OES/SEO 2001 Rome Workshop, Luiss Publications.

Development of Web Applications from Web Enhanced Conceptual Schemas*

Joan Fons, Vicente Pelechano, Manoli Albert, and Óscar Pastor

Department of Information Systems and Computation
Valencia University of Technology
Cami de Vera s/n, E-46022, Spain
{jjfons,pele,malbert,opastor}@dsic.upv.es

Abstract. This work presents an OO software production method that defines a systematic process for conceptual modelling of web applications. The paper discusses a set of minimum primitives to capture the essentials of dynamic web applications and it discusses how to introduce them in a classical model-centered OO method that provides systematic code generation. Finally, the paper presents some ideas to extend this generation process for developing web solutions taking as an input these web enhanced conceptual schemas.

1 Introduction

The advance of Internet and the emerging technologies associated to the web are universalizing information systems, allowing access to any connected potential user. The term "Web Application" refers to this new family of software applications specially designed to be executed on the web. The current development of those web applications require a methodological support to assure the quality of the final product. "Web Engineering" [1] deals with the methods, techniques and tools that should be used to undertake the development of such applications. In this context, it becomes indispensable to have development methods that provide solutions to the problem of modelling, designing and implementing web applications in a systematic and structured way.

Approaches of this kind (1) introduce new models and abstraction mechanisms to capture the essentials of web applications and (2) give support for the full development of a web solution [2]. Some representative efforts to introduce web features into classical conceptual modelling approaches are OOHDM [3], WebML [4], UWE [5] and WSDM [6].

Our proposal provides a concrete contribution in this context. We introduce a conceptual modelling centered method that integrates navigational and presentational design with a classical OO conceptual modelling that provides systematic code generation. In this conceptual modelling approach, the essential expressiveness is introduced in our graphical schemas in order to properly

---

* This work has been partially supported by the MCYT Project with ref. TIC2001-3530-C02-01 and the Valencia University of Technology, Spain.

I.-Y. Song et al. (Eds.): ER 2003, LNCS 2813, pp. 232–245, 2003.

specify navigation and presentation features, using high level abstraction primitives. Taking conceptual schemas as an input, a precise methodological guide is defined for going systematically from the problem space to the solution space by defining a set of correspondences between the conceptual modelling abstractions and the final software components.

The work introduced in this paper focuses on the required extensions needed to enhance "classical" OO software production methods (in particular the OO-Method [7]) in order to define a systematic web modelling method. It is also discussed the high level abstraction primitives to capture web applications features extending conceptual schemas.

The structure of this work is the following. Section 2 presents the methodological approach to model web applications. It extends the OO-Method introducing two models: the navigational model, which captures the navigation semantics of a web application, and the presentational model, which specifies some aspects related to user interfaces layout with a set of basic patterns. In section 3 it is briefly discussed how to extend the generation process of the OO-Method to create web clients using web enhanced conceptual schemas. Finally, section 4 presents the conclusions and future work.

2   A Method to Model Web Applications

OOWS (Object Oriented Web Solutions) is the extension of an object-oriented software production method (OO-Method) that introduces the required expressivity to capture the navigational and presentational requirements of web applications. This extended view of the OO-Method provides a full software development method that defines a set of activities to properly specify the functional, navigational and presentational dimensions of web applications requirements.

The proposed software production method comprises two major steps: *system specification* and *solution development*. A full specification of the system functional requirements is built in the *system specification* step. A strategy oriented towards generating the software components that constitute the solution (the final software product) is defined in the second step.

This paper presents the introduction of two new models in the OO-Method conceptual modelling step (the navigational and presentation models) and it discusses the strategy to extend the systematic generation process with respect to the interface of web applications.

To better understand the proposal, we use a case study of a web application for University Research Groups Management (URGM System). Different kind of users (anonymous, group members, guests and administrators) can use this application to access, query and manipulate information about research groups with its members, research projects, resources, performed activities (seminars, conferences, courses, etc.) and publications (articles, books, theses, technical reports, etc.).

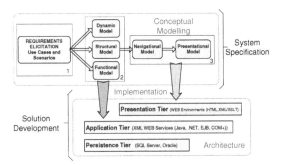

Fig. 1. Methodological Approach

2.1   OO-Method Conceptual Modelling

OO-Method [7] is an OO software production method that provides model-based code generation capabilities and integrates formal specification techniques with conventional OO modelling notations.

In the *"System Specification"* step, a conceptual schema is built to represent the application requirements. The modelling tools that are used by the method allow to specify structural and functional requirements of dynamic applications. The modelling process is divided into two steps:

1. **Functional Requirements Elicitation**. Techniques based on use cases and scenarios are applied to build a conceptual schema (class, sequence and state diagrams are built). An extensive work have been developed in our research group in the OO-Method context [8] (see box number 1 in Figure 1).
2. **Conceptual Modelling**. A set of models allow to capture and represent a software system from three different points of view (see box number 2):
   - a **Structural Model** that defines the system structure (its classes, operations and attributes) and relationships between classes (specialization, association and aggregation) by means of a *Class Diagram*,
   - a **Dynamic** Model that describes the different valid object-life sequence for each class of the system using *State Diagrams*. Also in this model object interactions (communications between objects) are represented by *Sequence diagrams*,
   - a **Functional Model** that captures the semantics of state changes to define service effects using a textual formal specification [7].

Figure 2 shows the portion of the URGM class diagram related to publications information. It shows a set of classes representing publications, its subtypes (articles, books, theses, etc.) and its signers using a standard UML notation. The Dynamic and Functional Models are not shown because they are out of the scope of this paper.

As it is stated in [9], web applications have additional properties that should be modelled. We want to extend the OO-Method to deal with navigation specification, user interface definition and user categorization and personalization, in

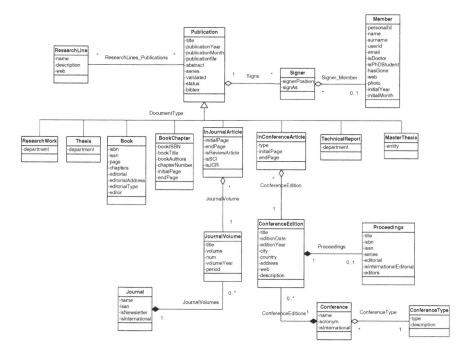

Fig. 2. Class Diagram of the URGM system

order to properly capture web application requirements. Next sections explain these extensions.

2.2 Navigational Modelling

This section discusses the conceptual modelling primitives for capturing the navigational semantics of web applications at the system specification step (see box number 3 in Figure 1). These primitives are represented within a graphical model that we call **Navigational Model** that define the system user types and how they access the system information and functionality. Two diagrams are introduced: the *user diagram* and the *navigational diagram*.

User Identification and Categorization. Before modelling navigation, the method provides a *user diagram* to express which kind of users can interact with the system and what visibility they would have over class attributes and operations. This diagram provides mechanisms to properly cope with additional user management capabilities, such as the *user specialization* that allows to define user taxonomies (see Figure 3) to improve navigational specification reuse [10].

Representing Navigation. Once users have been identified, a structured and organized system view for each user type must be specified. These views are

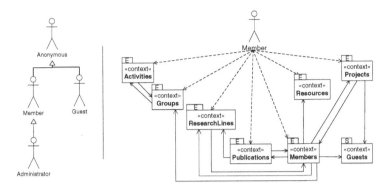

Fig. 3. URGM system User Diagram and Navigational Map of the Member user

defined over the class diagram, in terms of the visibility of class attributes, operations and relationships.

We capture the navigation specification in two steps: the "Authoring-in-the-large" (global view) and the "Authoring-in-the-small" (detailed view).

The "Authoring-in-the-large" step refers to the specification and design of global and structural aspects of the web application. It is achieved by defining a set of system-user abstract interaction units and how the user can navigate from one to another. These requirements are specified in a **Navigational Map** that provides the system view and accessibility that each kind of user have. It is represented using a directed graph whose nodes are navigational contexts (forward defined) and its arcs denote navigational links or valid navigational paths (see Figure 3).

These navigational contexts (graphically represented as UML packages stereotyped with the «context» keyword) represent the user interaction units that provide a set of cohesive data and operations to perform certain activity. In order to define the context reachability, we propose contexts of two types:

- *Exploration navigational contexts* (depicted with the *"E"* label) are reachable nodes from any node[1]. These contexts define implicit navigational links from any node and explicitly (using dashed arrows) from the root of the map (represented by the user, see Figure 3), contexts Resources, Publications, Activities, etc.). One exploration context can be marked as *default* or *home* (depicted with an *"H"* label).
- *Sequence navigational contexts* (depicted with the *"S"* label) can only be accessed via a predefined navigational path by selecting a sequence link (forward defined). For instance, the Guests context (see Figure 3) can only be reached from the Projects and Members contexts.

The *navigational links* (navigational map arcs) represent context reachabilities or *"navigational paths"*. There are navigational links of two types:

---

[1] *Landmark* pattern in [11]

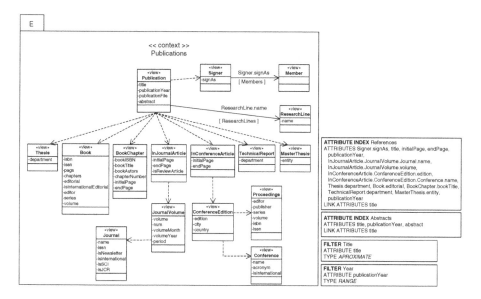

Fig. 4. Publications Navigational Context for the Member user

- *Sequence links* or *"contextual links"* (represented with solid arrows) define a *semantical* navigation between contexts. Selecting a sequence link implies carrying contextual information to the target context (the object that has been selected, the source navigational context, etc.).
- *Exploration links* or *"non contextual links"* (represented with dashed arrows) represent a user intentional change of task. They are implicitly defined from the root of the navigational map (depicted as a user) to any exploration context. When an exploration link is crossed, no contextual information is carried to the target context.

Figure 3 shows the navigational map of the Member user. This map structures its access to the system by providing a group of contexts to manage and query information about projects, publications, activities, resources, members, etc., defining, for instance, that the user can navigate to the ResearchLines context from the Publications context.

The "Authoring-in-the-small" step refers to the detailed specification of the contents of the nodes (navigational contexts[2]). To specify this content, each navigational context is made up of a set of **navigational classes** that represent *class views* (including attributes and operations). These classes are stereotyped with the ≪view≫ keyword (see Figure 4).

Each navigational context has one *mandatory* navigational class, called **manager class** and optional navigational classes to provide complementary information of the manager class, called **complementary classes**.

---

[2] OOHDM call them Navigational Classes

Figure 4 shows an example of the Publications navigational context. The purpose of this context is to provide detailed information about publications, their signers and the research lines that are related to the publication. To satisfy this requirements, the following navigational classes has been defined in that context: Publication *manager class* and its subclasses (InJournalArticle, Book, ...), Signer, Member, ResearchLine, etc (*complementary classes*). All these classes include the subset of the visible attributes and operations that the user can see or activate in this context.

Service links can also be attached to a service representing a target node that the user would reach after a service execution. Moreover, a **population filter** for each navigational class can be specified, defining an object retrieval filter depending on an OCL formula.

All navigational classes must be related by unidirectional binary relationships, called **navigational relationships**. They are defined over existing aggregation/association/composition or specialization/generalization relationships representing the retrieval of the related instances by these relationships. When more than one structural relationship exists between two classes, the role name of the relationship must be provided (depicted as */role-attribute/*). Two kind of navigational relationships can be defined, depending on if they define (or not) a navigation capability:

1. A *context dependency relationship* (graphically represented using dashed arrows) represents a basic information recovery by crossing a structural relationship between classes. When a context dependency relationship is defined, all the related instances to the origin class are retrieved. Relationships of this kind do not define any navigation.
   Figure 4 shows thirteen context dependency relationships, specifying that the context retrieves the related information for each publication, such as its signers, detailed information depending on the publication type (book, article, thesis, ...), etc.
2. A *context relationship* (graphically represented using solid arrows) represents the same information recovery as a context dependency relationship does plus a navigation capability to a target navigational context, creating a sequence link in the navigational map. They have the following properties:
   - A *context attribute* that indicates the target context of the navigation (depicted as [targetContext]).
   - A *link attribute* that specifies the attribute (usually an attribute of the target navigational class) used as the *"anchor"* to activate the navigation to the target context.
   Figure 4 shows two context relationships: Publication - ResearchLine and Signer - Member. They retrieve information about the involved lines of research in a publication and the group members that signs that publication. These contextual relationships create links to the target (ResearchLines and Members) contexts, using the link attribute (name of the line of research or name of the signer) as the "anchor" and carrying information about the selected instance ResearchLine or Member object. Figure 8 shows a possible implementation for this context.

We consider that this specification of the navigational semantics can be enriched by introducing mechanisms to help the user to explore and filter the huge amount of information in a context. Next section presents how to introduce access structures and search mechanisms taking as basis [3,4] adapted to our approach.

Advanced Navigational Features. Additional mechanisms to structure the access and to filter the population *in a navigational context* might be defined. This information is captured in the specification of the navigational context (see Figure 4). These mechanisms are the following:

1. An **index** is a structure that provides an *indexed access* to the population of the manager class. Indexes create a list of summarized information allowing the user to choose one item (instance) from the list. This selection causes this instance to become active in the navigational context. At least one of these attributes must act as the *link attribute* (*"anchor"*) to the context.
   For instance, in the URGM System, we have defined two indexes (References index and Abstracts index) in the Publications context (see Figure 4) to create a list of summarized information about publications: the first presents publications as bibliographic references and the second shows publications' title, year and abstract. When an element of the active index list is chosen (using the publication title as the anchor), all specified information of the selected instance becomes visible in the Publication navigational context (Figure 7 shows an implementation of this *indexed* context).
2. **Search mechanisms** define *population filters* to filter the space of objects to be retrieved. Filters must be defined by selecting one attribute of the *manager* class. We provide three types of searching mechanisms:
   a) *exact* filters take one attribute value and return all the instances that match it exactly
   b) *approximate* filters take one attribute value and return all the instances whose attribute values include this value as a substring
   c) *range* filters take two values (a maximum and a minimum) and return all the instances whose attribute values fit within the range. If we specify only one value, it is only bounded on one side
   Optionally, a *population condition* can be specified to a population filter to statically specify some predefined filtering conditions.

Figure 4 shows two filters: one *approximated* filter that allows the user to search publications by title, and one *range* filter that allows the user to search publications within a range of years. Implemented web pages of Figures 7 and 8 provide access to these filters.

2.3   Presentational Modelling

Once the navigational model is built, we must specify presentational requirements of web applications using a **Presentation Model** (see Figure 1). It is strongly based on the navigational model and it uses its navigational contexts (system-user interaction units) to define the presentation properties.

Presentation requirements are specified by means of patterns that are associated to the primitives of the navigational context (navigational classes, navigational links, access structures, searching mechanisms, etc.). These presentation patterns are:

1. **Information Paging**. This pattern allows to define information "scrolling". All the instances are "broken" into "logical blocks", so that only one block is visible at a time. Mechanisms to move forward or backward are provided. The required information for this pattern is:
   - **Cardinality** represents the number of instances that make a block.
   - **Access mode**. Two values can be specified for this property:
     a) *sequential* access provides mechanisms to go to the next, previous, first and last logical block
     b) *random* access mode allows the user to go directly to a desired block
   - **Circularity**. When this property is active, the set of blocks behaves as a circular buffer.

   This pattern can be applied to:
   - *the manager class*. In this case, the blocks are made up of instances from the manager class
   - *a navigational relationship*. In this case, the blocks are made up of instances related to the manager class through a navigational relationship
   - *an index or a filter*. The blocks are made of the retrieved instances

2. **Ordering**. This pattern defines a class population ordering (*ASC*endant or *DESC*endant) according to the value of one or more attributes. It can be applied to navigational classes, specifying how the retrieved instances will be ordered, or it can be applied to access structures and search mechanisms to order the obtained results.

3. **Layout**. We provide 4 layout patterns: *register, tabular, master-detail* (with a presentation pattern for the detail) and *tree*. They can be applied to:
   - the *manager class*, defining the way its instances are presented.
   - a *navigation relationship*, defining how instances of the target related class are presented with respect to the source class.

Figure 5 shows the presentation requirements specified for the Publications navigational context. Note that this context is the Publications navigational context (see Figure 4) with the presentation patterns applied to the navigational primitives. This context specifies that Publications are shown in a register way, being only possible to see one at a time (cardinality to one is specified) and the publications are sorted by year in a descendant way (the newest publications are shown first). The relationship between publications and signers is shown applying the master-detail pattern. The master role is played by the publications that are shown applying the register pattern. The detail role is played by the signers that are shown with the tabular pattern. As can be seen in Figure 5, these signers are shown ordered by the position in the publication.

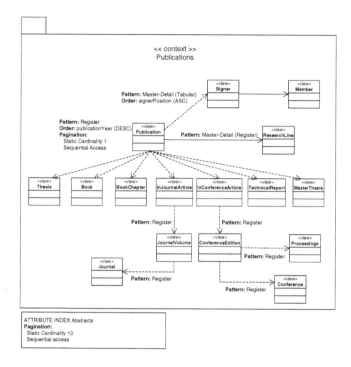

Fig. 5. Publications Context with Presentation

These presentation patterns, together with the specified navigation features, capture the essential requirements for the construction of web interfaces. The next step of our proposal ("solution development") is to define how to systematically implement a web application taking these models as an input.

3   A Strategy to Develop the Web Solution

OOWS follows the OO-Method strategy for systematically going from the problem space to the solution space. Although this is not the most important paper contribution, it is basic to introduce the main ideas that will guide the reification of a OOWS conceptual schema into a software product.

In order to develop the web solution, we define a two step process that (1) proposes a multi-tier architectural style, based on a classical three tier architecture, and (2) defines a set of correspondences between the conceptual abstractions and the software elements that implement each tier of the architecture, making use of design patterns. The tiers of the selected architectural style are the following (see Figure 1):

- **Presentation Tier**. It includes the graphical user interface components for interacting with the user.

Fig. 6. *Home* page of the web application for the *Member* kind of user

- **Application Tier**. This tier is divided into the *Business Facade* that publicizes the interfaces provided the *Business Logic* that implements the structure and the functionality of the classes in the conceptual schema.
- **Persistence Tier**. It implements the persistence and the access to persistent data in order to hide the details of data repositories to upper tiers.

Taking into account the new features introduced in our enhanced web schemas, the OOWS approach enriches the OO-Method generation process [7] providing a new translation process to systematically generate the *Presentation Tier* for web applications.

3.1   Implementing Web Application Presentation Tier from Navigational and Presentational Models

Starting from the navigational and presentational models, a group of connected web pages for each kind of user can be obtained in a systematic way. These web pages define the web application user interface for navigating, visualizing the data and accessing to the web application functionality. Let's show an example of how web pages are obtained for the Member.

A web page is created for each navigational context in the navigational map. This web page is responsible for retrieving the specified information in its navigational context by sending web services requests to the application tier. Marking as *home* one exploration context causes that the user automatically navigates to that web page when the user logs into the system. Otherwise, a web page that provides a link to each navigational exploration context (page) is created to play the role of the *home* page. Figure 6 shows an example of a created *home* page.

Clicking on a link, the application *navigates* to the web page that represents the target context. For instance, if we select the Publications link in the *home* page, we reach the Publications web page (related to the Publications context. As this context has defined an index, when we reach the web page (using an exploration link), the index gets activated, creating a list of instances with the specified information (see Figure 7).

Selecting one of these indexed instances (using the name of the publication as the link attribute), the web page shows all the information specified in the

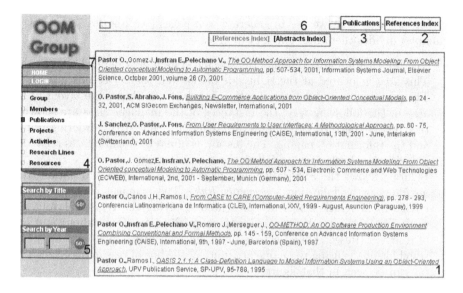

Fig. 7. Index for the web page of the Publications context

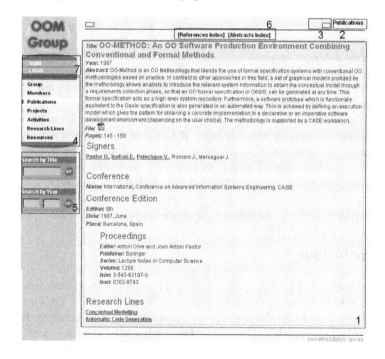

Fig. 8. Web page of the Publications context

context. The web page of Figure 8 presents the Publications context. It shows the publications (title, publicationYear, . . .), its signers and other information depending on the subtype of publication.

The strategy that we use to generate web pages (see Figures 7 and 8 as an example) divides them into two logical areas:

- The *information* area presents the specific system view defined by a context. This area is located at the right side of the web pages (see box number 1). The presentation model specification is applied to obtain the layout of this area in the following way: the instances of the manager class are shown as their layout pattern determines, applying (if defined) the ordering criteria and the information paging. The instances of navigational classes related by a navigational relationship follow the same strategy.
  Figure 8 shows the Publication web page with a selected publication (from an *index* or by following a *sequence link*). The manager class and all the navigational relationships are presented applying the register layout pattern. The context relationship between publication (Publication) and lines of research (ResearchLine) classes defines a navigation capability to the ResearchLine page using the name attribute of the line of research as the anchor (as can be seen in that figure).
- The *navigation* area provides navigation meta-information to the user, in order to improve some aspects of the quality (usability) of the final application [12]:
  - *Where the user is* (see box number 2). It is stated which web page (context) is being currently shown to the user.
  - *How the user reached here* (see box number 3). It is shown the navigational path that has been followed to reach that page.
  - *Where the user can go to* (see box number 4). A link to any exploration context appears in this area.
  - *Which filters and index mechanisms can be used by the user* (see boxes number 5 and 6, respectively). If the context has defined any filter or index mechanism, it is shown in this logical area. The figure shows the two specified filters (search members by *name* and publications between years) and the two available indexes (References and Abstracts).
  - *Applicational links* (see box number 7). Additional applicational links are provided to navigate to the home page and to log into the system.

4   Conclusions

The work presented in this paper incorporates new conceptual modelling facilities to OO-Method in order to model web applications. Two models have been discussed to properly capture web application requirements (navigation and presentation models). They have been integrated into an existing model-driven approach (OO-Method) that is capable of systematically generating code from conceptual schemas. Also this generation process have been extended to generate web applications.

Currently, we are applying this method to several web projects. These experiences are providing us the necessary feedback to extend conceptual modelling primitives related to web applications (personalization and adaptation features, security requirements, specification reuse mechanisms) and allow us to define their corresponding translation patterns.

We are also working on extending classical requirement elicitation techniques to extract navigational requirements providing guidelines to obtain navigational models starting from early navigational requirements. A CASE tool is being developed to support the full development process of web applications using our integrated model-driven approach.

References

1. Muruguesan, S., Desphande, Y.: Web Engineering. Software Engineering and Web Application Development. Springer LNCS – Hot Topics (2001)
2. Fraternali, P.: Tools and approaches for developing data-intensive Web applications: a survey. ACM Computing Surveys, ACM Press **31** (1999) 227–263 ISSN:0360-0300.
3. Schwabe, D., Rossi, G., Barbosa, S.: Systematic Hypermedia Design with OOHDM. In: ACM Conference on Hypertext, Washington, USA (1996)
4. Ceri, S., Fraternali, P., Bongio, A.: Web Modeling Language (WebML): a Modeling Language for Designing Web Sites. In: Proc. of the 9th International World Wide Web Conference, WWW9, Elsevier (2000) 137–157
5. Koch, N., Wirsing, M.: Software Engineering for Adaptive Hypermedia Applications. In: 3rd Workshop on Adaptive Hypertext and Hypermedia. (2001)
6. De Troyer, O., Leune, C.: WSDM: A User-centered Design Method for Web sites. In: Proc. of the 7th International World Wide Web Conference. (1997) 85–94
7. Pastor, O., Gómez, J., Insfrán, E., Pelechano, V.: The OO-Method Approach for Information Systems Modelling: From Object-Oriented Conceptual Modeling to Automated Programming. Information Systems **26** (2001) 507–534
8. Insfrán, E., Pastor, O., Wieringa, R.: Requirements Engineering-Based Conceptual Modelling. Requirements Engineering **7** (2002) 61–72
9. Rossi, G., Schwabe, D., Lyardet, F.: Web Application Models are More than Conceptual Models. In: 19th International Conference on Conceptual Modeling (ER'00), Salt Lake City, USA, Springer-Verlag (2000)
10. Fons, J., Valderas, P., Pastor, O.: Specialization in Navigational Models. In: Argentine Conference on Computer Science and Operacional Research. Subserie ICWE, Iberoamerican Conference on Web Engineering. Volume 31 of Anales JAIO., Santa Fe, Argentina (2002) 16–31 ISSN: 1666-6526.
11. Lyardet, F., Rossi, G., Schwabe, D.: Patterns for Dynamic Websites. In: Proc. of PloP98, Allerton, USA (1998)
12. Olsina, L.: Metodologia Cuantitativa para la Evaluacion y Comparacion de la Calidad de Sitios Web. PhD thesis, Facultad de Ciencias Excatas de la Universidad Nacional de La Plata (1999) In spanish.

Extending Hypertext Conceptual Models with Process-Oriented Primitives*

Marco Brambilla

Dipartimento di Elettronica e Informazione, Politecnico di Milano
Via Ponzio 34/5, 20133 Milano, Italy
mbrambil@elet.polimi.it

Abstract. Web conceptual modeling is a young discipline, which is gaining popularity among Web developers and CASE tool vendors. However, most conceptual models for the Web proposed so far are an evolution of hypermedia models, and pay attention mostly to the specification of data structures and navigation primitives. As the Web becomes a vehicle for implementing B2B applications, the need arises of extending Web conceptual modeling from data-centric applications to data- and process-centric applications. This paper presents a pragmatic approach to incorporate classical process modeling primitives within a Web modeling framework and comments on the experience gained applying the resulting methodology to an industrial case.

1 Introduction

Conceptual modeling has been widely recognized as one of the key ingredients of modern software engineering, because it permits developers to formalize their knowledge about the application in a high-level, platform-independent, yet formal and rigorous way. Conceptual models, originated in the database field (E-R model), have spread in the object-oriented community (UML), and have been recently proposed also for Web application development [3, 5].

The first generation of conceptual models for the Web [2, 3, 6, 10] essentially considered Web applications as a variant of traditional hypermedia applications, where the content to be published resides in a database and browsing takes place on the Internet. Therefore, the modeling focus of these methods is capturing the structure of content, e.g., as a set of object classes or entities connected by associations or relationships, and the navigation primitives, represented by such concepts as pages, content nodes, and links.

However, a second generation of conceptual models is required, because the Web is more and more being used as the implementation platform for B2B applications, whose goal is not only the navigation of content, but also supporting the business processes occurring within an organization and between the organization and its partners. These second generation models should cope with process and workflow

---

* This research is part of the WebSI (Web Service Integration) project, funded by the EC in the Fifth Framework.

I.-Y. Song et al. (Eds.): ER 2003, LNCS 2813, pp. 246–262, 2003.

modeling, support Web service interaction[1], and integrate data-centric and process-centric modeling primitives into a mix suited to the development of advanced B2B Web applications.

This paper reports on an experience of extending a first-generation Web modeling language [3, 4] to support the specification, design and implementation of B2B applications. The proposed approach is lightweight and pragmatic and relies on the following assumptions and objectives:

- We are interested in extending Web modeling concepts to cope with process and workflow modeling, not to adapt workflow management systems to the Web. This approach is justified in all those (numerous) contexts where Web B2B applications originate from a previous data-centric Web application. The typical case is an intranet application that is extended to support a complex content management lifecycle or is opened to business partners outside the company. In this case it should be possible to reuse the conceptual model of the original application and extend it to support inter- or intra-organization processes.

- We assume that the business processes behind the Web interface can be schematized as sequences of elementary operations, with a simple control logic based on decision points. More sophisticated business logic (e.g., the algorithm for the explosion of a bill of materials) are not modeled, but treated as a black box. This assumption is true in most content management workflows, where the actions are content production, deletion, and update, and the control logic reduces to the scheduling and approval of changes, and also in most inter-organization processes (e.g., supply chain management), where partners exchange pieces of data (e.g., orders or credit notes) and make decisions based on the status or content of such information.

- We want to reuse as far as possible the implementation techniques and tools matured for data-centric Web hypertexts, extending such techniques and tools only in those aspects directly connected to the implementation of multi-organizational process, e.g., the cooperation of application users belonging to different organizations via Web services.

In the light of the above assumptions, our contribution can be summarized in the following points:

- A web development process that adapts a classic software engineering paradigm (the RUP process model [6]) to the case of process-and data-centric Web applications.

- A mix of notations and modeling concepts that supports both the requirements analysis and the conceptual design phases.

- A set of extension to a specific Web modeling language, WebML, extending the expressive power of the language to cover process modeling. WebML has been chosen for tactical reasons (we know the language and an extensible CASE tool is available for experimentation), but the proposed approach is of general validity and can be restated in the context of other "first-generation" Web modeling languages.

---

[1] Web services are emerging as the technical means of implementing inter-organizational workflows over the Web, where human users and software programs collaborate in the fulfillment of a business process.

- An implementation architecture, whereby the existing code generation techniques and runtime framework for producing data-centric Web applications from WebML specifications are extended to support B2B applications.

The paper is organized as follows: Section 2 briefly outlines the development process underlying our proposal and overviews the mix of notations and techniques that will be addressed in the paper; Section 3 introduces a running case used throughout the paper, which is a simplified version of an industrial application we are implementing; Section 4 presents the requirements specification tasks, including user, process, data, and interface specification; Section 5 addresses the conceptual design phase, which is the core of the entire process. For space reasons, after a brief overview of WebML (Section 5.1), we concentrate on the aspects related to the integration of process modeling within "classical" Web modeling, by showing: 1) how to use data modeling to represent process data (Section 5.2.1); 2) how to extend the WebML hypertext modeling language to capture process enactment requirements (Section 5.2.2); 3) how to map process specifications into hypertexts targeted to the various actors involved in the process (Section 5.2.3). Section 6 discusses the implementation of the proposed modeling primitives in the context of a commercial CASE tool. Finally, Section 7 reviews related works and Section 8 draws some conclusions and presents our ongoing and future work.

2 Development Process of Web Applications

Fig. 1 shows the lifecycle of a data- and process-centric Web application, which consists of requirements specification, conceptual design, the technical tasks of architecture design and implementation, and the steps of testing and evaluation, which may spin-off other iterations over the lifecycle or lead to the deployment of the application and its successive maintenance and evolution.

With respect to a purely data-centric Web application, the lifecycle of Fig. 1 augments the conceptual design phase with Process Design, which addresses the high-level schematization of the processes assisted by the application. Process Design influences the role and content of data and hypertext design, which should take into account process requirements, as we explain in Section 5.2.

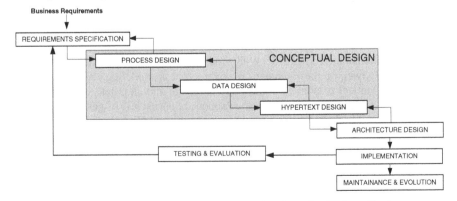

Fig. 1. Phases in the development process of data-intensive Web applications

Table 1. Development notations and techniques, charted by process phase and development perspective

Focus Activity	DATA	HYPERTEXT	PROCESS
ANALYSIS	Data dictionary	Site maps	- User groups - Use cases - Workflow diagrams
DESIGN	Entity – Relationship	Hypertext diagrams	Hypertextual process primitives
IMPLEMENTATION	Relational schemas	Server side languages (JSP, .NET, ...)	Server-side components, Web services

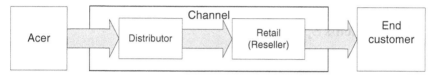

Fig. 2. The product flow of the Acer distribution channel

Table 1 overviews the notations and techniques used to support the lifecycle of Fig. 1: for each major phase of the development process (requirements specification, conceptual design, and implementation) we list the notations used for each application perspective (process, data, hypertext).

For some of these activities, we adopt widely consolidated standards and notations. In particular, data requirements analysis is performed using standard data dictionaries, data design exploits the traditional E-R model, and data implementation is typically obtained through relational technology, although different data implementations can be used. These aspects are quite consolidated and are addressed in this paper only to show how they are affected by the functional requirements about the business processes to support.

3   Running Example

To concretely illustrate our approach, we will use as a running example an application called Acer Business Portal, developed in collaboration with the European branch of Acer, the international computer manufacturing company. The application aims at providing services to the operators of the Acer's distribution channel, which includes distributors and retailers.

Fig. 2 shows the different stages of the supply chain: gray arrows represent the products flow from the producer to the end user and white boxes represent the involved actors. Acer provides products to the channel operators, who are in charge of distributing it. Distributors can be small local entities, country-wide operators, or international distributors. Retailers are the selling points, which allow the final customer to buy products.

The ultimate goal of the Business Portal is to standardize the communication processes of the various channel operators, especially in the area of inventory and sales management, presently managed "off-line" using different data exchange formats, communication and information systems, and technological supports. The Business Portal will serve various user groups, including Acer Europe top and middle managers, Acer's national subsidiaries, distributors, and resellers. In this paper, we consider only a small subset of the real requirements, to exemplify the main aspects of the development methodology. Besides the sales reports exchange, the portal must make distributors and resellers able to electronically submit their refunding requests for stock protection, in case the price of some product falls. The portal should support refunding management, both from the distributor's side and from the internal Acer personnel's side.

4   Requirements Specification

Requirements analysis is the phase in which the business goals of the application are translated into the precise specifications of the application users, of the required data, of the supported processes, and of the application interfaces. We will examine each aspect in turn, paying particular attention to process and interface requirements.

4.1 User and Data Requirements

The specification of user and data requirements can be performed using traditional means: users are clustered into groups, possibly organized in specialization hierarchies, and data requirements are formalized as a dictionary, which lists the main concepts of the application domain, their essential attributes and relationships. Fig. 3 shows the user taxonomy of the Business Portal application, whereas Table 2 illustrates an excerpt of the data dictionary.

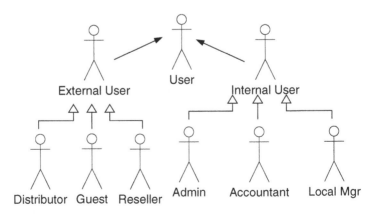

Fig. 3. User taxonomy of the Business Portal application

Table 2. Fragment of the data dictionary of the Business Portal application

Name	RefundingRequest
Synonyms	None.
Description	Is the request of refunding that a distributor submits to Acer
Properties	
Quantity	Number of sold pieces.
Old price	Old price of the goods
New price	New price of the goods
Document No.	Identifier of the sales document about which the refunding is asked
Request Date	Day in which the refunding request is submitted
Document Date	Date of the sales document about which the refunding is asked
Status	Status of the request: not yet evaluated, under consideration, approved
Relationships	
RequestToProduct	It relates the refunding request to the product for which the refunding is asked
RequestToDistributor	It relates the refunding request to the user that submitted it

4.2 Functional and Process Requirements

Functional and process requirements formalize the functions required by the users of the application and the structure of the processes where such functions are executed. UML use-case diagrams can be exploited to enumerate the relevant processes and process diagrams to express the flow of activities within a specific use case.

For specifying processes, we adopt the terminology and notation defined by the Workflow Management Coalition [13], which is particularly effective in the description of multi-actor workflows. The WFMC workflow model is based on the concepts of *Processes*, i.e., the description of the supported workflows; *Cases*, i.e., the process instances; *Activities*, i.e., the units of works composing a process; *Activity instances*, i.e., the individual instantiations of an activity within a case; *Actors*, i.e. the roles intervening in the process, and *Constraints*, i.e., the logical precedence among activities.

Processes can be internally structured using a variety of constructs: sequences of activities, AND-splits (i.e., points where a single thread of control splits into two or more threads, which can proceed autonomously and independently), AND-joins (points where two or more parallel activities converge), OR-splits (points where a single thread of control makes a decision upon which branch to take among multiple alternative workflow branches), OR-joins (points where two or more alternative branches re-converge to a single common thread of control), iterations for repeating the execution of one or more activities, pre- and post-conditions (entry and exit criteria to/from a particular activity, respectively).

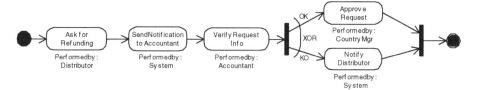

Fig. 4. Workflow diagram of the refunding request process supported by the Business Portal

Fig. 4 exemplifies a WFMC process model specifying the way in which distributors submit requests of refunding for stock protection. A distributor submits a refunding request through the Web portal interface. A notification is sent by the system to the Acer internal accountant in charge of managing the Distributor, who verifies the request. If everything is correct, the request is passed to the Country Manager, who approves it and makes the refunding payable; otherwise the Distributor who applied for refunding is automatically notified by email that his request has been rejected.

The functional and process requirements help the specification of the application hypertextual interfaces, as shown in the next section.

4.3 Interface Requirements

Interface requirements pin down the application interfaces (called *site views*) needed for accomplishing the requirements of the identified groups and in particular for supporting the identified processes. A site view serves the use cases associated to one or more user groups, offers access or content management functions over selected data elements, and publishes the interfaces for executing the activities of a process. For each site view, a specification sheet is filled, as shown in Table 3.

Table 3. Site view specification sheet for the Distributors site view

Site View Name	Distributor Site View	
Description	In order to access this site view, Distributors need to login. Then, they can browse the complete Acer products catalog, submit refunding requests, and check their status.	
User Groups	Distributor	
Use Cases	"Login", "Browse Products", "Ask for refunding", "Check refunding status".	
Site View Map		
Area Name	**Area Description**	**Accessed objects**
Products browsing	This area allows distributors to browse the products catalog in a top-down fashion, from ProductGroups to ProductBrands and Products	Product, ProductBrand, ProductGroup
Mailing list subscription	This area allows distributors to subscribe to the Acer marketing mailing list	Distributor
Stock protection refunding	This area implements the process of refunding management for the distributor. The user can submit a request through a page containing a form.	RefundingRequest

5 Conceptual Design

Conceptual design is the phase in which requirements are turned into a high-level, platform-independent specification of the application, which can be used to drive the subsequent implementation phase. Our approach to conceptual design relies on the following guidelines: *data requirements* are used to produce an Entity-Relationship diagram modeling the data stored, manipulated, and exchanged by the application actors, plus the metadata required for the management of the business processes; *process diagrams* are treated as a higher-level specification and are used to derive a set of hypertext models that "realizes" them. These hypertext models belong to the site views of the user groups involved in the process and must offer them the interface needed for performing the various activities specified in the process diagram.

For space limitations, we focus the illustration of the conceptual design phase to the process-related aspects. We start by giving a brief overview of WebML, the notation adopted for modeling the hypertextual interfaces.

5.1 Overview of WebML Hypertext Modeling Primitives

WebML [3, 4, 11] is a conceptual language originally conceived for specifying Web applications developed on top of database content described using the E-R model. A WebML schema consists of one or more hypertexts (called *site views*), expressing the Web interface used to publish or manipulate the data specified in the underlying E-R schema.

A *site view* is a graph of *pages* to be presented on the Web. Pages enclose *content units*, representing atomic pieces of information to be published (e.g., indexes listing items from which the user may select a particular object, details of a single object, entry forms, and so on); content units may have a *selector*, which is a predicate identifying the entity instances to be extracted from the underlying database and displayed by the unit. Pages and units can be connected with *links* to express a variety of navigation effects.

Besides content publishing, WebML allows specifying *operations*, like the filling of a shopping cart or the update of content. Basic data update operations are: the creation, modification and deletion of instances of an entity, or the creation and deletion of instances of a relationship. Operations do not display data and are placed outside of pages; user-defined operations can be specified, such as sending e-mail, login and logout, e-payment, and so on.

Fig. 5 shows a simplified version of the first two areas of the Distributor site view of the Business Portal, whose map have been illustrated in Table 3: the *Products* area allows guests to browse products, by first selecting in the *Home* page the product group from an index (*ProductGroups*) and then by looking at the group details and selecting a specific brand in page *ProductBrands*. Once a brand is selected, all the products of that brand are shown in page *Products*. The *Mailing List Subscription* area allows the user to subscribe to a mailing list through a form. The submitted data (email address and so on) are used to modify the profile of the Distributor. This is obtained by means of a modify operation called *Modify Subscr*, which updates the instance of entity *Distributor* currently logged[2].

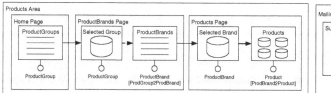
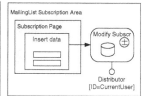

Fig. 5. WebML site view diagram featuring areas, pages, content units, and operations.

---

[2] The selector [ID = CurrentUser] specifies that the object to modify is the instance of entity Distributor having ID = CurrentUser, where CurrentUser is a session variable identifying the currently logged user.

5.2 Extending Data and Hypertext Modeling to Capture Processes

In the specification of a Web application for supporting business processes, the data model, which is normally used to describe the domain objects, is extended with user-related and workflow-related data, and the hypertext model is enriched by a set of primitives that enables the content of pages to be adapted to the status of the workflow.

5.2.1 Extending the Data Model with Process Metadata

Data modeling is extended with the metadata used to represent the runtime evolution of processes. Fig. 6 shows an E-R model encompassing all the main concepts of the WFMC process model. The schema includes entities representing the elements of a process, and relationships expressing the semantic connections of the process elements.

Entity *Process* is associated with entity *ActivityType*, to represent the classes of activities that can be executed in a process. Entity *Case* denotes an instance of a process, whose status can be: initiated, active, or completed. Entity *ActivityInstance* denotes the occurrence of an activity, whose current status can be: inactive, active and completed. Entities *User* and *Group* represent the workflow actors, as individual users organized within groups. A user may belong to different groups, and one of such groups is chosen as his default group, to facilitate access control when the user logs in.

Activities are "assigned to" user groups: this means that users of that group can perform the activity. Instead, concrete activity instances are "assigned to" individual users, who actually perform them.

Application data is a usual E-R model of the information involved in the current application. In our example, as depicted in the boxed part of Fig. 6, we model the three levels product catalog hierarchy (in which each *Product* belongs to a *ProductBrand*, and *ProductBrands* are categorized into *ProductGroups*), the *RefundingRequest* and the *Distributor* profile. *RefundingRequest* is related to the *Distributor* who submitted it, and to the *Product* it refers to.

The designer can specify an arbitrary number of relationships between the application data and the workflow data, which may be required to connect the activities to the data items they use. This connection can be expressed as a relationship (generically called *RelatedTo* in Fig. 6), which connects the instances of the application entities with the activity instances where they are used.

5.2.2 Extending the Hypertext Model with Process Enactment Primitives

Besides modeling the metadata for recording the status of processes, it is also necessary to design interfaces capable of producing and consuming such metadata, in order to correctly enact the processes. To ease the specification of hypertexts for executing workflows, a few additional primitives are introduced in WebML for updating process data as a result of activity execution, for accessing the data associated with a specific activity instance, and for expressing the assignment of data objects to an activity instance to be executed in the future.

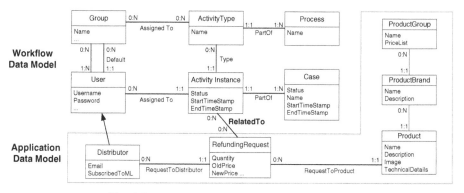

Fig. 6. Data model incorporating workflow concepts

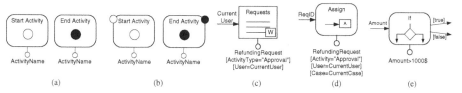

Fig. 7. *Start Activity* and *End Activity* operations (a), eventually denoted with start and end case notations (b); workflow-aware content unit notation(c); graphical notation of the *Assign* operation (d) and of the conditional operation (e)

The portion of hypertext devoted to the execution of a process activity must be enclosed between the two workflow-related operations shown in Fig. 7(a): *Start Activity* and *end activity*[3].

These operations delimit a portion of the hypertext devoted to the execution of an activity and have the side effect of updating the workflow data. Specifically, starting an activity implies creating an activity instance, recording the activity instance activation timestamp, connecting the activity instance to the current case (using relationship PartOf), to the current user (using relationship AssignedTo), and to the proper activity type, and setting the status of the activity instance to "active". Symmetrically, ending an activity implies setting the status of the current activity instance to "completed" and recording the completion timestamp.

The *Start Activity* operation can also be tagged as the *start of the case*, when the activity to start is the first one of the entire process; dually, the *End Activity* operation can be tagged as the *end of the case*. At case start, a new case instance is created with status="running"; when the case ends, its status is set to "terminated". Fig. 7(b) shows the graphic notation for case start / end.

For retrieving the data objects related to the instances of a particular activity, *workflow-aware content units* can be used. These units are like the regular WebML content unit but are tagged with a "W" symbol denoting a simplified syntax for their

---

[3] This means that the link(s) entering the portion of hypertext associated with the activity must trigger the *Start Activity* operation and the link(s) exiting such portion of hypertext must trigger the *end activity* operation.

selector, which shortens the expression of predicates involving both application data and workflow data. For example, Fig. 7(c) shows a workflow-aware index unit that retrieves all the instances of entity *RefundingRequest*, relevant to the user passed as a parameter to the unit and related to activities of type "Approval".

The *assign operation* is a WebML operation unit conceived for connecting application object(s) to an activity instance, for which an activity type, a case and possibly a user are specified. Fig. 7(d) shows the graphical representation of the assign operation, which assigns a RefundingRequest to the activity called "Approval", for the current case and for the currently logged user. Thus, the assign unit permits the specification of a "data connection" between activities.

The navigation of a hypertext may need to be conditioned by the status of activities, to reflect the constraints imposed by the workflow. Two dedicated operations called *if* and *switch* operations allow conditional navigation, performing the necessary status tests and deciding the destination of a navigable link. Fig. 7(e) shows an example of *if* operation: when the incoming link transporting the *Amount* parameter is navigated, the condition is tested, and the appropriate link is followed.

5.2.3 Mapping Process Diagrams to Hypertexts Supporting Process Enactment

Workflow activities are realized in the hypertext model by suitable configurations of pages and units representing the interfaces for executing them, enclosed between *Start / End activity* operations. Activity precedence constraints are turned into content publication and navigation constraints among the pages of the activities, ensuring that the data shown by the application and user navigation respect the constraints described by the process specification.

To better understand this design phase, we exemplify the hypertext realization of the *sequence*, the simplest WFMC constraint, and of the *AND-split/ AND-join* connectors.

Sequence. Given two activities A and B, the constraint expressing that activity B must be performed <u>after</u> activity A can be realized as a hypertext specification as illustrated in Fig. 8. Fig. 8(a) shows a first realization based on an explicit link going out of the page implementing the interface of Activity A[4]: navigating the link terminates activity A, starts activity B and opens the page for executing B; Fig. 8(b) shows an alternative realization based on data coordination: when the link outgoing the page of Activity A is navigated, it assigns some data to activity B; the page of activity B can be accessed at any time, but activity B can be performed only when some data assigned from activity A is available in a workflow-aware content unit, like the index unit shown in Fig. 8(b). If no data has been assigned to activity B, the index remains empty and thus the link for stating activity B cannot be navigated.

AND-split/ AND-join. Fig. 9 shows an hypertext diagram representing AND-split/ AND-join. In this realization, activities A and B can be performed by the same user in any order; when both activities have been terminated, activity C can start. From the initial page the user may either choose activity A or activity B; after termination of activity A (B) a test condition checks if activity B (A) has not been executed yet. If

---

[4] The example uses empty rectangles to denote the interface of an activity. In reality, an activity interface contains specific pages, units, and operations linked to yield a concrete hypertext for performing the activity.

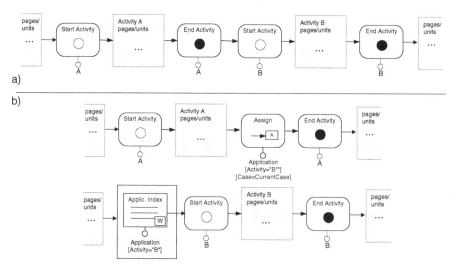

Fig. 8. Hypertext realization of the sequence

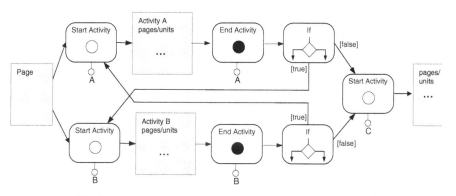

Fig. 9. Hypertext realization of the AND-split AND-join structures

this condition is true, a navigation link leads the user to the starting point of activity B (A), so that also activity B can be executed; instead, if both activities have been completed, the next activity C is started. It is important to notice that in this example parallelism is achieved through serialization to facilitate the user, which is the same for the two activities. However, it is possible to set up hypertextual schemas which grants real parallelism between activities, both for single and for multiple users.

Similarly, pre-conditions, post-conditions, OR-splits and OR-joins can be represented in hypertext diagrams. Pre- and post-conditions are modeled using *if* and *switch* operations, leading the user to the right activity depending on the status of the current case.

Splits can be modeled in different ways depending on the actor who takes the choice: if a human user chooses the branch to be executed, this will be modeled through links exiting from the pages where the choice is taken; if the system must

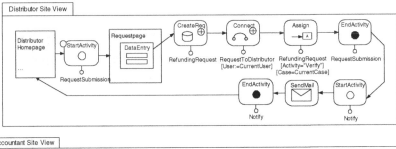

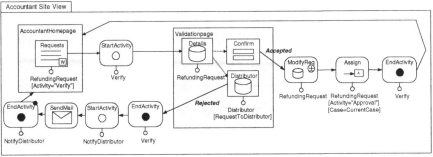

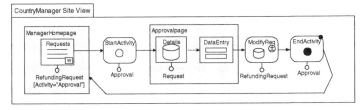

Fig. 10. Three site views realizing the refunding request process specified in Fig. 4

choose automatically, this will be modeled by means of conditional operations (*if* and *switch* operations), automatically executed by the system.

Fig. 10 shows the complete hypertext schema corresponding to the process specified in Fig. 4, representing the submission of refunding requests. Relevant actors are Distributors, Acer Accountants and Acer Country Managers. For each of them, a site view is designed.

From his *Home page*, the Distributor can follow a link to refunding request submission page. The navigation of the link triggers the *Start Activity* operation for the *RequestSubmission*. Since this activity starts a new process case, the *Start Activity* operation is marked as start case with a small white circle on the left. Once the activity is started, the distributor reaches the *Request page*, where he can submit the request data through a form(called *Data Entry*). When the user navigates the outgoing link of the *Data Entry* unit, an operations chain[5] is lauched. A new *RefundingRequest* object is instantiated in the database by the *CreateReq* operation (with the proper

---

[5] An operation chain consists of a set of operations directly connected each other through links. The chain can be activated by a click of the user, that triggers the start of the first operation. Once an operation is terminated, the link to the next one is automatically navigated and the next operation is executed.

attributes values) and connected to currently logged user through the *RequestToDistributor* relationship. The request is then assigned to the next activity in which it is involved (the *Verify* activity, to be performed by the Accountant). The *RefundingRequest* is then ended, and the *Notify* activity, that sends a notification email to Acer Accountant, is automatically performed by the system, since links between operations are always automatically navigated.

The Accountant can see in his home page the list of the *RefundingRequests* to be processed (i.e., assigned to the *Verify* activity). By choosing one, he starts the *Verify* activity on it, and is led to the *Validation page*, in which he can accept or reject the *RefundingRequest*. The page shows the details of the request and of the *Distributor* who submitted it. If he accepts the request, by clicking on the submit button in the *Confirm* form, the *RefundingRequest* status is modified to accepted, then the request is assigned to the *Approval* activity, and the *Verify* activity is ended. If he rejects the request, the *Verify* activity is ended as well, but then the *NotifyDistributor* activity is automatically performed. In this example, the choice between the two branches of the split in the process is manually performed by the Accountant, and therefore no decisions must be taken by the system by means of *if / switch* units. This activity is the last of the process, therefore the *End Activity* operation is marked with the black circle on the right that denotes the EndCase property.

The Country Manager can see in his *Home page* all the requests that have been verified by an Accountant, and that are now assigned to the *Approval* activity. He can definitively approve a request, by selecting it from the index in his *Home page*, and changing its status to approved in the *Approval page*. This is achieved by means of the *Modify Req* operation, which updates the *Status* attribute of the current *RefundingRequest*. Since the *Approval* activity is the last of the process, the corresponding *End Activity* operation is marked as EndCase.

6   Implementation and Experience

The modeling approach discussed in this paper has been implemented in the context of a commercial CASE tool, called WebRatio [12], which supports the model-driven development of data-intensive Web applications. WebRatio has an extensible architecture, where new modeling primitives can be plugged into the design environment, code generator, and runtime framework, by writing Java or C Sharp components and wrapping them using XML descriptors and XSL style sheets. The conceptual modeling approach proposed in this paper has been implemented by performing several extensions of WebRatio:

- The default data schema of WebRatio applications has been augmented to incorporate the workflow-related entities and relationships shown in the upper part of Fig. 6.
- The WebML diagram editor has been extended to support the specification of WFMC process diagrams. The code generator has also been extended to translate process diagrams into the skeletons of the site views associated with the actors involved in the process. This translation implements the mapping rules between process and hypertext diagrams exemplified in Fig. 8 and produces empty activity interfaces, plus all the auxiliary operations needed for activity synchronization (*Start Activity/ End Activity, start case/ end case*). The XSL translator covers a

subset of the WFMC primitives including activity sequences, AND/OR splits and joins, and conditional branching. The designer can extend the automatically produced site views by "filling-in" the empty activity pages with the content units and operations needed for performing activity-specific tasks, like content creation, approval, modification, message sending, and so on.

- The workflow-related units shown in Fig. 7 have been implemented as a package of custom content units and operations, which add up to the built-in hypertext-modeling primitives of WebML. The code generator has been consequently extended to translate workflow-related units into sequences of native WebML content and operation services, executable in the WebRatio runtime framework.

The ideas discussed in the paper is being benchmarked in the development of the Acer Business Portal Web application, which is being implemented as an extension of a previous application, modeled in WebML. The original application was limited to offering information browsing functions to the channel operators and Acer personnel. The new version supports a number of business processes, which are being integrated into the exiting portal by adding new site views for the novel user groups and new hypertextual interfaces to the site views of existing user groups, devoted to performing the activities of the newly identified business processes. The embedding of process-oriented modeling in the context of a structured Web development methodology eases the management of changes, because designers can analyze the novel requirements and redesign the application at the conceptual level, leveraging the already existing data and hypertext models.

7   Related Work

WebML [3, 4, 11] is one of a family of proposals for the model-driven development of Web sites, which includes also other approaches, e.g., Araneus [8], Strudel[6], OO-HDM [10], W2000 [2]. Among these, only Araneus has been extended with a workflow conceptual model and a workflow management system. Differently from our proposal, Araneus extensions offer a conceptual business process model and aim at allowing the interaction between the hypertext and an underlying workflow management system. In other words, the Web site is used as an interface to the WFMS. With this philosophy, the data-access and the process-execution layers are at the same level, and are accessed through the hypertext exactly in the same way. This is a good solution for all the cases in which a WFMS is already in place, and only the interface has to be redesigned for the Web context.

Many commercial enterprise toolsuite, such as IBM MQSeries Workflow [8] and Oracle Workflow 11i [9] implement complete workflow management systems, based on workflow engines. These tools aim at integrating different enterprise applications, often developed by the same vendor, but application and workflow Web publishing consists in re-building the application for the Web context (e.g., as Java applets) and applying workflow rules for their cooperation. This approach is completely different from our proposal, since we work at extending hypertext modeling with high-level workflow primitives, accompanied to a light-weight workflow implementation, whilst industrial WFMSs provide complete workflow engines as native feature, and extend them through Web technologies. The main drawback of this philosophy is that the hypertext navigation power is not completely exploited in the resulting applications, because they often consists in a re-building of the legacy enterprise software.

On the other hand, our proposal does not provide a workflow engine, but a methodology and a high-level modeling framework for a homogeneous description of a Web application with workflow constraints, helping the designer conceptualize and organize an application involving roles and workflow-style paradigms. Our approach is suitable for lightweight applications, which are very common on the Web, and is based on simple concepts, whose code can be automatically generated.

8   Conclusions and Future Work

In this paper, we have discussed the adaptation of data-centric Web conceptual modeling to process-oriented applications, such as B2B Web applications. This adaptation requires complementing the activities and artifacts of Web requirement analysis and conceptual design with notations and techniques for capturing the constraints that stem from the process structure and for embodying such constraints in the hypertextual interfaces of the application. To do so, we have extended an existing Web modeling language (WebML) and its underlying development process, incorporating process modeling and the translation of process models into suitable metadata and hypertext structures. This extension permits a smooth integration of process modeling within Web design methodologies, by standardizing the way in which process diagrams are transformed into the hypertext diagrams that realize the process.

The main advantage of our approach consist of the easy definition of process-driven Web applications. With respect to traditional Web applications the new primitives grant an immediate help in activity tracking, process status checking and workflow-related data extraction. The result of the design can be a real workflow application, exploiting all the power of complex hypertexts. This is a typical requirement of most Web applications, e.g., enterprise content publishing sites, self-registration wizards, e-commerce payments, event and travel booking and purchase, and so on.

Our future work will proceed along four directions: more complex process modeling features will be considered, to widen the spectrum of process diagrams to which the proposed approach can be applied; further experiments will be conducted with CASE tools, to better automate the derivation of hypertext from process models; scouting of methods for failure and consistency management in processes execution on traditional WFMS is going on, to prepare the basis for the failure and recovery analysis in the context of Web applications; finally, verification rules for keeping the hypertext model aligned with the process model during evolution and maintenance will be studied and implemented.

Orthogonally, we are experimenting novel architectural paradigms for deploying process-centric applications. The current implementation assumes that all the site views are deployed as dynamic page templates and server-side components running in a centralized host, which also contains the database storing the application data and the process metadata. Each party in the process must log into the central host for participating to the process. We have started implementing a different architecture based on data distribution and Web services, where both the application data and the process metadata can reside at the premises of the organizations involved in the B2B application (e.g., at Acer's central site and at the sites of the various channel operators). Synchronization is achieved by Web service calls: a given party A can expose Web services whereby other remote parties can selectively update A's data and the process-related metadata relevant to A's view of the ongoing process. In this way, the central data repository is replaced by several distributed local repositories and process synchronization takes place through asynchronous messaging rather than by updates performed in a central database.

Acknowledgments. We are grateful to Stefano Ceri, Piero Fraternali, Ioana Manolescu, Sara Comai and the whole team of the WebSI project for the stimulating discussions and ideas on workflow and hypertext integration. We wish to thank also Emanuele Tosetti of Acer Europe for providing the specifications of the Business Portal application and all the Acer personnel who collaborate to the development.

References

1. Atzeni, P., Mecca, G., Merialdo, P.: Design and Maintenance of Data-Intensive Web Sites. EDBT 1998: 436–450.
2. Baresi, L., Garzotto, F., Paolini, P.: From Web Sites to Web Applications: New Issues for Conceptual Modeling. ER Workshops 2000: 89–100.
3. Ceri, S., Fraternali, P., Bongio, A.: Web Modeling Language (WebML): a modeling language for designing Web sites. WWW9/Computer Networks 33(1–6): 137–157 (2000)
4. Ceri, S., Fraternali, P., Bongio, A., Brambilla, M., Comai, S., Matera, M.: Designing Data-Intensive Web Applications, Morgan-Kaufmann, December 2002.
5. Conallen, J.: Building Web Applications with UML. Addison Wesley (Object Technology Series), 2000.
6. Fernandez, M. F., Florescu, D., Kang, J., Levy, A.Y., Suciu, D.: Catching the Boat with Strudel: Experiences with a Web-Site Management System. SIGMOD 1998: 414–425.
7. Jacobson, I., Booch, G., Rumbaugh, J.: The Unified Software Development Process. Addison Wesley, 1999.
8. IBM MQSeries Workflow Homepage: http://www.ibm.com/software/ts/mqseries/workflow/v332/
9. Oracle Workflow 11i: http://www.oracle.com/appsnet/technology/products/docs/workflow.html
10. Schwabe, D., Rossi, G.: An Object Oriented Approach to Web Applications Design. TAPOS 4(4): (1998).
11. WebML Project Homepage: http://www.webml.org
12. WebRatio Homepage: http://www.webratio.com/
13. Workflow Management Coalition Homepage: http://www.wfmc.org

Requirement Engineering Meets Security: A Case Study on Modelling Secure Electronic Transactions by VISA and Mastercard

Paolo Giorgini[1], Fabio Massacci[1], and John Mylopoulos[1,2]

[1] Department of Information and Communication Technology
University of Trento – Italy
{massacci,giorgini}@dit.unitn.it
[2] Deptartment of Computer Science
University of Toronto – Canada
jm@cs.toronto.edu

Abstract. Computer Security is one of today's hot topic and the need for conceptual models of security features have brought up a number of proposals ranging from UML extensions to novel conceptual models. What is still missing, however, are models that focus on high-level security requirements, without forcing the modeler to immediately get down to security mechanisms. The modeling process itself should make it clear why encryption, authentication or access control are necessary, and what are the tradeoffs, if they are selected. In this paper we show that the *i**/Tropos framework lacks the ability to capture these essential features and needs to be augmented. To motivate our proposal, we build upon a substantial case study – the modeling of the Secure Electronic Transactions e-commerce suites by VISA and MasterCard – to identify missing modeling features. In a nutshell, the key missing concept is the separation of the notion of offering a service (of a handling data, performing a task or fulfilling a goal) and ownership of the very same service. This separation is what makes security essential. The ability of the methodology to model a clear dependency relation between those offering a service (the merchant processing a credit card number), those requesting the service (the bank debiting the payment), and those owning the very same data (the cardholder), make security solutions emerge as a natural consequence of the modeling process.

1 Introduction

"... Is there such a thing anymore as a software system that doesn't need to be secure? Almost every software controlled system faces threats from potential adversaries, from Internet-aware client applications running on PCs, to complex telecommunications and power systems accessible over the Internet, to commodity software with copy protection mechanisms. Software engineers must be cognizant of these threats and engineer systems with credible defenses, while still delivering value to customers.

I.-Y. Song et al. (Eds.): ER 2003, LNCS 2813, pp. 263–276, 2003.

... security concerns must inform every phase of software development, from requirements engineering to design, implementation, testing and deployment..."

In 2000, Devambu and Stubblebine introduced with these words their ICSE article on security and software engineering [5]. The article marked a surfacing need in the IT community: security is not just about securing protocols and communication lines, it is also about software [1,16]. Indeed, the need of securing software is even more pressing than the need of securing communication. Almost no attack has been reported in the literature where hackers harvesting credit card numbers by snooping communication lines, whereas exploits of software security bugs are constantly among the headlines [20].

It has also clearly emerged that security concerns must be tackled from the very beginning because looking at them as an afterthought often leads to problems [1,16]. In their ICSE article, Devambu and Stubblebine posed a challenge of integrating security concerns with requirements engineering, and in particular with UML.

Part of this challenge has been answered, and indeed we have a number of proposals for UML models that incorporate security features [9,8,10,7,13], as well as early requirements models of security concerns [17,22,12]. What is still missing is capturing the high-level security requirements, without getting suddenly bogged down into security solutions or cryptographic algorithms. If we look at the requirement refinement process of many proposals, we find out that at certain stage a leap is made: we have a system with no security features consisting of high-level functionalities, and then the next refinement shows encryption, access control, authentication and the like. The need for these features is indeed explained by the English text but this is hardly satisfactory. The modelling process itself should make it clear why encryption, authentication or access control are necessary.

In this paper we propose a solution that is based on augmenting the i*/Tropos framework [4,21] to take into account security considerations. Our decision to augment the language has been mainly driven by a major case study, the modelling of the Secure Electronic Transactions e-commerce suite[1] by VISA and MasterCard [14,15] that one of us has contributed to formally verify [2,3]. The industrial relevance of the case study is clear but the topic is challenging also for technical reasons. At first because the proposal is accompanied by a massive documentation spanning from an high-level business description to bit-oriented programming guide. However, if we look to the documentation we find out that the business case is described in a totally informal way and the programming guide is fairly operational, in many points a good example of bit-oriented programming. It is not possible to trace back the requirements from the 1000+ pages of the system description, except from the English text. In particular, the documentation contains no such thing as a UML process model.

---

[1] A new proposal superseding SET and encompassing also features related to smartcards, the VISA and Mastercard 3-D Secure initiative, has been launched this year.

Analysis has shown that the key to modelling security features is the separation of the notion of offering a service (of a handling data, performing a task or fulfilling a goal) and ownership of the very same service. Our enhancement of the Tropos/i* methodology is based exactly on this idea.

The ability of the methodology to model a clear dependency relation between those offering a service (for example, the merchant processing a credit card number), those requesting the service (e.g., the bank debiting the payment), and those owning the very same data (the cardholder), is what make security solutions emerge as a natural consequence of the modelling process. Indeed, our proposal ensures that security mechanisms are not introduced early on into a software system design. We believe that this early introduction is what creates gaps in the requirements analysis process and makes unclear the reason behind the introduction of these security mechanisms.

In the rest of the paper we give a quick introduction to the SET e-commerce suite (Section 2) and the Tropos/i* methodology (Section 3) with some examples drawn from the case study (Section 4). Then we present an initial model using Tropos (Section 5) and note its unsatisfactory character in explaining why some security mechanisms have emerged. We then introduce our enhanced version of Tropos/i* (Section 6) and show how we can capture more appropriately the (missing) trust relationships that are behind the SET design (Section 7). Finally, we discuss related works and conclude (Section 8).

2   A SET Primer

With the boom of internet shopping in the mid 90s, a consortium led by credit card companies (VISA and Mastercard) and major software vendors (Netscape and Microsoft among them) have put forward an architecture for securing electronic payments.

The need for a secure solution payment solution was spurred by the current unsatisfactory protection offered to customers and merchants dealing on-line. Indeed, people normally pay for goods purchased over the Internet using a credit card. Customers give their card number to the merchant, who claims the cost of the goods against it. To prevent eavesdroppers on the net from stealing the card number, the transaction is encrypted using the SSL protocol. Basically, this is what happen when the browser shows the closed lock on the screen. However this arrangement has many serious limitations:

- The cardholder is protected from eavesdroppers but not from dishonest merchants (pornographers have charged more than the advertised price, expecting their customers to be too embarrassed to complain), nor incompetent ones (a million credit card numbers have been stolen from Internet sites whose managers had not applied security patches) [20].
- The merchant has no protection against dishonest customers who supply an invalid credit card number or who claim a refund from their bank without cause. In most countries, legislation shields customers rather than merchants. So, upon receiving a claim, the banks will go to the merchant asking for a

signed receipt and if it does not exist (as it is obviously the case), tough luck for the merchant.

The proposal of the consortium, called SET (Secure Electronic Transactions) aims to "provide confidentiality of information, ensure payment integrity and authenticate both merchants and cardholders", according to the *Business Description* [14, p. 3].

SET's participants are *cardholders* and *merchants*. Their financial institutions are called *issuers* and *acquirers* respectively. Other participants are *payment gateways* (PG), who play the traditional role of clearing-houses in settling the payment requests made by merchants and cardholders during a purchase. There is also a hierarchy of *certificate authorities* (CA), rooted in a trusted *root certificate authority* (RCA).

Cardholder Registration. This is the initial phase for cardholders. It lets each cardholder register by providing him with a certificate for his signature key. A cardholder begins a session by sending his credit card details to a CA, which replies with a registration form. The cardholder completes the form and choose an asymmetric key pair and send the public part to a CA. The CA checks whether the request is valid (the protocol does not define how) and issues a certificate, signed by the CA, that binds the public key to the cardholder's name. He will have to use the corresponding private key to sign purchase requests. Few points are noteworthy:

- A merchant should not be able to verify a cardholder's account details from his certificate [14, pp. 7, 12 and 25]. Indeed, the cardholder's certificate does not store the account detail. The name of the certificate holder in the X.509 certificate standard [15, pp. 210, 213] is replaced by the hash of his *primary account number* (PAN), loosely speaking the credit card number, and of a secret nonce (PANSecret).
- Still the certificates must assure the merchant during the payment phase (without his having to see the PAN) that a link exists between a cardholder, and a valid PAN, and that the link was validated by the card issuer [14, pp. 8 and 25].

Merchant Registration. This phase performs the analogous function for merchants. Unlike cardholders, merchants register both a signature key and an encryption key. Each merchant gets two certificates.

Purchase Request. The cardholder sends the order information and the payment instructions to a merchant, who may run **Payment Authorization** (see below) before accepting the order. A trusting merchant can batch the payment authorizations and run them later. It is worth noticing that the cardholder invokes **Purchase Request** *after* he has agreed with the merchant to buy certain goods or services (the Order Description) for a certain amount. SET is concerned with payment, not with shopping.

Payment Authorization. When a merchant receives an order, he does not receive the cardholder's PAN. So, he cannot just use that number, as done with credit card transactions conducted via the telephone [19], to settle directly with the card issuer. Instead, the merchant forwards the payment instructions to a PG. The PG, in cooperation with the card issuer, checks that everything is fine, and sends the payment authorization to the merchant.

Payment Capture. The merchant sends to the PG one or more payment requests and the corresponding "capture tokens" obtained during the previous steps. The PG checks that everything is satisfactory and replies to the merchant. The actual funds transfer from the cardholder to the merchant is done outside the protocol. This step, for the finalization of the trasnfer of money from the bank to the merchant is explained by a business need: payments can be authorized on-line but captured (finalised) much later, such as at time of delivery. Another example comes from "Buy on Christmas, Pay on Easter" schemes or the like. All we expect is that payment is captured only if previously authorized.

3   The Tropos/i* Methodology for Requirement Analysis

We start by selecting the appropriate methodology for analysis. Among the competing alternatives we have chosen the Tropos/i* methodology, which has been already applied to model some security properties [12,22].

Tropos [4,21] is an agent-oriented software system development methodology, tailored to describe both the organisational environment of a system and the system itself, employing the same concepts throughout the development process. Tropos adopts the i* modelling framework, which uses the concepts of actor, goal, soft goal, task, resource and social dependency for defining the obligations of actors (dependees) to other actors (dependers). Actors have strategic goals and intentions within the system or the organisation and represent (social) agents (organisational, human or software), roles or positions (that represent a set of roles). A goal represents the strategic interests of an actor. In Tropos, we differentiate between hard (hereafter just "goals") and soft goals. The latter have no clear definition or criteria for deciding whether they are satisfied or not. A task represents a way of doing something. Thus, for example a task can be executed in order to satisfy a goal. A resource represents a physical or an informational entity. finally, a dependency between two actors indicates that one actor depends on another to accomplish a goal, execute a task, or deliver a resource.

These modelling concepts are particularly well suited to model business security requirements, which are usually expressed in natural language using notions such as agents and high level goals such confidentiality and authentication. Tropos features make also possible an explicit modelling of security as requirements without requiring an immediate discussion of sizes of cryptographic keys or deny vs access configuration of files.

The distinctive characteristic of Tropos (covering the very early phases of requirements analysis) allows for a deeper understanding of the environment

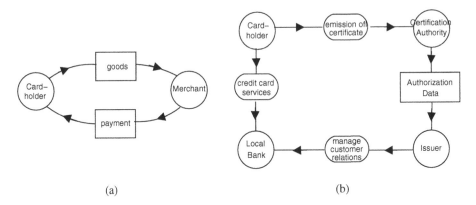

Fig. 1. (a) Merchant-Cardhodler Basic Dependencies; (b) Certification actor diagram

where the software must operate, and of the kind of interactions that should occur between software and human users. This understanding is often essential for having security features right [1,16]: technically perfect security solutions are typically hampered by lack of understanding of interactions. By considering early phases of the requirements analysis process, we can capture not only the *what* or the *how*, but also the *why* a piece of software is developed. This, in turn, supports a more refined analysis of system dependencies, covering both functional and non-functional requirements. Security requirements can, of course, be seen as a particular form of non-functional requirements.

4   Some Examples of Modelling Features

Let's now start from a simple example of a dependency in SET using plain Tropos.

Example 1 (Fig.1 - a). The Cardholder depends on the Merchant for obtaining some goods and the Merchant depends on the Cardholder for obtaining the payment.

The above example is fairly high level: a sort of first principle. We may want to model more complicated examples on interdepencies looking at some subsystems, for example Cardholder Registration.

Example 2 (Fig.1 - b). A Cardholder depends on the Certification Authority for the emission of certificates.The Authority itself depends on the Cardholder's credit card Issuer for authorization data. The Issuer of the credit card delegates to the local bank the management of customer relations, so that the Cardholder also depends on the local bank for the desired credit card services.

Another interesting feature of Tropos is the refinement analysis and the usage of rationale diagrams that explains dependencies.

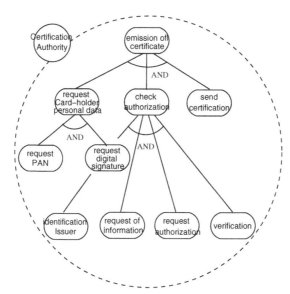

Fig. 2. Rationale diagram

Example 3 (Fig.2). Analyzing the goal of the emission of the certificate from example 2, it can be and-decomposed into three subgoals: Request of personal data from the cardholder, checking the authorization at the issuer and generating and sending back the certificate. The first subgoal can be further refined into requesting the PAN of the cardholder and requesting the digital signature. The subgoal for the authorization could be further sub-divided into subgoals: identification of the Issuer, request of information and authorization from the Issuer, verification from the authority internal database that no duplicate signature exists, etc.

5   First Attempt at Modelling SET with Tropos/i*

From an ideal perspective, we would like to start from the high level goal of electronic payments and show why the protocol itself is a possible solution and to what goals. So we start by refining the example 1. After all the merchant does not receive the money directly from the customer, the passage is mediated by the bank.

Example 4 (Fig.3). The Cardholder depends on the local Bank for banking services and credit and the Merchant for obtaining some goods. The Merchant depends on the Bank for obtaining the payment.

We can further refine this example as follows:

Example 5. The Cardholder depends on the local Bank for banking services and the Merchant for obtaining some goods. The local Bank depends on the Issuer for credit card transaction and the Issuer depends on the Bank for customer relations. The Merchant depends on his Bank for obtaining the payment and

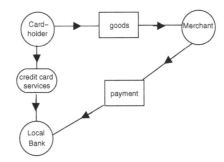

Fig. 3. Payment-2 actor diagram

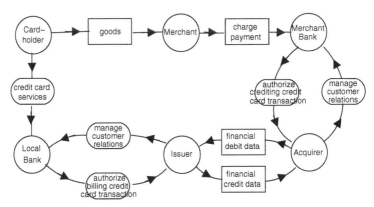

Fig. 4. Payment-3 diagram

the Bank depends on the Acquirer for payment of credit card transaction and the Acquirer depends on the Bank for customer service relations.

The next step clarifies the relations between various actors in the financial setting of the transaction.

Example 6 (Fig.4). The Cardholder depends on the local Bank for banking services and the Merchant for obtaining some goods. The local Bank depends on the Issuer for authorizing billing credit card transaction and the Issuer depends on the Bank for customer relations. The Merchant depends on his Bank for obtaining the payment and the Bank depends on the Acquirer for authorizing crediting of card transaction and the Acquirer depends on the Bank for customer service relations. The Issuer depends on the Acquirer for obtaining financial data for the transaction and viceversa.

Further analysis of the financial data between Acquirer and Issuers reveals that this is the client credit card number, the merchant account and the payment information.

At this stage one may jump to the conclusion that now we need to encrypt the credit card number so that the merchant cannot see it. Though possible, this conclusion, would not be immediately nor easily derivable from the present analysis. The distance between the analysis and the proposed solution is far too

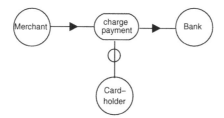

Fig. 5. Extendend dependency diagram

great. In Tropos, we could precisely model the protocol, but without explaining *why* encrypting a credit card number is a good solution and especially a solution for *which* problem.

6   Security-Enhanced Tropos

We now focus on what is missing in the "vanilla" version for Tropos. Looking at the above example, it is clear that we need to distinguish between the *servers* that manipulate some data (e.g., the Merchant) and the *owners* to whom the data ultimately belongs (e.g., the Cardholder). Indeed, inasmuch as the owner of a resource is also disposing of its use we have no need of security analysis. We need security as soon as the owner of some data must use the services of some other agent to use his own data.Looking at operating systems, we need operating system security because the user owns a file but the operating system, an agent distinct from the user, serves access to this file. So, we first extend the Tropos notion of *Actor* as follows:

Actor:= **Actor** *name [attributes] [creation-properties] [invar-properties] [actor-goals] [ownership] [services]*

We extend the notion of actor introducing the possibility that an actor can own resources, tasks and goals (*ownership*) and can provide *services* (task, goals and resources). Then we extend the notion of dependency introducing the notion of owner, as follows:

*Dependency:=***Dependency** *name type mode* **Depender** *name* **Dependee** *name [***Owner** *name] [attributes] [creation-properties] [invar-properties] [fulfill-properties]*

We can now model situations in which an agent (depender) depends on an another agent (dependee) for a resource (task and goal) and a third agent (owner) gives the permission to use such a resource (task and goal). Of course this includes also the fact that the dependee is able to provide the resource (task and goal), namely the resource is included in its service list, and that the owner owns the resource, namely the resource is included in the owned-resource list.

Figure 5 reports an example of such a dependency. The Merchant depends on the Bank for charging a payment to a specific credit card number, and the Card-holder has to give the permission for such a task (in figure the ownership is indicated as an "o").

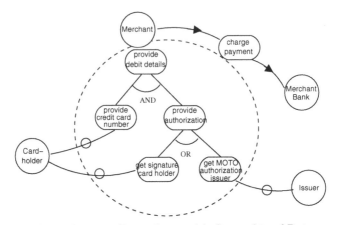

Fig. 6. Payment Dependency with Ownership of Data

The new model makes it possible to analyze the *trust relationship between clients, servers, and owners* and the consequent need for security solution. This is the missing gap between the high-level model and the low-level usage of cryptographic primitives. For example, suppose that we modelled some archival system where the owner of some data must give the data to somebody for storing it. The model will show the dependency relation. If the owner does not trust the storage server, we can change the model and encrypt the data. The trusted relation of the revised model can better address our desired trust relationships.

7   Modelling SET with Security Enhanced Tropos

Using this new ternary dependency we can refine the model presented in Fig. 4 with respect to the charge payment dependency between Merchant and Merchant Bank. Fig. 6 reports the new model.

In the new model, the problem is becoming clear: to obtain the money the Merchant must get a piece of data that belongs to somebody else. Since the Merchant and the Cardholder are not phisically close, the data must be trasmitted from the Cardholder to the Merchant via the network infrastructure. This is modelled in Fig. 7 and basically correspond to the typical usage of credit card for buying over the internet before the widespread adoption of SSL/TLS.

The analysis of the trust relationships in Fig. 7 shows by a glance that the cardholder must trust the network provider to safely and securely manage the credit card details. This situation is clearly unsatisfactory and thus we can revise the model to propose an alternative.

It is worth noting that the same analysis of the trust relationship also shows a potential vulnerability of the system that is not usually considered when discussing the security of internet payment systems. The cardholder must also trust the phone/network provider between the bank and merchant. This explains the need for additional protection on that side or the usage of a dedicated financial network. So we can devise a refinement alternative to Fig. 7 in which the data

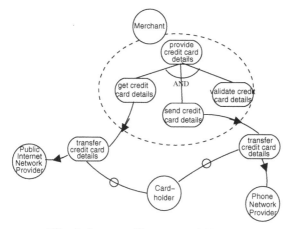

Fig. 7. Internet Shopping - Old Style

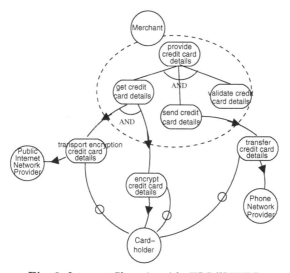

Fig. 8. Internet Shopping á la TLS/HTTPS

channelled through the network provider is encrypted. In a nutshell, we simply derive, the SSL/TLS idea of e-commerce. It is shown in Fig. 8. However, protection over Merchant and bank phone network is still necessary. Further details, down to the actual protocol can then be worked out, but there is no longer the big gap between the high level models and the sudden appearance of low level security mechanisms.

This solution can be still unsatisfactory for the cardholder. His data must still be processed by the merchant and there might be cases where this trust relationship is undesirable. Now we can define yet a different refinement in Fig. 9.

We now have a stepwise refinement process that makes it possible to understand why there is the need of enrypting and protecting credit card details. The refinement steps shows clearly how the trust relation is build, and what

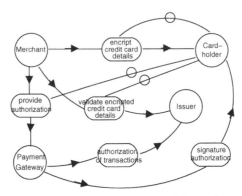

Fig. 9. Internete Shopping - SET-style

trust relations are created. The usage of encrytpion is now clearly motivated by the model itself: we have a owner of data that is forced to use the services of some other entity. Authentication and access control can be similarly introduced during the analysis of the depender-dependee model when the goal require some form of identification.

8   Related Work and Conclusions

A number of articles have discussed the usage of Tropos/i* methodology for modelling security concerns. For example, in [12] the authors show how modelling relationships among strategic actors can be used in order to elicit, identify and analyze security requirements. In particular, how actor dependency analysis helps in the identification of attackers and their potential threats, while actor goal analysis helps to elicit the dynamic decision making process of system players for security issues. [22] shows how goal models can be used to model privacy concerns and the different alternatives for operationalizing it. Using an example in the health care domain, the authors propose a framework based on a catalogue, to guide the software engineer through alternatives for achieving privacy. However, both proposals remain at an abstract level and stops before filling the missing gap that we noted.

A preliminary modification of the Tropos methodology to enable it to model security concerns throughout the whole software development process has been proposed in [18,17]. In particular, this extension proposes the use of security constraints and secure capabilities as basic concepts to be used in order to integrate security concerns throughout all phases of the software development process. Here, we find an operational description but still the notion of constraints is not sufficient to capture the trust relationship that we have been able to model in our enhanced Tropos model.

Down the line in the modelling paradigm, a number of proposals have proposed enhancements to UML to cope with security constraints. [9,10,11] propose an extension of UML where cryptographic and authentication features are explicitly modelled. The model is rich enough to allow for a detailed analysis and indeed has been driven by a similar case study of electronic payment systems [8]. In comparison to ours, the system is fairly low level and is therefore suited to more operational analysis. A challenging line of research may involve the integration of the two methodologies, so that one can start from a high level analysis of the system with our security-enhanced Tropos and then continue down the line to an operational specification using UML.

Another proposal of enhancing UML with security feature is the SecureUML language [7,13] which, however, is geared towards access control. The proposal is focused on providing concrete syntax for representing access control notions in UML so that access control policies can be directly modelled in UML and formal properties derived from that models. These modelling features are essential, but from our perspective only at the end of the system modelling process.

In this paper we have shown an enhancement of Tropos/i* that is based on the clear separation of roles in a dependency relation between those offering a service (the merchant processing a credit card number), those requesting the service (the bank debiting the payment), and those owning the very same data (the cardholder). This distinction makes it possible to capture the high-level security requirements of an industrial case study, without getting immediatley bogged down into cryptographic algorithms or security mechanisms, where purpose is obscured in a morass of details. The modelling process we envision makes it clear why encryption, authentication or access control are necessary and which trust relationships or requirements they address. The challenge is now to integrate this framework with other development phases, to ensure truly secure designs for software systems.

References

1. R. Anderson. *Security Engineering – a Guide to Building Dependable Distributed Systems.* Wiley and Sons, 2003.
2. G. Bella, F. Massacci, and L. C. Paulson. The verification of an industrial payment protocol: The SET purchase phase. In V. Atluri, editor, *9th ACM Conference on Computer and Communications Security*, pages 12–20. ACM Press, 2002.
3. G. Bella, F. Massacci, and L. C. Paulson. Verifying the SET registration protocols. *IEEE Journal on Selected Areas on Communications*, 21(1), 2003. in press.
4. J. Castro, M. Kolp, and J. Mylopoulos. Towards Requirements-Driven Information Systems Engineering: The Tropos Project. *Information Systems*, 2003. Elsevier, Amsterdam, the Netherlands, (to appear).
5. P. T. Devambu and S. Stubbelbine. Software engineering for security: a roadmap. In *Future of Software Engineering. Special volume of the proceedings of the 22nd International Conference on Software Engineering (ICSE 2000)*, pages 227–239, 2000.
6. J.-M. Jézéquel, H. Hußmann, and S. Cook, editors. *5th International Conference on the Unified Modeling Language (UML 2002)*, volume 2460 of *Lecture Notes in Computer Science*. Springer, 2002.
7. J.-M. Jézéquel, H. Hußmann, and S. Cook, editors. *SecureUML: A UML-Based Modeling Language for Model-Driven Security*, volume 2460 of *Lecture Notes in Computer Science*. Springer, 2002.

8. J. Jürjens. Modelling audit security for smart-card payment schemes with UMLsec. In *16th International Conference on Information Security (IFIP/SEC 2001)*. Kluwer AP, 2001.

9. J. Jürjens. Towards secure systems development with umlsec. In *Fundamental Approaches to Software Engineering (FASE/ETAPS 2001)*, LNCS. Springer-Verlag, 2001.

10. J. Jürjens. UMLsec: Extending UML for secure systems development. In Jézéquel et al. [6].

11. J. Jürjens. Using UMLsec and Goal-Trees for secure systems development. In *Symposium of Applied Computing (SAC 2002)*. ACM Press, 2002.

12. L. Liu, E. Yu, and J. Mylopoulos. Analyzing Security Requirements as Relationships Among Strategic Actors. In *Proceedings of the 2nd Symposium on Requirements Engineering for Information Security (SREIS-02)*, Raleigh, North Carolina, 2002.

13. T. Lodderstedt, D. A. Basin, and J. Doser. Model driven security for process-oriented systems. In *8th ACM Symposium on Access Control Models and Technologies*, 2003.

14. Mastercard & VISA. *SET Secure Electronic Transaction Specification: Business Description*, May 1997. Available electronically at
http://www.setco.org/set_specifications.html.

15. Mastercard & VISA. *SET Secure Electronic Transaction Specification: Programmer's Guide*, May 1997. Available electronically at
http://www.setco.org/set_specifications.html.

16. G. McGraw and J. Viega. *Building Secure Software*. Addison Wesley Professional computing, 2001.

17. H. Mouratidis, P. Giorgini, and G. Manson. Integrating security and systems engineering: Towards the modelling of secure information systems. In *Proceedings of the 15th Conference On Advanced Information Systems Engineering (CAiSE 2003)*, 2003.

18. H. Mouratidis, P. Giorgini, and G. Manson. Modelling secure multiagent systems. In *Proceedings of the 2nd International Joint Conference on Autonomous Agents and Multiagent Systems (AAMAS)*, 2003.

19. D. O'Mahony, M. Peirce, and H. Tewari. *Electronic payment systems*. The Artech House computer science library. Artech House, 1997.

20. A. Paller. Alert: Large criminal hacker attack on Windows NTE-banking and E-commerce sites. On the Internet at
http://www.sans.org/newlook/alerts/NTE-bank.htm, Mar. 2001. SANS Institute.

21. A. Perini, P. Bresciani, F. Giunchiglia, P. Giorgini, and J. Mylopoulos. A Knowledge Level Software Engineering Methodology for Agent Oriented Programming. In *Proc. of the 5th Int. Conference on Autonomous Agents*, Montreal CA, May 2001. ACM.

22. E. Yu and L. Cysneiros. Designing for Privacy and Other Competing Requirements. In *Proceedings of the 2nd Symposium on Requirements Engineering for Information Security (SREIS-02)*, Raleigh, North Carolina, 2002.

Goal-Based Business Modeling Oriented towards Late Requirements Generation*

Hugo Estrada[1,2], Alicia Martínez[1,3], and Óscar Pastor[1]

[1] Technical University of Valencia
Avenida de los Naranjos s/n, Valencia, Spain
{hestrada,alimartin,opastor}@dsic.upv.es
[2] CENIDET Cuernavaca, Mor. Mexico
[3] I.T. Zacatepec, Morelos, Mexico

Abstract. Recently, a lot of research efforts in software engineering have focused on integrating business modeling as a key piece in requirements engineering. In these research works, the business models are proposed as the source of the software requirements specification process. However, the majority of these works focus only on the definition of notations that permit the representation of the semantics of the organizational context, and only a few works define processes to generate business models and to use these to generate a requirements model. This lack of both generation methods and traceability relationships between models makes practical application in software development enterprises difficult. The objective of this paper is to define a goal-based methodological approach for the generation of business models and to use these models as the starting point for the process of software requirements specification. This will enable us to develop information systems that integrate the necessary functionality so that the business actors perform their tasks and fulfill their goals.

1 Introduction

Traditionally, requirements engineering has been defined as the systematic process of identification and specification of the expected functions of a software system. However, this approach has certain weaknesses. McDermind [Mcd94] indicates that when the functional specification of the software system is the focal point of the requirements analysis, requirements engineers tend to establish the scope of the software system before having a clear understanding of the user's real needs. It constitutes a very important reason why many of the systems developed from a requirements model that focuses only on the functionality of the software system do not comply with their correct role within the organization.

It is important to point out that the main objective of an information system is to automate certain tasks or activities of a business process, allowing the business actors to reach their individual goals, as well as the general goals of the organization. In this context, there are research works that highlight the importance of using business

---

* This project is partially funded by the Asociación Nacional de Universidades e Instituciones de Educación Superior ANUIES, Mexico.

I.-Y. Song et al. (Eds.): ER 2003, LNCS 2813, pp. 277–290, 2003.

models as a starting point in the development of information systems [Bub94][Ces02][Lou95][Cas02]. Unfortunately, the majority of these works focus only on the definition of notations that permit the representation of the semantics of the organizational context, and only a few works define processes to generate business models and use these to generate a requirements model.

In this paper, we present a novel method to create business models which are represented in the i* Framework. Specifications of information system requirements (use case and scenarios) are also derived from these business models. Hence, two important and complementary approaches are discussed in this paper. First, we begin by defining a goal-oriented method to be used to construct the business models. Later, we discuss an approach to generate a requirements model (represented through the uses cases and their corresponding scenarios) from the business model. This requirement specification is later used for the semi automatic creation of the user interface [San03].

The paper is structured as follows: Section 2 presents the background of the proposed method. Section 3 describes an overview of the proposal. Section 4 presents the Goal-based elicitation Method. Section 5 presents the construction of the i* Business Models. Section 6 presents the elicitation process of system requirements based on the business models. Finally, Section 7 presents the conclusions.

2 Background

This section presents the main concepts that are used in this paper: goal modeling and business modeling. Both approaches are combined to create a capture method of business requirements. The advantages of our proposal over other proposals are presented in this section.

2.1 Goal Modeling

The most significant works in Goal-oriented requirements engineering are: a) KAOS [Dar93]: a formal framework based on temporal logic to elicit and represent the goals that the system software should achieve. b) GBRAM: a Goal- Based Requirements Analysis Method [Ant96] to represent the goals in an approach that is less formal but more focused on user needs.

In these works and in other goal-based approaches [Bub94][Bol02], the software requirements are obtained directly from the operational goals that satisfy the goals. The operational goals are mapped into use case model specifications or into services of the information system. This approach allows us to carry out the elicitation process at a level which is closer to the final users. However, this approach does not allow us to carry out business analysis (business process reengineering analysis, dependency analysis, workflow analysis, task analysis), which are fundamental to obtaining requirements that reflect the functionality expected by the users of the information system.

2.2 Business Modeling

Business Modeling is a set of techniques used to represent and to structure the knowledge of a business enterprise [Bub94]. The enterprise analysis allows us to determine with great precision: the operations that satisfy each one of the goals, the network of dependencies among actors, the sequence in which the tasks of each business process should be executed, the dependency type, the task to be automated, etc. This information is fundamental for the generation of a requirements model that gives real support to the business tasks.

There is a lot of research being done in this field; however, the i* framework [Yu95] is one of the most well-known techniques today. The i* framework allows us to describe business models made up of social actors that have freedom of action, but that depend on other actors to achieve their objectives and goals. This information is useful for viewing the tasks that each actor is expected to perform, as well as for analyzing the repercussions of the fulfillment or non-fulfillment of the tasks assigned to the actors. The i* framework has a graphical notation with few elements, which allows us to represent the actors, dependencies, resources and the tasks of the business process in a unified view. The majority of business modeling techniques use multiple diagrams (each diagram represents a specific view of the business) to have the same expressivity as the i* framework. The i* notation also allows us to include software systems as actors inside the business model. These characteristics distinguish the i* framework from the rest of the business modeling techniques [Bub94], [Ces02], [Lou95].

The i*framework is made up of two business models that complement each other: the Strategic Dependency Model and the Strategic Rationale Model.

The *Strategic Dependency Model* (SD) shows the dependencies that exist between business actors to achieve their goals, carry out tasks and provide or request resources. A dependency describes an intentional relationship between two actors. It is composed by: a) *Depender*: the actor who is dependent on another actor, b) *Dependee*: the actor on whom another actor depends, c) *Dependum*: the task, goal, resource or softgoal on which the relationship is focused.

The SD model is represented by a graph where nodes represent actors (agents), and where the links represent dependencies. The combination of nodes and links in the SD Model create a network of dependencies that helps to graphically represent the external relationships between actors. There are directed arrows to link the *depender*, *dependum* and *dependee*. These arrows indicate the direction of the dependency, determining which actor is the *depender* and which is the *dependee*.

The SD model is composed by four types of dependencies: a) Goal dependency in which an actor depends on another actor to fulfill a goal, without prescribing the way in which it should be carried out. b) Resource dependency in which an actor depends on another actor to deliver a resource that can be either material or informational. c) Task dependency in which there exists a dependency for the carrying out of a task, establishing the way in which it should be performed. d) SoftGoal dependency. This is similar to the goal dependency, with the difference that the goal has not been precisely defined.

The Softgoal dependency, which corresponds to non-functional requirements, does not appear in our approach, because this paper is focused on generating Use Cases, that is a functional description of the information system.

The *Strategic Rationale Model* (SR) carries out a deeper reasoning of the motives that exist behind each dependency relationship. This is useful for representing tasks that have to be carried out by the actors to achieve the goals which are expected of them, as well as for rethinking new ways of working. This model is based on the elements of the dependency model, adding a) task decomposition links which allow us to represent the combination of necessary tasks to achieve a goal, and b) means-ends links whose objective is to present the diverse options that can be taken to fulfill a task or goal.

The i* framework has been used in several application areas, including requirements engineering, software processes and business process reengineering. However, in i* framework, there is still no method that creates an initial business models (Early requirements acquisition), to guide the analyst in eliciting the relevant information from the organizational context.

3   Description of the Proposal

The objective of the proposed method "Goal-based Business Modeling oriented towards late requirements generation" is to help to construct the software requirements specification using a business model as the starting point.

The steps of our proposed method are summarized as follows:
1. Use a Goal-Based Elicitation Method to construct a Goal-Refinement Tree (GRT) which captures the organizational context.
2. Use the GRT to create the Strategic Models of the i* Framework. These Models could then be used to perform business improvement analysis.
3. Use the Strategic Models to derive functional (use case) specifications with their corresponding scenarios [San03].

In order to illustrate our approach, we used the *Conference Review Process* case study. The purpose is to model the business process to obtain a software system that handles the process of submission, assignation, evaluation and selection of papers for a conference.

4   Goal-Based Elicitation Method

The Goal-Based Elicitation Method proposed in this paper allows us to elicit the business goals and to represent these in a goal structure. To do this, we propose a Goal Classification, which permits us to construct a Goal-Refinement Tree (GRT) using Refinement and Abstraction Strategies.

The root of the Tree represents one of the general goals of the organization. The intermediate nodes represent the groups of low-level goals for the satisfaction of a more general goal. Finally, all the leaves represent operational goals that satisfy the low-level goals.

4.1 Goal Classification

We propose a goal classification to structure the goals in the GRT. The goal classification was created to represent not only the internal goals or operations of the business actor, but also to represent the cases where there are relationships among actors. Relations of this kind imply that the actors depend on other actors to satisfy their goals or perform their operations. These relations are fundamental for creating the Strategic Models of the i* Framework. For this reason, the goal classification is not exhaustive; we classify only the goals necessary to create a i* business model.

Operational Goals: They are performed by the correct state transition of one of the business actors and change the state of one or more objects [Dar93]. They are characterized by pre-, post- and trigger- conditions. There are two types of Operational Goals:

- *Operation-Dependency*. In this case, the actor responsible for completing the operation depends on another actor to provide a resource or perform another operation. This kind of Operational Goal is represented in the GRT as OP-Dep.
- *Operation Without-Dependency*. In this case, the actor responsible for completing the operation does not depend on another actor to complete the operational goal. This kind of Operational Goal is represented in the GRT as OP-WDep.
- **Achievement Goals**: These goals are refined in Operations Without-Dependency or in other Achievement Goals. They are represented in the GRT as *AG*.
- **Achievement-Dependency Goals**: These goals are refined in Operational Goals, where at least one of these is an Operations-Dependency or in another Achievement-Dependency Goal. They are represented in the GRT as *ADG*.
- **General Goals**: These are high-level goals that are used to express the business manager's point of view. Goals of this type lead directly to General Goals, Achievement Goals or Achievement-Dependency Goals.

We have defined classes of relationships between goals to structure the Goal-Refinement Tree.

- **Conflict Goals**: This is the case where the achievement of a goal has a negative impact on the satisfaction of another goal or subgoal. They are represented by CG.
- **Decomposition links**: These represent the necessary Subgoals to satisfy a more general goal. These are represented using the link ──┼─ which links the subgoals with the goal.
- **Alternative links**: This is the case in which only one of the different alternatives to satisfy a goal could be satisfied. These represent a decision structure to show the alternatives that exist to achieve a goal. These goals are represented using the link ──▶ which links the alternative subgoals with the more general goal.

In this paper, we have determined that all the selected goals to model should be derived in operations (Operation-Dependency or Operation Without-Dependency), in the same way that all operations should be connected to goals. This restriction prevents the specification of goals that are not reflected in operations, as well as the specification of operations that do not satisfy any goal. The operationalization of the goals is one of the fundamental steps for construction in a goal model.

Figure 1 shows an example of a hierarchical configuration in the GRT.

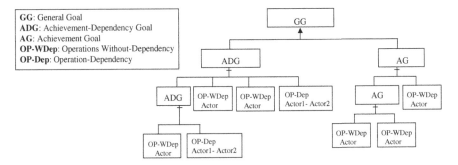

Fig. 1. Example of a hierarchical structure of the Goal-Refinement Tree

4.2 Goal Elicitation

To create the Goal-Refinement Tree, it is possible to use a strategy by refinement and/or by abstraction.

In the *refinement strategy*, it is necessary to select some of the general goals of the organization and determine the subset of subgoals that permit us to satisfy them. This information is used to construct the high levels of the Goal-Refinement Tree (General Goals). It is possible to continue the refinement to detect low-level goals or operations that satisfy the high-level goals. Once the low-level goals or the operations are determined, it is necessary to find the actors that are responsible for achieving them.

In the *abstraction strategy*, it is necessary to detect the actors that participate in the organization. Once the business actors are detected, their goals and operations need to be elicited. This information is used to construct the low levels of the Goal-Refinement Tree (Operational Goals). Later, it is necessary to determine the objective of the execution of the actor operations and to determine the more general goals that are satisfied by the more specific goals of the actors.

In the process of identifying the actors responsible for achieving the Operational Goal, there may be dependency relationships among actors. There are dependency relationships when another actor is needed to provide a resource or perform an operation. These dependencies must be represented in the Goal-Refinement Tree as Operation-Dependency.

To illustrate our case study, we have shown the textual description of the Goal-Refinement Tree (Table 1). The first column shows the identifying goals. The second column indicates the goal type. The third column shows the actors involved in reaching that goal or operation. If there are two actors in the third column, this indicate a relationship between actors.

The Goal-Refinement Tree can also be used to carry out obstacle analysis, conflict management and goal consolidation to generate a consistent and non-redundant goal structure. We propose using the methods and strategies proposed by KAOS [Dar93] and GBRAM [Ant96] to carry out these specific goal analyses.

As a result of this phase, we have a Goal-Refinement Tree, which represents the objectives of the organization.

Table 1. Goal-Refinement Tree for the Conference Review Process case study.

Name of the goal	Goal type	Actors
Goal: to perform a paper review process	GG	
Obtain the highest number of quality papers	ADG	PcChair - Author
• Send a call for papers	OP-Wdep	PcChair
• Obtain papers	OP-Dep	PcChair - Author
Assign papers to adequate PcMembers	ADG	PcMember - PcChair
• generate paper list	OP-Wdep	PcChair
• obtain interest list	OP-Dep	PcChair - PcMember
• select PcMembers	OP-WDep	PcChair
• identify and resolve conflicts	OP-WDep	PcChair
• send papers to PcMembers to review	OP-Dep	PcMember - PcChair
Assign papers to adequate Reviewers	ADG	PcMember - Reviewer
• select Reviewers	OP-Wdep	PcMember
• send papers to Reviewers to review	OP-Dep	PcMember - Reviewer
To do quality reviews	AG	PcMember
• assign qualifications	OP-WDep	PcMember
• assign commnents	OP-WDep	PcMember
• assign evaluation	OP-WDep	PcMember
Obtain quality reviews	ADG	PcChair - PcMember/ Reviewer
• obtain reviews	OP	PcChair - PcMember/ Reviewer
Give feedback to the Authors	GG	
• Send notifications to the Authors on time	ADG	PcChair - Author
• sort papers	*	
• resolve critical cases	*	
• send notifications and reviews	OP-Dep	PcChair - Author

5   Using the GRT to Create the Strategic Models of i* Framework

The objective of this phase is to use the knowledge elicited using the GRT to create the business models of the i* Framework.

In the current goal-based elicitation methods, the low-level goals are used to obtain the requirements of the information system. However, in this approach, the design decisions are taken too early, and the requirements are generated without the knowledge of the performance of the organization. This approach focuses on generating software specifications rather than on supporting reasoning and analysis about the performance of the business process.

Using only a goal-based structure, it is not possible to show: the order of execution of the operations, the work product flow, the workflow, the summarization of responsibilities of each business actor, etc. Therefore, it is not possible to improve the organization before generating the requirements of the information system.

We propose using the GRT to create a business model which allows us to perform this business analysis (business process reengineering analysis, dependency analysis, and task analysis) before taking decisions on the functionality of the information system. This allows us to have an improved business model that could be used to take design decisions.

This paper is focused on generating functional specifications of the system software. For this reason, the Softgoal Dependencies of the i* Framework, related to non-functional requirements are not consider in this paper.

5.1   Creation of the Strategic Dependency Model

The Goal-Refinement Tree is the starting point for the generation process of a business Model represented in the i* framework. The process begins with the creation of a Strategic Dependency Model (SD Model). The SD Model is focused on representing the dependency relationships that exist among the organizational actors. For this reason, this model must be constructed using a subset of the GRT (the goals in which a dependency exist between the actors).

The first step is to use the organizational actors of the GRT to create the actors of the SD Model. The actors identified with responsibilities to satisfy goals or achieve operations in our case study are: PcChair, PcMember, Reviewer and Author.

The second step is to use the Achievement-Dependency Goals of the GRT to create the goal dependencies in the Strategic Dependency Model. As was mentioned in 4.1, the Achievement-Dependency Goals are goals that are refined Operational Goals where at least one of these is an Operation-Dependency. Therefore, these kinds of goals represent dependency relationships between actors.   In our case study, for example, the Achievement-Dependency Goal *assign papers to adequate PcMembers* is translated into a goal dependency with the same name between the PcChair and the PcMember. In this dependency, the PcChair is the *dependee* actor because it executes the paper assignment operation. The PcMember is the *depender* actor because it depends on the assignment of the paper to be reviewed.

The third step is to use the Operation-Dependency of the GRT to create the resource and task dependencies of the Strategic Dependency Model. As was mentioned in 4.1, the Operation-Dependencies are goals that involve more than one actor for their execution. The Operational Goals performed by a single actor represent the internal actions of each actor in the Strategic Rationale Model. An Operation-Dependency must be translated into a task dependency if the actor that depends on the execution of the operation specifies a particular way of doing it. An Operation-Dependency must be translated into a resource dependency if the *depender* actor depends on the delivery of a resource to complete the operation. For example, in the GRT of the case study, the Operation-Dependency *obtain reviews* is translated into two dependencies: a) the task dependency *Send Reviews* between the PcChair and the PcMember, and b) the resource dependency *Reviews* between the PcChair and the PcMember. Figure 2 shows the result of the application of the translation process to the case study analyzed.

The SD Model is useful for detecting potential problems with the performance of the business model for finding: actors with a large number of dependencies, actors that represents bottlenecks, redundant dependency relationships, etc. This information can be used to improve the business model.

Once the SD Model is created, the Strategic Rationale Model must be created in order to detail the internal tasks that accomplish the dependencies.

5.2   Creation of the Strategic Rationale Model

The construction of the Strategic Rationale Model (SR Model) consists in defining the internal operations that all actors carry out in order to reach their dependencies. To do this, the Achievement Goals of the Goal-Refinement Tree are translated into internal goals or internal tasks in the Strategic Rationale Model. This is done using task

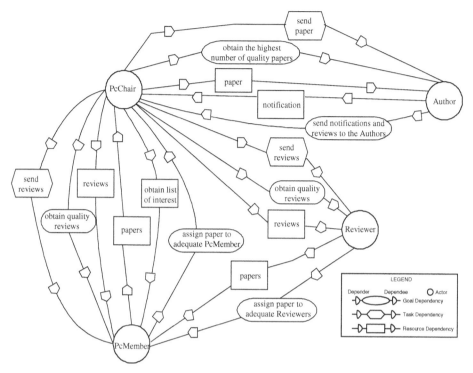

Fig. 2. Strategic Dependency Model of the Conference Review Process case study

decomposition to create internal task-refinement trees in each business actor. Some of these internal goals or tasks will be connected with the task dependencies or resource dependencies defined in the Strategic Dependency Model.

In our case study, for example (Figure 3), the Achievement Dependency Goal *assign papers to adequate PcMember* is translated into the root of an internal task-refinement tree (with the same name as the goal) inside the actor PcChair. Later, the Operational Goals *generate paper list, obtain interest list, select PcMembers, identify and resolve conflict* and *send papers to PcMember to review* are translated into tasks and linked with the root goal of the internal tree.

In the case of operations of the GRT that have been derived in resource dependencies, it is necessary to indicate the delivery of the resource in the *depender* actor. To do this, an internal task must be created in the *depender* actor to indicate the delivery of the resource and link it to the resource dependency. In our case study, resource dependency *Reviews* between the PcChair and the PcMember lead to the internal task *Obtain Reviews* in the actor PcChair. Figure 3 shows the SR Model generated. The internal goals of each actor are represented in this model.

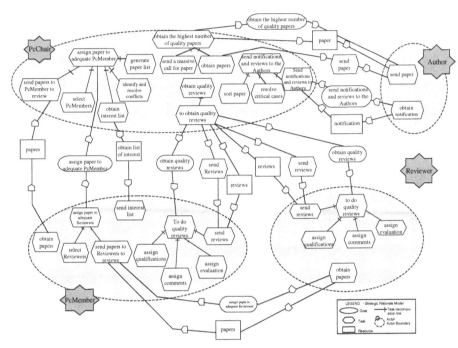

Fig. 3. SR Model of the Conference Review Process case study without system actor

6   Using the Business Models for Software Requirements Elicitation

The objective of this phase is to rely on the business model as the starting point of the process of requirements specification. The initial step in this process is to include a software system actor in the business model. In doing so, the candidate operations to be automated are isolated.

6.1   Process of Insertion of the System Actor

The strategy of this process consists of determining the type of interaction of each business actor model with the software system actor. An important concept used in this process is the "module". A module represents an internal task-refinement tree in an actor in the Strategic Rationale Model.

An actor may have more than one module. This indicates that the actor should fulfill more than one goal in the business model.

In our case study, for example, the PcChair has the modules *Send Notification* and *Assign Papers* (Figure 3).

We present a brief version of the guidelines that permit the insertion of the actor system into the business model. Figure 4 shows the result of the application of these guidelines to our case study.

Guideline 1. Insert the actor system into the organizational model and identify the modules that need to be delegated to the information system.

Guideline 2. Move these modules from the organizational actors to the system actor. This is only necessary when the main task (module root) needs to be automated. To move each module, it is necessary to apply two steps. The first step is to create a copy of the module root in the system actor. The second step is to create a task dependency (with the same name as the module) between the organizational actor and the system actor. This task dependency indicates that the software system actor is now responsible for completing the task. There may be manual operations in the modules, where the system can only be used to send or receive information. In these cases, it is necessary to leave these manual operations in the modules of the organizational actor.

Guideline 3. There are tasks that require information from the organizational actors when these tasks are transferred to modules in the system actor. In this case, it is necessary to create new resource dependencies between the system actor and the organizational actors. This is the case with the task *generate PcMember list*, which requires information from the PcChair (when transferred to the system actor), as the system cannot generate the PcMember List by itself, since it requires the information from the PcChair.

In the SR Model generated (Figure 4), the tasks selected to be automated have been redirected towards the system actor. In this way, the system actor has the following functions to help the users to accomplish the business task: *assign papers to adequate PcMembers, send notifications and reviews to Authors obtain papers*, and *to do quality reviews*. Each one of these functions is refined in a subtask in the SR Model.

The application of these guidelines allows business models to be naturally translated into requirements models which are based on use case models.

6.2   Use Case Generation from a Business Model

Santander and Castro [Sant01] have previously studied the generation of use case models from business models. This approach focuses only on the translation process of the business models in a use case model specification. Therefore, this work does not focus on the problem of business model generation. We place more emphasis on business model creation by providing guidelines that allow us to generate business models adapted for use case generation.

To guide the process of mapping between the business models and the use case model specified in UML, we defined a set of steps to establish the correspondence between the elements of the business model specified in the i* framework (with the system actor integrated in explicit form) and the use case model and the corresponding scenarios.

Obtaining a Use Case Model

The first step of the process is to determine the relevant goal dependencies that will be used to generate the use case model. The relevant dependencies are those goal dependencies which were translated into resource or task dependencies between a business actor and the system actor. If a goal dependency has not given rise to dependencies with the system actor, then it represents a manual activity in which there is no interaction between the user and the software system. For this reason, this goal does not need to be modeled as a use case.

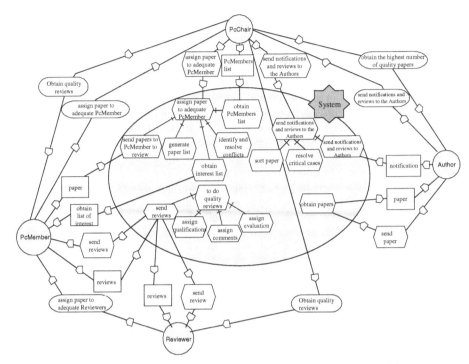

Fig. 4. Insertion of the software system actor into the business model

Fig. 5. Initial Model of the Conference Review System

Obtaining the Use Case Actors

The second step of the process is to determine the use case actors. In order to do this, it is necessary to analyze those resource and task dependencies which are derived from the relevant goal dependencies. The software system actor is always present at one end of the resource or task dependency, and the business actor is always present at the other end. Therefore, the business actor appears as a system user and also as a use case actor. The result of the application of these steps to our case study is shown in Figure 5.

Scenario Representation

It is necessary to create a description model for each goal dependency which has been chosen as a use case. Templates are used to show a sequence of events between the actors and the system. To do this, we use a variant of the template proposed by L. Constantine [Con99](for details, consult Sánchez [San01]).

Table 2. Specification of the use case *Send Review*

Use Case Name: Send Review	
Include:	None
Extend:	None
Preconditions	The PCMember has logged into the system.
Post conditions	The system saves a new review information
Primary Actor	PcMember
Secondary Actors	None
Roles	Reviewer

User intentions	System responsibilities
1. The PCMember selects "Enter Review"	2. The system asks for Paper ID.
3. The PCMember introduces Paper ID	4. The system verifies paper ID and the system displays paper title.
	5. The system asks for review data
6. The PCMember introduces values for Originality, Technical Quality, Relevance and Overall Rating.	7. The system asks for reviewer's comments
8. The PCMember introduces Author and Program Committee comments, and selects "Apply".	9. The system saves the review information.
Asynchronous extensions	
The Reviewer can select *Stop* at any point	
Synchronous extensions	
If there is no paper ID, the system displays an error message at point 4.	

It is necessary to detail the user intentions as well as the system responsibilities in the template. This division allows us to detect when the actors request services and when the system acts as a supplier of information. This information is obtained from the Strategic Rationale Model using the steps shown in [Mar02]. To illustrate the template, we select the use case *Send Reviews* shown in Table 2.

7 Conclusions

A goal-based business modeling method has been presented in this paper. We define a set of steps to generate business models that reflects the goals of each actor, as well as the general goals of the business. We also present the required steps to integrate the software system actor inside the business model. The software system actor integrates the business task to be automated by the information system. We have applied the guidelines for the business modeling to a case study, showing the graphic representation of each one of the business models generated. Finally, the steps to translate the business model into a compatible UML use case specification and its respective scenarios are also presented. The use case model generated serves as input to a semi automatic process that generates the specification of the system behavior, as well as the prototype of the user interface [Mar02]. This specification is used in the last phase of the method to simulate the interfaces generated. The simulation process is supported by a tool which is programmed in Delphi, and which has a relational repository in Interbase. The tool generates prototypes in the Delphi, Java and HTML languages. This tool is being reprogrammed in Java language.

References

[Ant96]   Anton Annie, "Goal Based Requirements Analysis", in Proceedings Second International Conference on Requirements Engineering. ICRE '96, pp. 136–144, April 1996.

[Bol02]   Davide Bochini, Paolo Paolini, "Capturing Web Application Requirements through Goal-Oriented Analysis", Proceedings of the Workshop on Requirements Engineering (WER 02), pp. 16–28, Valencia, Spain, 2002.

[Bub94]   Bubenko, J. A., Jr and M. Kirikova, "Worlds in Requirements Acquisition and Modelling", in: Information Modelling and Knowledge Bases VI. H.Kangassalo et al. (Eds.), IOS Press, pp. 159–174, Amsterdam, 1995.

[Cas02]   Castro J. Kolp M. Mylopoulos J. "Towards Requirements-Driven Information Systems Engineering: The Tropos Project". Information System Journal, Elsevier, Vol 27, pp 365–389, 2002.

[Ces02]   Cesare S. Mark Lycett, "Business Modelling with UML, distilling directions for future research", Proceedings of the Information Systems Analysis and Specification (ICEIS 2002), pp. 570–579, Ciudad-Real, Spain, 2002.

[Dar93]   Dardenne, A. Van Lamsweerde and S. Fickas, "Goal Directed Requirements Acquisition," Science of Computer Programming, vol. 20, pp. 3–50, North Holland, April 1993.

[Lou95]   Loucopoulos Pericles, Evangelia Kavakli, "Enterprise Modelling and the Teleological Approach to Requirements Engineering", International Journal of Cooperative Information Systems (IJCIS), pp. 45–79 , 1995.

[Mar02]   Martínez Alicia, Hugo Estrada, Juan Sánchez, "From Early Requirements to User Interface Prototyping: A methodological approach", Proceedings 17th IEEE International Conference on Automated Software Engineering (ASE 2002), pp. 257–260. Edinburgh, UK. September 2002.

[Mcd94]   McDermid, J..A, "Software Engineer's Reference Book", Edit. Butterworth-Heinenmann, 1994.

[San03]   J. Sánchez, O. Pastor, H. Estrada, A. Martínez, "Semi Automatic Generation of User Interfaces Prototypes from Early Requirements Models", Perspectives on Requirements Engineering. Editors: J. Leite; J. Doorn, Kluwer Academic Press, to appear in June 2003.

[San01]   Sánchez J; Pastor O, Fons J.J. "From User Requirements to User Interfaces: a methodological approach", Proceedings of the Fourteenth International Conference on Advanced Information Systems Engineering (CAISE 2001). pp. 60–75. Switzerland. 2001.

[Sant01]   Santander, V. F. A., Castro, J. B., "Developing Use Cases from Organizational Modeling", IV Workshop on Requirements Engineering (WER), Buenos Aires Argentina, 2001.

[Yu95]   Yu, Eric, "Modelling Strategic Relationships for Process Reengineering", PhD Thesis, University of Toronto, (1995).

Strategy for Database Application Evolution: The DB-MAIN Approach

Jean-Marc Hick and Jean-Luc Hainaut

University of Namur, Computer Sciences Department
Rue Grandgagnage 21, B-5000 Namur, Belgium
{jmh,jlh}@info.fundp.ac.be
http://www.info.fundp.ac.be/libd

Abstract. While recent data management technologies, e.g., object-oriented, address the problem of databases schema evolution, standard information systems currently in use raise challenging problems when evolution is concerned. This paper studies database evolution from the developer point of view. It shows how requirements changes are propagated to the database schemas, to the data and to the programs through a general strategy. This strategy requires the documentation of the database design. When absent, this documentation has to be rebuilt through reverse engineering techniques. The approach relies on a generic database model and on the transformational paradigm that states that database engineering processes can be modelled by schema transformations. Indeed, a transformation provides both structural and instance mappings that formally define how to modify database structures and contents. The paper then analyses the problem of program modification and describes a CASE tool that can assist developers in their task of system evolution.

1 Introduction

A database application is a software system that includes complex and high-volume persistent data stored in a set of files or in a genuine database. Such an application must evolve due to environment requirements changes.

The lack of support (methods and tools) in the database maintenance and evolution domain is now recognized. Systematic rules for translation of requirement modifications into technical modifications of the application are still unknown particularly when traceability of design and maintenance processes is missing. Current CASE[1] tools automatically generate incomplete DDL[2] code that must be modified to be truly operational. If database specifications change, these tools produce new code which is disconnected from the updated version. In addition, data conversion and program modification are up to the programmer.

Quite frustratingly, though schema evolution has been widely studied in the scientific literature, yielding interesting results, the latter still has to be implemented into practical technology and methodology. The problem of database evolution has first been studied for standard data structures. Direct relational schema modification

---

[1] Computer Aided Software Engineering.
[2] Data Definition Language.

I.-Y. Song et al. (Eds.): ER 2003, LNCS 2813, pp. 291–306, 2003.
© Springer-Verlag Berlin Heidelberg 2003

has been analysed by [2], [17] and [18], among others. The propagation of conceptual modifications on relational schemas are analysed in [17] and [20]. The object paradigm is a good framework to develop elegant solutions through the concepts of schema and instance versioning ([1], [4], [16]).

Several research projects have addressed the problem of change in information systems. For example, the NATURE project [14] has developed a requirement engineering framework playing an important role in modification management. The SEI-CMU project studied the evaluation of the evolution capacity of existing information systems [5]. Closer to our data-centric approach, the Varlet project [13] adopts a reverse engineering process that consists in two phases. In the first one, the different parts of the original database are analysed to obtain a logical schema for the implemented physical schema. In the second phase, this logical schema is transformed into a conceptual one that is the basis for modification activities.

This paper analyses the phenomenon of data evolution in database applications as the modification of three system components, namely the data structures, the data and the programs, as an answer to requirement changes at different levels of abstraction. After the problem statement (section 2), the paper introduces the methodological foundations (section 3). Finally, section 4 describes the evolution strategy of the DB-MAIN approach[3] and section 5 closes the paper.

2 Problem Statement

The phenomenon of evolution is analysed in the framework of classical modelling approaches, that are now familiar to database developers. These approaches consider the database design as a complex activity made up of elementary processes based on three abstraction levels, each of them dealing with homogeneous design requirements, i.e., the conceptual, logical and physical levels. One generally consider three kinds of requirements, namely functional (to meet the user requirements in terms of system functions), organizational (to answer the framework changes in a company) and technical (adaptation to the new technical or hardware constraints). In Fig. 1, the conceptual schema meets the organizational and functional requirements R1, while the logical schema satisfies the DBMS[4]-dependent technical requirements R2 and the physical schema integrates the physical requirements R3. The operational system contains the database (structures and data) and the programs. According to the most commonly agreed approaches, the conceptual schema is translated into a DBMS model-dependent logical schema, which is in turn enriched into the physical schema. These translation processes are basically of transformational nature.

We adopt the hypothesis that all the application specifications for each abstraction level and the trace of their design processes, i.e., the transformations, are available. This assumption is of course unrealistic in many situations, in which the program source code and DDL scripts (or DBMS data dictionary contents) are often the only available documentation. In this context, the strategies we are going to develop must be completed to take the lack of high-level specifications into account.

---

[3] DB-MAIN stands for *Database Maintenance and Evolution*. This approach has been grossly described in [7] and has been developed in detail in [12].

[4] DataBase Management System.

The database application evolution translates changes in the requirements into system changes. This paper focuses on the persistent data, i.e., the set of files or databases that store information on the application domain. More precisely, the problem can be summarised as following: how must a change in a schema be propagated to (1) the lower level schemas, including the DDL code, (2) the data and (3) the application programs.

This study relies on a *non-temporal* approach, according to which all the application components (i.e., the schemas, the data and the programs) are replaced by new versions. In particular, the data are transformed in such a way that they become unavailable in their previous form. The application programs can use the new data only after being transformed accordingly. This strategy applies on both legacy and modern database applications and contrasts with advanced systems where the modification of the database schema is translated into the addition of a new version. In such schema/data versioning approaches ([15],[17]), the old schema is preserved and the access to its data is stored or calculated.

For example, removing a property from a conceptual class is ultimately translated in our approach into the removal of the corresponding column through the query:
```
alter table <table_name> drop <column_name>.
```

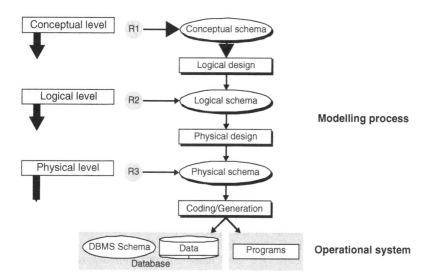

Fig. 1. Standard modelling approach divided into three abstraction levels.

3 Methodological Foundations

Requirement modification is translated into specification changes at the corresponding level (we ignore the translation rules in this paper). To ensure specification consistency, these changes must be propagated upwards and downward to other abstraction levels. Due to the complexity of the process, it must be supported by a CASE tool, which must meet three conditions.

- Genericity: the environment must offer a generic model of specification representation whatever the abstraction level, the technology or the paradigm on which the application relies.
- Formality: it must describe formally the database engineering activities.
- Traceability: the links between specifications must be rigorously recorded. They must be analysed to provide the information necessary for the modification propagation.

The DB-MAIN approach to database evolution is based on three concepts that implement these requirements: generic representation model (section 3.1), transformational approach (section 3.2) and history management (section 3.3).

3.1   Generic Model of Specification Representation

The DB-MAIN model has generic characteristics according to two dimensions:
- specification representation at each abstraction level: conceptual, logical and physical;
- coverage of the main modelling paradigms or technologies such as ERA, UML, ORM, objects, relational, CODASYL, IMS, standard files or XML models.

It is based on the Generic Entity/Relationship model and supports all the operational models through a specialization mechanism. Each model is defined as a sub-model of the generic model. A sub-model is obtained by restriction, i.e., by selecting the relevant objects, by defining the legal assemblies through structural predicates, by renaming the object according to the model taxonomy and by choosing a suitable graphical representation. Fig. 2 presents schemas according to classical sub-models for the three abstraction levels: ERA (Merise style), relational and Oracle 8.

In Fig. 2a, *PERSON, CUSTOMER, SUPPLIER, ORDER* and *ITEM* are entity types or object classes (ET). *CUSTOMER* and *SUPPLIER* are subtypes of *PERSON* (supertype). Totality and disjunction constraints (P = partition) are defined on these subtypes. Attributes *NumPers, Name, Address* and *Telephone* characterize *PERSON* (as well as *CUSTOMER* and *SUPPLIER*). *Address* is a compound attribute while *Telephone* is multivalued. Attributes *Number, Street* and *City* are components of *Address. Number* is optional. *place, reference* and *offer* are binary relationship types (RT). *reference* has an attribute. *ORDER* plays two roles in *place* and *reference*. Each role has minimal and maximal cardinalities (N stands for *infinity*). *reference* is called a many-to-many relationship type and *place* an one-to-many relationship type. *CUSTOMER* is identified by *NumCus*.

Fig. 2b depicts a relational schema in which *PERSON, CUSTOMER, SUPPLIER, TELEPHONE, ORDER, ...* are tables. *NumPers, NumCus* and *Name* are columns of *PERSON. Name* is mandatory and *Adr_Number* is optional (nullable). *PERSON* has a primary identifier (primary key) *NumPers* and two secondary identifiers *NumCus* and *NumSup. ORDER.NumCus*, as well as *PERSON.NumCus*, are *foreign keys* (*ref* or *equ*) targeting *CUSTOMER*. All the values of *CUSTOMER.NumCus* also appear as non-null values of *PERSON.NumCus*. This inclusion constraint forms with the foreign key an equality constraint (*equ*). *PERSON* is submitted to an *exactly-one* constraint (*exact-1*), i.e., for each row of this table, only one column among *NumSup* and *NumCus* has a non-null value.

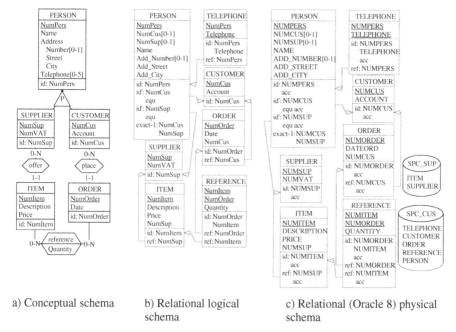

a) Conceptual schema

b) Relational logical schema

c) Relational (Oracle 8) physical schema

Fig. 2. Graphical views of conceptual, logical and physical schemas.

In Fig. 2c, the names of tables and columns are compliant with the SQL syntax and includes physical, performance-oriented constructs. For example, *Date* (reserved word) becomes *DATEORD* in *ORDER*. Indexes (*access* keys) are defined on columns such as *NUMPERS* of *PERSON* and *NUMSUP* of *ITEM*. Storage spaces (called TABLESPACE in Oracle) are defined: *SPC_SUP* contains the rows of tables *ITEM* and *SUPPLIER*.

3.2   Transformational Approach

Database engineering processes can be defined as a sequence of *data structure transformations* [3]. Adding an entity type, renaming an attribute, translating a relationship type into a foreign key are elementary transformations. They can be combined to build more complex processes such as schema normalization, logical schema optimization or DDL code generation. The concept of transformation used in this paper is formally described in [8], but we will briefly present some of its principles.

A transformation consists in deriving a target schema S' from a source schema S by replacing construct C (possibly empty) in S with a new construct C' (possibly empty). More formally, a transformation Σ is defined as a couple of mappings <T,t> such as: C' = T(C) and c' = t(c), where c is any instance of C and c' the corresponding instance of C'. Structural mapping T explains how to modify the schema while instance mapping t states how to compute the instance set of C' from the instances of C (Fig. 3). Structural mapping T is a couple of predicates <P,Q> where P are the minimal preconditions C must satisfy and Q the maximal postconditions observed in C'. We obtain: $\Sigma = <P,Q,t>$. P (resp. Q) are second order predicates that define the properties of structure C (resp. C').

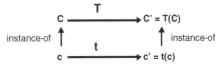

Fig. 3. General transformation pattern.

Fig. 4. The relationship type reference is transformed into an entity type REFERENCE.

Any transformation Σ can be given an inverse transformation $\Sigma' = <T',t'>$ such as $T'(T(C))=C$. If, in addition, we also are provided with instance mapping t' such as: $t'(t(c))=c$, then Σ (and Σ') are said semantics-preserving or *reversible*. If $<T',t'>$ is also reversible, Σ and Σ' are called *symmetrically reversible*.

Fig. 4 graphically illustrates the structural mapping T of the transformation of a relationship type into an entity type. This classical transformation appears in logical design, where complex structures, such as n-ary or many-to-many relationship types must be replaced with simple, flat structures. In this example, the relationship type *reference* is transformed into the entity type *REFERENCE* and the one-to-many relationship types *ro* and *ri*. The precondition of this transformation is void (all RT can be transformed). The postcondition states the properties of the resulting entity type, relationship types and constraints. The instance mapping explains how each *REFERENCE* entity derives from a *reference* relationship. The inverse transformation, denoted T' in Fig. 4, transforms the entity type *REFERENCE* into the relationship type *reference*. A complete formal description of this transformation can be found in [8].

A transformation is entirely specified by its signature, which gives the name of the transformation, the name of the objects concerned in the source schema and the name of the new objects in the target schema. For example, the signatures of the transformations represented in Fig. 4 are:

```
T:    (REFERENCE, {ro,ri})  ← RT-to-ET(reference)
```

```
T':  reference  ← ET-to-RT(REFERENCE)
```

The first expression reads as following: by application of the RT-to-ET transformation on the relationship type *reference*, a new entity type *REFERENCE* and two new relationship types *ri* and *ro* are created. Note that all objects must not be mentioned in a signature. Such is the case of relationship types *ri* and *ro* to which *REFERENCE* participates.

The notion of *semantics* of a schema has no generally agreed upon definition. We assume that the semantics of S1 include the semantics of S2 *iff the application domain described by S2 is a part of the domain represented by S1*. Though intuitive and informal, this definition is sufficient for this presentation. In this context, three transformation categories can be distinguished:

- T+ collects the transformations that augment the semantics of the schema (for example adding an entity type).
- T- includes the transformations that decrease the semantics of the schema (for example adding an identifier).
- T= is the category of transformations that preserve the semantics of the schema (for example the transformation of a relationship type into an entity type).

Transformations in T= are mainly used in logical and physical schema production, while T+ and T- transformations make up the basis of specification evolution process.

3.3 History

For the sake of consistency, we consider that the requirement modifications applied at a given abstraction level must be propagated at the other levels. For example, adding a column to a table must imply the addition of the corresponding attribute to the entity type implemented by this table. Conversely, removing a one-to-many relationship type must be followed by the removal of the corresponding foreign key in the logical and physical schemas. As far as evolution is concerned, keeping track of the design transformations is a necessity, as we will see, to avoid manually the reformulation of the design transformation sequence for each evolution modification [7].

The trace of the transformations that produce the schema Sj from schema Si is called the *history* of the transformation process, and is noted *Hij*. The composition of a sequence of elementary transformations *Hij* is also a (macro-)transformation, so that we can use the functional notation: $Sj = Hij(Si)$ with $Hij = Tn°...°T2°T1$, that will be noted <T1 T2 ... Tn> in the following.

Using the signature notation, the following history, named *LD0*, describes how the conceptual schema of Fig. 2a has been transformed into the relational schema of Fig. 2b.

```
LD0 = <
 T1:(pers_cus,pers_sup) ← ISA-to-
RT(PERSON,{CUSTOMER,SUPPLIER})
 T2:(REFERENCE,{ord_ref,ite_ref}) ← RT-to-ET(reference)
 T3:(TELEPHONE,have) ← Att-to-ET-inst(PERSON.Telephone)
 T4:(Add_Number,Add_Street,Add_City)
← disaggregate(PERSON.Address)
 T5:(PERSON.NumCus) ← RT-to-FK(pers_cus)
 T6:(PERSON.NumSup) ← RT-to-FK(pers_sup)
 T7:(TELEPHONE.NumPers) ← RT-to-FK(have)
 T8:(ORDER.NumCus) ← RT-to-FK(place)
 T9:(ITEM.NumSup) ← RT-to-FK(offer)
 T10:(REFERENCE.NumOrder) ← RT-to-FK(ord_ref)
 T11:(REFERENCE.NumItem) ← RT-to-FK(ite_ref)
>
```

When the transformations recorded in *Hij* are applied to Si, *Hij* is said to be *replayed* on Si. A history can be manipulated if several rules are respected (see [9] for more details):

- Exhaustivity: the transformations are recorded precisely and completely to allow the inversion of non semantics-preserving transformations (reversing a delete transformation requires a description of all aspects of the deleted objects).
- Normalization: the history is monotonous (no rollback) and linear (no multiple branch).
- Non-competition: a history is attached to one schema and only one user can modify it.

4 Evolution Strategy

Our approach has been developed for evolution of relational database applications, but other models can be coped with minimal efforts thanks to the genericity of the model and of the transformational approach. This choice allows us to build a modification typology and to design concrete conversion tools that can be used with systems developed in a third-generation language such as COBOL/SQL or C/SQL.

To make database applications evolve, the design history must be available. In particular, the three levels of specification must exist and are documented, together with the histories of the inter-level transformation processes. In other words, the database is fully documented through its conceptual, logical and physical schemas and the histories of the conceptual-to-logical and logical-to-physical processes. In most cases, this hypothesis is not met: some (or all) levels are missing, incomplete or obsolete. Sometimes, only the source code of the programs and of the data structures are available. In these cases, the documentation and the histories must be rebuilt thanks to reverse engineering techniques that are not addressed in this paper. The reverse engineering approach we have defined is described in [6] and [10] while the process of rebuilding histories has been developed in [9].

4.1   Evolution Scenarios

Three scenarios, one for each abstraction level, have been defined (Fig. 5). The initial specifications are available as the three standard schemas: conceptual (CS0), logical (LS0) and physical (PS0) schema. The operational components are the database (D0: data and structures) and the programs (P0). LD0 (resp. PD0) are the histories that describe the transformations applied to CS0 (resp. LS0) to obtain LS0 (resp. PS0). The scenarios are constrained by the following hypothesis: the change must be applied on the relevant level. For instance, adding a new property to an application class must be translated into the addition of an attribute to a conceptual entity type, in CS0, and not by adding a column to a table in LS0.

In the first scenario (Fig. 5a), the modifications translate changes in the functional requirement into conceptual schema updates. This new state is called CS1. The problem is the propagation of modifications towards the logical, physical and operational layers, leading to the new components LS1, PS1, P1 and D1, and to the revised histories LS1 and PS1. The second scenario (Fig. 5b) addresses logical schema modifications. Though the conceptual schema is kept unchanged (CS1 = CS0), the logical design history LD0 must be updated as LD1 and the modifications must be propagated in the physical and operational layers. In the third scenario (Fig. 5c), the designer modifies the physical schema to meet, e.g., new performance requirements. The physical design history is updated and the operational layer is converted.

The evolution strategy comprises four steps: *database schema modification* (section 4.2), *schema modification propagation* (section 4.3), *database conversion* (section 4.4) and *program modification* (section 4.5).

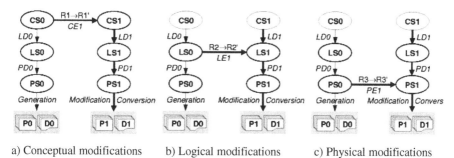

a) Conceptual modifications   b) Logical modifications   c) Physical modifications

Fig. 5. Propagation of modifications at each abstraction level.

4.2   Database Schema Modification

In Fig. 5a, the requirements met by CS0 evolve from R1 to R1'. The analyst copies the schema CS0 into CS1 and translates the changes into modifications of CS1. The transformations applied to CS0 to obtain CS1 are recorded into history CE1, so that CS1 = CE1(CS0). In Fig. 5b, the schema LS0 is modified to obtain LS1. The logical evolution transformations are recorded in the history LE1. Note that the designer can also modify the logical schema by using other transformations than those used in LD0, without modifying the conceptual objects. For example, a multivalued attribute transformed into a series of single-valued columns will now be transformed into an autonomous table. In this case, though the conceptual schema does not change, the first scenario is used. CE1 is empty and CS1 is equivalent to CS0, but the logical design history LD1 contains the new transformation (cf. section 4.3). In Fig. 5c, the physical schema PS0 is transformed into PS1 and the modification transformations are recorded in PE1.

Our approach is based on a set of standard schema modifications that accounts for most evolution needs. A detailed study of modification typology in conceptual, logical and physical levels is proposed in [12] and [17].

Thereafter, we are considering the first scenario for the following change: *the cardinality of the multivalued attribute Telephone becomes [0-2] in the conceptual schema of Fig. 2a*. This example will be analysed for each step of the evolution strategy process. The conceptual evolution history CE1 contains one signature: `change-max-card(PERSON.Telephone,2)`.

4.3   Schema Modification Propagation

At this level, all the specifications and the histories must be updated according to the modifications described in section 4.2.

In the first scenario, the new conceptual schema CS1 is transformed into a logical schema LS1 that is as close as possible to the former version LS0 and that integrates the conceptual modifications. The LD0 history is replayed on a copy of CS1 renamed LS1. This history contains the necessary operations to transform a conceptual schema into a relational logical one (for example Fig. 2b). The relational transformations belong essentially to the T= category.

When the LD0 history is replayed on the new conceptual schema CS1, four situations are possible according to the type of modification:

1. Unchanged object: the transformations of LD0 concerning this object are executed without modification.
2. Created object: the transformations of LD0 have no effect. The designer must specifically process the new object.
3. Removed object: the transformations of LD0 concerning this object can be applied but they have no effect.
4. Modified object: for minor modifications, the transformations concerning this object are executed. For major modifications, these transformations are no longer adapted and processing this object is under the designer responsibility.

The transformations of LD0 augmented with those applied on the new or modified objects and without the useless transformations make up the new logical design process recorded as LD1 history.

After that, we proceed in the same way by replaying history PD0 on LS1 to obtain the new physical schema PS1. PD1 contains the transformations (on physical structures: indexes and storage spaces) such as: PS1=PD1(LS1).

In the second scenario, the propagation starts at the logical level but is based on similar principles. The new logical design history LD1 is made up of LD0 augmented by the trace of the new transformations (LE1): LD1 = LD0 ° LE1. The propagation of modifications to the physical level is similar to that of the first scenario. If the evolution involves the application of other transformations than those used formerly to produce the logical schema from the conceptual specifications, then LS0 is replayed step by step and the designer replaces, when needed, the former transformations by the new ones. A second set of schema modifications includes the most useful conceptual-to-logical transformations for relational schemas [12].

The third scenario is similar to the second one, applied on the the physical schema. The new physical design history PD1 is made up of PD0 augmented by the trace of the new transformations (PE1): PD1 = PD0 ° PE1. The physical design only copes with indexes and storage spaces, which in most cases is sufficient to describe physical design and tuning scenarios. The logical design stays unchanged (LD1 = LD0).

In the example, when the LD0 history (section 3.3) is replayed on a new conceptual schema CS1, the designer does not transform the attribute *Telephone* into an entity type, that will become the table *TELEPHONE* (Fig. 6a). He decides to apply the instantiation transformation, according to which a single-valued attribute is introduced to store each value. *Telephone* is therefore replaced with two optional single-valued attributes: *Telephone1* and *Telephone2* (Fig. 6b). The new logical design history LD1 is equivalent to LD0 except that the signature

(Telephone1,Telephone2) ← instanciate(Telephone) replaces the T3 signature and the T7 signature is removed. By simply replaying PD0 on the new logical schema, a new physical design history PD1 is obtained, in which the indexes and storage space specifications related to the old *TELEPHONE* table have been automatically discarded.

a) *Telephone* represented by a table in LS0   b) *Telephone* represented by two columns in LS1

Fig. 6. Two popular representations of multivalued attribute Telephone.

4.4   Database Conversion

Once the specifications have been updated, the database structure and contents D0 can be converted. The data conversion can be automated thanks to a converter generator. The study of the evolution histories (CE1, LE1 or PE1) allows the generator to locate the modifications in the three abstraction levels. A differential analysis of the design histories (LD0, LD1, PD0 and PD1) gives the information to derive the removed, modified or added physical structures. To shorten the notation, let us call E any evolution history, C0 and C1 any elementary or composed history in the old and in the new branch. In the first scenario, we have: PS0 = PD0(LD0(CS0)) = C0(CS0) and PS1 = PD1(LD1(CS1)) = C1(CS1). In the second scenario, we have: PS0 = PD0(LS0) = C0(LS0) and PS1 = PD1(LS1) = C1(LS1). In the third scenario, C0 and C1 are empty.

According to a definite type of modification appearing in E, three distinct behaviours are possible:
1. In case of creation, the analysis of C1 gives the new physical structures according to the possible transformations applied successively on this object.
2. In case of suppression, the analysis of C0 provides the old physical structures to re-move according to the possible transformations applied on this object.
3. The case of modification is more complex. Initially, the new structures are created on the basis of C1. Then, the data instances are transferred from the old structures to the new ones. And finally, the old physical structures are removed according to the analysis of C0.

The analysis of E, C0 and C1 let us derive the transformation of data structures and instances of PS0 (i.e., D0) into structures and instances of PS1 (D1). The chain of structural mappings (T parts) drives the schema modification while the chain of instance mappings defines the way data have to be transformed. These transformations are translated into a converter made up of SQL scripts or programs[5] in more complex cases. The translation of schema transformations into SQL scripts has been described in [12].

Some modifications bring about information losses and constraint violations. In these cases, the conversion script produces a query to verify the violation of the constraint and to ensure data consistency. For example, if the designer creates a primary identifier on a previously non-unique column, the table contents can violate the uniqueness constraint, so that the script must store the inconsistent rows, as well as the possible dependent rows in other tables, in temporary *error* tables. Automating the generation of conversion scripts is always possible, but an user intervention is sometimes necessary to manage ambiguous or conflicting instances.

In the example, the analysis of CE1, C0 and C1 shows that the old table *TELEPHONE* (in source schema PS0) must be replaced by the columns *TELEPHONE1* and *TELEPHONE2* (in target schema PS1). A converter translates this transformation into the following Oracle script, which converts both the database structure and contents, and which stores the conflicting data, if any, into the table *TEL_ERROR*.

```
-- Creation of Telephone1 and Telephone2
ALTER TABLE PERSON ADD TELEPHONE1 CHAR(12);
ALTER TABLE PERSON ADD TELEPHONE2 CHAR(12);
-- Creation of table TEL_ERROR
CREATE TABLE TEL_ERROR(NUMPERS INT, TELEPHONE CHAR(12));
-- Transfert of data
CREATE OR REPLACE PROCEDURE Trf_data IS
  CURSOR c1 IS SELECT * FROM PERSON P
    WHERE exists(select * from TELEPHONE where NUMPERS=
                                         P.NUMPERS);
  CURSOR c2 IS SELECT * FROM TELEPHONE where NUMPERS=num;
  tP c1%ROWTYPE; tT c2%ROWTYPE; num INT; comp NUMBER;
  BEGIN
    FOR tP IN c1 LOOP
      comp := 1; num := tP.NUMPERS;
      FOR tT IN c2 LOOP
        IF comp=1 THEN
          UPDATE PERSON SET TELEPHONE1=tT.TELEPHONE WHERE
                                  NUMPERS=tP.NUMPERS; END IF;
        IF comp=2 THEN
          UPDATE PERSON SET TELEPHONE2=tT.TELEPHONE WHERE
                                  NUMPERS=tP.NUMPERS; END IF;
        IF comp>2 THEN INSERT INTO TEL_ERROR VALUES
                            (tP.NUMPERS,tT.TELEPHONE); END IF;
        comp := comp + 1;
      END LOOP;
    END LOOP;
  END;
-- TELEPHONE destruction
DROP TABLE PHONE CASCADE CONSTRAINT;
```

---

[5] Such a converter is a variant of Extract-Transform-Load, or ETL, processors.

4.5   Program Modification

Modifying the application programs P0 following database structure modification is clearly a complex task that cannot be completely automated or only in simple cases where the modifications are minor. To characterize the impact of data structure modifications on programs, we defined three kinds of modifications:

- Some structure modifications do not require any modification on the programs. For example adding or modifying physical constructs (on indexes and storage spaces) has no impact on the programs, at least for RDBMS[6]. The same is valid for the addition of a table or of columns for which no new constraints, such as *not null*, are defined.[7] Some more complex modifications can be absorbed through the *view* mechanism, if it can rebuild the former data structures.

- Other structure modifications only require minor, and easily automated, modifications of the programs. Such is the case of a table renaming or a value domain extension.

- However, many modifications involve deeper modification of the program structure. They often require a thorough knowledge of the application. In Fig. 2a, if the attribute *CUSTOMER.Account* becomes multivalued, it translates into a table in the corresponding logical schema. Following this extension of the schema semantics, the program must either keep its former specification (one must decide how to select the unique account value) or process the multiple accounts of each customer (generally by introducing a processing loop). In either case, the very meaning of the program must be coped with, possibly through program understanding techniques. The difficulty lies in the determination of code lines that must belong to the new loop.

In most cases, the program modification is under the responsibility of the programmer. However, it is possible to prepare this work by a code analysis that allows locating the critical sections of code. Techniques of program analysis such as pattern searching, dependency graphs and program slicing make it possible to locate with a good precision the code to be modified. These techniques have been detailed in [10] and [21].

On the basis of E, C1 and C0 analysis (section 4.4), the schema constructs that have changed can be identified and supplied to the program analysers (dependency graphs analysers and program slicers). The latter locates the code sections depending on these modified constructs. A generator examines the results of the program analysis and produces a report of modifications which would be advisable to apply to the programs under the programmer control.

In the example of the attribute *TELEPHONE*, the database conversion requires modifications of the program structure. Before the modification, the extraction of the telephone numbers of a person required a join operator, while in the new structure, the values are available in two distinct columns of the current *PERSON* row. Clearly, the processing of these values must be rewritten manually unless the program had been written in a particularly disciplined way. To locate the code to be modified, the program analysers use parameters based on the table *TELEPHONE*, its columns and the variables which depend on it.

---

[6] This would not be true for legacy databases, such as standard files.
[7] Provided the *select* and *insert* statements use explicit column names.

Despite the intrinsic complexity of program evolution, new approaches are being developed, and can prove promising. One of them is based on wrapper technology[8] that isolates the application programs from the data management technology. A wrapper is used to simulate the source schema PS0 on top of the new database (schema PS1). The mappings T and t of the history E are encapsulated in the wrapper instead of being translated into program changes. In this way, the programs access the new data through the old schema, so that the application logic must not be changed. File I/O primitives have to be replaced with wrapper calls in a one-to-one way, a process that can be easily automated. This approach has been described and explored in [11].

5   Conclusions

The problem of the evolution of an information system, or data-centred application, includes that of the database which is at its core. The requirement evolution is translated technically into the modification of specifications at the corresponding abstraction level. The difficulty lies in the propagation of these modifications towards the other levels and especially to the operational components, namely the database and the programs.

The concepts (transformational modelling, generic specification representation and process traceability) of the DB-MAIN approach are a formal basis for the understanding and resolution of the evolution problems. If the documentation of the system design is available or can be rebuilt by reverse engineering, then the evolution control becomes a formal process. This process can widely be automated as far as the database is concerned. Unfortunately, program modification remains an open problem in the general case. It is however possible to help the programmer to modify the code by automatically locating the sections where occurrences of modified object types are processed.

We have developed a prototype CASE tool for relational database evolution according to the strategy and the scenarios described in this paper. The prototype is developed in Voyager 2 as an add-on of the DB-MAIN platform [22]. It automatically generates the database converters corresponding to any transformation sequence. It also generates the rules to be used by the DB-MAIN program analysers to identify the program code sections that should be modified.

An experiment has been carried out on a medium size database (326 tables and 4850 columns) in a distribution company. The application programs were made up of 180.000 COBOL lines of code distributed among 270 modules (a table appears in seven modules on average). The experiment showed that the time of assisted conversion of the structure, the data and the programs was less than one third of that of the manual process. With the assisted method, an engineer propagated one

---

[8] A data wrapper is a procedural component that transforms a database from a legacy model to another, generally more modern model. It appears as a data server to client applications and makes them independent of the legacy model technology. For instance a set of COBOL files can be dynamically transformed into an object store or into a relational database. Wrappers can automatically be generated by the transformational approach described in this paper. See [19] for more details.

elementary database modification into the database and the programs in one day versus three days with the manual process. The company saved forty working days for twenty modifications a year while decreasing the risk of error. However, the assisted method required an initial investment of thirty days to rebuild a correct and up-to-date database documentation and to adapt the data conversion and program analysis tools.

References

1. Al-Jadir, L., Estier, T., Falquet, G., Léonard, M., Evolution features of the F2 OODBMS, in Proc. of 4th Int. Conf. on Database Systems for Advanced Applications, Singapore, 1995.
2. Andany, J., Léonard, M., Palisser, C., Management of Schema Evolution in Databases, in Proc. of 17th Int. Conf. on VLDB, Barcelona, 1991.
3. Batini, C., Ceri, S., Navathe, S.B., Conceptual Database Design – An Entity-Relationship Approach, Benjamin/Cummings, 1992.
4. Bellahsene, Z., An Active Meta-Model for Knowledge Evolution in an Object-oriented Database, in Proc. of CAiSE, Springer-Verlag, 1993.
5. Brown, A., Morris, E., Tilley, S., Assessing the evolvability of a legacy system, Software Engineering Institute, Carnegie Mellon University, Technical Report, 1996.
6. Hainaut, J.-L., Chandelon, M., Tonneau, C., Joris, M., Contribution to a theory of database reverse engineering, in Proc. of WCRE, IEEE Computer Society Press, Baltimore, 1993.
7. Hainaut, J.-L., Englebert, V., Henrard, J., Hick, J.-M., Roland, D., Evolution of database Applications: the DB-MAIN Approach, in Proc. of 13th Int. Conf. on ER Approach, Manchester, 1994.
8. Hainaut, J.-L., Specification Preservation in Schema transformations – Application to Semantics and Statistics, Data & Knowledge Engineering, Vol. 19, pp. 99–134, Elsevier, 1996.
9. Hainaut, J.-L., Henrard, J., Hick, J.-M., Roland, D., Englebert, V., Database Design Recovery, in Proc. of 8th CAiSE, 1996.
10. Henrard, J., Englebert, V., Hick, J.-M., Roland, D., Hainaut, J.-L., Program understanding in databases reverse engineering, in Proc. of Int. Conf. on DEXA, Vienna, 1998.
11. Henrard, J., Hick, J-M. Thiran, Ph., Hainaut, J.-L., Strategies for Data Reengineering, in Proc. of WCRE'02, IEEE Computer Society Press, 2002
12. Hick, J.-M., Evolution of relational database applications: Methods and Tools, PhD Thesis, University of Namur, 2001. [in French]
13. Jahnke, J.-H., Wadsack, J. P., Varlet: Human-Centered Tool Support for Database Reengineering, in Proc. of Workshop on Software-Reengineering, 1999.
14. Jarke, M., Nissen, H.W., Pohl, K., Tool integration in evolving information systems environments, in Proc. of 3rd GI Workshop Information Systems and Artificial Intelligence: Administration and Processing of Complex Structures, Hamburg, 1994.
15. Jensen, C., and al., A consensus glossary of temporal database concepts, in Proc. of Int. Workshop on an Infrastructure for Temporal Databases, Arlington, 1994.
16. Nguyen, G.T., Rieu, D., Schema evolution in object-oriented database systems, in Data & Knowledge Engineering (4), Elsevier Science Publishers, 1989.
17. Roddick, J.F., Craske, N.G., Richards, T.J., A Taxonomy for Schema Versioning Based on the Relational and Entity Relationship Models, in Proc. of 12th Int. Conf. on the ER Approach, Arlington, 1993.
18. Shneiderman, B., Thomas, G., An architecture for automatic relational database system conversion, ACM Transactions on Database Systems, 7 (2): 235–257, 1982.

19. Thiran, Ph., Hainaut, J-L., Wrapper Development for Legacy Data Reuse, in Proc. of WCRE, IEEE Computer Society Press, 2001
20. van Bommel, P., Database Design Modifications based on Conceptual Modelling, in Information Modelling and Knowledge Bases V: Principles and Formal Techniques, pp 275–286, Amsterdam, 1994.
21. Weiser, M., Program Slicing, IEEE TSE, Vol. 10, pp 352–357, 1984.
22. http://www.db-main.be/ and http://www.info.fundp.ac.be/libd.

A UML Based Approach for Modeling ETL Processes in Data Warehouses*

Juan Trujillo and Sergio Luján-Mora

Dept. de Lenguajes y Sistemas Informáticos
Universidad de Alicante (Spain)
{jtrujillo,slujan}@dlsi.ua.es

Abstract. Data warehouses (DWs) are complex computer systems whose main goal is to facilitate the decision making process of knowledge workers. ETL (Extraction-Transformation-Loading) processes are responsible for the *extraction* of data from heterogeneous operational data sources, their *transformation* (conversion, cleaning, normalization, etc.) and their *loading* into DWs. ETL processes are a key component of DWs because incorrect or misleading data will produce wrong business decisions, and therefore, a correct design of these processes at early stages of a DW project is absolutely necessary to improve data quality. However, not much research has dealt with the modeling of ETL processes. In this paper, we present our approach, based on the Unified Modeling Language (UML), which allows us to accomplish the conceptual modeling of these ETL processes. We provide the necessary mechanisms for an easy and quick specification of the common operations defined in these ETL processes such as, the integration of different data sources, the transformation between source and target attributes, the generation of surrogate keys and so on. Another advantage of our proposal is the use of the UML (standardization, ease-of-use and functionality) and the seamless integration of the design of the ETL processes with the DW conceptual schema.

Keywords: ETL processes, Data warehouses, conceptual modeling, UML

1 Introduction

In the early nineties, Inmon [1] coined the term "data warehouse" (DW): "A data warehouse is a subject-oriented, integrated, time-variant, nonvolatile collection of data in support of management's decisions". A DW is "integrated" because data are gathered into the DW from a variety of sources (legacy systems, relational databases, COBOL files and so on) and merged into a coherent whole. ETL (Extraction-Transformation-Loading) processes are responsible for

---

* This paper has been partially supported by the Spanish Ministry of Science and Technology, project number TIC2001-3530-C02-02.

I.-Y. Song et al. (Eds.): ER 2003, LNCS 2813, pp. 307–320, 2003.

the extraction of data from heterogeneous operational data sources, their transformation (conversion, cleaning, etc.) and their loading into DWs. Therefore, it is highly recognized that the design and maintenance of these ETL processes is a key factor of success in DW projects [2,3].

Moreover, data from the operational systems are usually specified in different schemas and have to be extracted and transformed to collect them into a common DW repository [4]. Some of the more common technical tasks that have to be accomplished with these data are as follows. Data usually have to be aggregated in order to facilitate the definition of the queries and improve the performance of the DW. Data are usually in different types and formats and they need to be converted into a common format. Data in the operational systems are usually managed by different primary keys, and in DWs we usually use surrogate keys, and therefore, we need an efficient mechanism to assign surrogate keys to the operational data in the DW repository. Furthermore, as data are coming from different sources, we usually need to check the different primary and foreign keys to assure a high quality of data. Moreover, we also need a high number of filters to verify the right data to be uploaded in the DW and many more problems.

Due to the high difficulty in designing and managing these ETL processes, there has lately been a proliferation in the number of available ETL tools that try to simplify this task [5,6]. During 2001, the ETL market grew to about $667 million [7]. Currently, companies expend more than thirty percent out of the total budget for DW projects in expensive ETL tools, but "It's not unusual for the ETL effort to occupy 60 percent to 80 percent of a data warehouse's implementation effort" [3]. Nevertheless, it is widely recognized that the design and maintenance of these ETL processes has not yet been solved [7].

Therefore, we argue that a model and methodology are needed to help the design and maintenance of these ETL processes from the early stages of a DW project; as Kimball states, "Our job as data warehouse designers is to star with existing sources of used data" [8]. However, little effort has been dedicated to propose a conceptual model to formally define these ETL processes.

In this paper, we present a conceptual model based on the Unified Modeling Language (UML) [9] for the design of ETL processes which deals with the more common technical problems above-presented. As the UML has been widely accepted as the standard for object-oriented analysis and design, we believe that our approach will minimize the efforts of developers in learning new diagrams for modeling ETL processes. Furthermore, as we accomplish the conceptual modeling of the target DW schema following our multidimensional modeling approach, also based in the UML [10,11,12], the conceptual modeling of these ETL processes is totally integrated in a global approach. Therefore, our approach reduces the development time of a DW, facilitates managing data repositories, DW administration, and allows the designer to perform dependency analysis (i.e. to estimate the impact of a change in the data sources in the global DW schema).

The rest of the paper is organized as follows. Section 2 provides an overview of ETL processes and their surrounding data quality problems. Section 3 describes in detail how to accomplish the conceptual modeling of ETL processes using our proposal. Section 4 presents the related work. Finally, Section 5 presents the main conclusions and future works.

2   ETL

In an ETL process, the data extracted from a source system pass through a sequence of transformations before they are loaded into a DW. The repertoire of source systems that contribute data to a DW is likely to vary from standalone spreadsheets to mainframe-based systems many decades old. Complex transformations are usually implemented in procedural programs, either outside the database (in C, Java, Pascal, etc.) or inside the database (by using any 4GL). The design of an ETL process is usually composed of six tasks:

1. Select the sources for extraction: the data sources (usually several different heterogeneous data sources) to be used in the ETL process are defined.
2. Transform the sources: once the data have been extracted from the data sources, they can be transformed or new data can be derived. Some of the common tasks of this step are: filtering data, converting codes, calculating derived values, transforming between different data formats, automatic generation of sequence numbers (surrogate keys), etc.
3. Join the sources: different sources can be joined in order to load together the data in a unique target.
4. Select the target to load: the target (or targets) to be loaded is selected.
5. Map source attributes to target attributes: the attributes (fields) to be extracted from the data sources are mapped to the corresponding target ones.
6. Load the data: the target is populated with the transformed data.

The transformation step of the ETL processes can also perform data cleaning tasks, although ETL tools typically have little built-in data cleaning capabilities. Data cleaning deals with detecting and removing errors and inconsistencies from data in order to improve the data quality [4]. Data quality problems are very significant: it has been estimated that poor quality customer data cost U.S. businesses $611 billion a year in postage, printing, and staff overhead [13].

The manual creation and maintenance of ETL processes increases the cost of development, deployment, running, and maintenance of a DW. That is why the conceptual modeling of ETL processes can be of a crucial help.

3   Modeling ETL Processes with UML

In this section, we present our ETL modeling proposal that allows the designer to decompose a complex ETL process into a set of simple processes. This approach helps the designer to easily design and maintain ETL processes. Moreover, our approach allows the DW designer to tackle the design of ETL processes from different detail levels: (i) the designer can define a general overview of the process and let the database programmer to specify them or, (ii) the designer can provide a detailed description of each one of the attribute transformations.

Based on our personal experience, we have defined a reduced and yet highly powerful set of ETL mechanisms. We have decided to reduce the number of mechanisms in order to reduce the complexity of our proposal. We have summarized these mechanisms in Table 1. We consider that these mechanisms process data in the form of records composed of attributes[1]. Therefore, we provide the Wrapper mechanism to transform any source into a record based source.

In our approach, ETL processes are modelled by using the UML class diagram instead of considering any other UML object-interaction diagram as we are not interested in showing the run-time communication structure of these processes (i.e. the sending of messages between ETL processes). In particular, an ETL process is composed of UML packages, which allow the user to decompose the design of an ETL process into different logical units. Every particular ETL mechanism is represented by means of a stereotyped class[2]. Moreover, we have defined a different icon for each ETL mechanism (Table 1). This icon can be used in a UML model instead of the standard representation of a class.

The ETL mechanisms are related to each other by means of UML dependencies. A dependency in the UML is represented as a dashed line with an arrowhead. The model element at the tail of the arrow (the client) depends on the model element at the arrowhead (the supplier). A dependency states that the implementation or functioning of one or more elements requires the presence of one or more other elements. This implies that if the source is somehow modified, the dependents must be probably modified.

A UML note can be attached to every ETL mechanism to (i) explain the functioning of the mechanism and, (ii) define the mappings between source and target attributes of the ETL mechanisms[3]. These mappings conform to the following syntax: target_attribute = source_attribute. To avoid overloading the diagram with long notes, when source and target attributes' names match, the corresponding mappings can be omitted. Moreover, when some kind of ambiguity may exist, the name of the source can be indicated together with name of the attribute (e.g., Customers.Name and Suppliers.Name). We do not impose any restriction on the content of these notes in order to allow the designer the greatest flexibility, but we highly recommend a particular content for each mechanism. The designer can use the notes to define ETL processes at the desired detail level. For example, the description can be general, specified by means of a natural language, or even specified by means of a programming language.

In the following, we provide a deeper description of each one of the ETL mechanisms presented in Table 1 together with the more appropriated contents for the corresponding attached notes.

---

[1] In our approach, the concept of attribute is similar to the concepts of column, property or field.

[2] Due to the lack of space, we do not include the formal definition of each stereotype with their corresponding OCL constraints.

[3] The connection between a note and the element it applies to is shown by a dashed line without an arrowhead as this is not a dependency [9].

Table 1. ETL mechanisms and icons

ETL Mechanism (Stereotype)	Description	Icon
Aggregation	Aggregates data based on some criteria	
Conversion	Changes data type and format or derives new data from existing data	A → B
Filter	Filters and verifies data	
Incorrect	Reroutes incorrect data	!!!
Join	Joins two data sources related to each other with some attributes	
Loader	Loads data into the target of an ETL process	
Log	Logs activity of an ETL mechanism	LOG
Merge	Integrates two or more data sources with compatible attributes	
Surrogate	Generates unique surrogate keys	123 →
Wrapper	Transforms a native data source into a record based data source	

3.1 Aggregation

The Aggregation mechanism aggregates data based on some criteria. This mechanism is useful to increase the aggregation level of a data source[4]. The designer can define the grouping criteria and the aggregation functions employed (SUM, AVG, MAX/MIN, COUNT, and so on) in the attached note to this mechanism.

For example, in Fig. 1 (a), we have represented a portion of a loading process in a DW[5] by using standard UML notation in which the stereotype icons are placed in the upper right-hand corner of the corresponding class. It may also be observed that the icon used in the Sales class corresponds to the Table stereotype icon defined in the UML profile for database design [14]. As the grain of Sales is ticket line, we need the daily total sales in the DW. Therefore, Sales are grouped and summed up by product and date in SummedSales. We have decided

---

[4] Partial summarization of data under different criteria is a very common technique used in DWs to facilitate complex analysis. Summarization helps to reduce the size of the resulting DW and increase the query performance [8].

[5] From now on, partial examples are used to describe each ETL mechanism.

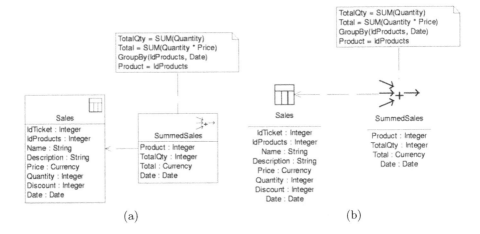

Fig. 1. Aggregation example by using standard UML class notation and the defined stereotype icons

to specify these aggregation tasks in the corresponding attached note. Fig. 1 (b) represents the same ETL process using our ETL icons. From now on, we will use this representation throughout the paper.

3.2 Conversion

The Conversion mechanism is used to change data types and formats or to calculate and derive new data from existing data. The conversions are defined in the attached note by means of conversion functions applied to source attributes. The syntax of these conversions is target_attribute = Function(source_attributes), where Function is any kind of function that can be applied to source attributes.

Based on our experience, we have defined conversion functions for the most common situations. However, this is not a closed set as the designer can define their own user-defined functions for more particular and complex situations:

- Data type conversions: convert data from a data type into another data type. For example: Price = StringToCurrency(Price).
- Arithmetic conversions: perform arithmetic operations (add, multiply, etc.) with data. For example: Total = Quantity * Price.
- Format conversions: convert a value (currency, date, length, etc.) from one format into another one. For example: Price = DollarToEuro(Price).
- String conversions: transform strings (upper and lower-case, concatenate, replace, substring, etc.), e.g. Name = Concatenate(FirstName, " ", Surname).
- Split conversions: break a value into different elements. For example, the following expression breaks a name ("John Doe") into first name ("John") and surname ("Doe"): FName = FirstName(Name); SName = Surname(Name).

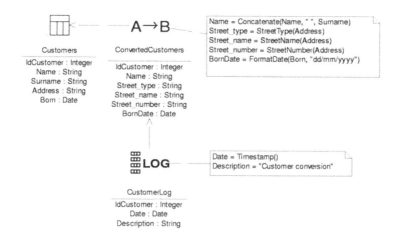

Fig. 2. An example of Conversion and Log processes

- Standardization conversions: standardize attributes to contain identical values for equivalent data elements. We can use a set of rules or look-up tables to search for valid values. For example, the following expression substitutes "Jan." or "1" with "January": Month = StdMonth(Month).
- Value generator: generates a constant value or a variable value from a function with no dependency on any source attribute, e.g., Date = Timestamp().
- Default value: when a value is missing (null, empty string, etc.), it is possible to define a default value. The syntax of this option is target_attribute ?= value. For example: Type ?= "unknown".

Fig. 2 presents an example in which different conversions are applied through the ConvertedCustomers stereotype. As it can be easily seen from the attached note, Name and Surname are concatenated; Address is split into street type, name and number; and Born is converted using a date format. Furthermore, all the activity is audited by CustomerLog (see next section).

3.3 Log

The Log mechanism can be connected to any ETL mechanism as it controls the activity of another ETL mechanism. This mechanism is useful to audit and produce operational reports for each transformation. The designer can add any kind of additional information in the note attached to this mechanism.

For example, in Fig. 2, the activity of a Conversion mechanism is controlled by the Log mechanism called CustomerLog.

3.4 Filter

The Filter mechanism filters unwanted data and verifies the correctness of data based on constraints. In this way, this mechanism allows the designer to load

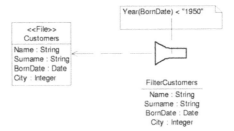

Fig. 3. An example of Filter process

only the required data or the data that meet an established quality level in the DW. The verification process is defined in the attached note by means of a set of Boolean expressions that must be satisfied. The Boolean expressions can be expressed by means of a set of rules or by means of look-up tables that contain the correct data. Some common tasks for this mechanism are checks for null values or missing values and so on. The data that do not satisfy the verification can be rerouted to an `Incorrect` mechanism (see Section 3.7).

For example, in Fig. 3, Customers are filtered and only those that were born before 1950 are accepted for a subsequent processing.

3.5 Join

The `Join` mechanism is used to join two data sources related to each other with some attributes (defined by means of a restrictive condition). The designer can define the following information in the attached note:

- The type of join: `Join(conditional_expression)`, where `Join` can be `InnerJoin` (includes only the records that match the conditional expression), `LeftJoin` (includes all of the records from the first (left) of the two data sources, even if there are no matching values for records in the second (right) data source), `RightJoin` (includes all of the records from the second (right) of the two data sources, even if there are no matching values for records in the first (left) data source), and `FullJoin` (includes all of the records from both data sources, even if there are no matching values between them).
- If `LeftJoin`, `RightJoin` or `FullJoin` are used, then the designer can define the values that substitute the non-existing values. The syntax of this option is `target_attribute ?= value`.

In Fig. 4, we have represented an ETL process that joins three data sources. Due to the fact that `Join` can only be applied to two sources, and we are dealing with three sources in this example, two `Join` mechanisms are needed. In the CitiesStates join, a LeftJoin is performed to join cities' and states' names. When it is not possible to join a city with a state (because Cities.State is missing or incorrect), the corresponding state name is replaced by "unknown". Finally,

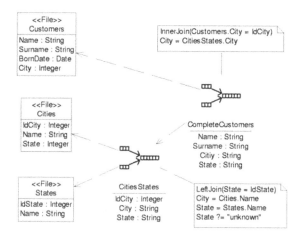

Fig. 4. An example of Join process

in the CompleteCustomers join, the result of the previous join is joined with Customers.

3.6   Loader

The Loader mechanism loads data into the target of an ETL process such as a dimension or a fact in a DW. Every ETL process should have at least one Loader mechanism. Two operation modes are supported in the Loader:

− Free loading: the Loader mechanism does not verify any constraint as the target applies its own constraints to the new data.
− Constrained loading: the designer can apply primary and foreign key constraints during the loading process. Moreover, the designer can also define how to manage existing data in the target. The following information can be attached to the Loader mechanism:
  • PK(source_attributes): defines the attributes of the source data that define a unique record in the target. This information is used for both constraining the loading process and detecting the old data that should be updated.
  • FK(target_attributes; source_attributes): defines the attributes of the source data that should previously exist in a target.
  • Append: the target need not be empty before loading the new data; new data are loaded and old data are updated.
  • Delete: the target need be empty before loading the data.
  • Insert: only new data are loaded in the target; old data are not loaded again or updated, although they have changed.
  • Update: only existing data in the target are updated with the corresponding data, but new data are not loaded.

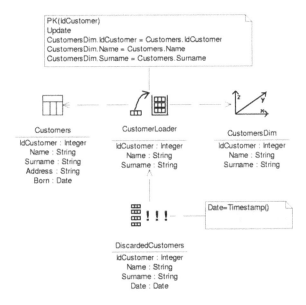

Fig. 5. An example of Loader and Incorrect processes

Append, Delete, Insert, and Update are mutually exclusive, i.e. only one of them can be used in a Loader mechanism.

For example, in Fig. 5, CustomerLoader updates existing data in Customers-Dim with data coming from Customers. Furthermore, due to the high probability of errors when making the loading process, those records that do not satisfy the constraints are rerouted to DiscardedCustomers. CustomersDim represents a dimension in our DW schema; the icon corresponds to the Dimension stereotype defined in our multidimensional modeling approach [11].

3.7 Incorrect

The Incorrect mechanism is used to reroute bad or discarded records and exceptions to a separate target. In this way, the DW designer can track different errors. This mechanism can only be used with the Filter, Loader, and Wrapper, because these mechanisms constrain the data they process. The designer can add additional information in the note attached to this mechanism, such as a description of the error or a timestamp of the event.

For example, in Fig. 5, the records that do not satisfy the constraints of CustomerLoader (primary key constraint on IdCustomer and only update existing data in the target) are rerouted to DiscardedCustomers, which collects the erroneous data and adds the Date attribute that is a timestamp of the event.

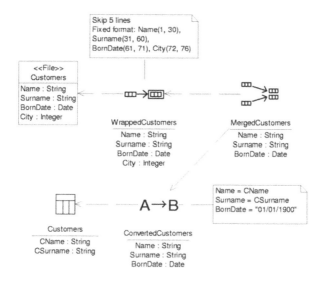

Fig. 6. An example of Merge and Wrapper processes

3.8   Merge

The Merge mechanism integrates two or more data sources with compatible attributes. Two data sources are compatible as long as both of them contain a subset of the attributes defined in the target: the attributes used in the integration must have the same names in all the data sources. If the attributes do not have the same names, the Conversion mechanism can be previously applied in order to standardize them. The attached note to this mechanism is used to define the mapping between the data sources and the target.

For example, in Fig. 6, MergedCustomers is used to integrate data coming from a file and from a database table. Firstly, WrappedCustomers is used to transform a file into a record based source (see next section). Then, Converted-Customers changes the names of the attributes (CName and CSurname) and adds a new attribute (BornDate) with a default value.

3.9   Wrapper

The Wrapper mechanism allows us to define the required transformation from a native data source into a record based data source. Different native sources are possible in an ETL process: fixed and variable format sources, COBOL files (line sequential, record sequential, relative files, and indexed files), multiline sources, XML documents, and so on. The needed code to implement the Wrapper is not relevant as we are at the conceptual level, although the designer can define in the attached note all the information that considers relevant to help the programmer at the implementation phase.

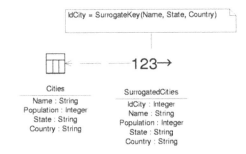

Fig. 7. An example of Surrogate process

In Fig. 6, WrappedCustomers is used to transform data from a fixed format file (more information on the format of the file is included in the attached note).

3.10   Surrogate

The Surrogate mechanism generates unique surrogate keys. Surrogate key assignment is a common process in DWs, employed in order to replace the original keys of the data sources with a uniform key. The attached note to this mechanism is used to define the source attributes used to define the surrogate key. Surrogate keys could have been defined in the Conversion mechanism, however, due to the importance that surrogate keys represent in DWs, we have decided to define an own mechanism.

For example, in Fig. 7, SurrogatedCities adds a surrogate key (IdCity) based on the attributes Name, State, and Country before loading the data into the DW.

4   Related Work

Little effort has been dedicated to propose a conceptual model that allows the DW designer to formally define ETL processes. Various approaches for the conceptual design of DWs have been proposed in the last few years [15,16,17,18,19]. However, none of them has addressed the modeling of ETL processes.

To the best of our knowledge, the best advance in this research line has been accomplished by the Knowledge and Database Systems Laboratory from NTUA [20]. In particular, they have proposed a conceptual model that provides its own graphical notation that allows the designer to formally define most of the usual technical problems regarding ETL processes [21]. Furthermore, this approach is accompanied by an ETL tool called ARKTOS as an easy framework for the design and maintenance of these ETL processes [22].

The main differences, and advantages, of our approach in contrast to Vassiliadis' are the use of a standard modeling language (UML), the use of a grouping mechanism (UML packages) that facilitates the creation and maintenance of complex ETL processes, and the integration of the design of ETL processes in a global and integrated approach for DW design based on the UML. On the other hand, Vassiliadis *et al.* do not employ standard UML notation because they need to treat attributes as "first class citizens" of their model, what we believe complicates the resulting ETL models: a DW usually contains hundreds of attributes, and therefore, an ETL model can become exceedingly complex if every attribute is individually represented as a model element.

5   Conclusions and Future Works

In this paper, we have presented a conceptual approach, based on the UML, for the modeling of ETL processes. Thanks to the use of the UML, we can seamlessly model different aspects of a DW architecture such as operational data sources, the target DW conceptual schema and ETL processes in an integrated manner by using the same notation.

In our approach for modeling ETL processes, we define a set of UML stereotypes that represents the most common ETL tasks such as the integration of different data sources, the transformation between source and target attributes, the generation of surrogate keys, and so on. Furthermore, thanks to the use of the UML package mechanism, large ETL processes can be easily modeled in different ETL packages obtaining a very simple but yet powerful approach. Thanks to its simplicity, our approach facilitates the design and subsequent maintenance of ETL processes at any modeling phase.

Regarding future works, we are working on a methodology to allow us to integrate all models and schemas we use for a DW design (the target DW schema, data source schemas, ETL processes, etc.) in a formal approach. On the other hand, in our approach, any required cleaning operation is embedded within a note attached to any other ETL mechanism used such as the `Login`, `join`, or `incorrect` mechanisms and so on. Thus, we are currently working on the proposal of a `clean` stereotype where any clean operation can be explicitly and formally defined. Finally, the UML profile for ETL processes (stereotype definitions together with their corresponding OCL formulas) is also being programmed in Rational Rose 2002 through the Rose Extensibility Interface (REI).

References

1. Inmon, W.H.: Building the Data Warehouse. QED Press/John Wiley (1992) (Last edition: 3rd edition, John Wiley & Sons, 2002).
2. SQL Power Group: How do I ensure the success of my DW? Internet: http://www.sqlpower.ca/page/dw_best_practices (2002)
3. Strange, K.: ETL Was the Key to this Data Warehouse's Success. Technical Report CS-15-3143, Gartner (2002)
4. Rahm, E., Do, H.: Data Cleaning: Problems and Current Approaches. IEEE Bulletin of the Technical Committee on Data Engineering **23** (2000) 3–13
5. Friedman, T.: ETL Magic Quadrant Update: Market Pressure Increases. Technical Report M-19-1108, Gartner (2003)

6. L. Greenfield: Data Extraction, Transforming, Loading (ETL) Tools. The Data Warehousing Information Center. Internet: http://www.dwinfocenter.org/clean.html (2003)
7. Agosta, L.: Market Overview Update: ETL. Technical Report RPA-032002-00021, Giga Information Group (2002)
8. Kimball, R.: The Data Warehouse Toolkit. John Wiley & Sons (1996) (Last edition: 2nd edition, John Wiley & Sons, 2002).
9. Object Management Group (OMG): Unified Modeling Language Specification 1.4. Internet: http://www.omg.org/cgi-bin/doc?formal/01-09-67 (2001)
10. Trujillo, J., Palomar, M., Gómez, J., Song, I.: Designing Data Warehouses with OO Conceptual Models. IEEE Computer, special issue on Data Warehouses **34** (2001) 66–75
11. Luján-Mora, S., Trujillo, J., Song, I.: Extending UML for Multidimensional Modeling. In: Proc. of the 5th International Conference on the Unified Modeling Language (UML 2002). Volume 2460 of LNCS., Dresden, Germany, Springer-Verlag (2002) 290–304
12. Luján-Mora, S., Trujillo, J., Song, I.: Multidimensional Modeling with UML Package Diagrams. In: Proc. of the 21st International Conference on Conceptual Modeling (ER 2002). Volume 2503 of LNCS., Tampere, Finland, Springer-Verlag (2002) 199–213
13. Eckerson, W.: Data Quality and the Bottom Line. Technical report, The Data Warehousing Institute (2002)
14. Naiburg, E., Maksimchuk, R.: UML for Database Design. Addison-Wesley (2001)
15. Golfarelli, M., Rizzi, S.: A methodological Framework for Data Warehouse Design. In: Proc. of the ACM 1st Intl. Workshop on Data warehousing and OLAP (DOLAP'98), Washington D.C., USA (1998) 3–9
16. Sapia, C., Blaschka, M., Höfling, G., Dinter, B.: Extending the E/R Model for the Multidimensional Paradigm. In: Proc. of the 1st Intl. Workshop on Data Warehouse and Data Mining (DWDM'98). Volume 1552 of LNCS., Springer-Verlag (1998) 105–116
17. Tryfona, N., Busborg, F., Christiansen, J.: starER: A Conceptual Model for Data Warehouse Design. In: Proc. of the ACM 2nd Intl. Workshop on Data warehousing and OLAP (DOLAP'99), Kansas City, Missouri, USA (1999)
18. Husemann, B., Lechtenborger, J., Vossen, G.: Conceptual Data Warehouse Design. In: Proc. of the 2nd. Intl. Workshop on Design and Management of Data Warehouses (DMDW'2000), Stockholm, Sweden (2000) 3–9
19. Abelló, A., Samos, J., Saltor, F.: YAM2 (Yet Another Multidimensional Model): An Extension of UML. In: International Database Engineering & Applications Symposium (IDEAS 2002), Edmonton, Canada (2002) 172–181
20. National Technical University of Athens (Greece): Knowledge and Database Systems Laboratory. Internet: http://www.dblab.ntua.gr/ (2003)
21. Vassiliadis, P., Simitsis, A., Skiadopoulos, S.: Conceptual Modeling for ETL Processes. In: 5th ACM International Workshop on Data Warehousing and OLAP (DOLAP 2002), McLean, USA (2002) 14–21
22. Vassiliadis, P., Vagena, Z., Skiadopoulos, S., Karayannidis, N., Sellis, T.: ARKTOS: towards the modeling, design, control and execution of ETL processes. Information Systems (2001) 537–561

A General Model for Online Analytical Processing of Complex Data

Jian Pei

Department of Computer Science and Engineering
State University of New York at Buffalo
Buffalo, NY 14260-2000, USA
jianpei@cse.buffalo.edu
http://www.cse.buffalo.edu/faculty/jianpei

Abstract. It has been well recognized that online analytical processing (OLAP) can provide important insights into huge archives of data.
While the conventional OLAP model is capable of analyzing relational
business data, it often cannot fit many kinds of complex data in emerging
applications, such as bio-medical data, time series and semi-structured
data.

In this paper, we propose *GOLAP*, a general OLAP model. We show
that GOLAP is consistent with the conventional OLAP model on multidimensional databases. Moreover, we show that the model can be applied
to complex data as well. As an example, we illustrate a research prototype
system, GeneXplorer, which enables OLAP over gene expression data.

1 Introduction

It has been well recognized that *online analytical processing* (OLAP) is an essential data analysis service and can provide critical insights into huge archives of
application data. In contrast to online transactional processing (OLTP), OLAP
supports queries about multi-dimensional, multi-level aggregates and summarizations of the data. Moreover, the users are enabled to browse the summarizations of the data at various granularities to identify trends, exceptions and
interesting regions.

While many previous studies on efficient and effective OLAP over relational
business data (e.g., [8,18,27,26,19,2,4,7,12,9,28,25,23,20]), few of them systematically studies how to extend the OLAP model to handle complex data, such as
bio-medical data, time series and semi-structured data. To motivate the study
and appreciate the challenges, let us look at the problems in OLAP of gene
expression data.

Recently, the DNA microarray technology enables simultaneously monitoring
the expression levels of thousands of genes during important biological processes
and cross collections of related samples. Figure 1 shows the typical structure
of microarray gene expression data. Usually, a row in the matrices represents
a gene and a column represents a sample or condition. The numeric value in

I.-Y. Song et al. (Eds.): ER 2003, LNCS 2813, pp. 321–334, 2003.

sample/condition

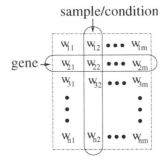

Fig. 1. A gene expression matrix.

each cell characterizes the expression level of a specific gene in a particular sample/condition.

Many previous studies have highlighted the importance of online analysis of gene expression data in bio-medical applications. As more and more gene expression data are accumulated, in addition to analyzing individual genes and samples/conditions, it is important to answer analytical queries about various "summarizations" over the gene expression data, e.g., the patterns and the trends. For example, in a gene expression database, with a new gene expression data sample, an analyst may want an online answer to the query *"with respect to the samples in the database whose gene expressions are similar to the new sample, what are the major patterns?"* This is a typical online analytical query.

Most of the previous studies on analysis of gene expression data focus on techniques of answering some specific queries, such as similarity search, alignments and clustering. However, there does not exist a general model in which the summarization-oriented OLAP queries can be specified and answered effectively.

Can we extend OLAP to handle complex data? While many algorithms for various analyses are available, the core problem is to *develop a general conceptual model* such that OLAP of complex data can be specified and evaluated effectively.

In this paper, we study the general model for OLAP of complex data. We make the following contributions.

- We illustrate that the conventional OLAP model does not work well for complex data. A typical example, the processing of gene expression data, is shown. It motivates our proposal of a new model.
- A general OLAP model, GOLAP, is proposed. We show that the model is a generalization of the conventional OLAP model.
- We elaborate how the GOLAP model can handle complex data.
- As an application, we demonstrate an OLAP system for gene expression data based on the GOLAP model. It shows that our model is effective.

The remainder of the paper is organized as follows. Section 2 introduces the preliminaries and motivates our study by showing the problems of the conventional OLAP model on complex data. Our GOLAP model is developed in

Store	Product	Season	Sale
S_1	P_1	Spring	6
S_1	P_2	Spring	12
S_2	P_1	Fall	9

Fig. 2. Base table `sales` for a data warehouse.

Section 3. It is shown that GOLAP is compatible to the conventional OLAP model on multidimensional databases. In Section 4, we present how to apply GOLAP to complex data and use time series gene expression data as an example. GeneXplorer, a research prototype OLAP system for gene expression data based on the GOLAP model, is also demonstrated. Section 5 discusses related work. The paper is concluded in Section 6.

2   Preliminaries and Motivations

In this section, we first revisit the conventional OLAP model briefly. Then, using gene expression data as an example, we illustrate why the conventional model cannot support effective OLAP over complex data.

2.1   OLAP Operations in the Multidimensional Data Model

For the sake of simplicity, we illustrate the ideas of OLAP using the following example.

Suppose that, in a marketing management department, data are collected under the schema `sales(Store, Product, Season, Sale)`. The **base table**, which holds the sales records, is shown in Figure 2. Attributes `Store`, `Product` and `Season` are called **dimension attributes** (or **dimensions** in short), while attribute `Sale` is called a **measure attribute** (or a **measure** in short).

A **data cube** [10,11] grouped by dimensions `Store`, `Product` and `Season` using an **aggregate function** (`AVG(Sale)` in this example) is the set of results returned from the 8 group-by queries with each dimension subset of {`Store`, `Product`, `Season`} forming the group-by. Each group-by corresponds to a set of **cells**, described as tuples over the group-by dimensions, identifying those tuples in the base table `sales` that match the conditions. The tuples in the data cube $Cube_{Sales}$ is shown in Figure 3(a). Here, symbol "$*$" in a dimension means that the dimension is generalized such that it matches any value in the domain of this dimension.

As shown, a data cube is the n-dimensional generalization of the `group-by` operator. It computes group-bys corresponding to all possible combinations of a set of dimensions. A record in a data cube is also called an **aggregate cell**.

Two basic OLAP operations are *roll up* and its dual, *drill down*. A cell c_1 is **rolled up** from cell c_2, and c_2 is **drilled down** from cell c_1, if c_1 generalizes c_2 in some dimensions, that is, in all dimensions where c_1 and c_2 have different values, c_1 has values "$*$". In other words, cell c_2 is a contributor to the aggregate of cell

Store	Product	Season	AVG(Sales)
S_1	P_1	Spring	6
S_1	P_2	Spring	12
S_2	P_1	Fall	9
S_1	*	Spring	9
S_1	P_1	*	6
*	P_1	Spring	6
...	...	...	...
*	*	Fall	9
S_2	*	*	9
*	*	*	9

(a) Cells in data cube $Cube_{Sales}$.

(b) The lattice of cells.

Fig. 3. Data cube $Cube_{Sales}$

c_1. For example, in the data cube in Figure 3(a), cell $(S_1, *, Spring)$ is a roll-up from cell $(S_1, P_1, Spring)$, and the latter cell is a drill-down to the former one. Cell $(S_1, *, Spring)$ represents a higher level aggregate (i.e., the sales of *ALL products* in store S_1 and in the spring) than cell $(S_1, P_1, Spring)$ does (i.e, the sales of product P_1 in store S_1 and in the spring).

All cells in a data cube form a lattice according to the roll-up/drill-down relation. Figure 3(b) shows the lattice for the data cube cells in Figure 3(a), while the top element, *false*, is not shown. Conceptually, OLAP provides a set of operations in the data cube space.

In addition to roll up and drill down, some other OLAP operations can be defined. For example, the **slice** operation performs a selection on one dimension of the data cube, and thus returns a sub-cube. The **dice** operation defines a sub-cube by selections on multiple dimensions, i.e., a composition of a set of slice operations. **Pivot** (also known as **rotate**) is a visualization operation that rotates the data axes in the presentation.

2.2   Challenges in OLAP of Complex Data

To examine the challenges in OLAP on complex data, let us consider an example: OLAP on gene expression data. As shown in Figure 1, gene expression data are in the form of matrices. *Can we treat a gene expression matrix with n genes and m conditions as a base table with n records and m dimensions or vice versa so that the conventional OLAP operations can be applied?* Unfortunately, such a naïve extension is unacceptable in both syntax and semantics.

In syntax, it is hard to define the measure and the aggregate function for gene expression matrices if the columns and the rows are treated as dimensions and tuples, respectively. Unlike the analysis of business data, where the common numeric aggregate functions (e.g., SUM, MAX, MIN and AVG) work well, the analysis of gene expression data often looks at the patterns, i.e., the common features approximately shared by similar genes or samples/conditions. There is no appropriate measure existing in the matrix. The numerical aggregate functions may not make sense in practice.

In semantics, the brute-force extension of roll up and drill down operation is meaningless in analyzing gene expression data. For example, suppose we take the samples/conditions as dimensions. Then, a roll up operation removes one or more samples/conditions from our analysis. The samples/conditions cannot be generalized. Similar problems exist if genes are treated as dimensions. That is, semantically, treating genes or samples/conditions as dimensions cannot achieve meaningful summarization of the data.

Similar problems exist in OLAP over other kinds of complex data, such as sequences, time series and semi-structured data. To make the situation even more challenging, in some kinds of data, such as semi-structured data, there can be even no explicitly existing dimension at all.

To conduct effective OLAP over complex data, we need to design a meaningful model. Based on the above analysis, we can obtain the following observations.

– There are two major issues in defining an OLAP model. On the one hand, it is essential to *define how to partition the data into summarization units at various levels*. On the other hand, it is critical to *define how to summarize the data*.
– *The summarization units for OLAP should yield to some nice hierarchical structure*, such as a lattice. That may facilitate the generation of concept hierarchies from OLAP analysis, and also support the users to browse the semantic summarizations of the data at various levels.

3   GOLAP: A General OLAP Model

In this section, we develop GOLAP, a general model for OLAP. We show that the model is a generalization of the conventional OLAP model.

3.1   The GOLAP Model

Let $\mathcal{D}$ be the space of data objects. A **base database** $B \subseteq \mathcal{D}$ is a set of data objects on which the OLAP is conducted. The concept of base database is the generalization of base table in the conventional model. In OLAP, we partition the objects in a base database into groups such that each group is a unit for summarization and all the groups form a hierarchy. The idea is formulated as follows.

Definition 1 (Grouping function). A **grouping function** is a function $g : 2^{\mathcal{D}} \times 2^{\mathcal{D}} \to 2^{\mathcal{D}}$. Given a base database B and a set of **query objects** Q (i.e., the set of objects need to be summarized) such that $Q \subseteq B$, $g(Q, B)$ is the subset of objects in B such that $g(Q, B)$ is the smallest summarization unit containing Q. $g(Q, B)$ is undefined for $Q \not\subseteq B$. A grouping function g should satisfy the following requirements.

1. **Containment.** For any sets of objects B and Q, $Q \subseteq g(B, Q) \subseteq B$. In words, the summarization unit should contain all query objects, and be in the base database B.
2. **Monotonicity.** For any sets of objects B, Q_1 and Q_2 such that $Q_1 \subseteq Q_2 \subseteq B$, $g(B, Q_1) \subseteq g(B, Q_2)$. In words, a larger query set needs a larger summarization unit.
3. **Closure.** For any sets of objects B and Q such that $Q \subseteq B$, $g(B, Q) = g(B, g(B, Q))$. In words, a summarization unit is self-closed.   ∎

A grouping function defines how data objects should be partitioned. Based on a grouping function, we can partition a base database into classes.

Definition 2 (Class). Given a grouping function g and a base database B. A subset of objects $S \subseteq B$ is said a **class** if $g(B, S) = S$.   ∎

In words, we use the closure of g (with respect to a given base database B) to define classes, the summarization units. We have the following result.

Theorem 1. *Given a base database B and a grouping function g. Let C be the set of classes with respect to B and g. Then, $(C, \subseteq)$ is a lattice.*
Proof sketch. The theorem follows the facts (1) $g(B, B) = B$ and $g(B, \emptyset)$ are the top and the bottom elements of the lattice, respectively[1]; and (2) lattice $(C, \subseteq)$ is a quotient lattice of $(2^B, \subseteq)$.   ∎

Moreover, we define a **member function** $member : C \to 2^D$ with respect to a lattice of classes as follows. Given a class $c \in C$, where C is the set of classes with respect to a base database B and a grouping function g, $member(c)$ returns the complete set of objects of class c in the base database.

So far, we define how to partition the data objects into summarization units (i.e., classes) and the summarization units yield to a nice hierarchical structure, a lattice. Now, we formalize the summarization of a set of data objects.

Definition 3 (Summarization function). Let M be the domain of summary over sets of objects. A **summarization function** is $f : D \to M$. In words, a summarization function returns a summary for a set of data objects.   ∎

Now, we are ready to define the OLAP operations in our model.

Definition 4 (OLAP operations). Given a base database B, a grouping function g and a summarization function f. Let C be the set of classes. There are three **basic OLAP operations** in the GOLAP model.

– **Summarize.** A **summarize** operation takes a set of objects Q as input and returns a duple

$$(g(B, Q), f(g(B, Q))).$$

That is, it returns the smallest class containing Q and the summary of the class.

---

[1] Please note that, in general, it is unnecessary $g(B, \emptyset) = \emptyset$.

- **Roll up**. A `roll up` operation takes a class c and a set of objects Q as parameters, and returns a duple

$$(g(B, member(c) \cup Q), f(g(B, member(c) \cup Q))).$$

That is, a roll up operation starts from a class c and returns the smallest class summarizing both the objects in class c and the objects in Q.
- **Drill down**. A `drill down` operation takes a class c and a set of objects Q as parameters, and returns

$$(g(B, member(c) - Q), f(g(B, member(c) - Q))).$$

That is, a drill down operation starts from a class c and returns the smallest class summarizing only the object in c but not in Q.   ∎

Based on the above, we have the GOLAP model and the corresponding data warehouse.

Definition 5 (GOLAP and G-warehouse model). Given a data object space $\mathcal{D}$, (g, f) is a **GOLAP model** in $\mathcal{D}$ if g and f are a grouping function and a summarization function, respectively.

In a data object space $\mathcal{D}$, given a GOLAP model (g, f), $\mathcal{W} = \{(c, f(c)) | c \in \mathcal{C}\}$ is said the **general data warehouse**, or **G-warehouse** in short, with respect to a base database B, where $\mathcal{C}$ is the complete set of classes with respect to g and B.   ∎

As can be seen, the essentials for a GOLAP model is the grouping function and the summarization function. Moreover, the classes with respect to a grouping function and a base database form a lattice. These properties are intuitive and consistent to our observations in Section 2.2.

Moreover, the GOLAP model has the following nice property: the product of two GOLAP models is still a GOLAP model, as stated below.

Theorem 2 (Product of GOLAP models). *Let (g_1, f_1) and (g_2, f_2) be two GOLAP models on data space $\mathcal{D}_1$ and $\mathcal{D}_2$, respectively. Then, $((g_1, g_2), (f_1, f_2))$ is a GOLAP model on data space $\mathcal{D}_1 \times \mathcal{D}_2$.*

Proof sketch. The proof follows the corresponding definitions. To illustrate the correctness, let us consider joining two base tables and the corresponding data cube lattices. Clearly, the product of the lattices is still a cube lattice on the joined table.   ∎

Theorem 2 is essential in GOLAP model. It indicates that we can construct advanced OLAP model from simple ones. Moreover, it provides an approach to achieve integration of multiple OLAP models and data warehouses.

3.2   Applying the GOLAP Model to Multi-dimensional Databases

In this section, we apply the GOLAP model to multi-dimensional databases to check whether it is consistent with the conventional OLAP model.

Let $\mathcal{D} = (D_1, \ldots, D_n, M)$ be the schema of a base table as defined in Section 2.1. $\mathcal{D}$ is also the space of the tuples.

First, we define the summarization function f_r as follows. Given an aggregate function $aggr$ over domain M. For any set of tuples T, let $V_T = \{t.M | t \in T\}$ be the multiple set (i.e., a bag) containing all the measure values in T. We define $f_r(T) = aggr(V_T)$.

Then, the grouping function can be defined as follows. Given any tuples $t_x = (x_1, \ldots, x_n, m_x)$ and $t_y = (y_1, \ldots, y_n, m_y)$. We define $t_x \wedge t_y = (z_1, \ldots, z_n, m_z)$ such that $m_z = aggr(m_x, m_y)$ and, for $(1 \le i \le n)$, $z_i = x_i$ if $x_i = y_i$, otherwise, $z_i = *$.

Given a base database (i.e., the base table) B and a set of query tuples Q. Let $t = (x_1, \ldots, x_n, m) = \bigwedge_{t_j \in Q} t_j$, and $x_{i_1}, \ldots, x_{i_k}$ are those dimension values not equaling to $*$. Then, $g_r(B, Q)$ is defined as the result of the following query in SQL.

```
SELECT  D_1, ..., D_n, M
FROM    B
WHERE   D_{i_1} = x_{i_1} AND ... AND D_{i_k} = x_{i_k}
```

It is easy to show that g_r is a grouping function. That is, g_r satisfies the requirements of containment, monotonicity and closure in Definition 1.

Clearly, the GOLAP model (g_r, f_r) is consistent with the conventional OLAP model for multi-dimensional databases, as illustrated in Section 2.1. A data warehouse is the materialization of the classes descriptions and their summary (i.e., aggregate measures).

4   Applying GOLAP on Complex Data

In Section 3, we developed GOLAP, a general OLAP model. It is a generalization of the conventional OLAP model. Now, the problem becomes *how the GOLAP model can be applied to complex data*.

4.1   GOLAP Based on Hierarchical Clustering

The key of applying GOLAP to complex data is to find appropriate grouping functions and summarization functions. The general idea is that we can define such functions based on hierarchical clustering of the data objects. Here, the term **clustering** refers to the methods partitioning the data objects into clusters as well as to the set of all clusters, while the term **cluster** refers to a specific group of data objects.

Given $\mathcal{D}$, the space of the data objects. Let $\mathcal{CL}$ be a **hierarchical clustering** of data objects. For any base database B containing a set of objects, $\mathcal{CL}(B)$ is a hierarchy of clusters such that

1. each cluster is a subset of objects in B;
2. the hierarchy covers every object in B, i.e., each object appears in at least one cluster;
3. the base database B itself is a cluster in the hierarchy;
4. the ancestor/descendant relation in the hierarchy is based on the containment of the sets of objects in the clusters; and
5. for any two clusters c_1 and c_2, if $c_1 \neq c_2$ and $c_1 \cap c_2 \neq \emptyset$, then $c_1 \cap c_2$ is a cluster.

Then, a grouping function g_c can be defined as follows. Given a base database B and a set of query objects Q, $g_c(B, Q)$ returns the smallest cluster c in $\mathcal{CL}(B)$ such that $Q \in c$. It can be shown that g_c is a grouping function as defined in Definition 1.

Please note that not every clustering satisfies the above condition. For example, some clustering may allow overlaps among clusters. If the non-empty intersection of two clusters is not a cluster, then such a clustering fails the above requirements. However, given a clustering, it can always be fixed to meet the above requirements by inserting some "intermediate clusters" into the hierarchy. The general idea is that we can always make the non-empty intersections of clusters as "intermediate clusters". Limited by space, we omit the details here.

The definition of summarization function f_c is application-oriented. In general, given a class c of objects, $f_c(c)$ returns the summary of the class. The summary can be the pattern(s) in the class, the regression, etc.

According to the above analysis, (g_c, f_c) is a GOLAP model over data objects in $\mathcal{D}$. Moreover, based on Theorem 2, we can conduct OLAP on a database containing multi-dimensional data and multiple kinds of complex data.

4.2 An Example

While GOLAP is general for complex data looks elegant, *what is the effect of applying the GOLAP model to complex data?*

To examine the effect of the GOLAP model, we apply it to time-series gene expression data. In [15], we developed a hierarchical clustering method for time-series gene expression data. The clustering satisfies the requirements in Section 4.1. For example, Figure 4 shows the hierarchical clustering in the Iyer's data set [14].

We define the grouping function g_{gene} according to the hierarchical clustering. Given a set Q of objects, $g_{gene}(B, Q)$ returns the smallest cluster in the hierarchy that is a superset of Q.

To summarize the objects, we use the *coherent patterns* in the clusters. A **coherent pattern** characterizes the common trend of expression levels for a group of co-expressed genes in a cluster. In other words, a coherent pattern is a "template", while the genes in the cluster yield to the pattern with small divergence. Figure 5 shows some examples. We define the summarization function f_{gene} as mapping a cluster of objects into the coherent pattern in the cluster.

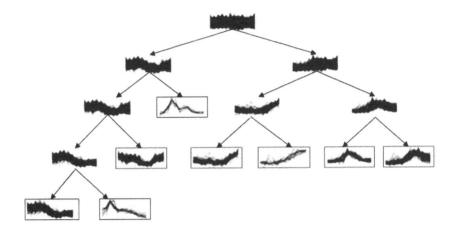

Fig. 4. The hierarchy of co-expressed gene groups in the Iyer's data set

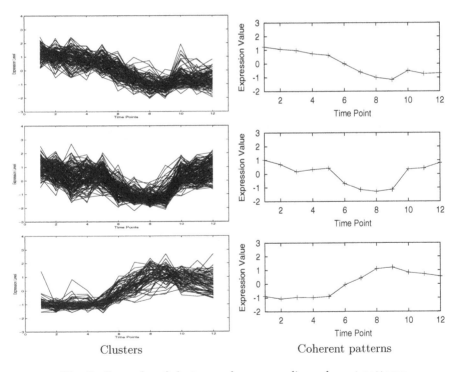

Clusters   Coherent patterns

Fig. 5. Examples of clusters and corresponding coherent patterns

(g_{gene}, f_{gene}) forms a GOLAP model for time series gene expression data. Based on this model, we develop **GeneXplorer**, an interactive OLAP system for time series gene expression data. The major OLAP operations in GeneXplorer are described as follows, where B is the base database (e.g., the Iyer's data set).

- **Summarization**. A user can submit a subset of genes Q. GeneXplorer returns $g_{gene}(B, Q)$ as well as $f_{gene}(g_{gene}(B, Q))$.
- **Roll up**. Starting from a current cluster c, a user can move to c's parent, and browse the genes and the coherent pattern in c's parent.
- **Drill down**. Starting from a current cluster c, a user can select one child of c, and browse the genes and the coherent pattern in that child.
- **Slice**. A user can compare the coherent patterns of the current cluster and its siblings.
- **Dice**. A user can select a subset of genes and apply the clustering. A hierarchy of clusters within the subset will be presented and the user can conduct the OLAP on the subset.
- **Pattern search**. A user can specify a coherent pattern, or some features of a pattern, the system returns the clusters and patterns that are similar to the specification within a user-specified similarity threshold.

As can be seen, the above OLAP operations are based on the GOLAP model (g_{gene}, f_{gene}). Some extensions are provided to facilitate the user's interactions.

To facilitate the above OLAP operations, GeneXplorer maintains a data structure (attraction tree) as the materialization of the clusters and the patterns. That can be regarded as a data warehouse.[2]

In summary, we illustrate how to use the GOLAP model to conduct OLAP on time series gene expression data. By carrying the similar idea, GOLAP can be extended to handle many other kinds of complex data, including sequences and semi-structured data (e.g., XML documents). Therefore, the GOLAP model based on hierarchical clustering as presented in Section 4.1 is general enough for those complex data.

Moreover, we also integrate the multi-dimensional data and the time series gene expression data in GeneXplorer. That is, each gene may have some attributes. As supported by Theorem 2, the attributes and the time series data are treated consistently in a uniform framework.

The idea of applying GOLAP model to complex data based on hierarchical clustering is general for many other applications. For example, hierarchical clustering is often available in document archives. Thus, with appropriate organization, GOLAP model can be applied. Moreover, when more than one hierarchical clustering theme presents, Theorem 2 indicates that we can construct a OLAP system containing more than one "*dimensions*". Here, one dimension corresponds to one hierarchical clustering theme.

---

[2] Precisely, an attraction tree is not exactly the materialization of the clusters and the patterns. Instead, it stores the objects and their relations (similarity) so that the clusters and patterns based on users' queries can be derived quickly on the fly. To this extent, an attraction tree is an index structure supporting the data warehouse.

5   Related Work

OLAP and data warehousing started from managerial practices. Some classical readings include [5,13,16,17,22]. It has been well recognized that OLAP is more efficient if a data warehouse is used. In [6], Colliat discusses how to support OLAP by relational and multidimensional databases. [4] is an excellent overview of the major technical progresses and research problems in 90's. In [29], Widom discusses some interesting research problems in data warehousing.

The data cube operator was firstly proposed by Gray et al. in [10,11]. Since it has been proposed, it became one of the most influential operator in OLAP. Several researches have been dedicated to the foundation and modelling of multidimensional databases and OLAP operations. [1,3,19,21] are some typical examples. However, most of them focus on multidimensional data. There is no systematic study on general OLAP model on complex data, like sequences, time series and semi-structured data.

Some recent studies aim at supporting advanced analysis in data warehouses and data cubes, such as discovery-driven exploration for online analysis of the exceptions in a data cube [25], online explanation of the differences in multidimensional aggregates [24], user-adaptive exploration in a data cube [26], finding the most general contexts under which the observed patterns occur [27], and answering hypothetical queries [2]. However, all these studies focus on specific analytical queries. There is no a general model. Again, they are based on multidimensional data.

6   Conclusions

In this paper, we study the problem of modelling for OLAP on complex data. We propose GOLAP, a general OLAP model. We show that GOLAP is consistent with the conventional OLAP model and, at the same time, general enough to support effective OLAP over complex data.

This study sheds light on the OLAP over complex data. Instead of conducting ad hoc, specific query oriented OLAP operations, we can have a uniform model for OLAP and develop the meaningful operations systematically.

Furthermore, the study opens the doors to some interesting future studies. For example, it is interesting to study how to model advanced OLAP operations specific to complex data. How to handle the changes in the base table, such as in the OLAP of XML document streams, is a challenging problem. Moreover, how to develop general techniques to implement a GOLAP model is important for warehousing complex data.

Acknowledgements. The author is grateful to Mr. Daxin Jiang and Ms. Chun Tang for their helps in the implementation of GeneXplorer. The author also thanks the anonymous reviewers for their invaluable comments.

References

1. R. Agrawal, A. Gupta, and S. Sarawagi. Modeling multidimensional databases. In *Proc. 1997 Int. Conf. Data Engineering (ICDE'97)*, pages 232–243, Birmingham, England, April 1997.
2. Andrey Balmin, Thanos Papadimitriou, and Yannis Papakonstantinou. Hypothetical queries in an olap environment. In Amr El Abbadi, Michael L. Brodie, Sharma Chakravarthy, Umeshwar Dayal, Nabil Kamel, Gunter Schlageter, and Kyu-Young Whang, editors, *VLDB 2000, Proceedings of 26th International Conference on Very Large Data Bases, September 10–14, 2000, Cairo, Egypt*, pages 220–231. Morgan Kaufmann, 2000.
3. Luca Cabibbo and Riccardo Torlone. A logical approach to multidimensional databases. In Hans-Jörg Schek, Fèlix Saltor, Isidro Ramos, and Gustavo Alonso, editors, *Advances in Database Technology – EDBT'98, 6th International Conference on Extending Database Technology, Valencia, Spain, March 23–27, 1998, Proceedings*, volume 1377 of *Lecture Notes in Computer Science*, pages 183–197. Springer, 1998.
4. S. Chaudhuri and U. Dayal. An overview of data warehousing and OLAP technology. *SIGMOD Record*, 26:65–74, 1997.
5. E.F. Codd. Providing olap (on-line analytical processing) to user-analysis: An it mandate. In *Technical Report, E.F. Codd and Associates*, 1993.
6. George Colliat. Olap, relational, and multidimensional database systems. *SIGMOD Record*, 25(3):64–69, 1996.
7. P. Deshpande, J. Naughton, K. Ramasamy, A. Shukla, K. Tufte, and Y. Zhao. Cubing algorithms, storage estimation, and storage and processing alternatives for OLAP. *Data Engineering Bulletin*, 20:3–11, 1997.
8. S. Geffner, D. Agrawal, A. El Abbadi, and T. R. Smith. Relative prefix sums: An efficient approach for querying dynamic OLAP data cubes. In *Proc. 1999 Int. Conf. Data Engineering (ICDE'99)*, pages 328–335, Sydney, Australia, Mar. 1999.
9. F. Gingras and L.V.S. Lakshmanan. nD-SQL: A multi-dimensional language for interoperability and OLAP. In *Proc. 1998 Int. Conf. Very Large Data Bases (VLDB'98)*, pages 134–145, New York, NY, Aug. 1998.
10. J. Gray, A. Bosworth, A. Layman, and H. Pirahesh. Data cube: A relational operator generalizing group-by, cross-tab and sub-totals. In *Proc. 1996 Int. Conf. Data Engineering (ICDE'96)*, pages 152–159, New Orleans, Louisiana, Feb. 1996.
11. J. Gray, S. Chaudhuri, A. Bosworth, A. Layman, D. Reichart, M. Venkatrao, F. Pellow, and H. Pirahesh. Data cube: A relational aggregation operator generalizing group-by, cross-tab and sub-totals. *Data Mining and Knowledge Discovery*, 1:29–54, 1997.
12. H. Gupta, V. Harinarayan, A. Rajaraman, and J. D. Ullman. Index selection for OLAP. In *Technical Note 1996 available at http://db.stanford.edu/ ullman/ullman-papers.html#dc*, Stanford University, Computer Science, 1996.
13. W. H. Inmon. *Building the Data Warehouse*. John Wiley & Sons, 1996.
14. Iyer V.R., Eisen M.B., Ross D.T., Schuler G., Moore T., Lee J.C.F., Trent J.M., Staudt L.M., Hudson Jr. J., Boguski M.S., Lashkari D., Shalon D., Botstein D. and Brown P.O. The transcriptional program in the response of human fibroblasts to serum. *Science*, 283:83–87, 1999.
15. D. Jiang, J. Pei, and A. Zhang. Interactive exploration of coherent patterns in time-series gene expression data. In *Submitted to the Nineth ACM SIGKDD International Conference on Knowledge Discovery and Data Mining (KDD'03)*, 2003.

16. Ralph Kimball. *The Data Warehouse Toolkit: Practical Techniques for Building Dimensional Data Warehouses*. John Wiley & Sons, 1996.
17. Ralph Kimball and Kevin Strehlo. Why decision support fails and how to fix it. *SIGMOD Record*, 24(3):92–97, 1995.
18. L.V.S. Lashmanan, J. Pei, and Y. Zhao. Qc-trees: An efficient summary structure for semantic OLAP. In *Proc. 2003 ACM SIGMOD Int. Conf. on Management of Data (SIGMOD'03)*, June 2003.
19. Wolfgang Lehner. Modelling large scale olap scenarios. In Hans-Jörg Schek, Fèlix Saltor, Isidro Ramos, and Gustavo Alonso, editors, *Advances in Database Technology – EDBT'98, 6th International Conference on Extending Database Technology, Valencia, Spain, March 23–27, 1998, Proceedings*, volume 1377 of *Lecture Notes in Computer Science*, pages 153–167. Springer, 1998.
20. Alberto O. Mendelzon and Alejandro A. Vaisman. Temporal queries in olap. In Amr El Abbadi, Michael L. Brodie, Sharma Chakravarthy, Umeshwar Dayal, Nabil Kamel, Gunter Schlageter, and Kyu-Young Whang, editors, *VLDB 2000, Proceedings of 26th International Conference on Very Large Data Bases, September 10–14, 2000, Cairo, Egypt*, pages 242–253. Morgan Kaufmann, 2000.
21. Torben Bach Pedersen and Christian S. Jensen. Multidimensional data modeling for complex data. In *Proceedings of the 15th International Conference on Data Engineering, 23–26 March 1999, Sydney, Austrialia*, pages 336–345. IEEE Computer Society, 1999.
22. N. Pendse and R. Creeth. The olap report. In *Technical Report, Business Intelligence*, 1995.
23. S. Sarawagi. Indexing OLAP data. *Bulletin of the Technical Committee on Data Engineering*, 20:36–43, 1997.
24. S. Sarawagi. Explaining differences in multidimensional aggregates. In *Proc. 1999 Int. Conf. Very Large Data Bases (VLDB'99)*, pages 42–53, Edinburgh, UK, Sept. 1999.
25. S. Sarawagi, R. Agrawal, and N. Megiddo. Discovery-driven exploration of OLAP data cubes. In *Proc. Int. Conf. of Extending Database Technology (EDBT'98)*, pages 168–182, Valencia, Spain, Mar. 1998.
26. S. Sarawagi and G. Sathe. Intelligent, interactive investigaton of OLAP data cubes. In *Proc. 2000 ACM-SIGMOD Int. Conf. Management of Data (SIGMOD'00)*, page 589, Dallas, TX, May 2000.
27. G. Sathe and S. Sarawagi. Intelligent rollups in multidimensional OLAP data. In *Proc. 2001 Int. Conf. on Very Large Data Bases (VLDB'01)*, pages 531–540, Rome, Italy, Sept. 2001.
28. Jayavel Shanmugasundaram, Usama Fayyad, and P. S. Bradley. Compressed data cubes for olap aggregate query approximation on continuous dimensions. In *Proceedings of the fifth ACM SIGKDD international conference on Knowledge discovery and data mining*, pages 223–232. ACM Press, 1999.
29. J. Widom. Research problems in data warehousing. In *Proc. 4th Int. Conf. Information and Knowledge Management*, pages 25–30, Baltimore, Maryland, Nov. 1995.

An Interpolated Volume Model for Databases

Tianqiu Wang[1], Simone Santini[2], and Amarnath Gupta[3]

[1] Department of Computer Science and Engineering,
University of California San Diego
9500 Gilman Drive, La Jolla, CA 92093, USA
tiwang@cs.ucsd.edu
[2] Biomedical Informatics Research Network,
Department of Neuroscience,
University of California San Diego
9500 Gilman Drive, La Jolla, CA 92093, USA
ssantini@ncmir.ucsd.edu,
[3] San Diego Supercomputer Center,
University of California San Diego
9500 Gilman Drive, La Jolla, CA 92093, USA
gupta@sdsc.edu

Abstract. In this paper we present a volume data model amenable to querying volumes in databases. Unlike most existing volume models, which are directed towards specific applications (notably, volume displaying) and are therefore directed towards executing with the greatest possible efficiency a small set of operations, we are interested in defining a *volume algebra* through which generic query conditions can be composed.

We argue that a general volume model should have two characteristics: (1) it should consider volumes as first class data types that can be returned as results of queries, and (2) it should model volumes as continua, hiding the discrete nature of the measurements inside the representation.

1 Introduction

Data representing volumes are common in many fields such as magnetic resonance imaging [1] and computed tomography in medicine [2], seismic data analysis in the oil and gas industry [3], and various areas of biology, chemistry, and nuclear physics. All these data have certain characteristics in common: they represent continua of points with (continuously varying) quantifiable properties at every point, and they are acquired in the form of a discrete, finite sample of measurement taken over the continuum where the properties are defined.

Considerable research efforts have been directed at modeling volume data, the majority of which have considered visualization problems [4,5]. In [6], a variety of methods is presented to represent volumes, and some related research topics are discussed.

There appears to be considerably less work available on models and data types for volumes intended as objects of computation. In particular, there isn't much work that we are aware of on data models for storing volumes in databases and querying them.

I.-Y. Song et al. (Eds.): ER 2003, LNCS 2813, pp. 335–348, 2003.

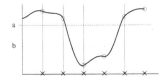

Fig. 1. A simple "one dimensional" volume.

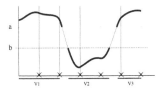

Fig. 2. Results of the query on the one dimensional volume example.

The issues in this case are quite different from those that are faced by the visualization researchers. While in visualization one must face the problem of performing a relatively small number of operations on one volume at a time (and consequently, of finding the correct data structures to perform those relatively few operations with the greatest efficiency), in databases, our problem is to deal with large sets of volumes and to create a generic *volume algebra* that can support many types of queries.

A good data model should represent a volume as first class data type with reasonable accuracy, provide means to create, manipulate, and query volume data intuitively, while preserving the unique characteristics of a volume. Users should be freed from dealing with lower level primitives so that they don't have to understand the details of how the volume is represented at the physical level.

We define a *volume* as a function $V : D \rightarrow S$ from a three-dimensional compact domain D to a property space S. It is the continuity of D that makes discrete models inaccurate, since these models fail to represent D as a continuum.

In order to exemplify the potential problems that a discrete model can cause, let us consider a simple example: a "one dimensional volume" that is, an interval on a line. Assume that the measurements available for this volume consist of a single real value v, so that the volume and its properties can be represented as a curve in the Cartesian plane, as in Figure 1. The discrete representation of the volume is constituted by the points marked by crosses. Assume now that the following query is posed:

return all the sub-volumes for which it is $v < b$ or $v > a$

where a and b are suitable constants. A query on the discrete set would return all the points in the data model that is, it would return a single, connected volume. In reality, by considering the volume as a continuum (which allows us to introduce the further hypothesis of continuity of the volume functions), it is clear that the query should return three separate pieces, as in Figure 2. In two or three dimensions, using the discrete model at the abstract data type level can result not only in the union of disconnected components, but in other topological defects as well. In particular, holes may disappear,

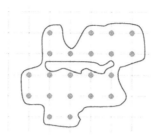

Fig. 3. Topological defect (the disappearing of a hole) consequent to the discrete representation of a two-dimensional volume.

as exemplified in the surface in Figure 3. In three dimension, other topological defects are possible, such as an incorrect homothopy number (which happens, for instance, when the "hole" of a torus is filled).

One obvious way of obtaining a continuous model is by interpolating the measurements, a solution that is proposed by several researchers for representing infinite relation in database [7,8].

It is very important to capture the continuous nature of volumes because in many cases a user needs to know the value of a property at a point where no measurement is available. As another example of possible problems caused by discrete models, consider a discrete volume created by measuring a property v in a portion of space. We have a query asking to return the sub-volume for which $v \geq 0$. Note that the boundary of this volume is composed of points for which $v = 0$ but, in general, for no point on the grid it will be $v = 0$ (theoretically, this is true with probability 1). Using changes in the sign of v and with a suitable continuity hypothesis, we can individuate the points on the grid adjacent to the "real" boundary of the required volume. The problem is that, with a discrete model, we have no way of representing such a boundary, and the best we can do is to return the set of points for which $v > 0$: the condition that holds true for the points on the boundary is not what one would expect from the query.

To make things worse, let us now take the result of the previous query, and let ϵ be the smallest value of v among all the points. We ask now for the sub-volume such that $v \leq \epsilon/2$. The query will obviously return the empty set, that is, the empty volume. But, of course, for every volume for which there is at least a point $v > \epsilon$, the condition

$$v \geq 0 \wedge v \leq \frac{\epsilon}{2}$$

should return a non-empty volume.

We propose a model in which volumes can be defined on continua, and an algebra for this data model. In addition to the modeling advantages mentioned above, modeling a volume as a continuum provides the right framework to solve certain issues that are hard to deal with in discrete models, since they require changing the underlying representation. For example, in our model it is easy to join volumes even if the underlying grids of properties values do not coincide (e.g. one is more dense than the other).

2   Related Work

Regular grids of point measurements are a fairly common representation of volume data [9]; it is the easiest way to model a volume in the common case in which the property values are on a regular grid to begin with [10]. An alternative representation is to consider the volume as a collection of finite volume, regular elements called "voxels." Each element has an associated value. In this case, unless additional hypotheses are made, the measurements are not associated with any point inside the element, but only with the whole element.

A regular, parallelepipedal grid can be stored in a three-dimensional array. There have been several proposals of array data models for databases, and several array languages have been defined such as the *Array Manipulation Language* (AML) and the *Array Query Language* (AQL). The AML [11] is a declarative language for optimizing the non-relational sub-expressions on the array data type (i.e. the one appears in the select clause) in a relational query. As the name Array Manipulation Language suggests, the AML is mainly designed to do array manipulations and transformations based on index patterns and sub-arrays. Its focus is not on selection and retrieval based on properties of the values stored in the array.

Unlike the AML, AQL [12] also supports queries. The AQL is a high level language language based on a comprehension syntax and nested relational calculus for arrays, which is an extension of the nested relational calculus. The user has the possibility to define new functions and register them as AQL primitives. The uniqueness of the AQL is the point of view that arrays are functions rather than collection types.

In general, most existing array based models do not have a rich set of query support based on content or property value of volumes. An exception is the model from [9], where some value selection primitives are provided.

In modern databases, volume data can be stored as spatial data [13]. Spatial data types have good support for geometric operations, but they don't allow operations on properties.

Interpolation has been proposed as a possibility for representing continuous functions because it can represent any point in a continuum using a finite representation [7,8]. While in [7], interpolated and sampled data are modeled differently at the logical level, leaving to the user the task of managing the interpolation, in [8], it is suggested that samples and interpolation functions should be hidden from the logical level, and that only the continuous model should be visible in the abstract data type. While an equal treatment of interpolated and sampled data is applicable in volume data, from the point of view of our application, volumes are not infinite relations, but data types. This means that, at least conceptually, they are not tables, but elements that are stored in columns of tables. They are, in other words, first class values and, among other things, can be returned as results of queries. The model in [8] suffers, from our point of view, from two drawbacks. First, while the continuum (which is there considered as an infinite relation) is used in the query condition, there appears to be no way to return it as the result of a query: only finite relations are returned. Second, the model in [8] doesn't include the explicit representation of the boundaries of a bounded continuum, so that the topology problems outlined previously would not disappear.

A similar continuous model for volume visualization has been proposed [14]. Volume is modeled as a scalar filed $F(p)$ which offers representations that defines data for every point p in E^3. It also uses a discrete physical representation consisting of a set of sampled points, their topological relationships, and an interpolation function. The recommended algebra used for this model is Constructive Volume Geometry [15]. However, this algebra framework is designed for modeling complex spatial objects for visualization. It is not based on a continuous domain, and its geometric operations are designed to rearrange volumes in a scene.

The problem we are considering in this paper is not solved by any of the models mentioned above. We are interested in a framework to perform general computation on large sets of volumes, and at the same time, to use these operations to identify volumes that satisfies certain requirements either based on geometry or content. From this perspective, it is obvious not only that databases have an important role to play, but also that we must develop a conceptual model of volume data broad enough to support general query operations. It is the goal of this paper to introduce such a model.

3   The Volume Model

In this section, we introduce the abstract model that we are going to use for our volume algebra, as well as some relevant associated concepts.

All the definitions are relative to the three-dimensional Euclidean space, since this is the case in which we are interested. In particular, a *point* is a triple $(x, y, z) \in \mathbb{R}^3$. Many of the definitions below, and many of the properties of the model, however, generalize to higher dimensional spaces.

Definition 1. *A* volume domain *(or, simply, a* domain*) is a compact, closed subset of* $\mathbb{R}^3$. *The measure of the domain* D *is*

$$m(D) = \int_V dx dy dz$$

We give this definition essentially to establish our terminology. In many cases, confusion may arise because the word "volume" is used to denote quite different things. For instance, both the entities that we have called domain and its measure are occasionally referred to as volumes. Since to us, a volume is yet another concept, it is worth risking being pedantic now to avoid confusion later.

Definition 2. *A* volume *is a continuous function* $V : D \rightarrow S$, *where* D *is a domain, and* S *is a* property space *that we will assumed endowed with the structure of a vector space and such that all the components of* S *are named. That is,* S *is represented as* $S = \{N_1 : T_1, \ldots, N_n : T_n\}$, *where* N_i *are the names of the content measurement and* T_i *are their data types.*

The property space S is specific to each volume, and it goes without saying that two volumes $V_1 : D \rightarrow S_1$ and $V_2 : D \rightarrow S_2$ which share the same domain but map into different measurement spaces should be regarded as instances of two different data types. A special volume type is what we call the *mask*. Formally, a mask is a volume

Table 1. Operations of the volume algebra

Name	Use	Description
affine	$V_{result} = \texttt{affine}(A, V_{src})$	Applies an affine transform to a volume
proj	$V_{result} = \texttt{proj}(V_{src}, [N_1, \ldots, N_n])$	Projects out columns in the property space.
intrs	$R = \texttt{intrs}(V_{src1}, V_{src2}, op)$	Apply op to the intersection
cut	$R = \texttt{cut}(V_{src}, Cg)$	Selects from a volume based on the geometric condition Cg.
sel	$R = \texttt{sel}(V_{src}, Cp)$	Selects from a volume based on the property condition Cp.
val	$v = \texttt{val}(p, V_{src})$	Value of a volume at point p.
vol	$m = \texttt{vol}(V_{src})$	Measurement of a volume's size.

that maps to the data type *unit* (the "bottom" data type, with one value only). A mask is uniquely identified by its domain D and will be used mostly to "cut" pieces from other volumes.

Note that in our model, we take what one might call a "functional" view of a volume, that is, our primary objects are functions from a domain to a measurement space, rather than compact sets in $\mathbb{R}^3$. We argue that this view models more accurately the way in which volumetric data are used in practice.

4   An Algebra for Volume Data

In this section, we introduce our volume algebra. Due to our view of a volume as a function, our algebra is a hybrid between a function algebra (which operates on the function types $D \to S$), an algebra for sets in space (which operates on the domains D), and a subset of relational algebra (which operates on the property spaces S).

A few boolean topological primitives need to be defined so that they can be used in volume queries. They are all defined based on the basic topological primitive **inside**: $inside(p, V)$ is true if the point p is contained in the domain D of the volume V.

disjoint: $disjoint(V_1, V_2) \iff \forall p, inside(p, V_1) \Rightarrow \neg inside(p, V_2)$.
overlap: $overlap(V_1, V_2) \iff \exists p, inside(p, V_1) \wedge inside(p, V_2)$.
enclose: $encloses(V_1, V_2) \iff \forall p, inside(p, V_2) \Rightarrow inside(p, V_1)$.

4.1   Operators

Our operators take either one or two volumes as operands. The common results types of these operations are volumes, sets of volumes, and scalar measurement values.

The most important operations of the volume algebra are summarized in Table 1. Other operations are defined for determining the bounding box of a volume, returning the points in its representation, creating a source volume, determining its homothopy number, and so on, but we will not consider them in this paper. Also, although we will not prove it in this paper, our model has the following completeness property: assume that a "volume table" is created in a relational database, with columns for x, y, and z, and for all the properties of the volume. Also, assume that we restrict the operations on this table to those which return a similar volume representation (for instance, we don't allow to project out y and z, as this would not produce a volume). Then any operation that can be expressed using relational operators and operators on the data types that constitute the columns can be executed on our volume model using our algebra.

The rest of this section is dedicated to an analysis of the operations in Table 1.

Affine. The *affine* operator is used to rotate, transform, scale, and shear a volume. It takes a volume and an affine transformation matrix and returns a new volume with the domain obtained by applying the matrix $A \in \mathbb{R}^{4 \times 4}$ to the domain of the argument volume. The general form is:

$$V_{result} = \text{affine}(A, V_{src})$$

where V_{src} is a volume and A is a 4×4 affine transformation matrix [16].

Projection. A volume is designed to have multiple properties or multiple measurements at each point. A projection on the volume measurement space is provided to select only a subset of these properties. The projection operator takes a volume and one or more names of measurements of that volume, and returns a volume with the same domain but now with only the projected measurements. The general form is:

$$V_r = \text{proj}(V, \{N_1, \ldots, N_n\}) \tag{1}$$

where V is a volume, and $N_1, \ldots, N_n$ are names of components in the measurement space of V. If $V : D \to S$, where $S = \{N_1 : T_1, \ldots, N_n : T_n, N_{n+1} : T_{n+1}, \ldots, N_p : T_p\}$, then $V_r : D \to S'$, where $S' = \{N_1 : T_1, \ldots, N_n : T_n\}$, that is V_r has the same domain as the V but with the property space restricted to the components named in the projection.

Intersection. The intersection operator takes the intersection of two source volumes and then applies a operation. The general form is:

$$R = \text{intrs}(V_1, V_2, \text{op}) \tag{2}$$

where V_1, V_2 are volumes, op is an operator on property spaces. If $V_1 : D_1 \to S_1$, $V_2 : D_2 \to S_2$, and op $: S_1 \times S_2 \to S_r$, then

$$\begin{aligned} R &= \{V_1, \ldots, V_q\} \\ V_i &: D_i \to S_r \\ \bigcup D_i &= D_1 \cap D_2 \end{aligned} \tag{3}$$

that is, the domain of the set of volumes R is given by the intersection of the domains of V_1 and V_2, and the property space is obtained by applying the operator *op* pairwise to elements of S_1 and S_2 corresponding to points in V_1 and V_2. Note that our definition of volume requires its domain to be connected. Since the intersection of two connected domains is not necessarily connected, this operation returns a set of volumes rather than a single volume. The operators that our algebra supported are element-wise addition ("+"), element-wise subtraction ("-"), element-wise multiplication ("*"), Cartesian product ($\times$), and the null function (nil $: \alpha \times \beta \to$ unit, for all data types α and β). Note that intersection is commutative (resp. associative) if and only if the operator *op* is commutative (associative). This operation can also be used as a way to select part of a volume by intersecting it with a mask volume.

Cut. The cut operator changes the domain of a volume by putting restrictions on the coordinates (x, y, z) of the points, expressed as a set of conditions that the coordinates are required to satisfy. Because in our definition, points in a volume must be connected, the result of *cut* could be more than one volume, therefore, *cut* returns a set of volumes,

$$R = \text{cut}(V, C) \tag{4}$$

where V is a volume, and C is a set of predicates on the point coordinates. If $V : D \to S$, $C = \{c_1, \dots, c_n\}$, then

$$\begin{aligned} R &= \{V_1, \dots, V_q\} \\ V_i &: D_i \to S \\ \bigcup D_i &: \{p | \forall i, i \le n \Rightarrow c_i(p)\} \end{aligned} \tag{5}$$

The predicates c_i often takes the form of polynomial equalities or inequalities: $c_i \equiv \mathbb{P}(x, y, z)$, which describes portions of space delimitated by polynomial surfaces. In this case, the operation corresponds to "cutting" (hence its name) the source volume with the given polynomial surface.

Selection. The select operator takes a volume and select a portion of it based on properties. Just like in **Intersection** and **Cut**, this also changes the domain, and may lead to several disjointed volumes. The general form is:

$$R = \text{sel}(V, c) \tag{6}$$

where V is a volumes, and C contains predicates based on the properties of the volume. If $V : D \to S$, then

$$\begin{aligned} R &= \{V_1, \dots, V_q\} \\ V_i &: D_i \to S \\ \forall p \, \exists i &: \text{inside}(p, V_i) \Rightarrow c(V_i(p)) \end{aligned} \tag{7}$$

The essential difference between **Cut** and **Selection** is that **Cut** picks portions of the source volume based on the conditions on the domain, while **Selection** does based on conditions on the properties.

Some properties of the algebra that can be used, for instance, for query rewriting, are the following:

- $\text{sel}(\text{cut}(V, C_1), C_2) = \text{cut}(\text{sel}(V, C_2), C_1)$;
- $\text{intrs}(\text{affine}(A, V_1), \text{affine}(A, V_2)) = \text{affine}(A, \text{intrs}(V_1, V_2))$;
- $\text{intrs}(\text{proj}(V_1, C_1), \text{proj}(V_2, C_2), \times) = \text{proj}(\text{intrs}(V_1, V_2), C_1 \cup C_2)$;
- $\text{intrs}(\text{proj}(V_1, C), \text{proj}(V_2, C), \text{op}) = \text{proj}(\text{intrs}(V_1, V_2), C)$ (if V_1 and V_2 have the same schema);
- $\text{cut}(\text{proj}(V, C_1), C_2) = \text{proj}(\text{cut}(V, C_2), C_1)$;
- $\text{sel}(\text{proj}(V, C_1), C_2) = \text{proj}(\text{sel}(V, C_2), C_1)$ (if none of the names in C_1 appears in the conditions C_2);

as well as some obvious extensions (for example, "affine" commutes with both selection and cut).

5 Representation

Our abstract data model is compatible with a number of finite representations: the only requirement is that the representation allows the definition of a suitable interpolation function. This is true, in general, for all representations that considers point measurements, while doesn't hold for "voxel" models, in which each measurement is associated with a finite volume, unless some additional assumption is made as to the location of the measurement inside the volume. Several measurement structures accommodate this model, from a regular grid of points, to an irregular tetrahedral grid, to a set of disconnected points (also called a "point cloud").

In our current implementation, the measurements are arranged in a regular parallelepipedal grid. We will use the expression "grid point" to refer to a point on the sampled grid. Whenever there is no danger of confusion with the points of the domain as defined in the previous section, we will simply call them "points".

The discrete representation is transformed into a function defined on a continuum with the introduction of an *interpolation function*, which allows us to determine the property values of the volume between sampled points. The interpolation function used is a configuration parameter determined during the installation of the system; in the following we will always make reference to the common case of a tri-linear function. When a volume is created, its boundaries are determined naturally by the grid on which the volume is defined, as exemplified, for a two-dimensional volume, in Figure 4. Any topological error with respect to the real data introduced by this representation would fall below the measurement precision, and would be undetectable.

The grid of points is stored in a three-dimensional array PS of dimension $N_1 \times N_2 \times N_3$. The *physical address* of a grid point p is the triple of non-negative integer $L = (i, j, k)$.

The translation between the physical address L of a point and its coordinates in the domain is done by keeping an affine transform matrix $\mathbf{A}$ alongside the volume. The transformation between domain coordinates (x, y, z) and physical address is given by:

$$\begin{bmatrix} i \\ j \\ k \\ 1 \end{bmatrix} = \mathbf{A} \cdot \begin{bmatrix} x \\ y \\ z \\ 1 \end{bmatrix} \tag{8}$$

(rounding to the greatest integer smaller than the computed value is implicit here).

Note that with this representation, the algebra operator *affine* doesn't need to operate on the point array: all it has to do is to change the matrix $\mathbf{A}$. Other components of the representation are connected to the problem of representing the boundary of the domain, about which we will make a little digression.

When a volume is obtained by cutting pieces of another volume, for example with a selection operation, the boundaries of the new volume will not in general be aligned with the grid. In order to return a more accurate volume and—more importantly—to avoid the topological defects mentioned in the introduction, we allow the boundary of the volume to be displaced with respect to the data grid. We do this by registering, for each boundary cell, the position of the boundary inside it. The resulting model is that of a piecewise linear boundary, as exemplified for a two-dimensional volume, in Figure 5.

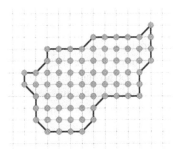

Fig. 4. Boundaries of a volume at creation time.

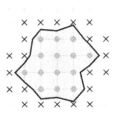

Fig. 5. Boundaries of a volume displaced with respect to the grid.

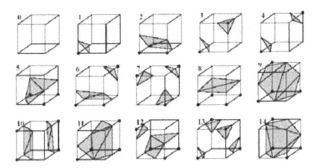

Fig. 6. Boundaries of three-dimensional volume.

In volumes, the specification of the boundary is a bit more complicated. First, the boundary itself is a piecewise linear surface rather than a piecewise linear curve; second, the relation between a portion of the boundary and a parallelepipedal cell must take into account a larger number of possibilities which are illustrated in Figure 6. This boundary surface can be constructed in many ways (see, for example, the Marching Cubes algorithm [17]). If we classify the values at each corner of the boundary cell as either being below or above the boundary condition, there are 256 possible configurations. If we account for symmetries, there are only 14 unique configurations. For each one of these configurations, we need to store the points at which the boundary surface intersects the edges of the cube. Once the various possibilities have been accounted for, we have the

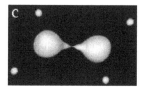

Fig. 7. spatial distribution of the electron density in the plane containing the two carbon and four hydrogen nuclei of the ethene molecule.

representation of a continuous piecewise bi-linear surface up to which we can interpolate the volume values, and that can be placed at arbitrary positions with respect to the grid points.

This model of boundary entails an additional complication, also illustrated in Figure 5. In order to extend the interpolated function to the geometric boundary of the domain, it is necessary to retain a number of points outside the volume so that every boundary cell have a full set of eight measurements on which the interpolation can be built. These points are called *phantom points* and are kept as part of the sampled grid with an indication that they do not belong to the volume.

6 Query Examples

In this section, we will present some examples of queries on our volume model. We will consider examples from quantum chemistry and biology, which are the domains to which we are currently applying our volume model.

6.1 Zero-Flux Surface Extraction

Background. The electrons of an atom are distributed around it in the attractive filed exerted by the nucleus. Although we often represent an atom as a sphere, its shape is actually determined by the electron density $\rho(p)$ which describes the manner in which the electronic charge is distributed in space. Certain physical properties of the molecular configuration are derived not from the electron density itself, but from those properties of the vector field generated by the gradient of the electron density. Starting at any point, one determines the gradient of $\rho(p)$, $\nabla\rho$. This is a vector that points in the direction of maximum increase in the density. In quantum mechanics, an atom can be defined as a region of space bounded by the so-called *zero flux surface*. The zero-flux surface is the locus of points for where the gradient of electron density equals to 0, and this inter-atomic surface separates the atoms in a molecule.

The problem. Let's assume that our volume V_e contains measurements of the electron density. If we need to find the zero-flux surfaces, the first step is to create a gradient volume. Since we are interested finding where gradient equals 0, we can use the modulo of the gradient (which is a scalar field) in lieu of the complete gradient.

The sequence of volume algebra operators that determines our surface is as follows.

1. Using an affine operator to create a volume V_{exp} which is the V_e shifted by one on the positive x direction.
2. Using intersection to produce a gradient volume V_{gxp} which is result of subtracting V_{exp} from V_e. This gradient volume contains the complete gradient volume's positive x direction component.
3. Repeat step 1 and 2, except now create a gradient volume containing the gradient's negative x direction component.
4. Using intersection again to produce a gradient volume V_{gx} which is result of subtracting V_{gxp} from V_{gxn}. This gradient volume contains the complete gradient volume's x direction component.
5. Continue to produce the y and z gradient volumes.
6. Now we intersects V_{gx} and V_{gy} using cartesian product, then intersects again with V_{gz} using cartesian product. The result of these intersects is V_g.

This is synthesized in the following query condition:

$$V_g = \text{intrs}(\text{intrs}(\text{intrs}(V_{gxp}, V_{gxn}, -), \text{intrs}(V_{gyp}, V_{gyn}, -), \times), \text{intrs}(V_{gzp}, V_{gzn}, -), \times) \quad (9)$$

Now we can search for zero-flux surfaces from V_g. Since zero flux surfaces are the same as the boundaries of the volumes containing gradient ≥ 0, we can use the following query operation:

$$\text{sel}(V_g, (V_{gx} \geq 0 \wedge V_{gy} \geq 0 \wedge V_{gz} \geq 0)) \quad (10)$$

6.2   Brain Neuron Density Comparison

Background. These days, volume data are quite common in the neurophysiological research and clinical practice because of the popularity of apparatuses such as magnetic imaging devices that produce volumetric "maps" of certain characteristics of the brain. Many problems in medical research and clinical practice involve tracking certain features of the brain over time, since abnormal changes are believed to be connected to the insurgence of certain diseases of neural origin such as Alzheimer's disease.

The problem. A problem that can be regarded as a good exemplification of the kind of queries that neuroscientists do is the following. Assume that for a group of patients, we have a number of neuron density measurements taken at a certain distance in time. Let's say that, for each patient, we have two measurements taken 10 years apart. The measurements are in a form of a volumetric model. For the sake of exposition, let's also assume we are only interested in the hippocampus. A legitimate scientific question is to analyze the region of the hippocampus in which the neuron density is abnormal (let us say that, for the purpose of this example, "abnormal" means no greater than a certain value α). A query might then be to select all the patients for which the ratio of the overlap of the abnormal regions in the two scans with the abnormal region in the new scan is less than or equal β. If a patient's condition is worse, this ratio is small.

In order to solve the problem, we need to first use **cut** to pick the hippocampus from each brain by $V_h = \text{cut}(V_b, c_g)$ (An alternative is to intersect with a mask volume which defines the hippocampus region: $V_h = intr(V_b, V_m, \text{nil})$.)

Now, we can use intersection to express the query condition. To find the desired overlap, we need to first select the part of hippocampus from each brain where the neuron density is no greater than α, then find and measure their intersection.

$$V_{n1} = \text{sel}(V_{h1}, \text{density} < \alpha)$$
$$V_{n2} = \text{sel}(V_{h2}, \text{density} < \alpha) \tag{11}$$
$$f(V_1, V_2) = \frac{\text{vol}(intr(V_1, V_2, \text{nil}))}{\text{vol}(V_2)}$$

(remember that $m(V)$ is the measure of a volume). Now the final query can be constructed as:

```
SELECT    *
FROM      patient
WHERE     diagnosis="alzheimer"
AND       f(V_{n1}, V_{n2}) ≤ β
```

7 Conclusions

In this paper we have introduced a volume data model amenable to database use, and an algebra for expressing conditions on such volumes. The salient characteristics of our volume model are the retention, in the abstract data model, of the continuous nature of the domain in which volumes are defined, the fact that volumes are first class data types (and, therefore, that can be returned as results of queries), and the fact that our volume algebra is sufficiently general and amenable to operating on sets of volume (rather than on a volume at the time) to make it a suitable model for databases of volume data.

Acknowledgments. The work presented in this paper was done under the auspices and with the funding of NIH project NCRR RR08 605, *Biomedical Imaging Research Network*, which the authors gratefully acknowledge.

References

1. A. Pommert, M. Bomans, and K. H. Hohne, "Volume visualization in magnetic resonance angiography," *IEEE Computer Graphics and Applications*, vol. 12, no. 5, pp. 12–13, 1992.
2. D. Ebert and P. Rheingans, "Volume illustration: Non-photorealistic rendering of volume models," in *Proceedings Visualization 2000* (T. Ertl, B. Hamann, and A. Varshney, eds.), pp. 195–202, 2000.
3. L. A. Lima and R. Bastos, "Seismic data volume rendering," Tech. Rep. TR98-004, 23, 1998.
4. C. S. Gitlin and C. R. Johnson, "Techniques for visualizing 3D unstructured meshes," Tech. Rep. UUCS-94-018, 1994.
5. V. Ranjan and A. Fournier, "Volume models for volumetric data," Tech. Rep. TR-93-50, 30, 1993.
6. G. Nielson, "Volume modelling," 1999.

7. L. Neugebauer, "Optimization and evaluation of database queries including embedded interpolation procedures," in *Proceedings of the 1991 ACM SIGMOD International Conference on Management of Data, Denver, Colorado, May 29–31, 1991* (J. Clifford and R. King, eds.), pp. 118–127, ACM Press, 1991.

8. S. Grumbach, P. Rigaux, and L. Segoufin, "Manipulating interpolated data is easier than you thought," in *The VLDB Journal*, pp. 156–165, 2000.

9. B. S. Lee, R. R. Snapp, L. Chen, and I.-Y. Song, "Modeling and querying scientific simulation mesh data," Tech. Rep. CS-02-7, February 2002.

10. T. T. Elvins, "A survey of algorithms for volume visualization," *Computer Graphics*, vol. 26, no. 3, pp. 194–201, 1992.

11. A. P. Marathe and K. Salem, "A language for manipulating arrays," in *The VLDB Journal*, pp. 46–55, 1997.

12. L. Libkin, R. Machlin, and L. Wong, "A query language for multidimensional arrays: design, implementation, and optimization techniques," pp. 228–239, 1996.

13. R. H. Güting, "Spatial database systems."

14. M. Chen, A. Winter, D. Rodgman, and S. Treavett, "Enriching volume modelling with scalar fields," 2002.

15. M. Chen and J. V. Tucker, "Constructive volume geometry," *Computer Graphics Forum*, vol. 19, no. 4, pp. 281–293, 2000.

16. J. D. Foley, A. V. Dam, and S. K. Feiner, *Introduction to Computer Graphics*. Addison-Wesley Pub Co, 1 ed., August 1993.

17. W. E. Lorensen and H. E. Cline, "Marching cubes: A high resolution 3d surface construction algorithm," in *Proceedings of the 1987 ACM Conference on Computer Graphics (SIGGRAPH'87), Anaheim, USA, pp. 163–169, July 1987*, pp. 163–169, ACM Press, 1987.

Integrity Constraints Definition in Object-Oriented Conceptual Modeling Languages

Antoni Olivé

Dept. Llenguatges i Sistemes Informàtics
Universitat Politècnica de Catalunya
08034 Barcelona (Catalonia)
olive@lsi.upc.es

Abstract. We propose two new methods for the definition of integrity constraints in object-oriented conceptual modeling languages. The first method applies to static constraints, and consists in representing them by special operations, that we call constraint operations. The specification of these operations is then the definition of the corresponding constraints. The second method, which is a slight variant of the previous one, applies to creation-time constraints, a particular class of temporal constraints. Both methods allow the specialization of constraints and the definition of exceptions. We include also an adaptation of the two methods to the UML.

1 Introduction

A complete conceptual schema must include the definition of all relevant integrity constraints [15]. The form of the definition of such constraints depends on the conceptual modeling language used. Some constraints are inherent in the conceptual model in which the language is based, but almost all constraints require an explicit definition [22, ch. 5]. Almost all conceptual modeling languages offer a number of special constructs for defining some popular constraints, such as cardinality constraints, population inclusion, etc. However, there are many constraints that cannot be expressed using only these constructs. These are general constraints whose definition requires the use of a general-purpose sublanguage [13, ch.2].

Many conceptual modeling languages include a formal sublanguage for the definition of general constraints. Among them, we mention here: Telos [17], Morse [4], Syntropy [10], Description Logics [8], Chimera [9], ORM [14], UML [19] and Catalysis [12].

The methods used by the above languages for defining general constraints are diverse, even within the same family of languages. In this paper, we focus on a particular family, the object-oriented (O-O) conceptual modeling languages, and we propose a method for the definition of general constraints in them. The method can be adapted to any particular O-O language, including the UML.

In essence, our method consists in representing the static constraints by special operations, that we call constraint operations. The specification of these operations is then the definition of the corresponding constraints. Such specification can be done in

I.-Y. Song et al. (Eds.): ER 2003, LNCS 2813, pp. 349–362, 2003.

the style and sublanguage most appropriate in each language. In the particular case of the UML, we propose to specify the postconditions, and to use for this purpose the OCL language [19, ch. 6]. We believe that the method provides some advantages that may make it appropriate in some cases, particularly in industrial projects.

The method can be adapted to temporal constraints, although this will not be explored in this paper. However, we have identified a special kind of constraint which lies in between the static and the temporal ones. We call them creation-time constraints, because they must hold when objects are created. These constraints involve facts that hold at the time an object is created. We have found, surprisingly, that these constraints occur frequently in practice. In the paper, we characterize them, and show how a variant of the previous method can be used to define those constraints in non-temporal O-O languages. In particular, we describe its adaptation to the UML.

The paper is structured as follows. Section 2 reviews the logical basis and notation of integrity constraints. Section 3 deals with the definition of static constraints. We describe a new method for their definition in O-O languages, and we include a suggestion for its adaptation to the UML. Section 4 deals with constraint specialization and exceptions. Section 5 describes the method for creation-time constraints, a subclass of temporal constraints. Finally, section 6 gives the conclusions and points out future work. Throughout the paper, we use examples from a hypothetical meeting management system. The system deals with committees (formed by members) that organize meetings that take place in rooms.

2 Basic Concepts and Notation

We adopt here a logical and temporal view of the information base (IB), and assume that entities and relationships are instances of their types at particular time points. By lifespan of an information system we mean the time interval during which the system operates. We represent by $Time(t)$ the fact that t is a time point of the lifespan. In the information base, if t is a time point of the life span, we represent by $E(e,t)$ the fact that e is instance of entity type E at t. For example, if *Committee* is an entity type then *Committee* (com,t) means that *com* is an instance of *Committee* at time t.

We denote by $R(p_1{:}E_1, ..., p_n{:}E_n)$ the schema of a relationship type named R with entity type participants $E_1, ..., E_n$, playing roles $p_1, ..., p_n$, respectively. When the role name is omitted, it is assumed to be the same as the corresponding entity type. In the logical representation, attributes will be considered as ordinary binary relationship types. In the IB, if t is a time point of the lifespan, we represent by $R(e_1,...,e_n,t)$ the fact that entities $e_1,...,e_n$ participate in a relationship instance of R at t. For example, if we have in the schema the relationship type:

HoldsMeeting (organizer:Committee, Meeting)

then a fact *HoldsMeeting* (com,m,t) means that, at time t, committee *com* is the organizer of meeting m.

In logic, integrity constraints can be defined by formulas that the information base must satisfy (must be true) or, equivalently, they can be defined by derived predicates, called inconsistency predicates, that cannot have any fact in the information base. We will call *condition* constraint a constraint defined by a formula, and *inconsistency* constraint a constraint defined by an inconsistency predicate.

Constraints may be static or temporal. Static constraints must be satisfied at each time t in the lifespan of the information system, and their evaluation involves only facts holding at the same time t. Temporal constraints involve facts holding at different times and/or must be satisfied only at some particular times [2]. In this section, we deal exclusively with static constraints.

In logic, a static condition constraint is defined by a closed first-order formula:
$$\forall t \ (\text{Time}(t) \rightarrow \phi(t))$$
that the IB is required to satisfy. The formula states that for each time t of the lifespan, the subformula $\phi(t)$ must be true in the information base. Subformula $\phi(t)$ can involve only facts holding at time t. Obviously, the temporal argument t is unnecessary for static constraints, but the notation used allows a unified treatment of static and temporal constraints. For example, the static constraint:

IC1: A committee cannot hold two meetings on the same day
can be defined by the formula:

$\forall t \ (\text{Time}(t) \rightarrow \forall \text{com},\text{m1},\text{m2},\text{st1},\text{st2}$

(HoldsMeeting (com,m1,t) $\wedge$ HoldsMeeting (com,m2,t) $\wedge$ m1 $\neq$ m2 $\wedge$

StartTime(m1,st1,t) $\wedge$ StartTime(m2,st2,t) $\rightarrow$ date(st1) $\neq$ date(st2)))

where a fact *StartTime* (m,st,t) means that, at time t, the (scheduled or actual) starting time of meeting m is st; and *date* (st) is a function that gives the date corresponding to a time st.

We will find it very useful to distinguish between targeted and untargeted condition constraints [9, p. 27]. A condition constraint is *targeted* at entity type E if it can be expressed in the form:
$$\forall t \ (\text{Time}(t) \rightarrow \forall e \ (E(e,t) \rightarrow \varphi(e,t)))$$
which, given that $E(e,t) \rightarrow Time(t)$, is equivalent to:
$$\forall e,t \ (E(e,t) \rightarrow \varphi(e,t))$$
That is, subformula $\varphi(e,t)$ must be true in the information base for any e instance of E at any time t. A condition constraint is *untargeted* if it cannot be targeted at any existing entity type. For example, IC1 can be expressed as targeted at *Committee*:

$\forall \text{com},t \ (\text{Committee (com},t) \rightarrow \forall \text{m1},\text{m2},\text{st1},\text{st2}$

(HoldsMeeting (com,m1,t) $\wedge$ HoldsMeeting (com,m2,t) $\wedge$ m1 $\neq$ m2 $\wedge$

StartTime(m1,st1,t) $\wedge$ StartTime(m2,st2,t) $\rightarrow$ date(st1) $\neq$ date(st2)))

Most condition constraints are targeted, and often they can be targeted at several entity types. IC1, for example, can be expressed also as targeted at *Meeting*. An example of untargeted condition constraint may be:

IC2: There must be at least one large room
which is defined by the formula:

$\forall t \ (\text{Time (t)} \rightarrow \exists r \ (\text{Room (r,t)} \wedge \text{Size(r,Large,t)}))$

Inconsistency constraints are used mainly in the logic programming and deductive databases fields [11, ch.12+]. The idea is to define an inconsistency predicate *Inc* for each constraint, and to require that no *Inc* fact may hold in the IB at any time [16]. Formally, *Inc* is a derived predicate defined by:
$$\forall x_1,\dots,x_m,t \ (\text{Inc}(x_1,\dots,x_m,t) \leftrightarrow \text{Time}(t) \wedge \phi'(x_1,\dots,x_m,t))$$
In general, an inconsistency predicate may have any number of arguments. A fact of an inconsistency predicate corresponds to a violation of the corresponding constraint. The arguments give the values for which such violation exists. This is an advantage over condition constraints, whose evaluation only returns true or false.

Another advantage of inconsistency predicates is that they have the same form as ordinary derived predicates, defined by derivation rules.

For example, the definition of IC1 by inconsistency predicate *OverlappingMeetings* could be:

$\forall$com,m1,m2,t (OverlappingMeetings (com,m1,m2,t) $\leftrightarrow$ Time(t) $\wedge$

HoldsMeeting (com,m1,t) $\wedge$ HoldsMeeting (com,m2,t) $\wedge$ m1 $\neq$ m2 $\wedge$

StartTime(m1,st1,t) $\wedge$ StartTime(m2,st2,t) $\wedge$ date(st1) = date(st2))

The meaning of a fact *OverlappingMeetings (com,m1,m2)* is that committee *com* holds meetings *m1* and *m2* on the same day.

The distinction between targeted and untargeted constraints applies also to inconsistency constraints. An inconsistency constraint is targeted at entity type E if it can be expressed in the form:

$\forall$e,x_1,...,x_m,t (Inc(e,x_1,...,x_m,t) $\leftrightarrow$ Time(t) $\wedge$ E(e,t) $\wedge$ φ'(e,x_1,...,x_m,t))

which, given that $E(e,t) \rightarrow Time(t)$, is equivalent to:

$\forall$e,x_1,...,x_m,t (Inc(e,x_1,...,x_m,t) $\leftrightarrow$ E(e,t) $\wedge$ φ'(e,x_1,...,x_m,t))

An inconsistency constraint is *untargeted* if it cannot be targeted at any existing entity type. For example, IC1 can be expressed as targeted at *Committee*:

$\forall$com,m1,m2,t (OverlappingMeetings (com,m1,m2,t) $\leftrightarrow$

Committee (com,t) $\wedge$

HoldsMeeting (com,m1,t) $\wedge$ HoldsMeeting (com,m2,t) $\wedge$ m1 $\neq$ m2 $\wedge$

StartTime(m1,st1,t) $\wedge$ StartTime(m2,st2,t) $\wedge$ date(st1) = date(st2))

3 Static Constraints

We now focus on the definition of static integrity constraints in non-temporal O-O conceptual modeling languages. Traditionally, as we will review in Subsection 3.3, these languages provide specific constructs for the purpose of constraint definition. However, we show in the following that there is an alternative method of definition, which (re)uses the standard concept of operation.

3.1 Static Constraints in O-O Languages

We deal first with condition constraints. The key point of the method we propose consists in representing these constraints by operations, that we call *constraint* operations. These operations are query operations (also called query functions), which return a value but do not alter the information base. The only purpose of a constraint operation is to specify the corresponding constraint. Constraint operations are purely conceptual; they may or may not be part of the implementation.

The constraint operation corresponding to a condition constraint targeted at E:

$\forall$e,t (E(e,t) $\rightarrow$ φ(e,t))

is defined as an instance operation of E, and its signature has the general form:

conditionName () : Boolean

where *conditionName* is a name that identifies the constraint. The semantics is that the result of the evaluation of this operation at any time t, for any instance e of E, must be the same as the result of the evaluation of $\varphi(e,t)$ in the information base. On the other hand, this result must be *true*. Note that, in this method, it is implicit that the result of the operation must be true for each time *t* of the lifespan, and for all instances of the hosting entity type (*E*) at each time *t*.

For example, IC1, as a condition constraint targeted at *Committee*, could be defined by a constraint operation of *Committee* with signature:

meetingsOnDistinctDays () : Boolean

Constraint operations may be specified formally in the style and the (sub)language most appropriate to the corresponding O-O language. In general, the preferred style could be the use of postconditions. For query operations, postconditions specify the value of the result.

If a condition constraint can be targeted at two or more entity types, we have then the choice of where to host the constraint operation. From a conceptual point of view all alternatives are valid. The designer may choose the place (s)he thinks is more natural or easier to specify. A factor that may influence the decision is the possibility of refinement and exceptions, as explained in the next section. In any case, the cross-references and indexes provided by documentation tools may be of some help in this respect. In the example, IC1 can be targeted also at *Meeting*. We could then define the constraint operation in *Meeting*, with signature:

noOtherMeetingsOnTheSameDay () : Boolean

which must give the result *true* for all instances of *Meeting*.

The constraint operation corresponding to an untargeted condition constraint is defined as a *class* operation of some entity type, and its signature has the general form:

conditionName () : Boolean

where, as before, *conditionName* is a name that identifies the constraint. The operation is intended to be evaluated only once and, as before, it must give the result *true*. In principle, the operation corresponding to an untargeted condition constraint could be hosted in any entity type. In particular, all of them could be grouped in a special-purpose entity type, if so desired. However, in practice, it may be sensible to host them in the entity types felt semantically more natural. For example, the untargeted constraint IC2 could be a class operation of entity type *Room*, with signature:

atLeastOneLargeRoom () : Boolean

The operation is intended to be evaluated at class level, and must return *true* at any time.

Inconsistency constraints can be defined similarly. The main difference is that now the result of the constraint operation must give the values for which the corresponding constraint is violated. For example, if IC1 is defined as an inconsistency constraint targeted at *Committee*, the constraint operation would then be an instance operation of *Committee*, with signature:

overlappingMeetings () : Set (Meeting)

The result is the set of (two or more) meetings of the corresponding committee that would be held on the same day. The constraint will be satisfied if the operation returns the empty set for all committees.

Fig. 1. Three examples of constraint operations in the UML

3.2 Adaptation to the UML

The above method is easily adaptable to any O-O conceptual modeling language. The main decisions to be made are: (1) How to specify the constraint operations; (2) The language of this specification; and (3)   How to indicate that an operation is a constraint operation.

In the case of the UML, we propose to specify the constraint operations by means of postconditions, using the OCL language, and to indicate that an operation is a constraint operation by means of the stereotype <<*IC*>>. All operations stereotyped by <<*IC*>> represent constraints. The difference between condition and inconsistency constraint is indicated by the operation result type: if the result is *Boolean* then it represents a condition; otherwise it represents an inconsistency.

Consider, as an example, the condition constraint IC1 targeted at *Committee*. Figure 1 shows the corresponding operation in entity type *Committee*, stereotyped with <<*IC*>>. The formal specification in OCL is:

```
context Committee :: meetingsOnDistinctDays () : Boolean
  post: result = self.meeting -> forAll (m1,m2 |
      m1 <> m2 implies m1.startTime.date <> m2.startTime.date)
```

For illustration purposes, in this paper we show the constraint operations in class diagrams. In practice, a designer could choose not to show them.

Figure 1 shows also a class operation (shown underlined) in entity type *Room*, corresponding to the untargeted condition constraint IC2. The operation has also stereotype <<*IC*>>. The formal specification in OCL is:

```
context Room :: atLeastOneLargeRoom () : Boolean
  post: result = Room.allInstances ->
                      select (size = Large) -> size () > 0
```

As a new example of inconsistency constraint consider:

IC3: Two meetings cannot share the same room at the same time

This constraint can be targeted at *Meeting*. Figure 1 shows also the corresponding constraint operation in *Meeting*, with stereotype <<*IC*>>. The formal specification in OCL would be:

```
context Meeting :: hasRoomConflictWith () : Set (Meeting)
  post: result = Meeting.allInstances -> select (m | m <> self
        and m.location = self.location and self.overlaps(m))
```

The operation must give the empty set for all meetings. We use an auxiliary operation (*overlaps*) to check whether the intervals defined by *startTime* and *duration* of two meetings overlap.

3.3   Comparison with Other Methods

We now compare our method with the methods used by other languages. Given that the focus of this paper is on the definition of integrity constraints in O-O languages, here we only compare with languages that may be considered more or less object-oriented and that include, in particular, the concept of redefinable query operation, or similar. This explains why we do not include in the comparison other conceptual modeling languages such as Telos [17], Morse [4], Syntropy [10], Description Logics [8], or ORM [14].

We start the comparison with the UML and the methods that use it, such as Catalysis. In UML, a constraint is a semantic condition or restriction expressed as a linguistic statement in some textual language. In the schema, a constraint is a model element instance of the metaclass *Constraint*. Each constraint has a body (a boolean expression) and a language of interpretation. UML provides the OCL language, but other languages can also be used [21, p. 235+]. There are three main predefined stereotypes of constraints: <<*invariant*>> (corresponding to our static constraints), <<*postcondition*>> and <<*precondition*>> [19, p. 2-36].

For example, a usual definition of a condition constraint like IC1 above would be the invariant:

```
context Committee inv meetingsOnDistinctDays:
    self.meeting -> forAll (m1,m2 |
    m1 <> m2 implies m1.startTime.date <> m2.startTime.date)
```

It can be seen that the body of this constraint is almost the same as our postcondition. The context is also the same, and we have used the same name for the constraint and for the operation. The (formal) difference is that this expression is a constraint stereotyped <<*invariant*>>, while in our method it is the specification of the postcondition of an operation.

We believe that our method has three main advantages over the UML method. The first is the economy, because we require one language construct less (i.e., invariants). Our method makes the language and its supporting tools simpler, which is important in many respects. In particular, in the framework of the Model Driven Architecture (MDA) [20], our approach eases the development of mappings from conceptual schemas to platform specific models, because now integrity constraints become just a particular case of operations. The second advantage is that in our method the designer may choose to specify a constraint as a condition or as an inconsistency. In the UML, constraints can be specified only as conditions. The third advantage is obtained by the use of the standard mechanism of operation redefinition, with its well-defined semantics. As we show below, this mechanism may simplify the definition of some integrity constraints and at the same time allows the definition of exceptions. Redefinition of UML constraints is not possible.

Chimera [9] defines constraints by inconsistency predicates, with the corresponding deductive rules. They can be targeted to a class, or untargeted. Constraints cannot be redefined. Our method can be adapted to Chimera. We would associate to each constraint an accessor operation with some predefined name. In this way, deductive rules for inconsistency constraint definition would not be needed, thus making the language simpler and, at the same time, allowing redefinition.

4 Constraint Specialization and Exceptions

As we have seen, the main idea of our method for constraints definition in O-O languages consists in defining them as (special) operations, that we have called constraint operations. However, a distinguishing feature of O-O languages is that an instance operation defined in an entity type may be redefined in its subtypes. This leads naturally to the question of the meaning of redefinition of constraint operations. The answer must be: constraint specialization or exception.

4.1 Constraint Specialization

By constraint specialization (or refinement) we mean that a constraint defined in an entity type is strengthened in some subtype (i.e. replacement of a constraint ϕ of the parent type with a stronger one ϕ' such that ϕ' implies ϕ) [7]. In our method, constraint specialization is achieved by redefining the corresponding constraint operation.

For example, assume that *Committee* has attribute *maxNumberOfMembers*, which indicates the maximum number of members that a committee may have at any time. In general the value for this attribute must be less than 100, but for *TaskForce*, a subtype of *Committee*, the value of that attribute must be less than 10. Figure 2 shows the condition constraint operation *validMaximum* defined in *Committee* and redefined in *TaskForce*. The formal specification of both operations in the OCL could be:

```
context Committee :: validMaximum () : Boolean
  post result = maxNumberOfMembers < 100

context TaskForce :: validMaximum () : Boolean
post result = maxNumberOfMembers < 10
```

The main advantages of constraint specialization are: (1) it eases the definition of constraints, and shows explicitly that a constraint in a subtype is an specialization of the same constraint in the supertype, and (2) it allows a more efficient implementation by showing the constraint that must be checked in each case (the constraint defined in the supertype needs not to be checked for the instances of the subtypes).

4.2 Exceptions

By exception we mean here that a constraint ϕ defined in an entity type must be redefined as ϕ' in some subtype, and such that ϕ' does not imply ϕ. In our method, exceptions can be defined also as redefinitions of the corresponding constraint operations.

As an example, assume that, in general, meetings are organized by exactly one committee. However there is an exception: for *JointMeeting*, a subtype of *Meeting*, the number of organizers must be greater than one. Figure 2 shows the representation of the constraint and its exception in our method. We have defined the condition constraint operation *validNumberOfOrganizers* in *Meeting*, and redefined it in *JointMeeting*. The formal specification of both operations in the OCL could be:

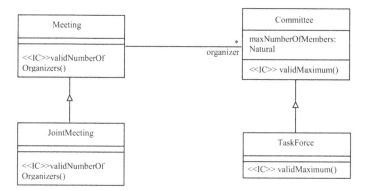

Fig. 2. Examples of constraint specialization and of exception

```
context Meeting :: validNumberOfOrganizers () : Boolean
post result = organizer -> size() = 1
context JointMeeting :: validNumberOfOrganizers () : Boolean
post result = organizer -> size() > 1
```

4.3   Comparison with Previous Work

Constraint specialization and exceptions have not attracted yet too much attention in conceptual modeling. Most languages allow only the specialization of attribute types in subtypes. To the best of our knowledge, the work closest to ours is represented by [6] and [1]. [6] distinguishes between exceptional individuals and exceptional classes. The former are dealt with run-time exception handling mechanisms (such as those described in [5]). Exceptional classes allow subclasses to redefine some attribute, as opposed to refining it. The typical example is:

```
class Patient is a Person
                  treatedBy: Physician
class Alcoholic is a Patient
                  treatedBy: Psychologist
```

where psychologists usually are not physicians. The author proposes a new construct (*excuses*) to handle such exceptions. In our method, excuses can be represented as redefinitions of constraint operations. On the other hand, we admit a much broader class of exceptions.

[1] represents constraints in O-O databases as objects, instance of a special class called *Constraint*. This class includes several attributes that allow defining specializations and exceptions. It is assumed that an O-O DBMS will include a run-time algorithm that analyzes the instances of *Constraint* and determines which constraints must be checked after each particular update. We believe that our method provides a similar expressiveness (with respect to constraint specialization and exceptions), but reusing the semantics of an existing construct (operations).

5   Creation-Time Constraints

The method described in the previous section can be extended easily to deal with a particular class of temporal integrity constraints. These are the constraints that must hold when the instances of some entity type are created. We have found that these constraints appear several times in most conceptual schemas. In this section, we define this class of constraints and propose a method for their definition in non-temporal O-O languages.

5.1   Definition

Assume, in our example, that there are two subtypes of *Meeting*: *ScheduledMeeting* and *FinishedMeeting*, and that the actual participants of a meeting are given when the meeting becomes instance of *FinishedMeeting*. In this context, consider the constraint:

IC4: "The participants of a finished meeting must be members of its organizing committee"

The formula:

$\forall fm,p,com,t$ (FinishedMeeting (fm,t) $\land$

Participant (fm,p,t) $\land$ HoldsMeeting (com,fm,t) $\rightarrow$ Member (com,p,t))

would define IC4 incorrectly, because it requires that *p* is member of *com* at any time *t* in which *fm* is a finished meeting. A meeting *fm* becomes instance of *FinishedMeeting* at a time t_0, and then remains in this situation forever. IC4 must not hold at each time *fm* is instance of *FinishedMeeting*. It must hold only at time t_0, the creation time of *fm* in *FinishedMeeting*. The participants must be members of the organizing committee at this creation time only. Later, the membership of committee *com* may change, but the changes must not affect the constraint.

Assuming a predicate:

FinishedMeetingCreatedAt (FinishedMeeting,Time)

that gives the instant when a finished meeting is created, the correct formula for IC4 would then be:

$\forall fm,p,com,t_0$ (FinishedMeetingCreatedAt (fm,t_0) $\land$

Participant (fm,p,t_0) $\land$ HoldsMeeting (com,fm,t_0) $\rightarrow$ Member (com,p,t_0))

Formally, we say that constraint ϕ is a creation-time constraint if it can be expressed in the form:

$$\phi \equiv \forall e,t_0 \text{ (ECreatedAt(e,}t_0\text{)} \rightarrow \phi(e,t_0))$$

where ϕ (e,t_0) is a formula that can be evaluated at time t_0 with facts holding at that time. Note that creation-time constraints can be considered as targeted. In the example above, we have:

$\forall fm,t_0$ (FinishedMeetingCreatedAt (fm,t_0) $\rightarrow$ ϕ(fm,t_0))

with:

ϕ(fm,t_0)) $\equiv$ $\forall p,com$

(Participant (fm,p,t_0) $\land$ HoldsMeeting (fm,com,t_0) $\rightarrow$ Member (com,p,t_0))

The distinction between condition and inconsistency constraints we made for static constraints in subsection 2.1 applies also to creation-time constraints. Formally, we say that constraint ϕ' is an inconsistency creation-time constraint if it can be expressed the form:

$$\forall e, x_1, \ldots, x_m, t_0 \ (Inc(e, t_0, x_1, \ldots, x_m) \leftrightarrow ECreatedAt(e, t_0) \land \phi'(e, t_0, x_1, \ldots, x_m))$$

where $\phi'(e, t_0, x_1, \ldots, x_m)$ is a conjunction of literals that can be evaluated at time t_0 with facts holding at that time.

5.2   Creation-Time Constraints in O-O Languages

Now, we focus on how to define creation-time constraints in non-temporal O-O languages. Most non-temporal O-O languages use a concept, *object creation*, which we will use too to define creation-time constraints. That concept is used, among other things, to define the initial value for attributes, which is the value an attribute takes when an object is created, if no explicit value is given. In the UML, such initial value is, in general, an expression that is meant to be evaluated at the time the object is initialized [19, p. 2-26].

There is an analogy between initial values for attributes and creation-time constraints, because both are meant to be evaluated when an object is created. The analogy justifies the method we propose to define creation-time constraints: The constraint operation corresponding to a creation-time condition constraint:

$$\forall e, t_0 \ (ECreatedAt(e, t_0) \rightarrow \phi(e, t_0))$$

is defined as an instance operation of E, and its signature has the general form:

conditionName () : Boolean

where *conditionName* is a name that identifies the constraint. In constraint IC4, we would define the operation in *FinishedMeeting*. Now the semantics is that the operation must be evaluated at the time t_0 when an entity e becomes instance of entity type E. The result of the evaluation must be the same as the result of the evaluation of $\phi(e, t_0)$ in the information base. On the other hand, this result must be *true*. Note that, in this method, it is implicit that the result of the operation must be *true* at the time entities become instance of the hosting entity type (E).

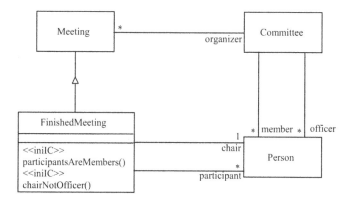

Fig. 3. Two examples of creation time constraint operations in the UML

5.3 Adaptation to the UML

The adaptation of our method to a particular O-O language is similar to the one described in the previous section. We indicate that an operation represents a creation-time constraint with the stereotype <<*iniIC*>>. Figure 3 shows two examples of the use of this stereotype. The first, is the constraint operation corresponding to the condition creation-time constraint IC4. The name of the operation is *participantsAreMembers*. Its formal specification in the OCL is:

```
context FinishedMeeting :: participantsAreMembers () : Boolean
  post result = self.participant ->
              forAll (p|self.organizer.member -> includes (p))
```

An example of inconsistency creation-time constraint could be:

IC5: The chair of a (finished) meeting must be one of the officers of the organizing committee.

Again, IC5 is a creation-time constraint because it must hold only when the finished meeting is created. The officers of the organizing committee may change later, but the changes cannot have any effect on past meetings. We define a new constraint operation of *FinishedMeeting*, called *chairNotOfficer*, with the OCL specification:

```
context FinishedMeeting :: chairNotOfficer () : Person
  post: result = if self.organizer.officer ->
                    excludes (self.chair) then
                      self.chair
              endif
```

5.4 Comparison with Other Methods

As far as we know, creation-time constraints have received some attention only in the deductive databases field. They were formalized for the first time by [18]. The approach (also followed by [11, ch. 16]) consists in defining "action relations" which, for insertions, have a tuple for each insertion performed in a given relation. These relations are similar to our *ECreatedAt* predicate. The main difference is that we deal with these constraints in object-oriented languages, instead of logic-relational ones.

6 Conclusions

We have proposed two related methods for the definition of integrity constraints in non-temporal O-O conceptual modeling languages. The first method applies to static constraints, and associates each constraint with a constraint operation. The specification of this operation is then the definition of the corresponding constraint. The second method applies to creation-time constraints, a particular class of temporal constraints. We have described a variant of the previous method to deal with these constraints.

The two methods have been formalized in logic and described independently of any particular O-O language. We have proposed also adaptations of the two methods to the UML. The methods are fully compatible with the UML-based CASE tools, and thus they can be adopted in industrial projects, if it is felt appropriate.

We hope that our methods will ease the definition of integrity constraints. The need of including integrity constraints in conceptual schemas has always been considered important, but nowadays, in the framework of the emerging Model Driven Architecture, it is becoming mandatory. On the other hand, we hope that our methods will ease the implementation of integrity constraints.

Our work can be continued in several directions. We mention two of them here. The first is the adaptation of our methods to other languages. Of particular interest may be the adaptation to temporal O-O conceptual modeling languages, such as [3]. The second direction is to develop mappings for transforming our constraint operations to the appropriate constructs of other platform independent and/or platform specific models, including database checks, assertions, triggers, operations or transaction pre/postconditions. Naturally, the mappings should draw upon the large body of available knowledge.

Acknowledgements. I would like to thank the anonymous referees and the GMC group (Jordi Cabot, Jordi Conesa, Dolors Costal, Xavier de Palol, Cristina Gómez, Maria-Ribera Sancho and Ernest Teniente) for many useful comments to previous drafts of this paper. This work has been partially supported by the Ministerio de Ciencia y Tecnologia and FEDER under project TIC2002-00744.

References

1. Bassiliades, N., Vlahavas, I. "Modelling Constraints with Exceptions in Object-Oriented Databases". Proc. ER'94, LNCS 881, pp. 189–204.
2. Boman, M.; Bubenko, J.A. jr.; Johannesson, P.; Wangler, B. Conceptual Modelling. Prentice Hall, 269 p., 1997.
3. Bertino, E.; Ferrari,E.; Guerrini, G. "T_Chimera: A Temporal ObjectOriented Data Model". Theory and Practice of Object Systems, 3(2), pp. 103–125.
4. Bouzeghoub, M.; Métais, E. "Semantic Modeling of Object Oriented Databases". Proc. 17th. VLDB, 1991, Barcelona, pp. 3–14.
5. Borgida, A. "Language Features for Flexible Handling of Exceptions in Information Systems". ACM TODS 10(4), December, pp. 565–603.
6. Borgida, A. "Modeling Class Hierarchies with Contradictions". Proc. ACM SIGMOD 88, pp. 434–443.
7. Borgida, A.; Mylopoulos, J.; Wong, H.K.T. "Generalization/Specialization as a Basis for Software Specification". In Michael L. Brodie, John Mylopoulos, Joachim W. Schmidt (Eds.): On Conceptual Modelling. Springer, pp. 87–117
8. Calvanese, D.; Lenzerini, M.; Nardi, D. "Description Logics for Conceptual Data Modeling". In Chomicki, J.; Saake, G. (eds). Logics for Databases and Information Systems, Kluwer, 1998, pp. 229–263.
9. Ceri, S.; Fraternali, P. Designing Database Applications with Objects and Rules. The IDEA Methodology. Addison-Wesley, 1997, 579 p.
10. Cook, S.; Daniels, J. Designing Object Systems. Object-Oriented Modelling with Syntropy. Prentice Hall, 1994, 389 p.
11. Das, S.K. Deductive Databases and Logic Programming. Addison-Wesley, 1992, 432 p.
12. D'Souza, D.F.; Wills, A.C. Objects, Components and Frameworks with UML. The Catalysis Approach. Addison-Wesley, 1999, 785 p.
13. Embley, D.W.; Kurtz, B.D.; Woodfield, S.N. Object-Oriented Systems Analysis. A Model-Driven Approach. Yourdon Press, 1992, 302 p.

14. Halpin, T. Information Modeling and Relational Databases. From Conceptual Analysis to Logical Design. Morgan Kaufmann Pub., 2001, 761 p.
15. ISO/TC97/SC5/WG3. "Concepts and Terminology for the Conceptual Schema and the Information Base", J.J. van Griethuysen (ed.), March 1982.
16. Kowalski, R. "Logic for Data Description". In "Logic and Data Bases", Gallaire, H.; Minker, J. (Eds). Plenum Press, 1978, pp. 77–103
17. Mylopoulos, J.; Borgida, A.; Jarke, M.; Koubarakis, M. "Telos: a language for representing knowledge about information systems". ACM TOIS, 8(4),1990, pp. 327–362.
18. Nicolas, J.M.; Yazdanian, K. "Integrity Checking in Deductive Databases". In "Logic and Data Bases", Gallaire, H.; Minker, J. (Eds). Plenum Press, 19878, pp. 325–344.
19. OMG. "Unified Modeling Language Specification", Version 1.4, September 2001, http://www.omg.org/technology/documents/formal/uml.htm.
20. OMG. "Model Driven Architecture (MDA)", Doc. number ORMSC/2001-07-01, http://cgi.omg.org/docs/ormsc/01-07-01.pdf
21. Rumbaugh, J.; Jacobson, I.; Booch, G. The Unified Modeling Language Reference Manual. Addison-Wesley, 1999, 550 p.
22. Thalheim, B. Entity-Relationship Modeling. Foundations of Database Technology. Springer, 627 p.

Conceptual Treatment of Multivalued Dependencies

Bernhard Thalheim

Computer Science Institute,
Brandenburg University of Technology at Cottbus,
PostBox 101344, D-03013 Cottbus
thalheim@informatik.tu-cottbus.de

Abstract. Multivalued dependencies are considered to be difficult to teach, to handle and to model. This observation is true if multivalued dependencies are treated in the classical approach. We introduce another treatment of multivalued dependencies based on ER modeling techniques and show that multivalued dependenices can be handled in a more natural and intuitive way within our framework. Based on the concept of competing multivalued dependencies we can prove in which case a unique ER schema representation exists. If multivalued dependencies are competing then either one of the competing schemata is chosen or an approximation which combines the competing schemata can be used.

1 Introduction

Multivalued dependencies (MVD) have been thoroughly investigated at the end of the 70ies and during the 80ies. The research led to a deep insight into the relational model and to five equivalent definitions of MVD's. [Thal91] surveys more than threescore papers directly concerned with MVD's. At the same time it surprises that multivalued dependencies did not find their place in the ER model, except[ChNC81,Ling85,Ling85']. We claim that ER models handle MVD's in a more sophisticated, better understandable, and more natural form. This paper aims in proving this claim. We are able to provide a natural treatment for MVD's which more flexible and more natural than that one which has been developed for the relational model.

1.1 Multivalued Dependencies Are Difficult to Model, to Teach, to Learn, and to Handle

Multivalued dependencies are introduced in almost any database book. The classical introduction is based on the tuple-generating definition of the multivalued dependency $X \twoheadrightarrow Y|Z$. It requires that whenever two tuples have the same value on the left-hand side then there also exist a tuple in the relation which matches to the first tuple by the left-hand side and the first element of the right-hand side and which matches to the second tuple by the left-hand side and the second element of the right-hand side.

I.-Y. Song et al. (Eds.): ER 2003, LNCS 2813, pp. 363–375, 2003.

More formally, given a type R, two sets X, Y of components of R and the set Z of remaining components of R. The statement $X \twoheadrightarrow Y|Z$ *is called* multivalued dependency.

The multivalued dependency $X \twoheadrightarrow Y|Z$ *is valid in a class R^C defined over the type R (denoted by* $R^C \models X \twoheadrightarrow Y|Z$ *) if for all objects $t, t' \in R^C$ with $t =_X t'$ an object $t'' \in R^C$ can be found for which the equalities $t'' =_{X \cup Y} t$ and $t'' =_{X \cup Y} t'$ are valid.*

This definition has the clarity of a mathematical definition and the problematic treatment often observed for other mathematical constructs.

It has been stated (e.g., [Mood01,Sims94]) in a number of practitioner reports that modeling MVD is rather difficult and often confuses people in practice. Modeling MVD's in teams becomes a nightmare. For this reason, modelers try to stay away from MVD's.

At the same time, MVD's are extensively used whenever normalization is concerned. In this case, they express that a certain normalization step is based on (vertical) decomposition, i.e. $R^C = R^C[X \cup Y] \bowtie R^C[X \cup Z]$.

Functional dependency normalization is mainly based on synthesis approaches. Currently, no synthesis approach is known for multivalued dependencies. Normalization based on multivalued dependencies is based on the decomposition approach. Unfortunately, the two normalization approaches are incompatible [Thal91]. Therefore, sets of multivalued and functional dependencies must be treated by the decomposition approach.

1.2   The Outline of the Paper

In Section 2 we introduce multivalued dependencies through the extended entity-relationship model. It is demonstrated that this treatment is far more natural and much simpler. A logical implication theory for the ER treatment of sets of multivalued dependencies is provided. In Section 3 we introduce the notion of competing schemata. We show that competing equivalent schema naturally appear and outline a way how to find a unique schema. Finally, a schema approximation approach is proposed for the case that competition among schemata cannot be resolved.

2   The ER Approach to Dependencies

2.1   Multivalued Dependencies within ER Schemata

J. Biskup [Bisk95] introduces three heuristical principles of conceptual modeling. The first principle is Separation of Application Aspects. Each type in the conceptual schema describes one and only one aspect. The type describes one and only one class of existing things. This principle allows to give another definition of validity of multivalued dependencies in the context of extended entity-relationship models [Thal00].

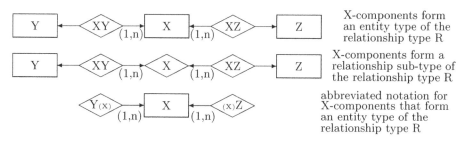

Fig. 1. Three ER representations of a MVD

Definition 1 *Given a type R, the partition of components of R into X, Y and Z. The multivalued dependency $X \twoheadrightarrow Y|Z$ is ER-valid in a class R^C defined over the type R (denoted by $R^C \models_{ER} X \twoheadrightarrow Y|Z$) if the type can be decomposed into three types representing X, Y, and Z and two mandatory relationship types defined on $X \cup Y$ and $X \cup Z$, respectively.*

The MVD can be represented by a decomposition of the type R displayed in Figure 1. We use the last figure whenever we want to use compact schemata. In this case, the relationship type with the components $_{(X)}Z$ is based on the X-components. It allows to show the direct decomposition imposed by the multivalued dependency.

Example 1. *(Running example)*
Let us consider a relationship type EmployeeAssociation defined on the entity types: StaffMember, DependentPerson, Project, Supplier, Product.
    We observe a number of MVDs, e.g. "A staff member determines the department he is working for and members of his family in dependently on the projects and products and their suppliers."
    { *StaffMember* } $\twoheadrightarrow$ { *Department, DependentPerson* }|
                    { *Project, Product, Supplier* }
This MVD can be represented by following picture. We shall see later that other MVD's allow to decompose the association of the type EmployeeAssociation into types representing the relationship between staff member and their dependent people, between staff member and departments and between staff members and projects, products and suppliers.

(Department, DependentPerson)   (Project, Product, Supplier)

2.2   ER-Schema-Based Derivation Rules for Multivalued Dependencies

It is now our interest to reason on ER-validity of multivalued dependencies within the ER schema. In this case we can directly display the results of the type decomposition within the ER schema.

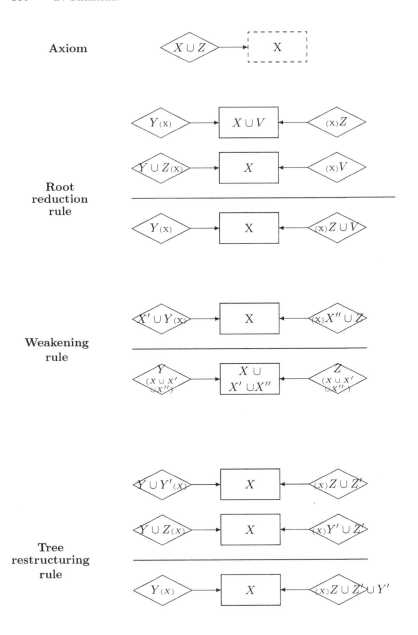

Fig. 2. The deductive system for ER schema derivation based on MVD's

We introduce a deductive system in Figure 2 that allows to derive ER-schema decompositions based on the knowledge of ER-validity of MVD's.

The axiom enables in introducing any component clustering for any relationship type. For rules of our calculus[1] we use subsets $X, X', X'', Y, Y', Z, Z', V, W \subseteq R$ and assume that the sets in one multivalued dependency constitute a cover of R.

The following three rules is based on the ER-validity of MVD's.

We remember the following statement of [Thal91]:

Proposition 1 *The deductive system consisting of the trivial MVD, the root reduction rule, and the weakening rule is correct and complete for inference of multivalued dependencies.*

The tree restructuring rule is correct too but does not form together with the trivial MVD and the weakening rule a complete system.

This proposition allows to deduce the following theorem[2].

Theorem 1 *The axiom and the weakening, root reduction and tree restructuring rules are sound and complete for inference of ER-validity of multivalued dependencies.*

We observe that the axiomatization of functional and multivalued dependencies can be derived in a similar way.

2.3   ER Treatment of Horizontal Dependencies

ER diagrams are not restricted to entity types which have not more than two associated relationship types. Therefore, multivalued dependencies are not powerful enough. We may use, however, hierarchical dependencies.

Given a cover $X, Y_1, ..., Y_m$ of components of (R) where the sets $Y_1, ..., Y_m$ are pairwise disjoint.

The *hierarchical dependency* $X \twoheadrightarrow Y_1 \mid Y_2 \mid ... \mid Y_m$ is valid in R^C if for object $t_1, t_2, ..., t_m$ from R^C which are equal on X an object t exists in R^C for which $t[X \cup Y_i] = t_i[X \cup Y_i]$ for all $i\,(1 \leq i \leq m)$.

Obviously, if $m = 2$ the hierarchical dependency is a multivalued dependency.

The hierarchical dependency can be represented in the ER diagram. The following picture shows this representation for the case that the set X of components forms an entity type.

This star unfolding rule in Figure 4 is a very powerful rule. It leads directly to *star* or *snowflake* schemata [Thal02]. We conclude based on [Thal00]:

Corollary 1 *The star unfolding rule is sound.*

---

[1] Derivation rules are displayed in the Hilbert style, i.e. using a dividing line. The formulas (in our case the sub-schemata) above the line are the prerequisites of the rule. The formula (in our case the sub-schema) below the line represents the conclusion of the rule.

[2] Proofs of theorems in this paper are based on the classical relational theory and can be derived directly by applying classical approaches [PDGG89]. Further, the full paper is available [Thal03].

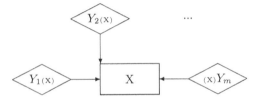

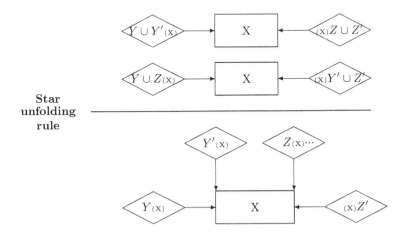

Fig. 3. The ER representation of a hierarchical dependency

Fig. 4. The star unfolding rule for hierarchical dependencies

Star unfolding provides an insight into the finest separation of types associated with a type through a set of multivalued dependencies. Based on hierarchical dependencies we can generalize the the dependency basis defined for multivalued dependencies to the dependency basis for functional, multivalued and hierarchical dependencies.

Define now $X^+ = \{ A \in U \mid \Sigma \models X \longrightarrow \{A\} \}$.

The *dependency basis* of a set Σ of functional, multivalued and hierarchical dependencies is given by

$$Dep^{M,H}(X,\Sigma) = \{ Y_i \mid \Sigma \models X \twoheadrightarrow Y_i , \; Y_i \cap X^+ = \emptyset,$$
$$\nexists Y_i' \subset Y_i (Y_i' \neq Y_i \wedge \Sigma \models X \twoheadrightarrow Y_i') \}$$
$$Dep^{M,H,F}(X,\Sigma) = Dep^M(X,\Sigma) \cup \{ X^+ \setminus X \} .$$

It defines the finest separation among components of the type.

Similar to the proof for the classical dependency basis in [Thal91] we can proof the following statement.

Proposition 2 *For any set Σ of functional, multivalued and hierarchical dependencies and any multivalued or hierarchical dependency $X \twoheadrightarrow Z_1 \mid ... \mid Z_m$, the set Σ implies $X \twoheadrightarrow Z_1 \mid ... \mid Z_r$ if and only if either $Y_i \subseteq Z_j$ or $Y_i \cap Z_j = \emptyset$ for all $i, j (1 \leq i \leq n, 1 \leq j \leq m)$ and for the dependency basis $Dep^{M,H}(X,\Sigma) = \{Y_1, ..., Y_n\}$ of X.*
Furthermore, $\Sigma \models X \longrightarrow Z$ if and only if $Z \subseteq X^+$.

3   Competing Schemata Due to MVD's

So far only local decomposition based on one component set has been investigated. Another component set may lead to another decomposition of the same type.

Example 2. *(Continuation of the running example by additional MVD's)*
{ StaffMember } ↠ { DependentPerson }|
                { Department, Project, Product, Supplier }
{ Project } ↠ { StaffMember, Department, DependentPerson }|
                { Product, Supplier }
{ Product } ↠ { Department, StaffMember, DependentPerson, Project }|
                { Supplier }
The dependency basis for StaffMember is the set
    $Dep^{M,H}($ StaffMember,$\Sigma) = \{\{$ Department $\}, \{$ DependentPerson $\},$
                { Project, Product, Supplier }}
Therefore, the following ER schema can be derived.

Staff Member Point of View

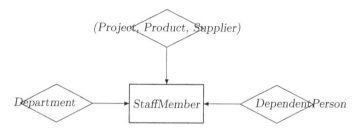

Computing the dependency basis for Project
    $Dep^{M,H}($ Product, $\Sigma) = \{\{$ Supplier $\}, \{$ StaffMember, Department,
                DependentPerson }}
we derive the point of view in the following figure:

Project Point of View

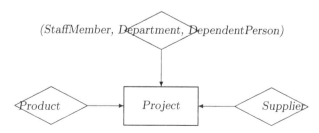

Which point is the correct one? Is there any unifying point of view? The schemata are somehow competing. Therefore, we need a *competition resolution technique*. Let us consider the reduced cover of all multivalued and hierarchical dependencies by

$$\Sigma^* = \{ X \twoheadrightarrow Y|Z \mid \Sigma \models X \twoheadrightarrow Y|Z,$$
$$X \cap Y = X \cap Z = Y \cap Z = \emptyset, \; Y \neq \emptyset, \; Z \neq \emptyset \} \quad .$$

Definition 2 *Given two partitions X, Z, V and Y, U, W of components of R. Two multivalued dependencies $X \twoheadrightarrow Z|V$ and $Y \twoheadrightarrow U|W$ from Σ are competing if*
(1) $\Sigma \not\models X \cap Y \twoheadrightarrow Z|V \cup W$ for $Z = U$ or
(2) $X \cap U \neq \emptyset$ and $X \cap W \neq \emptyset$.

Competing schemata offer different points of views. It might be the case that we find a *unifying point of view* that resolves competition. One solution for competing schemata is the introduction of an artificial separator type. [Scio81] gave it in the context of conflicting dependency bases.

Definition 3 *Given a type R and two partitions $\{X, V_1, ..., V_n, X_1, ..., X_m\}$ and $\{Y, V_1, ..., V_n, Y_1, ..., Y_k\}$ of components of R which both form a dependency basis, i.e.*
$$Dep^M(X, \Sigma) = \{V_1, ..., V_n, X_1, ..., X_m\}$$
$$Dep^M(Y, \Sigma) = \{V_1, ..., V_n, Y_1, ..., Y_k\} \; .$$
The two dependency bases are conflicting if $\Sigma \not\models X \cap Y \twoheadrightarrow \cup_{i=1}^{n} V_i$.

The solution given by [Scio81] is based on the introduction of an artificial separator type $P_{X,Y}$ into R combined with the additional functional dependencies $X \longrightarrow P_{X,Y}$ and $Y \longrightarrow P_{X,Y}$ and the hierarchical dependencies
$$(X \cap Y) \cup \{P_{X,Y}\} \twoheadrightarrow V_1|....|V_n \;,$$
$$X \cup \{P_{X,Y}\} \twoheadrightarrow V_1|....|V_n|X_1|...|X_m \quad \text{and}$$
$$Y \cup \{P_{X,Y}\} \twoheadrightarrow V_1|....|V_n|Y_1|...|Y_k \; .$$

This solution may be adequate in some cases. In most practical situations the solutions is not adequate for conceptual modeling since conceptual modeling aims in developing conceptually minimal schemata which use only types that are meaningful in the application. The solution may be however used as an implementation trick.

This idea can be however further developed. We introduce a new rule[3] displayed in the Figure 5.

Proposition 3 *The tree separation rule is sound.*

Proof sketch. First we observe that root reduction allows to derive a convenient generalized root split rule in Figure 5. Another rule that can be derived from

---

[3] The tree separation rules uses a property of the extended entity-relationship model: Entity types are of order 0, relationship types are ordered by orders 1, 2, 3,... The lowest order in any schema is 0. Therefore, the orders can be adapted whenever we wish to have a dense order.

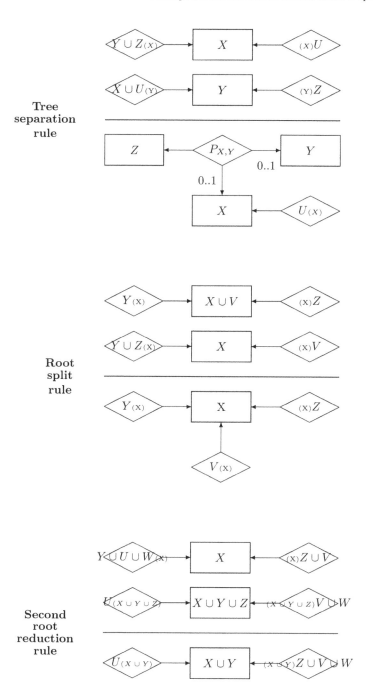

Fig. 5. Three derived rules for resolution of competition

the theory of MVD's is the second root reduction rule shows in Figure 5. The combination of the three rules proves the proposition.   □

We finally obtain a very serious argument in favor of non-competing sets of multivalued dependencies.

Theorem 2 *If a set of multivalued dependencies is not competing then there exists a unique decomposition which can be pictured entirely by a higher-order entity-relationship schema without additional multivalued or path dependencies.*

Example 3. *(Continuation of the running example)*
We can now resolve the competition among schemata. The application of the tree separation rules leads to the schema in the following picture which is the most detailed view and lies underneath of the two competing schemata discussed before. Let us use the name 'Working' for denoting the new type $P_{Product, Department\ StaffMember}$.

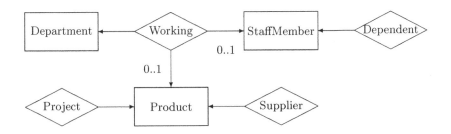

4   Approximation and Weakening of Competing Schemata

So far we considered only the case that multivalued dependency sets can be represented by a unique minimal schema. There are however cases in which competing dependency sets cannot be resolved to a unique minimal schema.

Example 4. *(Example from [LevL99]: Competing dependency set without resolution)*
Given a schema with a relationship type
    Engaged = (Employee, Project, Manager, Location, Σ)
and the multivalued dependencies
    { Employee, Manager, } $\twoheadrightarrow$ { Location } | { Project } ,
    { Project, Location } $\twoheadrightarrow$ { Employee} | { Manager} .
    The relationship type can be represented by two competing sub-schemata. The competition stresses two different points of view:

– The Engaged relationship type is differentiated by the working association and the leadership association. The last one related Mangers with employees at different project. The first one associates workers with the location and with the leadership. Additionally, the decomposition generates an inclusion constraint Works[Employee, Manager] $\subseteq \supseteq$ Leads [Employee, Manager].

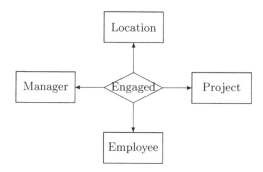

- The 'Engaged' relationship type is decomposed into the relationship types 'WorkingAt' and 'ManagingAt'. We observe the same kind of inclusion constraint WorkingAt[Project, Location] $\subseteq\supseteq$ MangagingAt [Project, Location].
  This inclusion constraint show again that the decomposition is not the most appropriate one. Second-order relationship types improve the situation.

The inclusion constraints directly lead to another decomposition which is more appropriate and much simpler to maintain. These decompositions are more appropriate and better reflect the sense of the multivalued dependencies.

We may, however, find stronger decompositions which are not entirely supported by the multivalued dependencies and weaker schemata which do not reflect the full power of the multivalued dependencies.

Definition 4 *Given a set of multivalued dependencies Σ for a relationship type R. Let*
$$weaker_M(\Sigma) = \{\ \Sigma' \subset MVD \mid \Sigma \models \Sigma' \wedge \Sigma' \not\models \Sigma \quad \text{and}$$
$$stronger_M(\Sigma) = \{\ \Sigma' \subset MVD \mid \Sigma' \models \Sigma \wedge \Sigma \not\models \Sigma'\ \}$$
the sets of weaker or stronger sets of multivalued dependencies for a set of multivalued dependencies.
 We define now the set $\underline{approx}_M(\Sigma)$ of maximal elements of $weaker_M(\Sigma)$ and the set $\overline{approx}_M(\Sigma)$ of minimal elements of $stronger_M(\Sigma)$ as approximations of Σ.

If we discover in an application sets of competing schemata then we might either stress whether

- one of the elements of $\overline{approx}_M(\Sigma)$ is valid as well (strengthening the specification) or
- one of sets in $\underline{approx}_M(\Sigma)$ can be used instead of Σ (weakening the specification).

Both approaches have their merits.

Proposition 4 *Approximations have the following regularity properties:*

- $\overline{approx}_M(\Sigma_1 \cup \Sigma_2)\ \supseteq\ \overline{approx}_M(\Sigma_1) \cup \overline{approx}_M(\Sigma)$

- $\Sigma \subseteq \Sigma'$ for some $\Sigma' \in \overline{\text{approx}}_M(\Sigma)$
- $\overline{\text{approx}}_M(\overline{\text{approx}}_M(\Sigma)) = \overline{\text{approx}}_M(\Sigma)$
- $\underline{\text{approx}}_M(\Sigma_1 \cap \Sigma_2) \subseteq \underline{\text{approx}}_M(\Sigma_1) \cup \underline{\text{approx}}_M(\Sigma)$
- $\Sigma \supseteq \underline{\Sigma'}$ for some $\Sigma' \in \underline{\text{approx}}_M(\Sigma)$
- $\underline{\text{approx}}_M(\underline{\text{approx}}_M(\Sigma)) = \underline{\text{approx}}_M(\Sigma)$

The proof is based on the properties of approximations and the monotonicity of derivable sets.   □

These regularity properties allow to weaken or strengthen one of the multivalued dependencies. Therefore, we can restrict our attention to those multivalued dependencies which do not have *strong support* or which are a bit *too strict*. This idea invokes the idea of Lukasiewicz of assigning fractional truth values to formulas and sets of formulas depending on their support. Especially, weakening leads to singleton sets of multivalued dependencies in most cases. Since the theory is rather complex in this case we demonstrate this property for second example.

Example 5. *(Resolving the example from [LevL99] by approximation)*
The example has a convincing weakening which is based on a fact-association based modeling approach [Thal00] and uses the association by relating the left-hand sides of the two multivalued dependencies.

Weakening the Set of Multivalued Dependencies
for the Point of View that Stresses Work Association

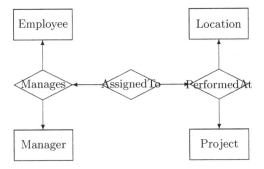

We note that the multivalued dependencies may be easily maintained by triggers in our weaker schema. Furthermore, cardinality constraints such as $card(\text{Manages}, \text{Employee}) = (1,1)$ *can easily be integrated.*

The set of upper approximations has a similar convenient property. It is characterized by strengthening one of the dependencies used in the decomposition. For instance, if we are more interested in work association then strengthening the second multivalued dependency to the functional dependency $\{\text{Project}, \text{Location}\} \longrightarrow \{\text{Manager}\}$ then we obtain a unique decomposition through applying results in the previous section.

5   Conclusion

Multivalued dependencies are a stepchild of database practice. Their specification is often error-prone. Sets of multivalued dependencies are difficult to survey and to understand.

In reality, multivalued dependencies specify **relative separation** of aspects of concern. Therefore, the most natural way to reflect them is their usage for decomposition of types in ER schemata. In this case we obtain a view on the set of multivalued dependencies that is simple and which is easy to survey, to maintain and to extend. Therefore, multivalued dependencies should be treated at the level of ER schemata rather than at the level of logical schemata.

It is an open problem whether competing schemata can be unified by critical pair resolution similar to term rewriting systems.

References

[Bisk95]   J. Biskup: Foundations of Information Systems. Vieweg, Braunschweig, 1995 (in German).

[ChNC81]   I. Chung, F. Nakamura and P.P. Chen: A Decomposition of Relations Using the Entity-Relationship Approach. Proc. ER 1981: 149–171

[LevL99]   M. Levene and G. Loizou: A Guided Tour of Relational Databases and Beyond. Springer, Berlin , 1999

[Ling85]   T.W. Ling: An Analysis of Multivalued and Join Dependencies Based on the Entity-Relationship Approach. Data and Knowledge Engineering, 1985,1: 3.

[Ling85']   T.W. Ling: A Normal Form for Entity-Relationship Diagram. Proc. 4th ER Conference, IEEE Computer Science Press, Silver Spring, 1985: 24–35.

[Mood01]   D.L. Moody: Dealing with Complexity: A Practical Method for Representing Large Entity-Relationship Models. PhD., Dept. of Information Systems, University of Melbourne, 2001

[PDGG89]   J. Paredaens, P. De Bra, M. Gyssens, and D. Van Gucht: The Structure of the Relational Database Model. Springer, Berlin, 1989.

[Scio81]   E. Sciore: Real-world MVD's. Proc. Int. Conf. on Data Management, 1981: 121–132

[Sims94]   G.C. Simsion, Data Modeling Essential – Analysis, Design, and Innovation. Van Nostrand Reinhold, New York 1994

[Thal91]   B. Thalheim: Dependencies in Relational Databases. Teubner, Leipzig, 1991

[Thal00]   B. Thalheim: Entity-Relationship Modeling – Fundamentals of Database Technology. Springer, Berlin, 2000
http://www.informatik.tu-cottbus.de/thalheim/HERM.htm

[Thal02]   B. Thalheim: Component Construction of Database Schemes. Proc. ER'02, LNCS 2503, Springer, 2002: 20–34

[Thal03]   B. Thalheim: Scrutinizing Multivalued Dependencies through the Higher-Order Entity-Relationship Model. Preprint BTU Cottbus, Informatik – 06 – 2003

Entity Types Derived by Symbol-Generating Rules

Jordi Cabot, Antoni Olivé, and Ernest Teniente

Universitat Politècnica de Catalunya
Dept. Llenguatges i Sistemes Informàtics
Jordi Girona 1-3, 08034 Barcelona (Catalonia)
{jcabot,olive,teniente}@lsi.upc.es

Abstract. We review the definition of entity types derived by symbol-generating rules. These types appear frequently in conceptual schemas. However, up to now they have received very little attention in the field of conceptual modeling of information systems. Most conceptual modeling languages, like the UML and ORM, do not allow their formal definition.
In this paper, we propose a new method for the definition of entity types derived by symbol-generating rules. Our method is based on the fact that these types can always be expressed as the result of the reification of a derived relationship type. Many languages, like the UML and ORM, allow defining derived relationship types and, at the same time, provide support for reification. Using our method, these languages can directly deal with those derived entity types.

1 Introduction

A fundamental principle that governs the contents of conceptual schemas is the well-known "100 Percent" (or completeness) principle, which states that "All relevant general static and dynamic aspects, i.e. all rules, laws, etc., of the universe of discourse should be described in the conceptual schema" [6]. The relevant "aspects" include, among others, derived entity and relationship types and their derivation rules. Many conceptual modeling languages provide constructs for the definition of those rules.

Most derived entity types are defined by what may be called "symbol-preserving" rules. The name comes from the object-oriented database field, in which a distinction is made between "object-preserving" and "object-generating" views. The former are those that only extract objects from existing classes, while the latter are those that create new objects [3]. For example, if *Person* is an entity type derived by the union of *Man* and *Woman*, then the derivation rule is "symbol preserving" because the symbols in the information base (IB) that denote people are the same as those that denote men or women. The rule does not create new symbols in the IB.

However, there are many derived entity types whose rule is not "symbol-preserving", but "symbol-generating". A typical example may be *PurchaseOrder*. Assuming that an information system must generate automatically a purchase order for a product to a vendor when the product satisfies some condition (quantity on hand below reorder level, etc.) then *PurchaseOrder* is derived, and its rule is "symbol-generating". The symbols in the IB that denote purchase orders are quite distinct from

I.-Y. Song et al. (Eds.): ER 2003, LNCS 2813, pp. 376–389, 2003.

those used to denote products or vendors. The rule must "invent" symbols for the purchase orders it derives.

Most conceptual modeling languages, including the UML [11, 9] and ORM [5], do not allow defining entity types derived by symbol-generating rules. In these languages, designers must define those types as base ones since the rules cannot be defined declaratively in a single place of the schema. For this reason, the designer must determine which external events (operations, transactions) may change the value of the condition (from true to false, or the other way around) and ensure that their effects include the generation or deletion of the corresponding entities.

In the previous example, the events that may change the value of the condition are those that reduce the quantity on hand, increase the reorder level, etc. The effects of these events must include checking whether the resulting state changes the value of the condition and, if it is so, generating the corresponding instances of *PurchaseOrder*.

One of the few conceptual modeling languages that deal with symbol-preserving and symbol-generating rules is ERCLog [13,14], a logic language based on ERC+ [12]. In ERCLog, both entity and relationship types can be derived by the two kinds of rules. The rules are distinguished by syntactical criteria.

The main contribution of this paper is a new method that allows defining derived entity types with symbol-generating rules, in languages that do not admit such rules. The method can be used in any conceptual modeling language that allows defining derived relationship types, and that allows the reification of relationship types [8]. Both the UML and ORM meet these requirements: associations and attributes can be derived, their derivation rules can be defined easily in a particular language (OCL in the UML, ConQuer in ORM) and association classes are the construct used to reify associations.

The rationale of our method is that a derived entity type, whose derivation rule is symbol-generating, can always be defined as the result of the reification of a derived relationship type. Therefore, if a language allows defining derived relationship types and their reification, then –using our method- the own language (without any extension) allows also defining derived entity types with symbol-generating rules. As a consequence, there is no need to develop nor to extend a graphical tool to support them since they can be defined already in any CASE tool available for these languages.

The main advantage of our method is its simplicity since it is based on the use of reification, a classical and well-known conceptual modeling construct, and it does not require to extend a language with a new construct (like a new kind of derivation rule).

The structure of the paper is as follows. The next section introduces basic concepts and notation used throughout the paper. Section 3, based on [10], defines, in logic, the concept of entity type derived by a symbol-generating rule. Section 4 reviews, also in the logic language, the concept of reification and shows that any entity type derived by a symbol-generating rule can be expressed as the reification of a relationship type. Section 5 applies this result to the UML and ORM languages. Finally, we present our conclusions and point out future work in Section 6.

2 Basic Concepts

We assume that entities and relationships are instances of their types at particular time points [2], which are expressed in a common base time unit such as second or day. We make this assumption for the sake of generality, but our work is also applicable when a temporal view is not needed.

We represent by $E(e,t)$ the fact entity e is instance of entity type E at time t. For instance, *Employee(Marta,D1)* means that *Marta* is an instance of *Employee* at time *D1* (day in this case). The population of E at t is defined as the set of entities that are instances of E at t.

A relationship type has a name and a set of n participants, with $n \geq 2$. A *participant* is an entity type that plays a certain role in the relationship type. $R(p_1{:}E_1,...,p_n{:}E_n)$ denotes a relationship type named R with entity type participants $E_1,...,E_n$ playing the roles $p_1,...,p_n$, respectively.

We say that $R(p_1{:}E_1,...,p_n{:}E_n)$ is the *schema* of the relationship type and that $p_1{:}E_1$, ..., $p_n{:}E_n$ are their participants. The order of the participants in the schema is irrelevant. Two different participants may be of the same entity type, but two different participants may not have the same role. When the role name is omitted, it is assumed to be the same as the corresponding entity type.

We represent by $R(e_1,...,e_n,t)$ the fact that entities $e_1,...,e_n$ participate in an instance of R at time t. The referential integrity constraints associated with R guarantee that e_1, ..., e_n are instance of their corresponding types $E_1,...,E_n$.

3 Entity Types Derived by Symbol-Generating Rules

This section formalizes entity types derived by symbol-generating rules in temporal conceptual models of information systems and extends our work presented in [10] in two different directions. First, we compare entity types derived by symbol-generating rules with object-generating views in object-oriented databases. Second, we state the inconveniences of not specifying explicitly such derived entity types.

We introduce entity types derived by symbol-generating rules by means of an example aimed at issuing automatically purchase orders for products. Assume that we have entity types *Product* and *PurchaseOrder*. Clearly, the symbols that denote purchase orders are different from those that denote products. Moreover, entity type *PurchaseOrder* can be derived from *Product* and *Date* if we assume that one purchase order is generated at a date when the quantity on hand of the product is below its reorder level at some moment of the date. To keep the example simple, we assume that all purchase orders are generated in this way.

Then, *PurchaseOrder* can be formally defined by means of the symbol-generating rule:

$$\exists!o \ (PurchaseOrder(o,t) \wedge HasPurchase(o,p,t) \wedge IssuedAt(o,d,t)) \leftrightarrow$$

$$Product(p,t) \wedge QuantityOnHand(p,nq,t) \wedge ReorderLevel(p,nr,t) \wedge nq{<}nr \wedge date(t){=}d$$

The right part of the rule defines the identifiers (p,d) for which there is one (and only one) purchase order (o). Moreover, it includes the necessary conditions to generate purchase orders. The entity fact *PurchaseOrder(o,t)* states that o is a symbol representing a purchase order at time *t*. *HasPurchase(PurchaseOrder,Product)* states the correspondence between products and purchase orders while the one among dates and purchase orders is represented by *IssuedAt(PurchaseOrder, Date)*, as shown in Fig. 1. We underline entity types derived by symbol-generating rules to graphically distinguish them from other entity types.

Fig. 1. Automatic generation of purchase orders for a product

Note that *HasPurchase(PurchaseOrder, Product)* and *IssuedAt(PurchaseOrder, Date)* is a compound reference [5] for *PurchaseOrder*. This means that a given product (*p*) and date (*d*) identify a purchase order (*o*).

Formally, if relationship types $R_1(E,E_1)$, ..., $R_n(E,E_n)$ are a compound reference for entity type *E*, and *E* is derived by a symbol-generating rule, then the conceptual schema must include a rule with the general form:

$$\exists! e \; (E(e,t) \land R_1(e,e_1,t) \land ... \land R_n(e,e_n,t)) \leftrightarrow \varphi(e_1,...,e_n,t)$$

The right part of the rule gives the identifiers $e_1,...,e_n$ of entities instance of $E_1,...,E_n$. The left part gives the entities *e*, instance of *E*, that must be generated, and the relationships between them and the identifiers.

In the particular case of n=1, $R_1(E,E_1)$ is a simple reference [7, pp 186+] for *E* and, therefore, the instances of *E* may be identified just by the instances of E_1.

We call the previous rule symbol-generating because, to maintain a model of such a domain, the information system must generate symbols for the instances of the derived entity type *PurchaseOrder*. Note that the symbol *o* appearing in the left part of the symbol-generating rule does not appear in the right part.

There is a close relationship between symbol-generating rules and "object-generating" views in object-oriented databases, although the latter do not consider a temporal perspective. First, both define new objects from existing objects. Second, both can be syntactically recognized because the symbol used to represent the defined objects appears only in one part of the rule (in the head of object-generating views; in the left part in our case). Third, both define the relationships between the defined entities and their external identifiers (explicitly in the left part of the rule in our case; implicitly as attributes of the view in object-oriented databases).

The information system can choose any symbol to represent symbol-generating derived entities, provided that they are immutable and new. By *immutable* we mean that the identifiers $e_1,...,e_n$ always refer to the same entity *e*. This is captured by the formal condition:

$$R_1(e,e_1,t_i) \land ... \land R_n(e,e_n,t_i) \land R_1(e',e_1,t_j) \land ... \land R_n(e',e_n,t_j) \rightarrow e = e'$$

The condition of immutable symbols is required also by most of the oid generation mechanisms used in object-generating views. For instance, [14, p. 270] requires the oid to be tied to the values where it comes from so that if the same values are used again, the result will be the same oid.

By *new*, we mean that the information system must generate symbols not used previously by other entities. Formally:

$$E(e,t_i) \wedge \neg \exists t_{before}(E(e,t_{before}) \wedge t_{before} < t_i) \rightarrow \neg \exists t_j(Entity(e,t_j) \wedge t_j < t_i)$$

where *Entity* is the supertype of all entity types. The condition states that if t_i is the first time that e is instance of E, then e cannot be instance of any entity type before t_i. Note that those conditions also apply to the symbols chosen to represent base entity types.

Fig. 2 shows a more complex example which extends the previous one by defining products as an entity type derived by a symbol-generating rule. *Group* and *Store* are base entity types. Group products are sold at stores. If we assume that a store sells only all products belonging to its groups, *ProductInStore* may be defined by means of the following symbol-generating rule:

$$\exists! ps\ (ProductInStore(ps,t) \wedge IsOf(ps,p,t) \wedge IsIn(ps,s,t))$$
$$\leftrightarrow Group(g,t) \wedge BelongsTo(p,g,t) \wedge SoldAt(g,s,t)$$

Now, *PurchaseOrder* may be derived as in the previous example but considering *ProductInStore* instead of *Product* in its symbol-generating rule.

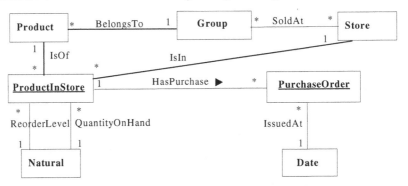

Fig. 2. ProductInStore and PurchaseOrder are derived by symbol-generating rules

If entity types derived by symbol-generating rules are not defined as such in a conceptual schema but as base entity types, the designer must determine which external events (operations, transactions) may change the value of the condition (from true to false, or the other way around) and ensure that their effects include the generation or deletion of the corresponding entities.

In the example of Fig. 2, several events may change the values of the condition of any of the rules that define the derived entity types:

- Including a new product in a group
- Removing a product from a group
- Changing the group of a product
- (Des)assigning a group to a store
- Increasing the reorder level
- Selling a product.

To define a complete specification, the effects of all these events must include checking whether the resulting state changes the value of the condition and, if it is so, generating the corresponding instances of ProductInStore and/or PurchaseOrder.

For instance, if *PurchaseOrder* is defined as a base entity type the contract of the operation *SellProduct (p-code:String, store-name:String, n-units: integer)* should be the following:

Operation: SellProduct   (p-code:String,   store-name:String,   n-units:integer):
              Boolean

Pre:

Post: 1.If there is no ProductInStore for the given product p-code at the given store store-name or if it exists but its quantity on hand is lower than n-units, then the operation is invalid and it returns false.

        2.Otherwise, the operation is valid and it returns true. Moreover:

            2.1 The Quantity on Hand of ProductInStore is reduced in n-units units.

            2.2 If the new value of Quantity on Hand is below its ReorderLevel and no PurchaseOrder of the ProductInStore exists for the current date, then a new PurchaseOrder is created.

Similar modifications, and even more complex, should also be performed on the other operations.

We see at least two important drawbacks regarding the definition of entity types derived by symbol-generating rules as base entity types. The first one is the difficulty to ensure that the designer performs all required changes in the contracts and that performs them correctly. The second one relies on the difficulty of changing the definition of those entity types if it evolves through time since we should change all operation contracts taking care of its contents instead of changing only the rule that defines them. We believe that these reasons are enough to justify the definition of entity types derived by symbol-generating rules as such in conceptual modelling.

4   Entity Types Obtained by Relationship Reification

We find many entity types derived by symbol-generating rules in real domains. In particular, an entity type obtained as a reification of a relationship type can also be regarded as a derived entity type with a symbol-generating rule as we will show in this section.

4.1   Relationship Reification

Relationship reification applies to an *n*-ary ($n \geq 2$) relationship type $R(E_1,...,E_n)$ and produces a new entity type E, and a set of n intrinsic relationship types $R_i(E,E_i)$, ($i = 1,...,n$), which connect instances of E with the n participant entities in the instances of R. Moreover, there is a one-to-one correspondence between the populations of R and E at any time t since there is an entity $E(e,t)$ for each relationship $R(e_1,...,e_n,t)$.

An example is given in Fig. 3, where the entity type *Enrolment* is defined as a reification of the base relationship type *EnrolledIn(Student,Subject)*.

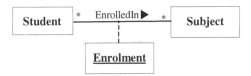

Fig. 3. Enrolment as a reification of a base relationship type

In temporal conceptual models, a student *st* may be enrolled in a certain subject *sub* during different time intervals. For instance, John can be enrolled in Medieval History from 1/2/2001 to 1/7/2001 and from 1/9/2001 to 1/2/2002.

The time-varying instances of a relationship type may be reified in three different ways [8]: reification per instant, reification per classification interval and reification per life span, the latter two being the most useful and usual ones.

Intuitively, reification per interval reifies a relationship *r* into a different entity *e* for each temporal interval in which *r* holds. In this way, the two previous enrolments of John in Medieval History would be different entities and, thus, be identified by two different symbols.

On the other hand, reification per life span reifies a relationship *r* into a single entity *e*, which is the same during the whole life span of *r*. In this case, both enrolments of John in Medieval History would be identified by the same symbol.

Given a relationship type $R(p_1{:}E_1,...,p_n{:}E_n)$ and an entity type $E(e,t)$ obtained as a reification of *R*, the one-to-one correspondence between the populations of *R* and *E* at any time *t* can be formally specified by means of the following symbol-generating rule:

$$\exists! e\ E(e,t) \leftrightarrow R(e_1,...,e_n,t)$$

This rule follows the general form of symbol-generating rules except that the relationships between the entities *e* that are generated and their compound reference $R_1(e,e_1,t), ..., R_n(e,e_n,t)$ are not explicitly stated in its left part. Note, however, that no information is lost since these relationships are already implicitly provided by the *n* intrinsic relationship types required by the reification.

As before, the information system can choose any symbol to represent the entities that are generated by the previous rule. The particular approach we apply to generate these symbols will make us follow a certain type of temporal reification. We will have reification per life span if the system generates always the same symbol for each compound reference, and we will have reification per interval if the system generates a different symbol for each temporal interval in which the relationship *R* among the entities defining the compound reference holds.

The same ideas can be applied to entity types obtained as a reification of a derived relationship type. For instance, we could specify the tickets that a theatre may sell in terms of the seat numbers of the theatre, its sessions, and the dates in which it is opened. This information may be captured by means of the derived relationship type *HasTicket(Theater,Date,Session,SeatNumber)* that can be defined by means of the following rule (to simplify the example, we assume that seats in a theatre are identified with a single number):

$$HasTicket(th,d,s,num,t) \leftrightarrow Theater(th,t) \wedge HasSession(th,s,t) \wedge NumSeats(th,n,t)$$
$$\wedge\ OpensOn(th,d,t) \wedge Natural(num) \wedge num{>}0 \wedge num{<}{=}n$$

In general we will require to reify the derived relationship type *HasTicket* to specify additional information regarding the tickets that theatres may sell (like whether they are sold or not, the method of payment, etc.). We show this reification in Fig. 4. We distinguish derived relationship types by means of a slash in front of its name.

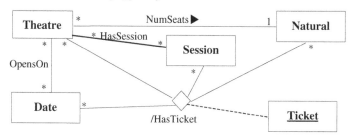

Fig. 4. Theatre tickets as a reification of a derived relationship type

The population of *Ticket* can be computed from the population of *HasTicket* by means of the rule:

$$\exists!k \; Ticket(k,t) \leftrightarrow HasTicket(th,s,d,num,t)$$

To specify a derived relationship type $R(p_1{:}E_1,...,p_n{:}E_n)$ and the entity type $E(e,t)$ obtained as a reification of R, we require two different rules: a rule to define R and a symbol-generating rule to specify the one-to-one correspondence between the populations of R and E at any time t. Formally, they can be respectively defined as:

$$R(e_1,...,e_n,t) \leftrightarrow \varphi(e_1,...,e_n,t)$$
$$\exists!e \; E(e,t) \leftrightarrow R(e_1,...,e_n,t)$$

4.2 Entity Types Derived by Symbol-Generating Rules vs Reification

Once we have seen that entity types obtained by reification can be regarded also as entity types derived by symbol-generating rules, we may wonder about the existing differences and similarities between these two different kinds of entity types.

It is not difficult to see that any entity type obtained by reification of a derived relationship type can also be specified as a non-reified entity type derived by a symbol-generating rule. Intuitively, this can be done by using the formula that defines the derived relationship type in the symbol-generating rule of the non-reified entity type, and by making explicit in this rule the intrinsic relationships that are implicit in the reification construct.

Formally, if we have a reification of a derived relationship type defined by the rules:

$$R(e_1,...,e_n,t) \leftrightarrow \varphi(e_1,...,e_n,t)$$
$$\exists!e \; E(e,t) \leftrightarrow R(e_1,...,e_n,t)$$

with the n intrinsic relationship types $R_1(E,E_1,t), ..., R_n(E,E_n,t)$, we can define $E(e,t)$ as a non-reified entity type by means of the following symbol-generating rule:

$$\exists!e \; (E(e,t) \wedge R_1(e,e_1,t) \wedge ... \wedge R_n(e,e_n,t)) \leftrightarrow \varphi(e_1,...,e_n,t)$$

As an example we apply this transformation to show that the entity type *Ticket*, as defined in Fig. 4, can also be stated as a non-reified entity type derived by a symbol-generating rule. The graphical representation of this example is given in Fig. 5 and the rule we obtain is:

$\exists!ti$ (Ticket(ti,t) $\land$ BelTo(ti,th,t) $\land$ HasNum(ti,n,t) $\land$ Of(ti,s,t) $\land$ AtDate(ti,d,t) $\leftrightarrow$
    Theater(th,t) $\land$ HasSession(th,s,t) $\land$ NumSeats(th,n,t) $\land$ OpensOn(th,d,t) $\land$
    Natural(num) $\land$ num>0 $\land$ num<=n

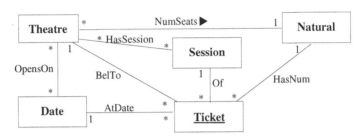

Fig. 5. Theatre tickets are derived by a symbol-generating rule

In a similar way, entity types obtained by reification of a base relationship type may be specified as non-reified entity types derived by symbol-generating rules.

Moreover, non-reified entity types derived by symbol-generating rules with a compound reference can be specified by reification of a derived relationship type. Intuitively, we must create a new derived relationship type having as participants the entity types that form the compound reference and whose derivation rule is defined by the formula of the symbol-generating rule. The reification of this relationship type will correspond to the initial non-reified entity type.

Formally, if we have an entity type $E(e,t)$ derived by the symbol-generating rule:

$\exists!e$ (E(e,t) $\land$ R$_1$(e,e$_1$,t) $\land$ ... $\land$ R$_n$(e,e$_n$,t)) $\leftrightarrow$ φ(e$_1$,...,e$_n$,t) with n $\geq$ 2

we can define $E(e,t)$ as an entity type obtained by reification of a new derived relationship type $R(e_1,...,e_n,t)$ by considering the following two rules:

R(e$_1$,...,e$_n$,t) $\leftrightarrow$ φ(e$_1$,...,e$_n$,t)
$\exists!e$ E(e,t) $\leftrightarrow$ R(e$_1$,...,e$_n$,t)

As an example, consider the conceptual schema of Fig. 1 where *PurchaseOrder* was a non-reified entity type. Fig. 6 defines it as a reification of a derived relationship type.

We need the following rule to define the derived relationship type *PurchasedAt*:

PurchasedAt(p,d,t) $\leftrightarrow$ Product(p,t) $\land$ QuantityOnHand(p,nq,t) $\land$
    ReorderLevel(p,nr,t) $\land$ nq<nr $\land$ date(t)=d

The reification of this relationship type defines the entity type *PurchaseOrder*, as given by the following symbol-generating rule:

$\exists!o$ PurchaseOrder(o, t) $\leftrightarrow$ PurchasedAt(p,d,t)

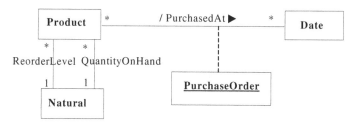

Fig. 6. *PurhcaseOrder* as an entity type defined by reification

In the particular case of non-reified entity types identified by a simple reference, we cannot naturally transform them into a reified entity type since we need at least two references to define a derived relationship type (unless the modeling language we use supports unary relationship types).

To overcome this limitation, if $R_i(E,E_i)$ is a simple reference for E, we may create a new recursive derived relationship type R by connecting each entity of E_i with itself. The reification of this new relationship type R specifies the same concept as the initial non-reified entity type E. Formally, if we have an entity type $E(e,t)$ derived by the symbol-generating rule:

$$\exists!e\ (E(e,t) \wedge R_i(e,e_i,t)) \leftrightarrow \varphi(e_i,t)$$

we can define E as an entity type obtained by reification of a new derived relationship type R by considering the following two rules:

$$R(e_i,e_i,t) \leftrightarrow \varphi(e_i,t)$$
$$\exists!e\ E(e,t) \leftrightarrow R(e_i,e_i,t)$$

We illustrate this transformation by means of a simple example, shown in Fig. 7, of an information system that must issue automatically invoices once the orders for goods are satisfied.

Fig. 7. Relationship type InvoicedBy is a simple reference for Invoice

Invoice is a derived entity type defined by the rule:

$$\exists!inv\ (Invoice(inv,t) \wedge InvoicedBy(inv,ord,t)\ ) \leftrightarrow SatisfiedOrder(ord,t)$$

We can define *Invoice* as a reification of a derived relationship type (see Fig. 8) if we consider the following rules:

$$RelatedToItself(ord,ord,t) \leftrightarrow SatisfiedOrder(ord,t)$$
$$\exists!inv\ Invoice(inv,t) \leftrightarrow RelatedToItself(ord,ord,t)$$

Fig. 8. Invoice as a reification of a derived relationship type

From the previous discussion we may conclude that entity types derived by symbol-generating rules can always be defined as a reification of a derived relationship type. This allows to define those derived entity types as such and, at the same time, to model them by means of a well-known construct, reification, that has shown to be very useful in conceptual modeling and many languages provide specific constructs for modeling it.

5 Defining Entity Types Derived by Symbol-Generating Rules

Most conceptual modeling languages do not support entity types derived by symbol-generating rules. Nevertheless, we have just seen that these entity types can be always specified as a reification of a derived relationship type. Therefore, if a language allows defining derived relationship types and its reification, then –using our method– the language itself allows also to define derived entity types with symbol-generating rules, without requiring any extension to the language.

In this section we describe how to apply this idea to two widely used conceptual modeling languages: the UML and ORM.

5.1 Entity Types Derived by Symbol-Generating Rules in the UML

In the UML metamodel, reification is specified by means of the *AssociationClass* metaclass. An association class is a single model element that inherits from both the *Class* and the *Association* metaclasses [9, p.2-22]. Thus, it represents at the same time the relationship type and the reified entity type. It is drawn using a class symbol attached by a dashed line to an association path. It has a unique name, which can be placed either in the association part or in the class part.

A derived model element is defined in the UML metamodel as a model element with the tag derived (tag defined in the metaclass *ModelElement*) set to true. Graphically, UML distinguishes derived from non-derived elements by placing a slash in front of the name of the derived ones.

The derivation relationship between the derived element and its providers is specified by an abstraction dependency (instance of the *Abstraction* metaclass) with the stereotype <<derive>>. The *Abstraction* metaclass has an attribute called *Mapping* where the computation of the derived element is specified [9, pp. 2-18].

The correspondence among the population of the derived relationship type R and its reification E (which is given by the rule $\exists! e\, E(e,t) \leftrightarrow R(e_1,...,e_n,t)$) does not need to be specified in the UML because, in this language, an association class is a single model element that represents both the relationship type and the reified entity type. That is, the previous rule is not needed because it is already enforced by the UML metamodel.

As a conclusion, we may say that to represent entity types derived by symbol-generating rules in the UML we only have to specify the derived relationship type, together with its derivation rule, and to reify it. The UML does not restrict the derivation rule to be expressed in any particular language although the OCL is probably the most popular one. We must also note that, since the UML is not a temporal language, the reification will necessarily be reification per classification interval [8].

Fig. 9 shows how to define in the UML the *ProductInStore* entity type we have presented in Fig. 2.

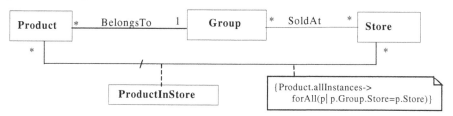

Fig. 9. *ProductInStore* in the UML

A more complex example is shown in Fig. 10, where the entity type *Ticket* (see Fig. 4) is defined as the reification of a quaternary relationship type.

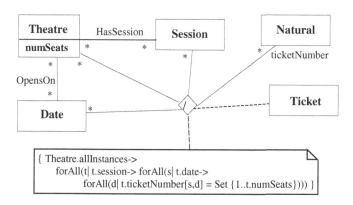

Fig. 10. *Ticket* in the UML

5.2 Entity Types Derived by Symbol-Generating Rules in ORM

In a similar way, we can define this kind of entity types in ORM, Object Role Modeling [5], since ORM supports both the reification (*nesting* according to ORM terminology) of a relationship type and the definition of derived relationship types.

In ORM, reification can be considered as an instance of the *ObjectifiedRelationship* object type [4], a single model element that corresponds to a metaclass according to our terminology and that represents both the relationship type and the reified entity type (which is called *objectified relationship* or *nested object type* in ORM). A reified entity type is depicted in ORM by a rounded rectangle around the relationship type.

Moreover, the derivation rule of a derived relationship type is specified using ConQuer [1], an ORM conceptual query language. Derived relationship types are distinguished graphically in ORM by means of an asterisk placed besides them.

As it happens in the UML, we do not need to explicitly specify in ORM the correspondence among the population of the derived relationship type *R* and its reification *E* because it is already enforced by the ORM metamodel.

To summarize, to represent entity types derived by symbol-generating rules in ORM we only have to specify the new derived relationship type, together with its derivation rule, and reify it. As an example, Fig. 11 shows the specification in ORM of the entity type *ProductInStore*.

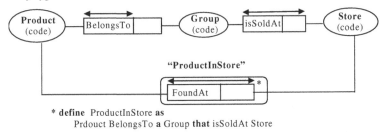

* define ProductInStore **as**
         Prdouct BelongsTo **a** Group **that** isSoldAt Store

Fig 11. ProductInStore in ORM

6   Conclusions and Further Work

We have reviewed the formal definition of entity types derived by symbol-generating rules and we have seen that they appear frequently in conceptual schemas. However, up to now they have received very little attention in the field of conceptual modeling of information systems and very few languages provide modeling support for them. The consequence is that designers cannot define declaratively the rules in the schema, and that they are forced to define those types as base, and to handle the evolution of their population (insertions, deletions) as part of the effects of the relevant external events.

We have shown, formally, that entity types derived by symbol-generating rules can be expressed as the reification of a derived relationship type. This fact is the main result of our paper, and the basis of our method. We believe that the method has great interest because many conceptual modeling languages, including the UML and ORM, allow the definition of derived relationship types and, at the same time, provide support for reification. Using our method, these languages can deal perfectly with those derived entity types, without requiring any extension.

We have not sketched the issues that arise in the object-oriented design of the reifications obtained by our method. This is a direction in which our work should be continued. The ideal would be a procedure able to transform automatically a reification of a derived relationship type in a conceptual schema into an equivalent, efficient and easy to implement, construct in an object-oriented design.

Acknowledgements. We would like to thank Dolors Costal, Cristina Gómez and Maria Ribera Sancho for their many useful comments to previous drafts of this paper.

This work has been partially supported by the Ministerio de Ciencia y Tecnologia and FEDER under project TIC2002-00744.

References

1. A.C. Bloesch, T.A. Halpin, Conceptual Queries using ConQuer-II, 16th Int. Conf. on Conceptual Modeling (ER'97), LNCS 1331, Springer, pp. 113–126
2. J.A. Bubenko jr, The Temporal Dimension in Information Modelling. In Architecture and Models in Data Base Management Systems. North-Holland, 1977, pp. 93–113.
3. G. Guerrini, E. Bertino, B. Catania, J. Garcia-Molina, A Formal View of Object-Oriented Database Systems, Theory and Practice of Object Systems (TAPOS), 3(3), 1997, pp. 157–183.
4. T.A. Halpin, An ORM Metamodel, Journal of Conceptual Modeling, 16, October 2000.
5. T.A. Halpin, Information Modeling and Relational Databases, Morgan Kaufmann, 2001.
6. ISO/TC97/SC5/WG3. "Concepts and Terminology for the Conceptual Schema and Information Base", J.J. van Griethuysen (ed.), March.
7. J. Martin, J.J. Odell, Object-Oriented Methods: A Foundation, Prentice Hall, 1995.
8. A. Olivé, Relationship Reification: A Temporal View, in: M. Jarke, A. Oberweis (Eds.), 11th International Conference on Advanced Information Systems Engineering (CAiSE'99), LNCS 1626, Springer, pp. 396–410.
9. OMG. "Unified Modeling Language Specification", Version 1.4, September 2001
10. A. Olivé, E. Teniente, Derived Types and Taxonomic Constraints in Conceptual Modeling, Information Systems, 27(6), 2002, pp. 391–409.
11. J. Rumbaugh, I. Jacobson, G. Booch, The Unified Modeling Language Reference Manual, Addison-Wesley, 1999.
12. S. Spaccapietra, C. Parent, ERC+: an object based entity relationship approach, in Conceptual Modeling, Database and CASE: An Integrated View of Information Systems Development, John Wiley, 1992.
13. X. Ye, C. Parent, S. Spaccapietra, On the Specification of Views in DOOD Systems, 4th Int. Conf. on Deductive and Object-Oriented Databases (DOOD), LNCS 1013, Springer, 1995, pp. 539–556.
14. X. Ye, C. Parent, S. Spaccapietra, View Definition and Positioning in DOOD Systems, Journal of Systems Integration, 7, 1997, pp. 263–290.

DAISY, an RER Model Based Interface for RDB to ILP

Keiko Shimazu[1], Atsuhito Momma[1], and Koichi Furukawa[2]

[1] Information Media Laboratory, Corporate Research Group, Fuji Xerox Co., Ltd.
430 Sakai, Nakai-machi, Ashigarakami-gun, Kanagawa 259-0157 Japan
{Keiko.Shimazu,Atsuhito.Momma}@fujixerox.co.jp
[2] Graduate School of Media and Governance, Keio University
5322 Endo, Fujisawa-shi, Kanagawa 252-8520 Japan
furukawa@sfc.keio.ac.jp

Abstract. In this paper, we propose an RER (Refined-Entity-Relationship) model, an extension of the ER (Entity-Relationship) model, which has an added feature of each entity attribute as well as each relationship being one indicating whether it can be derived from others or not. The purpose of an RER model is to apply ILP (Inductive Logic Programming), one of the most expressive machine-learning algorithms, to data mining by directly connecting RDB (relational databases) and ILP systems. We believe that the interface based on our model enables to easily make ILP systems access RDB in order to realize a powerful data mining system incorporating ILP. We examined the accuracy of the interface with benchmark data for evaluation of learning algorithms in artificial intelligence fields. Further, we tested our model on an email database to be supplied to an ILP system called PROGOL which in turn successfully derived a set of rules to assign each newly arrived email to the most suitable classification class based on its contents.

1 Introduction

Application of data mining to real-world data has drawn a great deal of attention. Data mining techniques acquire regularities and rules among data that cannot be discovered without trial-and-error of complicated database operations [8]. From the 1990s, a series of research achievements have been reported from such fields as statistics, database management, and machine learning. Accordingly, machine-learning systems are often employed as a data-mining engine. Among them, Inductive Logic Programming, or ILP for short, systems are effective for inducing rules from qualitative and structural data.

However, most applications of machine learning algorithms to data mining were based on propositional logic. Representative examples are decision tree induction algorithms such as C4.5, which have been widely applied to the financial industry as the basis of practical systems [2]. ILP have been applied to only a few business databases until now, despite its expressiveness [11, 4, 22, 20, 6, 7].

In this study, we propose a method to convert a database to ILP input files by capturing qualitative and structural aspects of data by means of semantic data. Our method is based on the ER (Entity Relationship) model [5], a popular data modeling method.

I.-Y. Song et al. (Eds.): ER 2003, LNCS 2813, pp. 390–404, 2003.
© Springer-Verlag Berlin Heidelberg 2003

From a database design perspective, there are two types of data models: a syntactic model and a semantic model [12]. Syntactic models include the relational model and the network model, while the ER model is a kind of semantic models. Recently, many CASE tools to automatically convert ER-model data to relational-model data have been developed, pursuing practical database design. This proves the semantic expressiveness of the ER model in representing information structure and its qualification as a framework to share common understanding of system requirements between users and designers [17].

The ER model is suitable for ILP systems since the expressive power of the model is potentially rich enough for ILP systems. Based on observations, we developed an RER model, an enhancement of the ER model, and adopted it to database representation. The RER model is an extended ER model which has an added feature of each entity attribute as well as each relationship, being one indicating whether it can be derived from others or not. As a result, it enabled input data identification for Progol, a representative ILP system.

We developed an interface that connects Progol with database systems, based on the RER model. Here, Progol is selected as the data-mining engine. This interface corresponds to the automation of the preprocessing step in the KDD process [8]. We also examined the practicality of our method by incorporating the interface into an expert system in an enterprise as a module.

The remainder of this paper is structured as follows. Section 2 summarizes related work on an ILP system and its interface to RDB. Section 3 introduces an RER model. Section 4 explains our DAISY's algorithms while Section 5 reports on an examination of them. Section 6 demonstrates our application of DAISY to a practical system. Finally, Section 7 presents conclusions and future directions.

2 Preliminary and Related Work

2.1 Inductive Logic Programming

ILP (Inductive Logic Programming) is a machine-learning algorithm that conducts inductive learning based on predicate logic. ILP is allowed to define relationships among predicates relevant to a target concept and to utilize them as background knowledge. Many propositional logic-based machine-learning systems generate classification trees in the form of a decision tree. While these systems are able to employ relational data without preprocessing, their acceptable data structure is limited to a single two-dimensional relational table. By contrast, ILP systems are able to induce rules from multiple two-dimensional relational tables, and are effective in extracting meaningful features by taking advantage of complex structures in the target domains.

However, decision tree induction algorithms, such as C4.5, tend to be employed in mining applications. Their popularity has not faded even though the application domain is limited to classification problems and input is limited to a single relation. Although it has a wide range of application domains in the experimental stage due to its expressiveness, applications of ILP to business domains are still limited. The difficulty in generating input files for ILP systems prevents their applications across a wide range of real-world domains. Figure 1 shows an input file example for PROGOL, which is one of the most powerful ILP systems.

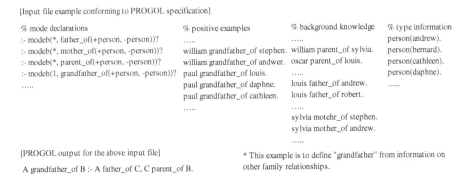

[Input file example conforming to PROGOL specification]

% mode declarations
:- modeb(*, father_of(+person, -person))?
:- modeb(*, mother_of(+person, -person))?
:- modeb(*, parent_of(+person, -person))?
:- modeh(1, grandfather_of(+person, -person))?
......

% positive examples
.....
william grandfather_of stephen.
william grandfather_of andwer.
paul grandfather_of louis.
paul grandfather_of daphne.
paul grandfather_of cathleen.
.....

% background knowledge
.....
william parent_of sylvia.
oscar parent_of louis.
.....
louis father_of andrew.
louis father_of robert.
.....
sylvia motehr_of stephen.
sylvia mother_of andrew.
.....

% type information
person(andrew).
person(bernard).
person(cathleen).
person(daphne).
.....

[PROGOL output for the above input file]

A grandfather_of B :- A father_of C, C parent_of B.

* This example is to define "grandfather" from information on other family relationships.

Fig. 1. Input File for PROGOL and Its Output

2.2 ILP-RDB Interface

To reduce the burden of generating input files for ILP systems, studies on methods to automatically deliver database contents to ILP systems have been variously conducted. Among them, we believe that a series of studies by Morik et al. [3, 9, 10] are predominant. They have proposed an interpreter that directly accesses data in relational databases in each hypothesis evaluation.

By contrast, we employed a compiler-based approach that converts a database into an ILP input file in preprocessing. Our method enables utilization of semantic information in a database during the conversion by means of an extension of an ER model. The advantages of our methods are twofold: (1) it is able to generate unique input files for the ILP system from a specific database, despite variations in database design, and (2) its generalized approach is applicable to future advanced ILP systems, not limited to a specific ILP system.

3 RER Model

3.1 Equivalence of ER Expression to ILP Input File

Our method is designed by taking qualitative and structural aspects of databases into account when converting them to ILP input files. As a basis for our method, we adopted an ER model [5], a representative data modeling method. Since it has been proven to be possible to convert an ER model to a network model [5, 16], our ER-model-based design method is likely to be widely applicable to real-world databases with practical design. In addition, our method not only guarantees that the target domain can be uniquely converted to ILP input files, but also enables a decision as to whether the application of ILP systems is effective or not for analyzing the target domain in advance.

In [5], Chen captured the relationship among real-world entities in a top-down approach and represented the information structure as an ER model. Later, the concepts of normalization and generalization were introduced [15, 18, 17], as well as a standardized procedure to improve ER schema. In the ER model, information consists of three conceptual components: entity, relationship, and attribute values [17]. The fundamental element of the ER model is entity, which represents the essential real-world components in the target domain to be modeled, and is particularly unable to be further divided. Relationship relates to more than two entities. "E set" refers to a set of entities of the same type. Similarly, "R set" and "V set" refer to a set of relationships of the same type and a set of attribute values of the same type. Figure 2 illustrates a diagrammatic representation of the ER model (ER diagram). In an ER diagram E sets and R sets are represented as rectangles and lozenges. The fact that several E sets are connected by an R set is represented by solid lines connecting each E set and R set.

According to Chen [5], an E set is represented as $E (A_1 /V_1, A_2 /V_2, \dots , A_n /V_n)$, where E refers to the name (or label) of the E set, and A_i /V_i ($i = 1,2, \dots , n$) denotes a pair of attribute names (or label) and a V set. An attribute A_i refers to a feature of an E set and is defined as a function from E into V_i. If a minimal subset of an attribute set $X = \{A_1, A_2, \dots , A_k\}$ provides a one-to-one mapping from an E set into the direct product of the V set $V_1 \times V_2 \times \bullet \bullet \bullet \times V_k$, X is called an identifier of E. The identifier is often underscored in ER diagrams (see Figure 2). The notation of an E set is simplified as E $(A_1, A_2, \dots , A_k, A_{k+1}, \dots , A_n)$ [17]. In other words, once the values of the identifiers are specified, those of all other attributes are automatically fixed[1].

Similarly, an R set relates several E sets $E_1, E_2, \bullet \bullet \bullet, E_m$. A set of mutually related entities $(e_1, e_2, \dots ,e_m)$, where $e_i \in E_i (i = 1,2,\dots,m)$, is called a relation and an R set is a set of relations with the same type. An R set is denoted as $R (E_1 / L_1, E_2 / L_2,\dots, E_m / L_m$: $A_1 /V_1, A_2 /V_2, \dots , A_n / V_n)$, where R denotes the name (or label) of an R set, L_i denotes the role of E_i in an R set R, and E_i / L_i ($i = 1,2, \dots , m$) denotes a pair of E_i and L_i. Some R sets include pairs of an attribute and a V set A_i /V_i ($i = 1,2, \dots , n$). Similar to E sets, the notation of R sets is simplified as $R (E_1, E_2, \dots , E_m : A_1, A_2, \dots , A_n)$ [17].

When a relational database is generated from an ER model, the number of tables in the database is equal to $| E | + | R |$, where $| E |$ and $| R |$ denote the numbers of E sets and R sets. In practice, when the database is implemented in a DBMS, tables of the relevant number are further generated through generalization, instantiation, and typification operations.

We suppose that the adequacy (the effectiveness of the result) of a machine learning system to a target domain can be estimated with the number of optimal tables for the domain. Specifically, ILP-based learning is appropriate for a domain if the difference between the redundancy (i.e., the number of missing data) of a single table representation of the domain and that of a multiple table representation is significant.

In such situations, the corresponding ER diagrams include relationships among multiple entities, which ILP systems are effective in handling. Among the PROGOL example input files [13], the animal classification database is represented without redundancy by a single table. Meanwhile, the database for family relationship rule

---

[1] If every non-identifier attribute in an E set is functionally independent of other non-identifier attributes and is fully dependent on the identifiers of the E set in an ER model, the model is "normalized" [Sakai 78, Sakai 80]. In this paper, we assume that ER models are normalized.

induction is properly represented only by multiple tables. The size of its single table representation may increase up to infinity. These facts are more intuitively understood with the corresponding ER diagrams. Figure 3 indicates the ER diagrams. Note that the "family" relation is a binary relation between two persons, which is represented by a double link connecting them. An example of an RER diagram appears in Section 3.2 (Figure 4). If a database's normalized representation is a single entity, like the animal classification database, it can be represented as a single table and propositional logic learners are suitable for them. On the other hand, if a database's normalized representation includes relationships, like the family relationship database, one can obtain meaningful results only by employing predicate logic learners, such as ILP systems.

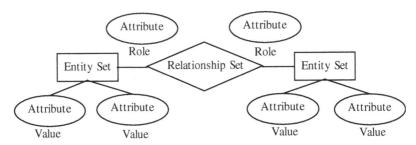

Fig. 2. ER Diagram

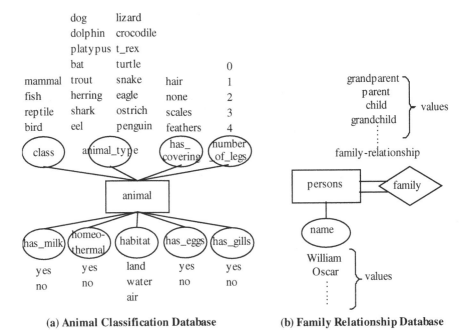

(a) **Animal Classification Database**   (b) **Family Relationship Database**

Fig. 3. ER Diagrams of PROGOL Sample Files

3.2 ER into RER Model

In this section, we introduce the RER (Refined ER) model. This model identifies specific attributes that are functionally dependent on other attributes, or whose values can be calculated with values of other attributes (and themselves). As mentioned in the previous section, values of attributes are determined by the values of the identifiers. Among them, we term those attributes whose functional dependency is defined as functional expressions "derived attributes." These functional expressions are included into the background knowledge in the input file generation for ILP systems.

A normalized form and an example of the RER model are shown in Figure 4. The left-hand side is the normalized form and the right-hand side shows the RER Diagram of "Responses" database, which will be utilized later in Section 6. In this example, "label_count" attribute and the "co-occurrence" attributes ("distance" and "in_front") are derived attributes.

The redundant attributes caused by functional dependency, introduced in the Extended Entity-Relationship (EER) model [21], are considered to be equivalent to derived attributes in this paper. However, their purpose, which is to eliminate such redundancy through normalization, differs from our position to utilize them for advantageous purposes.

4 DAISY

4.1 Design Principles of DAISY

We designed an interface module called DAISY (Data Arrangement Interface System) that connects ILP systems and relational databases. Here, we report a general-purpose method to directly connect ILP systems and relational databases for the first time. We adopted PROGOL as the ILP system because its tolerance of missing data makes it relatively easy to apply to real-world systems.

While connection of heterogeneous information systems is often achieved with individual interface modules that operate on demand, these modules may undermine the system's performance as overhead cost. Since ILP systems already have performance issues, additional overhead must be eliminated by all means. Based on the above observation, we set the following design principles for DAISY.

1. It must narrow down search space in advance by extracting optimum subset data from a database.
2. The functions of PROGOL must be fully utilized to avoid introducing additional overhead.
3. It must generate input files directly applicable to PROGOL.

Another design issue was system versatility. The following two principles were taken into account to enable the application of DAISY for various domains.

4. It must be applicable to any database that can be modeled by the ER model.
5. It must automate as much input file generation operations as possible to minimize manual operation by end users.

In our experiments, we explicitly distinguished databases that can be automatically converted to PROGOL input files from those that require manual operation, to achieve versatility in practical use.

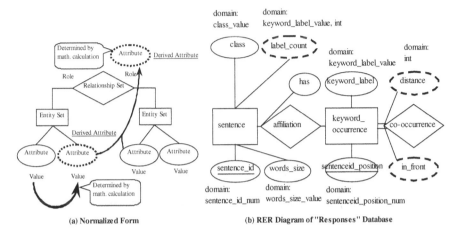

(a) Normalized Form   (b) RER Diagram of "Responses" Database

Fig. 4. Normalized Form and Example of RER Model

4.2 PROGOL Input File Generation Algorithms in DAISY

DAISY is a pioneering interface module that directly connects predicate logic learners and relational databases. A procedure to automatically convert an RER model to PROGOL input files is shown below.

(1) Initial Conversion (1): Generation of unary atoms from entities' identifier attributes

Let entities in the RER model be e_1, e_2, ..., e_m, and $e_i\_a_{id}$ the identifier attribute of e_i whose values are $e_i\_a_{id}\_v_{i1}$, $e_i\_a_{id}\_v_{i2}$, ..., $e_i\_a_{id}\_v_{in}$. Then, DAISY generates the following clause list as a part of the PROGOL input file, where $e_i\_a_{id}$ refers to a predicate name.

$$e_i\_a_{id}(e_i\_a_{id}\_v_{i1}).$$
$$e_i\_a_{id}(e_i\_a_{id}\_v_{i2}).$$
$$\vdots$$
$$e_i\_a_{id}(e_i\_a_{id}\_v_{in}).$$

(2) Initial Conversion (2): Generation of binary atoms from entities' non-identifier attributes

Let $e_i\_a_{id}$ be a non- identifier attribute of e_i, whose values are

$$e_i\_a_j\_v_{j1}, ei\_a_j\_v_{j2}, ..., e_i\_a_j\_v_{jn}.$$

Then, DAISY generates the following set of clauses as a part of the PROGOL input file, where ei_aj refers to the predicate name and the first argument $e_i\_a_{id}\_v_{ik}$ ($k = 1, ..., n$) denotes the value of the identifier of an entity e_i that the attribute $e_i\_a_j$ belongs to.

$$e_i\_a_j(e_i\_a_{id}\_v_{i1}, e_i\_a_j\_v_{j1}).$$
$$e_i\_a_j(e_i\_a_{id}\_v_{i2}, e_i\_a_j\_v_{j2}).$$
$$\vdots$$
$$e_i\_a_j(e_i\_a_{id}\_v_{in}, e_i\_a_j\_v_{jn}).$$

(3) Initial Conversion (3): Generation of $k+1$-any atoms from relationship attributes

Let a relationship among k ($k > 1$) entities in the RER model e_g, ..., e_h be $r\_e_g...e_h$ and their attribute names and attribute values be $r\_e_g...e_h\_a_1$, $r\_e_g...e_h\_a_2$, ...,

$r\_e_g...e_{h\_}a_n$, and $r\_e_g...e_{h\_}a_{l\_}v_l$, $r\_e_g...e_{h\_}a_{2\_}v_2$,   ... $r\_e_g...e_{h\_}a_{n\_}v_n$, respectively. Then, DAISY generates the following set of clauses as a part of the PROGOL input file, where $r\_e_g...e_{h\_}$ a_i refers to a predicate name and $e_{gn\_}a_{id\_}v_{id}$, ..., $e_{hn\_}a_{id\_}v_{id}$ refers to the identifier values of entities e_g ...., e_h.

$r\_e_g...e_{h\_}a_l$ $(e_g\_a_{id\_}v_{id}, ..., e_h\_a_{id\_}v_{id}, r\_e_g...e_{h\_}a_{l\_}v_l$).
$r\_e_g...e_{h\_}a_2$ $(e_g\_a_{id\_}v_{id}, ..., e_h\_a_{id\_}v_{id}, r\_e_g...e_{h\_}a_{2\_}v_2$).
:
$r\_e_g...e_{h\_}a_n$ $(e_g\_a_{id\_}v_{id}, ..., e_h\_a_{id\_}v_{id}, r\_e_g...e_{h\_}a_{n\_}v_n$).

(4) Initial Conversion (4): Generation of rules from derived attributes

When the value of an attribute $e_{i\_}a_q$ (or $r_{i\_}a_q$) in e_i (or r_i), denoted as $e_{i\_}a_{q\_}v_q$ (or $r_{i\_}a_{q\_}v_q$), can be calculated as a function of $a_{x\_}v_x$, ..., $a_{z\_}v_z$, denoted as $f(a_{x\_}v_x$, ..., $a_{z\_}v_z$), DAISY generates the following rule clause as a part of PROGOL input file[2]. Here, $e_{i\_}a_q$ and $r_{i\_}a_q$ refer to the predicate names and $f(a_{x\_}v_x$, ..., $a_{z\_}v_z$, $e_{i\_}a_{q\_}v_q$) refers to a predicate that calculates $f(a_{x\_}v_x$, ..., $a_{z\_}v_z)$ and assigns the result to $e_{i\_}a_{q\_}v_q$.

$e_{i\_}a_q$ $(e_{i\_}a_{q\_}v_q$) :- $f(a_{x\_}v_x$, ..., $a_{z\_}v_z, e_{i\_}a_{q\_}v_q$).

(5) Positive Example Identification

Among the predicates generated from step (1) to (3), DAISY selects the clauses that begin with the predicate corresponding to the target concept as positive examples. If a clause generated in step (1) does not begin with the predicate, it is deleted.

(6) Background Knowledge Identification

Among the predicates generated from step (1) to (4), DAISY selects all clauses other than those selected in step (5) as the background knowledge.

(7) Negative Example Identification/Generation

Negative examples are identified/generated by repeatedly replacing one of the arguments of a positive example obtained in step (5) with a value different from the original one. There are two types of candidates for replacement, depending on the source of the positive example. The following algorithm is a summary of the method to generate optimal negative examples for ILP systems proposed in Shimazu et al. [19].

If a positive example is identified either in step (1) or (2), a negative example candidate is generated by replacing the value of an arbitrary argument with a different value. In addition, an arbitrary element of any list argument is replaced by a different value from the original.

For example, if "$e_i\_a_j$ $(e_i\_a_{id\_}v_{in}, e_i\_a_{j\_}v_{jn})$." is generated in step (2) and is identified as a positive example in step (5), the value of an arbitrary argument (i.e., $e_i\_a_{id\_}v_{in}$ or $e_i\_a_{j\_}v_{jn}$) is replaced by a different value from the original. If the second argument (i.e., $e_i\_a_{j\_}v_{jn}$) is to be replaced, the new value is selected from its range ($e_i\_a_{j\_}v_{jl}, e_i\_a_{j\_}v_{j2}, ..., e_i\_a_{j\_}v_{jn}$). If the derived clause is not identical to any positive, DAISY selects it as a negative example.

(8) Mode Declaration creation

(A) Modeh declaration

The modeh declaration is derived from the format of positive examples identified in step (5). When the following clauses were identified as the positive examples ($i = 1..., n, j = 1 ..., m$) DAISY generates the mode

---

[2] This predicate is provided manually or automatically through the conversion of SQL statements for databases.

declaration, where arg_1k, arg_2k, ..., arg_tk denote the ranges of the corresponding arguments.

[modeh declaration]

:- modeh (n, predicate_i (+/–/*arg_1k, +/–/*arg_2k, ..., +/–/*arg_tk))?

Here, predicate_i is identical to the name of an attribute employed for predicate generation (i.e., a_i (i = 1, ..., n, j =1, ..., m)), and arg_xk (x = 1, 2, ..., t) denotes the range of attribute a_i and identifier attribute a_id, belonging to the entity that contains a_i. "+/–/*" specifies the input/output mode of the associated argument. "+"(input mode) is attached to arguments corresponding to identifier attributes, while "-"(output mode) or "#"(constant mode) is attached to others[3]. If all arguments are derived from identifiers, "+" is attached only to the first argument. If a_i is a derived attribute with a value, "+" is attached to all arguments generated from the range name of the identifier attribute. The first argument of the modeh, "n", is manually replaced by the recall number such as "1" or "*" which means unlimited repetition of backtracking (usually set to, say, 100).

(B) Modeb declaration(s)

The modeb declarations are generated by (i) applying the modeh declaration generation procedure to the clauses selected as background knowledge in step (6), and (ii) replacing all "modeh" occurrences to "modeb".

(9) Type Information Identification

Type information specifies the ranges of arguments in mode declarations. The application of the following procedure to each declaration generates type information for all arguments in the mode declarations:

Given the modeh declaration:

:- modeh (n, predicate_i (+/–/*arg_1k, +/–/*arg_2k, ..., +/–/*arg_tk))?

and the corresponding positive examples:

predicate_i (val_11, val_12, ..., val_1t).
predicate_i (val_21, val_22, ..., val_2t).
:

predicate_i (val_j1, val_j2, ..., val_jt).   ,

the following type information is generated:

arg_1k(val_11).   arg_1k(val_21).   ... arg_1k(val_j1).
arg_2k(val_12).   arg_2k (val_22).   ... arg_2k(val_j2).
:

arg_tk(val_1t).   arg_tk(val_2t).   ...arg_tk (val_jt).

Here, arg_ pk (p = 1, 2, ... , t) denotes the predicate name, which is identical to the name of an attribute employed for predicate generation (i.e., a_i (i = 1, ..., n, j =1, ..., m)), while val_qp (p = 1, 2, ...,j, q = 1, 2, ... , t) denotes all values that appear in the clauses generated between step (1) and step (4).

(10) Search Space Restriction

For effective learning within realistic time, search time must be minimized. We addressed this issue by restricting the domain of each argument of a predicate to the corresponding set of data appearing in positive examples. Accordingly, type information is defined solely with data within positive examples.

For example, a list with an arbitrary number of elements is usually defined as:

---

[3] Decisions whether "-" or "#" should be attached to each argument are made by the user.

list ([]).

list ([H|T]) :- list (T).

By adopting the above approach, the second clause is altered to:

list ([H|T]) :- db_instance (H), list (T). [4]

Here, H in db_instance (H) is an argument of the following predicates generated by DAISY in a preceding step, where e_1, e_2, ..., e_m denote all entities in the RER model, and $e_i\_a_{id}$ refers to the identifier of e_i:

$$e_i\_a_{id} (e_i\_a_{id}\_v_{i1})$$
$$e_i\_a_{id} (e_i\_a_{id}\_v_{i2})$$
$$:$$
$$e_i\_a_{id} (e_i\_a_{id}\_v_{in})$$

5 Examination of DAISY Algorithm

5.1 Data Mining Based on Input Files by DAISY Algorithm

We conducted data mining experiments to verify the functionality of DAISY. We obtained source data for DAISY by converting three sample input files [13] in PROGOL distribution to the relational table data. They consist of a file for classifying animals, a file for acquiring a definition of "grandfather" based on definitions of other family relationships, and a file for extracting the characteristics of eastbound trains[5]. The source data were then converted to RER model representation (see Figure 4). With the source data and the corresponding RER diagram, DAISY generated PROGOL input files.

Table 1 compares the input files that DAISY generated and the original sample files, as well as the characteristics/rules extracted by PROGOL and its processing time. While PROGOL outputs Prolog Horn-clause representations, these were translated to If/then statements for the sake of readability. The obtained characteristics/rules turned out to be identical, while the input files generated by DAISY tended to be more redundant, containing more background knowledge, than the corresponding original files. Also, the DAISY-generated input files tended to take greater processing time.

5.2 Discussions

The above result confirmed that (1) DAISY is able to generate a unique PROGOL input file, and (2) the characteristics of the target concept can be acquired in an optimum form by providing the generated input files to PROGOL. Hence, we believe that we successfully developed an algorithm to generate input files for ILP systems by representing the target domain with the RER model. Since our study aims to promote

---

[4] This clause should be given manually.

[5] The "Eastbound Train" input file is often employed for evaluation of machine learning systems. The fact that Quinlan used this file for evaluating the utility of a propositional logic learner FOIL in [Quinlan 79] boosted its popularity.

application of predicate logic-based learners to real-world systems, we expect that our achievement will boost the utility of ILP systems to real-world applications.

Table. 1. Data Mining based on Input Files generated by DAISY

		DAISY output files	Sample files
Num. of attributes for explaining the target concept (Num.of background knowledge)	Animal Classification	8	8
	Family Relationship	4	4
	Eastbound Train	12	11
Processing Time (in seconds)	Animal Classification	0.04	0.03
	Family Relationship	0.02	0.02
	Eastbound Train	0.04	0.03
Output	Animal Classification	If A is a mammal, then A has milk. If A is a fish, then A has gills. If A is a reptile, then A has scales. If A is a bird, then A is covered by feathers.	If A is a mammal, then A has milk. If A is a fish, then A has gills. If A is a reptile, then A has scales. If A is a bird, then A is covered by feathers.
	Family Relationship	If A is grandfather of B, then A is parent of C and C is parent of B.	If A is grandfather of B, then A is parent of C and C is parent of B.
	Eastbound Train	If A is bound east, then A has car B and B loads a triangle luggage.	If A is bound east, then A has car B and B loads a triangle luggage.

Relational database design is usually initiated with an ER diagram for the target domain. Therefore, RDT/DB [3, 9, 10] requires virtually identical operations to our method (i.e., conversion of attribute names in RER diagrams to predicates). DAISY further aspires to a higher versatility by pursuing independence from DBMS design and applicability to arbitrary ILP systems.

Since RDT/DB, an ILP system tightly connected to relational databases, employs an interpreter-like interface, its application to other ILP systems is not easy, while it is effective in dynamic recalculation in response to a database update. On the other hand, DAISY converts the target databases to ILP input files in advance. Although DAISY loses the dynamic feature of RDT/DB, it obtains potential applicability for various ILP systems in addition to PROGOL.

Another distinctive advantage of DAISY is its effectiveness in "debugging" trial-and-error modification of input files repeatedly performed until an acceptable result is obtained[6]. This operation is unavoidable because of the difficulty of intuitively grasping logical consistency in a predicate-logic-based description for practical data with many attributes. DAISY is able to generate a unique input file, as long as the target domain is represented as an RER diagram. Thus, the correctness of an input file can be determined solely by verifying its conversion procedure. We believe that this

---

[6] In practice, users become further confused because they do not recognize "an acceptable result" in advance!

feature enhances the reliability of the input files and contributes to the diffusion of ILP systems.

On the other hand, input files generated by DAISY contain redundancy and their processing time tends to be longer. We shall address this issue in our future research.

6   Application of DAISY to System in Practical Use

In this section, we verify that DAISY functions well in practical use. For this purpose, we developed an expert system AUTOMAIL. It supports call center operators in a company to promptly prepare near optimum responses to their customers by automatically classifying their inquiries.

AUTOMAIL is implemented as a data mining system that captures email classification rules by inducing typical patterns of past email inquiries. Associating a response template with each pattern can identify the optimum response for an email inquiry. Whenever an email arrives, candidate patterns that approximately represent its characteristics are selected. Then, the response templates associated with the patterns are provided to the operator, and then she/he selects the most appropriate one to construct an answer.

We designed AUTOMAIL so that it provides near optimal response candidates for an email according to the email classification rules induced from past email contents. Through usage of AUTOMAIL in daily operations of a call center, we confirmed that DAISY is able to connect databases and ILP systems in real-world systems.

6.1   "Responses" Database and Its RER Model

Figure 5 shows the design of "Responses" database, which is built on top of Oracle7. In this database, 2,085 email inquiries are classified into 86 groups by professionals and each inquiry record contains a classified group identifier in the "Corresponding Prototypical Sentence NO#" field. Body text of each inquiry is converted into a list of keywords by means of a dictionary dedicated for this system and is stored in the "Qkeyword" field in Figure 5. In the "Best Answer to the Prototypical Inquiry" field, body text of the actual responses to the inquiries, whose body text are in the "CONTEXT" field, are stored. The induction subsystem performs data mining on this database.

In the induction subsystem, DAISY functions as the interface module that directly connects the data mining engine PROGOL and databases. It interprets database structure according to the RER model and automatically converts a database to PROGOL input files. Figure 4 shows the semantic structure of "Responses" database as an RER diagram.

6.2   Data Mining with PROGOL

Classification rules for all 86 classes are acquired from the input file generated in Section 6.1. For example, the classification rule for the class "Prototypical Question 85" is as follows (translated into English):

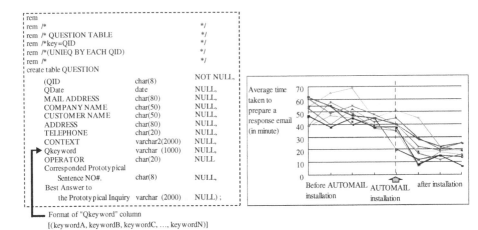

```
rem
rem /*                                    */
rem /* QUESTION TABLE                     */
rem /*key=QID                             */
rem /*(UNIEQ BY EACH QID)                 */
rem /*                                    */
create table QUESTION
  (QID                    char(8)          NOT NULL,
   QDate                  date             NULL,
   MAIL ADDRESS           char(80)         NULL,
   COMPANY NAME           char(50)         NULL,
   CUSTOMER NAME          char(50)         NULL,
   ADDRESS                char(80)         NULL,
   TELEPHONE              char(20)         NULL,
   CONTEXT                varchar2(2000)   NULL,
 → Qkeyword               varchar (1000)   NULL,
   OPERATOR               char(20)         NULL
   Corresponded Prototypical
       Sentence NO#.      char(8)          NULL,
   Best Answer to
       the Prototypical Inquiry  varchar (2000)  NULL) ;
```

Format of "Qkeyword" column
[(keywordA, keywordB, keywordC, ..., keywordN)]

Fig. 5. "Responses" Database Design

Fig. 6. Changes in Operating Time

sentence 85 (A) :-	have (A, 'method'),
	in_order (A, 'MFPrn', 'mode'),
	not_have (A, 'NewMFPrn').
sentence 85 (A) :-	in_order (A, 'MFPrn', 'automatic operation')
sentence 85 (A) :-	in_order (A, 'turning off power supply', 'method').

Here, this prototypical question asks for the procedure to automatically switch the operation mode of the product "MFPrn." Since this function is not taken over by its successor "NewMFPrn," a totally different response must be prepared for inquiries concerning "NewMFPrn," even if their content is similar to those for "MFPrn."

If the keyword list derived from a newly arrived email inquiry conforms to one of the three rules above, this inquiry is classified as "Prototypical Question 85" class.

6.3 Evaluation

We measured the effect of AUTOMAIL with a change in operation time of call center operators. Figure 6 compares the average operation time for responding to a single inquiry email in a day by 10 randomly selected operators. While a surge is observed just after installation, all users successfully reduced operation time by 1/3, over the long run.

6.4 Discussion

We demonstrated DAISY's adequacy for systems in practical use through an experiment with AUTOMAIL, as described above. We also confirmed that the DAISY algorithm enables ILP systems to conduct effective data mining for real-world data. These results demonstrate the versatility of DAISY and the RER model in preprocessing structured database information for a data mining engine.

In the above experiment, AUTOMAIL contributed to call center operations by providing near-optimal response candidates. Overall system quality can be enhanced by incremental rule acquisition in the knowledge base.

We believe that the above achievements promote expanded application domains for knowledge discovery in databases by means of ILP systems whose development has been restricted despite its expressiveness.

7 Conclusions

In this paper, we proposed the RER (Refined Entity Relationship) model. By converting relational databases to RER model representations, databases can be uniquely converted to input files for ILP systems, which can be employed as expressive data mining engines. DAISY is an algorithm to convert relational databases to ILP input. In other words, DAISY is designed to effectively perform preprocessing in a KDD process where ILP systems are employed as data mining engines.

We verified and confirmed the expressiveness of the RER model and the soundness of DAISY. With test data often employed in machine learning studies, input files were generated in which the ILP system functioned correctly and provided the desired results.

Furthermore, we developed an expert system AUTOMAIL which automatically classified newly arrived inquiry emails based on classification criteria of past inquiries. With this system, time required for call center operators within a company to send desirable responses to inquiries was reduced by 1/3. This result demonstrated that DAISY is effective even within systems in practical use. We stress that the distinctive feature of AUTOMAIL is that it is able to enhance the quality of the whole system by gradually increasing rules in the knowledge base by storing the results of data mining in the knowledge base in the form of rules for future reuse. We believe that our study is among the leading-edge studies in active mining research [1], which has gained attention within the data mining community.

Acknowledgements. We express our deep gratitude to Mr. Takemi Yamazaki, director of Information Media Laboratory, who has provided invaluable support and consideration in our research and experiments. In addition, we thank Mr. Takuo Shigetani for his support in the early stages of our experiments, and Mr. Tetsushi Sakurai for his help in the later stages of the experiments.

References

1. ICDM2002 WORKSHOP, International Workshop on Active Mining (AM–2002). http://www.ar.sanken.osaka-u.ac.jp/activemining/am2002.html
2. Brachman, R. J., Khabaza, T., Kloesgen W., Piatetsky-Shapiro, G., Simoudis, E.: Mining business databases. Commun. ACM 39, 11 (November 1996) 42–48

3. Brockhausen, P., Morick K.: Direct Access of an ILP Algorithm to a Database Management System. In Proceedings of the MLnet Familiarization Workshop on Data Mining with Inductive Logic Programming (1996) 95–110
4. Califf, E. M., Mooney, R.: Relational Learning of Pattern-Match Rules for Information Extraction. ACL–97 Workshop in Natural Language Learning (1997) 6–11
5. Chen, P.: The Entity-Relationship Model – Toward a Unified View of Data. ACM Transactions on Database Systems 1, 1 (1976) 9–36
6. Craven, M., DiPasquo, D., Freitag, D., McCallum, A.: Learning to Extract Symbolic Knowledge from the World Wide Web. In Proceedings of the 15th National Conference on Artificial Intelligence (Madison WI, July 1998) 509–516
7. Dastani, M., Jacobs, N., Jonker, C. M., and Treur, J.: Modeling User Preferences and Mediating Agents in Electronic Commerce. Agent-Mediated Electronic Commerce III. Springer-Verlag (2002) 163–193
8. Fayyad, U., Piatetsky-Shapiro, G. and Smyth, P.: From Data Mining to Knowledge Discovery in Databases. AI Magazine 17, 3 (Fall 1996) 37–52
9. Morik, K., Brockhausen, P.: A Multistrategy Approach to Relational Knowledge Discovery in Databases. Machine Learning 27 (1997) 287–312
10. Morik, K.: Knowledge Discovery in Databases – An Inductive Logic Programming Approach. Foundations of Computer Science – Theory, Cognition, Applications. Springer-Verlag (1997) 429–326
11. Muggleton, S.: Inverse Entailment and Progol. New Generation Computing 13 3&4 (1995) 245–286
12. Parsaye, K., Chignell, M., Khoshafian, S., Wong, H., Chingnell, M. Intelligent Databases: Object Oriented, Deductive Hypermedia Technologies. John Wiley & Sons (1989)
13. Progol. http://www.doc.ic.ac.uk/~shm/Software/
14. Quinlan, J. R.: Discovering Rules from Large Collections of Examples: a Case Study. In Expert Systems in the Micro-electronic Age. Edinburgh University Press (1979) 168–201
15. Sakai, H.: On the Optimization of the Entity-Relationship Model. In Proceedings of the 3rd USA–JAPAN Computer Conference (1978) 145–149
16. Sakai, H.: A Unified Approach to the Logical Design of a Hierarchical Data Model. In Proceedings of the International Conference on Entity-Relationship Approach to Systems Analysis and Design (Santa Monica CA, 1979) 61–74
17. Sakai, H.: Entity-Relationship Approach to the Conceptual Schema Design. In Proceedings of the 1980 ACM SIGMOD International Conference on Management of Data (Santa Monica CA, May 1980) 1–8
18. Scheuermann, P., Schiffner, G., Weber, H.: Abstraction Capabilities and Invariant Properties Modeling within the Entity-Relationship Approach. In Proceedings of the International Conference on Entity-Relationship Approach to Systems Analysis and Design (Santa Monica CA, 1979) 121–140
19. Shimazu, K., Furukawa, K. and Yagi, N.: Design of Negative Examples for Input Data to Progol. In Proceedings of the ICLP '95 Post-Conference Workshop on Inductive Logic Programming (Tokyo Japan, June 1995) 145–144
20. Slattery, S., Craven, M.: Combining Statistical and Relational Methods for Learning in Hypertext Domains. In Proceedings of the 8th International Conference on Inductive Logic Programming (Madison WI, July 1998), 38–52
21. Teorey, T. J., Yang D., Fry J. P.: A Logical Design Methodology for Relational Databases Using the Extended Entity-Relationship Model. ACM Computing Surveys 18, 2 (1986), 197–222
22. Zelle, J. M., Thompson, A. C., Califf, E. M., Mooney, J. R.: Inductive Logic Programs without Explicit Negative Examples. In Proceedings of the Fifth International Workshop on Inductive Logic Programming (Leuven Belgium, September 1995), 403–416

Context-Based Data Mining Using Ontologies

Sachin Singh, Pravin Vajirkar, and Yugyung Lee

School of Computing and Engineering,
University of Missouri–Kansas City,
Kansas City, MO 64110 USA.
{sbs7vc,ppv22e,leeyu}@umkc.edu

Abstract. Data mining, which aims at extracting interesting information from large collections of data, has been widely used as an active decision making tool. Real-world applications of data mining require a dynamic and resilient model that is aware of a wide variety of diverse and unpredictable contexts. Contexts consist of circumstantial aspects of the user and domain that may affect the data mining process. The underlying motivation is mining datasets in the presence of context factors may improve performance and efficacy of data mining as identifying the factors, which are not easily detectable with typical data mining techniques. This paper proposes a *context-aware* data mining framework, where context will (1) be represented in an ontology, (2) be automatically captured during data mining process, and (3) allow the adaptive behavior to carry over to powerful data mining. We have shown that the different behaviors and functionalities of our context-aware data mining framework dynamically generate information in dynamic, uncertain, and distributed medical applications.

1 Introduction

Real world applications are laden with huge amount of data and encompass entities that evolve over time. However, this data-rich environment does not guaranty for information-rich environment. Due to dynamic nature of environment, data must be interpreted differently depending upon situation (context). For instance, the meaning of a cold patient's high fever might be different from the fever of a pneumonia patient.

Context is a powerful, long-standing concept. It can be helpful in computer-human interaction which is running mostly via explicit contexts of communication (e.g., user query input). Implicit context factors (e.g., physical environmental conditions, location, time etc.) are normally ignored by the computer due to absence of knowledge base or appropriate model. Context-aware computing work has been carried out by many researchers [2,1,3,11]. Many of them have been working on defining context-awareness and some of them have also focused on building context-aware applications. However, little has been done towards building data mining framework based on context-awareness, leading to useful and accurate information extraction.

I.-Y. Song et al. (Eds.): ER 2003, LNCS 2813, pp. 405–418, 2003.
© Springer-Verlag Berlin Heidelberg 2003

Data mining is a process that discovers useful information in data that may be used for valid predictions [5]. Context-aware data mining is related to how the attributes should be interpreted under specific request criteria. Current data mining approaches do not provide adequate support for handling context-aware data mining. The main reason for this is the lack of rich context that specifies when and how a data mining should be applied to its context.

We fervently believe implicit context factors could be used to interpret and enhance explicit user input and thereby affecting data mining results to deliver accurate and precise prediction results. Different behaviors and functionalities of data mining are highly useful and required in generating information in dynamic, uncertain, and distributed environments. It is because such behaviors and capabilities can help to increase the various degrees of effectiveness and flexibility of data mining process. In this paper, we tried to mimic such aspects wherever feasible and show such sophisticated functionality to significantly enhance the quality of data mining.

Ontologies provide a means to represent information or knowledge that is machine processable and can be communicated between different agents. The Framework represents the context factors in carefully crafted ontologies. Context is a very subjective term and is dependent on the domain under consideration. Thus, we can differentiate the context aware data mining into two parts; the actual representation of the context factor for a domain in a corresponding ontology and a generic framework which can query this ontology and invoke the mining processes and coordinate them according to the ontology design. Knowledge representation in an ontology can a building block in context based data mining.

The paper is organized as follows. In Section 2 we define the concept of Context-awareness to suit the need of our unique integrated model which recognizes various Context factors that are generic for all domains. Section 3 discusses how the context factors can be applied to data mining through a carefully selected motivating example. Section 4 proposes a framework which applies context factors to data mining process. Section 5 explains the design of the ontology used by the framework. Section 6 demonstrates the experimental results performed using the framework, bringing out the affect of context on data mining. Medical data has been used to test with the proposed model. Section 7 concludes this paper.

2   What Is Context-Awareness?

The concept of *Context* has often been interwoven and used in many different fields. When the information has to be conveyed from one element to another we need to let the receiving element know the reference of our discussion. Dey and Abowd [4] defined it as a piece of information that can be used to characterize the situation of a participant in an interaction. Similarly, [2,1] defined context as location, environment, identity of people and time. By sensing context information, context enabled applications can present context information to users, or modify their behavior according to changes in the environment [10]. Chen and Kotz [3] defines context as the set of environmental states and rules that either determines an application behavior or describes where the event occurs. It is very similar to our definition. Schilit and Theimer [12] emphasized the importance of applications which get adapt themselves to context.

Lack of context-awareness leads to missing a lot of critical and useful information that would affect the data mining process and thereby, affecting the data mining results. In real-world and live data sets, the context factors that constitute Context awareness changes rapidly and therefore the factors tend to become subjective and very domain specific. There are some definition which were too broad to apply to any application. The context will make the system understand and adapt the data mine process and thereby providing the users with a time sensitive data accurately, efficiently and in a precise manner.

Now we define the types of context factors specific to our framework:

Domain Context describes domain specific context which is patient-centric in our case. The Target (Patient) Context captures the personal and medical history of the patient. It also records the immediate family members and their medical history. This could be useful in scenarios where the diagnosis and the treatment of a patient is affected by the medical history of his/her family. For example, an important factor in predicting whether a patient has diabetes is if anyone in his immediate family has diabetes. In such a case, it is important to get the patient context before making predictions in this regard.

Location context: The datasets primary formed from the population living near a certain location. Living area is related to health issues. For example, people living in coastal regions have less probability of getting goiter. Similar, people living in the country side have fewer tendencies to get high blood pressure as compared to suburban folks. It would be a good idea to pick the appropriate data sets depending on the location context of the patient.

Data Context: It is important to figure out which of the available datasets to pick for mining for a given service. This context helps us to figure out which dataset to pickup and how to combine them to get useful mining results. Here the combination of datasets is at a semantic level rather than at a structural level. For example, from domain knowledge we know that making predictions for heart attack also involves checking his diabetes. In such a case the two structurally disjoint data sets are combined at semantic level before mining the resulting dataset.

User Context: (1) User Identity Context describes the information of user responsible for the query including his/her field of expertise, authorization of tasks or data sets, his/her team members and their expertise fields. (2) User History Context describes the history (i.e., user-profiling) built up for each user when he/she queries for a particular information. This helps when the user frequently queries with a similar query or uses the same piece of information.

3   A Motivating Example of Context-Aware Data Mining

The effect of context factors can be explained in the light of a carefully selected scenario. The scenario explains a typical situation when a doctor wants to know the likelihood of a patient having the major blood vessels $< 50\%$ or $> 50\%$ narrowing as a measure of heart attack risk. Data mining based application is a natural choice, for building a prediction model by mining the existing data warehouse containing large amount of data. A typical data mining application would require a big set of input parameters to query the prediction model to result into the predicted value. However, by carefully selecting the context factors the user is made to give only a small set of input [14] while system deduces the rest based on context factors.

Let us look into the attributes of the dataset in details:
1. (age) Age in years
2. (sex)Sex
   - Value 1: Male and Value 0: Female)
3. (chest_pain) chest pain type
   - Value 1: Typical angina, Value 2: Atypical angina
   - Value 3: Non-anginal pain, Value 4: Asymptomatic
4. (trestbps) resting blood pressure (in mm Hg on admission to the hospital)
5. (chol) Serum cholestoral in mg/dl
6. (fbs) (Fasting blood sugar >120 mg/dl)
   - Value 1: True and Value 0: False
7. (restecg)resting electrocardiographic results
   - Value 0: Normal
   - Value 1: Having ST-T wave abnormality (T wave inversions and/or ST elevation or depression of >0.05 mV)
   - Value 2: Showing probable or definite left ventricular hypertrophy by Estes' criteria 8. (thalach) Maximum heart rate achieved
9. (exang) Exercise induced angina (1 = yes; 0 = no)
10.(oldpeak) ST depression induced by exercise relative to rest
11.(slope) The slope of the peak exercise ST segment
   - Value 1: upsloping, Value 2: flat, Value 3: downsloping
12.(ca) Number of major vessels (0-3) colored by flourosopy
13.(thal) the heart status
   - Value 3: Normal, Value 6: Fixed defect, Value 7: Reversable defect
14.(Family-Hist)- History of any heart disease within immediate family
   - Value 1: True, Value 0: False
15.(Smoke-Disease) - Symptoms of smoke disease
16.(Location) - Location of the person where he lives.
17.(num)Diagnosis of heart disease (angiographic disease status)
   - Value 0: <50% Diameter narrowing
   - Value 1: >50% Diameter narrowing
(in any major vessel: attributes 59 through 68 are vessels)

In this scenario the doctor might be interested in determining whether the major blood vessel is <50% or >50% narrowing to evaluate the measure of heart attack risk. This could form the basis of further action that the doctor may take in treating the person. So the attribute 17 becomes the pivot element (also called as class attribute), forming the prediction value in the prediction tree. All other parameters are required as the query parameters to reach to a prediction value. As is apparent in the dataset lots of factors are required to determine the value of the pivot element. Now most of the elements from attribute 4 through attribute 13 are standard clinical tests and are available to doctors at their disposal. Attribute 1 and 2 are trivial. Consider other attributes.

Location: Logically location doesn't seem to affect this data directly. So it is less likely that this attribute will affect as a significant node in the classification tree. However the importance of this attribute lies in the fact that it can be used to cluster data records based on that. For example, if we have collected the data set from different zones/countries/states etc. If the patient under consideration falls in any one of the *zones*, then the system could extract a set of records, which correspond to that particular zone and then use this sub data set to mine for the classification tree. This may improve the accuracy of the system, wherein we just concentrate on the data more relevant to him than the *generic* data. If the patient doesn't fall in any one of the zone then it's on the system to decide whether it can approximate his dataset to the zone closest to him or use the entire dataset or combination of two zones etc. This is an example of how we can use the *Location Context*. This is true because Location here is not an input to the data mining process but a context factor which will affect the output given same other input parameters

Family-History: This input parameter demands an input, which is beyond the standard clinical tests. This is an example, which uses *historical personal data* as input. The system stores information corresponds to the immediate family members of the given patient based on his or her user profile. Then for each of these members it can access the *Historical patient repository*. Hospitals usually, maintain some kind of medical record of each patient in history about what disease they had in past. Thus, this is a specific case of *Domain context*, which is called as *Patient context*.

Smoke-Disease: This parameter refers to any health affects caused by smoking. Determining whether a person has smoking ill effects is in itself a sub-problem. Here we refer to another data set which has information like (1) Smoking from when (2) Cigs per day (3) When quit (period) etc. Based on these input parameters from the user, the system picks up another dataset referring to smoking say *Smoking Effects*, mine this dataset and builds the classification tree, which predicts whether the person has smoking problems. Now using the input parameter for the given patient, the system will query this tree and predict whether the patient has smoking problems. The predicted output is the input to the original query and is then used to query the original tree for the heart disease. This is an example of the *Data Context*. It is so because one of the input to the original query is output after selecting another dataset. The system will select the auxiliary dataset only if the patient ever smoked. Thus based on the context a different dataset(s) is selected, queried and used in cascade to identify implicit context factors.

4   Context-Aware Data Mining Framework

We propose a new framework for an application which mines real life datasets to build effective data mining models taking into consideration all the relevant context factors. It is worth mentioning here that the system is not focusing on how the context factors are collected but on how these factors are utilized to obtain relevant and correct results. The objective of the framework is the use of context factors to achieve better prediction and accuracy of the data mining process. The context factors are applied through a set of carefully designed ontology concepts described in details in Section 5.

The framework is oriented towards medical datasets and the examples used refer to using the mining, especially classification models to build decision support systems related to medical field. However, the idea of this framework is generic and is applicable to other important application areas of data mining like e-commerce, stock trading etc.

4.1   Context-Aware Data Mining Model

In the context-aware data mining framework, different context factors engage in a number of different types of data mining behaviors. First, let us consider a set of context factors which may affect the behavior of data mining: $C = \{c_1, c_2, \ldots, c_n\}$. The different mining behaviors are employed according to whether or not some tuples, attributes or values of given datasets are related to computing the contexts. Suppose that a context factor takes values in the set $\{c_1, c_2, \ldots, c_k\}$. Let D a dataset composed of a set of tuples, $T = \{t_1, t_2, \ldots, t_n\}$, a set of attributes, $A = \{a_1, a_2, \ldots, a_m\}$, a set of values for a given attribute a_j, $V = \{v_1, v_2, \ldots, v_l\}$.

In relation to the set of the context factors, C, we briefly describe two main processes of data mining. Please refer to [9] for details.

Phase 1. Preprocessing: datasets to be mined are prepared using different schemas *Pick*, *Join*, or *Trim* against tuples (T), attributes (A) or values (V) of available datasets (D). The preprocessing schemas can be specified as follows:

- **Pick** determines how to pick a particular tuple(s), a particular field or a particular value from the given dataset(s) for a particular context(s) c_k. Picking particular tuples (rows), fields (columns) is called *horizontal pick* denoted by $hPick(T_i, c_k)$, *vertical pick* denoted by $vPick(T_i, c_k)$, respectively.
- **Join** determines how to join a particular tuple(s), a particular field or a particular value picked from the source dataset(s) T_i to a target dataset T_j. Joining particular tuples (rows), fields (columns) is called *horizontal join* denoted by $hJoin(T_i, T_j, c_k)$ and *vertical join* denoted by $vJoin(T_i, T_j, c_k)$, respectively.

- **Trim** determines how to trim a particular tuple(s), a particular field or a particular value from a particular dataset T_i. Triming particular tuples (rows), fields (columns) is called *horizontal trim* denoted by $hTrim(T_i, c_k)$, *vertical trim* denoted by $vTrim(T_i, c_k)$, respectively.

Phase 2. Data Mining: Different types of mining processes can be invoked.

- *Cascading mining process* comprises of a main process which acquires some of its inputs by recursively invoking other process and obtaining their output to complete the input set required to execute itself.
- *Sequential mining process* specifies requiring the output of a process being the input of the subsequent process.
- *Iterative mining process* represents a repetitive execution of a set of activities.
- *Parallel fork process* partition a process into a set of the subsequent processes.
- *Aggregating Mining Process* aggregates the outputs from the previous processes.

A typical data mining behavior is a hybrid form where the system employs data mining processes as combination of some behaviors mentioned above and then computes the value by using the proposed schemas. As an example, the context of height/weight ratio picks height and weight as two different values and then compute this ratio. In all these cases the system is *aware* of the domain and the mining processes dealing with implicit contexts. The domain knowledge and processes are specified in ontologies as described in Section 5.

4.2   Architecture

Fig. 1 shows the architecture of the proposed framework. *User Profile* is a collection of information about the users of the system. The user context denotes all or some of this user information, reference to the current, query. For instance, current user is obtained by the user login information. As the system is used by the user, the system *learns* more about the user and maintains a user profile. The *User Profile* could contain information like types of queries he is mostly interested in, which can help the system to provide a better service to the user.

The *User Interface* component is the one which interacts with the client subsystems. It is essentially a client interface component which interacts with the client. The User Interface component refers to the *Service Ontology* which provides a listing of all services offered by the system and the input required by the user for providing that service. Once it receives a request from the user, it forwards it to the query analyzer.

The *Query Analyzer* refers to the *Process Ontology* to get additional information about the process to be executed to fulfill the service. This information is typical of what additional context factors to consider for the query; where to get additional implicit input to complete the input for the given process. The *Query Analyzer* will fetch all the implicit information to complete the query parameters. It then passes the complete (explicit and implicit) input list to the *Query Processor*. The *Query Processor* carries out the actual data mining operation

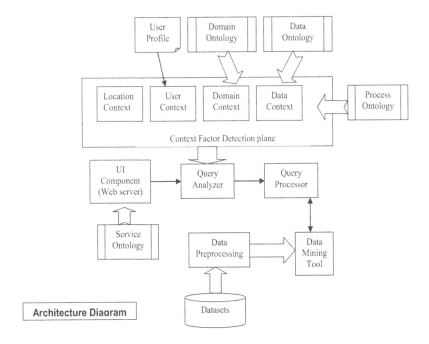

Fig. 1. Architecture of Context-Aware Data Mining Framework

when invoked with complete set of input from the *Query Analyzer*. The implicit information could be picked up from a dataset record or it could be a result of a sub mining task. In such a case, the query analyzer will invoke the query processor to execute such sub mining tasks individually, consolidate the results and then pass it back to *Query Processor* to execute the main mining task. Thus the query analyzer can be considered as a Meta task manager, managing multiple atomic tasks which are part of the same high level tasks.

The *Domain Ontology* stores knowledge about the existing datasets like relationships between datasets not only at structural level but more so at the semantic level. For example, if one gives a query which requires to mine a diabetes data set, from the *Data Ontology* we also know that anybody who has diabetes should also be queried for kidney disease, and so we also have to mine other dataset apart from the primary one. Thus this ontology can be used to semantically integrate the datasets for a *consolidated* mining on multiple physical datasets.

The actual data mining consists of two components. The first one is a *Data Preprocessing* component which converts the existing dataset formats into the one that is accepted by the data mining tool. The second component is the actual *Data Mining tool*, which will mine the dataset, given all the input parameters, like the dataset name, query element etc. this component accepts the preprocessed dataset, the other query parameters and returns the queried result. We implement the data mining using WEKA [6] as part of our framework. The

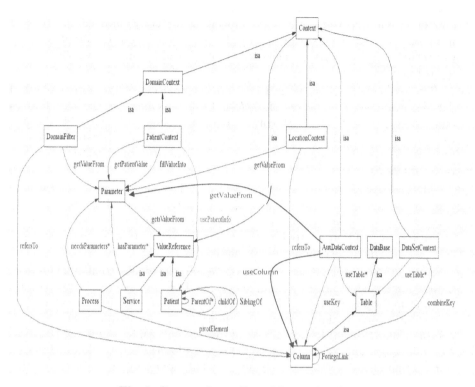

Fig. 2. Context-Aware Data Mining Ontology

Query Generator may use the output of one query as an input to other query and so on till it gets all the input required for the primary query that the user had requested. After the Meta task is executed the final result is returned to the user.

5 Ontology Design

The system supports the application of context through a carefully designed ontology. The ontology is shown in Fig. 2. The main concepts in the ontology are *Service* and *Process*. The service concept represents the services that the system offers to the user along with the description. The service is linked to the concept of parameters which represent the input required for the data mining process. The concept of parameter is generic and it represents all input; explicit from the user and implicit to the context. The concept of *Process* represents the idea of processes inside the system. It can be considered as a process which needs to be executed to provide a given service. Process keeps all information about the process that needs to be executed; that is the data Mining process that has to be executed to fulfill the described service. It keeps a track of all the parameters that are needed for the mining process. Some of these parameters are obtained from user, while others are implicit or indirectly obtained as discussed in Section 4. Thus *Process* can be thought as a reference to the complete set of parameters while the service refers only to the set of Parameters which the user needs to enter.

The concept of *Database* is a semantic abstraction of the actual physical datasets available. The concept of *Table* and *Columns* represent the actual tables and columns respectively. Each column refers to column of other table through the *Foreign Key* attribute, which can be used to combine the tables based on these references. This link is an abstraction of the structural relationships between tables.

The concept of *Context* is an abstraction of the context factors. All the context factors defined for our framework above are represented as concepts too. The *Data context* concept refers to the datasets that are required for the mining operation. In addition it provides the *Combine Key* attribute which refers the columns on which the combine operation is to be done.

As mentioned earlier a data mining operation may require combining physical datasets before starting the mining operation. This combination is however different from the former one in a sense that it is a semantic combination rather than a structural combination as was the case in foreign key attribute. For example a dataset may be represented in form of two physical tables as part of Database Normalization. This combination is done on the foreign key attribute. However, some of that datasets are physically unrelated like for example a dataset denoting symptoms of heart attack and other for diabetes.

To predict a diabetes has to take into consideration the kidney failure symptoms too. Thus the two physically unrelated datasets are now semantically associated. This relationship is represented in the form of *Combine Key* attribute. *Auxiliary Dataset* represents the implicit parameters that can be picked up directly from a given dataset. It refers to the table from where to pick the data, the column consisting of the data *useColumn*; and the parameter which will give the *foriegnKey* Value, which will be used to query the dataset. The *Location Context* refers to the actual column which has some location related information, like zone, country, state etc. Physically the name could be different, but this one semantically abstracts the notion of a region in general as location. It also refers to the parameter which provides the value. Using this information the system will filter the dataset(s) to get a relevant mining data.

The concept of *Domain Context* abstracts all the concepts that represent domain centric context factors. As in our case, the patient context refers to the *Patient Ontology*. The patient ontology describes a patient, through its relationship with with other patients, like immediate family members. As described in Section 3, the Patient Ontology is used to determine the medical history of related patients. In addition the ontology supports the idea of *Domain Filters*, which are any factors specific to a process used to filter a given dataset(s) and refers to a column which will be used to filter and the parameter from which it gets the value. Each parameter refers to *ValueReference* which denotes the place from which the parameter gets its value. *ValueReference* is a concept which is an abstraction of all entities from which a parameter can get its value; Service means value comes from user, context means it comes from one of the context factors.

Most important point to note is that the parameter may refer to another process, which is also a *ValueReference* to get its value. This denotes the *Cascading Mining* discussed in Section 4, where the main mining process would require one or more sub mining tasks and prediction outputs of each would form the input for the main task. Each of these sub-mining task is represented as different *Process* and hence a parameter referring to a process means that the output of such a process is the input value for the given parameter.

The framework also supports multiple domain specific contexts. Our example patient context is such a domain context. The *Patient Ontology* stores knowledge about patient. It stores knowledge like possible relationship between patients, like family relationships. This can be used in determining past family health problems for a patient during data mining process. In addition one could plug in additional contexts like if one needs to filter a dataset on a given attribute before mining the resulting dataset. For example, as mentioned in the example later, one could use *sex* as a filtering attribute to get relevant data before mining.

Our initial investigation for developing ontologies has led us to the tool environment Protégé [7]. This knowledge-editing environment is found to be excellent environment for our purpose to create and maintain models of concepts and relations in the context-aware data mining process.

6   Experimental Results

Now we will show the experimental results regarding the heart attack risk case. The data set selected is same as described in Section 3 that stores the history of patients with heart diseases. The dataset consists of following attributes:

- Personal details: *age* in years and *sex* (1 = male; 0 = female)
- Cardiac Details: *painloc* : chest pain location (1: substernal; 0: otherwise)
- The prediction output for this dataset is *num*: the diameter of the artery (angiographic disease status) (0: < 50% diameter narrowing; 1: > 50% diameter narrowing)

The user requests a query, which consists of input. He/she expects an outcome prediction value *num*. The system performs data mining using all attributes and entire datasets to construct the model. Using this model, it will apply the query variables to get the prediction result. We applied the J48 algorithm [13] and build a decision tree using C4.5 [8] on the heart dataset.

Fig. 3 (Case 1) shows the classification tree generated using C4.5 tree. Case 1 specifies the tree generated when the mining is done on the entire data set as it is. However context aware data mining will be different in that. Using the meta-level understanding (which we will have eventually), we know that the personal detail attributes can be patient-contexts. If we use them as context we achieve interesting results.

Case 1: Classification Tree
exang= no
    oldpeak _ 1: < 50 (190.0/27.0)
    oldpeak > 1
        slope = down: > 50 1 (0.0)
        slope= flat
            sex = female: < 50 (3.0/1.0)
            sex = male: > 50 1 (8.0)
        slope = up: < 50 (3.7)
exang = yes: > 50 1 (89.3/19.3)

Case 2: Classification Tree
exang= no
    oldpeak _ 1: < 50 (129.0/24.0)
    oldpeak > 1
        slope = down: > 50 1 (0.0)
        slope = flat: > 50 1 (8.0)
        slope = up: < 50 (2.0)
exang= yes
        chest pain = typ angina: > 50 1 (0.0)
        chest pain = asympt: > 50 1 (62.0/6.0)
        chest pain = non anginal
            age _ 55: > 50 1 (3.0/1.0)
            age > 55: < 50 (2.0)
        chest pain = atyp angina
            oldpeak _ 1.5: < 50 (4.0/1.0)
            oldpeak > 1.5: > 50 1 (3.0)

Case 3: Classification Tree
exang = no: < 50 (64.82/4.0)
exang = yes
    thalach _ 108: > 50 1 (3.04/0.04)
    thalach> 108
        chol _ 254: < 50 (4.0)
        chol > 254
    thalach _ 127: < 50 (4.08/1.0)
    thalach > 127: > 50 1 (3.06/0.06)

Fig. 3. The Experimental Results

In our case we considered *Sex* as a context factor. The user enters the query variables as he does previously. The application is now *context-aware* so it knows that part of the query the *Sex* variable is actually a context input. Using *Sex* as context is just like saying, if we need to predict the risk of heart disease, why should we mix data. Male persons can have different factors affecting more predominantly as compared to female ones. If we mine the datasets differently we may get interesting results. So if the user query variable is *Sex=male*, then it may not make sense to mine the entire dataset and then query the model and get the results. Instead retrieve only those records that are Male, and then mine the dataset excluding the sex column. That is we do vertical and horizontal trimming of data. The data model mined out of this could be *specialized* information. Our experiments we mined the datasets separating on basis of Sex as context information and the classification tree corresponding to males is shown in Fig. 3 (Case 2).

As is evident from the figure the new model shows emergence of some new factors in the decision making tree which were not appearing in the *generalized* domains. This shows how using Context factors can achieve different results and also give more insight of the trend in the dataset and their interrelations. In another example we considered input as *Sex=female* and we get a different data model shown in Fig. 3 (Case 3). From this simple query variance it is obvious that considering context factors can greatly affect the efficacy of the results of data mining applications.

7   Conclusion

In this paper we introduced a context aware data mining framework which provides accuracy and efficacy to data mining outcomes. Context factors were modelled using Ontological representation. Although the context aware framework proposed is generic in nature and can be applied to most of the fields, the medical scenario provided was like a proof of concept to our proposed model. An experimental result confirmed the effectiveness of use of context factor in data mining.

References

1. Brown, P.J.: The Stick-e Document: a Framework for Creating Context-Aware Applications. Electronic Publishing '96, 259–272 (1996)
2. Brown, P.J., Bovey, J.D. Chen, X.: Context-Aware Applications: From the Laboratory to the Marketplace. IEEE Personal Communications, **4(5)** 58–64 (1997).
3. Chen, G., Kotz, D.: A Survey of Context-Aware Mobile Computing Research. Dartmouth Computer Science Technical Report TR2000-381 (2000).
4. Dey, A.K., Abowd, G.D.: Towards a better understanding of Context and Context-Awareness. GVU Technical Report GITGVU-99-22, College of Computing, Georgia Institute of Technology. **2**, 2–14 (1999).
5. Edelstein, H. A.: Introduction to Data Mining and Knowledge Discovery, Third Edition, Two Crows Corporation, 1999. ISBN: 1-892095-02-5.
6. Machine Learning Software in Java. The University of Waikato (http://www.cs.waikato.ac.nz/ ml/weka/index.html).
7. The Protégé Project Website, http://protege.stanford.edu/.
8. Ragone, A.: Machine Learning C4.5 Decision Tree Generator.
9. Singh, S., Lee, Y.: Intelligent Data Mining Framework, Twelfth International Conference on Information and Knowledge Management (CIKM03) (submitted) (2003).
10. Salber, D., Dey, A.K., Orr, R.J., Abowd, G.D.: Designing For Ubiquitous Computing: A Case Study in Context Sensing, GVU Technical Report GIT-GVU 99–129, (http://www.gvu.gatech.edu/) (1999).
11. Schilit, B., Adams, N., Want, R.: Context-Aware computing applications. In Proceedings of IEEE Workshop on Mobile Computing Systems and Applications, 85–90, Santa Cruz, California, December (1994).

12. Schilit, B., Theimer, M.: Disseminating Active Map Information to Mobile Hosts. IEEE Network,**8(5)**, 22–32 (1994).
13. Witten, I.H., Frank, E.: Data Mining: Practical Machine Learning Tools and Techniques with Java Implementations. Morgan Kaufmann (1999).
14. UCI Knowledge Discovery in Databases Archive, Information and Computer Science University of California, Irvine, CA 92697-3425 (http://kdd.ics.uci.edu/)

Mining Typical Preferences of Collaborative User Groups

Su-Jeong Ko and Jiawei Han

Department of Computer Science
University of Illinois at Urbana-Champaign,
Urbana, Illinois 61801 U.S.A.
sjko@uiuc.edu
hanj@cs.uiuc.edu

Abstract. Collaborative filtering systems have the problems of sparsity--providing a recommendation by correlation between only two customers' preferences, and being unable to recommend a unique item owing to the recommendation based on preference rather than on the content of the item. The native feature space consists of unique words with single dimension when it occurs in documents as items, which can be tens or hundreds of thousands of words for even a moderate-sized text collection. This is prohibitively high for many learning algorithms. Since the feature extraction method using association word mining does not use the profile, it needs not update the profile, and it automatically generates noun phrases by using confidence and support of the Apriori algorithm without calculating the probability for index. However, in case that the feature extraction method is based on a set of association words, it makes an error of judging different documents identically. This paper proposes an association word mining method with weighted word, which reflects not only the preference rating of items but also information on the items. The proposed method is capable of creating the profile of the collaborative users, in which users are grouped according to the vector space model and Kmeans algorithm. Thus, the new method eliminates the existing collaborative filtering system's problems of sparsity and of recommendations based on the degree of correlation of user preferences. Entropy is used in order to address the said system's shortcoming whereby items are recommended according to the degree of correlation of the two most similar users within a group. Thus, the typical preference of the group is extracted. Since user preferences cannot be automatically regarded as accurate data, users within the group who have entropies beyond the threshold are selected as typical users. After this selection, the typical preference can be extracted by assigning typical user preferences in the form of weights. By using the typical preference of the group, the method also reduces the time required for retrieving the most similar users within the group.

1 Introduction

Collaborative filtering systems such as Ringo and GroupLens use person correlation to compare the information preferences of users and to find similar users by computing their degree of correlation[6, 8, 14]. To obtain the degree of correlation

I.-Y. Song et al. (Eds.): ER 2003, LNCS 2813, pp. 419–432, 2003.

between two users, these systems compute only the two users' item preferences. They thus incur the following problems[3, 9, 19]. Studies have been conducted to address the problem of sparsity in such a case. One such study explores a method that uses one of the EM algorithms[14], Kmeans algorithm[2,10], entropy weighting, and SVD, which groups users by the feature selection of a group[5, 18, 12]. This method does not find similar users by grouping users who have similar item preferences, but applies the item preferences of similar users to all the users within a group. It cannot thus address the problem of sparsity[12]. The method has another shortcoming, though, in that a recommendation is made depending on the correlation match between only two users, and it cannot be made when there is a low degree of preference correlation[15]. This paper uses a document as an item. The native feature space consists of unique words with single dimension when it occurs in documents, which can be tens or hundreds of thousands of words for even a moderate-sized text collection. This is prohibitively high for many learning algorithms. Since the feature extraction method using association word mining does not use the profile, it needs not update the profile, and it automatically generates noun phrases by using confidence and support of the Apriori algorithm without calculating the probability for index. Besides, since this method is representing document as a set of association words, it prevents users from being confused by word sense disambiguation, and thus, it has an advantage of representing a document in detail. However, in case that the feature extraction method is based on a set of association words, it makes an error of judging different documents identically.

This paper extracts the feature with higher dimension from item by using association word mining and then selects a weighted word with single dimension from association word by using TF.IDF. Using this method, the profile of the collaborative user is created, and based on this profile, users are grouped according to the vector space model and Kmeans algorithm. Consequently, the collaborative filtering system's problems of sparsity and of recommendations based on the degree of correlation of user preferences are eliminated. Moreover, entropy is used to address the system's shortcomings whereby items are recommended according to the degree of correlation of the two most similar users within a group. Thus, the typical preference of the group is extracted. Since user preferences cannot be automatically regarded as accurate data, users within the group who have entropies beyond the threshold are selected as typical users. The user preference means the value that user rates for an item. After this selection, the typical preference can be extracted by assigning typical user preferences in the form of weights. The method enables dynamic recommendation because it reduces the time for retrieving the most similar users within the group.

2   System Diagram for Mining the Typical Preference

Fig. 1 shows the system diagram for mining the typical preference of a collaborative user group in the recommender system. The system consists of three steps: Step A, in which the collaborative user profile of the {user-item} matrix is composed; Step B, in which collaborative users are grouped; and Step C, in which the typical preference is mined from within the group.

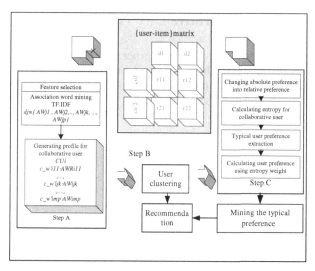

Fig. 1. System diagram for mining the typical preference of a collaborative user group in the recommender system

In Step A, the profile of collaborative users is created on the basis of the {user-item} matrix. The item feature is selected through association word mining with the weighted word to reflect the item information. Consequently, an item is a set of association words. A collaborative user specifies his/her preference rating for the items as the initial weight of the association word, and computes and merges the frequency statistics. The final result becomes the weight for the association word. With the weight of association word computed, the result becomes the basis for the collaborative user's profile. In Step B, users are grouped according to the weighted collaborative user profile. Similarities between users are computed using the vector space model and Kmeans algorithm, which is the typical clustering algorithm. In Step C, the typical preference of each group is extracted. To extract the typical preference, the entropy of each user within the group is computed. As a pre-processing step prior to computing the entropy, the user preference based on the {user-item} matrix must be converted into the relative preference. Since entropy utilizes the user preference distribution chart, it can be computed inaccurately when the absolute preference is used. There must thus be a step in which the absolute preference is converted into the relative preference. After computing the user entropy based on the relative preference, typical users are selected. The preference is recomputed by reflecting the entropy of the corresponding user on the absolute preference of the typical users. Lastly, since the recomputed preference is not suitable for the {user-item} matrix, the conversion process is required. After these processes are completed, the final typical preference of the group can be mined.

3 Generating the Collaborative User Profile

In section 3, a collaborative user profile is generated to mine the typical preference first. The collaborative user profile is generated based on {user-item} matrix. For the generation of collaborative user profile, the feature extraction should be done first. This paper uses web documents as items.

3.1 Feature Extraction with Typical Word

In this paper, we use a more effective feature extraction method applying association word mining[5] to express the characteristics of the documents as either a bag-of–words or a bag-of-associated-words. The association word mining method, by using Apriori algorithm[1], represents a feature for document not as single words but as association-word-vectors. Since the feature extraction method using association word mining does not use the profile, it needs not update the profile, and it automatically generates noun phrases by using confidence and support at Apriori algorithm without calculating the probability for index. Besides, since this method is representing document as an association word set, it prevents users from being confused by word sense disambiguation, and thus, it has an advantage of representing a document in detail. However, because this feature extraction method is based on a word set of association words, it makes an error of judging different documents identically. This problem decreases the accuracy of document classification. In the case of inserting a new document into database, this method has a problem that the database should be updated each time. This paper proposes a method of giving the weight to a word in association word by using TF•IDF. TF•IDF is defined to be the weight of the words in the document. We select the word that has the largest TF•IDF in association word. Both the association word and the typical word are selected as features, and it solves the problem, which is caused by using only association words. The Apriori algorithm[1] is used to mine associated data from the words extracted from morphological analysis. The association word mining algorithm, Apriori, is used to find the associative rules of items out of the set of transactions. The mined data, or the set of associated words from each document, are represented as an association-word-vector model. As a result, documents are represented in Table 1 in the form of an association-word-vector model.

Table 1. An example of features extracted from Web document

Web document	Features
document₁	game&participation&popularity operation&selection&match game&rank&name user&access&event
document₂	data&program&music figure&data&program game&explanation&provision game&utilization&technology

The words in association word at Table 1 are weighted using by TF•IDF. First, feature selection using TF•IDF makes morphological analysis of the document to extract characteristics of the document, and then extracts only nouns from its outcome. TF•IDF of all extracted nouns can be obtained through Equation (1).

$$W_{nk} = f_{nk} \bullet [log_2 \frac{n}{DF} + 1] \tag{1}$$

In Equation (1), fn_k is the relative frequency of word n_k against all words within the document, and n is the number of study documents, and DF is the number of training documents where word n_k appeared. It extracts only higher frequency words by aligning them from higher TF•IDF words to lower ones. If characteristic of experiment document(D) is $\{n_1,n_2,...,n_k,..,n_m\}$, it is compared with words in association word in Table 1. As a result, the words, which are belonged to association word, are weighted by TF•IDF. The word with the highest weight is selected as the typical word of the association word. If the typical word of (data&program&music) in Table 1 is 'data', we represent it as (*data*&program&music). Equation (2) defines the features of document d_j that is composed of p association words.

$$d_j = \{ AW_{j1}, AW_{j2},..., AW_{jk}, ..., AW_{jp}\} \tag{2}$$

In Equation (2), each of $\{AW_{j1}, AW_{j2}, AW_{jk}, AW_{jp}\}$ means association word that is extracted from document d_j. For the best results in extracting the association words, the data must have a confidence of over 85 and a support of less than 20[11].

3.2 Collaborative User Profile

The collaborative filtering system based on web documents recommends a document to users according to {user-item} matrix. The user in collaborative filtering system does not rate preference on all documents. Therefore, the missing value occurs in the {user-item} matrix. The missing value causes the sparsity of {user-item} matrix. In this section, the collaborative user profile is generated to reduce the sparsity of {user-item} matrix caused by the missing value. If we define m items composed of p feature vectors and a group of n users, the user group is expressed as $U=\{cu_i\}(i=1,2,...,n)$, and the document group is expressed as $I=\{d_j\}(j=1,2,...,m)$. We define the users in collaborative filtering database to be 'collaborative user'. And $R=\{r_{ij}\}(i=1,2,...,n$ $j=1,2,...,m)$ is a matrix of {user-item}. The element in matrix r_{ij} means user cu_i's preference to document d_j. Table 2 is the matrix of {user-item} in collaborative filtering system.

Table 2. {user-item} matrix in collaborative filtering system

	d_1	d_2	d_3	d_4	...	d_j	...	d_m
cu_1	r_{11}	r_{12}	r_{13}	r_{14}	...	r_{1j}	...	r_{1m}
cu_2	r_{21}	r_{22}	r_{23}	r_{24}	...	r_{2j}	...	r_{2m}
cu_i	r_{i1}	r_{i2}	r_{i3}	r_{i4}	...	r_{ij}	...	r_{im}
cu_n	r_{n1}	r_{n2}	r_{n3}	r_{n4}	...	r_{nj}	...	r_{nm}

The collaborative filtering system uses the information on how the user rates the preference for web pages. Preference levels are represented on a scale of 0~1.0 in increments of 0.2, a total of 6 degrees, and only when the value is higher than 0.5 is the user classified as showing interest. The web documents used in this paper are computer-related documents gleaned by an http down loader. The features of web documents are extracted by association word mining described in section 3.1. r_{ij} in

Table 2 is the preference rated by user. Namely, the element of matrix r_{ij} is in one of 6 degrees or no rating.

The profile of collaborative filtering user cu_i is generated based on the document features. In case a collaborative user rates preference low, the weight of rated document is given low. In case a collaborative user rates preference high, the weight of rated document is given high. Therefore, the preference of association words expressed in features indicates various values according to the weight. As a collaborative user cu_i defines the preference rating r_{ij} on the document d_j, the weight of each association word extracted from document d_j is weighted as r_{ij}. The weight of association word AW_{ijk} is defined as c_w_{ijk}. In case a collaborative user cu_i rates for document d_j, AW_{ijk} is the kth association word from Equation (2). Equation (3) defines the initial weight AW_{ijk}, which are structural elements, to generate the user cu_i's profile. The initial weight of AW_{ijk} of association words, c_w_{ijk}, is defined as the initial preference, the elements of the {user-item} matrix. The preference that the user rates directly is the most correct and important data for automatic preference rating.

$$c\_w_{ijk} = \text{Preference}(AW_{ijk}) = r_{ij}\ (user{:}cu_i, 1 \leqslant j \leqslant m, 1 \leqslant k \leqslant p) \tag{3}$$

Table 3 shows the detailed calculating method to get the initial weight c_w_{ijk} obtained by the definition of Equation (3). Each of documents d_i, d_j, and d_m is rated the value of 0.2, 0.8, 1 by the collaborative user cu_i in Table 3. The word in italics in association word is a typical word.

Table 3. Giving initial weight for profile generation

Document	Initial weight	Association word
d_i (preference r_{ii}=0.2)	$c\_w_{i1}(0.2)$	AW_{i1} *game*&configuration&user&selection
	$c\_w_{il2}(0.2)$	AW_{il2} interior&newest&*technology*& installation
	$c\_w_{ilk}(0.2)$	AW_{ilk} figure&popularity&*service*&music
	$c\_w_{ilp}(0.2)$	AW_{ilp} *Utilization*&technology&development
d_j (preference r_{ij}=0.8)	$c\_w_{ij1}(0.8)$	AW_{ij1} *Utilization*&technology&development
	$c\_w_{ij2}(0.8)$	AW_{ij2} *game*&organization&selection&rank
	$c\_w_{ijk}(0.8)$	AW_{ijk} interior&newest&*technology*& installation
	$c\_w_{ijp}(0.8)$	AW_{ijp} organization&user&*rank*
d_m (preference r_{im}=1.0)	$c\_w_{im1}(1.0)$	AW_{im1} provision&illustation&*explanation*
	$c\_w_{im2}(1.0)$	AW_{im2} *Utilization*&technology&development
	$c\_w_{imk}(1.0)$	AW_{imk} development&*rank*&sports
	$c\_w_{imp}(1.0)$	AW_{imp} figure&data&*service*&engine

In Table 3 based on Equation (3), the weights of $\{AW_{i1}...\}, \{AW_{ij1}...\}, \{AW_{im1}...\}$ are defined to be 0.2, 0.8, 1, respectively. Although AW_{ijl}, AW_{im2}, AW_{ilp} in Table 3 are the same association word, their initial Weights, 0.2, 0.8, 1, are different. It needs combining these different initial weights to generate a collaborative user profile. The weight of the same association word is multiplied after retrieving all association words. Table 4 shows the detailed weighting procedures and examples based on Table 3. For example, the final weights of $\{AW_{il2}, AW_{ijk}\}$, $c\_w'_{il2}$ and $c\_w'_{ijk}$, are $c\_w_{il2} \times c\_w_{ijk}$ because they are the same.

Table 4. The final weight given to association words

Association Word	Weight to association word
AW_{ij1} , AW_{im2}, AW_{ilp}	$c\_w'_{ij1 <= }c\_w_{ij1}\mathrm{x}c\_w_{im2}\mathrm{x}c\_w_{ilp}$ $c\_w'_{im2 <= }c\_w_{ij1}\mathrm{x}c\_w_{im2}\mathrm{x}c\_w_{ilp}$ $c\_w'_{ilp <= }c\_w_{ij1}\mathrm{x}c\_w_{im2}\mathrm{x}c\_w_{ilp}$
AW_{il2}, AW_{ijk}	$c\_w'_{il2 <= }c\_w_{il2}\mathrm{x}c\_w_{ijk}$ $c\_w'_{ijk <= }c\_w_{il2}\mathrm{x}c\_w_{ijk}$

Equation (4) based on Table 4 is applied in changing a weight according to the frequency of the association word extracted from all documents rated by the user, after giving initial weight to association word by Equation (3) as in Table 3. All association words extracted from documents, which are rated by the collaborative user cu_i, are saved in database($AWDB$). Then, an association word(AW_{ijk}) is the same as another association word($AW_{ij'k'}$) after retrieving $AWDB$, c_w_{ijk} is multiplied by $c\_w_{ij'k'}$. The final weight of association word AW_{ijk} is defined to be $c\_w'_{ijk}$. In Equation (4), $j \neq j'$ or $k \neq k'$ means that the same association word like $AW_{111}=AW_{111}$ is excluded from computing.

$$c\_w'_{ijk} = \prod_{AW_{ijk},AW_{ij'k'} \in AWDB} c\_w_{ijk} \cdot c\_w_{ij'k'} \mid (AW_{ijk}=AW_{ij'k'})(1 \leq j,j' \leq m, 1 \leq k,k' \leq p)|j \neq j \, or \, k \neq k',user:cu_i, (4)$$

Table 5 defines the structure of a collaborative user profile to be CU_i based on Table 4 and Equation (4). By definition in Equation (4), the final weight $c\_w'_{ijk}$ is given to association word AW_{ijk}.

Table 5. The structure of a collaborative user profile CU_i

User ID	Weight	Association word	...	Weight	Association word	...	Weight	Association word
CU_i $(user:cu_i 1 \leq j \leq$ $m, 1 \leq k \leq p)$	$c\_w'_{i11}$	AW_{i11}	...	$c\_w'_{ijk}$	AW_{ijk}	...	$c\_w'_{imp}$	AW_{imp}

4   Mining Typical Preference of Group

In section 4, we describe the method for clustering users into groups and extracting group typical preference based on collaborative user profile in section 3. In order to cluster users, we compute similarity between users by using vector space model and cluster users into groups by using Kmeans algorithm based on the results.

To determine similarities between users, this paper uses the vector space model, which is widely used in the information retrieval field when grouping users that show similar inclinations. Moreover, this paper uses Kmeans algorithm to group users. In the vector space model, all information - such as stored text and natural information requests - is represented as a set of words and a vector[2]. According to the vector space model, the collaborative user profile CU_i of the collaborative user cu_i in Table 5 is defined as a vector in the dimension p. When computing similarities between users according to the vector space model using the collaborative user profile in Table 5, the vector length normalization process is required[17]. When there are many association words in the form of profiles, the vector length normalization process sets the length of the collaborative user vector at 1 in order to solve the imbalance problem through the influence of the word count. This process divides the weight of each word by the square root of the sum of the square of the weight. Kmeans algorithm[2] groups users according to similarities between collaborative users. Kmeans clustering algorithm is a simplified form of the Maximum-Likelihood(ML) method in data classification and does not guarantee absolute convergence[2]. Moreover, it has a shortcoming in that the number of groups must first be determined for the algorithm to perform well, and the convergence of clustering results differs depending on the group center's initial value. The algorithm has been efficiently applied, however, to user grouping because of its simplicity[2].

This section predicts the typical preference of users within a group using the distribution of user preferences. The distribution of user preferences for items is very significant in the collaborative filtering system. For instance, if a user has rated all items 0.8, it is impossible to predict the typical preference based on this value. If all items are rated 0.8, it is very probable that the user rated the items very carelessly because of the tedious rating system or lack of time. Thus, since these data cannot accurately represent the user's preferences, using these data to predict the typical preference will decrease the accuracy of the recommendation. The typical preference of users within a group must be based on the more carefully chosen preferences of the users. Carefully chosen user preferences are more accurate than identical preferences because users cannot have identical tastes for all items in which they are interested. If the values of the preferences of users within a group range uniformly between 0 and 1, such data can be used to predict the typical preference within the group. If the values are identical, however, such data will decrease the accuracy of the recommendation.

To apply the abovementioned theory, entropy is used to predict the typical preference of users within a group. Assume that the collaborative user cu_i has indicated different preference ratings -- $x1, x2, x3, \dots$ -- for the given items. As the distribution of $x1, x2, x3, \dots$ becomes more uniform, the uncertainty increases and entropy increases as well. On the other hand, as the probability variable becomes smaller and only a few concentrated values appear, the uncertainty decreases and entropy decreases as well.

The process of dynamic recommendation by predicting the typical preference of a group using entropy involves Step 1, in which the absolute preference is converted into the relative preference; Step 2, in which the entropy of the collaborative user is computed; Step 3, in which collaborative users are sorted; Step 4, in which the typical preference of the group is predicted; Step 5, in which the typical preference in Step 4 is converted into the typical preference that can be used for recommendation; and Step 5, in which a recommendation is dynamically made using the typical preference.

In Step 1, the absolute user preference is converted into the relative preference. When the entropy of a collaborative user is computed based on the absolute preference, accurate values cannot be computed because the computation is greatly influenced by the absolute value of the preference rather than the preference distribution. Thus, the process of converting the absolute preference into the relative preference is required. Equation (5) is applied in converting the absolute preference ($p_{cui,j}$) into the relative preference ($Rp_{cui,j}$).

$$Rp_{cui,j} = p_{cui,j} - MIN_j\, p_{cui,j} \qquad (5)$$

Equation (5) finds the minimum preference out of all the preference values indicated by the user cu_i. Then, the preference rating of each item minus the minimum preference is specified as the relative preference. Table 6 lists the relative preference ratings for given items as a result of substituting, in Equation (5), the absolute preference ratings for the items.

Table 6. Conversion of absolute preference into relative preference

	Item1	Item2	Item3	Item4	Item5	Item6
UserA	0.8	0.6	0.4	0.2	1	0
UserB	0	0	0	0	0	0
UserC	0	0.2	0	0.2	0.8	0.2
UserD	0	0.6	0.4	0.8	0.2	0.8
UserE	0	0	0.2	0	0	0.2
UserF	0	0	0.2	0.2	0.4	0
UserG	0	0	0	0	0	0
UserH	0	0	0	0	0	0

In Step 2, the entropy of the collaborative user is obtained based on the relative preference converted as shown in Table 6. Equation (6) computes the entropy (H_{cui}) of a user within the group. $Rp_{cui,j}$ in Equation (6) indicates the relative preference of the collaborative user cu_i for the item j.

$$H_{cui} = \sum_j (Rp_{cui,j} + 1) \cdot log_2 (Rp_{cui,j} + 1) \tag{6}$$

1 is added to the relative preference in Equation (6) because the relative preference for items is often 0, as Table 6 shows. Since in this case, 0 cannot be substituted in the log equation, the entropy of the collaborative user is computed with 1 added to the relative preference

In Step 3, to predict the typical preference of the group, users with high numerical values, as computed in Equation (6), are extracted. In this step, the threshold for the entropy of the collaborative users is set, users beyond the threshold are extracted, and users with low entropy are excluded. To determine the threshold, 200 users were experimented on with different thresholds. As a result, when a numerical value under 1 was set as a threshold, too many typical users were extracted, which reduced the accuracy of the typical preference prediction. On the other hand, when a numerical value greater than 1 was set as a threshold, too few typical users were extracted, which also reduced the accuracy of the predicted typical preference. Thus, this paper has set the threshold at 1 and excluded collaborative users with entropies under 1 in the typical preference prediction. If the threshold of 1 is applied for the users in Table 6, users A, C, D and F will become the subjects of the typical preference prediction.

Step 4 predicts the typical preference of the group. The typical preference is predicted by multiplying the users' absolute preferences with their entropy weighting. The entropy of a collaborative user must be lowered to a decimal fraction so that it may be applied as a weight. When an entropy value over 1 is used, the predicted typical preference turns out the same, and the predicted typical preference cannot be used for recommendation. Thus, this paper divides by 10 the entropy value of the users shown in Equation (6). Equation (7) is applied for obtaining a user's entropy weighting (wH_{cui}).

$$wH_{cui} = H_{cui} / 10 \tag{7}$$

To predict the typical preference for an item, the entropy of a collaborative user, defined as in Equation (7), must be merged with the absolute preference of the collaborative user. The missing value in collaborative filtering matrix is estimated through absolute preference being reflected the entropy value. The equation for this is shown in Equation (8), which is the typical preference (Rd_j) of the item d_j.

$$Rd_j = \sum_i P_{cui,j} \cdot wH_{cui} \qquad (8)$$

Equation (8) sums up all the items of the absolute preferences of all collaborative users within the group for item d_j to be multiplied with the entropy weighting of the collaborative users. Table 7 lists the absolute preference and the user entropy weighting by Equation (6). It also shows the results of the substitution of the typical preference per item in Equation (8).

Step 5 converts the typical preference in Step 4 into the typical preference that may be used for recommendation. The typical preference by Equation (8) in Table 7 is not the value 0, 0.2, 0.4, 0.6, 0.8 or 1 used in the collaborative filtering matrix. Thus, the process of converting the typical preference predicted in Step 4 into the preference that may be used for actual recommendation is required. Fig. 2 shows the algorithm that computes the typical preference (Rd_j') of the item d_j. The function INT () removes the fractional part of a number and leaves only the resulting integer value, and the function REMAINDER (A, B) divides A by B and leaves only the remainder.

> *temp= INT(Rd_j x 10)*
> *temp1= REMAINDER(temp,2)*
> If (temp1 ==1)
> *Rd_j'=(temp+1)/10*
>   Else
> *Rd_j'=temp/10*
>   Endif

Fig. 2. Algorithm for computing the typical preference (Rd_j') of item d_j

Table 7 shows the results of converting the typical preference by Equation (8) into the typical preference that may be used for recommendation, using the algorithm in Fig. 2.

Table 7. Weighting entropy of users and typical preferences for given items

	Item1	Item2	Item3	Item4	Item5	Item6	Entropy	Entropy weight
UserA	0.8	0.6	0.4	0.2	1	0	5.606	0.5606
UserC	0.2	0.4	0.2	0.4	1	0.4	2.473	0.2473
UserD	0.2	0.8	0.6	1	0.4	1	5.132	0.5132
UserF	0.2	0.2	0.4	0.4	0.6	0.2	1.310	0.1310
Typical preference By Equation (8)	0.63	0.87	0.63	0.78	1.09	0.64		
Typical preference by Fig. 3	0.6	0.8	0.6	0.8	1	0.6		

In Step 5, a dynamic recommendation for an item is made using the typical preference. To give dynamic recommendations to users, the process of classifying users receiving recommendations into the most suitable group takes precedence.

5 Performance Evaluation

The database for collaborative filter recommendations was created from the data of 200 users and 1600 web documents. Users evaluated a minimum of 10 of the 1600 web documents. The database for content_based filter recommendations was created from 1600 web documents. These 1600 web documents were collected from URLs related to computer by an http downloader, then hand-classified into 8 areas of computer information. The 8 areas were classified under the labels of the following classes: {Games, Graphics, News and media, Semiconductors, Security, Internet, Electronic publishing, and Hardware}. The basis for this classification comes from search engines such as AltaVista and Yahoo that have statistically analyzed and classified computer related web documents. Of the 200 users, 100 were used as the training group, and the remaining users were used as the test group.

In this paper, mean absolute error(MAE) and rank score measure(RSM), both suggested by paper[4] are used to gauge performance. MAE is used to evaluate single item recommendation systems. RSM is used to evaluate the performance of systems that recommend items from ranked lists. The accuracy of the MAE, expressed as Equation (9), is determined by the absolute value of the difference between the predicted value and real value of user evaluation.

$$S_a = \frac{1}{m_a} \sum_{j \in p_a} | p_{a,j} - v_{a,j} | \qquad (9)$$

In Equation (9), $p_{a,j}$ is the predicted preference, $v_{a,j}$ the real preference, and m_a the number of items that have been evaluated by the new user.

The RSM of an item in a ranked list is determined by user evaluation or user visits. RSM is measured under the premise that the probability of choosing an item lower in the list decreases exponentially. Suppose that each item is put in a decreasing order of value j, based on the weight of user preference. Equation (10) calculates the expected utility of user U_a's RSM on the ranked item list.

$$R_a = \sum_j \frac{\max(V_{a,j} - d, 0)}{2^{(j-1)/(\alpha-1)}}$$

$$(10)$$

In Equation (10), d is the mid-average value of the item, and α is its the halflife. The halflife is the number of items in a list that has a 50/50 chance of either review or visit. In the evaluation phase of this paper the halflife value of 5 shall be used. In Equation (11), the RSM is used to measure the accuracy of predictions about the new user.

$$R = 100 \times \frac{\sum_u R_u}{\sum_u R_u^{max}}$$

$$(11)$$

In Equation (11), if the user has evaluated or visited a item that ranks highly in a ranked list, R_u^{max} is the maximum expected utility of the RSM.

For evaluation, this paper uses all of the following methods: the proposed method using typical preference(RecoMine), the method of recommendation using K-means user clustering (K-means)[10], the method of recommendation using feature of group(Feature_G)[12]. These methods are compared by changing the number of clustered users. Also, the proposed method was compared with the previous method using memory based collaborative filtering technique (Memory_Coll)[8] by changing the number of user evaluations on items. Fig. 3 shows the MAE of RecoMine, K-means, and Feature_G based on Equation (9) and Equation (11). In Fig. 3, as the number of users increases, the performance of the RecoMine increases, whereas K-means and Feature_G show no notable change in performance. Fig. 4 shows the time required for recommendation by changing the number of clustered users.

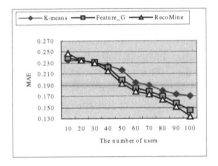

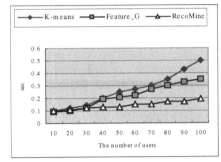

Fig. 3. MAE varying at the number of users

Fig. 4. The time required for recommendation by changing the number of clustered users.

It is evident that method RecoMine is more superior to others. On the other side, in case that the number of users is small, the performance of RecoMine decreases a little. In Fig. 4, although the number of users increases, RecoMine is more superior to others. Fig. 5 shows the MAE of RecoMine and Memory_Coll when the number of user's evaluations is increased. Fig. 6 shows the time required for recommendation when the number of user's evaluations is increased. In Fig. 5 the RecoMine outperforms the other in accuracy. In Fig. 6, RecoMine needs the smaller time than Memory_Coll.

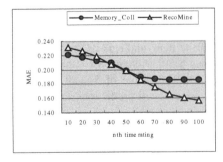

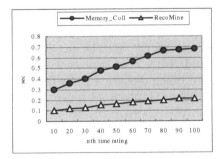

Fig. 5. MAE at n'th rating

Fig. 6. The time required for recommendation at n'th rating

6 Conclusion

The collaborative filtering system does not directly analyze the contents of the information but utilizes similarities between users. This paper proposed an association word mining method with the weighted word, which reflects not only the preference rating of items but also information on the items. Using this method, the profile of the collaborative user is created, and based on this profile. Users are grouped according to the vector space model and Kmeans algorithm. Consequently, the existing collaborative filtering system's problems of sparsity and of recommendations based on the degree of correlation of user preferences are eliminated. Moreover, entropy is used to address the said system's shortcomings whereby items are recommended according to the degree of correlation of the two most similar users within a group. Thus, the typical preference of the group is extracted. Since user preferences cannot be automatically regarded as accurate data, users within the group who have entropies beyond the threshold are selected as typical users. After this selection, the typical preference can be extracted by assigning typical user preferences in the form of weights. The method enabled dynamic recommendation because it decreases the inaccuracy of recommendations based on unproven user preferences, by using the typical preference of the group. The method also reduced the time for retrieving the most similar users within the group.

Reference

[1] R. Agrawal and R. Srikant, "Fast Algorithms for Mining Association Rules," Proceedings of the 20th VLDB Conference, Santiago, Chile, 1994.

[2] K. Alsabti, S. Ranka, and V. Singh, "An Efficient K-Means Clustering Algorithm," http://www.cise.ufl.edu/ranka/, 1997.

[3] C. Basu, H. Hirsh, and W. W. Cohen, "Recommendation as classification:Using social and content-based information in recommendation," In proceedings of the Fifteenth National Conference on Artificial Intelligence, pp. 714–720, Madison, WI, 1998.

[4] John. S. Breese and C. Kadie, "Empirical Analysis of Predictive Algorithms for Collaborative Filtering," Proceedings of the Conference on Uncertainty in Artificial Intelligence, Madison, WI, 1998.

[5] D. Billsus and M. J. Pazzani, "Learning collaborative information filters," In proceedings of the International Conference on Machine Learning, 1998.

[6] J. Delgado and N. Ishii, "Formal Models for Learning of User Preferences, a Preliminary Report," In Proceedings of International Joint Conference on Artificial Intelligence (IJCAI-99), Stockholm, Sweden, July, 1999.

[7] Inha University, "Intelligent Information Retrieval System centering User", Technical research report, 1997.

[8] A. Kohrs and B. Merialdo, "USING CATEGORY-BASED COLLABORATIVE FILTERING IN THE ACTIVE WEBMUSEUM," Proceedings of the IEEE International Conference on Multimedia and Expo – Vol. 1 , 2000.

[9] Sarwar, B. M., Karypis, G., Konstan, J. A., and Riedl, J., "Application of Dimensionality Reduction in Recommender System – A Case Study," In ACM WebKDD 200 Web Mining for E-Commerce Workshop, 2000.

[10] Taek-Hun Kim, Young-Suk Ryu, Seok-In Park, Sung-Bong Yang, "An Improved Recommendation Algorithm in Collaborative Filtering," EC-Web 2002, pp. 254–261, 2002.

[11] S. J. Ko and J. H. Lee, "Feature Selection using Association Word Mining for Classification," In Proceedings of the Conference on DEXA2001, LNCS2113, pp. 211–220, 2001.

[12] Y. S. Lee and S. W. Lee, "Group Feature Selection using Entropy Weight and SVD," Transaction of KISS(B), Vol. 29, No. 4, 2002.

[13] W. S. Lee, "Collaborative learning for recommender systems," In Proceedings of the Conference on Machine Learning, 1997.

[14] G. J. McLachlan and T. Krishnan, The EM Algorithm and Extensions, New York: John Wiley and Sons, 1997.

[15] M. Pazzani, D. Billsus, Learning and Revising User Profiles: The Identification of Interesting Web Sites, Machine Learning, Kluwer Academic Publishers, pp. 313–331, 1997.

[16] Badrul Sarwar, George Karypis, Josephp Konstan, and John Ridedl, "Analysis of Recommendation Algorithms for E-Commerce," Proc. Of The ACM E-Commerce 2000, 2000.

[17] G. Salton and M. J. McGill, Introduction to Modern Information Retrieval, McGraw-Hill, 1983.

[18] I. Soboroff and C. Nicholas, "Combining content and collaboration in text filtering," In Proceedings of the IJCAI'99 Workshop on Machine Learning in Information filtering, pp. 86–91, 1999.

[19] L. H. Ungar and D. P. Foster, "Clustering Methods for Collaborative Filtering," AAAI Workshop on Recommendation Systems, 1998.

Conceptual Modeling of Concurrent Systems through Stepwise Abstraction and Refinement Using Petri Net Morphisms

Boleslaw Mikolajczak[1,2] and Zuyan Wang[1]

[1] University of Massachusetts Dartmouth, Dartmouth, MA, USA
[2] Polish-Japanese School of Information Technology, Warsaw, Poland

Abstract. Development of complex concurrent systems is very often performed in a top-down or bottom-up approach depending on design circumstances. Such design reflects vertical conceptual modeling of concurrent systems with certain number of abstraction/ refinement layers. Petri net morphisms have been proven to be useful in this process as long as certain desired structural and behavioral properties of such systems are preserved. We use example of a renting agency to illustrate applicability of morphisms in systematic development of distributed systems. Preservation of structural and behavioral properties of Petri net morphisms is also discussed.

1 Motivation and Introduction

Petri nets are formal, graphical, and executable mathematical models that are appropriate for the development of concurrent, discrete-event dynamic systems. It has been under development since the beginning of the 1960's. After forty years of research and development, Petri nets have been proven to be applicable to a variety of areas. It can be used in design and analysis of concurrent and distributed systems, workflow management systems, requirement specifications in software engineering, specifications of communication protocols, and so on.

Usually there are two different approaches in Petri net system modeling. One is the top-down approach and the other is the bottom-up approach. In top-down approach, one can start modeling a system from the highest conceptual level of abstraction, then refine the system using techniques such as rule-based refinement [11], general refinement [4], and hierarchical modeling [5] until reaching a satisfying level of detail of the system. In bottom-up approach, one starts the modeling of a system at the lowest level of abstraction, then abstracts the system model step by step until reaching the highest level of abstraction.

In practice, the top-down approach is relatively easy to achieve. Yet modeling a system using the bottom-up approach is very difficult, because there are very few techniques about 'how to shrink' a system model to a higher level of abstraction without losing the structural and behavioral properties of the system. However, this approach is practically very important in system modeling.

I.-Y. Song et al. (Eds.): ER 2003, LNCS 2813, pp. 433–445, 2003.

On one hand, for large and complex systems, it is necessary to have models for different levels of abstraction and notions for refinement and abstraction to formulate relations between these models. Petri nets are methods of modeling using graphic representation to specify events and state changes. In practice, such kind of graph is easy to understand when the graph contains only a small number of elements. But when the net becomes larger, the graph becomes so complicated that it is difficult to understand and extract useful information from it. Thus if we have a large system model at a detailed level, then to understand essential logical relations among the elements or between different parts of the system, we must abstract the system to achieve a satisfying level of detail such that it is easy to understand the essential properties of the system.

On the other hand, in formal object-oriented software engineering, rigorous software development requires continuous verification during all phases of the software development process. However, resources are often very restricted and a totally new verification at each step is usually too expensive and time consuming. Thus, vertical structuring techniques that can preserve desired properties for both top-down and bottom-up approaches will be very helpful.

Moreover, the concept of morphisms originated from the category theory and algebras in mathematics, it can be applied to state machines [8] as well as Petri nets [9]. There exist several different concepts of Petri net morphisms which have already been introduced in literature, such as vicinity respecting morphisms [2], Winskel's morphisms [16], Lakos' net morphisms and system morphisms [7], and general morphisms [1]. These morphisms respect different types of Petri nets and preserve different structural and behavioral properties of Petri nets. The properties of Petri net morphisms make them useful in the refinement and abstraction of Petri net system modeling and analysis of the system being modeled [15].

In this paper, we will focus on the abstraction of Petri net model, and try to provide a solution to the following problem using vicinity respecting morphisms of Petri nets: Suppose we have a detailed system modeled using Petri nets, how can we abstract the system model so that some desired properties of the system can be preserved. In section two, we will give some basic definitions about Petri nets and Petri net morphisms, section three will be an example of conceptual modeling of distributed systems using vicinity respecting morphisms of Petri nets, section four discusses structural and behavioral properties of Petri nets with morphisms, section five is the conclusions.

2   Petri Nets and Petri Net Morphisms

2.1   Petri Nets

Petri nets are directed bipartite graphs with two node types called places and transitions. The nodes are connected via directed arcs. Connections between two nodes of the same type are not allowed. Graphically, circles represent places and rectangles represent transitions. There are two different approaches in defining

Petri nets. One respects the structure of Petri nets, the other extends the first one and emphasizes the behavioral aspect of Petri nets.

[Def.2.1.1] (Structure Respecting Petri Nets) A Petri net is a triple $N = (P, T, F)$ satisfying:

1. P is a finite non-empty set of places,
2. T is a finite non-empty set of transitions satisfying $P \cap T = \emptyset$,
3. $F \subseteq (P \times T) \cup (T \times P)$ is a set of arcs called the flow relation,

[Def.2.1.2] (Behavior Respecting Petri Nets) A Petri net is a 4-tuple $N = (P, T, F, M_0)$ satisfying condition (1), (2) of Def.2.1.1 and the following conditions:

1. F is a multiset of $(P \times T) \cup (T \times P)$, called the flow relation,
2. M_0 is a non-empty multiset of places, called *initial marking*.

In both definitions $X = P \cup T$ denotes the set of all elements of a Petri net. We call the set $\{y \in X | (y, x) \in F\}$ the *pre-set* of x, the set $\{y \in X | (x, y) \in F\}$ the *post-set* of x , denoted by $^\bullet x$ and $x^\bullet$, respectively. We will use the notation $^\circ x = ^\bullet x \cup \{x\}$ to represent *pre-vicinity* and $x^\circ = x^\bullet \cup \{x\}$ to represent *post-vicinity*, too.

Here, initial marking is introduced in Def.2.1.2 and the definition uses a multiset [9] of $(P \times T) \cup (T \times P)$ to specify the change of marking when a transition t *fires* [13]. By doing this, the behavioral aspects of Petri nets are defined.

2.2   Petri Net Morphisms

The abstraction of Petri nets is not a new idea and can date back to Petri [10]. The method of relating a Petri net and its abstraction net is called a Petri net morphism. Roughly speaking, A Petri net morphism is a mapping from elements of a source net to elements of a target net that preserves some properties of the source net. There are two types of Petri net morphisms. One focuses on the structural relationship between source and destination nets, i.e. how places and transitions are connected via arcs in both nets. The other one respects the behavioral relationship, i.e. the relationship between different markings caused by firing of transitions in a Petri net. In our discussion, we will talk about both structure and behavior respecting Petri net morphisms.

[Def.2.2.1] (Structure Respecting Petri Net Morphisms) Let $N = (P, T, F)$, $N' = (P', T', F')$ be Petri nets. A mapping $\varphi : P \times T \to P' \times T'$ is called a Petri net morphism, denoted by $\varphi : N \to N'$, if for every edge $(x, y) \in F$ holds:

1. If $(x, y) \in F \cap (P \times T)$ then either $(\varphi(x), \varphi(y)) \in F' \cap (P' \times T')$ or $\varphi(x) = \varphi(y)$ and
2. If $(x, y) \in F \cap (T \times P)$ then either $(\varphi(x), \varphi(y)) \in F' \cap (T' \times P')$ or $\varphi(x) = \varphi(y)$

[Def.2.2.2] (Vicinity Respecting Morphisms) Let $\varphi : N \to N'$ be a Petri net morphism as defined in Def.2.2.1,

1. φ is S-vicinity respecting if, for every $x \in P$:
   a) $\varphi(^\circ x) =^\circ (\varphi(x))$ or $\varphi(^\circ x) = \varphi(x)$ and
   b) $\varphi(x^\circ) = (\varphi(x))^\circ$ or $\varphi(x^\circ) = \varphi(x)$
2. φ is T-vicinity respecting if, for every $x \in T$:
   a) $\varphi(^\circ x) =^\circ (\varphi(x))$ or $\varphi(^\circ x) = \varphi(x)$ and
   b) $\varphi(x^\circ) = (\varphi(x))^\circ$ or $\varphi(x^\circ) = \varphi(x)$
3. φ is vicinity respecting if it is both S-vicinity respecting and T-vicinity respecting.

The above definitions are based on the definition of structure respecting Petri nets and respect the structural properties of Petri nets. Vicinity respecting morphisms are special class of structure respecting Petri net morphisms. In vicinity respecting morphisms, φ is S-vicinity respecting means that the pre-vicinity (post-vicinity) of a place x is mapped to either the pre-vicinity (post-vicinity) of the image of place x or the image of place x itself. This is dual to transitions. It can preserve many structure respecting properties of Petri nets, such as connectivity and strong connectedness, path, vicinity of places and transitions, strongly connected place or transition bordered subnet, S-components and T-components, covering by S-component and T-component, minimal trap and minimal siphon [3].

[Def.2.2.3] (Winskel's homomorphisms) Let $N = (P, T, F, M_0)$ and $N' = (P', T', F', M'_0)$ be Petri nets. A homomorphism from N to N' is a pair of multirelations (η, β) with $\eta : T \to_\mu T'$ and $\beta : P \to_\mu P'$ such that

1. $\beta M_0 = M'_0$,
2. $\forall A \in \mu T,\ ^\bullet(\eta A) = \beta(^\bullet A)$ and $(\eta A)^\bullet = \beta(A^\bullet)$

[Def.2.2.4] (Winskel's morphisms) A morphism from Petri net N to N' is a homomorphism $(\eta, \beta) : N \to N'$, in which η is a partial function, that is, the matrix of η satisfies

1. $\eta_{t,t'} \leq 1$,
2. $\eta_{t,t'} = 1$ and $\eta_{t,t''} = 1 \Rightarrow t' = t''$

for transitions $t \in T$, $t' \in T'$ and $t'' \in T'$.

These two definitions are based on the definition of behavior respecting Petri nets and respects behavioral aspects of Petri nets. In the definition of homomorphisms, η and β refer to multirelation between T and T', P and P', respectively. "A" refers to a multiset of transitions, $^\bullet A$ refers to the pre-set of A, $A^\bullet$ refers to the post-set of A. Such Petri net homomorphisms preserve initial marking and the environments of transitions, that is, the pre-set of the image of a transition set is equal to the image of the pre-set of that transition set, the post-set of the image of a transition set is equal to the image of the post-set of that transition set.

In Def.2.2.3, η is a multirelation from T to T', yet in Def.2.2.4, η is a partial function from T to T'. It satisfies the condition that a transition can be mapped to either nothing ($\eta t = \emptyset$) or a single transition in the destination net. If a transition is mapped to two transitions in the destination net, the two transitions in the destination net should be the same transition. Comparing with Def.2.2.3, Def.2.2.4 eliminates the possibility that a transition in source net can be mapped to two coincident transitions using a single morphism and allows a source net to refine or shrink as needed. It is more useful and meaningful in modeling practice. [Def.2.2.5] Let $N = (P, T, F, M_0, \mathbf{M})$ and $N' = (P', T', F', M'_0, \mathbf{M'})$ be two augmented Petri nets. A general morphism $f : N \rightarrow N'$ between N and N' consists of a partial function $\eta : T \rightarrow T'$ and a multirelation $\beta : P \rightarrow P'$ which together fulfill the following conditions:

1. $\beta M_0 = M'_0$,
2. $M \in \mathbf{M}$ implies $\beta M \in \mathbf{M'}$,
3. ${}^\bullet(\eta t) \leq \beta({}^\bullet t)$,
4. $\beta(t^\bullet) = \beta({}^\bullet t) -{}^\bullet (\eta t) + (\eta t)^\bullet$

In this definition (P, T, F, M_0) is a classical Petri net, and $\mathbf{M} \subseteq \mu P$ is a set of markings of a Petri Net satisfying the following conditions: $M_0 \in \mathbf{M}$, and $M \in \mathbf{M}$ and $M[e\rangle M'$ implies $M' \in \mathbf{M}$.

Other fundamental concepts concerning Petri nets that are not defined here can be found in [13] and [14].

3   Conceptual Modeling of Concurrrent Systems with Vicinity Respecting Petri Net Morphisms

Vicinity respecting morphisms can preserve many structural respecting properties of Petri nets and can be a useful means to refine and abstract concurrent systems modeled with Petri nets. By refining and abstracting a system model using vicinity respecting morphisms, we can gain better understanding of the system.

An example of conceptual modeling of concurrent systems with vicinity respecting morphisms of Petri nets: the renting agency example will be presented here. We will do the modeling using RENEW software tool [12].

The renting agency example concerns the concurrent modeling of a car renting service, seen from three different perspectives: the customer perspective, the insurance company perspective and the car renting service perspective. The customer perspective emphasizes the different possible states of the customer, with the car renting service viewed as some form of transition with which customers interact. The emphasis of the insurance company perspective is to be able to track down cars and customer authorizations. The insurance company perspective emphasizes that the transition *Fetch car* puts together an authorized customer (determined by the car renting service) and a car (from the parking area). The car renting service perspective emphasizes the renting procedure and the record keeping from the business perspective.

Fig.1 presents the Petri net model of renting agency system that merges together the three perspectives mentioned above. Places and transitions have names that implicitly give their semantics. Using the concept of Petri net vicinity respecting morphisms, we can get the abstraction of the renting agency system from the customer perspective, shown in Fig.2. In this case we applied

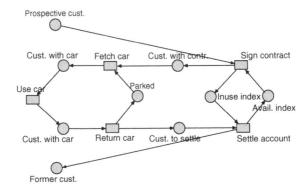

Fig. 1. Detailed Petri net model of the renting agency system

twice vicinity morphism-based transformations. First, we represent as a single transition, two places (*Inuse index* and *Avail. index*) and two transitions (*Sign contract* and *Settle account*). This new unnamed transition shall have direct connections with four places: *Prospective cust.*, *Former cust.*, *Cust. with contr.*, *Cust. to settle*. This new transition is called in Fig.2 as *Work on CHS issue*. Secondly, two transitions (*Fetch car* and *Return car*) and one place (*Parked*) are combined into a single transition, called *Working on assur. Issue*. When these two abstraction transformations are completed one can combine a subnet composed of these two new transitions and two places, *Cust. With contr.* and *Cust. To settle*, that links them together into a single transition. This new transition has a name *Work on CHS issue*. So, from the customer perspective there are only two transitions: *Use car* and *Work on CHS issue*. Customer can be in one of four states: *Prospective cust.*, *Cust. With car* (car not used yet), *Cust. With car* (already used), and *Former cust*. One can note that a sequence of morphic transformations performed is somewhat flexible as long as the final Petri net reflects intentions of having a Petri net that presents relevant states and actions of a customer. Differently speaking, this final Petri net can be achieved by several abstracting transformation sequences.

Similarly, we can get both the insurance company perspective and the car renting service perspective in Fig.3 and Fig.4, respectively. In all these cases Petri net subnets that are combined into a single place or transition are denoted by a surrounding larger oval or larger rectangle. In this manner it is straightforward to trace consecutive transformation steps. Furthermore, using the result in Fig.2 together with the concept of vicinity respecting morphisms, we can achieve the highest level of abstraction of the system being modeled as shown in Fig.5. Here, we represent a pool of customers as a single place called *Customers*, and these customers change their status as a result of a single transition *Work on CHS issue*.

In Fig.2 we show two abstraction transformations of a Petri net from Fig.1 (the Customer perspective).

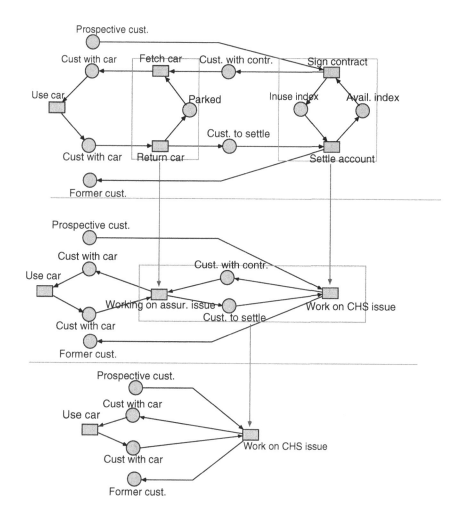

Fig. 2. Process of achieving the customer perspective of renting agnecy system

In Fig.3 we present two abstraction transformations of a Petri net from Fig.1 (the insurance company perspective).

In Fig.4 we present four abstraction transformations of a Petri net from Fig.1 (the car renting service perspective). In Fig.4 two actions, *Sign contract* and *Settle account*, are at the center of renting agency perspective. A contract can be signed only when there are customers and there are cars available in the index. Similarly to settle an account, the customer with used car is needed and a record of the car as being in use.

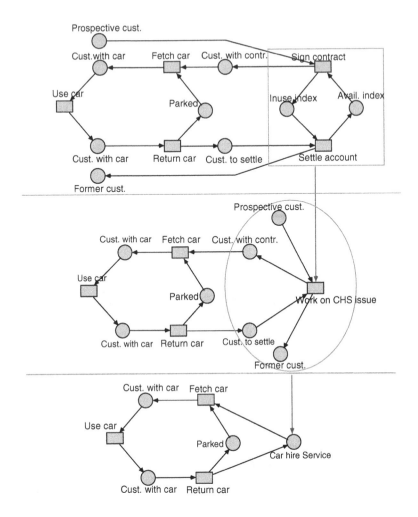

Fig. 3. Process of achieving the insurance company perspective of renting agency system

4   Structural and Behavioral Properties of Petri Net Morphisms

Vicinity respecting morphisms, Winskel's morphisms and general morphisms of petri nets can all preserve structure or behavior of Petri nets. If some important properties of source Petri net can be preserved in the destination Petri net, it will not only be useful in conceptual modeling of concurrent systems but also simplify the verification process of the system model.

In this section, two discovery matrixes will be constructed to achieve exhausted information on structural and behavioral properties of Petri nets with

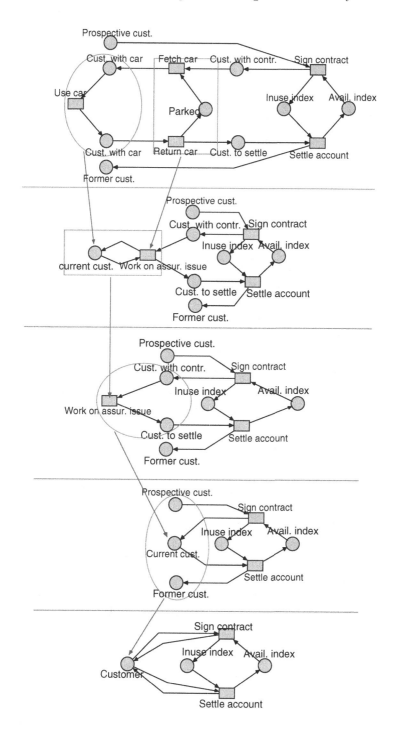

Fig. 4. Process of achieving the car renting service perspective of renting agency system

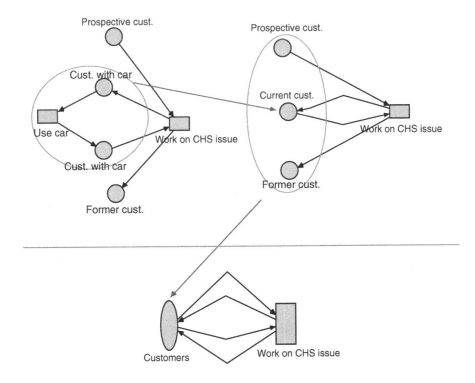

Fig. 5. Process of reaching highest level of abstraction of renting agency system from customer perspective of the system

vicinity respecting morphisms, Winskel's morphisms and general morphisms, respectively. Then we will discuss some of the unproved problems in the matrixes.

In the matrixes, columns represent different types of Petri net morphisms, "VRM" means vicinity respecting morphisms, "WM" means Winskel's morphisms and "GM" means general morphisms; rows represent structural or behavioral properties of Petri nets. Here, "Yes" means the property in a row will be preserved by the corresponding morphisms. "No" means the property will not be preserved by the corresponding morphisms. "Proved" means the property in a row has been proved to be preserved by the corresponding morphisms in the column in other literatures. In the matrixes, the properties mentioned refer to those properties that if it is satisfied in the source net of a morphism, it should also be held in the destination net of the morphism. We will discuss some of those "Yes" and "No" (unproved) problems next.

[Proposition 4.1] Every Winskel's morphism is a vicinity respecting morphism.

Suppose $\varphi = (\eta, \beta) : N = (P, T, F, M_0) \to N' = (P', T', F', M_0')$ is a Winskel's morphism, which means $\varphi(x) = \beta(x)$, when $x \in P$; $\varphi(x) = \eta(x)$, when $x \in T$. $\forall (a, b) \in F \cap (P \times T)$, we have $b \in T$. According to the definition of Winskel's homomorphisms, we get ${}^{\bullet}\eta(b) = \beta(a)$, that is $(\beta(a), \eta(b)) \in$

Table 1. Discovery matrix concerning behavioral properties of Petri nets

	VRM	WM	GM
Minimal Siphon	Proved	Yes	No
Minimal Trap	Proved	Yes	No
Free Choice Net	Proved	Yes	No
Liveness	No	Yes	Yes
Boundedness	No	Yes	Yes
Safety	No	Yes	yes
Initial Marking	No	Yes	Yes
Reachable Marking	No	Yes	Yes
Case Graph	No	Yes	Proved

Table 2. Discovery matrix concerning structural properties of Petri nets

	VRM	WM	GM
Edge	No	No	No
Connectivity	Yes	Yes	No
Path	Yes	Yes	No
Strong Connectedness	Yes	Yes	No
Pre and Post Vicinity of Place	Yes	Yes	No
Pre and Post Vicinity of Transition	Yes	Yes	No
Subnet	Yes	Yes	No
Transition or Place Bordered Subnet	Yes	Yes	No
Strongly Connected Transition or Place Bordered Subnet	Proved	Yes	No
S or T component	Proved	Yes	No
Covering by S or T Component	Proved	Yes	No

$F' \cap (P' \times T')$. Besides, according to the definition of Winskel's morphisms, we can see $\eta(b) = \beta(a)$, when $\eta_{b,b'} = 0$. So, we have $\varphi(a) = \varphi(b)$, when $\eta_{b,b'} = 0$, else $(\varphi(a), \varphi(b)) \in F' \cap (P' \times T')$. Similarly, we can prove that $\forall(a, b) \in F \cap (T \times P)$, either $(\varphi(a), \varphi(b)) \in F' \cap (T' \times P')$ or $\varphi(a) = \varphi(b)$. Thus we know that a Winskel's morphism is a structure respecting Petri net morphism.

For any Winskel morphism $\varphi = (\eta, \beta)$, we know $0 \leq \eta_{t,t'} \leq 1$. $\forall a \in P$, if $\eta_{t,t'} = 0$, if $t \in^\bullet a$, we have $\varphi(^\circ a) = \eta(^\circ a) = \varphi(a)$; if $\eta_{t,t'} \neq 0$, we have $\varphi(^\circ a) = \eta(^\circ a) =^\circ \varphi(a)$, thus a Winskel's morphism is a S- vicinity respecting morphism. And we can prove that a Winskel's morphism is a T-vicinity respecting morphism too. Therefore we get the conclusion that every Winskel's morphism is a vicinity respecting morphism.

[**Proposition 4.2**] In discovery matrix, no structural property is preserved by general morphisms.

From [1], we know that every Winskel's morphism is a general morphism but not vice verse. That means that general morphisms are generalized version of Winskel's morphisms, it does not guarantee that elements that are connected in source net must be connected in the destination net. If there is not guarantee of the connectivity property, there is no need to discuss the preservation of other structural properties mentioned in the discovery matrix, as they are all based on the connectivity of the net.

[**Proposition 4.3**] Winskel's morphisms preserve boundedness property of Petri nets. That is, given a Winskel's morphism $(\eta, \beta) : N = (P, T, F, M_0) \to N' = (P', T', F', M'_0)$, if β is finite and N is bounded, then N' is bounded.

Proof.

What we know is:$\forall p \in P, \exists n \in \mathbf{N}, \forall M \in [M_0 >, M(p) \leq n$.

What we want to prove is: $\forall p' \in P', \exists n' \in \mathbf{N}', \forall M' \in [M'_0 >, M'(p') \leq n'$.

As we knew that Winskel's morphisms preserve reachable marking of Petri nets, we could see, $\forall M' \in [M'_0 >, \exists M \in [M_0 >, M' = \beta(M)$. (Otherwise $\exists M' \in [M'_0 >, \forall M \in [M_0 >, M' \neq \beta(M)$, thus we will violate the definition of Winskel's morphisms). So $\forall p' \in P'$, we have $M'(p') = \beta(M(p))$, as β is finite and $M(p) \leq n$, there must exist some $n' \in \mathbf{N}$, $M'(p') = \beta(M(p)) \leq n'$.

[**Proposition 4.4**] Winskel's morphisms preserve safety property of Petri nets. That is, given a Winskel morphism $(\eta, \beta) : N = (P, T, F, M_0) \to N' = (P', T', F', M'_0)$, N is safe $\Rightarrow N'$ is safe if $\beta_{p,p'} \leq 1$.

Proof.

What we know is:$\forall p \in P, \forall M \in [M_0 >, M(p) \leq 1$.

What we want to prove is:$\forall p' \in P', \forall M' \in [M'_0 >, M'(p') \leq 1$,

We have proved in the Proposition 4.3, $\forall p' \in P', \exists n' \in \mathbf{N}, \forall M' \in [M'_0 >, M'(p') = \beta(M(p))$. now $M(p) \leq 1$ and $\beta_{p,p'} \leq 1$, so $M'(p') = \beta(M(p)) \leq 1$.

[**Proposition 4.5**] Winskel's morphisms preserve liveness property of Petri nets. That is, given a Winskel morphism $(\eta, \beta) : N = (P, T, F, M_0) \to N' = (P', T', F', M'_0)$, N is live $\Rightarrow N'$ is live.

Proof.

What we know is:$\forall M \in [M_0 >, \exists t \in T, \exists M_1 \in [M > t$

What we want to prove is:$\forall M' \in [M'_0 >, \exists t' \in T', \exists M'_1 \in [M' > t'$

According to the definition of Winskel's morphisms and proposition 4.4, we could see that $\forall M' \in [M'_0 >, \exists M \in [M_0 >$ in N, so that $\beta(M) = M'$ (otherwise we will violate the definition of Winskel's morphisms). For $t' = \eta t, \beta(M_1) = M'_1$, because $M_1 \in [M > t$, so from $M \to_t \dots \to M_1$, we could get $\beta(M) \to_{\eta t} \dots \to \beta(M_1)$, that is $M'_1 \in [M' > t'$, so N' is live too.

Similarly, we can prove that general morphisms preserve boundedness, safety and liveness properties too.

5   Conclusions

In this paper, vicinity respecting Petri net morphisms were applied to conceptual stepwise abstraction of concurrent systems by using a renting agency example. Structural and behavioral properties of vicinity respecting morphisms, Winskel's morphisms and general morphisms were discussed. The structural and behavioral properties of Petri net morphisms make them very important in stepwise conceptual modeling of concurrent systems, their proeperties are also very useful in simplifying the verification process of Petri net models.

Continuous works could be done on using Petri net morphisms in simplifying verification process of Petri net models and on discussing the verification of the equivalence and effectiveness of the morphisms.

Besides, in the research process, we found currently no Petri net software tool explicitly supports Petri net-based morphic transformations. Integration of morphic transformations of Petri nets into Petri net-based software development tools would be a desired addition to the functionality of these tools. An algorithm that computes the set of all net morphisms between two Petri nets is unknown as of today. Its computational complexity would be excessive taking into account complexity of computing morphisms between two deterministic automata [8].

References

1. Bednarczyk, M. A.; Borzyszkowski, A. M., General Morphisms of Petri nets, Lecture Notes in Computer Science, vol. 1644: Automata, Languages and Programming, Springer-Verlag 1999.
2. Desel, J, Merceron, A., Vicinity Rrespecting Net Morphisms Lecture Notes in Computer Science, vol. 483: Advances in Petri nets, pp. 165–185, Springer-Verlag, 1991.
3. Desel, J., Merceron, A., Vicinity Rrespecting Homomorphisms for Abstracting System Requirements, Bericht 337., Karlsruhe, 1996.
4. Devillers, R., Klaudel, H., Riemann, R. C., General Refinement for High Level Petri Nets, Lecture Notes in Computer Science, vol. 1346, Foundations of Software Technology and Computer Science pp. 297–311, Springer-Verlag, 1997.
5. Fehling, R., A Concept of Hierarchical Petri nets with Building Blocks, The 12th International Conference on Application and Theory of Petri Nets, 1991, Gjern, Denmark, pp. 370–389, June 1991.
6. Girault, C., Valk, R., Petri Nets for Systems Engineering: a Guide to Modeling, Verification, and Applications, Springer, 2003.
7. Lakos, C., Composing Abstraction of Colored Petri nets, Lecture Notes in Computer Science, vol. 1825: Application and Theory of Petri nets, pp. 323–345, Springer-Verlag, 2000.
8. Mikolajczak, B. A Parallel Algorithm for Computing all Homomorphisms of Deterministic Finite Automata, in DIMACS Series in Discrete Mathematics and Theoretical Computer Science, vol.22, Parallel Processing of Discrete Optimization Problems, American Mathematical Society, 1994.
9. http://www.nist.gov/dads
10. Petri, C.A., Introduction to General Net Theory Net and Applications, Lecture Notes in Computer Science, W. Brauer (ed.), pp. 1–19, Springer-Verlag, 1980.
11. Padberg, J., Gajewsky, M.;, Ermel, C., Rule-based Refinement of High-level Nets Preserving Safety Properties, Lecture Notes in Computer Science, vol. 1382, Fundamental Approaches to Software Engineering, pp. 221–238, Springer-Verlag, 1998.
12. www.renew.de
13. Reisig, W., Petri Nets,An Iintroduction, Springer-Verlag, 1985.
14. Reisig, W., Elements of Distributed Algorithms: Modeling and Analysis with Petri Nets, Springer Verlag, 1998.
15. Wang, Zuyan, Morphisms of Petri Nets and their Role in Formal Modeling of Concurrent Systems, Master Project, UMASS Dartmouth, May 2002.
16. Winskel, G. Petri Nets, Algebras, Morphisms and Compositionality, Information and Computation, 72: pp. 197–238, 1987.

Taxonomy-Based Conceptual Modeling for Peer-to-Peer Networks

Yannis Tzitzikas[1]*, Carlo Meghini[1], and Nicolas Spyratos[2]

[1] Istituto di Scienza e Tecnologie dell' Informazione [ISTI]
Consiglio Nazionale delle Ricerche [CNR], Pisa, Italy
{tzitzik,meghini}@isti.cnr.it

[2] Laboratoire de Recherche en Informatique, Universite de Paris-Sud, France
spyratos@lri.fr

Abstract. We present a taxonomy-based conceptual modeling approach for building P2P systems that support semantic-based retrieval services. We adopt this simple conceptual modeling approach due to its advantages in terms of ease of use, uniformity, scalability and efficiency. As each peer uses its own taxonomy for describing the contents of its objects and for formulating queries to the other peers, peers are equipped with *articulations*, i.e. inter-taxonomy mappings, in order to carry out the required translation tasks. We describe various kinds of articulations and we give the semantics for each case. Then we discuss the differences between query evaluation in mediators and query evaluation in P2P systems, and finally we identify issues for further research.

1 Introduction

There is a growing research and industrial interest on peer-to-peer (P2P) systems. A peer-to-peer system is a distributed system in which participants (the peers) rely on one another for service, rather than solely relying on dedicated and often centralized servers. Many examples of P2P systems have emerged recently, most of which are wide-area, large-scale systems that provide content sharing (e.g. Napster), storage services [7,20], or distributed "grid" computation (e.g. Entropia, Legion). Smaller-scale P2P systems also exist, such as federated, server-less file systems [3,2] and collaborative workgroup tools (e.g. Groove). Existing peer-to-peer (P2P) systems have focused on specific application domains (e.g. music file sharing) or on providing file-system-like capabilities. These systems do not yet provide semantic-based retrieval services. In most of the cases, the name of the object (e.g. the title of a music file) is the only means for describing the contents of the object.

Semantic-based retrieval in P2P networks is a great challenge that raises questions about data models, conceptual modeling, query languages and techniques for query evaluation and dynamic schema mapping. Roughly, the language that

---

* Work done during the postdoctoral studies of the author at CNR-ISTI as an ERCIM fellow.

I.-Y. Song et al. (Eds.): ER 2003, LNCS 2813, pp. 446–460, 2003.

can be used for indexing the objects of the domain and for formulating semantic-based queries, can be *free* (e.g natural language) or *controlled*, i.e. object descriptions and queries may have to conform to a specific vocabulary and syntax. The former case, resembles distributed Information Retrieval (IR) systems and this approach is applicable in the case where the objects of the domain have a textual content (e.g. [10]). In this paper we focus on the latter case where the objects of a peer are indexed according to a specific conceptual model represented in a particular data model (e.g. relational, object-oriented, logic-based, etc), and content searches are formulated using a specific query language. A P2P system might impose a single conceptual model on all participants to enforce uniform, global access, but this will be too restrictive. Alternatively, a limited number of conceptual models may be allowed (e.g. see [13]), so that traditional information mediation and integration techniques will likely apply (with the restriction that there is no central authority). The case of fully heterogeneous conceptual models makes uniform global access extremely challenging and this is the case that we are interested in.

In this paper we propose an approach which is based on *taxonomies*. Taxonomies are very easy to build in comparison to other kinds of conceptual models. Moreover, as we shall see, if the conceptualization of the domain is a set of objects (e.g. a set of music files, images, etc) then this approach is as expressive as other more sophisticated conceptual modeling approaches. Peers can construct their taxonomies either from scratch or by extracting them from existing taxonomies (e.g. from the taxonomy of Open Directory or Yahoo!) using special-purpose languages and tools (e.g. like the one presented in [19]). In addition to its taxonomy, a source can have an object base, i.e. a database that indexes the objects of the domain under the terms of the taxonomy. Information integration, reconcilement and personalization is achieved through *mediators*, i.e. through sources which in addition to their taxonomies are enriched with *articulations* to the other sources of the network, where an articulation is actually a mapping between the terms of the mediator and the terms of the sources. Of course, in a pure P2P system we cannot partition sources to primary and secondary (i.e. mediators) as we may have mutually articulated sources. We describe the semantics of P2P systems of this kind and we identify issues that require further research concerning query evaluation and optimization.

The remaining of this paper is organized as follows: Section 2 discusses the benefits of taxonomies with respect to the P2P paradigm. Section 3 describes the building blocks of a network of articulated sources, i.e. sources, mediators and articulated sources. Section 4 describes the semantics of the network. Section 5 discusses query evaluation issues. Finally, Section 6 concludes the paper and identifies issues for further research.

2   Taxonomies

Taxonomies is probably the oldest conceptual modeling tool. Nevertheless, it is a powerful tool still used is in libraries, in very large collections of objects (e.g. see

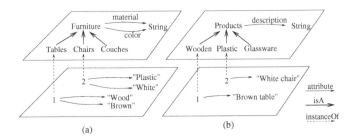

Fig. 1. Two different conceptual models for the same domain

[17]) and the Web (e.g. Yahoo!, Open Directory). Although more sophisticated conceptual models (including concepts, attributes, relations and axioms) have emerged and are recently employed even for meta-tagging in the Web [11,25], almost all of them have a backbone consisting of a subsumption hierarchy, i.e. a taxonomy.

What we want to emphasize here, is that in a very broad domain, such as the set of all Web pages or in large scale P2P system, it is not easy to identify the classes of the domain because the domain is too wide and different users, or applications, conceptualize it differently, e.g. one class of the conceptual model according to one user may correspond to a value of an attribute of a class of the conceptual model according to another user. For example, Figure 1 shows two different conceptual models for the same domain. We consider only two objects of the domain, denoted by the natural numbers 1 and 2. The conceptual model of Figure 1.(a) is appropriate for building an information system for a furniture store, while the conceptual model of Figure 1.(b) is appropriate for building an information system for a department store. The classes of model (a), i.e. the classes **Tables**, **Chairs** and **Couches**, have been defined so as to distinguish the objects of the domain according to their *use*. On the other hand, the classes of model (b), i.e. the classes **Wooden**, **Plastic** and **Glassware**, have been defined so as to distinguish the objects of the domain according to their *material*. This kind of distinction is useful for a department store, as it determines (up to some degree) the placement of the objects in the various departments of the store.

Figure 2 shows a taxonomy for the same domain which consists of terms and subsumption links only. This taxonomy seems to be more application independent. All criteria (characteristics) for distinguishing the objects are equally "honoured".

A simple conceptual modeling approach where each conceptual model is a taxonomy, has two main advantages. The first is that it is very easy to create the conceptual model of a source or a mediator. Even ordinary Web users can design this kind of conceptual models. Furthermore, the design can be done more systematically if done following a faceted approach (e.g. see [15,14]). In addition, thanks to techniques that have emerged recently [21], taxonomies of compound terms can be also defined in a flexible and systematic manner.

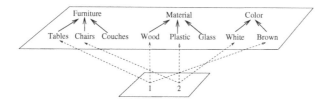

Fig. 2. A taxonomy that consists of terms and subsumption links only

The second, and more important for P2P systems, advantage is that the simplicity and modeling uniformity of taxonomies allows integrating the contents of several sources without having to tackle complex structural differences. Indeed, as it will be seen in the subsequent sections inter-taxonomy mappings offer a *uniform* method to bridge *naming, contextual* and *granularity* heterogeneities between the taxonomies of the sources. Given this conceptual modeling approach, a mediator does not have to tackle complex structural differences between the sources, as happens with relational mediators (e.g. see [9,8]) and Description Logics-based mediators (e.g. see [6,4]). Moreover, it allows the integration of *schema* and *data* in a uniform manner. Another advantage of this conceptual modeling approach is that query evaluation in taxonomy-based sources and mediators can be done efficiently (polynomial time).

Due to the above benefits (conceptual modeling simplicity, integration flexibility, query evaluation efficiently), taxonomies seem appropriate for large scale pure P2P systems. The only assumption that we make is that the domain is a set of objects which we want to index and subsequently retrieve, without being interested in the relationships that may hold between the objects of the domain.

3   The Network

Let *Obj* denote the set of all objects of a domain common to several sources. A typical example of such a domain is the set of all pointers to Web pages. A network of articulated sources over *Obj* is a set of sources $U = \{S_1, ... S_n\}$ where each S_i falls into one of the following categories:

Simple sources: they consist of a taxonomy and an object base, i.e. a database that indexes objects of *Obj* under the terms of the taxonomy. A simple source accepts queries over its taxonomy and returns the objects whose index "matches" the query.

Mediators: they consist of a taxonomy plus a number of articulations to other sources of the network. Again, a mediator accepts queries over its taxonomy but as it does not maintain an object base, query answering requires sending queries to the underlying sources and combining the returned results.

Articulated sources: they are both simple sources and mediators, i.e. they consist of a taxonomy, an object base and a number of articulations to other sources of the network. An articulated source can behave like a simple source,

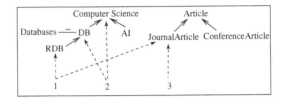

Fig. 3. Graphical representation of a source

like a mediator, or like a mediator which in addition to the external sources can also use its own simple source for query answering.

Clearly, simple sources and mediators are special cases (or roles) of articulated sources. Each kind of source is described in detail below.

3.1   Simple Sources

A simple source S is a pair $\langle (T, \preceq), I \rangle$ where $(T, \preceq)$ is a taxonomy and I is an interpretation of T.

Definition 1. A taxonomy is a pair $(T, \preceq)$ where T is a *terminology*, i.e. a finite and non empty set of names, or *terms*, and $\preceq$ is a reflexive and transitive relation over T called *subsumption*.

If a and b are terms of T and $a \preceq b$ we say that a is *subsumed* by b, or that b *subsumes* a; for example, Databases $\preceq$ Informatics, Canaries $\preceq$ Birds. We say that two terms a and b are *equivalent*, and write $a \sim b$, if both $a \preceq b$ and $b \preceq a$ hold, e.g., Computer Science $\sim$ Informatics. Note that the subsumption relation is a preorder over T and that $\sim$ is an equivalence relation over the terms T. Moreover $\preceq$ is a partial order over the equivalence classes of terms induced by $\sim$.

In addition to its taxonomy, each source has a stored *interpretation* I of its terminology, i.e. a total function $I : T \rightarrow 2^{Obj}$ that associates each term of T with a set of objects. Here, we use the symbol 2^{Obj} to denote the powerset of Obj. Figure 3 shows an example of a simple source. In this and subsequent figures the objects are represented by natural numbers and membership of objects to the interpretation of a term is indicated by a dotted arrow from the object to that term. For example, the objects 1 and 3 in Figure 3 are members of the interpretation of the term JournalArticle, i.e. $I(\text{JournalArticle}) = \{1, 3\}$. Subsumption of terms is indicated by a continuous-line arrow from the subsumed term to the subsuming term. Note that we do not represent the entire subsumption relation but its Hasse diagram, in which the reflexive and the transitive arrows are omitted. Equivalence of terms is indicated by a continuous non-oriented line segment. Note that equivalence captures the notion of synonymy, and that each equivalence class simply contains alternative terms for naming a set of objects.

3.2   Mediators and Articulated Sources

A *mediator* is a secondary source that bridges the heterogeneities that may exist between two or more sources in order to provide a uniform query interface to an integrated view of these sources. According to the model presented in [23], a mediator has a taxonomy with terminology and structuring that reflects the needs of its potential users, but does *not* maintain a database of objects. Instead, the mediator maintains a number of *articulations* to the sources. An articulation to a source is a set of relationships between the terms of the mediator and the terms of that source.

These relationships can be defined manually by the designer of the mediator, or they can be constructed automatically or semi-automatically following a model-driven approach (e.g. [18,12]) or a data-driven approach (e.g. [22,5,16,1]). In this paper we do not focus on articulation design or construction (we treat this issue in [22]).

Users formulate queries over the taxonomy of the mediator and it is the task of the mediator to choose the sources to be queried, and to formulate the query to be sent to each source. To this end, the mediator uses the articulations in order to translate queries over its own taxonomy to queries over the taxonomies of the articulated sources. Then it is again the task of the mediator to combine appropriately the results returned by the sources in order to produce the final answer.

Definition 2. An *articulation* from a taxonomy $(T_i, \preceq_i)$ to a taxonomy $(T_j, \preceq_j)$, denoted by $\preceq_{a_{i,j}}$, or just $a_{i,j}$, is any set of relationships $t_j \preceq t_i$ where $t_i \in T_i$ and $t_j \in T_j$.

We assume that each term has a unique identity over the network and that all terminologies are pairwise disjoint.

Definition 3. A *mediator* M over k sources $S_1, ..., S_k$ consists of:
1) a taxonomy $(T_M, \preceq_M)$, and
2) a set $\{a_{M,1}, ..., a_{M,k}\}$, where each $a_{M,i}$ is an *articulation* from $(T_M, \preceq_M)$ to $(T_i, \preceq_i)$.

Figure 4.(a) shows an example of a mediator over two sources that provide access to electronic products. The articulation $a_{M,1}$ shown in this figure is the following sets of subsumption relationships: $a_{M,1} = \{$PhotoCameras$_1 \preceq$ Cameras, Miniature$_1 \preceq$ StillCameras, Instant$_1 \preceq$ StillCameras, Reflex$_1 \preceq$ Reflex $\}$ while the articulation $a_{M,2}$ is $a_{M,2} = \{$Products$_2 \preceq$ Electronics, SLRCams$_2 \preceq$ Reflex, VideoCams$_2 \preceq$ MovingPictureCams$\}$.

Integrating objects from several sources often requires *restoring the context* of these objects, i.e. adding information that is missing from the original representation of the objects which concerns the context of the objects. An example that demonstrates how the articulations can restore the context of the objects is shown in Figure 4.(b). The illustrated mediator provides access to electronic products according to the *type* of the products and according to the *location*

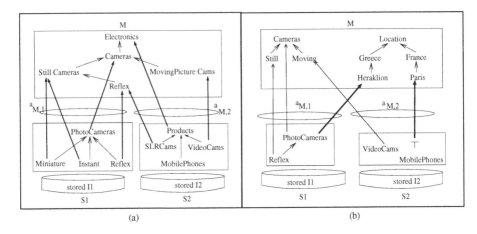

Fig. 4. Two examples of a mediator

of the stores that sell these products. The mediator has two underlying sources S_1 and S_2, where the former corresponds to a store located in Heraklion, while the latter corresponds to a store located in Paris. The context of the objects of each source, here the location of the store that sells each product, can be restored by adding to the articulations appropriate relationships. Specifically, for defining that all PhotoCameras of the source S_1 are available through a store located in Heraklion, it suffices to put in the articulation $a_{M,1}$ the relationship PhotoCameras$_1$ $\preceq$ Heraklion, while for defining that all products of the source S_2 are available through a store located in Paris, it suffices to put in the articulation $a_{M,2}$ the following relationship $\top_2$ $\preceq$ Paris, where $\top_2$ denotes the maximal element of the subsumption relation of S_2.

An articulated source is a source that is both simple and mediator.

Definition 4. An *articulated source* M over k sources $S_1, ..., S_k$ consists of:
1) a taxonomy $(T_M, \preceq_M)$,
2) a stored interpretation I_s of T_M, and
3) one *articulation* $a_{M,i}$ for each source S_i, $1 \leq i \leq k$.

4   Semantics and Queries

Suppose that a source S receives a query q. In this section we shall give answer to the following question: what answer S should return ? We will answer this question for the cases where S is: (a) a simple source, (b) a mediator, (c) an articulated source, and (d) a source (mediator or articulated source) that participates in a P2P system.

4.1   Simple Sources

A simple source $\langle (T, \preceq), I \rangle$ answers queries based on the stored interpretation of its terminology. However, in order for query answering to make sense, the interpretation that a source uses for answering queries must respect the structure of the source's taxonomy (i.e. the relation $\preceq$) in the following sense: if $t \preceq t'$ then $I(t) \subseteq I(t')$.

Definition 5. An interpretation I is a *model* of a taxonomy $(T, \preceq)$ if for all t, t' in T, if $t \preceq t'$ then $I(t) \subseteq I(t')$.

Definition 6. Given an interpretation I of T we define the model of $(T, \preceq)$ *generated* by I, denoted $\bar{I}$, as follows: $\bar{I}(t) = \bigcup \{I(s) \mid s \preceq t)\}$.

The set of interpretations of a given terminology T can be ordered using pointwise set inclusion, i.e. given two interpretations I, I' of T, we call I less than or equal to I', and we write $I \leq I'$, if $I(t) \subseteq I'(t)$ for each term $t \in T$. Note that $\leq$ is a partial order over interpretations. It can be easily seen that if I is an interpretation of T then $\bar{I}$ is the unique minimal model of $(T, \preceq)$ which is greater than or equal to I.

Definition 7. A *query* over a terminology T is any string derived by the following grammar, where t is a term of T: $q ::= t \mid q \wedge q' \mid q \vee q' \mid q \wedge \neg q' \mid (q) \mid \epsilon$ We will denote by Q_T the set of all queries over T.

A simple source responds to queries over its own terminology.

Definition 8. Any interpretation I of T can be extended to an interpretation $\hat{I}$ over the set of all queries in Q_T as follows: $I(q \wedge q') = I(q) \cap I(q'), I(q \vee q') = I(q) \cup I(q'), I(q \wedge \neg q') = I(q) \setminus I(q')$. For brevity we use I to denote both I and its extension over Q_T.

We shall use $ans_i(q)$ to denote the answer that a source S_i will return for the query q, i.e. the set $\bar{I}_i(q)$. Query evaluation in taxonomy-based sources can be done in polynomial time with respect the size of T, specifically the computation of $\bar{I}(q)$ can be done in $O(|T| * |Obj|)$ in the case where the transitive closure of $\preceq$ is stored.

4.2   Mediators and Articulated Sources

A mediator $\langle (T_M, \preceq_M), \{a_{M,1}, ..., a_{M,k}\} \rangle$ receives queries (boolean expressions) over its own terminology T_M. As it does not have a stored interpretation of T_M, the mediator answers queries using an interpretation of T_M obtained by *querying* the underlying sources. To proceed we need to introduce some notations. If A is a binary relation over a set T then we shall use A^* to denote the transitive closure of A, e.g. if $A = \{(a, b), (b, c)\}$ then $A^* = \{(a, b), (b, c), (a, c)\}$. If S is a subset of T then the restriction of A on S, denoted by $A_{|S}$, consists of those relationships in A that relate only elements of S. For example if $T = \{a, b, c\}$, $S = \{a, c\}$ and $A = \{(a, b), (b, c)\}$ then $A_{|S} = \emptyset$ while $A^*_{|S} = \{(a, c)\}$.

We define the *total subsumption* of the mediator, denoted by $\sqsubseteq_M$, by taking the transitive closure of the union of the subsumption relation $\preceq_M$ with all articulations of the mediator, that is: $\sqsubseteq_M = (\preceq_M \cup a_{M,1} \ldots \cup a_{M,k})^*$. Clearly, $\sqsubseteq_M$ is a subsumption relation over $T_M \cup F$, where F consists of all terms that appear in the articulations and are not elements of T_M ($F \subseteq T_1 \cup \ldots \cup T_k$). Clearly it holds: $(\sqsubseteq_M)_{|T_M} = \preceq_M$.

We can define an interpretation I of the terminology $T_M \cup F$ as follows:

$$I(t) = \begin{cases} \emptyset & \text{if } t \in T_m \\ ans_i(t) & \text{if } t \in T_i \end{cases}$$

Now let $\bar{I}$ denote the model of the taxonomy $(T_M \cup F, \sqsubseteq_M)$ that is generated by I, and let I_M denote the restriction of $\bar{I}$ on T_M, i.e. $\bar{I}_{|T_M}$. Clearly, I_M is a model of $(T_M, \preceq_M)$, and this is the model that the mediator has to use for answering queries. It can be easily seen that the mediator can compute this as follows:

$$I_M(t) = \bigcup_{i=1}^{k} (\cup\{\, ans_i(s) \mid s \in T_i, s \sqsubseteq_M t\}) \tag{1}$$

where t is a term of T_M. For example the interpretation of term Cameras of Figure 4.(a) is computed as follows:
$I_M(\text{Cameras}) = (\cup\{\, ans_1(s) \mid s \in T_1, s \sqsubseteq_M \text{Cameras}\}) \bigcup (\cup\{\, ans_2(s) \mid s \in T_2, s \sqsubseteq_M \text{Cameras}\}) = ans_1(\text{PhotoCameras}) \cup ans_1(\text{Miniature}) \cup ans_1(\text{Instant}) \cup ans_1(\text{Reflex}) \cup ans_2(\text{VideoCams}) \cup ans_2(\text{SLRCams})$

It worths mentioning here that as the articulations contain relationships between single terms these kinds of mappings enjoy the benefits of both *global-as-view* (*GAV*) and *local-as-view* (*LAV*) approach (see [4,8] for a comparison). Specifically, we have (a) the query processing simplicity of the *GAV* approach, as query processing basically reduces to unfolding the query using the definitions specified in the mapping, so as to translate the query in terms of accesses (i.e. queries) to the sources, and (b) the modeling scalability of the *LAV* approach, i.e. the addition of a new underlying source does not require changing the previous mappings.

Now, an articulated source behaves like a mediator, except that now, in addition to the k external sources $S_1, ..., S_k$, we have the mediator's own simple source $S_M = \langle (T_M, \preceq_M), I_s \rangle$ acting as a $(k + 1)$-th source. The interpretation I_M of T_M that is used for answering queries is defined by

$$I_M(t) = \bigcup_{i=1}^{k+1} (\cup\{\, ans_i(s) \mid s \in T_i, s \sqsubseteq_M t\}) \tag{2}$$

Here we assume that $T_{k+1} = T_M$, $I_{k+1} = I_s$, and thus $ans_{k+1}(t) = \bar{I}_{k+1}(t) = \cup\{\, I_s(s) \mid s \preceq_M t\}$.

4.3   Mediators and Articulated Sources in a P2P System

Figure 5 shows an example of a P2P network consisting of four sources $S_1, ..., S_4$; two simple sources (S_3 and S_4), one mediator (S_2) and one articulated source

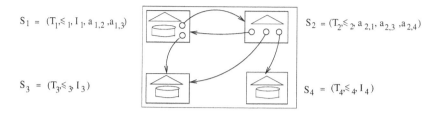

$S_1 = (T_1, \leqslant_1, I_1, a_{1,2}, a_{1,3})$

$S_2 = (T_2, \leqslant_2, a_{2,1}, a_{2,3}, a_{2,4})$

$S_3 = (T_3, \leqslant_3, I_3)$

$S_4 = (T_4, \leqslant_4, I_4)$

Fig. 5. A network of articulated sources

(S_1). In a P2P system we can no longer distinguish sources to primary and secondary (i.e. mediators), as we can have mutually articulated sources, e.g. notice the mutually articulated sources S_1 and S_2. Due to this characteristic, we have to consider the entire network in order to define semantics and query answers.

We can view the entire network as a single simple source. Let T denote the union of the terminologies of all sources in the network, i.e. $T = \bigcup_{i=1}^{n} T_i$. An interpretation of the network is any interpretation of the terminology T, i.e. any function $I : T \rightarrow 2^{Obj}$. At any given time point, we can define *the* interpretation of the network by taking the union of the interpretations that are stored in the sources of the network, i.e. $I = I_1 \cup ... \cup I_n$. Reversely, we can consider that there is one interpretation $I : T \rightarrow 2^{Obj}$ which is stored distributed in k sources $S_1, ..., S_k$ where each source S_i stores a part of I, i.e. a function $I_i : T_i \rightarrow 2^{Obj}$, where the sets $T_1, ..., T_k$ constitute a partition of T. We can define *the* subsumption relation of the network, denoted by $\sqsubseteq$, by taking the union of the total subsumption relations of the sources, i.e.: $\sqsubseteq = (\bigcup_{i=1}^{n} \sqsubseteq_i)^*$.

Now, a model of the network is any model of the taxonomy $(T, \sqsubseteq)$. Analogously to the simple source case, the minimal model that is greater than the interpretation of the network I, denoted by $\bar{I}$, is defined as follows: $\bar{I}(t) = \bigcup \{ I(t') \mid t' \sqsubseteq t \}$.

It is reasonable to use $\bar{I}$ as the model for answering queries. This means that if a source S_i receives a query q_i over T_i, then it should return the set $\bar{I}(q_i)$. For deriving the set $\bar{I}(t)$, where t is any term of T, each source has to contribute. Specifically, the contribution of each source S_i, denoted by $Contr_i(t)$, is the following: $Contr_i(t) = \bigcup \{ I_i(t') \mid t' \in T_i, \ t' \sqsubseteq t \}$ Thus we can also write: $\bar{I}(t) = Contr_1(t) \cup ... \cup Contr_n(t)$.

4.4   Extending the Form of Articulations

Before describing query evaluation in P2P systems let us first study a more general case where an articulation $a_{i,j}$ can contain subsumption relationships between terms of T_i and *queries* in Q_{T_j}. We call such articulations *term-to-query* (*t2q*) articulations and the former *term-to-term* (*t2t*) articulations. Clearly, a *t2q* articulation can contain relationships that we *cannot* express in a *t2t* articulation, e.g.: $\texttt{DBArticles}_i \succeq_{a_{i,j}} (\texttt{Databases}_j \wedge \texttt{Articles}_j)$,

`FlyingObject`$_i \succeq_{a_{i,j}}$ (`Birds`$_j \wedge \neg$ (`Ostrich`$_j \vee$ `Penguin`$_j$)).
Formally, a *t2q* articulation is defined as follows:

Definition 9. A *term-to-query articulation* $a_{i,j}$ is any set of relationships $q_j \preceq t_i$ where $t_i \in T_i$ and $q_j \in Q_{T_j}$.

Below we discuss the consequences of this extension. The relation $\sqsubseteq_M$ of a mediator over k sources $S_1, ..., S_k$ is defined similarly to the case of *t2t* articulations, but now $\sqsubseteq_M$ is a subsumption relation over $T_M \cup Q_{T_1} \cup ... \cup Q_{T_k}$. The interpretation I_M of the mediator can be defined as follows: $I_M(t) = \bigcup_{i=1}^{k}(\cup\{ ans_i(q) \mid q \in Q_{T_i}, q \sqsubseteq_M t\})$. Notice that since the articulations now contain relationships between terms of the mediator and source queries, we are in a *global-as-view* (*GAV*) approach.

Analogously to the case of *t2t* articulations, we can view the entire network as one simple source. However, the subsumption relation of the network, i.e. $\sqsubseteq$, now is not a relation over T, but a relation over V, where $V = T \cup \{q \in Q_T \mid q$ appears in an articulation$\}$. Consequently, the models of the network are defined as:

Definition 10. An interpretation I of T is a *model* of $(V, \sqsubseteq)$ if:
(a) if $t \sqsubseteq t'$ then $I(t) \subseteq I(t')$, and (b) if $q \sqsubseteq t$ then $\hat{I}(q) \subseteq I(t)$.

We can consider that the model of the network is the minimal model of $(V, \sqsubseteq)$ which is greater than the stored interpretation I. If the queries that appear in the articulations do not contain negation, then certainly there is always a unique minimal model. Indeed, we can view the entire network as a distributed Datalog program whose rules contain only monadic predicates. Specifically, we can view each $o \in I(t)$ as a fact $t(o)$ (where o is a constant), each $t \preceq t'$ as a rule $t'(X) :\!\!- t(X)$, and each *t2q* articulation as a set of rules, e.g. the relationship $t \succeq (t_1 \wedge t_2) \vee (t_3 \wedge \neg t_4)$ corresponds to the rules $t(X) :\!\!- t_1(X), t_2(X)$ and $t(X) :\!\!- t_3(X), \neg t_4(X)$. It is known that this kind of programs have always a unique minimal model. However, if the queries of the articulations have negation, then the corresponding Datalog program has rules with negation in their bodies, and such programs may not have a unique minimal model (e.g. see [24]). This is also illustrated by the example shown in Figure 6. The table shown in (b) of this figure shows the stored interpretation I of the network and two interpretation which are greater than I, namely I_a and I_b. Note that both are models and both are minimal.

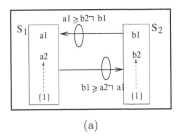

term/query	I	I_a	I_b
$a1$	$\emptyset$	$\{1\}$	$\emptyset$
$a2$	$\{1\}$	$\{1\}$	$\{1\}$
$b1$	$\emptyset$	$\emptyset$	$\{1\}$
$b2$	$\{1\}$	$\{1\}$	$\{1\}$
$b2 \wedge \neg b1$	$\{1\}$	$\{1\}$	$\emptyset$
$a2 \wedge \neg a1$	$\{1\}$	$\emptyset$	$\{1\}$

(a)   (b)

Fig. 6. A network with *t2q* articulations which has not a unique minimal model

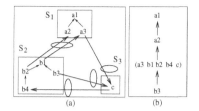

Fig. 7. A network of articulated sources

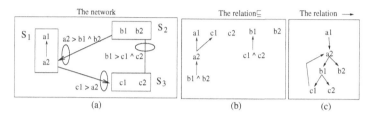

Fig. 8. A network with term-to-query articulations

5   Query Evaluation in P2P Systems

One can easily see that a straightforward query evaluation approach in which each mediator acts without taking into account that it participates in a P2P system is not appropriate as the external cycles (those that contain terms from two or more different sources) in the graph of the relation $\sqsubseteq$ may cause *endless query loops* as it happens in the network shown in Figure 7.(a). Notice the cycle $(a3, c, b4, b2, b1, a3)$ which is also shown in the Hasse diagram of the relation $\sqsubseteq$ that is shown in Figure 7.(a). Let use $q_{i,j}$ to denote a query which is submitted by a source S_i to a source S_j. The first part of the sequence of queries that will be exchanged between the sources, for answering the query $q = a2$, follows: $q_{1,2} = b2$, $q_{2,3} = c$, $q_{3,2} = b3$, $q_{3,1} = a3$, $q_{1,2} = b1$, $q_{2,3} = c$, and so on. Clearly, the query evaluation will never terminate. It can be easily proved that the cycles of $\sqsubseteq$ that contain terms from two or more sources cause this phenomenon.

Let us now consider the networks with $t2q$ articulations with no negation, like the one shown in Figure 8.(a). Notice that endless query loops can arise in this network. Indeed, if S_1 receives the query $q_1 = a1$ then we will have: $q_{1,2} = b1 \wedge b2$, $q_{2,3} = c1 \wedge c2$, $q_{3,1} = a2$, $q_{1,2} = b1 \wedge b2$, and so on. In networks with $t2t$ articulations we can identify the cases where endless query loops arise using the relation $\sqsubseteq$. However, in our case the relation $\sqsubseteq$ of the network (shown in Figure 8.(b)) does not allow us to detect this phenomenon as $\sqsubseteq$ does not have any external term cycle. For this reason, we can define an auxiliary relation over the set T of the network:

Definition 11. Let t, t' be two terms of T. We say that t *requires* t' and we write $t \rightarrow t'$, if one of the following holds:
(a) $t \succeq_i t'$ for an $i = 1, .., k$,

(b) $\exists\, q$ such that $t \sqsupseteq q$ and t' appears in q,

(c) $\exists\, t"$ such that $t \rightarrow t" \rightarrow t'$.

It follows directly from the above definition that if a term t requires a term t' then the computation of $\bar{I}(t)$ requires the computation of $\bar{I}(t')$. This implies that an external term cycle in the relation $\rightarrow$ certainly causes endless query loops. In our example the cycle $a2 \rightarrow b1 \rightarrow c1 \rightarrow a2$ (shown in Figure 8.(c)) is responsible for the endless query loops. Note that in networks with only $t2t$ articulations the relation $\rightarrow$ coincides with the relation $\sqsupseteq$, i.e. $t \rightarrow t'$ iff $t \sqsupseteq t'$.

Below we describe a simple (not optimized) query evaluation method that avoids the endless query loops. At first notice that each source in the network can receive *two* kinds of queries: (a) queries submitted by the *users* of the source, and (b) queries submitted by other *sources* of the network. We may call the former *external queries* and the latter *internal queries*. At first we assume that all external queries are single-term queries. Whenever a source S receives an external query q, it assigns to it a *network-unique identifier* denoted by q_{id}. This identifier will accompany all internal queries that will be exchanged in the network during the evaluation of q. Now consider the following operation mode:

- Each source keeps a log file of the queries that it has received. The log file stores pairs of the form: $(Query, QueryId)$.
- whenever a source S receives an internal query (q', q_{id}) from a source S' which matches a row of the log file, i.e. if (q', q_{id}) is already stored in the log file, then it replies by sending to S' the empty set and it does not query any other underlying source

It can be easily proved that if each source operates in this way, no endless query loops appear and that every external query is answered correctly. This is true for both $t2t$ and $t2q$ articulations with no negation.

However, techniques for reducing the number of queries that have to be exchanged between the sources of the network have to be designed. Furthermore, techniques that allow a source to identify the global relationships, i.e. the relationships of $\sqsubseteq$, are also very important as they can be exploited for query optimization and for enforcing integrity constraints. This kind of issues are still unexplored and are subject of further research.

6 Concluding Remarks

This paper describes an approach for building P2P systems that support semantic-based retrieval services by extending the mediator model presented in [23]. The contents of the objects and the queries are expressed in terms of taxonomies. As each peer uses its own taxonomy for describing the contents of its objects and for formulating queries to the other peers, peers are equipped with inter-taxonomy mappings in order to carry out the required translation tasks. The adopted conceptual modeling approach (taxonomies, and inter-taxonomy mappings) has three main advantages: First, it is very easy to create the conceptual model of a source. Second, the integration of information from multiple sources can be done easily. Third, automatic articulation using data-driven methods is possible.

We gave the semantics for this kind of systems and identified the differences between query evaluation in mediators and query evaluation in P2P systems. Issues for further research include techniques for query optimization and for identification of the global relationships. Another important and very interesting issue for further research is the automatic or semi-automatic construction of articulations. Currently, we are investigating an ostensive data-driven method for automatic articulation [22].

References

1. S. Amba. "Automatic Linking of Thesauri". In *SIGIR'96*, Zurich, Switzerland, 1996.
2. T.E. Anderson, M. Dahlin, J. M. Neefe, D. A. Patterson, D. S. Roselli, and R. Wang. "Serveless Network File Systems". *SOSP*, 29(5), 1995.
3. W. J. Bolosky, J. R. Douceur, D. Ely, and M. Theimer. "Feasibility of a Serveless Distributed File System Deployed on an Existing Set of Desktop PCs". In *Procs. of Measurement and Modeling of Computer Systems*, June 2000.
4. D. Calvanese, G. De Giacomo, and M. Lenzerini. A framework for ontology integration. In *SWWS'2001*, 2001.
5. A. Doan, J. Madhavan, P. Domingos, and A. Halevy. "Learning to Map between Ontologies on the Semantic Web". In *WWW-2002*, 2002.
6. V. Kashyap and A. Sheth. "Semantic Heterogeneity in Global Information Systems: the Role of Metadata, Context and Ontologies ". In *Cooperative Information Systems: Trends and Directions*. Academic Press, 1998.
7. J. Kubiatowicz, D. Bindel, Y. Chen, S. Czerwinski, P. Eaton, D. Geels, R. Gummadi, S. Rhea, H. Weatherspoon, W. Weimer, C. Wells, and B. Zhao. "Oceanstore: An Architecture for Global-Scale Persistent Storage". In *ASPLOS*, November 2000.
8. M. Lenzerini. Data integration: A theoretical perspective. In *Proc. ACM PODS 2002*, Madison, Wisconsin, USA, June 2002.
9. A. Y. Levy. "Answering Queries Using Views: A Survey". *VLDB Journal*, 2001.
10. B. Ling, Z. Lu, W. Siong Ng, B. Ooi, Kian-Lee Tan, and A. Zhou. "A Content-Based Resource Location Mechanism in PeerIS". In *Procs. WISE'2002*, Singapore, Dec. 2002.
11. S. Luke, L. Spector, D. Rager, and J. Hendler. "Ontology-based Web Agents". In *Procs of 1st Int. Conf. on Autonomous Agents*, 1997.
12. P. Mitra, G. Wiederhold, and J. Jannink. "Semi-automatic Integration of Knowledge sources". In *Proc. of the 2nd Int. Conf. On Information FUSION*, 1999.
13. W. Nejdl, B. Wolf, C. Qu, S. Decker, M. Sintek, A. Naeve, M. Nilsson, M. Palmer, and T. Risch. "EDUTELLA: A P2P networking infrastructure based on RDF". In *WWW'2002*, 2002.
14. R. Prieto-Diaz. "Implementing Faceted Classification for Software Reuse". *Communications of the ACM*, 34(5), 1991.
15. S. R. Ranganathan. "The Colon Classification". In Susan Artandi, editor, *Vol IV of the Rutgers Series on Systems for the Intellectual Organization of Information*. New Brunswick, NJ: Graduate School of Library Science, Rutgers University, 1965.

16. I. Ryutaro, T. Hideaki, and H. Shinichi. "Rule Induction for Concept Hierarchy Allignment". In *Procs. of the 2nd Workshop on Ontology Learning at the 17th Int. Conf. on AI (IJCAI)*, 2001.
17. G. M. Sacco. "Dynamic Taxonomies: A Model for Large Information Bases". *IEEE Transactions on Knowledge and Data Engineering*, 12(3), May 2000.
18. M. Sintichakis and P. Constantopoulos. "A Method for Monolingual Thesauri Merging". In *SIGIR'97*, Philadelphia, PA, USA, July 1997.
19. N. Spyratos, Y. Tzitzikas, and V. Christophides. "On Personalizing the Catalogs of Web Portals". In *FLAIRS'02*, Pensacola, Florida, May 2002.
20. I. Stoica, R. Morris, D. Karger, M. F. Kaashoek, and H. Balakrishnan. "Chord: A Scalable Peer-to-peer Lookup Service for Internet Applications". In *SIGCOMM'2001*, 2001.
21. Y. Tzitzikas, A. Analyti, N. Spyratos, and P. Constantopoulos. "An Algebraic Approach for Specifying Compound Terms in Faceted Taxonomies". In *13th Europ.-Jap. Conf. on Information Modelling and Knowledge Bases*, Japan, June 2003.
22. Y. Tzitzikas and C. Meghini. "Ostensive Automatic Schema Mapping for Taxonomy-based Peer-to-Peer Systems". In *CIA-2003*, Helsinki, Finland, August 2003.
23. Y. Tzitzikas, N. Spyratos, and P. Constantopoulos. "Mediators over Ontology-based Information Sources". In *WISE'2001*, Kyoto, Japan, December 2001.
24. J. D. Ullman. *"Principles of Database and Knowledge-Base Systems, Vol. I"*. Computer Science Press, 1988.
25. F. v. Harmelen and D. Fensel. "Practical Knowledge Representation for the Web". In *Workshop on Intelligent Information Integration, IJCAI'99*, 1999.

EITH – A Unifying Representation for Database Schema and Application Code in Enterprise Knowledge Extraction

Mark S. Schmalz, Joachim Hammer, MingXi Wu, and Oguzhan Topsakal

Department of CISE, University of Florida
Gainesville, FL 32611-6120, USA
{mssz,jhammer,mingxi,topsaka}@cise.ufl.edu

Abstract. The integration of heterogeneous legacy databases requires understanding of database structure and content. We previously developed a theoretical and software infrastructure to support the extraction of schema and business rule information from legacy sources, combining database reverse engineering with semantic analysis of associated application code (DRE/SA). In this paper, we present a compact formalism called EITH that unifies the representation of database schema and application code. EITH can be efficiently derived from various types of schema representations, particularly the relational model, and supports comparison of a wide variety of schema and code constructs to enable interoperation. Unlike UML or E/R diagrams, for example, EITH has compact notation, is unambiguous, and uses a small set of efficient heuristics. We show how EITH is employed in the context of SEEK, using a construction project management example. We also show how EITH can represent various structures in relational databases, and can serve as an efficient representation for E/R diagrams. This suggests that EITH can support efficient matching of more complex, hierarchical structures via indexed tree representations, without compromising the EITH design philosophy or formalism.

1 Introduction

Inherent in numerous techniques for integrating heterogeneous legacy data sources is the concept of *logical integration of data* [15] in terms of a unifying model that supports analysis and decision making procedures convenient to the user. Logical integration requires transformation of legacy source structure and content to meet or match the structure and content requirements of an *analysis model* (AM), as well as translation of user queries or data updates mediated through the AM. Common to this integration process is the development of wrappers that perform data and query transformation between a legacy source and the AM. This paper presents an efficient formalism that supports the logical integration of heterogeneous databases, in particular, efficient wrapper design and production. Our previous work in this area provided formalisms for wrapper description and semi-automatic wrapper generation, with understanding of database structure, content, and associated data manipulation rules [7, 9, 14]. Here, we extend this work to provide a formalism called EITH that

I.-Y. Song et al. (Eds.): ER 2003, LNCS 2813, pp. 461–475, 2003.

supports schema comparison and transformation, thereby facilitating more accurate and efficient automated wrapper generation. EITH serves as an efficient representation for E/R diagrams – we show how EITH can be used to represent diverse constructs in relational databases described by E/R diagrams. We also suggest that EITH can be employed in the generation and recursive updating of ontological formalisms to support enterprise domain extension and eventual cross-domain semantic understanding.

Current implementations of database interoperability and integration rely on technologies developed as part of the TSIMMIS [2] or Garlic [4] projects, for example, which primarily emphasize distributed query processing and data transformation. In contrast, our SEEK and EITH approaches support deeper *semantic understanding* of legacy data, which is synergistic with the following objectives:

1. Unified EITH representation of database structure in terms of schema, business rules in application code, and relationships between these entities;
2. Understanding of functional relationships between data objects in the context of an application domain, which is simplified by the EITH formalism;
3. Comparison between data objects ranging from the schema-entity or code-operand level up to relations or schema (data model) as well as business rules or body of code (rule model), again simplified by EITH; and
4. Eventual automatic or semi-automatic construction or augmentation of domain-descriptive ontologies from extracted legacy schema and code represented in terms of EITH.

Our approach differs from previous structural-based wrapper generation techniques in using schema, business rules, and semantic relationships between these entities to drive design and implementation of the underlying EITH representation. This approach, combined with proven theory and software development practice, produces a representation that is efficient spatially and computationally, tractably unifies both data and code, and supports semantic operations such as schema comparison, schema and code understanding, as well as eventual ontology building and merging.

The remainder of this paper is organized as follows. Sect. 2 reviews previous work in data reverse engineering and wrapper generation that motivates our current research. We show how EITH evolved from this work, and how it supports representation of schema and code at multiple levels of abstraction. Sect. 3 presents EITH theory, which is shown to represent numerous schema structures. Sect. 4 exemplifies application of EITH to (a) represent different schemas or application code in disparate legacy sources and (b) show how this representation facilitates source comparison with respect to a prespecified analysis model also represented in terms of EITH. Sect. 5 discusses future uses of EITH in semantic understanding and cross-domain database interoperability. Conclusions and suggestions for future work are presented in Sect. 6.

2   Extraction and Representation of Database Knowledge

2.1   Review of Our Previous Work in Enterprise Knowledge Extraction

This section presents a brief overview of our research in enterprise knowledge extraction and integration, further elaborated in [10]. A high-level view of the SEEK architecture (Fig. 1), which follows established mediation/wrapper methodologies (e.g., TSIMMIS [2], Garlic [4]) and provides a middleware layer that connects legacy information sources and decision makers/decision support applications. The Hub provides decision support for an extended enterprise of firms (e.g., a construction supply chain). Decision support information is gathered from firms via SEEK connection tools. The Analysis Module (AM) performs knowledge composition or mediation [16] on legacy data extracted from the Firm. The AM does not cache data, but connects in real time with source wrappers, which translate between data representations and query formalisms of the Hub/AM and underlying source(s).

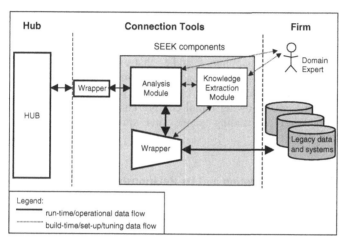

Fig. 1. Schematic diagram of the conceptual architecture of the SEEK system and related components

In practice, multiple Hubs can have diverse internal data formats and languages. However, SEEK is limited to specific forms of data extraction constrained by decision support capabilities provided by each class of Hubs. Thus, Hub-AM wrappers are simple to implement and can support multiple Hubs, increasing SEEK's scalability.

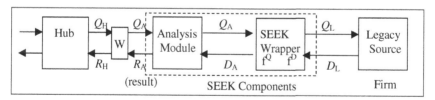

Fig. 2. Overview of the interactions between Hub, SEEK components and Firm

At runtime, (i.e., after the SEEK wrapper W and analysis module AM are configured), the AM accepts a query issued by the Hub (Q_H in Fig. 2) that has been converted into a query (Q_A) which the AM can understand using W. The AM processes a Hub request and issues one or more queries (Q_A) to W to obtain legacy data needed to satisfy the Hub's request. The SEEK wrapper produces one or more queries (Q_L) in a format that the legacy source can understand. The legacy source processes Q_L and returns legacy data (D_L) that is transformed by the SEEK wrapper into data (D_A) that is tractable to the AM. The AM processes this data and returns a result (R_H) via the wrapper W to the Hub that fulfills the original Hub query (Q_H).

As SEEK tools must be instantiated for each firm, it is important to provide rapid configuration with minimal human support. Instantiation is accomplished semi-automatically during build-time by SEEK's knowledge extraction module (KEM) that directs wrapper configuration. A SEEK-specific representation of operational knowledge in the sources is obtained via domain specific templates that describe semantics of commonly-used structures and schemas. KEM queries a legacy source using the initial instantiation of a simple (generic) SEEK wrapper. Via data reverse engineering (DRE), KEM constructs a legacy schema representation that includes legacy data semantics determined, for example, from queries, data samples, application code, and user input (as required). Using an iterative, step-wise refinement process, KEM constructs mappings f^Q and f^D that extend the initial SEEK wrapper to perform the aforementioned query and data translations (per Fig. 2). A wrapper generation toolkit [6] implements the customized wrappers. Human domain experts can assist this process following initial configuration, compensating for poor legacy documentation while expanding scope and quality of the SEEK knowledge representation.

2.2   The EITH Representation and Its Relationship to SEEK

To support SEEK's unified representation of diverse data sources, the EITH representation of a database has the following levels of abstraction:

- *High-Level Semantics* describe the types of entities within a schema and their high-level meanings in a context that is a superset of the domain semantics. For example, in the SEEK project management model, we have defined *physical objects*, *abstract objects*, and *constraints*. The former include people and materials, while abstractions include objects such as Project and Task.
- *Constraint Layer* describes constraints on entities and relationships between constraints. For example, in a SEEK project management model, a Schedule is a high-level constraint, while its constituents (e.g., abstractions such as Time Interval and Cost) are low-level constraints. Other constraints include variables such as Flag and Type.
- *Schema Layer* describes database structure in terms of a schema with data instances. This is determined primarily by SEEK's KEM.
- *Formulaic Layer* contains mathematical relationships between data objects, which are typically found in application code. For example, total project cost is the sum of the individual task costs, since a project is comprised of its tasks.

The high-level semantics and constraints comprise instances of an ontological framework for a superset of the legacy data. For example, a project management model could be associated with an ontology that would include but not be limited to Entities, Relationships between Entities, Constraints on Entities, and Constraints on Relationships. Additional information in the ontology would include business rules and generic information that would be specialized in the Formulaic Layer. The challenges in representing such information include (a) compact but sufficiently expressive formalisms lacking ambiguities that confound interpretation of knowledge represented in terms of the formalism; (b) unification of data and code representations using one set of representational building blocks, for efficiency; and (c) representation of ontological layers and knowledge partitions within layers via well-established data structures whose processing is well understood, and which are represented by a rigorous, concise, and unified formalism.

We next overview EITH, and discuss its Schema Layer representation in terms of the EITH formalism, then illustrate EITH's unifying capabilities in terms of code representation in the Formulaic Layer (Fig. 4). For readers unfamiliar with schema representation, theory and more complex representation issues are discussed in Sect. 3, while EITH's relationship to High-Level Semantics and Constraint Layers is clarified in Sect. 5.

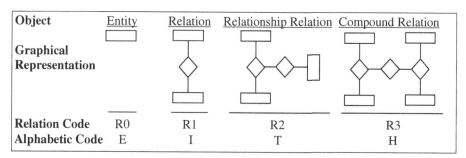

Fig. 3. High-level graphical representation of building blocks for description of database structure: entity, relation, relationship relation, and compound relation

The structures shown in Fig. 3 can represent typical structures in a database schema, for example, entities, relations, relationship relations, and compound relations. To support efficient comparison of structures within or between schemas, compact names were devised for EITH constructs (shown at the bottom of Fig. 3).

The problem of representing programs has been studied extensively in the context of software engineering [1]. For example, in traditional interprocedural analysis, a program is abstracted by a *call graph* [5]. Compilers use a variety of intermediate representations of programs, such as *abstract syntax trees* (AST), *control flow graphs*, *def-use chains*, etc. For more complex manipulations of programs, the *program dependence graph* (PDG) [3] and the *dependence flow graph* (DPG) [12] have been used. Finally, in program pattern matching [11], interesting programming patterns are stored in templates using a so-called '*pattern language*'. These templates are then compared to patterns in the source code. The majority of published representations were developed in the context of program compilation and program manipulation problems such as slicing but are not adequate for representing the deep semantics of both code constructs as well as their relationships to database entities in a compact yet unambiguous and easy-to-use format.

2.2.1 Example: Schema Representation. Consider the construction project schema shown in Fig. 4a, and its graphical EITH representation shown in Fig. 4b. The high-level alphabetic EITH representation is given by $S = \{I,I,I,I,I\}$, which denotes an unordered set of relations. Note that the mapping which produces S is irreversible, in the sense that the schema cannot be completely reconstructed from S because the entity and relation names, and cardinality of the relations, are missing. However, we are implementing a frame-based elaboration of EITH, whereby each entity and relation can be described in terms of its attributes, similar to UML [13]. This approach is advantageous because design and implementational details are retained but migrated to the next-lower level of the graphical representation, thereby facilitating comprehension and ease of maintenance.

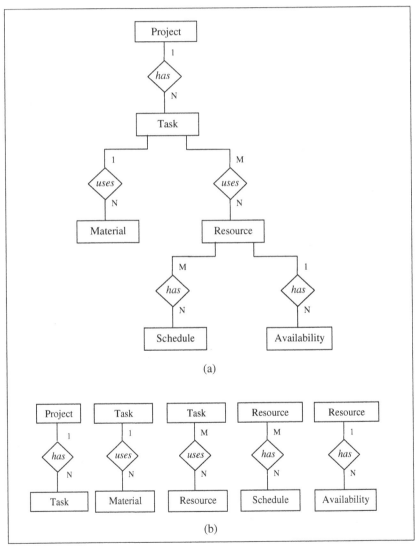

Fig. 4. Construction project schema (a) E/R diagram and (b) graphical EITH representation

EITH can be extended to represent database application code by observing that a leaf (internal node) in a hierarchical relationship such as an abstract syntax tree or AST can correspond to an entity (resp. relationship) in Fig. 3. We thus discovered

EITH representations for code constructs such as unary operations of assignment, binary operations with assignment, control structures such as if-then-else and loops, as well as sequences or concurrently executable collections of operations. A key advantage of this approach is that ASTs can represent both schema and code, which supports efficient translation of source representations into XML format.

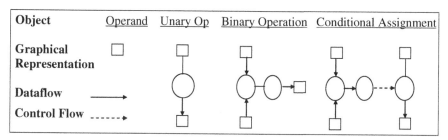

Fig. 5. Graphical representation of building blocks for description of constructs in code: operand, unary operation, binary operation with assignment to a result, and a conditional assignment. Data and control flow links elaborate the schema objects of Fig. 3

Slight modifications to the EITH schema objects portrayed in Fig. 3 produce the code objects shown in Fig. 5, which include the following:

- *Operands* in code (EITH symbol: *O*) are conceptually similar to database Entities, although represented by a square instead of a rectangle;
- *Operations* in code (*U*, *B*, or *C* for unary, binary, or conditional operations), similar to schema Relations, are represented graphically by a circle or oval, versus a diamond for a database relation;
- *Data transfer link* (–) indicates dataflow from left to right.
- *Causal link* (dashed arrow in graphics, > in text) illustrates control flow within a structure such as a loop (*L*), multiple *if* statement, or case statement (aggregation of *C*-type primitives); and

Multi-operator groups of operations executed sequentially (denoted by [ ] or *S*), versus unordered collections ({ }), thus representing control dependency.

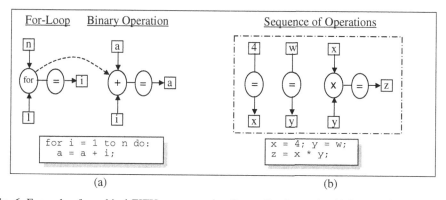

Fig. 6. Example of graphical EITH representation for application code: (a) loop and (b) multi-operator sequence. Note the transfer of control in the loop indicated by the dashed arc

2.2.2 Example Application Code Representation. Consider the loop in Fig. 6a, where the *for* operator transfers control to the addition operation. Control transfers to the *for* operator when the addition operation completes, then back to the addition operation following index incrementation, until the condition $i > n$ signals loop exit. The sequence of operations itself does not transfer control from the statement $x = 4$ to the statement $y = w$, since no dependencies exist between these statements. Although one could construct a control arc from either of these statements to $z = x + y$, this would be superfluous and misleading, since these statements and $z = x + y$ have no control dependencies. Instead, data dependencies exist among the three statements depicted in Fig. 6b, which can be detected during the code slicing performed as part of the DRE/SA operation in SEEK's KEM. Also, because EITH is modular, a sequence of operations such as shown in Fig. 6b can be substituted for the addition operation comprising the loop body in Fig. 6a.

2.2.3 Implementation Issues in SEEK. Note that the graphical constructs in Figs. 4 and 6 resemble ASTs, albeit with some lack of reduction. ASTs provide a convenient representation for low-level EITH primitives (e.g., I, T, H, U, B, or C) and higher-level data structures such as acyclic directed graphs. Techniques for derivation of an AST from a well-specified formal language are well documented in the literature of programming languages. Algorithms for manipulating or comparing ASTs are well represented in the literature.

The graphical EITH representation and AST representation are isomorphic: inspection of Fig. 7 discloses that an AST is obtained by renaming the entities (operands) and relations (operators) of the database-specific (resp. code-specific) primitives shown in Figs. 3 and 4. Salient examples are presented in Fig. 7. In practice, we obtain code primitives as subtrees of an AST by parsing application code (e.g., in the DRE/SA phase of SEEK knowledge extraction). Similarly, the database primitives shown in Fig. 3 can be thought of as subtrees of an E/R diagram obtained from applying SEEK's DRE process to a database schema.

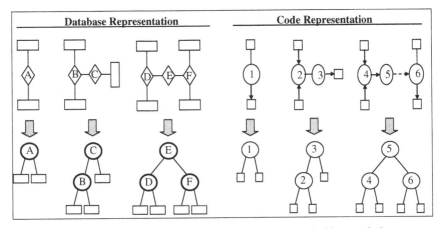

Fig. 7. Examples of correspondence between representational primitives and abstract syntax tree representation, where database relations are graphically distinguished from code operations (which mathematically are relations) by the boldness of the internal node border.

By viewing the E/R diagram (parse tree) as a graphical representation of a schema (resp. code fragment), and by representing these concisely with the EITH alphabet Σ = {B, C, E, H, I, L, O, S, T, U, >, [ ], { }}, we can structurally compare objects within and between databases. Due to isomorphism between data and code primitives (e.g., between E and O, I and U, T and B, H and C) EITH provides a unifying description of database and application code structure. This has the practical advantage that the same manipulation and comparison algorithms can be applied to schema or code representations in SEEK, thus reducing software duplication and maintenance overhead. Since SEEK focuses on schema and code objects that are typically small, these comparison algorithms can be small and efficient. As discussed in Sec. 3, EITH can be used to represent complex structures, for which similar claims hold. We next discuss the theoretical basis, notation, and coverage of the EITH representation.

3 Theory of EITH

3.1 Background

3.1.1 Definition. A *relation* $r : E \rightarrow E$ that associates two entities in a set E is written in EITH as *ErE*. If e is a particular entity in E, then $r = ere$ is appropriate.

3.1.2 Observation. Since relations can be aggregated, a *relationship relation* r that associates a relation q with an entity is written as $(E\ q\ E)\ r\ E$, and a *compound relation* r that associates two relations p and q is written as $(E\ p\ E)\ r\ (E\ q\ E)$. For purposes of simplicity, we hereafter write $(E\ r\ E)\ r\ E$ instead of $(E\ q\ E)\ r\ E$ and $(E\ r\ E)\ r\ (E\ r\ E)$ instead of $(E\ p\ E)\ r\ (E\ q\ E)$.

3.1.3 Definition. The EITH symbols for relational objects are elaborated as
- $I \equiv ErE$ for a relation
- $T \equiv (ErE)\ r\ E$ for a relationship relation
- $H \equiv (ErE)\ r\ (ErE)$ for a compound relation

3.1.4 Definition. A *unary operation* $o : O \rightarrow O$ on a set of operands O can be written in infix notation as *OoO*.

3.1.5 Definition. A *binary operation* $o : O \times O \rightarrow O$ can be expressed as $(O\tau O)\ o\ O$, where τ denotes the infix form of the aggregation operator Ψ.

3.1.6 Observation. A conditional operation c such as implication, which associates a relation r with an operation o, can be written as $(E\ r\ E)\ c\ (O\ o\ E)$. For example, in the code fragment `if Cost < Limit then ExpenseIncrement := 1000`, we have $r = <$, $c = \rightarrow$ (implication), and o equals `:=` (assignment).

3.1.7 Definition. Denoting a set of operands as O, and observing the notational generality of Definition 3.1.2, the EITH constructs for code primitives are given by:

- $U \equiv OoO$ for a unary operation
- $B \equiv (O\tau O)oO$ for a binary operation
- $C \equiv (OoO)o(OoO)$ for a conditional or compound operation

3.1.8 Example. The code fragment in Fig. 6a could be represented as $L{>}B$. Although L has the form of a binary operation and could thus be represented by B, its specific function is that of an iterative control structure or loop, so we employ L to reduce ambiguity. Similarly, the sequence of operations depicted in Fig. 6b could be represented by $[UUB]$. Under loop control, this sequence would be represented as $L{>}[UUB]$ or $L{>}S$, depending on the desired level of abstraction. Under conditional control of the sequence, the corresponding code fragment is represented as $C{>}[UUB]$ or $C{>}S$. If both data and control dependencies exist, then we write $C{-}{>}S$.

3.1.9 Observation. It can be claimed that the T and H constructs in Fig. 3, while useful as high-level abstractions, inaccurately portray the implementation of relationship relations and compound relations in actual schema. This problem is solved by the use of a construct called a super-relation.

3.1.10 Definition. An EITH *super-relation*, denoted by ($'$) following the relation designator (e.g., T'), is an aggregate relationship that associates two relations with an entity, such that R' is of form rEr. As exemplified in Fig. 8a, R' is defined in terms of an entity (e_2), where $e_1r_1e_2$, $e_2r_2e_3$, and $e_2r_3e_4$ exist. Then, $R' = (r_1e_2r_2)$ if and only if the aggregation of $e_1R'e_3$ and e_4r_3R' comprises a relationship relation.

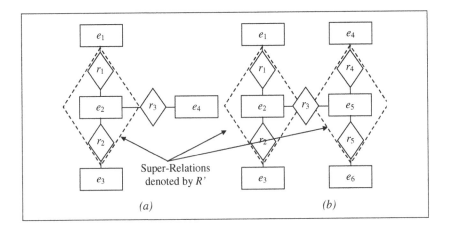

Fig. 8. EITH representation of low-level schema structure using super-relation R' to represent (a) T-type relation as T' = (e_1 R'e_3) r_3e_4, and (b) H-type relation as H' = (e_1 R'e_3) r_3 (e_4 R'e_6).

3.1.11 Example. In Fig. 8a, the super-relation $R' = r_1 e_2 r_2$ supports expression of the T-type construct implementationally as $T' = (e_1 R' e_3) r_3 e_4$. Similarly, in Fig. 8b, the use of R' in both the left and right I-type sub-constructs of $H = I r I$ allows us to express the H-type construct implementationally as $H' = (e_1 R' e_3) r_3 (e_4 R' e_6)$.

3.1.12 Observation. The super-relation thus enables representation of EITH constructs at the Schema and Formulaic Levels of our ontology, and maintains rigor with respect to database implementation practice. In practice, T' in Figure 8a would be constructed by a postprocessor, which is designed to (1) input the results of SEEK DRE/SA, (2) find the common entity (e.g., e_2), (3) determine if $e_1 r_1 e_2$, $e_2 r_2 e_3$, and $e_2 r_3 e_4$ exist in the schema, (4) aggregate $(r_1 e_2 r_2)$ to form R', then (5) verify that the aggregation $(e_1 R' e_3,\ e_4 r_3 R')$ comprises a relationship relation. The latter step can be performed with heuristics from our DRE/SA module. The postprocessor is currently being implemented as part of SEEK's KEM.

3.1.13 Remark. The rules shown in Definition 3.1.3 also apply to I', T', and H' representations of I, T, and H constructs, per Example 3.1.11. We next show that super-relations enable EITH to represent a wide variety of schema structures.

3.2 Coverage of EITH in Realistic Database Applications

In order to represent schema structures as complex and diverse as snowflakes, stars, or rings, we use a super-relation to reduce these configurations to a hierarchical collection of I, T, and H relations. For example, as shown in Fig. 9a, a four-petaled snowflake S_4 that has a central super-relation R' can be expressed as $S_4 \equiv E r (E R' E) r E$. From Definition 3.1.3 and Remark 3.1.13, we have $I \equiv E R' E$. Thus, we can express the four-petaled snowflake as $S_4 \equiv E r I' r E \equiv E r T'$.

Note that these different expressions are equivalent, and thus do not introduce ambiguity into the EITH representation, since $E r T'$ can be expanded as $E r (I' r E)$, which can, in turn be expanded to yield $E r ((E R' E) r E)$, where parentheses merely illustrate hierarchical levels. This result suggests the EITH representation of an n-petaled snowflake S_n comprised, for example, of a central fact node e_0 and n relations denoted by r_i, each of which associates a dimension e_i with e_0, where $i = 1, \ldots, n$ and $n > 2$. Letting the symbol Ψ denote aggregation, we write

$$S_n \equiv \overset{n}{\underset{i=3}{\Psi}}\ e_i\, r_i\, (e_1 R' e_2),$$

since e_1 and e_2 are contained in R'. For example, given entities e_1, e_2, and e_3 with relations p and r, the aggregation of relations $e_1 r e_2$ and $e_2 p e_3$ would result in $e_1 r e_2 p e_3$.

Similarly, the ring P shown in Fig. 9b can be expressed as $P = E r I r E$, with the initial and terminal E's being identical. A question arises: *Can EITH also represent a ternary relation X, shown in Fig. 9c?* The answer is yes, if we insert the null relation λ to form a T-type construct, as shown in the right-hand part of Fig. 9c. The formula is given by

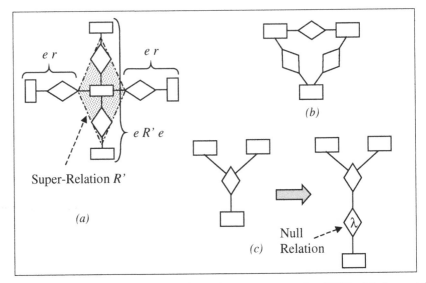

Fig. 9. Representation of more complex schema structures by EITH: (a) four-petaled snowflake, (b) ring, and (c) ternary relation

$$X \equiv e\,\lambda\,(e\,r\,e) \equiv T,$$

Note that this technique can readily be extended to *n*-ary relations, where $n > 3$, although these are not customarily found in legacy schema.

4 Applicative Example

Consider management of a construction project with multiple `Tasks`, each of which is comprised of `Activities` that require effort (`Resources`) and, for convenience, infinitely available `Materials`. Note that `Resources` must be scheduled. `Materials` and `resources` have cost metrics (e.g., cost per unit weight, volume, or time), allocated during scheduling to produce task costs, which are summed to product project cost. Given an analysis model based on the E/R diagram shown in Fig. 4a, SEEK attempts to reconcile knowledge contained in a legacy source (e.g., Primavera Project) to answer user questions about optimal scheduling under project cost constraints. This requires comparison of legacy schema entities and relations, or rules in application code, with corresponding AM (or Hub) knowledge representations. We call this *semantic matching* (SM).

EITH directly supports SM at the Formulaic and Schema ontological layers (Sect. 2.2), as only simple schema/code constructs are typically compared. For example, the relationship between `project` and `tasks` is described by an I-type construct (e.g., `Project has Task`) in both AM and legacy sources thus far studied. Similarly, business rules (e.g., determination of project cost) are typically expressed in *C*-type constructs supported by *U*-type initialization statements. For accumulation, one encounters *B*-type statements under loop control, e.g.,

U-type:	**Limit = 10,000;**
C-type:	**if Task_Cost < Limit, then**
> *L-type*:	**for I = 1 to N_tasks do**
- *B-type*:	**Project_Cost := Project_cost + Task_Cost[i];**

One obtains the EITH representation [*U-C*>[*L-B*]], because the *U*-type statement transfers data to the *C*-type, which controls the *L*-type that is linked to the *B*-type statement. Similar graphical examples are given in Figs. 10–12.

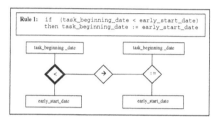

Fig. 10. EITH representation of SEEK business rule 1 (simple scheduling rule)

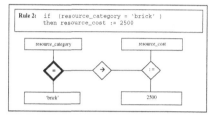

Fig. 11. EITH representation of SEEK business rule 2 (resource costing rule)

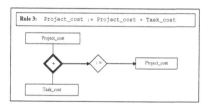

Fig. 12. EITH representation of SEEK business rule 3 (cost accumulation rule)

5   Comparison of Complex Structures with EITH

Published research indicates that complex constructs occur infrequently in legacy sources, and their interpretation or comparison often requires human expertise. We are currently developing theory and algorithms to address the problem of (1) identifying complex structures in an AST representation *A* of database schema and code, then (2) partitioning them into EITH-representable sequences to be (3) compared using a schema structure similarity metric [8]. This would allow large sources (e.g., 10^3 to 10^5 relations and 10^4 to 10^7 lines of code) to be accommodated in SEEK.

In particular, after Step 1 traverses *A*, bidirectionally indexing all nodes to a symbol table S_D, and Step 2 similarly builds a structure table S_S, then Step 3 does the following:

a) Compares a legacy structure s_L with an AM structure s_A, by first lexically comparing all s_L nodes with all s_A nodes using S_D (e.g., compare legacy table name *Task_MSP* with AM table name *Task*), resulting in a node score $M_{nd}(s_L, s_A)$.

b) Compares the EITH-encoded structure of s_L (from structure table S_S) with that of s_A, to yield a structure metric $M_{st}(s_L, s_A)$.

c) M_{st} is combined with M_{nd} to yield composite matching score M.

d) Matches with high M are reviewed by a domain expert; this knowledge is accumulated to eventually support more automated processing.

e) If the list of M-scores indicates inconclusive match, then a partition of S_S is queried using M_{st} scores derived from comparisons of all s_L's with s_A that have high M_{nd} scores, to find subtrees of A which structurally resemble s_A.

Because S_D and S_S are constructed at build-time, and because Steps 1-3 are build-time activities, the computational complexity is less important than for runtime processing. Our research indicates that EITH helps decrease computational costs and increases comparison accuracy, versus traditional AST traversal and subtree comparison approaches. Additionally, EITH facilitates comparison of business rules across multiple programming languages (PLs), due to the use of the parse tree as a unifying construct. That is, the parse tree of a business rule expressed at the statement level (e.g., if..then..else statement) has the same form whether the rule is written in Java, C, Pascal, or FORTRAN. This concept is basic to PL translation in software reverse engineering applications [17] as well as in program comparison systems such as the well-known *moss* plagiarism detection program.

6 Conclusion

We have presented a novel formalism called EITH that unifies the representation of database schema and application code. EITH can be efficiently derived from various types of schema representations, particularly the relational model, and supports comparison of a wide variety of schema and code constructs (e.g., relations, relationship relations, assignment, arithmetic, or flow control statements). Unlike UML or E/R diagrams, for example, EITH has compact notation, is unambiguous, and uses a small set of efficient heuristics. We have shown how EITH is employed in the context of SEEK, using a construction project management example. We have also shown how EITH can represent various structures in relational databases, and can serve as an efficient representation for E/R diagrams. We believe that EITH can support efficient matching of more complex, hierarchical structures via indexed tree representations, without compromising the EITH design philosophy or formalism. We are currently in the process of integrating EITH with the SEEK toolkit to demonstrate its usefulness in the context of legacy system integration.

References

1. D. C. Atkinson and W. G. Griswold, "The design of whole-program analysis tools," *18th International Conference on Software Engineering*, 1996.
2. S. Chawathe, H. Garcia-Molina, J. Hammer, K. Ireland, Y. Papakonstantinou, J. Ullman, and J. Widom, "The TSIMMIS Project: Integration of Heterogeneous Information Sources," *10th Meeting of the Information Processing Society of Japan*, Tokyo, Japan, 1994.
3. J. Ferrante, K. J. Ottenstein, and J. D. Warren, "The program dependence graph and its uses in optimization," *ACM TOPLS*, vol. 9, pp. 319–349, 1987.
4. L. Haas, R. J. Miller, B. Niswonger, M. T. Roth, P. M. Schwarz, and E. L. Wimmers, "Transforming heterogeneous data with database middleware: Beyond integration.," *IEEE Data Engineering Bulletin*, vol. 22, pp. 31–36, 1999.
5. M. Hall, J. M. M. Crummey, A. Carle, and R. G. Rodriguez, "FIAT: A framework for interprocedural analysis and transformations," *6th Workshop on Languages and Compilers for Parallel Computing*, 1993.
6. J. Hammer, M. Breunig, H. Garcia-Molina, S. Nestorov, V. Vassalos, and R. Yerneni, "Template-Based Wrappers in the TSIMMIS System," *Twenty-Third ACM SIGMOD International Conference on Management of Data*, Tucson, Arizona, 1997.
7. J. Hammer, H. Garcia-Molina, S. Nestorov, R. Yerneni, M. Breunig, and V. Vassalos, "Template-Based Wrappers in the TSIMMIS System," *SIGMOD Record (ACM Special Interest Group on Management of Data)*, vol. 26, pp. 532–535, 1997.
8. J. Hammer and C. Pluempitiwiriyawej, "Element Matching across Data-oriented XML Sources using a Multi-strategy Clustering Technique," *Data and Knowledge Engineering (DKE), Elsevier Science*, 2004.
9. J. Hammer, M. Schmalz, W. O'Brien, S. Shekar, and N. Haldavnekar, "SEEKing Knowledge in Legacy Information Systems to Support Interoperability," *ECAI–02 International Workshop on Ontologies and Semantic Interoperability*, Lyon, France, 2002.
10. W. O'Brien, R. R. Issa, J. Hammer, M. S. Schmalz, J. Geunes, and S. X. Bai, "SEEK: Accomplishing Enterprise Information Integration Across Heterogeneous Sources," *ITCON – Journal of Information Technology in Construction*, vol. 7, pp. 101–124, 2002.
11. S. Paul and A. Prakash, "A Framework for Source Code Search Using Program Patterns," *Software Engineering*, vol. 20, pp. 463–475, 1994.
12. K. Pingali, M. Beck, R. Johnson, M. Moudgill, and P. Stodghill, "Dependence Flow Graphs: An Algebraic Approach to Program Dependencies," *18th ACM Symposium on Principles of Programming Languages*, 1991.
13. Rational Software Corp., *Unified Modeling Language Summary 1.1*, 1997.
14. S. Shekar, J. Hammer, and M. Schmalz, "Extracting Meaning from Legacy Code through Pattern Matching," Department of CISE, University of Florida, Gainesville, FL 32611–6120, TR03–003, January 2003.
15. A. Sheth and J. A. Larson, "Federated Database Systems for Managing Distributed, Heterogeneous, and Autonomous Databases," *ACM Computing Surveys*, vol. 22, pp. 183–236, 1990.
16. G. Wiederhold, "Weaving data into information," *Database Programming and Design*, vol. 11, 1998.
17. L. Willis and P. Newcomp, "Reverse Engineering." Boston, MA: Kluwer, 1996.

A Heuristic-Based Methodology for Semantic Augmentation of User Queries on the Web*

Andrew Burton-Jones[1], Veda C. Storey[1], Vijayan Sugumaran[2], and Sandeep Purao[3]

[1] J. Mack Robinson College of Business, Georgia State University,
Atlanta, GA 30302,
{vstorey,abjones}@gsu.edu
[2] School of Business Administration, Oakland University
Rochester, MI 48309
sugumara@oakland.edu
[3] School of Information Sciences & Technology, The Pennsylvania State University,
University Park, PA 16801-3857
spurao@ist.psu.edu

Abstract. As the World Wide Web continues to grow, so does the need for effective approaches to processing users' queries that retrieve the most relevant information. Most search engines provide the user with many web pages, but at varying levels of relevancy. The Semantic Web has been proposed to retrieve and use more semantic information from the web. However, the capture and processing of semantic information is a difficult task because of the well-known problems that machines have with processing semantics. This research proposes a heuristic-based methodology for building context aware web queries. The methodology expands a user's query to identify possible word senses and then makes the query more relevant by restricting it using relevant information from the WordNet lexicon and the DARPA DAML library of domain ontologies. The methodology is implemented in a prototype. Initial testing of the prototype and comparison to results obtained from Google show that this heuristic based approach to processing queries can provide more relevant results to users, especially when query terms are ambiguous and/or when the methodology's heuristics are invoked.

1 Introduction

It is increasingly difficult to retrieve relevant web pages for queries from the World Wide Web due to its rapid growth and lack of structure [31, 32]. In response, the Semantic Web has been proposed to extend the WWW by giving information well-defined meaning [3, 10]. The Semantic Web relies heavily on ontologies to provide taxonomies of domain specific terms and inference rules that serve as surrogates for semantics [3]. Berners-Lee et al. describe the Semantic Web as "not a new web but an extension of the current one, in which information is given well-defined meaning" [3]. Unfortunately, it is difficult to capture and represent meaning in machine-

---

* This research was partially supported by J. Mack Robinson College of Business, Georgia State University and Office of Research & Graduate Study, Oakland University.

I.-Y. Song et al. (Eds.): ER 2003, LNCS 2813, pp. 476–489, 2003.

readable form, even though understanding more of the semantics of a user's application or query would help process users' queries more effectively.

There is wide agreement that a critical mass of ontologies is needed for representing semantics on the Semantic Web [6, 27]. Libraries of ontologies are being developed for this purpose, with the most well-known being the DARPA DAML library with approximately 200 ontologies and over 25,000 classes http://www.daml.org/ontologies/. Although significant effort has gone into building these ontologies, there is little research on methodologies for retrieving information using them. Thus, the development of a methodology for doing so would greatly assist in realizing the full potential of the Semantic Web.

The objective of this research, therefore, is to: *develop a heuristic-based methodology for an intelligent agent to process queries on the Semantic Web so that the processing takes into account the semantics of the user's request.* This is done through the use of WordNet [15] (http://www.cogsci.princeton.edu/cgi-bin/webwn) to obtain senses for query terms and WordNet and the DAML ontologies to augment a query by expanding and shrinking the set of query terms to achieve a more precise, context-specific query.

The contribution of this research is to develop a methodology that more effectively processes queries by capturing and augmenting the semantics of a user's query. The methodology has been implemented in a prototype and its effectiveness verified. Results of this research should help realize the potential of the Semantic Web, while demonstrating useful applications of lexicons and ontology libraries.

2 Related Work

2.1 Semantic Web

The unstructured nature of the web makes it difficult to query and difficult for applications to use. The Semantic Web is a vision of the web in which these problems will be solved by 'marking-up' terms on web pages with links to online ontologies that provide a machine-readable definition of the terms and their relationship with other terms [3]. This is intended to make the web machine-readable and, thus, easier to process for both humans and their applications (e.g., agents). Consider a prototypical query (adapted from [3]): *Find Mom a specialist who can provide a series of bi-weekly physical therapy sessions.* To complete this query on the Semantic Web, agents will use online ontologies to interpret relevant semantics on web pages (e.g., specialist, series, etc) [16, 25]. The proliferation of ontologies is crucial for the Semantic Web, hence the creation of large ontology libraries [10, 47]. Hendler [25] predicts: *"The Semantic Web...will not primarily consist of neat ontologies...I envision a complex Web of semantics ruled by the same sort of anarchy that rules the rest of the Web."* Therefore, research is needed to determine how useful these ontologies will be for helping users and agents query the Semantic Web.

2.2 Ontologies

An ontology should be a way of describing one's world [50]. Ontologies generally consist of terms, their definitions, and axioms relating them [19]. However, there are many different definitions, descriptions, and types of ontologies [20, 39, 40]. In knowledge representation, well known contributions include Ontolingua [14], SHOE [23], Cyc [21] and the XML based schemes such as OIL [16], and DAML [24]. Ontologies can be characterized as either formal/top-level ontologies that describe the world in general or material/domain ontologies that describe specific domains [20]. Semantic Web ontologies (e.g., at the DAML library) are primarily domain ontologies. The development of domain ontologies was motivated by the need to develop systems that could reason with common sense knowledge of the real world [19]. More formally, a domain ontology is a catalog of the types of things that are assumed to exist in the domain of interest, D, from the perspective of a certain language, L, for the purpose of talking about that domain, D [45]. Conceptual modeling researchers have contributed extensively to the development and application of both formal and domain ontologies [2, 11, 13, 30, 50].

2.3 Information Retrieval

Methods from the information retrieval (IR) field [42] can inform the process of querying the Semantic Web and the role of domain ontologies. A core problem in IR is word-sense disambiguation: a word may have multiple meanings (homonymy), yet several words can have the same meaning (synonymy) [26, 36]. Resolving homonymy increases the relevance of the results returned (precision) by eliminating results of the wrong word-sense; resolving synonymy increases the proportion of relevant results in the collection returned (recall) by including terms that have the same meaning.

In IR, word-sense disambiguation involves two steps: 1. identifying the user's intended meaning of query terms, and 2. altering the query so that it achieves high precision and recall. In IR, the first step is usually achieved by automatically deducing a term's meaning from other terms in the query [1]. This is feasible because IR queries are typically long, e.g., 15 terms for short queries [9] and 50-85 for long queries [22]. On the Semantic Web, however, this appears infeasible. Most web queries are only two words long [46] and this is an insufficient length to identify context [9, 49]. Therefore, some user interaction will be required to accurately identify the intended sense of query-terms [1].

The second step (altering the query) is generally achieved in IR through a combination of:

- query constraints, such as requiring pages to include all query terms (possibly near each other) [22, 37].
- query expansion with 'local context,' in which additional terms are added to the query based on a subset of documents that the user identifies as relevant [37, 43]
- query expansion with 'global context,' in which additional terms are added to the query from thesauri, from terms in the document collection, or from past queries [9, 18, 29, 41, 49]

Of these methods, query constraints should be useful on the Semantic Web because they improve web search [38]. Query expansion with local context is less likely to be effective because reports indicate that web users rarely provide relevance feedback [8, 46]. Finally, query expansion with global context will remain relevant, but the sources used in global context analysis will be largely superseded by ontologies. For example, rather than use a thesaurus to add synonyms to a query so that relevant pages were not missed, a Semantic Web query could be left unexpanded and could simply rely on web pages referencing the terms on their pages to ontologies that defined each term and its synonyms. Recall, however, that ontologies will be of mixed quality [25]. Therefore, thesauri will likely remain important on the Semantic Web. The IR field suggests that two thesauri should be used (ideally in combination) [29, 34, 38, 49]: (1) general lexical thesauri that detail lexically related terms (e.g., synonyms), and (2) domain-specific thesauri that detail related terms in a specific domain. The preferred lexical thesaurus is WordNet, a comprehensive on-line catalog of English terms [15]. WordNet classifies the English language into synonym sets with underlying word senses (e.g., the noun "chair" has 4 word senses). WordNet has been found useful for traditional and web IR [38, 49]. It is difficult, however, to identify domain-specific thesauri for all domains on the web [18]. A solution is to use the domain ontology libraries on the Semantic Web. Stephens and Huhns [47] have shown that large ontology libraries can provide useful knowledge even in the presence of individual ontologies that are incomplete or inaccurate. Ontology libraries, therefore, have a dual role on the Semantic Web: 1) as a source of definitions of terms on specific web pages, and 2) as a source of semantics that can assist query expansion.

In summary, the IR field provides several insights into methods that will be required for querying the Semantic Web. The following insights, in particular, have influenced the development of the methodology presented in this paper:

- the need for user-interaction to identify the context of terms in short web queries,
- the continued relevance of query expansion using global context analysis,
- the need to use lexical and domain thesauri in combination, and
- the important role of large libraries of domain ontologies as sources of semantics.

3 Methodology for Retrieving Information from Semantic Web

Semantic Web languages and query schemes are still being developed [7, 10]. Nonetheless, the usefulness of Semantic Web ontologies for querying can be tested on the current web. Consider Berners-Lee's et al. query: *Find Mom a specialist who can provide a series of bi-weekly physical therapy sessions.* The need for disambiguation is clear if the query is transformed into a short, more ambiguous query, more closely approximating queries on the web [46]: *Find doctors providing physical therapy.*

3.1 Overview of Methodology

A methodology for processing the query above is presented in Figure 1, above. Steps 1 to 3 identify the query context, as outlined below.

Identify Query Context →	Build Knowledge Base →	Execute Query
Step 1: Identify noun phrases	Step 4: Exclude incorrect sense	Step 7: Construct Boolean query
Step 2: Build synonym sets	Step 5: Include hypernyms	Step 8: Run query on search engine
Step 3: Select word sense	Step 6: Resolve inconsistencies	Step 9: Retrieve and present results

Fig. 1. Methodology for Disambiguating, Augmenting, and Executing Query

Step 1 – Identify noun phrases. The methodology assumes that users enter their queries in natural language form, as users often have difficulty using Boolean logic or other query syntax [33, 46]. Nouns are identified using a modified form of the Qtag part-of-speech tagger [35]. Identifying phrases can significantly improve query precision [9, 33]. Thus, noun phrases are identified by querying each consecutive word-pair in WordNet. For example, "physical therapy" is a phrase in WordNet, so this step would find two noun phrases ('doctor' and 'physical therapy'). These noun phrases form the base nodes for expansion of the query. They are represented by a semantic network (see Figure 2). Initially, the terms are lined by a 'candidate' relationship, indicating that the terms have not yet been identified as relating in a lexical or domain-specific way. In the following stages, the semantic network will be augmented with three additional relationships: synonym (X is the same as Y), hypernym (X is a subclass of Y), and negation (X is not Y).

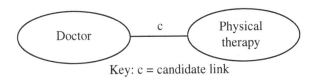

Key: c = candidate link

Fig. 2. Semantic Network of Query Terms after Step 1

Step 2 – Build synonym sets. To identify the different senses for each noun-phrase, synonym sets for each context are obtained from WordNet. For example, the term "doctor" has four senses in WordNet: 1. a medical practitioner, 2. a theologian, 3. a game played by children, and 4. an academician. "Physical therapy" has just one sense in WordNet. Each synonym set comprises one to many synonyms. These synonym sets for the query terms are incorporated into the knowledge base.

Step 3 – Select word sense. As the query does not contain enough terms to automatically deduce the word sense, user interaction is required [1, 49]. The user is presented with synsets for terms with multiple senses (e.g., "doctor") from which the user selects the most appropriate sense. Once the word-sense of terms has been identified, steps 4-6 build the knowledge base with additional terms to expand and constrain the query. The emphasis is on building a query that is biased towards precision, i.e., gives greater weighting to precision than recall [9, 22].

Step 4 – Exclude incorrect sense. To ensure that the results returned for a query are accurate, it is important to filter out those pages that contain incorrect senses of the term. Traditional query expansion does not include negative terms as filters [12, 18, 49]. Studies of web-query expansion have similarly not considered incorrect senses [28, 38]. Excluding incorrect senses is important on the web because of the vast number of results returned. Given that WordNet can return multiple synsets for each query term, incorrect senses can be inferred from the user's chosen word sense. For example, if a user selects the "medical practitioner" sense of 'Doctor,' then, a correct inference is that the user does not want pages associated with the other three senses of the term (theologians, children's games, or academics). Furthermore, because WordNet orders its synsets by estimated frequency of usage, terms can be chosen that are most likely to be successful in eliminating irrelevant results. We therefore use the following exclusion heuristic: *For each noun phrase, if a user identifies a synset as relevant, select the synonyms from the highest-ordered remaining synset, and include them in the knowledge base as negative knowledge* (see, e.g., Figure 3).

Step 5 – Including hypernyms. Past research has added hypernyms (or superclasses) to queries as a recall-enhancing technique, retrieving pages that contain either the search term (e.g., physical therapy) or its superclass (e.g., therapy) [18, 49]. Because precision is preferred over recall on the web [9, 22], our methodology uses hypernyms to increase the precision of queries by including them as mandatory terms. For example, rather than searching for *doctor OR "medical practitioner,"* pages would be searched that contain *doctor AND "medical practitioner."* Of course, some 'doctor' pages that are relevant to the user may not include the hypernym "medical practitioner." Nevertheless, pages that contain 'doctor' and 'medical practitioner' are expected to be more likely to be consistent with the medical sense of the term 'doctor' than if the page only contained the 'doctor' term alone. Recall is, thus, sacrificed for precision. Following this approach, hypernyms are obtained from both WordNet and the DAML ontology library. WordNet provides the hypernyms for each synset automatically. The hypernyms from the DAML ontology library are obtained by querying the library for each noun phrase. The hypernyms from DAML and WordNet are then incorporated into the knowledge base. Table 1 shows the terms extracted from WordNet and the DAML ontology library from this step based upon the example. Figure 3 illustrates the expanded semantic network of terms after completing this step.

Step 6 – Resolve inconsistencies. The ability of query expansion to improve a query is dependent upon the quality of the terms added. Inconsistent terms could be added to the knowledge base when: (a) the synonym sets in WordNet are not orthogonal so a word-sense may be partially relevant but excluded by our methodology in step 4, (b) the DAML ontologies are of mixed quality so might contain inaccurate information [25], and (c) WordNet and the domain ontologies represent the contribution of many individuals who may have conflicting views of a domain. To identify inconsistencies, the methodology uses the following heuristic: *Check the hypernyms of the query terms (from DAML and WordNet) against the synonyms of the query term (from WordNet) that the user did not select as the desired word sense. Upon finding a match, ask the user if the term is desired. Adjust the knowledge base accordingly.*

Once the knowledge-base has been expanded, steps 7–9 are used to build and execute the query.

Table 1. Extraction of Hypernyms from WordNet and the DAML Ontology Library

Knowledge from WordNet		
Term	Word-sense (defined by synsets)	Hypernym (superclass)
Doctor	Doc, Physician, MD, Dr, medico	Medical practitioner, medical man
	Doctor of Church	Theologian, Roman Catholic
	Doctor	Play
	Dr	Scholar, scholarly person, student
Physical Therapy	Physiotherapy, physiatrics	Therapy
Knowledge from DAML ontology library		
Term	Hypernym (superclass)	
Doctor	Qualification, Medical care professional, Health professional	
Physical therapy	Rehabilitation, Medical practice	

Step 7 – Construct Boolean query. Following [22, 38], we construct the query using Boolean constraints to improve precision. Three heuristics are used:

(a) Synonym: *Automatically include the first synonym in the synset selected by the user and include it in the query with an OR, e.g., (query term OR synonym).*

(b) Hypernym: *Automatically include the first hypernym from WordNet for the user's selected word-sense. Allow the user to select up to one hypernym from those from the DAML library. Require the results to include either one or both hypernyms, e.g., query term AND (WordNet hypernym OR DAML hypernym).*

(c) Negation: *Automatically include the first synonym from the first synset in WordNet's list that was not selected by the user with a Boolean NOT, e.g., (query term NOT synonym).*

The rationale for each heuristic is to improve precision while minimizing user interaction. The synonym heuristic is used because the user may not have selected the most precise query term for that word sense. While this heuristic on its own could increase recall at the cost of precision [18], the use of a synonym in combination with a hypernym should improve precision. Because WordNet lists terms in estimated order of frequency of use, the first synonym is likely the best alternative for that term.

The hypernym heuristic is used to force pages to include the query term (or synonym) as well as the hypernym should increase the likelihood that the page contains the sense of the term the user desires. Following [34], WordNet and the DAML ontology are used in combination by allowing either of their hypernyms to be found. Because the DAML ontologies can be of mixed quality and because they do not provide hypernyms by word sense, user interaction is required to select the appropriate hypernym obtained from the domain ontologies.

Finally, the negation heuristic is used to filter out unwanted word senses. As WordNet can provide many synonyms in each synset and because terms are listed in estimated order of frequent usage, the first synonym from the first remaining synset is chosen as the most useful term for excluding pages.

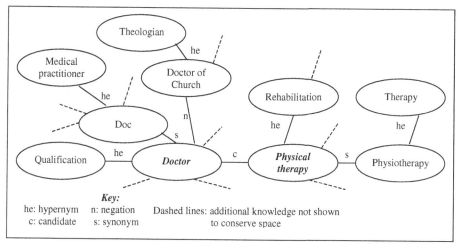

Fig. 3. Semantic Network of Query-Terms After Building Knowledge-Base

Applying these heuristics to the example, the following query is constructed:
(Doctor or Doc) and ("Medical practitioner" or Qualification) –"Doctor of church" and ("Physical therapy" or physiotherapy) and (therapy or "medical practice").

Step 8 – Run query on search engine. Although a number of IR search engines have been developed, (e.g., for TREC), there is evidence that web search engines are more effective for web querying [44]. The methodology, therefore, submits the query to one or more web search engines (in their required syntax) for processing. The query construction heuristics are designed to work with most search engines. For example, while Altavista.com allows queries to use a NEAR constraint, this is unavailable on other search engines (e.g., Google.com, Alltheweb.com), so it is not used. Likewise, query expansion methodologies in IR can add up to 800 terms to the query with varying weights [41]. This approach is not used in our methodology because web search engines limit the number of query terms (e.g. Google has a limit of ten terms).

Step 9 – Retrieve and present results. In the final step, the results from the search engine (URLs and 'snippets' provided from the web pages) are retrieved and presented to the user. The user can either accept the query or revise the query to get more relevant results.

    A pilot-test of the methodology indicated that the approach is feasible [5]. Queries using the above steps returned fewer results of equal or more relevance, with results dependent on the length and ambiguity of the query. A prototype was thus implemented to enable more detailed testing.

4 Implementation

A prototype called ISRA (Intelligent Semantic web Retrieval Agent) has been developed using J2EE technologies and informally tested [48]. ISRA uses the traditional client-server architecture as shown in Figure 4. The client is a basic web browser, through which the user specifies search queries in natural language. The server contains Java application code and the WordNet database. The prototype also provides an interface to several search engines including Google (www.google.com), Alltheweb (www.alltheweb.com) and AltaVista (www.altavista.com).

The prototype consists of three agents: a) Input-Output-Parser Agent, b) WordNet Agent, and c) Query Refinement and Execution Agent. These were implemented using a combination of jsp pages and servlets. The input-output-parser agent is responsible for capturing the user's input, parsing the natural language query, and returning results. The agent uses "QTAG", a *probabilistic parts-of-speech tagger* (available at http://web.bham.ac.uk/o.mason/software/tagger/index.html), to parse the user's input. It returns the part-of-speech for each word in the text. Based on the noun phrases (propositions) identified, an initial search query is created.

The WordNet Agent interfaces with the WordNet lexical database via JWordNet (a pure Java standalone object-oriented interface available at http://sourceforge.net/projects/jwn/). The prototype uses WordNet 1.6 (PC). For each noun phrase, the agent queries the database for different word senses and requests that the user select the most appropriate sense for the query. The agent extracts word senses, synonyms and hypernyms (superclasses) from the lexical database and forwards them to the query refinement agent to augment the initial query.

The Query Refinement and Execution (QRE) agent expands the initial query based on word senses, and synonyms obtained from WordNet. The refined query is then submitted to the search engine using appropriate syntax and constraints, and the results returned to the user. For example, the agent interacts with Google through its Web API service and adheres to the ten word limit for query length and displays ten hits at a time. Essentially, the QRE agent applies the steps shown in Figure 1 to augment the initial query. For example, it searches for phrases (word pairs) and includes them within double quotes, adds synonyms (from the WordNet synset) to the query based on the word sense selected by the user, and adds negative knowledge (terms) from the remaining word senses (e.g., would exclude the theologian sense of doctor if a query was for a medical doctor). For each term, the hypernym corresponding to the selected word sense is also retrieved from WordNet and DAML ontology and added to the query. The refined query is then sent to the search engine.

5 Testing

The effectiveness of the methodology was assessed by carrying out a laboratory study in which the results obtained using ISRA were compared to those obtained using the Google search engine alone. As the control group (Google) and the experimental group (Google plus methodology) used the same search engine, the experiment directly tests the benefit of the methodology and its heuristics.

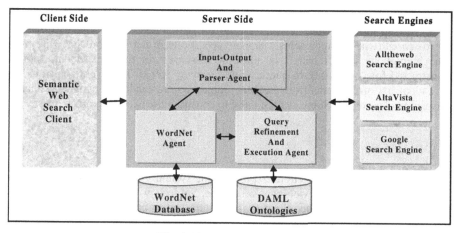

Fig. 4. ISRA Prototype Design

Forty-nine students from two universities participated voluntarily. All were experienced and frequent search engine users. Subjects were required to build their own queries and evaluate their own results since experimenters are unable to create as diverse a set of queries as users, can bias results, and cannot objectively determine whether a result is relevant to a user [17].

5.1 Dependent Variable and Hypothesis

Two measures of precision were used: the number of relevant pages in the first 10 and first 20 pages (Precision(10) and Precision(20)). These suit a web context because users do not view many results [4, 46]. Recall was not tested because it is less relevant and not strictly measurable on the web [12].

To test the flexibility of the methodology, the experiment tested the system's performance on two types of terms: ambiguous and clear. *Query term ambiguity* refers to the degree to which the query terms contain many word senses. Because the methodology aims to improve query precision, it should provide the most benefits when query terms have many word senses. Formally, the following hypothesis was tested:

Hypothesis: *ISRA will produce more relevant results than Google for queries with ambiguous terms.*

5.2 Query Sample

A large body of diverse user-developed queries was tested (per [4]). Some queries were expected to contain terms that did not exist in WordNet or the DAML library, e.g., 'instance' information such as product names. To alleviate this problem, and to test the hypothesis, the query sample was constructed as follows. First, all single-word classes in the DAML library were extracted. These were then pruned by excluding terms that (a) had no superclasses in the library, or (b) would be unknown to subjects (e.g., very specialized terms). 268 terms were obtained. These were divided into two groups based on their word-senses in WordNet. 131 terms (the clear group) had 0-2 word-senses (where 0 represents a domain-specific term not in WordNet). 137 terms (the ambiguous group) had 3 or more word-senses. In the experiment, subjects constructed four queries. Two queries could use any words. Two were constrained to a random list of 20 terms from DAML. Subjects were randomly assigned either 20 clear or unclear terms. Subjects used these to construct the two constrained queries.

5.3 Procedure

Each subject received instructions explaining the system's operation, how to construct queries, and how to grade web-page relevance. Subjects were first given a 10-minute training exercise to introduce them to the system and to practice developing a query and ranking results. Next, each participant developed his or her four queries. Each student's materials included the random list of clear or unclear terms for constructing their two constrained queries. The system provided the results from both ISRA and Google (in random order) and asked the subject for his or her ranking. Subjects were given three minutes to perform each query and four minutes to rank the first twenty pages returned for each query (two minutes to rank the results from ISRA and two minutes to rank the results from Google). A short time was given for assessment because this was considered to be typical web user behavior. Overall, the experiment took approximately 45 minutes.

5.4 Summary of Results

Table 2 summarizes the results. For each query, the methodology was expected to increase the number of relevant pages, decrease the number of irrelevant pages, and reduce the number of hits. Paired-sample t-tests identify the difference between groups. To assess the benefit of the heuristics, all subjects' queries were analyzed to determine if they invoked the query construction heuristics in section 3.1 (step 7) above. A more detailed analysis of each heuristic (e.g., to compare the contribution of terms from WordNet versus terms from DAML) is being examined in future research. The results for the experiment are:

All differences between the system and Google were in the expected direction

- For all queries, the methodology significantly reduced the number of pages returned
- For the full sample: the number of irrelevant pages in the top 10 was significantly reduced
- For the ambiguous queries: all results were significant and supported the hypothesis
- For the full sample, results were strong when heuristics were invoked. Using synonyms, hypernyms, and/or negative knowledge decreased the irrelevant pages. Using synonyms and/or negative knowledge increased the relevant pages.

Table 2. Summary of Results

Variable	Hypothesized Direction	All	Unclear	Syn	Hyp	Neg	SNH
R(10)	+	+.279	+.054*	+.091*	+.175	+.033**	+.003**
R(20)	+	+.371	+.014**	+.180	+.453	+.050*	+.006**
NR(10)	-	-.035**	-.003**	-.002**	-.007**	-.006**	-.000**
NR(20)	-	-.106	-.002**	-.011**	-.034**	-.007**	-.000**
Hits	-	-.000**	-.000**	-.000**	-.000**	-.000**	-.000**
N	NA	156	44	96	123	95	63

Key: Cell entries are p-values for paired sample t-tests (ISRA vs. Google).
** significant at $\alpha < 0.05$ one-tailed, * at $\alpha < 0.10$ one-tailed
R(10) = # relevant in top 10 , R(20) = # relevant in top 20, NR = # not relevant (in top 10 & 20), N = Sample size, All = full set of queries minus missing values, Unclear = subset of queries for the ambiguous group, Syn = subset of queries that invoked synonym heuristic, Hyp = subset of queries that invoked hypernym heuristic, Neg = subset of queries that invoked negation heuristic, SNH = subsets of queries that invoked synonym, hypernyms, and negation heuristics.

6   Conclusion

A significant body of research has emerged to investigate ways to facilitate the development of the Semantic Web. There have been few attempts, however, to develop methodologies for retrieving information from the Semantic Web. This paper presented a methodology for the development of an intelligent agent that makes effective use of lexicons and ontologies for processing queries on the Semantic Web. The methodology is based upon a desire to obtain good results from a query with minimal user intervention. The methodology builds upon research on natural language processing, knowledge-based systems, and information retrieval. Initial results show that the approach is beneficial. A prototype system was found to improve query results over a common search engine when (a) query terms were ambiguous, and/or (b) when the methodology's heuristics were invoked. Further work is needed to improve the scalability and customizability of the approach, and minimize user interaction.

References

1. Allan, J. and H. Raghavan. *Using Part-of-Speech Patterns to Reduce Query Ambiguity*. in *25th Annual International ACM SIGIR Conference on Research and Development in Information Retrieval*. 2002. Tampere, Finland: ACM Press, New York.
2. Bergholtz, M. and P. Johannesson. *Classifying the Semantics in Conceptual Modelling by Categorization of Roles*. NLDB'01. 2001. Madrid, Spain.
3. Berners-Lee, T., J. Hendler, and O. Lassila, *The Semantic Web*, in *Scientific American*. 2001. p. 1–19.
4. Buckley, C. and E.M. Voorhees. *Evaluating Evaluation Measure Stability*. in *SIGIR*. 2000. Athens, Greece: ACM.

5. Burton-Jones, A., S. Purao, and V.C. Storey. *Context-Aware Query Processing on the Semantic Web.* in *Proceedings of the 23rd International Conference on Information Systems.* 2002. Barcelona, Spain, Dec. 16–19.
6. CACM, *Special issue on ontology.* Communications of ACM, Feb. 2002. 45(2) p. 39–65.
7. Crow, L. and N. Shadbolt, *Extracting Focused Knowledge From the Semantic Web.* International Journal of Human-Computer Studies, 2001. 54: p. 155–184.
8. Cui, H., et al. *Probabilistic Query Expansion Using Query Logs.* in *Eleventh World Wide Web Conference (WWW 2002).* 2002. Honolulu, Hawaii.
9. de Lima, E.F. and J.O. Pedersen. *Phrase Recognition and Expansion for Short, Precision-biased Queries based on a Query Log.* in *22nd Annual International ACM SIGIR Conference on Research and Development in Information Retrieval.* 1999. Berkeley, CA.
10. Ding, Y., et al., *The Semantic Web: Yet Another Hip?* Data & Knowledge Engineering, 2002. 41: p. 205–227.
11. Dullea, J. and I.Y. Song. *A Taxonomy of Recursive Relationships and Their Structural Validity in ER Modeling.* Lecture Notes in Computer Science 1728. 1999. Paris, France.
12. Efthimiadis, E.N., *Interactive Query Expansion: A User-Based Evaluation in a Relevance Feedback Environment.* Jl. of American Society for Inf. Science, 2000. 51(11) p. 989–1003.
13. Embley, D.W., et al. *A Conceptual-Modeling Approach to Extracting Data from the Web.* in *17th International Conference on Conceptual Modeling, ER '98.* 1998. Singapore.
14. Farquhar, A., R. Fikes, and J. Rice. *The Ontolingua Server: a Tool for Collaborative Ontology Construction.* in *Tenth Knowledge Acquisition for Knowledge-Based Systems Workshop.* 1996. Banff, Canada.
15. Fellbaum, C. *WordNet: An Electronic Lexical Database.* 1998, MIT Press Cambridge, MA.
16. Fensel, D., et al., *OIL: An Ontology Infrastructure for the Semantic Web.* IEEE Intelligent Systems, 2001. March/April: p. 38–45.
17. Gordon, M. and P. Pathak, *Finding Information on the World Wide Web: The Retrieval Effectiveness of Search Engines.* Info. Processing & Management, 1999. 35: p. 141–180.
18. Greenberg, J., *Automatic Query Expansion via Lexical-Semantic Relationships.* Journal of the American Society for Information Science, 2001. 52(5): p. 402–415.
19. Gruber, T.R., *A Translation Approach to Portable Ontology Specifications.* Knowledge Acquisition, 1993. 5: p. 199–220.
20. Guarino, N. *Formal Ontology and Information Systems.* in *1st International Conference on Formal Ontology in Information Systems.* 1998. Trento, Italy: IOS Press.
21. Guha, R.V. and D.B. Lenat, *Enabling Agents to Work Together.* Communications of the ACM, 1994. 37(7): p. 127–142.
22. Hearst, M.A. *Improving Full-Text Precision on Short Queries using Simple Constraints.* in *SDAIR.* 1996. Las Vegas, NV.
23. Heflin, J., J. Hendler, and S. Luke, *SHOE: A Knowledge Representation Language for Internet Applications. Technical Report CS-TR-4078 (UMIACS TR-99-71).* 1999, Dept. of Computer Science, University of Maryland at College Park.
24. Hendler, J. and D.L. McGuinness, *The DARPA Agent Markup Language.* IEEE Intelligent Systems, 2000. 15(6): p. 67–73.
25. Hendler, J., *Agents and the Semantic Web.* IEEE Intelligent Systems, 2001. Mar p. 30–36.
26. Ide, N. and J. Veronis, *Introduction to the Special Issue on Word Sense Disambiguation: The State of the Art.* Computational Linguistics, 1998. 24(1): p. 1–40.
27. IEEE, *Special issue on the Semantic Web.* IEEE Intelligent Systems, Mar 2001: p. 32–79.
28. Jansen, B.J., *An Investigation Into the Use of Simple Queries on Web IR Systems.* Information Research: An Electronic Journal, 2000. 6(1): p. 1–13.
29. Jing, Y. and W.B. Croft. *An Association Thesaurus for Information Retrieval.* in *RIAO-94, 4th International Conference "Recherche d'Information Assistee par Ordinateur".* 1994.
30. Kedad, Z. and E. Metais. *Dealing with Semantic Heterogeneity During Data Integration. 18th Intl Conf on Conceptual Modeling, LNCS 1728.* 1999. Paris, France.

31. Kobayashi, M. and K. Takeda, *Information Retrieval on the Web.* ACM Computing Surveys, 2000. 32(2): p. 144–173.
32. Lawrence, S., *Context in Web Search.* IEEE Data Engg. Bulletin, 2000. 23(3) p. 25–32.
33. Lewis, D.D. and K. Spark Jones, *Natural Language Processing for Information Retrieval.* Communications of the ACM, 1996. 39(1): p. 92–101.
34. Mandala, R., T. Tokunaga, and H. Tanaka. *Combining Multiple Evidence from Different Types of Thesaurus for Query Expansion.* in *22nd Intl ACM SIGIR Conference on Research & Development in Information Retrieval.* 1999. Berkeley, CA.
35. Mason, O., *Qtag – a Portable POS Tagger.* 2003, online: http://web.bham.ac.uk/O.Mason/software/tagger/.
36. Miller, G.A., *Contextuality,* in *Mental Models in Cognitive Science,* J. Oakhill and A. Garnham, Editors. 1996, Psychology Press: East Sussex, UK. p. 1–18.
37. Mitra, M., A. Singhal, and C. Buckley. *Improving Automated Query Expansion.* in *21st Intl Conf on Research & Development on Information Retrieval.* 1998. Melbourne, Australia.
38. Moldovan, D.L. and R. Mihalcea, *Improving the Search on the Internet by using WordNet and Lexical Operators.* IEEE Internet Computing, 2000. 4(1): p. 34–43.
39. Mylopoulos, J., *Information Modeling in the Time of the Revolution.* Information Systems, 1998. 23(34): p. 127–155.
40. Noy, N.F. and C.D. Hafner, *The State of the Art in Ontology Design: A Survey and Comparative Review.* AI Magazine, 1997. 18(3/Fall): p. 53–74.
41. Qiu, Y. and H.-P. Frei. *Concept Based Query Expansion.* in *16th Annual Intl ACM SIGIR Conference on Research and Development in Information Retrieval.* 1993. Pittsburgh, PA.
42. Raghavan, P. *Information Retrieval Algorithms: A Survey, Eighth Annual ACM-SIAM Symp on Discrete Algorithms.* 1997. New Orleans, Louisiana: ACM Press, New York, NY.
43. Salton, G. and C. Buckley, *Improving Retrieval Performance by Relevance Feedback.* Journal of the American Society for Information Science, 1990. 41(4): p. 288–297.
44. Singhal, A. and M. Kaszkiel. *A Case Study in Web Search Using TREC Algorithms.* in *10th International World Wide Web Conference.* 2001. Hong Kong.
45. Sowa, J.F., *Knowledge Representation: Logical, Philosophical, and Computational Foundations.* 2000: Brooks Cole Publishing Co.
46. Spink, A., et al., *Searching the Web: The Public and Their Queries.* Journal of the American Society for Information Science, 2001. 52(3): p. 226–234.
47. Stephens, L.M. and M.N. Huhns, *Consensus Ontologies: Reconciling the Semantics of Web Pages and Agents.* IEEE Internet Computing, 2001. September–October: p. 92–95.
48. Sugumaran, V., A. Burton-Jones, and V.C. Storey. *A Multi-Agent Prototype for Intelligent Query Processing on the Semantic Web.* in *Proceedings of the 12th Annual Workshop on Information Technology and Systems (WITS).* 2002. Barcelona, Spain, Dec. 14–15.
49. Voorhees, E.M. *Query Expansion Using Lexical-Semantic Relations.* in *17th Annual International ACM/SIGIR Conference on Research and Development in Information Retrieval.* 1994. Dublin, Ireland.
50. Weber, R., *Ontological Foundations of Information Systems.* Coopers and Lybrand Accounting Research Methodology, Monograph No. 4. 1997, Melbourne: Coopers & Lybrand and Accounting Association of Australia and New Zealand. 212.

On Analysing Query Ambiguity for Query Refinement: The Librarian Agent Approach

Nenad Stojanovic

Institute AIFB,
Research Group Knowledge Management
University of Karlsruhe,
76128 Karlsruhe, Germany
nst@aifb.uni-karlsruhe.de
http://www.aifb.uni-karlsruhe.de/wbs

Abstract. In this paper, we present an approach for the disambiguation of ontology-based queries. The approach is based on measuring the ambiguity of a query with respect to the user's initial information need. We define several types of ambiguities concerning the structure of the underlying ontology and the content of the information repository. For each of these ambiguities we define a set of refinements/explanations, which helps in more efficient searching for information in an ontology-based information repository. We demonstrate the benefits of using our approach in an evaluation study.

1 Introduction

One of the main problems for achieving the high precision in the (web) information retrieval is the ambiguity of the users' queries, since the users tend to post very short queries. Consequently, the users try to refine their queries until their information need is satisfied. An efficient support for this query disambiguation is missing in the current IR systems, first of all because they only partially reflect the process which humans use in searching for goods in the bricks-and-mortar environment. Briefly, in the non-virtual search, there is a shop assistant, who helps the user express her need more clearly, and guides the user through the searching space. It means that the user refines her query incrementally according to the suggestions made by the shop assistant.

In this paper, we present the conceptual architecture of the Librarian Agent, an information portal management system, which simulates the role a human librarian plays in searching for information resources in a library. The Agent analyses the user's query based on: (i) the structure of the used vocabulary, (ii) the capacity of the information repository and (iii) the information about the past users' activities in the portal. The agent, through an interactive dialogue, guides the user in closing the initial query to the original user's information need, in the so-called query refinement process. Moreover, the Agent supports efficient ranking/clustering of retrieved results. The approach assumes the existence of a common vocabulary that is used for creating the queries, as well as for providing meta-information about the content of information resources. In order to simulate the background knowledge that a human

I.-Y. Song et al. (Eds.): ER 2003, LNCS 2813, pp. 490–505, 2003.

librarian uses in searching, we extend the vocabulary to the conceptual model of the given domain, i.e. an ontology.

The focus of the paper is on the problem of determining the ambiguity in the user's request, and providing corresponding refinements. We consider the realistic case when the users make Boolean queries using a controlled vocabulary provided by the ontology (it means that the query is not in the form of a logic formula and, therefore, various interpretations of a query term are possible). We define the notion ambiguity, provide a categorisation of the ambiguities which can be found in the users' queries, and develop methods for measuring and resolving these ambiguities. The approach is based on the analysis of the structure of the underlying vocabulary (ontology) and the content of the information repository, using formal concept analysis [1]. The benefits of using such a query-refinement process are demonstrated in an evaluation study. The approach has been implemented in our KAON framework (kaon.semanticweb.org).

The paper is organised as follows: In the second section, we describe the conceptual architecture of the Librarian Agent through a usage scenario. In the section 3, we present our query refinement approach. In the section 4, we present results from an evaluation study. In the section 5, we discuss some of the related works. The section 6 contains conclusion remarks.

2   The Librarian Agent – The Usage Scenario

The role of the Librarian Agent is (i) to resolve the disambiguation of the queries posted by users (query management), (ii) to enable efficient ranking and/or clustering of retrieved answers (ranking) and (iii) to enable the changes in the knowledge repository regarding the users' information needs (collection management).

Fig. 1 sketches the conceptual architecture of the Librarian Agent. In order to make the ideas behind the architecture more understandable, we describe it through several examples of querying the Information Portal of an Institute. It is assumed that the backbone of that Portal is the *ResearchInstitute* ontology, a part of which is depicted in the Fig. 2.

A user posts the query (cf. 1 in Fig. 1), which is processed firstly by the Librarian Agent. Let us assume that the query is "Researcher and Project and KM", e.g. the user is searching for the information resources about "researchers in projects related to the knowledge management (KM)". The Agent measures the ambiguity of the query (cf. 2 in Fig. 1) by considering the capacity of the knowledge repository and the domain vocabulary - ontology. The user is provided with an explanation what is ambiguous in the query and how this ambiguity can influence the result of the querying.

For the given query, the Agent might find the following ambiguities (more elaborations on these ambiguities are given in the next section):

1) The sense of the term KM is not clear: KM can be a research area or a lecture, see Fig.2;

2) The context of the query is not clear: since there are two relations between the terms Researcher and Project (i.e. worksIn and manages – see Fig.2.), the user should clarify which of these meaning she is interested in. Otherwise, she could get some irrelevant answers;

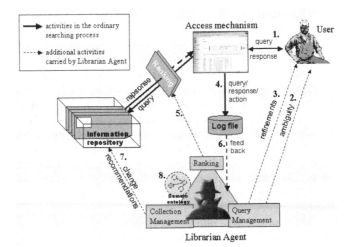

Fig. 1. The roles of the Librarian Agent in the process of searching for knowledge

3) The clarity of the term `Researcher` used in the query is not well determined: since there are two subtypes of `Researcher` (see Fig.2.), the user should specify which type of `Researchers` she is interested in. Otherwise, she could get some irrelevant results;

4) By analysing the information repository, it follows that the list of answers for the given query is the same as for the query "`Researcher and Project`", which means that all existing `Projects` are about `KM`.

synonyms(Researcher, Scientist, Forscher)	Researcher(rst)[2]	workIn(rst, LA)[3]
isA(PhDStudent, Researcher)[1]	Researcher(nst)	workIn(nst, LA)
	Researcher(ysu)	workIn(ysu, LA)
	Researcher(jan)	workIn(jan, LA)
isA(Professor, Researcher),	Researcher(meh)	workIn(meh, LA)
workIn(Researcher, Project)	Researcher(sha)	
manages(Researcher, Project)	project(LA)	ResearchArea(KM)
about(ResearchArea, Project)	Lecture(KM)	researchIn(rst, KM)[4]
		researchIn(ysu, KM)
researchIn(Researcher, ResearchArea)	PhDStudent(nst)	researchIn(nst, KM)
	PhDStudent(ysu)	researchIn(meh, KM)
teaches(Researcher, Lecture)	PhDStudent(meh)	researchIn(rst, CBR)
	Professor(rst)	researchIn(nst, CBR)
	Professor(jan)	researchIn(ysu, CBR)
		subtopic(KM, CBR)

Fig. 2. A part of the ontology we use for illustrating our approach

---

[1] It means that `PhDStudent` is a subtype of `Researcher`

[2] It means that `rst` is a `Researcher`

[3] It means that `rst` works in the project `LA`

[4] It means that `rst` researches in the `KM`

Moreover, the Agent recommends the user some changes (refinements) in the query (cf. 3 in Fig. 1), considering the underlying vocabulary, the information repository and the agent's experience (the past behaviour of the users). For example, beside the refinements related to the cases 1) - 3), the Agent can "recognise" that in the underlying repository there are a lot of resources about PhD_Students involved in projects in KM and it can probably be a suitable refinement of the given query (i.e. "PhD_Student and project and KM").

The Agent receives the feedback information about how many (and which) refinements' steps the user performed (cf. 4 in Fig. 1), and it uses this information to improve its own strategies for creating recommendations.

The **Query Management module** is responsible for the previous two tasks, i.e. for the ambiguity measurement and for the recommendations for the refinements of a query.

Let us assume that the user refined her query into "PhD_Student and Project and KM", and the retrieved results are meh, nst, ysu (see Fig.2.). The retrieved list of results is ranked according to the relevance for the given query. The **Ranking module** analyses the domain ontology, the underlying repository and the searching process in order to determine the relevance of the retrieved answers (cf. 5 in Fig. 1) For example, it finds that the answer nst is more relevant than the answer meh, since nst researches in the areas KM and CBR, whereas meh researches only in KM. Moreover, the results can be clustered into semantically related groups of results, in order to enhance searching.

The information about which of the retrieved results were clicked by the users can be used for the management of the searching process. In order to avoid disturbing the users by additional questioning, the feedback information is collected implicitly by analysing the activities of the users that are captured in the log file of the system.

Moreover, the list of queries is further analysed (cf. 6 in Fig. 1) by the Librarian Agent, in order to make recommendations for the changes in the collection (cf. 7 in Fig. 1). This is the task of the **Collection Management module**. This recommendation takes into account the analysis of the queries posted by users and the used vocabulary, as well. For example, if a lot of users post the query "Project and Coordination", which returns zero answers, then it can be interpreted as an unsatisfied information need of lots of users. Consequently, the repository should be extended with such an information resource. Or if there are a lot of queries containing only the term "Project", then it can be a sign to split (specialise) the concept Project in several subconcepts (e.g. national project, EU-projects, etc.), in order to support fine-tuning of users' queries.

The conceptual model of the given domain – the domain ontology (cf. 8 in Fig. 1) supports the processing of each step in this approach. Moreover, the searching mechanism and the information repository are based on the domain ontology.

In the rest of the paper, we present the query management's capabilities of the Librarian Agent in details. More information about the Collection Management Module can be found in [2].

3 Query Management Module

The Query management module performs two sequential tasks in processing the ambiguity of a query: (i) Ambiguity Measurement and (ii) Query Refinement, i.e. the discovery of ambiguities in the given query and the recommendation of corresponding refinements, respectively.

3.1 Ambiguity Measurement

The users often estimate the ambiguity of a query through the number of results: a lot of results can be an indicator that there are some irrelevant results, i.e. that some other information needs are covered by that query. In most of the existing IR system, the user gets only this information, i.e. the number of results, as the characterisation of the ambiguity. However, the ambiguity of a query is a more complex category and it requires handling by using a more formalised approach. We have found two main factors, which affect the ambiguities of a query: the used vocabulary (i.e. ontology) and. the information repository. Consequently, we define two types of the ambiguity of a query: (i) the *semantic ambiguity*, as the characteristic of the used vocabulary and (ii) the *content-related ambiguity*, as the characteristics of the repository.

3.1.1 The Semantic Ambiguity

As we already mentioned in the introduction, we consider that the users make Boolean queries (a list of terms concatenated with a logical operator[5]), because forcing users to make formal logic queries slows and constrains information retrieval process. However, we assume that these terms are selected from an ontology. Since an ontology vocabulary allows using synonyms and homonyms, the meaning of some terms in a query can be ambiguous. Therefore, the very first step in our approach is the disambiguation of the meaning of the terms in a query, done by measuring *SenseAmbiguity*. Next, we measure the clarity of the context (defined by relations with other terms) in which a term appears – *ContextClarity*. Finally, we estimate the generality/speciality of a query term by measuring its *Clarity*.

In the following, we define these three ambiguity parameters.

SenseAmbiguity

In order to combine formal modelling of a domain and the user-friendly searching, the abstract model of ontology we use in our research, presented in [3], contains an additional modelling layer, the so-called lexical layer, which is responsible for mapping the terms used by the users in searching into the formal entities of an ontology (i.e. concepts, relations and instances). Due to lack of the space, we omit here the formal definition of the ontology, which can be found in [3], and give an informal explanation. For instance, returning to the example shown in the Fig. 2., the user can use the terms "Researcher", "Scientist" or "Forscher" in searching for the

---

[5] Although our approach can be applied to disjunctive queries as well, in order to simplify the explanation of the approach, in the following examples, we use only conjunctive queries.

resources related to the (domain-specific) concept `Researcher` from the ontology. Moreover, a term can be used for encoding several ontology entities, i.e. for representing several meanings. For example, the term "`KM`" can be used for encoding a `Lecture` or a `ResearchArea`, and we say that the term "`KM`" has two senses[6]. Consequently, if a query contains the term "`KM`", then the Query Management Module has to clarify the sense of that term, i.e. if the query is about a `Lecture` or a `ResearchArea`. The sense can be clarified by analysing the relations between the senses of that term with the senses of other terms in the query. For example, in the query "`KM and Projects`", the meaning of the term "`KM`" should be the ontology concept `ResearchArea`, because in the *ResearchInstitute* ontology there is a relation between concepts `ResearchArea` and `Project`, but there is no relation between concepts `Lecture` and `Project`. In case more than one sense is possible, ranking of the senses is needed. It can be done by considering the information repository. For example, in the query "`KM and Researcher`", the meaning of the `KM` can be a `ResearchArea`, as well as a `Lecture`, since there are relations between both of these concepts (`ResearchArea`, `Lecture`) and the concept `Researcher`, i.e. researchIn and teaches, respectively. By considering the number of information resources which are about "researching in KM area" and "teaching KM course", the ranking of these two senses of the query "`KM and Researcher`" can be done. Such a discussion is out of the scope of this paper.

In order to estimate this ambiguity, we define *SenseAmbiguity* factor for the query Q = " $t_1, t_2, ... t_n$ " as follows:

$$\text{SenseAmbiguity}(Q) = \frac{\sum_{\forall t_i, t_j \in Q} \text{NumberOfSensesInContext}(t_i, t_j)}{\text{NumberOfSenses}(Q)} \text{ , where,}$$

$\text{NumberOfSensesInContext}(t_i, t_j) = \left| \{i_p \in \text{Sense}(t_i), i_k \in \text{Sense}(t_j) : \text{Relation}(i_p, i_k)\} \right|$,

$\text{NumberOfSenses}(Q) = \sum_{\forall t_i \in Q} \left| \text{Sense}(t_i) \right|$, $|a|$ denotes the cardinality of the set a.

$\text{Sense}(t_i)$ is the set of the senses of the term t_i in the ontology. For example, Sense(KM) = {lecture, researchArea} ;

$\text{Relation}(i_p, i_k)$ is the function that returns 1 if there is a relation between i_p and i_k in the given ontology, for the case that i_p and i_k are concepts. In case that i_p and i_k are instances $\text{Relation}(i_p, i_k)$ returns 1 if there is the relation between the ontology concepts which corresponds to the instances i_p and i_k. Analogy definition holds for the case that one of i_p, i_k is an instance and other is a concept.

For example, for the query $Q_{initial}$ = "`Researcher and Project and KM`", we get:

$$\text{SenseAmbiguity}(Q_{initial}) = \frac{2+2+1}{1+1+2} \text{ , since}$$

Sense(researcher) = {researcher }, Sense(project) = {project} and Sense(KM) = {lecture, researchArea}, i.e. `KM` is the term which is assigned to the instance of a `Lecture` or a `ResearchArea`, NumberOfSensesInContext(researcher, project) = 2, i.e. a `Researcher workIn` or `manages` a `Project`, NumberOfSensesInContext(researcher, KM) = 2, i.e. a `Researcher researchIn` a

---

[6] Similarly to WordNet [4] synsets

`ResearchArea (KM)` or `teaches` a `Lecture (KM)` and
$NumberOfSensesInContext(project, KM) = 1$, i.e. a `Project` is about a `ResearchAarea`.

ContextClarity

This parameter models the existence of incomplete information in a query, regarding the used concepts/relations. It means that the query can be *automatically* expanded, in order to clarify the meaning of the query. For the given ontology, the query "`Researcher and Project and KM`" is incomplete, because there are two relations between concept `Researcher` and `Project`, namely `workIn` and `manages`, which can be used to specify the query more precisely.

For measuring the context clarity of a query, we use the following formulas:

$$ContextClarity(Q) = \prod_{\substack{i=1,n \\ j=1,n}} Contextuality(Q, Ci, Cj) \text{ where } Ci, Cj \in Q \text{, where}$$

$$Contextuality(Q, C1, C2) = \begin{cases} \dfrac{1}{|Properties(C1, C2)| + 1}, & |Properties(C1, C2)| \geq 1 \wedge \forall x \in Properties(C1, C2), x \notin Q \\ \\ 1 & else \end{cases}$$

$Properties(C1, C2)$ is the function which returns the set of all properties between C1 and C2, Q is the given query.

For example, $ContextClarity(Q_{initial}) = \dfrac{1}{3} \cdot \dfrac{1}{2} \cdot \dfrac{1}{3}$, whereas each of multiplicands corresponds to the number of the senses calculated for the SenseAmbiguity. The values for NumberOfSensesInContext and Contextuality are similar, because there are no terms which correspond to a relation in the given query. In the case of the query "`Researcher and Project and KM and workIn`" the context of the `Researcher`-`Project` pair can be treated as "fixed" (i.e. `workIn`) and $ContextClarity(Q) = 1 \cdot \dfrac{1}{2} \cdot \dfrac{1}{3}$.

Clarity

The clarity factor represents the uncertainty to determine the user's interest in the given query. For example, when the user makes a query using the concept `Researcher`, which contains two subconcepts `Professor` and `PhDStudent`, it could be a matter of discussion whether she is interested in the concept `Researcher`, or in one of its subconcepts. Anyway, she failed to express it in a clear manner. The formula for the clarity factor depends on the entity type:

$$Clarity(Q) = \dfrac{\sum_{\forall t_i \in Q, i_p \in Sense(t_i)} TermClarity(i_p)}{NumberOfSenses(Q)} \text{, where}$$

$$TermClarity(E) = \begin{cases} \dfrac{1}{numSubConcepts(E) + 1} & E \text{ is a concept} \\ \\ \dfrac{1}{numSubPropeties(E) + 1} \cdot \dfrac{1}{numDomains(E)} & E \text{ is a propetry} \end{cases}$$

numSubConcepts(E) is the number of subconcepts[7] of a concept E, numSubProperties(E) is the number of subproperties of a property E and numDomains(E) is the number of domains defined for the property E.

For the given query $\mathrm{Clarity}(Q_{\mathrm{initial}}) = (\frac{1}{3}+1+\frac{1}{4})/4$, in case that the concept `Researcher` has two subconcepts and `KM` (as a research area) has 4 subtopics.

3.1.2 The Content-Related Ambiguity

The *content-related ambiguity* of a query depends on the capacity of the information repository. Since this capacity determines the list of the results for a query, the content-related ambiguity of a query can be defined by comparing the results of the given query with the results of other queries. In the rest of this subsection, we define several relations between queries, in order to estimate this type of the ambiguity of a query.

Let $Q = (M, O)$ be the query-answering pair, whereas M is an ontology-based query and O is the list of results for the query Q. M and O are called query_terms and query_objects, respectively. Further, we define:

1. *Structural equivalence* (=) by: $(M_1, O_1) = (M_2, O_2) \leftrightarrow O_1 = O_2$
Two query-answering pairs (queries)[8] are structurally equivalent if their result sets are the same.

2. *Structural subsumption* (parent-child): (<) by: $(M_1, O_1) < (M_2, O_2) \leftrightarrow O_1 \subset O_2$.
A query (M_2, O_2) subsumes another query (M_1, O_1) if the result set of the second query pair subsumes the results of the first one. For query-answering pairs Q_1, Q_2 we define two subsumption relations:

- direct_parent ($<_{\mathrm{dir}}$): If $Q_1 < Q_2 \wedge \neg \exists Q_i, Q_1 < Q_i < Q_2$, Q_2 is direct_parent of the Q_1;
- direct_child ($>_{\mathrm{dir}}$): If $Q_2 < Q_1 \wedge \neg \exists Q_i, Q_2 < Q_i < Q_1$, Q_2 is direct_child of the Q_1.

For a query Q_a, we define five properties which characterise its structural ambiguity: *Largest equivalent query*, *Smallest equivalent query*, *Uniqueness*, *Covering* and *CoveringTerms*.

The *Largest equivalent query* for the query Q_a is its equivalent query with the maximal query_terms. It is calculated in the following way: $Q_{a\,max} = (\bigcup_{Q_i <_{\mathrm{dir}} Q_a} M_i, O_a)$. It means that the largest equivalent query contains the union of query_term of all direct_child.

The *Smallest equivalent query* for the query Q_a is its equivalent query with minimal query_terms. There can be several such queries. They are calculated in the following way: $Q_{a\,min} \in \{(\times(M_i \cap M_a), O_a) \mid Q_a <_{\mathrm{dir}} Q_i, i = 1,..n\}$

---

[7] It holds for each transitive relation and not only for the isA relation. For example, `subTopic` is a transitive relation.
[8] Due to simplicity, in the rest of the text, we will use the term query for referring to a query-answering pair.

For a query Q_a, it is possible to define a subset of objects which are unique for that query, i.e. they cannot be obtained for any direct_child query. We call that the *Uniqueness* of the query, and it is calculated in the following way:

Uniqueness$(Q_a) = \{O_a / \{\cup O_i\} | Q_i <_{dir} Q_a, i = 1..n\}$

Covering and *CoveringTerms* are parameters which define the percent of identical answers and query_terms, respectively, in two queries. More formally, for two queries Q_a and Q_b we define:

Covering$(Q_a, Q_b) = |O_a \cap O_b| / \max\{|O_a|, |O_b|\}$

CoveringTerms$(Q_a, Q_b) = |M_a \cap M_b| / \max\{|M_a|, |M_b|\}$

It is clear that the calculation of the above-mentioned parameters could be time-consuming. In order to make this calculation more effective, we use formal concept analysis (FCA) [1] for organising data in the so-called concept lattices which correspond to the multi-inheritance hierarchical clusters. Each of these clusters can be considered a query posted to the repository and, consequently, the lattice represents the clustering of the query space. A cluster is called a formal concept and it contains query terms and resources retrieved for that query. By analysing such a lattice, many interesting relations between queries can be discovered and used for measuring the query ambiguity and/or for the query refinement.

Due to the lack of space, we omit here the detailed introduction of the FCA which can be found in [1]. We mention only the main concepts needed for the understanding of our approach. Formal Concept Analysis (FCA) is a technique derived from the lattice theory that has been successfully used for various analysis purposes. The organisation of the data is achieved via a mathematical entity called a formal context. A formal context is a triple (G, L, I) where G is a set of objects, L is a set of attributes, and I is a binary relation between the objects and the attributes. A formal concept of a formal context (G, L, I) is a pair (A, B) where $A \subseteq G$, $B \subseteq L$, $A = B' = \{g \in G \mid \forall l \in B: (g,l) \in I\}$ and $B = A' = \{l \in L \mid \forall g \in A: (g,l) \in I\}$. For a formal concept (A, B), A is called the extent, and is the set of all objects that have all the attributes defined in B. Similarly, B is called the intent, and is the set of all attributes possessed by all the objects in A. As the number of attributes in B increases, the concept becomes more specific, i.e. a specialisation ordering is defined over the concepts of a formal context.

In this representation, more specific concepts have larger intents and are considered "less than" (<) concepts with smaller intents. The same partial ordering is achieved by considering extents, in which case more specific concepts have smaller extents. The partial ordering over concepts is always a lattice.

Note: Since an ontology uses the three-dimensional space for presenting information (object-attribute-value), a transformation into the two-dimensional space (attribute-value) is needed. Due to the lack of the space, we avoid here the discussion about this transformation. For example, the information `rst[worksIn->>LA]` is represented as the pair `(rst,worksIn->>LA)` in the table. In order to enhance the readability of the table, we replace the relations with the name of the domain of that relation (for example - `LA:Project` is the replacement for the `workIn->>LA`, because the relation `workIn` has for the range the concept `Project`).

Table 1. A part of the *ResearchInstitute* ontology given in the section 2

Attr. Obj.	Resea rcher	Pro- fessor	Proje ct	workIn - >>LA (= LA: Project)	Resear ch Area	researchIn - >>CBR (= CBR: ResearchArea)	ResearchIn->>KM (=KM: ResearchArea)
rst	X	X	X	X	X	X	X
nst	X		X	X	X	X	X
ysu	X		X	X	X	X	X
jan	X	X	X	X	X		X
meh	X		X	X	X		X
sha	X						

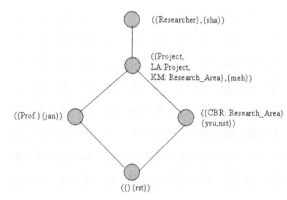

Fig.3. An example which shows the process of generating a concept lattice from a set of data given in the table 1. The concepts represented in the lattice should be read as in the following example: foremost left concept, ({Prof.}, {jan}), corresponds to the objects (jan, rst) and attributes (Researcher, Prof., Project, LA:Project, KM:ResearchArea) — some attributes are inherited from upper formal concepts.

Such a representation enables a very intuitive interpretation of a query: one can see a formal concept as a representation of a query state, where the intent of the formal concept represents the query itself, and the extent represents all resources that match the query. For example, the query "Researcher and Project and KM" will be mapped into the formal concept described as ({Project, LA:Project, KM:Research_Area}, {meh}) in the concept lattice. Note that a formal concept encompasses all objects from its super-concepts – i.e. the (attribute, object) set for that formal concept is: ({Researcher, Project, LA:Project, KM:Research_Area}, {meh, jan, nst, rst, ysu}).

Such an ordering in the query space enables a very easy interpretation of query results regarding their ambiguity. Moreover, the values for the content-related ambiguity parameters can be read directly from the concept lattice. For the given query "Researcher and Project and KM", these parameters are as follows:

Largest equivalent query: "Researcher and Project and KM *and* LA *and* ResearchArea"

Smallest equivalent query: "Researcher and Project"

Uniqueness: "meh"

Covering for upper formal concept: 6/5

CoveringTerms for upper formal concept: 1/3

These parameters are very useful for estimating the ambiguity. A user is provided with this information, in order to determine the position of her query with respect to other queries. That can enhance the efficiency of the query refinement process. For the given example, according to the *Largest equivalent query*, expanding the initial query with the term ResearchArea will not cause any changes in the set of answers. Moreover, the *Smallest equivalent query*, "Researcher and Project", means that the request KM in the query "Researcher and Project and KM" is redundant, because all the researchers research in the KM research area. Further, according to the *Covering* parameter, almost all results from the query "Researcher" are contained in the results of the query "Researcher and Project and KM", which means that the importance of the terms "Project" and "KM" for the given is not so high. In the next section, we give more details about using *content-related ambiguity* for the query refinement.

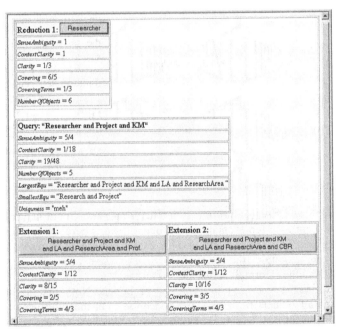

Fig. 4. Librarian Agent in the action: The neighborhood of a query. A screenshot from the Portal, which is used in the evaluation. The ambiguity parameters are calculated using formulas presented in the section 3.1.

3.2 Refinement

Our approach for query refinement tries to simulate reflect the refinement model which a human librarian (or a shop assistant) uses in her daily work. It means that we use three sources of information in suggesting query refinement: (i) the structure of the underlying ontology (vocabulary), (ii) the content of the knowledge repository and (iii) the users' behaviour (how users refine their queries on their own).

Since the first two sources are used for measuring the ambiguity of a query, the query refinements based on them are treated cooperatively as the *ambiguity-driven query refinement.* In the rest of the paper, we describe this refinement approach in more details

The third source for making the query's refinement recommendations requires an analysis of the users' activities in an ontology-based application. In [5], we presented a framework for capturing the user's activities in a semantic query log file. This query log is "mined", in order to discover query patterns (i.e. regularities in refining the queries). This analysis is out of the scope of this paper.

3.2.1 Ambiguity-Driven Query Refinement

The ambiguity parameters presented in the previous section are combined and presented to the user in case she wants to make a refinement of the initial query. Fig 4. presents the visual metaphor to present the information about the ambiguities of a query to the user. Each of ambiguity parameters has its role in quantifying ambiguity. Table 2 presents the most common cases of the ambiguities and their role in the query refinement process. For each of the parameters, query term(s) that affect the ambiguity most importantly are determined. In that way, the user receives the most specific suggestions.

The current version of the Query Management module allows the user to navigate through the query neighbourhood. By clicking on a neighbour, the focus of the map is changed, and all parameters are calculated for that query (Fig.4.). In that manner, the user can inspect the queries around the initial query, in order to find the most suitable refinement. This process is called querying by navigation [6]. More details are given in the evaluation section.

4   Evaluation

The research presented in this paper is a part of the Librarian Agent, a management system we have developed for the improvement of searching in an information portal. The Librarian Agent is developed using the KAON ontology engineering framework (kaon.semanticweb.org). As a test bed for presented research, we use the VISION Portal (www.km-vision.org), a semantics-driven portal that allows browsing and querying of the state-of-the-art information (researcher, projects, software, etc.) related to the knowledge management. It is developed in the scope of the EU-funded VISION project, which should provide a strategic roadmap towards the next-generation organisational knowledge management. The backbone of the system is the VISION ontology, which includes the *ResearchInstitute* ontology presented in the section 2. It is used as a common vocabulary for providing and searching for information. The ontology lexical layer contains about 1000 terms and the information repository consists of about 500 information resources (the web page of concrete person, project, etc.). Each of the information resources is related to a concrete instance in the ontology (e.g. to the person Dietmar Ratz). The query refinement system is implemented as an additional support in the searching process. When the refinement support is turned on, after posting a query, the user gets the query's neighbourhood, similarly to the situation presented in Fig.4.

Table 2. The suggestions for the query refinement, which are based on the analysis of the ambiguity parameters presented in the previous section.

Value of Ambiguity Parameters	Meaning	Action
High *SenseAmbiguity*	Too many interpretations of some terms from the query	To specify the meaning of some terms more precisely – to determine which sense of a term is valid
Low *ContexClarity*	Too many interpretations of the relation between (two) terms	To add a relation in the query in order to specify one of many possible relations between terms
Low *Clarity*	Too general query	To replace a term with a more specific term (from its isA hierarchy)
Big difference between *Smallest equivalent query* and given query	Query contains redundant terms	To reconsider whether the smallest equivalent queries correspond to the initial information need. If this is not the case, then change the query. Define which part of the query is missing in the smallest equivalent query
Big difference between *Largest equivalent query* and given query	Query is too general for the repository	To reconsider if the largest equivalent query corresponds to the initial information need. If this is not the case, then change the query. Define which part of the query is irrelevant in the largest equivalent query
Too low *Uniqueness*	The query shares almost all results with other queries (it contains very few of its own results)	If more results are needed replace the query with a neighbourhood query
Too high *Covering/CoveringTerms*	The query gives similar results as a query from its neighbourhood	If more results are needed move the query in the direction of that "similar" query

The goal of our experiment was to evaluate how the effectiveness of Boolean retrieval is changed when the query process is enhanced with the presented refinement facility. Actually, we evaluated the possibility of our system to help the user define her information need more precisely. To obtain the basic Boolean retrieval system with which to compare our system, we simply turned off the query-refinement support.

For the experiment, we randomly selected 20 queries which cannot be expressed precisely using the defined vocabulary, but whose answers are contained in the information repository. For example, a question was: "Find researchers with diverse experiences about Semantic Web", which cannot be directly expressed using the given ontology vocabulary, but it can be answered by considering the information repository. For example there are two persons who work in five projects related to the Semantic Web. They can be treated as the broadly experienced experts for the Semantic Web.

We tested six subjects in the experiment. The subjects were computer science students with little knowledge of the ontology domains (or domain) and no prior knowledge of the system. The six subjects were asked to retrieve the documents relevant to the 10 queries in one session using the two retrieval methods. For assigning the queries to the methods, we used a repeated-measures design, in which each subject searched each query using each method. To minimise sequence effects, we varied the order of the two methods. The subjects were asked to confirm explicitly when they found a relevant answer. Otherwise, the searching was treated as unsuccessful.

For each search, we considered four measures: success, quality, number of Boolean queries, and search time (i.e. the time needed by the user to perform her task). The quality (0 – 1) is the subjective judgment of the three domain experts about the relevance of the results which are proclaimed by the user as a success. The results are displayed in Table 3. The table shows that searching with query refinement support results in better evaluation scores for all measures. These results are not surprising, because our approach complements the basic capabilities of a Boolean retrieval system with additional useful features. In particular, it allows smooth query refinement/enlargement, which is likely to be the key factor for obtaining the improvement in the searching time [7]. Moreover, the experiment shows that our system can play the role of a query-assistant who, according to the user's query, provides more (quantified) information about the queries "around" the initial query, making the process of expressing/satisfying the user's needs more efficient (about 85% of searching was highly relevant).

Table 3. Average values of retrieval performance measures

Method	Success for the session	Quality for the session	Number of queries pro a question	Search time (sec) for session
Boolean	57%	0.6	10.3	2023
Our	85.7%	0.9	5.2	1203

5 Related Work

Query Ambiguity. The determination of an ambiguity in a query, as well as the sources of such an ambiguity, is the prerequisite for the efficient searching for information. Word sense disambiguation of the terms in the input query and words in the documents have shown to be useful for improving both precision and recall of an IR system [4]. In [8], the set of experiments using lexical relations from WordNet for the query expansion is described, but without treating the query ambiguity. Although some work has recently been done in quantifying the query ambiguity based on the language model of the knowledge repository [9], [10], the IR research community has not explored the problem of using a rich domain model in modelling the querying. Some very important results in the query analysis can be found in the deductive database community [11], namely semantic query optimisation. That approach, although revolutionary for using domain knowledge for the optimal compilation of the queries, does not consider the ambiguity of the query regarding the user's information need at all.

Query Refinement. There is a lot of research devoted to the query refinement in the Web IR community. In general, we see two directions of modifying queries or query results to the needs of users: query expansion and recommendation systems respectively. *The query expansion* is aimed at helping the users make a better query, i.e. it attempts to improve retrieval effectiveness by replacing or adding extra terms to an initial query. The *interactive query expansion* supports such an expansion task by suggesting candidate expansion terms to users, usually based on hyper-index [6] or concept-hierarchies [12] automatically constructed from the document repository. In [13] the model of the query-document space is used for the interactive query expansion. *Recommendation systems* [14] try to recommend items similar to those a given user has liked in the past (content-based recommendation), or try to identify users whose tastes are similar to those of the given user, and recommend items they have liked (collaborative recommendation). Personalised web agents, e.g. WebWatcher [15] track the users browsing, and formulate user profiles which are used in suggesting which links are worth following from the current web page. However, none of these approaches uses the rich domain model for the refinement of a query, i.e. the reasons for doing a refinement are not based on the deep understanding of the structure of a query, or the deep exploring of the interrelationships in the information repository. Moreover, none of them tries to determine (measure) the ambiguity in a query, and to suggest a refinement which will decrease such an ambiguity.

6 Conclusion

In this paper, we presented an approach for the query management in ontology-based IR systems. The system realises a library scenario in which users search for information resources in a repository. The so-called Librarian Agent plays the role of the human librarian in the traditional library – it uses all possible information about the domain vocabulary, the behaviour of previous users and the capacity of the knowledge repository, in order to help users find the resources they are interested in. Based on various analyses, the agent, through an interactive interface, guides the users in more efficient searching for information. We presented an evaluation study, which showed that this approach decreases the time, and enhances the precision of the retrieval process.

We find that our approach represents a very important step in using paradigms from searching in the brick-and-mortar environment for the improvement of searching for information in the virtual world. Moreover, this approach leads to the self-adaptive knowledge portals, which can discover some changes in the user's preferences automatically, and evolve the structure of the portal correspondingly.

Acknowledgement. The research presented in this paper would not have been possible without our colleagues and students in the research group Knowledge Management, at the Institute AIFB, University of Karlsruhe. Research for this paper was partially financed by BMBF in the project "SemIPort" (08C5939).

References

1. Ganter, B., Wille, R.: Formal Concept Analysis: Mathematical Foundations. Springer (1999)
2. Stojanovic, N., Stojanovic, L.: Usage-oriented Evolution of Ontology-based Knowledge Management Systems, ODBASE 2002, LNCS (2002)

3. Meadche, A.: Ontology Learning for the Semantic Web, Kluwer Academic Publishers (2002)
4. Rila, M.: The Use of WordNet in information retrieval. ACL Workshop on the Usage of WordNet in Natural Language Processing Systems (1998) 31–37.
5. Stojanovic, N., Stojanovic, L., Gonzalez, J.: More efficient searching in a knowledge portal – an approach based on the analysis of users' queries, PAKM 2002, Vienna, LCNS/LNAI (2002)
6. Bruza, P.D., Dennis, S.: Query Reformulation on the Internet: Empirical Data and the Hyperindex Search Engine. RIAO97, Computer-Assisted Information Searching on Internet, Montreal (1997)
7. Carpineto, C., Romano, G.: Effective re formulation of boolean queries with concept lattices. Flexible Query Answering Systems FQAS'98, Springer-Verlag (1998) 277–291
8. Voorhees, E.,: Query expansion using lexical-semantic relations, 17th ACM/SIGIR, Dublin, (1994)
9. Ponte, J., Croft, W.B.: A language modeling approach to information retrieval, ACM/ SIGIR'98 (1998) 275–28
10. Cronen-Townsend, S. and Croft, W.B., Quantifying Query Ambiguity, HLT 2002 (2002) 94–98.
11. Chakravarthy, U., Grant, J., Minker, J.: Logic-based approach to semantic query optimization. ACM Transactions on Database Systems, 15(2) (1990) 162–207
12. Joho, H., Coverson, C., Sanderson, M., Beaulieu, M.: Hierarchical presentation of expansion terms, ACM SAC, (2002)
13. Wen, J.-R., Nie, J.-Y. and Zhang, H.-J. Clustering User Queries of a Search Engine. WWW10, May 1–5, 2001, Hong Kong (2001)
14. Balabanovic, M., Shoham, Y: Content-Based, Collaborative Recommendation. CACM 40 (3): 66–72 (1997)
15. Joachims, T., Freitag, D., Mitchell, T.: Webwatcher: A tour guide for the World Wide Web. IJCAI–97 (1997)

A Declarative XML-RL Update Language

Mengchi Liu, Li Lu, and Guoren Wang

School of Computer Science
Carleton University
Ottawa, Ontario, Canada K1S 5B6
{mengchi,llu,wanggr}@scs.carleton.ca

Abstract. With the wide adoption of XML, it is a natural requirement to allow users to directly update XML documents. This paper formally presents a novel XML update language for updating XML documents based on the XML-RL language. Taking the advantages of XML-RL data model that give us the ability to comprehend XML data from database point of view, the XML-RL update language provides users with the ability to make change to XML documents in a simple, natural and effective way. It provides a uniform framework that is advantageous over other XML update languages in the following ways. (1) The binding variables that can refer to any kind of XML object provide a very powerful and intuitive way to express updates. Moreover, using such binding variable to bind object name, we do not need *rename* operation. (2) The user is not required to create an object before it can be inserted into the document. We can update not only object values, but also object name or both with the help of binding variable. (3) The multi-level update does not need nested query-update expressions. (4) The updates to more than one XML document can be expressed in just one update statement. (5) It supports IDREFS update which is lacking in other update languages. (6) It incorporates some of features of object oriented database and logic programming language, which make it easier for user to understand and to use.

1 Introduction

With the wide adoption of XML document, it is a natural requirement to allow users to update XML documents. The manipulation of XML document includes not only querying, but also updating. In recent years, there are a few proposals for updating XML document, such as Lorel [2,3], DB2 XML Extender [4], XML-GL [5], XQuery update extension [6], XUpdate [7].

The Lorel query language [2] from Stanford's Lorel semi-structured database system provides simple insertions and deletions of nodes in the Lorel data graph. Due to the lower level data model adopted, Lorel uses many built-in functions for updating operations, and the update operations cannot fully support the ordered XML document. The DB2 XML Extender [4] converts XML document into DB2 database before query and update operation are executed, then converts it back after the operations are completed. It uses XPath expressions [8] for

I.-Y. Song et al. (Eds.): ER 2003, LNCS 2813, pp. 506–519, 2003.

its SQL-like query and update statements and does not support variable bindings. The XML-GL [5] is a graphical query language which relies on a graphical representation of XML documents based on the edge-node relationship. It uses *I, D, U* to label nodes to be inserted, deleted, and updated, respectively. The data model used is not an abstract data model. Therefore, it cannot provide a mechanism to perform any type checking according to the XML DTD or XML Schema. Another limitation is that it does not support tag variable so that there is no way to update an XML tag using XML-GL. The XQuery update extension [6] extends XQuery's original FLWR expressions to accommodate update operations by introducing *"FOR ... LET ... WHERE ... UPDATE"*. It inherits the nested FLWR feature from XQuery to solve the multiple levels problem, which makes update languages too complicated to understand. The XUpdate [7] makes extensive use of the expression language defined by XPath to select elements for updating and itself is a pure descriptive language that is designed with references to the definition of XSLT. XUpdate is not based on any abstract data model and does not support variable bindings.

All above update languages have same limitations. First, to insert a new object, a create constructor must be called to create the object first. Also, most of them depend on built-in functions to complete update operations. This is because they are all based on a low level data model using tree-node based data graph to represent XML data. Furthermore, most of the languages do not support IDREFS update and multi-level update.

Using the graph-based or tree-based data model makes the query and data manipulation expressions complicated, non-intuitive and unnatural. In [9], a novel XML data model called XML-RL is proposed to model XML data in a way similar to complex object models [1]. Based on this higher level data model, a rule-based declarative XML query language, XML-RL, is presented as well.

In this paper, we formally presents a noval XML update language for updating XML documents based on XML-RL [9,10]. It treats XML documents directly as an extensional database. Thus it avoids mapping the XML document to a relational database before the operation can be performed on it, and does not need to create an object using a constructor before it can be inserted to the document, since it uses a high level data model to represent XML documents. In XML-RL update language, binding variables can be used to refer to any kind of XML object, such as *element object, attribute object, tuple object* as well as *attribute name, element name, attribute value, element value*. As a result, it provides a very powerful and intuitive way to express updates. Therefore, the multi-level update does not need nested query-update expressions. Also, it supports IDREFS updates and updates on more than one XML document at the same time, which are lacking in other update languages. Because the XML-RL update language incorporates some of features of object-oriented databases and logic programming, it is easy for users to understand and to use.

The remainder of this paper is organized as follows. Section 2 uses several examples to demonstrate the XML update language. Section 3 presents the syntax of the XML-RL update language. Section 4 defines the semantics for the XML-

RL update language. Section 5 concludes the paper and gives further research issues.

2   Examples

In this section, we give a brief description of the XML-RL update language and use several examples to demonstrate its usage and the intended semantics. The XML-RL update language extends the XML-RL query language according to XML Update Language Requirements [7]. We aim at a minimal set of primitive update operations to fulfill all the functions. All valid updates to XML data should be specifiable by one or a sequence of our primitive update operations.

The examples shown in this section are based on the sample DTD document in Figure 1, the sample XML document in Figure 2, and its XML-RL representation is in Figure 3. We assume the document is at *http://www.abc.edu/sc.xml*. To make our presentation simply, we use *URL* instead of the real URL in our examples.

The XML-RL update language uses update statements to update XML documents. An update statement is composed of two parts, *query* and *update*. The *query* part is a set of query expressions, which are used to query one or more XML documents. The query result could be bound to variables to hold various XML objects. These variables can be used in the *update* part. The *update* part is a set of update expressions, each of which is used to modify one or more XML objects in one or more XML documents. The order of update execution is in which they appear in the statement.

The XML-RL update language supports five kinds of update expressions: **insert before, insert after** and **insert into, delete** and **replace with**.

The **Insert before** and **insert after** operations allow users to directly insert one or more XML objects before or after an element in an XML document. These two operations support updates on ordered XML documents.

Example 1. Insert a new *student* element in the XML document shown in Figure 2 before *Jack*, with id *1000*, name *Anne* and age *25*.

> **query** (URL)/studentCourse/$s (student ⇒ [name⇒ Jack])
> **insert** student ⇒ [@id ⇒ 1000, name ⇒ Anne, age ⇒ 25] **before** $s

where variable *$s* holds the *student* element for *Jack*. After the update, a new *student* element for *Anne* is added before *Jack*.

In XML, ID values must be unique. If the element object to be inserted has a conflicting ID value with an element in the document, then the insertion is not allowed.

Compared with other XML update languages such as Lorel [2,3], DB2 XML Extender [4], XML-GL [5], XQuery update extension [6], and Xupdate [7], the XML-RL update language does not need a constructor to create a new element object for insertion.

```
<DOCTYPE StudentCourse[
    <!ELEMENT studentCourse (student*, course*)>
    <!ELEMENT student (name, age)>
    <!ATTLIST    student id ID #IMPLIED>
    <!ATTLIST    student coursesTaken IDREFS #IMPLIED>
    <!ELEMENT course (name, loc)>
    <!ATTLIST    course number ID #IMPLIED>
    <!ELEMENT name (#PCDATA)>
    <!ELEMENT age (#PCDATA)>
    <!ELEMENT loc (#PCDATA)>
]>
```

Fig. 1. Sample DTD

```
<studentCourse>
    <student id = "2000", coursesTaken = "cs300 cs400 mt200 mt300">
        <name> Jack </name>
        <age> 20 </age>
    </student>
    <student id = "3000", coursesTaken = "cs300 mt300">
        <name> Mary </name>
        <age> 30 </age>
    </student>
    <student id = "4000", coursesTaken = "cs300">
        <name> Tony </name>
    </student>
    <course number = "cs300">
        <name> Network </name>
        <Loc> CL200 </Loc>
    </course>
    <course number = "cs400">
        <name> Databases </name>
        <Loc> CL300 </Loc>
    </course>
    <course number = "mt200">
        <name> Algebra </name>
        <Loc> CL300 </Loc>
    </course>
    <course number = "mt300">
        <name> Calculus </name>
        <Loc> CL400 </Loc>
    </course>
</studentCourse>
```

Fig. 2. Sample XML document at http://www.abc.edu/sc.xml

It is possible that there might be more than one student whose name is *Jack* in the XML document. In this case, the new student is inserted into the XML document as the following sibling of each *Jack* student.

```
studentCourse ⇒ [
    student ⇒ [
        @id ⇒ 2000,
        @coursesTaken ⇒ {cs300,cs400,mt200,mt300},
        name ⇒ Jack,
        age ⇒ 20],
    student ⇒ [
        @id ⇒ 3000,
        @coursesTaken ⇒ {cs300, mt300},
        name ⇒ Mary,
        age ⇒ 30],
    student ⇒ [
        @id ⇒ 4000,
        @coursesTaken ⇒ {cs300},
        name ⇒ Tony],
    course ⇒ [
        @number ⇒ cs300,
        name ⇒ Network,
        Loc ⇒ CL200] ,
    course ⇒ [
        @number ⇒ cs400,
        name ⇒ Databases,
        Loc ⇒ CL300] ,
    course ⇒ [
        @number ⇒ mt200,
        name ⇒ Algebra,
        Loc ⇒ CL300] ,
    course ⇒ [
        @number ⇒ mt300,
        name ⇒ Calculus,
        Loc ⇒ CL400]
    ]
```

Fig. 3. Sample XML document in XML-RL representation

An XML-RL update statement can contain several update expressions for several updates at different levels, as shown in the following example.

Example 2. Insert a new *course* element before the *database* course element with course number *cs200*, course name *software*, and the same location as the database course, and an *age* element with value *20* to student *Tony* after the *name* element.

query (URL)/studentCourse/$c(course ⇒ [name ⇒ database, Loc ⇒ $l]),
        (URL)/studentCourse/student/$n(name ⇒ Tony)
insert course ⇒ [@number ⇒cs200, name ⇒software, Loc ⇒$l] **before** $c
insert age ⇒ 20 **after** $n

where the first query expression gets the *database* course element and binds the element to element variable $c and the *Loc* value to lexical variable $l while the second query expression gets the name element of student *Tony* and binds it to variable $n. The update expressions then add the new course and age elements into the XML document properly.

It is very flexible to use a list-valued variable to hold multiple query results with the same type. Some built-in functions are designed for such updates.

Example 3. Add the reference to the course *calculus* into the list of courses taken by *Tony*.

> **query** (URL)/studentCourse/
>   student ⇒ [@coursetaken ⇒ {$c}, name ⇒ Tony]
>   (URL)/studentCourse/course ⇒ [@number ⇒ $n, name ⇒ Calculus]
> **insert** $n **after** {$c}.position(1)

where the list-valued variable {$c} holds all course references that *Tony* takes and the built-in function *position(1)* returns the first reference. After the update, the references to *calculus* is added into *coursetaken* element at the second position.

In the XML-RL update language, we mention the consistency between ID values and IDREF/IDREFS. In the above example, {$c} is a list of IDREFS. If $n is not a ID value, then the insertion is not allowed.

Because attributes are unordered, **insert before** and **insert after** are not applicable for attribute updating. But if attribute type is IDREFS, its value is an ordered list object. In this case, *insert before* and *insert after* can be applicable for the attribute update.

Using the **insert before** and **insert after** operations together with the built-in position function, we can insert an element anywhere in the XML document: insert first, insert second, etc.

The **insert into** operation allows users to insert one or more XML objects as a child or children in the selected object. For ordered XML data, the new object is inserted in the last position in the selected object; for unordered XML data, the new object is inserted at arbitrary position in the selected object.

If we do not care its position, the **insert into** operation is very efficient to add an object into an XML document. It is especially useful if the selected parent object is a *null* value as **insert before** or **insert after** operations cannot be used according to their semantics.

It is often necessary to apply the same updating operation to each applicable object in a document that matches a certain criteria, as shown in the following example.

Example 4. Add a *credit* element with value 3 to each course.

> **query** (URL)/studentCourse/$c (course)
> **insert** credit ⇒ 3 **into** $c

From the above example, we can see that the **insert into** operation can ensure the *credit* object is inserted to each applicable object. This would not be true if we use **insert before** or **insert after** operation.

Example 5. Add the references to courses *Calculus* and *Databases* to the attribute *coursesTaken* of student *Ann.*

> **query** (URL)/studentCourse/$s (student⇒[name ⇒ Anne]),
>   (URL)/studentCourse/course⇒[@id⇒$id1, name⇒Calculus],
>   (URL)/studentCourse/course⇒[@id⇒$id2, name⇒Databases]
> **insert** @coursesTaken⇒{$id1,$id2} **into** $s

The **delete** operation allows users to remove objects from an XML document. The deleted object is usually the one returned by the *query* part, either object name and its value or object value only. When the value of an element is deleted, the value of object will be set to *null.*

Example 6. Delete the value of the element *age* in student *Mary:*

> **query** (URL)/studentCourse/student ⇒ [name ⇒ Mary, age ⇒ $a]
> **delete** $a

When an element object is deleted, its sub-elements and attributes are deleted recursively. If the object is referenced by other objects, a cascading deletion is performed.

Example 7. Delete the course *Calculus.*

> **query** (URL)/studentCourse/$c (course ⇒ [name ⇒ Calculus])
> **delete** $c

where the variable $c holds a course element whose value has sub-elements: *name* and *Loc,* and attribute *number.* The course is referred by students *Jack* and *Mary.* After the update, (1) the deleting operation will recursively delete all sub-elements and attribute of the course; (2) the course will no longer be references by the students.

The **replace with** operation can be used to modify the name or value of existing objects. The modified object must be returned by the *query* part before the *replace* operation can be applied. The **replace with** operation can replace name of an object, value of an object, or both, which depends on what variable binds to.

Example 8. Change the attribute name *id* of *student* to *sid* and the name of the *database* course to *inforbase.*

> **query** (URL)/studentCourse/student ⇒ [@$id ⇒ $i], $id = id,
>   (URL)/studentCourse/course ⇒ [name ⇒ $n], $n = database
> **replace** $id **with** sid,
> **replace** $n **with** inforbase

Lorel [2] can also support object name updating. The updating process is done in two steps. First, select value from existing object and assign it to a new object name; second, set the existing object to *null.* This is actually a combination of creation and deletion. Comparing to Lorel, the XML-RL updating language can complete name updating in one step. This is simpler and more efficient.

In XQuery [6], to change attribute value, a built-in function (new_attribute()) must be used. To change the name of object, XQuery uses pure XML form. XUpdate [7] does not support object name update.

In Figure 2, *studentCourse* is at the root level, *student* and *course* are at the second level, *@id, @coursesTaken, name* and *age* are at the third level. The following example shows how to update multiple levels at the same time.

Example 9. Change the student number from 4 digits to 5 digits and add a new course *Programming* with number *cs100* before cs200.

> **query** (URL)/studentCourse/student $\Rightarrow$ [@id $\Rightarrow$ $n],
>   (URL)/studentCourse/$c (course $\Rightarrow$ [@number $\Rightarrow$ cs200])
> **replace** $n **with** $n $\times$ 10
> **insert** course $\Rightarrow$ [@number $\Rightarrow$ cs100, name $\Rightarrow$ Programming] **before** $c

where the variable $n holds a student number at the third level while variable $c holds a *course* element at the second level. The update operations apply to the binding variables that refer to different level objects.

Multiple level updates are performed consecutively from innermost query result to outermost query result for each iteration of variable binding. See Section 4 for details.

In XQuery [6], updating multiple level object must use nested FOR WHERE UPDATE form, which makes it too complicated to understand and use.

3   Syntax of the XML-RL Update Language

In this section, we formalize the XML-RL update language. First, we introduce several important notions.

Objects : objects used in the XML-RL update language are defined recursively as follows.

1. A *lexical object* is a constant. For example, *name, id, Mary, Databases.*
2. An *attribute object* consists of attribute name and value pair. For example, *@id $\Rightarrow$ 3000, @coursesTaken $\Rightarrow$ {cs300, mt300}.*
3. An *element object* represents element name and value pair. For example, *name $\Rightarrow$ Jack, student $\Rightarrow$ [@coursesTaken $\Rightarrow$ {cs300,mt300}, name $\Rightarrow$ Mary].*
4. A *tuple object* represents the relationship among elements and attributes in XML. For example, [*@coursesTaken $\Rightarrow$ {cs300,mt300}, name $\Rightarrow$ Mary].*
5. A *list object* represents multiple values of an attribute or element. For example, *{1000,2000,3000}, {databases, network}.*

Variables : variables in the XML update language are logical variables that are place holders and are divided into two kinds, *single-valued* variable and *listed-valued* variable.

- A *single-valued* variable starts with '$' followed by a string.
- A *listed-valued* variable uses a pair of '{ }' with a *single-valued* variable inside.

Depending on where they occur, we can call them more specifically.

- Single-valued variable n in @$n \Rightarrow v$ is an *attribute name variable*.
- Single-valued variable n in $n \Rightarrow v$ is an *element name variable*
- Single-valued variable v in @$n \Rightarrow \$v$ or $n \Rightarrow \$v$ is an *attribute value variable* or *element value variable* respectively, and it binds one object at a time.
- List-valued variable $\{\$v\}$ in @$n \Rightarrow \{\$v\}$ or $n \Rightarrow \{\$v\}$ is an *attribute value variable* or *element value variable* respectively and it binds a list of object at a time.
- If a single-valued variable occurs in the place of an attribute object, then it is an *attribute variable*.
- If a single-valued variable occurs in the place of an element object, then it is an *element variable*.
- If a single-valued variable occurs in the place of a tuple, then it is a *tuple variable*.

Terms : terms used in the XML-RL update language are defined recursively using objects, variables and path expressions as follows:

1. A lexcial object is a *lexical* term.
2. A list object or a list-valued variable is a *list* term.
3. Let a be a constant or a variable and v a constant, a single-valued variable, a list of lexical objects, or a list-valued variable. Then @$a \Rightarrow v$ is an *attribute* term.
4. Let e be a constant or a variable and v a term. Then $e \Rightarrow v$ is an *element* term.
5. Let @A_1,...,@A_m be attribute terms, $E_1, ..., E_n$ be element and lexical terms with $m \geq 0, n > 0$. Then $[@A_1, ..., @A_m, E_1, ..., E_n]$ is a *tuple* term.
6. Let a be an attribute variable and s an attribute terms. Then $\$a(s)$ is an *attribute selection term*. For example, @$a(@id \Rightarrow \$i)$, @$a(@number \Rightarrow 1000)$.
7. Let e be an element variable and s an element terms. Then $\$e(s)$ is an *element selection term*. For example, $\$c(course \Rightarrow [name \Rightarrow Databases])$.
8. Let t be a tuple variable and s an element terms. Then $\$t(s)$ is a *tuple selection term*. For example, $student \Rightarrow \$v(name \Rightarrow Tony)$.
9. Let T_1, T_2, T be terms. Then T_1/T_2 and $/T$ are path terms, where T_1/T_2 stands for $T_1 \Rightarrow [T_2]$, and $/T$ stands for there exists $T_1', ..., T_n'$ for some $n \geq 0$ such that $T_1'/.../T_n'/T$. For example, $student/name \Rightarrow \$n$, $//name \Rightarrow \$n$, $//course/\$n(name \Rightarrow \$v)$.
10. A single-valued variable is either a lexical, attribute, element, or tuple term depending on the context.

Query expressions : the XML-RL update language supports two kinds of query expressions: document expression $(U)/T$, and arithmetic, logical, string, and list expressions defined using terms in the usual way, where U is a URL and T an element term. The following are examples:

$(URL)/\$s$
$(URL)/studentCourse/\$c(course)$
$(URL)//student \Rightarrow \{\$s\}$
$\$n \times 10 = \$m$
$\$a \neq Databases$
$\$a \ni XML$
$\{\$c\} = \{cs300, cs400\}$

Built-in functions : the XML-RL update language supports the same built-in functions as in XML-RL [10], such as *count, avg, min, max, sum, position(n)* etc.

Update expressions : the XML-RL update language supports the following five kinds of update expressions:

insert T **before** V	(1)
insert T **after** V	(2)
insert T **into** V	(3)
delete V	(4)
replace V **with** T	(5)

where V is either a variable or an invocation of some built-in function, and T is a term. The following are two examples of update expressions:

insert student $\Rightarrow$ [	**insert** student $\Rightarrow$ [
@id $\Rightarrow$ 1000,	@id $\Rightarrow$ 1000,
@coursesTaken $\Rightarrow$ {cs300,cs400},	@coursesTaken $\Rightarrow$ {cs300,cs400},
name $\Rightarrow$ Jack]	name $\Rightarrow$ Jack]
after \$t	**after** {\$t}.position(2)

where \$t is a single-valued variable referring to an element after which the insertion operation should occur, {\$t} is a list-valued variable referring to a list of elements and the built-in function *position(2)* denotes the second element in the list after which after which the insertion operation should occur, and everything after **insert** is the update content, which is a term that represents a new *student* element.

Update statements : an update statement has the following form:

query $exp_1, \cdots, exp_m$
$update_1, \cdots, update_n$

where $exp_1, \cdots, exp_m$ are query expressions and $update_1, \cdots, update_n$ are update expressions. We have seen many update statements in Section 2.

4   Semantics of the XML-RL Update Language

In this section, we define the semantics of the XML-RL update language. First, we assume the following notations.

1. $name(o)$ denotes the names of object o. For example, $name(@id \Rightarrow 1000) = id$, $name(Age \Rightarrow 20) = Age$.
2. $value(o)$ denotes the value of object o. For example, $name(@id \Rightarrow 1000) = 1000$, $name(Age \Rightarrow 20) = 20$.
3. $IDvalues^*(e)$ denotes the set of the values of the ID attribute within the element object e, and $IDValues^*$ denotes the set of the values of all the ID attribute in the XML document. For example $IDvalues^*(@id \Rightarrow 2000) = \{2000\}$, $IDvalues^*(student \Rightarrow [@id \Rightarrow 2000, name \Rightarrow Jack]) = \{2000\}$, $IDvalues^*(student \Rightarrow [@id \Rightarrow 2000, name \Rightarrow [@id \Rightarrow 10000, Jack]) = \{2000, 10000\}$.
4. $IDrefs^*(e)$ denotes the set of the IDREF/IDREFS values within the object e, and $IDrefs^*$ denotes the set of the all the IDREF/IDREFS values within the XML document. For example, $IDrefs^*(coursesTaken \Rightarrow \{cs300, cs400\}) = \{cs300, cs400\}$.
5. $attriNames(o)$ denotes the set of all attribute names in object o.

The semantics of the updating expressions are defined as follows:

1. **insert** T **before** V. Assume the parent object of V is p.
   a) V is an element object, $p = e \Rightarrow [@A_1,...,@A_m, E_1, ..., E_n]$ and $V = E_i$ for some $1 \leq i \leq n$, T is also an element object, $IDvalues^*(T) \cap IDvalues^* = \emptyset$, and $IDrefs^*(T) \subseteq IDrefs^*$. Then replace p with $p' = e \Rightarrow [@A_1,...,@A_m, E_1, ..., E_{i-1}, T, E_i, ..., E_n]$. In other words, the IDs T contains should not be used in the document and the ID references T refers to must be valid.
   b) V is an IDREF whose parent object is $p = \{id_1, ..., id_n\}$ and $V = id_i$ for some i, $T \in IDrefs^*$ and $T \notin p$, and $IDrefs^*(T) \subseteq IDrefs^*$. Then replace p with $p' = \{id_1, ..., id_{i-1}, T, id_i, ..., id_n\}$. That is, T is insert into p before V if T is also an IDREF and T is not in the list p.
   c) Otherwise, the insert operation is not prohibited.
2. **insert** T **after** V. The semantics for the **insert after** operation is similar to **insert before**.
3. **insert** T **into** V.
   a) V is an element object $V = e \Rightarrow [@A_1, ..., @A_m, E_1, ..., E_m]$, T is an element object, $IDvalues^*(T) \cap IDvalues^* = \emptyset$, and $IDrefs^*(T) \subseteq IDrefs^*$. Then replace V with $V' = e \Rightarrow [@A_1, ..., @A_m, E_1, ..., E_m, T]$.
   b) V is an element object $V = e \Rightarrow [@A_1, ..., @A_m, E_1, ..., E_m]$ and T is an attribute object, $name(T) \notin attriNames(V)$, and $IDvalues^*(T) \cap IDvalues^* = \emptyset$. Then replace V with $V' = e \Rightarrow [@A_1, ..., T, ..., @A_m, E_1, ..., E_m]$. That is, if V has an attribute with the same name as T or T uses an ID value that is alreay in the document, then the operation is not allowed.

c) V is a list object $V = \{C_1, ..., C_n\}$ and $T \notin V$. Then replace V with $V' = \{C_1, ..., T, ...C_n\}$ where the location of T in the list is a random number between 1 and n.

d) Otherwise, the insert operation is prohibited.

4. **delete V.**

a) V is the value of element object o. Then replace o with $o' = name(o) \Rightarrow null$. If $IDvalues^*(V) \subseteq IDrefs^*$, then delete every ID in $IDvalues^*(V)$ in the XML document so that $IDvalue^*(V) \subseteq IDrefs^*$ no longer holds.

b) V is an element object whose parent is $p = e \Rightarrow [@A_1, ..., @A_m, E_1, ..., E_n]$ and $V = E_i$. Then replace p with $p' = e \Rightarrow [@A_1, ..., @A_m, E_1, ..., E_{i-1}, E_{i+1}, E_n]$. If $IDvalues^*(V) \subseteq IDrefs^*$, then delete every ID in $IDvalues^*(V)$ in the XML document so that $IDvalue^*(V) \subseteq IDrefs^*$ no longer holds.

c) V is an attribute object whose parent is $p = e \Rightarrow [@A_1, ..., @A_m, E_1, ..., E_n]$ and $V = A_i$. Then replace p with $p' = e \Rightarrow [@A_1, ..., @A_{i-1}, @A_{i+1}, @A_m, E_1, ..., E_n]$. If $IDvalues^*(V) \subseteq IDrefs^*$, then delete every ID in $IDvalues^*(V)$ in the XML document so that $IDvalue^*(V) \subseteq IDrefs^*$ no longer holds.

d) Otherwise, the deletion operation is not prohibited.
   In other words, if V contains ID values, then all IDREF/IDREFS to them must be deleted as well.

5. **replace V with T.**

a) V is the name of object o. Then replace o with $o' = T \Rightarrow value(o)$.

b) V is the value of object o, $IDvalues^*(T) \cap (IDvalues^* - IDvalues^*(V)) = \emptyset$, and $IDrefs^*(T) \subseteq (IDrefs^* - IDvalues^*(V)) \cup IDvalues^*(T)$. Then replace o with $o' = name(o) \Rightarrow T$.

c) V is an object whose parent is $p = e \Rightarrow [@A_1, ..., @A_m, E_1, ..., E_n]$ and $V = @A_i$ for some $1 \le i \le m$, $name(T) \notin attriNames(p)$, $IDvalues^*(T) \cap (IDvalues^* - IDvalues^*(V)) = \emptyset$, and $IDrefs^*(T) \subseteq (IDrefs^* - IDvalues^*(V)) \cup IDvalues^*(T)$. Then replace p with $p' = e \Rightarrow [@A_1, ..., @A_{i-1}, @T, @A_i, ..., @A_m, E_1, ..., E_n]$.

d) V is an object whose parent is $p = e \Rightarrow [@A_1, ..., @A_m, E_1, ..., E_n]$ and $V = E_i$ for some $1 \le i \le n$, $IDvalues^*(T) \cap (IDvalues^* - IDvalues^*(V)) = \emptyset$, and $IDrefs^*(T) \subseteq (IDrefs^* - IDvalues^*(V)) \cup IDvalues^*(T)$. Then replace p with $p' = e \Rightarrow [@A_1, ..., @A_m, E_1, ..., E_{i-1}, T, E_i, ...E_n]$.

e) Otherwise, the replacement operation is not allowed.
   In other words, we delete V then insert T and consistency with the deletion and insertion must be maintained.

5 Conclusion and Future Work

In this paper, we first reviewed several XML update languages. We then presented our update extension to XML-RL language, called XML-RL update language. Based on the XML-RL data model, we presented the formal syntax and logic-based declarative semantics for the update language. Our update language incorporated some techniques and ideas from the existing updating languages within a uniform framework that is advantageous over other XML update languages. It supports update operation among different XML documents; it supports the multiple update at multiple level for the XML documents without nested operations; it supports update operation for both ordered or unordered XML document; it uses some of the features of object-oriented database and logic programming language, which make it very powerful but easy to understand.

We are now also implementing the XML-RL system that supports XML-RL query and update languages. A native XML database system is also underway.

Acknowledgement. Mengchi Liu's research is partially supported by National Science and Engineering Research Council of Canada. Guoren Wang's research is partially supported by the Teaching and Research Award Programme for Outstanding Young Teachers in Post-Secondary Institutions by the Ministry of Education, China (TRAPOYT) and National Natural Science Foundation of China under grant No. 60273079.

References

1. Abiteboul, S., Hull, R., and Vianu, V. Foundations of Databases. Addison Wesley, 1995.
2. Abiteboul, S., Quass, D., Mchug, J., Widom, J., Wiener, J.: The Lorel Query Language for semistructured Data. International Journal on Digital Libraries. **1** (1997) 5–19
3. Goldman, R., Mchugh, J., Widom, J.: From semistructured data to XML: Migrating the Lorel data model and guery language. In ACM SIGMOD WEBDB Workshop'99, Philadelphia, Pennsylyania. (1999) 25–30
4. Cheng, J., Xu, J.: DB2 XML Extender. http://www-3.ibm.com/software/data/db2/extenders/xmlext/xmlextbroch.pdf (2002)
5. Ceri, S., Comai, S., Damiani, E., Fraternali, P., Paraboschi, S., Tanca, L.: XML-GL: a Graphical Language for Querying and Restructuring XML Documents. http://www8.org/w8-papers/1c-xml/xml-gl/xml-gl.html (1999)
6. Tatarinov, I., Ives, Z.G., Halevy, A.Y., Weld, D.S.: Updating XML. In Proceedings of 2001 SIGMOD Conference, Santa Barbara, CA, USA (2001)
7. Laux, A., Martin, L.: XML:DB. XUpdate-XML WD. http://www.xmldb.org/xupdate/xupdate-wd.html#Nfeb48 (2000)
8. W3C Working Group. XML Path Language (XPath). http://www.w3.org/TR/xpath (2002)
9. Liu, M.: A Logical Foundation for XML. In Proceedings of the 14th International Conference on Advanced Information Systems Engineering (CAiSE '02), Toronto, Ontario, Lecture Notes in Computer Science, Vol. 2348, Springer 2002. (2002) 568–583
10. Liu, M., Ling, T.W.: Towards Declarative XML Querying. In Proceedings of the 3rd International Conference on Web Information System Engineering (WISE 2002), Singapore (2002)
11. Ceri, S., Gottlob, G., Tanca, L.: Logic Programming and Database. Springer-VerlagBerlin Heidelberg. (1990)

12. Daum, B., Merten, U.: System Architecture With XML. Morgan Kaufmenn Publishers (2002)
13. W3C Working Group. Xquery 1.0: An XML Query Language. http://www.w3.org/TR/xquery/ (2002)
14. eXcelon Team: Updating XML Data in eXcelon Explorer. EXcelon. http://support.exln.com/doc/full/xml/b2bps/doc/exug/topsetug.htm (2000)
15. W3C Working Group. DTD Tutorial. http://www.w3schools.com/dtd/default.asp (1999)
16. Chen, Y., Revese, P.: CXQuery: A Novel XML Query Language. http://www.ssgrr.it/en/ssgrr2002w/papers/216.pdf (2002)
17. W3C Working Group. XML Schema. http://www.w3.org/XML/Schema (1999)

Resolving Structural Conflicts in the Integration of XML Schemas: A Semantic Approach

Xia Yang, Mong Li Lee, and Tok Wang Ling

School of Computing, National University of Singapore
3 Science Drive 2, Singapore 117543
{yangxia,leeml,lingtw}@comp.nus.edu.sg

Abstract. While the Internet has facilitated access to information sources, the task of scalable integration of these heterogeneous data sources remains a challenge. The adoption of the eXtensible Markup Language (XML) as the standard for data representation and exchange has led to an increasing number of XML data sources, both native and non-native. Recent integration work has mainly focused on developing matching techniques to find equivalent elements and attributes among the different XML sources. In this paper, we introduce a semantic approach to resolve structural conflicts in the integration of XML schemas. We employ a data model called the ORA-SS (Object-Relationship-Attribute Model for Semi-Structured Data) to capture the implicit semantics in an XML schema. We present a comprehensive algorithm to integrate XML schemas. Compared to existing methods, our algorithm adopts an n-nary integration strategy that takes into account the data semantics, importance of a source, and how the majority of the sources model their data when resolving structural conflicts such as attribute/object class conflict and ancestor-descendant conflict. Further, redundant object classes and transitive relationship sets are removed to obtain a more concise integrated schema.

1 Introduction

Advances in the Internet infrastructure have facilitated access to large amounts of information sources. Many of these sources are heterogeneous, and an integrated access to these sources remains the focus of ongoing research. Much work has been done on the integration of relational databases, ranging from semantic enrichment using a semantic data model such as the Entity-Relationship model or the object-oriented data model, translation algorithms, and conflict resolution [8][9][10][22]. Integration systems such as [4][7][15][16][18][21] have also been developed.

The adoption of the eXtensible Markup Language (XML) as the standard for data representation and exchange has led to an increasing number of XML data sources, both native and non-native. Native XML data sources are essentially XML files with an associated XML schema, while non-native XML sources such as the relational database publish their data in XML format together with the XML schema. Given the semistructured nature of XML data that can be modeled as a tree or a graph, recent research in integrating XML data sources has mainly concentrated on schema matching [4][12][21].

I.-Y. Song et al. (Eds.): ER 2003, LNCS 2813, pp. 520–533, 2003.

The task of integrating XML data sources is non-trivial for the following reasons:
1. The XML Schema or DTD is lacking in semantics. While this has prompted proposals to augment the schema with information such as keys [3], and functional dependencies [11], it remains unclear whether the relationship between the element objects is binary or n-nary, and whether an attribute belongs to an element object class (e.g. title of an element book) or to the relationship set between elements (e.g. quantity of books supplied by a supplier to a bookshop).
2. The source schemas are heterogeneous, containing various conflicts involving naming conflict, cardinality conflict, and structural conflict such as attribute/object class conflict and ancestor-descendant conflict. There is no unique global schema, but it is subject to the needs of applications and the perspective of the users.

To address these issues, we develop a semantic approach to the integration of XML schemas. We employ the semantically rich model ORA-SS [5] for semistructured data to capture the semantics of the underlying XML data. An n-nary integration strategy that provides a global view of the source schemas is adopted. The integrated schema obtained takes into consideration underlying data semantics such as different relationship sets among equivalent object classes, the importance of the source schemas, and how the majority of the sources schemas modeled their data. Structural conflicts such as attribute-object class conflict and ancestor-descendant conflict are resolved in the process. Finally, redundant object classes and transitive relationship sets are identified and removed to obtain a more concise integrated schema.

The rest of the paper is organized as follows. Section 2 presents some background material including a brief description of the ORA-SS model. Section 3 gives a motivating example and highlights the various features that we consider in our integration strategy. Section 4 describes the details of the algorithm to integrate XML schemas. Section 5 discusses related work, and we conclude in Section 6.

2 Preliminaries

In this section, we first describe the ORA-SS model that we utilize in our integration strategy. This is followed by the assumptions we make in our integration approach.

2.1 ORA-SS Model

The ORA-SS model (Object-Relationship-Attribute model for Semi-Structured data) is a semantically rich data model that has been designed for semi-structured data [5]. The rich semantics of ORA-SS allows us to capture more of the real world semantics, and use them for integration. The ORA-SS model distinguishes between objects, relationships and attributes. The relationships between objects are expressed explicitly. An object class in the ORA-SS model is similar to the concept of entity type in an ER model and classes in the object-oriented model. They coincide with the concept of elements in XML. An object class may be related to another object class through a relationship set. Attributes are properties, and may belong to an object class or a relationship set.

Here, we use the ORA-SS Schema Diagram as the conceptual model for XML data. The object classes such as "project" and "part" in Fig 1(d) are represented by labeled rectangle. The relationship set between the object classes are denoted by *name, n, p, c*, where *name* denotes the name of the relationship, *n* is the degree of the relationship, *p* is the participation constraint of the parent object class in the relationship, and *c* is participation constraint of the child object. The participation constraints are defined using the min:max notation. The labeled circles denote attributes, and the filled circles denote keys. Attributes are properties of object class or the relationship set. For example, in Fig 1(d), "jno" is the attribute of object class "project", while "quantity" is the attribute of relationship set "jps". The degree of relationship set "jps" is 3, which is a ternary relationship set involving object classes "project", "part" and "supplier". For details on ORA-SS, please refer to [5].

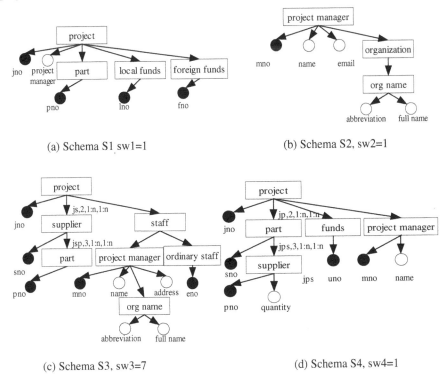

(a) Schema S1 sw1=1

(b) Schema S2, sw2=1

(c) Schema S3, sw3=7

(d) Schema S4, sw4=1

Fig. 1. ORA-SS Schema Diagrams for four XML sources

2.2 Assumptions

The input to the proposed integration algorithm is a set of ORA-SS schemas, which has been generated from XML schemas. Details of the transformation of XML schema to the ORA-SS model are given in [2]. Inputs from the users may be solicited to enrich the ORA-SS schema with the necessary semantics.

The output of the algorithm is an integrated schema, also modeled in ORA-SS. Since queries on the integrated schema will be subsequently mapped to equivalent queries on the data sources, the integrated schema should contain all the information modeled in the original schemas. Further, the integrated schema should be as simple and concise as possible to facilitate users' understanding.

For meaningful integration to occur, we assume that the various sources model similar domains. Object classes with the same label are considered to be semantically equivalent, that is, they refer to the same object class in the real world. Similarly, attributes of the same object class (or relationship set) with the same label are also semantically equivalent, that is, they refer to the same property of an object class (or relationship sets) in the real world. The object classes (or relationship sets) in the different original schemas that refer to the same real world object (or relationship) may have different names. We assume that the renaming step have been done before the integration process. Note that there may also exist different relationship sets between the same object classes. In such cases, we assume they will be assigned different labels.

3 Motivating Example

In this section, we illustrate some of the unique features of the integration strategy we offer. Consider the ORA-SS schema diagrams for four XML sources in Fig 1. The swi under each schema indicates the source weight, i.e., the importance of a source. This is determined by users or computed based on some statistic information.

A. Resolve Attribute-Object Class Conflict
This occurs when a concept has been modeled as an attribute in one schema, and as an object class in another schema. For example, the attribute "project manager" in schema S1 is semantically equivalent to the object class "project manager" in schema S2 of Fig 1. This conflict can be easily resolved by mapping the attribute to an object class (see Fig 2).

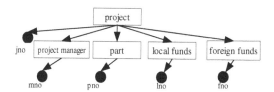

Fig. 2. Schema S1': Attribute "project manager" in schema S1 of Fig 1 has been transformed into an object class "project manager" in S1'

B. Resolve Generalizations and Specializations
A generalization exists when an object class in one schema is the union of several object classes in another schema. Consider again Fig 1. The object class "funds" in schema S4 is a generalization of the object classes "local funds" and "foreign funds" in schema S1. The integrated schema will include the generalization hierarchy as shown in Fig 3.

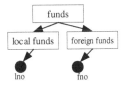

Fig. 3. Build a generalization hierarchy from S1 of Fig 1

C. Merge the Schemas to Obtain an Integrated Graph

Fig 4 shows the graph obtained from merging the schemas S1', S2, S3 and S4. Each node in the graph denotes an object class, and edges represent the relationship sets between the object classes. To facilitate processing, attributes are first omitted from the integrated graph. The attributes will be incorporated into the final integrated schema. Note that only the equivalent relationship sets will merged together. Semantically different relationship sets between the equivalent object classes will be treated as different relationship sets, as indicated by the different edges.

The edges in the integrated graph are weighted as follows. Since we have "project" as the parent of "part" in schemas S1 and S4, the weight of the edge from "project" to "part" is given by the sum of the weights of these schemas, that is, 1+1=2. In the same way, since "project" is the parent of "staff" in schema S3 only, the weight of this edge is 7. Since the edge from "supplier" to "part" in S3 is actually involved in two relationship sets jsp and sp, its edge weight would be given by 7*2=14.

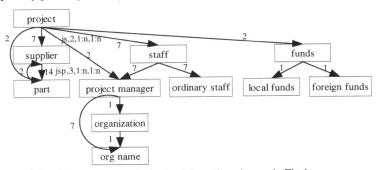

Fig. 4. Integrated graph obtained from the schemas in Fig 1

D. Transform Integrated Graph to Resolve Structural Conflicts and Remove Redundancy

We proceed to transform the graph to differentiate the semantically different relationships between equivalent object classes, identify cycles to resolve ancestor-descendant conflicts, remove redundant object classes and redundant relationship sets. Redundant relationship sets include relationship sets that are derived from projecting higher-degree relationships in the schema and transitive relationship sets.

D-1. Differentiate Semantically Different Relationship Sets between Equivalent Object Classes

Consider the schemas S5 and S6 in Fig 5 that are structurally the same, except for the additional object class "contract" in S6. The relationship sets between the same object classes are semantically different. The relationship set in schema S5 indicates that the person owns the house, while that in schema S6 indicates that the person rents the house. We first merge the two schemas to obtain the integrated graph G56 before transforming it to G56' (see Fig.5). The edges from object classes "house1" and "house2" to the object class "house" in G56' indicate foreign key-key references. Note that the relationship phc between the "person", "house" and "contract" is represented explicitly in the transformed graph.

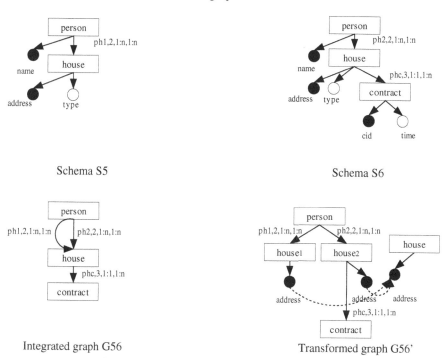

Fig. 5. Different relationship sets among equivalent object classes

D-2. Remove Relationship Sets That Are Projections of Higher Degree Relationship Sets

A schema may model a relationship set that is a projection of another relationship set in another schema. For instance, if we integrate the schemas S1 and S3, the integrated graph will contain the binary relationship set between "project" and "part" from schema S1, and the ternary relationship set between "project", "supplier" and "part" from schema S3. Since the former is a projection of latter relationship set, we remove the binary relationship set and keep the ternary relationship set in the integrated graph. Subsequently, we can issue a query "/project//part" on the integrated schema to retrieve all the "part" information.

D-3. Resolve Ancestor-Descendant Conflicts

An ancestor-descendant conflict arises when a schema models an object class A as an ancestor of another object class B, and the other schema models B as the ancestor of

A. The simplest form of this conflict is the parent-child conflict in schemas S3 and S4. We have "supplier" as the parent of "part" in S3, while "part" is the parent of "supplier" in S4. This conflict creates a cycle "supplier" → "part" → "supplier" in the integrated graph of Fig 4. One of the edges which represent the inverse relationship sets can be removed to break the cycle. We propose to remove the edge with the lowest edge weight, that is, the edge from the less important schema. In this case, the edge from "part" to "supplier" with an edge weight of 2 will be removed.

Fig 6 shows another example of an ancestor-descendant conflict. The object class "module" is the ancestor of "tutor" in schema S7, while "tutor" is the ancestor of "module" in S8. This conflict will create a cycle in the integrated graph G78. The conflict can be resolved by removing one of the edges that has the least weight. Further, the edge removed should represent a relationship set that can be derived by a series of joins and projections of the other relationship sets involved in the cycle.

If the source weights are sw7=2, sw8=1, then the weight of the edge from "tutor" to "module" is 1. Since this edge has the lowest edge weight, we will remove it from G78. The transformed graph obtained at this point will be G78'.

On the other hand, if the source weights are sw7=1, sw8=2, then the weight of the edge from "tutor" to "module" is 2, and will not be removed. The weights of the edges from "module" to "lecturer", and from "lecturer" to "tutor" are both 1. Since both of these edges have the lowest edge weight, we can remove either one of them, which will result in the transformed graph G78(a) or G78(b).

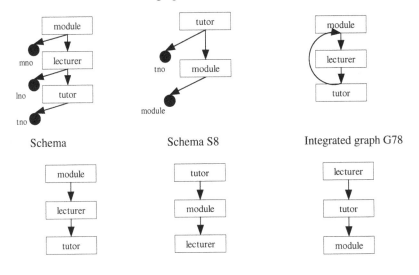

Fig. 6. Example of an ancestor-descendant conflict

D-4. Remove Transitive Relationship Sets
Transitive relationships sets are also redundant, and can be removed so that the resulting integrated graph will be concise. For example, the relationship set between "project" and "project manager" in Fig 4 is a transitive relationship set that can be

obtained from the relationship sets between "project" and "staff", and between "staff" and "project manager". Thus, we can remove the transitive relationship set from the integrated graph.

Fig. 4 also contains another transitive relationship set between "project manager" and "org name". We observe that the object class "organization" does not have any attribute, and has only one child object class "org name". This object class from schema S2 cannot contain any instances in the corresponding XML data files. Since "organization" is a redundant object class, we propose to remove it and its associated relationship sets from the integrated graph in Fig 4. As a result, the relationship set between "project manager" and "org name" is no longer a transitive relationship set.

D-5. Remove Multiple Parent Nodes

If a node has more than one incoming edges in an integrated graph, then it is called a *multiple parent* node. Consider the integrated graph G9-10 in Fig 7. The two incoming edges to "student" indicate two different relationship sets. The attribute "mark" can only belong to one of them, namely, the relationship set "jd". In the transformed graph G9-10', we will split the multiple parent node and represent these two relationship sets separately.

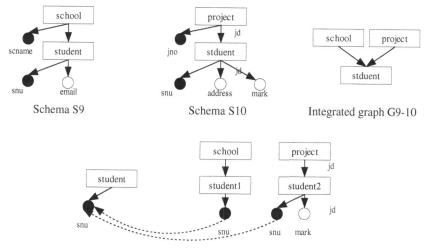

Schema S9   Schema S10   Integrated graph G9-10

Transformed Graph G9-10'

Fig. 7. Example of a multiple parent node

Fig 8 shows the transformed graph obtained for the source schemas in Fig 1 after addressing the above concerns. For instance, when solving ancestor-descendant conflict, the cycle "supplier"→"part"→"supplier" is detected and the edge "part"→"supplier" is deleted. The redundant object class "organization" and its associated edges are deleted. Transitive edges as "project"→"project manager" and "project"→"part" are also removed. The transformed graph is augmented with attributes such as "quantity" for the ternary relationship set "jsp". The final integrated schema is shown in Fig 9. Note that the attribute "quantity" belongs to the relationship set "jps" in schema S4 (see Fig. 1), which is a ternary relationship set associating object classes "project", " supplier" and "part". Since the node "part" is at the lowest level compared to "supplier" and "project", the attribute "quantity" becomes an attribute under "part".

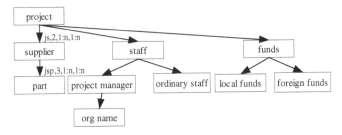

Fig. 8. Transformed graph obtained from Fig 4

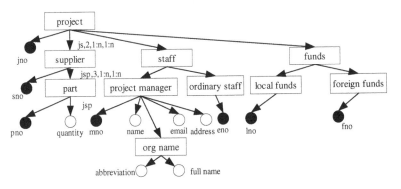

Fig. 9. Final integrated schema

4   Integration Algorithm

In this section, we first discuss some of the terms used before giving the details of the integration algorithm.

If a node i has more than one incoming edges in an integrated graph, then we called it a *multiple parent* node. If a directed edge sequence $<e_{i0,i1}, e_{i1,i2}, \cdots\cdots e_{im,i(m+1)}, e_{i(m+1),i0}>$ occurs in an integrated graph, then a *cycle* exists. We observe that an ancestor-descendant conflict occurs if and only if there is a cycle in the integrated graph.

There are essentially four main steps in our integration algorithm:

1. Preprocessing.
2. Construct integrated graph.
3. Transform graph.
4. Augment graph with attributes.

The input is a set of schemas modeled using the ORA-SS model. The output is an integrated ORA-SS schema. The third step *Transform Graph* aims to identify semantically different relationships among equivalent object classes, resolve ancestor-descendant conflicts, and remove redundant object classes and redundant relationship sets such as transitive relationship sets. The resulting integrated schema preserves data semantics in the sources, considers how the majority of the sources model the data, and is concise.

Step 1 Preprocessing

    1.1 Resolve attribute-object class conflict.

        If the same concept is expressed as an object class in one schema, and as an attribute in another schema, then convert the attribute to an equivalent object class. The attribute becomes the key of this new object class.

    1.2 Resolve generalizations and specializations.

        When one object class is the generalization object class of some object classes of other schemas, it becomes the parent node of these object classes.

Step 2 Construct Integrated Graph

    2.1 Merge the equivalent object classes and relationship sets from original schemas to obtain an integrated graph G such that each node is an object class, and edges denote relationship sets between the object classes. Note that attributes are not included in G.

    2.2 Compute the weights of the edges.

        For each edge e in G do

            Let $e_1, e_2, \ldots e_k$ be the equivalent edges in the original schemas $s_1, s_2, \ldots s_k$.
            Let $sw_1, sw_2, \ldots sw_k$ be the source weights of the schemas $s_1, s_2, \ldots s_k$ respectively.
            Let $n_1, n_2, \ldots n_k$ be the number of relationship sets the edge is involved in the schemas $s_1, s_2, \ldots s_k$
            Set the weight of the edge $ew = sw_1*n_1 + sw_2*n_2 + \ldots sw_k*n_k$.

Step 3 Transform Graph

    3.1 Differentiate semantically different relationship sets between equivalent object classes.

        For each node n_s in G do

            If n_s has k outgoing edges $\{e_{s1}, e_{s2}, \ldots, e_{sk}\}$ to the same node n_t Then
                Create k duplicate nodes $\{n_{t1}, \ldots, n_{tk}\}$ of n_t;
                Each edge e_{si} (from n_s to n_t), $1 \leq i \leq k$, becomes an edge from n_s to n_{ti};
                For each n_{ti}, $1 \leq i \leq k$, do
                    Create a foreign key-key reference from the key of n_{ti} to that of n_t.
                For each child node c of node n_t do
                    If c is involved in an n-nary relationship set that includes e_{si}
                    Then Move c and its descendent nodes from n_t to n_{ti}.

    3.2 Remove relationship sets that are projections of higher degree relationship sets.

        For each n-nary relationship set R in G do

Let $N = \{n_1, \ldots, n_k\}$ be the set of nodes involved in relationship R.
For each relationship set R' that involves a subset of nodes in N do
      If   R' is a projection of R
      Then   Remove R' from the integrated graph.

3.3 Resolve any ancestor-descendant conflicts which create cycles in G.
    For each cycle in G do
      Let e_{ij} be the edge with the smallest edge weight in the cycle.
      If e_{ij} can be derived from other relationship sets in the cycle.
      Then   Remove e_{ij} from G.

3.4 Remove redundant relationship sets and redundant object classes.
    For each multiple parent node n in G do
      Let P be the set of parent nodes of n.
      While $|P| > 1$ do
        Let $p_{max} \in P$
        Let $<n_0, n_1, \ldots, n_k>$ be the path from p_{max} to n, where $n_0 = p_{max}$, $n_k = n$,
        and $k > 1$.
        / remove redundant object classes with no attribute and only one*
        *child object class. */*
        For each node n_i in the path, $0 < i < k$, do
          If n_i has no attributes and no sub-object classes besides n_{i+1}
          Then Remove n_i and its associated edges from G;
                Create an edge between n_{i-1} and n_{i+1};
        $P = P - \{p_{max}\}$;
        If the edge from p_{max} to n can be derived from $<n_0, n_1, \ldots, n_k>$
        Then   Remove the transitive edge from p_{max} to n in G.

3.5 Remove multiple parent nodes.
    For each multiple parent node n_m in G do
      Let n_m have k incoming edges $e_1, e_2, \ldots, e_k$ from nodes $n_1, n_2, \ldots, n_k$
      respectively.
      Create k duplicate nodes $\{n_{m1}, \ldots, n_{mk}\}$ of n_m;
      Each edge e_i (from n_i to n_m), $1 \leq i \leq k$, becomes an edge from n_i to n_{mi};
      For each node n_{mi}, $1 \leq i \leq k$, do
        Create a foreign key-key reference from the key of n_{mi} to that of n_m.
      For each child node c of node n_m do
        If c is involved in an n-nary relationship set that includes e_i
        Then   Move c and its descendent nodes from n_m to n_i.

Step 4   Augment Graph with Attributes

4.1 Map the transformed graph G to an equivalent ORA-SS schema S.

4.2 Augment the schema with the attributes of object classes.

4.3 Augment the schema with attributes of relationship sets.

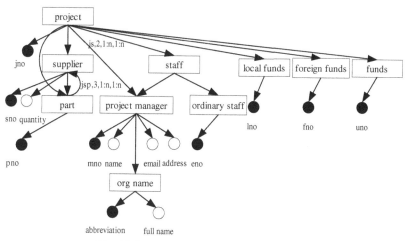

Fig. 10. Integrated schema obtained by [7]

5 Related Work

Research in data integration has focused on various aspects to integrate information from multiple sources. Most of the work has focused on the matching problem to find equivalent elements among the different sources. These work include XClust [12], CUPID [14], SKAT [16][17], and Xyleme [19]. A taxonomy and a survey of matching approaches are given in [6].

Having obtained a set of equivalent elements, the next step is to obtain an integrated schema. [7] use schema learning to generate a set of tree grammar rules from the DTDs in a class and optimizes the rules to transforms them into an integrated view. Fig 10 shows the integrated schema that [7] will obtain. Since the method does not take into account the underlying semantics of the data, the attribute "quantity" is considered to belong to "supplier". Further, the relationship set between "project" to "project manager" is transitive relationship set, which is redundant. The relationship set from "part" to "supplier" and "project" to "part" is redundant. In contrast, the integrated schema obtained by our approach preserves the underlying data semantics and is concise (see Fig 9).

LSD [4] employs instance information and machine learning techniques in their integration work. This is because instances contain more information than the schemas. For example, if the phone number of a given element have significant commonalities, the phone numbers are more likely to be the office phones of employees, rather than home phones. However, the number of instances is very much larger than that of the schemas, hence this method is very costly.

All these work do not take into consideration the importance of the individual data sources, and how the majority of the local schemas model their data. In contrast, our proposed method employs the ORA-SS conceptual model which is able to capture the semantics necessary for the resolution of structural conflict during integration. The n-nary strategy that we adopted provides a global view of the local sources, and is faster compared to the binary strategy, whose intermediate schemas will grow with the number of sources. The binary strategy will not be able to utilize the source importance and how the majority of the sources model the data.

6 Conclusion

In this paper, we have introduced a semantic approach to resolve structural conflicts in the integration of XML schemas. We employed the ORA-SS semantic data model to capture the implicit semantics in an XML schema. We presented a comprehensive n-nary algorithm to integrate XML schemas. Compared to existing methods, our algorithm takes into account the data semantics, the importance of a source, and how the majority of the sources model their data. Structural conflicts such as attribute/object class conflict, ancestor-descendant conflict are resolved in our approach. We also remove redundant object classes and relationship sets such as transitive relationship sets, and relationship sets, which are projections of higher degree relationship sets in order to obtain a concise integrated schema.

References

1. S. Castano, V. Antonellis, S. C. Vimercati, M. Melchiori. An XML-Based Framework for Information Integration over the Web. IIWAS, 2000.
2. Y.B. Chen, T.W. Ling, M.L. Lee. Designing Valid XML Views. ER, 2002.
3. P. Buneman, S. Davidson, W. Fan, C. Hara, W.C. Tan. Keys for XML. WWW, 2001.
4. A. Doan, P. Domingos, A. Levy. Learning Source Descriptions for Data Integration. WebDB, 2000.
5. G. Dobbie, X. Wu, T.W. Ling, M.L. Lee. ORA-SS: An Object-Relationship-Attribute Model for Semi-structured Data. Technical Report TR21/00, National University of Singapore, 2000.
6. E. Rahm, P. Bernstein. On Matching Schemas Automatically. MSR Tech. Report MSR-TR-2001-17, 2001.
7. E. Jeong, C.-N. Hsu. Induction of Integrated View for XML Data with Heterogeneous DTDs. ACM CIKM, 2001.
8. T.W. Ling, M.L. Lee. Relational to Entity-Relationship Schema Translation Using Semantic and Inclusion Dependencies, in Journal of Integrated Computer-Aided Engineering, John-Wiley Publishers, Vol 2, No 2, pages 125–145, 1995.
9. M.L. Lee, T.W. Ling. Resolving Structural Conflicts in the Integration of Entity-Relationship Schemas. OOER, 1995.
10. M.L. Lee, T.W. Ling. Resolving Constraint Conflicts in the Integration of Entity-Relationship Schemas. ER, 1997.
11. M.L. Lee, T.W. Ling, W.L. Low. Designing Functional Dependencies for XML, EDBT, 2002.
12. M.L. Lee, L.H. Yang, W. Hsu, X. Yang. XClust: Clustering XML Schemas for Effective Integration, ACM CIKM, 2002.
13. D. Maier. Theory of Relational Databases. Computer Science Press, 1983.
14. J. Madhavan, P.A. Bernstein, E. Rahm. Generic Schema Matching with Cupid. VLDB, 2001.
15. R. Mello, S. Castano, C.A. Heuser. A Method for the Unification of XML. Information and Software Technology Journal, 2002.

16. P. Mitra, G. Wiederhold and J. Jannink. Semi-automatic Integration of Knowledge Sources. Fusion, 1999.
17. P. Mitra, G. Wiederhold, M. Kersten. A Graph-Oriented Model for Articulation of Ontology Interdependencies. EDBT 2000.
18. F. Naumann, U. Leser, J.C. Freytag. Quality-driven Integration of Heterogeneous Information Systems. VLDB, 1999.
19. C. Reynaud, J.-P. Sirot, D. Vodislav. Semantic Integration of XML Heterogeneous Data Sources. IDEAS, 2001.
20. http://www.cogsci.princeton.edu/~wn
21. Xyleme. A dynamic warehouse for XML Data of the Web. IEEE Data Engineering Bulletin 24(2):40–47, 2001.
22. L.L. Yan, T.W. Ling. Translating Relational Schema with Constraints into OODB Schema. IFIP DS-5 Semantics of Interoperable Database Systems. 1992.

Operators and Classification for Data Mapping in Semantic Integration

Anca Dobre[1], Farshad Hakimpour[2]*, and Klaus R. Dittrich[1]

[1] Department of Information Technology,
[2] Department of Geography,
University of Zurich, Winterthurerstrasse 190, 8057 Zurich, Switzerland
{dobre,farshad,dittrich}@ifi.unizh.ch

Abstract. Adopting and reusing outsourced data is becoming increasingly popular. We consider that the integration of outsourced data has two phases, namely relating schemas and data mapping. The former refers to relating entities and attributes between the source and the target schema. The latter refers to the mechanisms for the transformation of data. In this paper we discuss issues related to the data mapping phase. We introduce a set of mapping operators for both entities and attributes. A classification of possible mapping cases is presented. For each of the possible cases of mapping we also suggest a resolution method using the introduced mapping operators.

1 Introduction

As the number of data providers and amount of data increases, reusing outsourced data raises many technical problems due to their semantic heterogeneity. Efficient mechanisms for transforming outsourced data into the internal format of applications are needed, as the provider and the user often do not share the same understanding of data. This transformation has two phases, namely relating schemas and data mapping. By relating schemas, we refer to relating entities and attributes in the provider's schema and the user's schema. Such relation are rooted in the semantics of the data at the provider's community and its interpretation at the user community. After establishing such relations between the schemas one should specify the data mapping mechanism according to the relations between the two schemas. The focus of our work presented here is the data mapping phase.

In this work, we assume semantic relations between schema elements (i.e. entities and attribute) are available and we elaborate on the data mapping issues. That is because, our original motivation is to complement prior work on semantic integration [4,5] in which we left the data mapping part open and focused on schema integration by means of formal ontologies. The major relations between schema elements treated in our approach in [5] are hypernymy, hyponymy

---

* The work of Farshad Hakimpour is funded by Swiss National Science Foundation (Project Number: 2100-053995).

I.-Y. Song et al. (Eds.): ER 2003, LNCS 2813, pp. 534–547, 2003.

and synonymy relations (as the main construction component of ontologies). Although we rely on the relations we find during our semantic matching, we keep a comprehensive view, rather than considering only the above mentioned semantic relations. A comprehensive view independent of the semantic relations can help us evaluate which possible cases of mapping can be detected using ontologies. We also show that if the semantic relations are received from other sources one can perform the mapping using a limited set of operators.

The structure of the paper is as follows. The next section introduces related work. Section 3 gives an overview of the work and introduces the sample schemas on which we identify the data mapping cases. Section 4 introduces the entity mapping operators and contains a classification of the entity mappings. Similarly, Section 5 treats the mappings of attributes. Section 6 concludes the paper.

2   Related Work

Attempts towards a generalized approach to data mapping go back to the early 70s. Applications used to keep their data in files of various structures. Format conversion was needed when moving data from one application to another. Initially, this was done by means of conversion programs written for every pair of formats (source format, target format). Later, systems and methodologies for restructuring a wide variety of hierarchical data were envisioned [7,11]. Nowadays, EXPRESS is an international standard providing a family of languages for schema definition and data mapping [6]. It proposes a reference architecture of a transformation system, which is supported by data definition languages (EXPRESS, EXPRESS-G) for describing data structures of source and target files and a data mapping language (EXPRESS-M) for specifying the data transformations. At the first glance one may see major similarities between the objectives of EXPRESS-M and our data mapping operators. However, the focus of this work is not to prepare a suite of tools for data mapping, but to find those aspects of data mapping that may be facilitated. That is, our aim is to explore those aspects of mapping that can be automatically invoked by a semantic matching module.

Starting with the 80s applications keep their data in databases. The challenge becomes the development of a mechanism to transparently access data from multiple heterogeneous databases. Global schema and federated schema are the main approaches and they have the goal of generating an integrated schema that is mapped to the component schemas [10]. The mappings between component schemas and the integrated schema are used for the translation of global queries into local queries, rather than for data migration between systems. Even if the mappings in the integration process are used differently at run-time from the mappings in the migration process, they are both defined in a schema mapping language.

The mapping identification and specification is presented in [10] as a key area for research, especially because mappings that are derived only from schema information cannot convey the whole semantic of underlying data and therefore mapping generation cannot be automated. Miller et al. [8] take the opposite approach and do not use at all schema level assertions, arguing that mapping discovery is best done at data level using an integration-by-example paradigm.

Model management [1,2] is an approach to metadata management, which defines operations on schemas like, for example, MATCH, COMPOSE, DIFF, MERGE. The operator that generates mappings is MATCH, which takes as input parameters two schemas and returns a mapping between them. The survey in [9] uses a taxonomy to characterize approaches to automation of the mapping generation, which are seen as implementations of the MATCH operator. The taxonomy does not specify a source and target schema for the mapping, as in data migration, but rather two input schemas, as in schema integration.

We address the gap indicated in [1], which is that the MATCH operation has to be further analyzed and refined. The existing approaches mentioned in [9] concentrate either on preparing a suite of tools for data mapping, or on generating mappings based on schema-level information. Our approach is to define a complete set of operators that can be composed to realize the function of MATCH.

3   Overview

Let $\mathcal{E}$ be the set of entities of the schema S, $\mathcal{A}$ the set of attributes of the schema S. We use the notation E for an entity, $E \in \mathcal{E}$, and A for an attribute, $A \in \mathcal{A}$. E is a subset of $\mathcal{A}$, $E = \{A_1, A_2, \ldots, Ap\}$. Every attribute A has an associated set of values Δ_A called A's domain. Δ is the union of domains of all attributes in $\mathcal{A}$. An instance e is a mapping from E into Δ, such that each A in E is mapped to an element of Δ_A. The extension of E is a finite set of e.

We assume that similarities between two schemas $S_Q = (E_1, E_2, \ldots, E_n)$ and $S_Z = (F_1, F_2, \ldots, F_m)$ are known and consequently the mappings between them are identified. The goal of the mapping process is to generate instances of the target schema S_Z out of instances of the source schema S_Q and the specification of mappings between S_Q and S_Z. We propose a set of mapping operators that can be invoked by a semantic matching process. Although the operators can be used manually, we pay special attention to find the general characteristics of the mapping operations. The mapping operations are applied according to the semantic relations detected by the semantic matching process.

Example. Assuming two entities *Railway* and *Eisenbahn* are synonym classes represented in the source schema as *Railway(length, Endstation[2])* and in the target schema as *Eisenbahn(start, end, type)*, the three phases of the mapping process are:

1. Entity mapping: *Railway* $\longmapsto$ *Eisenbahn*
2. Attribute mapping: *Endstation*[1] $\longmapsto$ *start*, *Endstation*[2] $\longmapsto$ *end*, *length* $\longmapsto$ *type*.
3. Data transformation: if *length* > 100 then *type*="Main railway", otherwise *type*="Secondary railway".

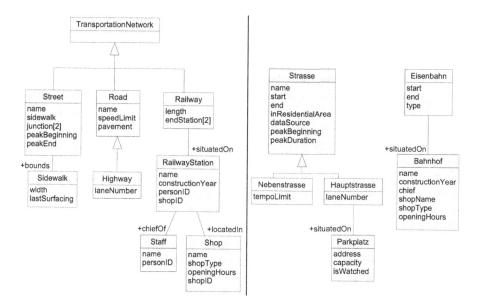

Fig. 1. The sample schemas involved in the data mapping

In the first phase, the entity *Railway* is mapped to the entity *Eisenbahn*. In the second phase, the components of the vector *Endstation* are mapped to the attributes *start* and *type*. The attribute *length* is mapped to the attribute *type*. The third phase specifies an algorithm to transform the values of the attribute *length* into the values of the attribute *type*. As no data transformation process is defined for the vector *Endstation*, the target attributes *start* and *end* will have the same values as the source attributes of the vector. We note that, although entity and attribute matching are bidirectional, data transformation is unidirectional (we cannot determine the length of the railway from the information "main or secondary railway").

Throughout this paper we will use the schemas illustrated in Fig. 1 involving transportation networks.[1] There exists a set of semantic similarities relating these two schemas. We introduce those needed while treating every category of data mapping.

4   Entity Matching

In this section we classify the required mappings between entities and between attributes. The classification criterion is the cardinality of the mapping, i.e. the number of source and target elements that are involved in the mapping. We consider the migration problem from a source schema to a target schema.

---

[1] The direction of migration between the schemas is not fixed. We assume it for every mapping example.

The mapping of entities is followed by the mapping of attributes and thus we analyze them separately.

4.1   Entity Mapping Operators

For schema matching and data transformation we need three types of algebra operators: (1) operators that generate instances for a target entity, (2) vertical operators, which create intermediate entities by modifying and composing the schema and extensions of existing entities, and (3) horizontal operators, which affect only the extensions of the entities.

The first category contains only one operator $map(F)$, which generates instances for the target entity F according to a specified mapping plan.

The second category contains the operators *project, join, apply,* and *rename.* *Projection* and *join* are inverse if the information about the join attribute is maintained.

Project. $I = \Pi_{A_i,...,A_j}(E)$ generates an entity I with the $A_i, ..., A_j$ attributes of entity E and the same extension as E.

Join. $I = join_{P(A_i,A_j)}(E_1, E_2)$, where $A_i \in E_1$, $A_j \in E_2$, and P a predicate, generates an entity I with (1) schema: all the non-join attributes of E_1 and E_2 and one of the join attributes and (2) extension: the cartesian product of E_1 and E_2 for which $P(A_i, A_j)$ is true.

Apply $I = apply_{A=f(A_i,...,A_j)}(E)$ generates an entity I whose schema contains all attributes of E plus a supplementary attribute A whose values are given by the function f of parameters $A_i, ..., A_j$.

Rename $I = rename_{A=A'}(E)$ generates an entity I whose schema contains all attributes of E, but the name of the attribute A is changed to A'.

The third category contains the operators *select, union,* and *eliminateDuplicates.*

Union. $I = union(E, F)$, where E and F are two entities that are union compatible, generates an entity I whose extension represents the union of the extensions of E and F. Two entities $E = \{A_1, A_2, ..., Ap\}$ and $F = \{B_1, B_2, ..., Bq\}$ are said to be union compatible if they have the same degree p=q and if for $\forall i \in \{1, ..., p\} \exists$ one and only one $j \in \{1, ..., q\}$ such that $\Delta_{A_i} = \Delta_{B_j}$ and for $\forall j \in \{1, ..., q\} \exists$ one and only one $i \in \{1, ..., p\}$ such that $\Delta_{B_j} = \Delta_{A_i}$.

Difference. $I = difference(E_1, E_2)$, where E_1 is the generalization of E_2, generates an entity I whose extension represents the extensions of E_1 in which no instance is of type E_2.

Select. $I = \sigma_P(E)$, where P is a predicate, generates an entity I whose extension is the extension of E restricted to the set of instances for which P(e) is true.

EliminateDuplicates. $I = eliminateDuplicates(E)$ generates an entity I whose extension does not contain two instances e_1 and e_2 such that e_1 has the same values as e_2.

4.2   Classification of Entity Mappings

Entity matching is concerned only with the correspondences between entities and does not regard the correspondences between attributes. Its goal is to define entity mappings for target entities, so that we determine map_F as the mapping for the target entity F. Source entities may be involved in more mappings. However, for a source or target entity at least one mapping must be defined.

For each type of mapping we describe (1) the cardinality of the mapping, (2) the number of instances that are generated in the target schema depending on the number of instances in the source schema, (3) the operators that realize the mapping, and (4) an example.

Case 1 (Homomorphic mapping). $E \longmapsto F$

(1) A 1:1 mapping between entities that are on the same level of abstraction and represent the same real-world entity.
(2) For each instance of E exactly one instance of F will be generated.
(3) map_F=mapAttributes(E,F).
(4) For the previous example Railway$\longmapsto$Eisenbahn,

$$map_{Eisenbahn} = mapAttributes(Railway, Eisenbahn).$$

Case 2 (Generalization mapping). $E \longmapsto F$

(1) A 1:1 mapping between entities, where the source entity is a specialization of the target entity. Similar to case 1.
(2) For each instance of E exactly one instance of F will be generated.
(3) map_F=mapAttributes(E,F).
(4) Assume Street$\longmapsto$Strasse,

$$map_{Strasse} = mapAttributes(Street, Strasse).$$

Case 3 (Specialization mapping). $E \longmapsto F$

(1) A 1:1 mapping between entities, where the source entity is a generalization of the target entity (i.e., F "is a" E). A predicate on the attributes or a classification attribute of E distinguishes between the instances of E that are in F or not.
(2) The extension of the target entity will contain all instances of the source entity for which the selection predicate is true.
(3) $I = \sigma_P(E)$, $map_F = mapAttributes(I, F)$.
(4) Assume $Road(name, speedLimit, pavement) \longmapsto Nebenstrasse$,

$$I = \sigma_{speedLimit<50}(Road),$$

$$map_{Nebenstrasse} = mapAttributes(I, Nebenstrasse).$$

Case 4 (Hierarchy mapping). $E_1, \ldots, E_n \longmapsto F$

There are two classes of entity relationships that describe hierarchies: the "is a" relationship and the "part of" relationship. "Is a" relationships describe generalization/specialization hierarchies, whereas "part of" relationships describe aggregation hierarchies. Semantically, for both types of hierarchies, the entities on the higher levels are said to have a higher level of abstraction than the entities on the lower levels [3].

We treat under "hierarchy mapping" only the generalization/specialization relationship, the aggregation relationship being subsumed in "association mapping".

Discussion for the Generalization/Specialization Relationship among $E_1, \ldots, E_n$

(1) A n:1 mapping between entities, where the source entities are in a generalization/specialization relationship (i.e., E_1 is a the superclass of E_2, which is the superclass of E_3 etc.). If the source schema describes one homogeneous database, the problem of duplicates in the target schema does not appear (it is taken care of in the source schema). If the source schema is an integrated schema, so that objects in it come from different databases, the problem of object identification and duplicate elimination occurs.

(2) The extension of the target entity will contain all instances of the source entities taken only once (i.e., no duplicates in the target extension).

(3) Preprocessing steps to make $(E_1, \ldots, E_n)$ union compatible,

$$I_1 = union(E_1, \ldots, E_n), map_F = mapAttributes(I_1, F).$$

If the schema is integrated, the union is followed by:

$$I_2 = eliminateDuplicates(I_1), map_F = mapAttributes(I_2, F).$$

(4) Assume *Highway(name, speedLimit, laneNumber, pavement)* is a specialization of *Road(name, speedLimit, pavement)*. *Road* has n_1 instances and *Highway* has n_2 instances. The entities *Road* and *Highway* are n:1 mapped to *Strasse* in the target schema.

If *Road* and *Highway* are of the same database, then *Strasse* will have n_1 instances, as the instances of *Highway* are counted among the instances of *Road*.

$$I_1 = apply_{laneNumber=NULL}(difference(Road, Highway)),$$

$$map_{Strasse} = mapAttributes(union(I_1, Highway), Strasse).$$

If *Road* and *Highway* come from different databases (i.e., the source schema is an integrated schema), such that an object of *Highway* might be also object of *Road*, then *Strasse* will have $n_1 + n_2 - numberDuplicates$ instances.

$$I_1 = apply_{laneNumber=NULL}(Road), I_2 = union(I_1, Highway),$$

$$I_3 = eliminateDuplicates(I_2), map_{Strasse} = mapAttributes(I_3, Strasse).$$

Case 5 (Association mapping). $E_1, \ldots, E_n \longmapsto F$

There is a third class of entity relationships, the association, which denotes a semantic connection among independent entities. From the implementation point of view, aggregation and association are similarly represented. In the context of XML, every association is represented as an aggregation. In the context of ODMG and object-oriented languages, every aggregation is represented as an association. Thus we treat association and aggregation together.

Discussion for the Association/Aggregation Relationship among $E_1, \ldots, E_n$.

(1) A n:1 mapping between entities, where the source entities are in an association relationship (i.e., E_1 is associated to $E_2, \ldots, E_n$).
(2) For each instance of E_1 exactly one instance of F will be generated.
(3) $I_1 = join_{P_1}(E_1, E_2), \ldots, I_{n-1} = join_{P_{n-1}}(I_{n-2}, E_n)$, $map_F = mapAttributes(I_{n-1}, F)$.
(4) Assume *RailwayStation*, *Staff*, and *Shop* in the source schema are n:1 mapped to *Bahnhof* in the target schema. *RailwayStation(name, constructionYear, personID, shopID)* is associated to *Staff* and *Shop*. The nature of the association is the same, no matter if the attributes *personID* and *shopID* contain a value (i.e. foreign key) or a reference to an object. In this example the association in done by value. The number of instances generated for *Bahnhof* equals the number of instances of *RailwayStation*.

$$I_1 = join_{P(personID)}(RailwayStation, Staff), I_2 = join_{P(shopID)}(I_1, Shop),$$

$$map_{Bahnhof} = mapAttributes(I_2, Bahnhof).$$

Case 6 (Hierarchy construction). $E \longmapsto F_1, \ldots, F_m$.

(1) A 1:n mapping between entities, where the target entities are in a generalization/specialization relationship and $F_1, \ldots, F_m$ are categories of E.
(2) The extensions of the target entities contain subsets of instances of the source entity.
(3) Apply the select operator with a predicate for each target entity $P_1, \ldots, P_m$. Usually, the predicates use one classification attribute of the source entity, e.g. type.

$$I_1 = \sigma_{P_1}(E), \ldots, I_m = \sigma_{P_m}(E).$$

$$map_{F_1} = mapAttributes(I_1, F_1), \ldots, map_{F_m} = mapAttributes(I_m, F_m).$$

(4) Assume *Strasse* is 1:n mapped to *Street* and *Road*. *Street* and *Road* are both subclasses of *TransportationNetwork*. We consider *Street* and *Road* as categories of *Strasse*. A *Street* "is a" *Strasse* located in a residential area (*inResidentialArea=true*), whereas a Road is "is a" *Strasse* outside residential areas (*inResidentialArea=false*).

$$I_1 = \sigma_{inResidentialArea=true}(Strasse),$$

$$I_2 = \sigma_{inResidentialArea=false}(Strasse),$$

$$map_{SecondaryStreet} = mapAttributes(I_1, SecondaryStreet),$$

$$map_{Mainstreet} = mapAttributes(I_2, Mainstreet).$$

Observation: Case 6 reduces to case 3 (specialization).

Case 7 (Association construction). $E \longmapsto F_1, \ldots, F_m$.

(1) A 1:n mapping between one source and many target entities, where the target entities are in an association relationship (i.e., F_1 is associated to $F_2, \ldots, F_m$).
(2) For each instance of E exactly one instance for each of $F_1, \ldots, F_m$ will be generated.
(3) Generate the association attributes for entity F_1, project the attributes of E into intermediate entities $I_1, \ldots, I_m$ that correspond to $F_1, \ldots, F_m$, and eliminate duplicates in the intermediate entities.
(4) Assume Bahnhof(name, constructionYear, chief, shopName, shopType, openingHours) is 1:n mapped to *RailwayStation, Staff, Shop*. The number of instances generated for each of *RailwayStation, Staff* and *Shop* equals the number of instances of *Bahnhof*. We have to generate the attributes that realize the association between *RailwayStation, Staff,* and *Shop*. We generate *personID* by applying a function f to *chief* and *shopID* by applying a function g to *shopName*.

$$I_1 = apply_{personID=f(chief)}(Bahnhof),$$

$$I_2 = apply_{shopID=g(shopName)}(I_1),$$

$$map_{RailwayStation} = \Pi_{name,constructionYear,personID,shopID}(I_2),$$

$$I_3 = \Pi_{personID,chief}(I_2),$$

$$I_4 = \Pi_{shopID,shopName,shopType,openingHours}(I_2),$$

$$map_{Staff} = eliminateDuplicates(rename_{chief=name}(I_3)),$$

$$map_{Shop} = eliminateDuplicates(rename_{shopName=name}(I_4)).$$

Case 8 (Preterition entity). $E \longmapsto \emptyset$

(1) A 1:0 mapping that involves only one source entity that has no correspondent in the target schema. We call this a preterition entity.
(2) This case represents information loss of the source schema, as no instances are generated in the target schema.
(3) No operators are involved.
(4) The entity *Sidewalk* is an example of preterition entity.

Case 9 (Abundant entity). $\emptyset \longmapsto F$

(1) A 0:1 mapping that involves only one target entity that has no correspondent in the source schema. We call this an abundant entity.

(2) This case represents a semantic enrichment of the source schema, as new values are generated in the target schema, e.g. out of metadata of the source data.

(3) $map_F = generateAttributes(F)$.

(4) The entity *Parkplatz* is an example of abundant entity.

5   Attribute Matching

The matching of entities is followed by the matching of attributes. We can specify mappings only between attributes that belong to entities that are mapped to each other.

5.1   Attribute Mapping Operators

The operators realizing the attribute mapping can be classified according to their arity in (1) unary operators, which compute their output value based on the values of one attribute value, (2) multivariate operators, which compute their output value based on the values of many attribute (e.g., binary operators). The operators may apply to (a) the value of attributes in a single entity instance, and (b) the value of attributes in many entity instances. The operators have a separate implementation for each arity and combination of data type of the parameters.

We consider as atomic data types *string*, *numeric* and *date*. As composite data types we consider *arrays*.

(A) Unary operators perform conversion tasks. The need for conversion arises when two attributes are mapped to each other, but their domains are different. The conversion may refer to data types (e.g., string to numeric), data formats (e.g., from dd/mm/yy to dd.mm.yyyy), measurement systems (e.g., from metric to imperial system), or may be arbitrary defined (e.g., from "LastName, First-Name" to "FirstName LastName").

Generic form: $operator1(A_Q)$.

Examples.

1. Data type conversion: $toString(A_Q)$, $toNumeric(A_Q)$.
2. Data format conversion:
   $toUpperCase(A_Q)$, $toLowerCase(A_Q)$, $toAmericanDate(A_Q)$.
3. Measurement system conversion: $yardToM(A_Q)$.
4. User defined conversion:

$$extract(A_Q, <regularExpression>), filter(A_Q, <regularExpression>),$$

$$replace(A_Q, <regularExpression>, <pattern>), sqrt(A_Q).$$

(B) Multivariate operators involve more attributes and realize their composition.

Generic form: $operator N(A_{Q_1}, \ldots, A_{Q_n})$.

Examples.

1. Arithmetic operations: $add, multiply$, for N=2 also $divide, subtract, modulo$.
2. String operations: $concatenate$.
3. User defined.

(C) Set operators involve a set of values of the same attribute.

Generic form:
$setOperator K(A_Q, P[k], f[k]) = (f[1](A_Q, P[1]), \ldots, f[k](A_Q, P[k]))$, where $P[i]$ is a predicate of A_Q and $f[i]$ is a grouping function. This operators determines k subsets of values of A_Q based on the predicates $P[1], \ldots, P[k]$ and applies to each of them a function $f[i]$.

Examples of f.

1. Group operations: $SUM, AVG, COUNT, MIN, MAX$.
2. String operations: $CONCATENATE$.
3. User defined.

The operators are pipeable, such that an attribute mapping may consist of a chain of operators. Every source attribute participates at least in one mapping. Every target attribute participates in exactly one mapping.

5.2   Classification of Attribute Mappings

Figure 2 presents all cases of attribute mappings for a 1:1 entity mapping. $lastSurfacing$ is a preterition attribute, whereas $dataSource$ and $inResidentialArea$ are abundant attributes. For each of the cases we describe (1) the nature of the mapping, (2) generic attribute operators used, and (3) operators used in the example of Fig. 2.

Case 1 (1:1 mapping of attributes). $a \longmapsto b$,
where $a \in E, b \in F, E \longmapsto F$.

(1) To an attribute in the source schema corresponds an attribute with the same structure in the target schema.
(2) $b = operator1(a)$.
(3) $name_{Strasse} = name_{Street}$.

Case 2 (n:1 mapping of attributes). $a_1, \ldots, a_n \longmapsto b$

(1) An attribute in the target schema is calculated according to a formula from many attributes of the source schema, or many simple source attributes are composed to a target attribute (e.g. $firstName, lastName \longmapsto name$).
(2) $b = operator N(a_1, \ldots, a_n)$.
(3) $peakDuration_{Strasse} = subtract(peakEnd_{Street}, peakBeginning_{Street})$.

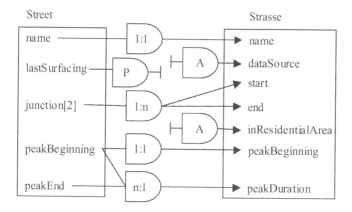

Fig. 2. Attribute matching for a 1:1 entity mapping

Case 3 (1:n mapping of attributes). $a \longmapsto b_1, \ldots, b_m$

(1) This case includes the following:

- Many attributes in the target schema are derived from one attribute of the source schema, or
- one composite source attribute is split in components that are mapped to many target attributes (e.g. $Name \longmapsto FirstName, LastName$), or
- subsets of the values of a single attribute are mapped to different target attributes, or
- one array is decomposed in atomic components.

(2) The above cases are resolved as follows:

- $b_1 = f_1(a), \ldots, b_m = f_m(a)$.
- e.g., for $a \longmapsto b_1, b_2$, $b_1 = extract(a, E_1)$, $2_2 = extract(a, E_2)$, where E_1, E_2 are regular expressions.
- $b_1 = setOperator_1(a, P_1), \ldots, b_m = setOperator_m(a, P_m)$.
- $b_1 = a[1], \ldots, b_m = a[m]$.

(3) $start = junction[1]$, $end = junction[2]$.

Case 4 (1:0 mapping of attributes). $a \longmapsto \emptyset$

1) If no mapping can be defined for a source attribute a of E, we call this a **preterition** attribute.

(2) No operators are involved.

(3) The information about $lastSurfacing$ gets lost.

Case 5 (0:1 mapping of attributes). $\emptyset \longmapsto b$

(1)If no mapping is specified to a target attribute b of F, we call this an **abundant** attribute.

(2) $b = constant$.

(3) $inResidentialArea = true$, $dataSource = $ "$Municipality\ database$".

6   Conclusion

One commonality between data migration and schema integration is the specification of mappings, which is a difficult process. The database community has addressed the problem of semi-automatically generating semantic mappings by providing tools that support the process of manually writing semantic mappings. In an attempt to make this process more transparent, our approach is to distinguish between entity mapping and attribute mapping. The mapping process follows the waterfall principle with 3 phases. Every mapping between entities must be followed by specifying mappings between attributes.The mapping between attributes may contain a data conversion process. We introduce a set of mapping operators for both entities and attributes. To verify the completeness of the operators set, a classification of possible mapping cases is presented and a resolution for every possible case of mapping is given using the introduced mapping operators.

It is too soon to evaluate the effectiveness of our approach for real-world mapping problems, since this work is currently at an early implementation stage. However, we are aware of the shortcomings of current semantic matching approaches. These approaches focus on finding specialization/generalization (i.e. hypernymy, hyponymy) relations when detecting the similarities between schema elements. They are capable of finding and providing information on subclass/superclass relations in schema definitions. A major difficulty obviously is the representational aggregation[2] and decomposition. As an example, the attributes of both classes *Shop* and *Staff* take part in the definition of the class *Bahnhof*. Detecting such relation between *Bahnhof* in the target schema and *RailwayStation*, *Shop* and *Staff* in the source schema is complicated for an automated semantic matching system and needs further investigation.

Acknowledgements. The authors are grateful to Matthias Trüb for invaluable comments and suggestions.

References

1. Bernstein, P.A.: Applying Model Management to Classical Meta Data Problems. Proceedings of the 1st Conference on Innovative Data Systems Research (2003)
2. Bernstein, P.A., Levy, A.Y., Pottinger, R.A.: A Vision for Management of Complex Models. Technical Report (MSR-TR-2000-53). Microsoft Research, Microsoft Corporation (2000)
3. Booch, G.: Object-Oriented Design with Applications. Benjamin/Cummings (1991)
4. Domenig, R., Dittrich, K.R.: A Query Based Approach for Integrating Heterogeneous Data Sources. Proceedings of the 9th International Conference on Information and Knowledge Management (2000) 453–460

---

[2] One may see *Shop* as "part-of" a *RailwayStation* (aggregation), while *Chief* is not "part-of" a *RailwayStation* and can only be regarded as representational aggregation.

5. Hakimpour, F., Geppert, A.: Global Schema Generation Using Formal Ontologies. Proceedings of the 21st International Conference on Conceptual Modeling (2002) 307–321
6. Kemmerer, S.J.: Step: the Great Experience. National Institute of Standards and Technology Special Publication (1999)
7. Lum, V.Y., Shu, N. C., Housel, B. C.: A General Methodology for Data Conversion and Restructuring. IBM J. Res. and Develop. **20(5)** (1976)
8. Miller, R.J., Haas, L.M., Hernández, M.A.: Schema Mapping as Query Discovery. Proceedings of the 26th International Conference on Very Large Data Bases (2000) 77–88
9. Rahm, E., Bernstein, P.A.: A Survey of Approaches to Automatic Schema Matching. VLDB Journal: Very Large Data Bases **10(4)** (2001) 334–350
10. Ram, S., Ramesh, V.: Schema Integration: Past, Current and Future. In: Elmagarmid, A., Rusinkiewicz, M., Sheth, A. (eds.): Management of Heterogeneous and Autonomous Database Systems. Morgan Kaufmann, The Morgan Kaufmann Series in Data Management Systems (1999)
11. Shu, N.C., Housel, B.C., Taylor, R.W., Ghosh, S.P., Lum, V.Y.: EXPRESS: A data EXtraction, Processing, and RESstructuring System. ACM Transactions on Database Systems. **2(2)** (1977)

Querying and Integrating Ontologies Viewed as Conceptual Schemas

Dimitri Theodoratos[1] and Theodore Dalamagas[2]

[1] Dept. of Computer Science
New Jersey Institute of Technology
USA
dth@cs.njit.edu
[2] Dept. of Elec. and Computer Engineering
National Technical University of Athens
Greece
dalamag@dblab.ece.ntua.gr

Abstract. Real-world ontologies have associated data sets. In order to exploit ontologies as a means to provide semantics to the data it is necessary not only to reason about concepts and their properties but also to be able to query the underlying data and efficiently obtain answers. We view ontologies as conceptual schemas that are populated with data. We define a generic graph-based representation for ontology schemas and provide a language for querying ontologies. This language is appropriate for ontology transformation and ontology integration. We show how ontologies can be integrated by defining views over multiple ontologies, and how user queries can be specified using views. Our approach can be easily implemented on top of a relational database management system.

1 Introduction

Ontologies aim at capturing domain knowledge and provide an understanding of that domain which may be used and shared across applications. The current development of the World Wide Web has promoted ontologies as a means to provide semantics to the data. Ontologies typically contain hierarchies of concepts and describe each concepts' features through properties and relations. Many real-world ontologies have associated data instances. In this sense, ontologies can be seen as instantiated conceptual schemas. In order to fully take advantage of ontologies it will be necessary not only to be able to reason with ontology schemas but also with the instances that populate these schemas. Current research efforts have concentrated on how to specify ontologies and on providing formal semantics to ontology languages. The issue of querying ontologies and efficiently obtaining answers over ontology instance sets has been neglected.

When we have various local ontologies, we are often required to build an integrated "global" ontology by extracting information from the local ones. A similar problem appears with data sources where a global schema needs to be constructed over multiple source schemas [15,13]. A typical approach to logical

I.-Y. Song et al. (Eds.): ER 2003, LNCS 2813, pp. 548–561, 2003.

data source integration uses mediators [19,8]. The mediators export a mediator schema which is an integrated representation of data sources. A mediator can be abstractly seen as a view defined over the data sources [17]. The users query the mediator schema, and the views transform these queries between the mediator schema and the data sources. These techniques for integrating data sources can be also applied to the integration of ontologies provided that a query language for ontologies is available.

The main contributions of this paper are the following:

- We present a model for ontologies. Ontologies in this model have schemas and instances. Isa hierarchies and axioms expressing constraints can be specified in a schema. We do not adhere to a specific representation language and we view an ontology schema as a graph.
- We provide a simple language for querying ontologies. Queries in this language are intuitive because they are ontology schemas annotated with relational algebra expressions and other characterizations. Queries can, in addition, specify isa-relationships and axioms.
- A notable feature of the language is that the answers of the queries are ontologies. Therefore, queries can also be used to transform ontologies.
- The query language allows the integration of ontologies through the definition of views over multiple local ontologies.
- We show how the query language can be extended so that queries can be defined using ontology integrating views.
- Since the instances of the ontologies are relations and the expressions that compute the answers of the queries are extended relational algebra expressions, the whole system can be easily implemented on top of a relational data base management system thus taking advantage of its storage and query optimization techniques.

Several formal languages to specify ontologies have been used or proposed, especially for the Semantic Web: Frame Logic [14], Resource Description Language Schema (RDFS) [2], Ontology Inference Layer (OIL) [6,3], DAML+OIL [10], an expressive description logic language SQOD(D) [11] etc. These representation languages differ in their terminology and expressive power but they model ontologies that share most of the features presented here. Query languages for ontologies in [4,12] are conjunctive languages based on description logic. B Amman et al. use a simple sub-language of OQL defining trees to query global schemas viewed as ontologies over local XML data sources [7,1]. All these query languages return only tuples of values and therefore, they are not appropriate for integrating ontologies through the definition of views. The query language in [16] allows querying graph represented schemas in a more general setting but does not take into account isa-relationships and constraints and is not adequate for ontologies.

The rest of the paper is organized as follows. Section 2 introduces ontologies and ontology instances. The query language for ontologies is presented in Section 3. Section 4 shows how ontologies can be integrated by defining views over multiple ontologies, and how queries can then be expressed using views. The last section contains concluding remarks and directions for further research.

2   Ontologies and Ontology Instances

In this section, we formally define ontologies. An ontology specifies a conceptualization of a domain in terms of concepts, properties, roles, isa-relationships and axioms. Ontologies are associated with instances.

We assume three sets $\mathbf{C}$, $\mathbf{P}$, and $\mathbf{R}$ of names called *concepts*, *properties*, and *roles* respectively. The concepts represent model entities of interest in the domain. The concepts can have properties. Concepts and properties are collectively called *constructs*. From a conceptual point of view, there is not a clear distinction between concepts and properties besides the fact that properties cannot have other properties. Every concept C in $\mathbf{C}$ is associated with a set $dom(C)$ of concept instances, common to all the concepts. Every property P in $\mathbf{P}$ is associated with a set $dom(P)$ of property instances. A *role* is the name of a binary relation between a concept and a property, or between two concepts. The meaning of a role between a concept C and a property P is that concept C can have property P. The meaning of role R between concepts C_1 and C_2 is that concepts C_1 and C_2 can be associated through R. An *isa-relationship* involves two concepts and is denoted $isa(C_1, C_2)$, where C_1 and C_2 are concepts. Isa-relationships are interpreted with subset semantics. Concept C_1 is called subconcept of C_2 and inherits the roles in which C_2 is involved. Isa-relationships are transitive, and can be combined to form hierarchies of concepts. *Axioms* are boolean expression that involve concepts, properties and roles. We consider a number of axioms of specific type. Axioms denoted $rigid(R)$, $unique(R)$, and $identity(R)$, where R is a role between a concept and a property, determine rigidity, uniquenesss and identity features of roles between concepts and properties [9,18]. Axioms denoted $one\text{-}to\text{-}many(R)$, $many\text{-}to\text{-}one(R)$, $one\text{-}to\text{-}one(R)$, where R is a role between two concepts, determine cardinality ratio constraints for roles between two concepts. Axioms denoted $total\text{-}to\text{-}partial(R)$, $partial\text{-}to\text{-}total(R)$ and $total\text{-}to\text{-}total(R)$, where R is a role between two concepts, determine participation constraints for roles between concepts. The meaning of the axioms will be explained later.

Definition 1. An *ontology schema* $\mathcal{S}$ is a quintuple $(\mathcal{C}, \mathcal{P}, \mathcal{R}, \mathcal{I}, \mathcal{A})$, where
(a) $\mathcal{C}$ is a set of concepts.
(b) $\mathcal{P}$ is a set of properties.
(c) $\mathcal{R}$ is a set of roles that does not include more than one role between a concept in $\mathcal{C}$ and a property in $\mathcal{P}$ (in contrast, $\mathcal{R}$ can include multiple roles between two concepts). In particular, for every concept $C \in \mathcal{C}$ (resp. property $P \in \mathcal{P}$), there is a role in $\mathcal{R}$ involving C (resp. P).[1]
(d) $\mathcal{I}$ is a set of isa-relationships $isa(C_1, C_2)$, where $C_1, C_2 \in \mathcal{C}$.
(e) $\mathcal{A}$ is a set of axioms of the type mentioned above where R is a role in $\mathcal{R}$. □

We do not stick with a specific language for ontologies of those that are recently suggested and we use a graph representation.

---

[1] We assume that roles are defined between distinct concepts. A *recursive* role, that is a role involving the same concept twice, can be modeled using a role between two distinct concepts and mutual isa-relationships between these concepts.

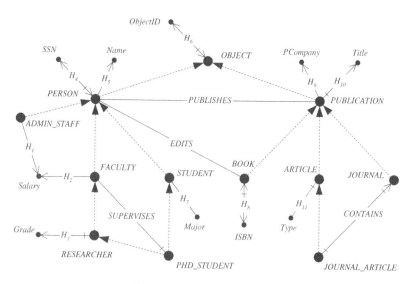

Fig. 1. An ontology schema

Example 1. Figure 1 shows an ontology schema of persons and publications inspired by an ontology presented in [5]. Nodes represent constructs. Nodes shown as bigger filled circles represent concepts, while smaller ones represent properties. Construct names are depicted close to the respective circles. For instance, *PERSON*, *STUDENT*, and *PUBLICATION* are concepts, and *SSN*, *Name*, and *ISBN* are properties. Edges between constructs represent roles. Their names are depicted on the edges. Symbolic names, H_1, H_2 etc. are used for roles between concepts and properties since the meaning of such roles is that a concept has a certain property. For instance, H_5 is a role between concept *PERSON* and property *Name*, and *PUBLISHES* is a role between concepts *PERSON* and *PUBLICATION*.

Dashed arcs represent isa-relationships. For instance the arc from concept *FACULTY* to concept *PERSON* identifies *FACULTY* as a subconcept of *PERSON*. Concept *PHD_STUDENT* is a subconcept of concepts *RESEARCHER* and *STUDENT* and inherits the roles of both of them.

An arrow on an edge (role) R between a concept and a property pointing to the concept (resp. property) denotes axiom *identity(R)* (resp. *unique(R)*). For instance the arrow on edge H_4 pointing to concept *PERSON* denotes axiom *identity(H_4)*, while the arrow on edge H_5 pointing to property *Name* denotes axiom *unique(H_5)*. A small perpendicular line by the concept on an edge (role) R between a concept and a property denotes axiom *rigid(R)*. For instance, the line on edge H_{10} denotes axiom *rigid(H_{10})*.

An arrow on an edge $R(C_1, C_2)$ between concepts C_1 and C_2 pointing to concept C_1 (resp. C_2) denotes axiom *one-to-many(R)* (resp. *many-to-one(R)*). For instance, the arrow on edge *CONTAINS(JOURNAL, JOURNAL_ARTICLE)* pointing to concept

$JOURNAL$ denotes axiom $one\text{-}to\text{-}many(CONTAINS)$. A perpendicular line on edge $R(C_1, C_2)$ by the concept C_1 (resp. C_2) denotes axiom $total\text{-}to\text{-}partial(R)$ (resp. $partial\text{-}to\text{-}total(R)$). For instance, the line on the edge $CONTAINS(JOURNAL, JOURNAL\_ARTICLE)$ by the concept $JOURNAL$ denotes axiom $total\text{-}to\text{-}partial(CONTAINS)$, while the line on the edge $SUPERVISES(FACULTY, PHD\_STUDENT)$ by the concept $PHD\_STUDENT$ denotes axiom $partial\text{-}to\text{-}total(SUPERVISES)$. The presence of a line by both concepts of edge R denotes axiom $total\text{-}to\text{-}total(R)$; e.g. the lines on edge $CONTAINS$ denote axiom $total\text{-}to\text{-}total(CONTAINS)$. □

Ontology instances are defined using exclusively role instance sets. The instance set of a role is a binary relation. We follow the approach to the relational model of data that uses attribute names. The names of the attributes are constructs (concepts or properties).

Definition 2. An *instance set of a role between a concept C and a property P* is a binary relation whose schema is (C, P) and whose instance is a finite set of tuples (c, p), where $c \in dom(C)$ and $p \in dom(P)$. An *instance set of a role between two concepts C_1 and C_2* is a binary relation whose schema is (C_1, C_2) and whose instance is a finite set of tuples (c_1, c_2), where $c_1 \in dom(C_1)$ and $c_2 \in dom(C_2)$. In the following we confound a role with its instance set. □

Consider an ontology schema $\mathcal{S} = (\mathcal{C}, \mathcal{P}, \mathcal{R}, \mathcal{I}, \mathcal{A})$. Let C, C_1, C_2 be concepts in $\mathcal{C}$. $\mathcal{R}_C$ denotes the set of roles in $\mathcal{R}$ between C and a property or a concept.

Definition 3. The *instance set* of concept C, denoted $inst(C)$, is the set of concept instances from $dom(C)$ that appear in instance sets of roles in $\mathcal{R}_C$. That is, $inst(C) = \bigcup_{R \in \mathcal{R}_C} \Pi_C(R)$, where Π_C denotes the relational projection operator on attribute C. □

An isa-relationship $isa(C_1, C_2)$ states that $inst(C_1) \subseteq inst(C_2)$. If concept C_2 is involved in a role $R(C_2, X)$, where X is a construct in $\mathcal{S}$, then R is inherited by C_1. The inherited role is denoted $R[C_1]$, if X is a property, and $R[C_1, X]$, if X is a concept. The schema of the instance set of this inherited role is (C_1, X) and its extension is the restriction of the extension of R to tuples that involve elements of $inst(C_1)$. For instance, in Figure 1, role H_4 inherited by concept $RESEARCHER$ is denoted $H_4[RESEARCHER]$, while role $PUBLISHES$ inherited by concepts $STUDENT$ and $ARTICLE$ is denoted $PUBLISHES[STUDENT, ARTICLE]$.

The association of instances of a concept in an ontology with instances of a certain property is not necessarily complete: let $R(C, P)$ be a role between a concept C and a property P; instances of C that are related with property instances of P in R, are not necessarily related to other property or concept instances in other roles involving C, and conversely. Axiom $rigid(R)$ states that for every role $R' \in \mathcal{R}$, $\Pi_C(R') \subseteq \Pi_C(R)$. This axiom requires property P of C to be rigid, that is essential to all instances of concept C. Indeed, $rigid(R)$ implies that $inst(C) = \Pi_C(R)$.

A property instance can be associated with more than one instance of a concept in an ontology. Axiom $identity(R)$ states that the same instance of

H_4

PERSON	SSN
p_1	123456789
p_2	987654321
p_3	567891234
p_4	678912345

H_5

PERSON	Name
p_1	Smith
p_2	Brown
p_3	Smith

PUBLISHES

PERSON	PUBLICATION
p_1	u_3
p_3	u_4

EDITS

PERSON	BOOK
p_1	$u1$
p_2	u_2

H_3

RESEARCHER	Grade
p_1	senior
p_2	senior
p_3	junior

H_8

BOOK	ISBN
u_1	$0 - 8053 - 1655 - 4$
u_2	$0 - 7762 - 2344 - 4$

H_{11}

ARTICLE	Type
u_3	research
u_4	review

H_9

PUBLICATION	PCompany
u_1	Springer
u_3	AW
u_4	IEEE

Fig. 2. Role instance sets

property P is not associated with distinct instances of concept C in R. In this sense, P can act as an identity of C (for those instances of C that are related to instances of P in R). More formally, $identity(R)$ is the boolean expression $\forall c, c' \in dom(C)\ \forall p \in dom(P)\ (R(c,p) \wedge R(c',p) \Rightarrow c = c')$. In relational terms, $identity(R)$ implies that P is a key of relation $R(C, P)$. If $rigid(R)$ holds in addition to $identity(R)$, property P is an identity of C for all instances in $inst(C)$.

A concept instance can be associated with more than one instance of a property in an ontology. Axiom $unique(R)$ states that property P is unique, that is, an instance of concept C is not associated with more than one instance of property P in R. More formally, $unique(R)$ is the boolean expression $\forall c \in dom(C)\ \forall p, p' \in dom(P)\ (R(c,p) \wedge R(c,p') \Rightarrow p = p')$. In relational terms, $unique(R)$ implies that C is a key of relation $R(C, P)$.

Let $R(C_1, C_2)$ be a role between concepts C_1 and C_2. Cardinality ratio axioms $one\text{-}to\text{-}many(R)$, $many\text{-}to\text{-}one(R)$, and $one\text{-}to\text{-}one(R)$ restrict the number of concept instances a concept instance can be related to in R. Axiom $one\text{-}to\text{-}many(R)$ is the boolean expression $\forall c_1, c_1' \in dom(C_1)\ \forall c_2 \in dom(C_2)\ (R(c_1,c_2) \wedge R(c_1', c_2) \Rightarrow c_1 = c_1')$. Axiom $many\text{-}to\text{-}one(R)$ is the symmetric expression. Axiom $one\text{-}to\text{-}one(R)$ is the expression $one\text{-}to\text{-}many(R) \wedge many\text{-}to\text{-}one(R)$.

Participation axioms $total\text{-}to\text{-}partial(R)$, $partial\text{-}to\text{-}total(R)$ and $total\text{-}to\text{-}total(R)$ specify whether all the instances in the instance set of a concept are related to another concept in R. Axiom $total\text{-}to\text{-}partial(R)$ states that $Inst(C_1) \subseteq \Pi_{C_1}(R)$. Axiom $partial\text{-}to\text{-}total(R)$ states that $Inst(C_2) \subseteq \Pi_{C_2}(R)$. Axiom $total\text{-}to\text{-}total(R)$ is the expression $partial\text{-}to\text{-}total(R) \wedge total\text{-}to\text{-}total(R)$.

Definition 4. An *instance* of an ontology schema $\mathcal{S} = (\mathcal{C}, \mathcal{P}, \mathcal{R}, \mathcal{I}, \mathcal{A})$, denoted $inst(\mathcal{S})$, is a set of instance sets of all the roles in $\mathcal{R}$ that satisfy the isa-relationships in $\mathcal{I}$ and the axioms in $\mathcal{A}$. An *ontology* $\mathcal{O}$ is a pair $(\mathcal{S}, inst(\mathcal{S}))$. $\square$

Example 2. Figure 2 shows part of the ontology schema of Figure 1. Only some of the instance sets of the roles are depicted. Clearly, $inst(PERSON) = \{p_1, p_2, p_3, p_4\}$, and $inst(RESEARCHER) = \{p_1, p_2, p_3\}$. Therefore, these role instance sets satisfy the isa-relationship $isa(RESEARCHER, PERSON)$ of the ontology schema of Figure 1. One can see that they also satisfy the axioms $rigid(H_4)$, $unique(H_5)$, and $identity(H_8)$ of this ontology schema.   □

3   A Query Language for Ontologies

We present in this section a query language for ontologies. This language adheres to the graph representation for ontologies shown in the previous section. Queries in this language are ontology schemas where roles are associated with expressions. Query answers are ontologies.

Syntax. We first present the syntax of the query language.

Definition 5. A *query* Q over an ontology schema $\mathcal{S}$ is an ontology schema such that:
1. Every property in Q is involved in exactly one role.
2. Every role $R(C, X)$ in Q, where C is a concept and X is a construct, is associated with a relational algebra expression that involves roles from $\mathcal{O}$. Given an instance for $\mathcal{S}$, this expression evaluates to a relation whose schema is (C, X).
3. The roles in Q are characterized as *restrictive* or *non-restrictive*.
4. The constructs in Q are characterized as *shown* or *hidden*. At least one construct in Q is shown. A role $R(C, X)$ in Q is called *shown* if both C and X are shown. Otherwise it is called *hidden*. A shown construct must be involved in at least one shown role.   □

Intuitively, shown concepts and roles (as opposed to hidden ones) appear in the answer of the query. Role expressions specify an initial instance set for the roles in this answer. Restrictive roles (as opposed to non-restrictive ones) force the instances in the instance sets of their concepts to be chosen from the instances appearing in their instance set. They do so by restricting the instance sets of the roles with whom they share concepts.

A role expression is built using the usual relational algebra operators: selection (σ_c, where c is a Boolean combination of selection predicates), projection (Π_X, where X is a set of attributes), join ($\bowtie_c$, where c is a conjunction of join predicates), union ($\cup$), intersection ($\cap$), difference ($-$), and attribute renaming ($\rho_{A \to B}$, where A and B are attribute names). Set theoretic operations ($\cup$, $\cap$, $-$) require the operand relations to be union compatible. Role expressions satisfy also the following restrictions: (1) The expression of a role between a concept and a property does not involve join operators. (2) The expression of a role between concepts does not involve selection operators. (3) Selection and join conditions in the expression of a role do not involve concepts.

Semantics. Let Q be a query over an ontology $\mathcal{O} = (\mathcal{S}, inst(\mathcal{S}))$. Let also $e_1, \ldots, e_n$, $n \geq 0$, be the expressions associated with restrictive roles in Q, and

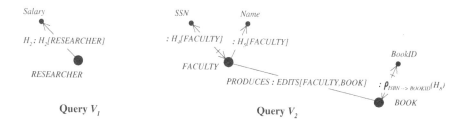

Fig. 3. Queries V_1 and V_2

$e'_1, \ldots, e'_m$, $m \geq 0$, be the expressions associated with non-restrictive roles in Q. We define expression $E = (e_1 \bowtie \ldots \bowtie e_n) \ltimes (e'_1 \ltimes \ldots \ltimes e'_m)$. The *instance set of a role* $R(C, X)$ *in* Q is the relation resulting by evaluating the expression $\Pi_{C,X}(E)$.

Definition 6. The *answer* of Q is the empty set, if the instance sets of the roles in Q do not satisfy the isa-relationships and the axioms in Q. Otherwise, the *answer* of Q is an ontology $\mathcal{O}' = (\mathcal{O}', inst(\mathcal{O}'))$ where:
(a) The ontology schema $\mathcal{O}'$ is defined by the shown constructs and roles and the isa-relationships between shown concepts of Q.
(b) The instance $inst(\mathcal{S}')$ of $\mathcal{S}'$ is the set of the instance sets of the shown roles in Q. □

An alternative representation for $inst(\mathcal{S}')$ in the form of a single relation (possibly containing null values) is provided by evaluating the expression $E' = P_Y(E)$, where P denotes the duplicate and null preserving projection operator, and Y is the set of constructs in S'. Clearly, the instance sets of the roles in S' can be derived from the resulting relation.

In the rest of this section we provide example queries over the ontology schema shown in Figure 1. The queries below involve simple operations and axioms.

Example 3. Figure 3 shows queries V_1 and V_2. The expression of a role follows the name of the role separated by a colon. All the constructs are shown constructs and the all the roles are restrictive. Query V_1 retrieves the researchers and their salaries. The expression that computes the instance of the resulting ontology (in the form of a single relation) is $P_{RESEARCHER,Salary}(H_2[RESEARCHER])$.

Query V_2 retrieves the SSN and the $Name$ of faculty members and the $ISBN$ of the books they have edited. The role between $FACULTY$ and $BOOK$ is renamed $PRODUCES$, and the property $ISBN$ is renamed $BookID$. In this query (and quite often in the following) we omit the names of some roles and we mention only their expression. The expression that computes the instance of the resulting ontology is $P_{SSN,Name,FACULTY,BookID}(H_4[FACULTY] \bowtie H_5[FACULTY] \bowtie EDITS[FACULTY,BOOK] \bowtie \rho_{ISBN \to BookID}(H_8))$. □

The next queries involve selection operations and hidden and shown edges.

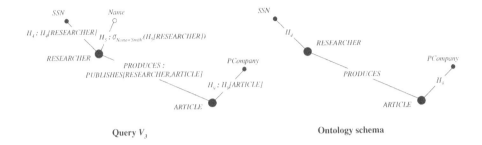

Fig. 4. Query V_3 and the resulting ontology schema

SSN	RESEARCHER	ARTICLE	PCompany
123456789	p_1	u_3	AW
567891234	p_3	u_4	IEEE

Fig. 5. Instance of the ontology resulting from query V_3

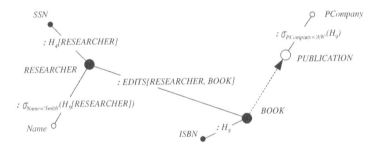

Fig. 6. Query V_4

Example 4. Query V_3 of Figure 4 retrieves the SSN of researchers named 'Smith' and the publishing company of the articles they have published. All the roles are restructive. Property $Name$ is hidden. Hidden constructs are depicted in the figures by white circles. The schema of the resulting ontology is also shown in Figure 4. The expression that computes the instance of the resulting ontology is $P_{SSN,RESEARCHER,ARTICLE,PCompany}(H_4[RESEARCHER] \bowtie \sigma_{Name='Smith'} (H_5[RESEARCHER]) \bowtie PUBLISHES [RESEARCHER, ARTICLE] \bowtie H_8[ARTICLE])$. This expression evaluated over the role instance sets of Figure 2 returns the relation shown in Figure 5.

Query V_4 (Figure 6) retrieves the SSN of researchers named 'Smith' and the $ISBN$ of the books they have edited but only if all these books are published by the company AW. Based on the role instance sets of Figure 2, one can see that $inst(BOOK) \not\subseteq inst(PUBLICATION)$ in V_4. Therefore the answer of query V_4 is the empty set. □

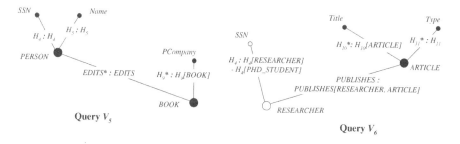

Fig. 7. Queries V_5 and V_6

SSN	Name	PERSON	BOOK	PCompany
123456789	Smith	p_1	u_3	AW
987654321	Brown	p_2	u_2	null
567891234	Smith	p_3	null	null

Fig. 8. Instance of the ontology resulting from query V_5

The queries below involve restrictive and non-restrictive roles and set theoretic operations.

Example 5. Query V_5 of Figure 7 retrieves the SSN and the name of all persons. Also, it retrieves the books they have edited if they happen to have edited a book, and the publishing company of these books if this information is available. Roles $EDIT$ and H_9 are non-restrictive. Non-restrictive roles are specified on the figures by suffixing their name by a '*'. The expression that computes the instance of the resulting ontology is $P_{SSN,Name,RESEARCHER,BOOK,PCompany}$ $((H_4 \bowtie H_5) \;\rtimes\; (EDITS \;\rtimes\; H_9[BOOK]))$. The resulting relation over the role instance sets of Figure 2 is shown in Figure 8.

Query V_6 of Figure 7 finds the type and the title of articles published by researchers that are not PhD students or just one of them if the other is missing. In fact, every instance of $ARTICLE$ in the resulting ontology instance is related to an instance of both properties $Type$ and $Title$ because of the axioms $rigid(H_{11})$ and $rigid(H_{10})$ and the isa-relationship $isa(ARTICLE, PUBLICATION)$ of the ontology of Figure 1. The instance of the resulting ontology can be computed by the expression $P_{ARTICLE,Type,Title}(((H_4[RESEARCHER] \; - \; H_4[STUDENT]) \bowtie PUBLISHES[RESEARCHER, ARTICLE]) \;\rtimes\; (H_{10}[ARTICLE] \;\rtimes\; H_{11}))$.   □

The instance of an ontology is a set of relations and can be stored in a relational database. The expressions associated with the roles of a query are relational algebra expressions, while those that compute the role instance sets of the answer are extended relational algebra expressions. There are two advantages related to these features: (a) queries over ontologies can be easily trans-

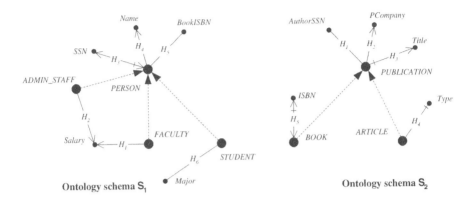

Fig. 9. Ontology schemas $\mathcal{S}_1$ and $\mathcal{S}_2$

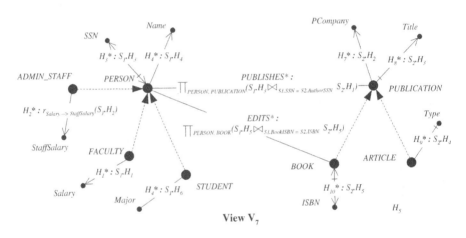

Fig. 10. View V_7 integrating the ontology schemas $\mathcal{S}_1$ and $\mathcal{S}_2$

lated to queries in a popular relational query language (e.g. SQL) over relational databases, and (b) well known query optimization techniques for centralized and distributed database systems can be employed for evaluating queries on ontologies.

4   Ontology Integration

We show in this section how we can express queries over multiple ontology schemas. Then, we define views and show how queries and views can be defined using views.

Queries can be defined over multiple ontology schemas. In order to do so the schema names precede the names of their roles and concepts separated by a period.

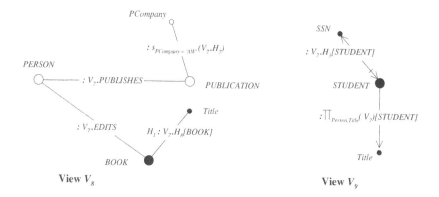

Fig. 11. Views V_8 and V_9 defined using view V_7

Example 6. Consider the ontology schemas of Figure 9. Schema S_1 is an ontology schema of persons which provides also information about the books edited by these people in the form of property $BookISBN$. Schema S_2 is an ontology schema of publications which provides also information about the identity of the authors of the publications in the form of property $AuthorSSN$. We assume that both ontologies are defined over the same sets of concept, property and role names and thus their respective domains are common.

Figure 10 shows a query that integrates the two ontologies into one global ontology. Roles H_5 from S_1, and H_1 from S_2 between concepts and properties are transformed into roles $EDITS$ and $PUBLISHES$ between concepts from different schemas. The expressions of the new roles in the query join expressions of roles between concepts and properties on properties with common domains. All the roles are non-restrictive. Therefore, no information is lost and the instance sets of the roles of the initial schemas can be recovered from the global ontology resulting by evaluating the integrating query V_7 (though this is not always required).   □

A view is a named query. Since the answer of a view is an ontology, a query (or another view) can be defined using exclusively or inclusively the schema of the answer ontology. Any shown edge of a view can be evoked in the expression of a role in a query preceded by the name of the view. The instance set of this role is the one in the instance of the answer of the query. Further, every two shown constructs C, X (two concepts, or a concept and a property) of a view V can be evoked in a role expression in a query even if there is no role in the query between these constructs. This "virtual" role is denoted $\Pi_{C,X}(V)$ in the role expressions and its instance set is $\Pi_{C,X}(A)$, where A is the single relation representation of the instance of the answer ontology.

Example 7. View V_8 of Figure 11 is defined exclusively using view V_7 of Figure 10. It retrieves the titles of the books edited by a person who has a publication published by the company 'AW'.

View V_9 (Figure 11) is also defined exclusively using view V_7 and computes the SSN of the students and the titles of their publications. Note that the expression of the role between student and title does not refer to an existing role in view V_7. $\square$

5 Conclusion

The proliferation of the use of ontologies and their population with data necessitate languages for querying ontologies. We have presented a model for ontologies that distinguishes between schemas and instances and we have provided a query language for this model. Queries in this language return ontologies. This feature allows the language to be used for both: transforming ontologies and obtaining answers. Further, the query language can be used for ontology integration by defining views over multiple ontologies. We have extended the query language so that users can define queries over integrating views.

We are currently working towards extending the query language with grouping and aggregation operations and with path expressions. We are also investigating how the language can be coupled with ontology transformation rules. Graduate students at NJIT have already implemented part of our approach on top of a relational database management system.

References

1. B. Amann, C. Beeri, I. Fundulaki, and M. Scholl. Ontology-Based Integration of XML Web Resources. In *Proc. of the International Semantic Web Conference*, pages 117–131, 2002.
2. D. Brickley and R. Guha. RDF Vocabulary Description Language 1.0: RDF Schema. *W3C Working Draft*, Jan. 23, 2003; available on line at http://www.w3.org/TR/2003/WD-rdf-schema-20030123/.
3. J. Broekstra, M. C. A. Klein, S. Decker, D. Fensel, and F. van Harmelen. Enabling Knowledge Representation on the Web by Extending RDF Schema. *Computer Networks*, 39(5):609–634, 2002.
4. D. Calvanese, G. D. Giacomo, and M. Lenzerini. A Framework for Ontology Integration. In *Proc. of the Semantic Web Working Symposium*, 2001.
5. M. Erdman and R. Studer. How to Structure and Access XML documents with Ontologies. *Data & Knowledge Engineering*, 36(3):317–335, 2001.
6. D. Fensel, I. Horrocks, F. van Harmelen, S. Decker, M. Erdmann, and M. C. A. Klein. OIL in a nutsell. In *Proc. of the 12th Intl. Conf. on Knowledge Acquisition, Modeling and Management (EKAW'00)*, volume 1937 of *Lecture Notes in Computer Science*, pages 1–16. Springer, 2000.
7. I. Fundulaki, B. Amann, M. Scholl, C. Beeri, and A.-M. Vercoustre. Mapping xml fragments to community web ontologies. In *Proc. of the Fourth International Workshop on the Web and Databases*, 2001.
8. H. Garcia-Molina, Y. Papakonstantinou, D. Quass, A. Rajaraman, Y. Sagiv, J. D. Ullman, V. Vassalos, and J. Widom. The TSIMMIS Approach to Mediation: Data Models and Languages. *Journal of Intelligent Information Systems*, 8(2):117–132, 1997.

9. N. Guarino and C. A. Welty. A Formal Ontology of Properties. In *Proc. of the 12th Intl. Conf. on Knowledge Engineering and Knowledge Management*, Lecture Notes in Computer Science. Springer, 2000.

10. I. Horrocks. DAML+OIL: a Reason-able Web Ontology Language. In *Proc. of the 5th Intl. Conf. on Extending Database Technology*, pages 2–13, 2002.

11. I. Horrocks and U. Sattler. Ontology Reasoning in the SHOQ(D) Description Logic. In *Proc. of the 17th Intl. Joint Conference on Artificial Intelligence*, pages 199–204, 2001.

12. I. Horrocks and S. Tessaris. Querying the Semantic Web: A Formal Approach. In *Proc. Of the International Semantic Web Conference*, pages 177–191, 2002.

13. R. Hull. Managing Semantic Heterogeneity in Databases: A Theoretical Perspective. In *Proc. of the 16th ACM Symp. on Principles of Database Systems*, pages 51–61, 1997.

14. M. Kifer, G. Lausen, and J. Wu. Logical Foundations of Object-Oriented and Frame-Based Languages. *Journal of the ACM*, 42(4):741–843, 1995.

15. M. Lenzerini. Data Integration: A Theoretical Perspective. In *Proc. of the 21st ACM Symp. on Principles of Database Systems*, pages 233–246, 2002.

16. D. Theodoratos. Semantic Integration and Querying of Heterogeneous Data Sources Using a Hypergraph Data Model. In *Proc. of the 19th British National Conference on Databases*, pages 166–182, 2002.

17. J. Ullman. Information Integration Using Logical Views. In *Proc. of the 6th Intl. Conf. on Database Theory*, 1997.

18. C. A. Welty and N. Guarino. Supporting Ontological Analysis of Taxonomic Relationships. *Data & Knowledge Engineering*, 39(1):51–74, 2001.

19. G. Wiederhold. Mediators in the Architecture of Future Information Systems. *Computer*, 25(3):38–49, 1992.

A Comparison of Frameworks for Enterprise Architecture Modeling

Richard Martin[1] and Edward Robertson[2]

1 Tinwisle Corporation
2 Indiana University

This presentation compares and contrasts two distinct approaches to the representation and management of models relating to enterprise complexity. The approaches share a common focus on describing the enterprise domain, although in different ways. Each approach has an audience of existing supporters. The first approach organizes models according to the perspectives of model users and is exemplified by the Zachman Framework for Enterprise Architecture, which has gained popularity over the past decade in a wide variety of commercial and government settings. The second approach uses life cycle as its organizing theme and is exemplified by three ISO standards related to industrial automation and systems engineering (15704:2000, 19439:2003, and 15288:2002), all of which build upon decades of practice. The two approaches are seen to use a framework structure with a common meta-meta-model [1] and are found to be complementary. Each approach serves a distinct and essential need in the effort to understand and realize a successful enterprise.

A framework approach presents the architecture of the enterprise as articulated by the models built to describe that enterprise. Each approach recognizes the importance of model representations as an enlightening way of describing complex enterprise reality. For each, the expression of such representations is considered critical to effective and efficient enterprise operation. These framework archetypes enable a better understanding of common themes in enterprise management observed over many years of practice. Whether the frameworks address manufacturing operations, process control, information systems, or government bureaucracy, the models produced to describe the enterprise comprise a valuable asset requiring its own distinct management. Management of that asset is the reason frameworks for enterprise architecture modeling are conceived, built and used.

Fundamental to the examination of frameworks for enterprise models are principles for enterprise architecture, principles that encompass any effort to adequately describe the complex system known as an enterprise in a framework context. We compare the two approaches and identify their unique contributions to organizing the complexity of enterprise models with respect to these principles. Among the principles are strategic aspects that lead to formalizable approaches amenable to computational methods.

We identify the dimensions of an enterprise domain addressed by each approach. These range from the interrogative questions of Zachman to the entire system life cycle of ISO 15704. Although each framework depicts the arrangement of models in a simple graphical form, the actual structure rises to meet the complexity associated with real enterprises.

I.-Y. Song et al. (Eds.): ER 2003, LNCS 2813, pp. 562–564, 2003.
© Springer-Verlag Berlin Heidelberg 2003

Structurally, items within these frameworks are arranged in one of two ways: (i) in an ordinant structure (i.e., a table, grid, or matrix) or (ii) in a decompositional structure (i.e., a tree). We call either of these a dimension of the arrangement. Dimensions of either kind are discrete and ordinant dimensions typically have only a few coordinate positions. The coordinate positions of an ordinant dimension may be ordered (e.g. ISO 19439 model phase) or unordered (e.g. Zachman interrogative) while only its containment relation orders a decompositional dimension.

There are (at least) three dimensions identified that roughly reflect conceptual (as opposed to physical) scale: (i) abstractness, ranging from abstract to concrete, (ii) scope, from general (generic) to special (specific), and (iii) detail, from coarse to fine. Using the previous terminology, abstractness and scope are ordinant-ordered and detail is decompositional.

We distinguish the thematic purpose for each framework approach from the various purposes for which frameworks are applied to enterprises. In the aspect of thematic purpose we begin to see the distinction each approach brings to enterprise understanding. Bound to this distinction are fundamental notions of representation with respect to time that correspond to methodological choices driven by modeling expectations. Comprehending this difference in thematic purpose is essential to the proper application of each approach and is the source of their complementary nature.

One, and typically only one, of a framework's ordinant-ordered dimensions reflects the thematic purpose expressed within a framework. For ISO 15704 this theme is "life-cycle" and for Zachman it is "perspective". Note that such a "purposive dimension" does not represent the purpose of the framework (which is to support a particular methodology or standard, and all dimensions should support that purpose) but instead represents the fact that artifacts derive their purpose from artifacts earlier in the dimension's order. The ordering of a purposive dimension often manifests itself as causality, dependency, or chronology. However, it is not merely a time dimension, even though purpose in a framework often leads to temporal ordering in enterprise operations.

It seems necessary, as one moves through a framework along its purposive dimension, from one place in the order to the next, that the entire framework structure at one coordinate is potentially relevant when describing an element at the next. This is not a claim that every element at one coordinate is in fact materially relevant for each element of the next; it is merely recognition that all of the models from prior coordinates can be useful in understanding and constructing the next. Moreover, it is sometimes as important to know which concerns are not needed as it is to know which are.

The decompositional "scale' dimension, detail, is fundamentally different in that it works (or a least works best) through decomposition and successive refinement. Thus frameworks should be recursive in their application. While neither archetype has an explicit recursive representation, presentations of both advocate recursive use. A major benefit of recursion in framework structure is that it directly supports a "drill-down" approach to framework development and exploration. Recursion is the structural mechanism for providing a layered approach and greatly facilitates building one unified framework out of several here-to-fore independent ones. Iteration is the procedural mechanism most often used to create recursive structures.

The complexity of an enterprise makes it impossible for a single descriptive representation to be humanly comprehensible in its entirety. Thus particular frameworks are often constructed with predefined views intended to usefully "package" subsets of their complex space. Such views are often described as if they comprise a distinct dimension, as is the case with ISO 15704 and ISO 19439, but such a collection of views is a result of the construction process rather than of the underlying model.

Views are not merely for viewing; they are used for constructing and populating frameworks. For example, entities are placed in the ER model through the "information view" of ISO 19439 rather than into the complete framework. Thus the "view update" problem from the world of relational database reappears in the context of frameworks.

Along a scope dimension, each approach brings a set of prototype or reference models that provide the basis for specific application of the framework to an enterprise. These range from simple associative prototypes to sophisticated reference model catalogs. Missing however is attention to critical needs for identifying model and enterprise components in ways that serve both the modelers and their audience in the complex context of an enterprise.

Essential to our assessment of each framework is the treatment of four defining aspects for formalization – structure, connections, views, and constraints. We assess the suitability of each framework for formal treatment and suggest mechanisms to achieve this formalization. Of particular interest is the restructuring of framework content to meet emerging needs and to provide for efficient population of the frameworks.

And finally we look at ways in which the two approaches can be used together in furthering the goals of enterprise operations. As a result of their complementary nature we observe an interesting possibility for transforming the contents of one framework approach into content for the other approach. Such transformations offer an opportunity to address the time-to-change function in enterprise operations by maintaining an "as is" enterprise condition for use in initiatives that are responding to changes in the enterprise environment.

References

1. R. Martin and E. Robertson: A Formal Enterprise Architecture Framework to Support Multi-model Analysis. Proceedings of the Fifth CAiSE/IFIP8.1 International Workshop on Evaluation of Modeling Methods in Systems Analysis and Design, Stockholm, 2000.

Bless the ODS

Michael Bryan and Ali M. Tafreshi

Nextel Communications
593 Herndon Parkway
Herndon, Virginia 20170, USA
{michael.bryan,ali.tafreshi}@nextel.com
http://www.nextel.com

Abstract. This article challenges the conventional role of operational data stores and staging areas in managing a corporate information factory (CIF). Vendors, consultants and industry publications have dedicated a lot of attention to the tools and uses of completely integrated data. Nextel's experience, however, suggests that the CIF's value and future may lie in its operational data store (ODS) rather than its integrated data warehouse. This article summarizes Nextel's experience in six misconceptions:

- Operational Data Responsibility - The ODS can serve as a data replication point among operational systems.

- Requirements - By sourcing more data than required, the ODS can isolate the CIF from requirements changes.

- Business Case - The ODS can justify the CIF with less discretionary and more persuasive business cases.

- Risk- The ODS can convert the CIF's data quality challenge from risk to service. Lost or incomplete business rules can be re-discovered from the behavior of source systems.

- Impact - The ODS can add smaller tactical impacts from operational reporting to the benefits of the CIF. It allows functional analysts to translate strategic decisions into operational actions.

- Sponsorship - The ODS allows a CIF's sponsorship to extend beyond an analytical champion.

The ODS may contain relationally transformed as well as staged source data without transformation. So, this article will use the term ODS to refer to both these forms of CIF data prior to updating an integrated data warehouse. Source data is a valuable asset, worth planning, measuring and formalizing. Imhoff, in the corporate information factory took the first step, introducing a legitimate architectural role for the operational data store. This article continues to advocate for and challenge conventional wisdom of an ODS' role in developing and managing a CIF environment.

Nextel launched its first data warehouse in 1996. In the last two years, however, several trends have shifted the mission and architecture of Nextel's CIF databases:

- Several systems were outsourced relieving the company of operational activities, but also isolating it from critical data resources. The CIF is now used to recover ownership of the relocated data, and validate the outsourced system.

I.-Y. Song et al. (Eds.): ER 2003, LNCS 2813, pp. 565–566, 2003.

- Client server and internet technologies dramatically changed the enterprise's data sources. The data warehouse now faces a data landscape that is highly fragmented and contains significant redundancy.

- Informational activities have become part of daily job. The data consumers now live in customer service, sales, collections, billing, and operations.

- Timeliness requirements have gone from monthly to daily and near-real time.

The impact of these trends on the CIF environment is shown in Table 1. These forces shifted Nextel's use of its CIF from a tactical and strategic role into much more of an operational one. They have also shifted the nature of the CIF from that of a valuable application to that of an architectural layer.

Table 1. Increased demand on the systems as a function of outsourced systems

Time	Data Size (trabytes)	Data feeds	No. of users	No. of outsourced Systems
1998	0.28	3	190	0
1999	0.40	8	270	0
2000	1.10	15	700	1
2001	6.30	28	1600	2
2002	23.80	40	3000	3

The data warehouse may contain organized data digestible by the end user. It may also be integrated with other data warehouses, but inherently it contains less "information" about the source systems and corporate operations. A data warehouse contains transformed data, which may have changed hands many times. The rules associated with each transformation may be lost, forgotten or changed. The data warehouse does hold a valuable place in the corporate data portfolio. The information from a data warehouse will lead to policies or campaigns, which will lead to strategic decisions. The impact of a strategic decision is measurable in longer time frames and ROI is difficult to calculate.

In order to take proper advantage of an ODS in a CIF environment, the mission of enterprise data modeling, data administration and management will become a CIF organization's responsibility. The value of a data organization to a corporation depends on leveraging the ODS. The ODS holds the true information on a corporation's operation. Any enhancements or investment on an ODS can be translated to value or actual dollars immediately.

Modeling Reactive Behavior in ORM

Terry Halpin[1] and Gerd Wagner[2]

[1] Northface University, Salt Lake City, Utah, USA
terry@northface.edu
[2] Eindhoven University of Technology Eindhoven, The Netherlands
G.Wagner@tm.tue.nl

1 Introduction

A system may exhibit proactive and reactive behavior. While proactive behavior is based on goal-directed action planning and execution, reactive behavior may be viewed as a set of reaction patterns that determine how the system reacts to events. Modeling reaction patterns is of particular importance for e-business systems, whose behavior is largely determined by their reactions to incoming messages.

Object-Role Modeling (ORM) is a fact-oriented approach for modeling information at a conceptual level. Unlike Entity-Relationship (ER) modeling and the class diagram technique of the Unified Modeling Language (UML), ORM makes no use of attributes as a base construct, instead expressing all fact types as relationships. This attribute-free approach leads to greater semantic stability in conceptual models and conceptual queries and enables ORM fact structures to be directly verbalized and populated using natural language sentences.

ORM supports mixfix predicates of any arity (unary, binary, ternary etc.), so its constraints and derivation rules may be directly verbalized in sentential form. ORM's graphic constraint notation is far more expressive than that of UML class diagrams or industrial ER. ORM is now supported by modeling tools that can automatically transform ORM schemas into physical database schemas. For such reasons, ORM is being increasingly used for conceptual analysis, as well as ontology specification.

Although ORM supports modeling of business terms, facts, and many *static* integrity constraints and derivation rules, ORM cannot model the *reactive behavior* of a system. Reaction patterns may be described using *dynamic* integrity constraints or *reaction rules*. These rules specify a triggering event type and a precondition, as well as a triggered action type and a postcondition. We discuss an extension of ORM, provisionally called ORM/RR, which allows one to model (action) events and reaction rules along with object types, fact types and static rules. This extension is inspired by the *Agent-Object-Relationship* (AOR) modeling language.

2 Extending ORM with Agents and Actions

Like ER modeling, ORM ignores dynamic aspects of information systems, such as communication, interaction, events, activities, and processes. ORM classifies objects into *entities* (non-lexical objects) and *values* (lexical objects). To capture semantic

I.-Y. Song et al. (Eds.): ER 2003, LNCS 2813, pp. 567–569, 2003.

aspects of the interaction dynamics, we further classify entities into *agents* and *passive entities*. Agents are sometimes called *actors*[1]. Unlike passive entities, agents can communicate, perceive, act, make commitments, and satisfy claims. Only agents may actively participate in business interactions.

Agents may interact with their inanimate environment (*non-social interaction*), or each other (*social interaction*). A simple example of a non-social interaction process is Gerd Wagner's reaction to turn on his office light when it becomes dark outside. Fig. 1 depicts a simple example of a social interaction process, where a library member requests a certain book from the library, the library confirms the request and delivers the book to that person, and he/she finally returns the book. This diagram is similar to a UML collaboration diagram, but the notation is based on ORM and AOR.

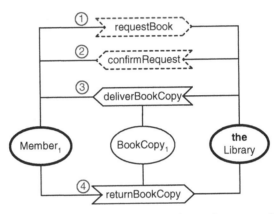

Fig. 1. An interaction sequence diagram for a social interaction process for library loans.

In ORM, object types are depicted as named ellipses (solid for entity types, and dashed for value types). *Object variables* (arbitrary instances of an object type) are subscripted, for example $Member_1$ and $BookCopy_1$. Prepending "the" to a type name indicates the type has only one instance, for example "**the** Library"—although such *unit object types* often feature in interaction diagrams, they are typically omitted from data models because their existence is implicit.

Agents are displayed with bold ellipses to distinguish them from passive entities. Events modeled as agent *actions* are depicted as named, wide arrows, directed from the agent performing the action to the agent perceiving the action. If the action is communicative (sending/receiving a message) the arrow border is dashed to reflect its lexical nature, for example requestBook. If the action is physical (non-lexical) in nature, the arrow border is solid, for example deliverBookCopy. A connection between an action and a passive entity (e.g. $BookCopy_1$) indicates the latter is involved in the action. Circled numbers depict the order in which actions take place.

---

[1] In UML, human and artificial agents that are users of a system appear as *actors* in *use cases* but remain external to the system model, while software agents within the boundaries of the system considered are called "active objects".

3   ORM and Reaction Rules

Interaction process types may be modeled using interaction patterns and associated *reaction rules*. Reaction rules may be used both for the *description* of the reactive behavior, and for the *executable specification* of the reaction patterns of an artificial agent to be built. An example reaction rule (expressed informally) is:

> *When the library receives a book request from a member, it checks whether a copy of that book is available, and if so, the request is confirmed, a new loan object is created, and a copy of the book is delivered to the faculty member*

Fig. 2 depicts an ORM model including a data-perspective of this reaction rule. Fact types are depicted as named sequences of role boxes (a role is a part played in a relationship). Derived fact types are marked by an asterisk, and formally specified by a derivation rule. To save space, some derivation rules are omitted here. The temporal order inherent in the interaction model (Fig. 1) and reaction rule is captured by subset constraints in either explicit (circled "⊆") or implicit form (e.g. implied by mandatory constraint). For example, a book request is confirmed only if it is fulfilled by a loan. Although temporal order may be modeled in ORM using mandatory, subset, equality, or subtype constraints, the corresponding dynamic processes are typically easier to understand and validate using interaction diagrams and reaction rule verbalizations. Such dynamic specifications may be used in conjunction with data use cases to seed ORM models.

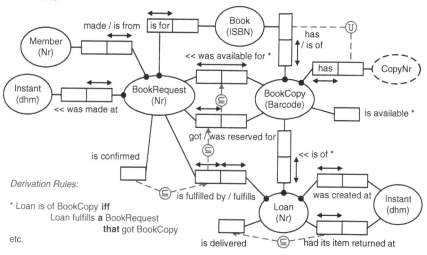

Fig. 2. ORM model for the library loan process depicted in Fig. 1.

To optimally integrate dynamic and static models, several research questions are under investigation. For example, to what extent can corresponding features of dynamic and static models be automatically transformed into one another? What formal logics are best for capturing the dynamic and language-act semantics of social interactions? How are information system viewpoints from the perspective of a single agent type best related to a global viewpoint of a system with multiple autonomous agents?

Developing Complex Systems with Object-Process Methodology Using OPCAT

Dov Dori, Iris Reinhartz-Berger, and Arnon Sturm

Technion, Israel Institute of Technology
Technion City, Haifa 32000, Israel
{dori@ie,ieiris@tx,sturm@tx}.technion.ac.il

Abstract. OPCAT – Object-Process CASE Tool – is an integrated systems engineering environment. It supports system lifecycle evolution using Object-Process Methodology (OPM). OPM integrates the object-oriented (structure) and process-oriented (behavior) paradigms into a single frame of reference through a combination of graphics and equivalent natural language. This short paper briefly describes OPM and demonstrates highlights of OPCAT and some of its capabilities.

1 The Basis: Object-Process Methodology

Object-Process Methodology (OPM) [1] is a holistic approach to the study and development of systems. It integrates the object-oriented and process-oriented paradigms into a single frame of reference. Structure and behavior, the two major aspects that each system exhibits, co-exist in the same OPM view without highlighting one at the expense of suppressing the other. The elements of the OPM ontology are entities (stateful objects and processes) and links. Objects are (physical or informatical) things that exist, while processes are things that transform objects. Links can be structural or procedural. Structural links express static relations between pairs of entities. Procedural links connect entities to describe the behavior of a system. The behavior is manifested in three major ways: processes can transform objects, objects can enable processes, and objects can trigger events that invoke processes.

Two semantically equivalent modalities, one graphic and the other textual, jointly express the same OPM model. A set of inter-related Object-Process Diagrams (OPDs) constitute the graphical, visual OPM formalism. Each OPM element is denoted in an OPD by a symbol, and the OPD syntax specifies correct and consistent ways by which entities can be linked. The Object-Process Language (OPL), defined by a grammar, is the textual counterpart modality of the graphical OPD-set. OPL is a dualpurpose language, oriented towards humans as well as machines. Catering to human needs, OPL is designed as a constrained subset of English, which serves domain experts and system architects engaged in analyzing and designing a system. Every OPD construct is expressed by a semantically equivalent OPL sentence or phrase. Designed also for machine interpretation, OPL provides a solid basis for automatically generating the designed application. This dual representation of OPM increases the processing capability of humans. Another advantage of OPM is its

I.-Y. Song et al. (Eds.): ER 2003, LNCS 2813, pp. 570–572, 2003.

complexity management mechanisms. OPM offers three refinement/abstraction mechanisms: (1) unfolding/folding is used for refining/abstracting the structural hierarchy of a thing; (2) in-zooming/out-zooming exposes/hides the inner details of a thing within its frame; and (3) state expressing/suppressing exposes/hides the states of an object. Using flexible combinations of these mechanisms, OPM enables specifying a system to any desired level of detail without losing legibility and comprehension of the resulting specification. The complete OPM system specification is a set of OPDs and their corresponding OPL paragraphs.

2 OPCAT Overview

Based on human cognition principles, OPCAT [2, 3] implements OPM and enables bimodal visual-lingual balanced modeling of the structural and behavioral aspects of systems in a single view. Due to this intuitive dual notation, the resulting model is comprehensible to both domain experts and system architects engaged in the development process. Due to OPM formality, OPCAT also provides a solid basis for implementation generation and an advanced simulation tool, which animates system behavior. OPCAT enables generic translation of the OPL (subset of English) script to various formal target languages. Currently we generate Java code from OPL.

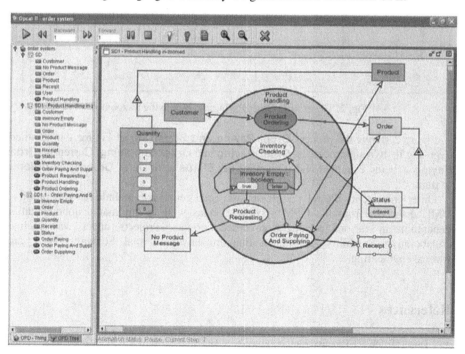

Fig. 1. A snapshot of OPCAT simulating an inventory system

Figure 1 is a snapshot of OPCAT simulating an inventory system. The OPD shows in dark green objects that already exist (e.g., **Customer, Product**), while light green, becoming dark, (e.g., **Order**) represents objects being generated. Dark blue is the process currently in action (**Product Ordering**), while light blue (**Product Handling**) is the higher-level process of which the current process is subprocess. The red dots indicate the progress of the control. For example, the red dot along the arrow (result link) from **Product Ordering** to **Order** indicates that **Product Ordering** is about half done so **Order** is about half ready.

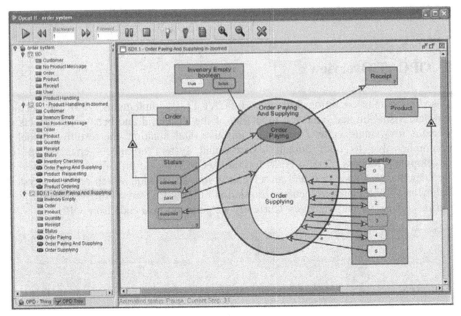

Fig. 2. The process Order Paying and Supplying in-zoomed

Figure 2 shows the process **Order Paying and Supplying** of Figure 1 in-zoomed, exposing its two subprocesses, **Order Paying** and **Order Supplying**. Currently, **Order Paying** is being executed and it changes the **Status** attribute of **Order** from **ordered** to **paid**.

Other prominent OPCAT features beside code generation include the generation of UML diagrams from the OPM specification as well as automated documentation generation in various parameter-governed formats. Projects under way include collaborative capability, automated diagram layout, Visual Semantic Web, and reverse engineering.

References

1. Dori, D. Object-Process Methodology – A Holistic Systems Paradigm, Springer-Verlag, Berlin, Heidelberg, New York, 2002.
2. Dori, D. Reinhartz-Berger, I. and Sturm A. *OPCAT* – A Bimodal Case Tool for Object-Process Based System Development. 5th International Conference on Enterprise Information Systems (ICEIS 2003), pp. 286–291, 2003.
3. OPCAT download site: http://www.ObjectProcess.org

Conceptual Data Models for Engineering Information Modeling and Formal Transformation of EER and EXPRESS-G

Z.M. Ma, Shiyong Lu, and Farshad Fotouhi

Department of Computer Science, Wayne State University,
Detroit, MI 48202, USA
{ma,shiyong,fotouhi}@cs.wayne.edu

1 Conceptual Data Models for Engineering Information Modeling

Nowadays computer-based information systems have become the nerve center of current manufacturing systems. The requirement on engineering information modeling is hereby potential [8]. Viewed from database systems, engineering information modeling can be identified at two levels: conceptual data modeling and logical database modeling, which result in conceptual data models and logical database models respectively. Engineering information modeling generally starts from conceptual data models which are then mapped into logical database models. Since conceptual data models can capture and represent richer and more complex semantics in engineering applications at a high abstract level, much attention has been paid to the conceptual data modeling of engineering information and some conceptual data models have been used for this purpose, e.g., ER/EER [3], IDEF1X [5], and EXPRESS [9].

Traditional ER/EER can be used for engineering information modeling at conceptual level. However, limited by their power in engineering modeling, some new conceptual data models have been developed. IDEF1X is a method for designing relational databases with a syntax designed to support the semantic constructs necessary in developing a conceptual schema applied in computer integrated manufacturing systems. In order to implement the sharing and exchange of product data, the Standard for the Exchange of Product Model Data (STEP) is being developed by the International Organization for Standardization (ISO). STEP provides a means to describe a product model throughout its life cycle and to exchange data between different units. STEP [6, 7] consists of 4 major categories: *description methods, implementation methods, conformance testing methodology and framework*, and *standardized application data models/schemata*. EXPRESS, being the description methods of STEP and a conceptual schema language, can model product design, manufacturing, and production data. EXPRESS model is now becoming a major conceptual data model for engineering information modeling [4].

I.-Y. Song et al. (Eds.): ER 2003, LNCS 2813, pp. 573–575, 2003.

2 The Requirement on Transformation of Conceptual Data Models

In contrast to ER/EER and IDEF1X, EXPRESS is not a graphical schema language. In order to construct EXPRESS data model at a higher level of abstract, EXPRESS-G is introduced as the graphical representation of EXPRESS. Here EXPRESS-G can only express a subset of the full language of EXPRESS, which provides supports for the notions of entity, type, relationship, cardinality, and schema. The functions, procedures, and rules in EXPRESS language are not supported by EXPRESS-G. In addition to EXPRESS-G, it is also suggested in STEP that IDEF1X or ER/EER can be used as one of the optional languages for EXPRESS data model design. Then EXPRESS-G, IDEF1X, ER/EER, or even UML [2] data model can be translated into EXPRESS data model.

That multiple graphical data models can be employed facilitates the designers with different background to design their EXPRESS models easily by using one of the graphical data models that they are familiar with. There are already some efforts for converting EXPRESS-G, IDEF1X, ER/EER, or UML data model into EXPRESS data model. However, a complex EXPRESS data model is generally completed cooperatively by a design group, in which each member may use a different graphical data model. All these graphical data models designed by different members should be converted into one consistent data model since:

- Creating EXPRESS data models. Then EXPRESS-G is chosen as the target data model and the other graphical data models should be converted into EXPRESS-G.
- Creating databases. Then one of no EXPRESS-G graphical data models, say EER model, is chosen as the target data model and EXPRESS-G as well as other graphical data models are converted into the target data model.

The last issue is essentially related to the implementation of EXPRESS data model in database systems, which is the foundation of achieving STEP goal that product data can be exchanged and shared among different applications.

So far, the data model conversions among EXPRESS-G, IDEF1X, ER/EER, and UML only receive few attentions although such conversions are crucial in engineering information modeling. In [1], a mapping from EXPRESS-G to UML was introduced in order to define a linking bridge and bring the best of worlds of product data technology and software engineering together.

3 Formal Transformation of EER and EXPRESS-G

EER and EXPRESS-G models are known well and popular in the areas of database design and engineering information modeling, respectively. To implement the formal transformation of EER and EXPRESS-G, it is necessary to compare their capabilities in data modeling and investigate how they match each other.

First of all, we introduce the constructs in each of these two data models briefly. In addition to *entity*, *relationship*, and *attribute*, the following notions are introduced in the EER: *specialization/generalization*, *category*, and *aggregation*. EXPRESS-G provides supports for the notions of *entity*, *type*, *relationship*, *cardinality*, and *schema*.

The notions *entity* in EER and *entity* in EXPRESS-G mean the same thing. There are three kinds of *relationship* in EXPRESS-G: *optional valued attributes of an entity*, *supertype/subtype relationships*, and *common attributes of an entity*, which are denoted by *dashed lines, thick solid lines*, and *thin solid lines*, respectively. The notion *attribute* in EER corresponds to *dashed lines* and *thin solid lines* in EXPRESS-G. The notion *specialization/generalization* in EER corresponds to *thick solid lines* in EXPRESS-G. In addition, the notion *relationship* in EER can be regarded as the *entity* in EXPRESS-G. Now let us focus on some incompatibilities between EER and EXPRESS-G. The notions *category* and *aggregation* are only supported by EER and the notions *type* and *schema* are only supported by EXPRESS-G.

For the compatibilities between EER and EXPRESS-G, we can map them from EXPRESS-G to EER as well as mapping from EER to EXPRESS-G. As to the incompatibilities between EER and EXPRESS-G, we can simulate *category* and *aggregation* in EXPRESS-G. But current EER cannot support *type* and *schema*. In order to model *type* and *schema*, EER should be extended.

Due to space limit, the generic rules for mapping from EXPRESS-G to EER as well as mapping from EER to EXPRESS-G are not provided in this paper. The details can be found in the separate industrial proceedings in which you can also find the mapping with examples is presented whereby several problematic cases are discussed and possible solutions presented.

References

1. Arnold, F. and Podehl, G.: Best of Both Worlds – A Mapping from EXPRESS-G to UML. Lecture Notes in Computer Science 1618 (1999) 49–63
2. Booch, G., Jacobson, I. and Rumbaugh, J.: The Unified Modeling Language, Documentation Set 1.1 (1997)
3. Chen, P. P.: The Entity-Relationship Model: Toward a Unified View of Data. ACM Transactions on Database Systems 1 (1976) 9–36
4. Eastman, C. M. and Fereshetian, N.: Information Models for Use in Product Design: A Comparison. Computer-Aide Design 26 (1994) 551–572
5. IDEF1X Overview (1993) http://www.idef.com/idef1x.html
6. ISO IS 10303-1 TC184/SC4: Product Data Representation and Exchange-Part 1: Overview and Fundamental Principles (1994) International Standard
7. ISO TC184/SC4 WG7 N392: Industrial Automation Systems and Integration – Product Data Representation and Exchange – Part 22: Implementation Methods: Standard Data Access Interface (1995)
8. Ma, Z. M. et al.: Database Models for Engineering Information Modeling: Needs and Construction. Computers in Industry (2002)
9. Schenck, D. A. and Wilson, P. R.: Information Modeling: the EXPRESS Way. Oxford University Press (1994)

AXIS: A XML Schema Integration System

Bipin Sakamuri[1], Sanjay Madria[1], K. Passi[2], Eric Chaudhry[2], Mukesh Mohania[3], and S. Bhowmick[4]

[1]Department of Computer Science, University of Missouri-Rolla, MO 65401
madrias@umr.edu
[2]Department of Computer Science, Laurentian University, Sudbury, ON P3E2C6
kpassi@cs.laurentian.ca
3 IBM India Research Lab, Block No. 1, IITD, New Delhi – 110016, India
mkmohania@in.ibm.com
[4]School of Computer Engineering, Nanyang Technological University, Singapore

1 Introduction

The availability of large amounts of heterogeneous distributed web data necessitates the integration and querying of XML data from multiple XML sources for many reasons. For example, currently many government agencies in US such as IRS, INS, FBI, CIA are integrating their system to deal with new security threats, and these different departments uses legacy database systems including relational data, flat files, spreadsheets, and html pages, and simple text data. Similarly, there are many e-commerce companies, which sell similar products but represent data using different XML schemas. When any two such companies merge, or make an effort to service customers in cooperation, there is a need for a uniform schema integration methodology [1,2]. In some applications like comparison-shopping, there is a need for an illusionary centralized homogeneous information system. Such systems need a uniform data representation and access platform, which is provided by XML. However, the XML schema and data are still heterogeneous and represent their constraints differently. To avoid the overhead of system integration and system specific data access mechanisms, applications should be provided with data in an integrated form. The idea is to use XML as an intermediate medium to achieve date integration from heterogeneous data resources. There are many efforts currently on generating views or representing data in only XML format, but internally stored in legacy databases. Using wrappers, applications can view the data in XML, instead of moving the data from their original format to XML. However, wrappers fail if the structure of the data is dynamically changed. Our approach is two phase; the integration of the local XML schemas into a global schema, and the integration of the resultant XML data produced in response to the queries to the local XML data sources. A global schema eliminates data model differences by integrating local schemas. The heterogeneous XML data sources need not be represented in an integrated fashion. This is because integrating the XML data and storing it in the new integrated schema occupies extra resources, and may result in duplication, and thus, creates the problems of multiple updates and data inconsistencies. For this reason, we present a dynamic mechanism, which can interface the different XML data and can present an integrated representation of the XML sources, rather than physically integration of data.

I.-Y. Song et al. (Eds.): ER 2003, LNCS 2813, pp. 576–578, 2003.

In this paper, we present a system design that use XML as an intermediate medium to achieve data integration from the heterogeneous data resources. For this purpose, an integrated view of the schemas of individual/local data sources is constructed, and a query mechanism that works on the integrated view is developed that helps in retrieving data from various local data sources. In this paper, we mainly focus on the following modules of the proposed system:

XSM (XML Schema Model)

In this phase, the schemas from the XML representation of the heterogeneous data sources are integrated to construct an integrated view of the schema. This view of the data is called the Integrated Schema. The schemas of the individual data sources are referred as the Local Schemas. We consider XSchema to represent each schema in our system. We defined an object-oriented data model called XSM (XML Schema Model) and present a graphical representation of XML Schema for the purpose of schema integration [1,2]. We used a three-layered architecture for XML schema integration Phase. The three layers included are namely *pre-integration, comparison* and *integration*. During *pre-integration*, the schema present in Xschema notation is read and is converted into the XSM notation. During *comparison*, correspondences as well as conflicts between elements are identified. During *integration*, conflict resolution, restructuring and merging of the initial schemas takes place to obtain the global schema. We define integration policies for integrating element definitions as well as their data types and attributes. In *comparison* layer, the correspondences are identified either using the ontologies between the data in various local schemas available, or by taking input from the data administrators. The correspondences entered by the data administrators are semantically validated using an ontologies mechanism. This information obtained is used to integrate the schemas. The information about the conflicts resolved is stored and is used in the querying phase of the data integration model.

Mapping of Global XQuery to Local XQueries

After the Schema Integration Phase, the user of the system has the integrated view of the global Schema. To access the data, the user is allowed to query the integrated global schema using the application. A user's query (XQuery) can be applied on the integrated global schema, called the global query. In this phase, the global query is parsed and local queries are generated so that they can be applied on the local XML data sources. To generate the local queries, the origin of Elements and Attributes present in the global schema are required which can be obtained from the XML schema model phase. Predicates in the global query, which cannot be applied on the local XML documents are resolved. Thus, so obtained local queries are executed on the local XML documents using XQuery engine.

This Phase has three modules. The first module, "*Global Query Parser and Modeler Module*" parses the user's XQuery and stores in an in built data structure which allows restructuring and mapping back to the data elements and attributes of the local schemas.

The second Module, *"Local Queries Generator Module"* uses the information from the XML schema model phase such as correspondences, and conflict resolutions to break the global predicates that cannot be applied on local XML documents and to generate the local queries.

The third module, *"Query Engine Interface"* acts an interface to the generated local queries on corresponding XML documents using any third party XQuery Engine. The reason to separate this module from the previous module is to decrease the dependency/interface of the system on third-party tools. In this implementation, the IPSI XQuery Demonstrator (IPSI-XQ) is used. The results of the local queries are passed to the next phase.

XML Data Integration

In this phase, the results of the local queries are integrated. This is the only phase where the integration of the XML data is performed, whereas in the earlier phases, only schema integration is done. Generally, the size of the query results, which is small as compared to the huge size of actual data and knowledge of the local schemas make the process of XML data integration feasible. To integrate the XML data, the ontologies are used and the data administrators' input received during the XML schema integration phase are used to resolve the conflicts. For example, in few cases, where a substitution element is present, while rewriting the global query into local queries these elements name in the local queries should be changed. After getting the results back, these element names should be converted back to the original names used in global query. Most of the XML data integration methodology is similar to the schema integration except in the case of global predicates. In case of global predicates, we need to get the result from local queries, integrate the results and then query the integrated result with global predicate. The integrated XML data is validated with the integrated schema. A sub module that allows the user to store the result of his query to any persistent storage is made available.

References

[1]   Kalpdrum Passi, Louise Lane, Sanjay Kumar Madria, Bipin C. Sakamuri, Mukesh K. Mohania, Sourav S. Bhowmick: A Model for XML Schema Integration. EC-Web 2002: 193–202.
[2]   L. Lane, K. Passi, S.K. Madria, M. Mohania, XML Data Integration to Facilitate E-commerce, Book Chapter in Web Enabled Systems and Integration, pp. 66–90, IDEA Group of Publisher, 2002

Episode-Based Conceptual Mining of Large Health Collections

Tatiana Semenova

Computer Science Laboratory
Australian National University
Canberra ACT 0200, Australia
tatiana@csl.anu.edu.au

In many countries, health care undustry is challenged by growth of costs associated with the use of new treatments or diagnostic techniques; wasteful or inefficient health care practices where funds are unnecessarily spent with no additional benefits to patients; health fraud where those who either provide or receive health services misrepresent those services to attract higher benefits. It has become very important for health service administrators to better understand current health care trends and patterns and associated costs to estimate health costs into the future. The key characteristics of a health system are hospital care, visits to medical practitioners, the consumption of pharmaceuticals calculated with regards to the particular cohorts of patients. One of the measure units for such calculations is episode of care, which has a variety of definitions. Episodes take into account various indices of patient care, for instance, a patient's age, ethnical background, gender, location, medical services provided, information about participating physicians, fees and some other. Aggregating these attributes is important for *Medicare* (Australia's universal health scheme) administrators because they can then produce extensive reports on utilisation. From a data mining point of view, applying some definition of episode is a way to preprocess data according to some temporal principle that is also clinically meaningful. Besides, it is an opportunity to filter out those irrelevant attributes that will not be included in data analyses. Episodic mining of health data is also a method to compress transactional dataset into a collection of health care episodes, that are not so diverse due to the nature of services and standardised medical practice.

We define episode of care as an abstract concept referring to a period during which a patient receives a particular type(s) of care from an identified doctor or service unit. It is a block of one or more medical services, received by an individual during a period of relatively continuous contact with one or more providers of service, in relation to a particular medical problem or situation. Episodes of care should be carefully distinguished from episodes of illness though. Care episodes focus on health care delivery whereas illness episodes focus on the patient experience. Episodes of care are the means through which the health care delivery system addresses episodes of illness. Construction of an episode of care begins with the first service for a particular condition and ends when there are no additional claims for a disease-specific number of days. In our case, an episode will be defined by the medical professional delivering the initial health care service(s) to an identified patient on the same day.

I.-Y. Song et al. (Eds.): ER 2003, LNCS 2813, pp. 579–581, 2003.
© Springer-Verlag Berlin Heidelberg 2003

In the database used for our analyses, for *3,617,556* distinct patients only *368,337* unique patient histories were matched. Applying our definition of a health care episode as a group of tests ordered for a patient by the same doctor on the same day, which in terms of database is the content of all records containing the same *Patient Identification Number*, the same *Referring Provider*, and the same *Date of Reference*, we represented one of the datasets originally containing *13,192,395* transactions as a set of *2,145,864* sequences (episodes). Amongst them only *62,319* sequences were unique. Our experience in processing administrative health data has shown that unique health care episodes normally occupy less than 10% of the total size of data, which makes episode-based representation an efficient technique of a database compression. Thus effective pruning of the original data is suggested to be a starting point in handling computations on large datasets. Besides that, the obtained knowledge about diversity and consistency in data is a valuable contribution in understanding the actual meaning of data. This also contributes to the knowledge representation in general.

One approach to identifying patterns in health data uses association rule mining. The *Apriori*-like approaches for discovering frequent associations in data achieve reasonable performance on a variety of datasets, but for large health records collections in particular this method is found limited. Another type of approaches has arised from *Formal Concept Analysis*, a field that focuses on the lattices structures extracted from binary data tables, or concepts, which have been shown to provide a theoretical framework for a number of practical problems in information retrieval, knowledge representation and management. In fundamental philosophies, concepts combine things that are different. Implicit in this is the knowledge that the *attributes* to which our concepts apply have many *qualities*. Thus, implicit in the nature of concepts is recognition that each referent of a *concept* differs quantitatively from the others. That is, implicit in grouping attributes into concepts is recognition that those attributes have various *qualities* in some *quantity*, but we do not consider the actual quantities. It is understood, that a *concept* is constituted by two parts: *extension*, consisting of all *objects* belonging to the concept and *intension*, containing all *attributes* shared by the objects. Such a view at a concept allows to detect all structures in a dataset containing complete information about attributes. Alltogether, these structures present a compact version of the dataset - a *lattice*. Building a lattice can be considered as a conceptual clustering technique as well because it describes a concept hierarchy. In this context, lattices appear to be a more informative representation comparing with trees, for instance, because they support a multiple inheritance process (e.g. various types of service by the same type of health care provider).

The classic and one of the most efficient techniques for frequent pattern mining is *FP-growth algorithm*. It is an unsupervised learning technique for discovering conceptual structures in data. Its benefits are *completness* and *compactness*, that is, the derived associations contain conclusive information about data, and their amount is reduced down to the number of *maximal* frequent patterns. However, on a large scale this technique may face memory problems due to a great *FP-tree* expansion. We suggest an alternative algorithm based on splitting the initial records into two or more sub-records, so that none of the sub-records contained irrelevant information. Such an expanded record is in fact a ministructure (or a *concept*) that already is or will become one of the components of a *formal concept* (or *Galois* lattice) later on.

The patterns of practice derived from administrative health data is a way to gain some insights into the clinical side of health care services. *Medicare* transactions do not contain information about any e.ects of clinical treatments. Neither do they contain information about pre-conditions of the treatments or duration of the disease. *Medicare* items combinations include various mixes of consultation, diagnostic and procedural services provided by health providers to patients for various pathological conditions. Thus, *Medicare* items and possibly other relevant attributes associated within one episode could reveal some clinical side of the event. For example, in our experience, a number of (at least more than one) blood group tests prescribed on the same day to the same patient by the same doctor indicates at very least the uncommonness of the provided medical treatment. But within one episode, there could be such pathology tests like *Quantitation of hormones and hormon building proteins* and *TSH quantitation*, which also includes tests on quantitation of hormones and makes it sufficient examination without the first one. This combination isn't obviously uncommon. Thus, in addition to discovering patterns of practice efficiently, there is also a need to interpret such patterns in order to assess the clinical necessity of the provided services, in other words, to apply knowledge-based data mining techniques.

The suggested technique is found more efficient than *FP-growth*, because its complexity is dependant mainly of the number of attributes in a database, whereas *FP-growth*'s complexity largely depends on both the number of attributes and the size of the database.

Author Index